MW01040724

Daxue and *Zhongyong*

Daxue and *Zhongyong*

Bilingual Edition

Translated and annotated by

Ian Johnston and Wang Ping

The Chinese University Press

Daxue and Zhongyong: Bilingual Edition
    Translated and annotated by Ian Johnston and Wang Ping

© **The Chinese University of Hong Kong** 2012

ISBN: 978-962-996-445-0

THE CHINESE UNIVERSITY PRESS
The Chinese University of Hong Kong
SHA TIN, N.T., HONG KONG
Fax: +852 2603 6692
Fax: +852 2603 7355
E-mail: cup@cuhk.edu.hk
Website: www.chineseupress.com

Printed in Hong Kong

Contents

Abbreviations vii

General Introduction. 1

Introduction: The *Daxue*. 19

Taixue 太學: The Highest Learning*. 41

    TX1 44

    TX2 46

    TX3 52

    TX4 58

    TX5 64

    TX6 66

    TX7 70

    TX8 74

    TX9 76

    TX10 80

    TX11 90

    TX12 96

    TX13 106

    TX14 114

    TX15 118

Daxue 大學: The Greater Learning. 125

    DX Text 134

    DX Comm. 1 138

    DX Comm. 2 140

    DX Comm. 3 142

    DX Comm. 4 148

    DX Comm. 5 150

    DX Comm. 6 152

    DX Comm. 7 156

    DX Comm. 8 158

DX Comm. 9 158
DX Comm. 10.1–10.5 164

Introduction: The *Zhongyong* 181

Zhongyong 中庸: Using the Centre 211
ZY1 214
ZY2–6 222
ZY7 240
ZY8–13 250
ZY14–19 290
ZY20–26 320
ZY27–29 348
ZY30–31 356
ZY32 368
ZY33 394

Zhongyong 中庸: Central and Constant 399
ZY1 406
ZY2–10 412
ZY11–12 424
ZY13–19 428
ZY20.1–20.6 446
ZY21–26 462
ZY27 472
ZY28–29 476
ZY30–32 480
ZY33 486

Appendices 495
Appendix 1—The Origin of the *Li ji* 禮記 495
Appendix 2—Commentaries and Translations 499
Appendix 3—Terminology 521

Bibliography 549

Index 555

---

* For more detail on the organisation of the texts in this volume, see the introductions for each work, and the Tables on pages 25 (*Taixue*/*Daxue*) and 193 (*Zhongyong*).

Abbreviations

CSJC:	*Congshu jicheng* 叢書集成
DMB:	*Dictionary of Ming Biography*
DX/TX:	*Daxue/Taixue* 大學/太學
ECCP:	*Eminent Chinese of the Ch'ing Period*
LCC:	*The Chinese Classics* (James Legge)
SB:	*A Sung Bibliography* (*Bibliographie des Sung*)
SBCK:	*Sibu congkan zhengbian* 四部叢刊正編
SKQS:	*Siku quanshu* 四庫全書
SSJZS:	*Shisanjing zhushu* 十三經注疏
SSZJ:	*Sishu zhangju (jizhu)* 四書章句集註
ZWDCD:	*Zhongwen da cidian* 中文大辭典
ZY:	*Zhongyong* 中庸

General Introduction

The *Daxue* 大學 and the *Zhongyong* 中庸 are two short texts of particular and enduring importance in Confucian philosophy. Despite the vicissitudes of social upheaval and philosophical fashion, they have retained their relevance for almost two millennia and remain, arguably, no less relevant today than when they were first written. They have been variously titled in translation but are probably most familiar in English as "The Great Learning" and "The Doctrine of the Mean" dating from Legge's translations which first appeared in 1861.[1] There have been four distinct periods in the history of these two texts:

1. From their original composition, possibly some time during the Zhou/Warring States period, to their incorporation into the *Li ji* 禮記 (*Rites Record*) which probably occurred sometime during the Later or Eastern Han dynasty (25–220 CE).[2]

2. From their inclusion in the *Li ji* redaction to their "elevation" to form the "bookends" of the Four Masters or Four Books (the *Daxue*, the *Lunyu* or *Analects* of Confucius, the *Mencius* and the *Zhongyong*) by Zhu Xi 朱熹 (1130–1200) in 1190.

3. From their inclusion in the Four Books, which became the foundation of the official examinations, until the end of the Imperial period: that is, from the end of the twelfth century to the end of the nineteenth century.

4. From the end of the traditional examinations until the present day: that is, the twentieth and twenty-first centuries.

---

[1] See James Legge, *The Chinese Classics,* 5 vols. (Hong Kong: University of Hong Kong Press, 1960), 1:355–81 and 382–434 respectively. Legge subsequently changed the title of the "The Doctrine of the Mean" to "The State of Equilibrium and Harmony" in his 1885 translation of the *Li ji* (*Book of Rites*). For a list of other translations of both titles, see Appendix 2, Table 1.

[2] A brief account of views on the origin of the *Li ji* is given in Appendix 1. It must be recognized that there are those who think the initial composition of the two tracts dates from the Han period—see the specific introduction to each text.

The distinctive features of their existence during each period will be considered before turning to an examination of their content and relevance.

The first stage might be deemed a period of obscurity. A traditional, and widely accepted, account of their authorship did emerge but this has remained without either significant supporting evidence or compelling contrary evidence. The putative author of the *Daxue* is the first generation Confucian disciple Zeng Shen 曾參 (Zengzi, c. 505–437 BCE). This attribution is particularly associated with Zhu Xi. It was Zhu Xi who divided the text into an opening statement by Confucius himself followed by a series of sections of commentary supposedly written by Zengzi. There is, however, no real evidence to support this attribution. Neither of the *Li ji* commentators makes any mention of Zengzi as the author. The putative author of the *Zhongyong* is Kong Ji 孔伋 (Zisi, c. 483–402 BCE), the grandson of Confucius and disciple of Zengzi. In this case there is some early written evidence of Zisi's role, both from the historians Sima Qian 司馬遷 (c. 145–86 BCE) and Ban Gu 班固 (32–92) and from the *Li ji* commentators. Although both Zengzi and Zisi have works listed in the *Han shu* "Yiwenzhi" (Catalogue of Literature),[3] neither entry can be identified with, or even certainly linked to the two tracts in question. Further, the recent discoveries of ancient manuscripts at Mawangdui and Guodian, which have particular relevance for the writings of Zisi, have not helped resolve the issue of authorship of either of these two tracts.[4] Finally, the problems associated with the identification of Zisi in early writings have recently been examined in detail by Csikszentmihalyi who highlights the complexity of attributing specific works to him.[5] In short, the matters of authorship and dating of these two texts remain more or less completely unresolved. What is clear, however, is that readers of the Zhu Xi edition post-1200 are likely, for the most part, to have accepted his views on these points whilst earlier readers presumably at least accepted Zisi's role in preparing the *Zhongyong*.

The second stage began with the definitive redaction of the *Li ji* in the Later Han period. Quite quickly commentary was added in the interlinear form, said to have been introduced by Ma Rong 馬融 (79–166) who himself may have prepared a commentary for this work. However, it has been his

---

3   *Han shu,* "Yiwenzhi," (Beijing: Zhonghua shuju, 1975), 6:30.1724.
4   See Kenneth W. Holloway, *The Newly Discovered Seeds of Chinese Religious and Political Philosophy* (New York: Oxford University Press, 2009).
5   See Mark Csikszentmihalyi, *Material Virtue: Ethics and the Body in Early China* (Leiden: Brill, 2004), 86–100.

student, Zheng Xuan's 鄭玄 (127–200) commentary which has survived from the Han period and still survives today in the *Shisanjing zhushu* 十三經注疏 (The Thirteen Classics with Notes and Commentaries—SSJZS) compiled during the Qing period by Ruan Yuan 阮元 (1764–1849) and based on Song editions.[6] To this was added the commentary attributed to Kong Yingda 孔穎達 (574–648), prepared as part of the editions of definitive texts of the Five Classics commissioned by the Tang emperor, Taizong (reigned 629–649)— the endeavour which produced the *Wujing zhengyi* 五經正義 (The Correct Meanings of the Five Classics) and also included material from Lu Deming 陸德明 (556–627). This is essentially the form in which these classics exist today in the SSJZS. There are also works specifically devoted to these two tracts in the "Catalogue of Books" in the *Sui shu*, as detailed in Appendix 2, but nothing of these survives. What do survive, however, are three essays from the Tang, which signal the beginning of a more concentrated focus on the two chapters as individual works. These essays, two by Han Yu 韓愈 (768–824) and one by Li Ao 李翱 (774–826), are briefly considered in Appendix 2. This focus intensified over the following four centuries, especially during the major development of Neo-Confucianism during the Song dynasty (960–1279).[7] It is important to remember that throughout this whole stage the two tracts, as chapters in the *San li* 三禮 (the three *Li* texts—*Zhou li*, *Yi li* and *Li ji*), were part of the curriculum for the official examinations.

The third stage dates from Zhu Xi's combining of these two texts with the *Lunyu* of Confucius and the *Mencius* in his edition of the Four Books first published in 1190. What Zhu Xi did with the two texts in question was, in summary, as follows:

1. He prepared new editions of both texts, isolating them from the *Li ji* and adding them to the *Lunyu* and *Mencius* to constitute the Four Books—his *Sishu zhangju* (The Four Books in Chapters and Sentences; SSZJ).

---

[6] The "Thirteen Classics" are, in their order in the SSJZS, the *Zhou yi* 周易 (*Book of Changes*), the *Shang shu* 尚書 (*Book of Documents*), the *Shi jing* 詩經 (*Book of Songs*), the *Zhou li* 周禮 (*Rites of Zhou*), the *Yi li* 儀禮 (*Book of Etiquette and Ceremonies*), the *Li ji* 禮記 (*Book of Rites*), the *Zuo zhuan* 左傳 (*The Zuo Commentary*), the *Gongyang zhuan* 公羊傳 (*Gongyang Commentary*), the *Guliang zhuan* 穀梁傳 (*Guliang Commentary*), the *Lunyu* 論語 (*Analects*), the *Xiaojing* 孝經 (*Book of Filial Piety*), the *Er ya* 爾雅 (*An Ancient Dictionary*) and the *Mengzi* 孟子 (*Mencius*). The "Five Classics" are *Changes*, *Documents*, *Odes*, *Rites*, and the *Spring and Autumn Annals*.

[7] A recent and important study of the development of Neo-Confucianism is that by Peter K. Bol, *Neo-Confucianism in History* (Cambridge, MA: Harvard University Press, 2008).

2. He made substantial rearrangements of the text of the *Daxue* and relatively minor rearrangements of the text of the *Zhongyong*.
3. He added an informative preface to each work.
4. He added a new interlinear commentary for each work, prepared by himself but also drawing on the work of earlier scholars including Zheng Xuan and his own Song period Neo-Confucian predecessors, in particular the Cheng brothers—Cheng Hao 程顥 (1032–1085), Cheng Yi 程頤 (1033–1108) and Lü Dalin 呂大臨 (1044–1093).
5. He established an account of authorship for both texts, which became the authorised version and elevated the two putative authors, Zengzi and Zisi, to a major position in the story of the orthodox transmission of the Master's teaching.

It was from this work, together with his other writings on the two texts, all of which represented a lifetime's endeavour,[8] that these two short tracts attained the great importance in Confucian philosophy they still enjoy today. Two notable and tangible results were shortly to follow. First, the Four Books became the basis of the official examinations when they were reinstituted in 1315, a position which they retained until the end of the Imperial period. Second, in their new form and elevated position, they spawned a large amount of further analysis and commentary which still continues. Much of this has been favourable to the orthodox interpretations, but there has also been a significant amount of opposition. A third consequence was that these texts came very early to the attention of Western scholars beginning with the Jesuit missionaries in the sixteenth century. These matters are examined more fully in Appendix 2.

The fourth stage, which covers the last hundred years or so, has obviously seen a decline in the importance of these tracts. With the end of the official examinations in 1905 they were no longer required reading for all aspiring scholars. There have, of course, also been other developments since, particularly in China itself—the continuing incursions of foreign powers, the Communist revolution and increasing Western influence generally—which have threatened to marginalise them. Nevertheless, new editions of the two enduring forms (the SSJZS and the SSZJ) continue to appear as do numerous specific studies of one or both tracts in Chinese and in other languages.

---

[8]   It is said that Zhu Xi was working on this material until a few days before his death.

As ethical tracts they have by no means been relegated to the category of "historical interest only."

What was it about these two short chapters that allowed them to achieve such a place of importance in the Confucian canon? First, they are clearly about the ethical development of the individual, presenting in an instructional and didactic way how to go about reaching the highest level of ethical excellence. Second, their key statements are illustrated and supported by the most authoritative of ancient sources—quotations from Confucius himself and passages from the *Documents* and the *Odes*. In contrast, whilst the other two of the Four Books are also primarily about ethics, their messages are expressed in the form of enlightening anecdotes, edifying dialogues and gnomic utterances without any clear sequential pattern. In a sense the student could open the *Lunyu* or the *Mencius* at any point and read with interest and possible edification, whereas in these other two texts he must begin at the beginning and follow the progression of the exposition systematically. Third, because they are so short and so structured, they particularly lend themselves to constant re-reading and memorisation. Moreover, a small group of key terms is recurringly and methodically considered, both in isolation and in their inter-connections, a point that will be taken up later in this introduction when examining the issue of their translation. The structure and arrangement of the two texts will be dealt with more fully in the specific introductions to each of them but an outline of these aspects is apposite here.

The opening section of the *Daxue*, which Zhu Xi attributes to Confucius himself, begins with a statement of the three components of the highest or greater learning; that is "the principles." These are: displaying enlightened virtue, loving (or restoring the virtue of) the people,[9] and coming to rest in the utmost goodness. These are the objectives. A sequence of consequences follows the achievement of these objectives: stability, calmness, tranquility, contemplation and attainment. A sorites of eight components is then set out which details the steps of the process of realising the desired self-cultivation and expressing it in the three levels of social organisation. The remaining sections of the short text are then devoted to exemplifying and clarifying the components of the sorites, borrowing from ancient texts as mentioned above.

The opening section of the *Zhongyong*, which is attributed to Zisi, begins by defining three key terms: nature (i.e. human nature), the Way and

---

[9] One major point of difference between the two commentarial traditions is the reading of *qin* 親 in the opening statement.

teaching. The remainder of the text might be characterised as describing how to perfect this nature (understood as being decreed by Heaven, itself a problematic concept) by following the Way, and how to beneficially influence others and the world in general by teaching. This teaching is achieved essentially by displaying and acting on the basis of one's own completed and perfected nature. A perfected nature is one which possesses the following seven key virtues:[10]

1. *Ren* 仁: mainly translated as benevolence or humanity but with a much wider and deeper range of meaning as is the case with the next three virtues listed.
2. *Yi* 義: mainly translated as righteousness, right action or justice.
3. *Li* 禮: mainly translated as propriety or rites.
4. *Cheng* 誠: mainly translated as sincerity or integrity.
5. *Zhi* 知: mainly translated as knowledge or wisdom. With this and the next two virtues the single-term English translation is relatively satisfactory.
6. *Xin* 信: mainly translated as trustworthiness, truthfulness or good faith.
7. *Yong* 勇: mainly translated as bravery or courage with moral courage implied in the Confucian ethical context.

Again the arguments are supported by quotations from authoritative ancient sources. The *Zhongyong* is undoubtedly a more complex text than the *Daxue* and certainly carries a hint of discontinuity in its composition. Much of the supporting material comes in the form of quotations from Confucius, only a small number of which have a clear correspondence to other extant texts. Seventeen such quotations follow the opening section and are, in turn, followed by Confucius' reply to a question from Duke Ai of Lu on government.[11] This is followed by a number of sections devoted to the explication of the term *cheng* 誠, a pivotal term which is raised by Confucius in his reply. Finally, there is a somewhat miscellaneous group of sections

---

10   In the translations the first four terms are transliterated for reasons considered later in this introduction and discussed further in Appendix 3.

11   This section is to be found in a slightly different form in the *Kongzi jiayu* 孔子家語 (*The Family Sayings of Confucius*), thought to be a forgery by Wang Su 王肅 (195–256), a scholar also mentioned in the *Li ji* commentary to the *Zhongyong*. Some of the material is also found in the *Mencius* IVA.12.

focusing in part on the distinction between the Way of Heaven and the Way of mankind, made earlier in the text. There is also a section devoted to praise of Confucius as the exemplar of perfect *sheng* 聖 (sagacity) and perfect *cheng* 誠 (purity, genuineness and sincerity).

The common features of the two works are, then, an opening statement expressing the fundamental arguments followed by a series of sections exemplifying and explaining the elements of these arguments. These supplementary sections utilise comments from the presumed authors of the texts, Zengzi and Zisi as described above, quotations from Confucius, quotations from two other ancient texts, the *Documents* and the *Odes*, as well as other quotations from unknown sources although the last are very few in number.

The three commentaries included with the present translations—those of Zheng Xuan and Kong Yingda for the *Li ji* text and that of Zhu Xi for his SSZJ text—have a long-established position as the most important of the preserved commentaries on these works. They are distinct in both form and focus quite apart from the specific differences in interpretation which do occur, particularly between the first two and the third. Thus, Zheng Xuan's commentary, which is the shortest of the three, concentrates predominantly on clarifying the meanings of individual characters and expressions. Although it does include some brief explanatory and summarising statements about overall meaning, it may be characterised as primarily philological. Kong Yingda's commentary, often referred to as a subcommentary, is the longest of the three. Apart from glosses on specific characters and expressions (which almost invariably agree with those of Zheng Xuan where both are given), there are paraphrastic clarifying restatements of almost every sentence as well as a considerable amount of literary and historical detail on many passages, but predominantly on the quotations from ancient texts. This commentary might be characterized as primarily literary-historical with a philological component. Zhu Xi's commentary also includes glosses on various characters oftentimes more or less at odds with those of the *Li ji* commentators. There is, however, a particular focus on philosophical issues especially pertaining to ethical terms and to questions about nature and the Way, and so it may be characterized as philosophical. The specific features and differences in the three commentaries in relation to individual passages are set out in some detail in the separate introductions to each work. In general, the three commentaries are much more complementary than conflicting. However, the differences that do occur in the interpretation of specific characters can lead to important variations in the readings of individual passages. A particular case in point is found in the variant readings of *qin* 親 in the opening statement of the *Daxue* referred to above.

Since the two main versions of these tracts were never without their respective commentaries over the many centuries of their existence, and since they were texts studied repeatedly and assiduously, especially after Zhu Xi's edition of the Four Books, it is critically important for Western readers who wish to study them in detail to have these commentaries available. This is the essential *raison d'etre* for the present work. But quite apart from the commentaries as aids to the understanding of the texts, there are also the important questions of how the readings of the texts may have changed with the passage of time and exactly what Zhu Xi did or did not do to the original *Li ji* texts in his singularly successful endeavour to bring them to the forefront of Neo-Confucian philosophy. On the first point, a full appreciation of the changes over time requires not only an appraisal of the three commentaries included here but also a study of the many other commentaries, analyses and rearrangements that followed Zhu Xi's work. This subject is briefly considered in Appendix 2 but is not treated in detail in the present work. Finally, and by no means of least importance, is the fact that Zhu Xi's full commentary coupled with his prefaces to the two works (both of which are included in the translations) represent a significant statement of his own mature philosophical views.

For the aspiring noble man who studies these two tracts with the aim of becoming a truly virtuous person, what are the issues within the texts that most need to be resolved? These are largely apparent in the opening statements of both texts which set out the basic argument. In the case of the *Daxue*, which is clearly the simpler of the two tracts, there are theoretical and practical issues. The theoretical issues emerge from the initial statement. First, what is meant by *ming ming de* 明明德? Is this a process of gradually acquiring virtue and then displaying it, as the remarks of the *Li ji* commentators suggest, or does it involve removing the accretions of impurity which come to overlie an already existing innate goodness that is in everyone? This latter view is Zhu Xi's reading, although he too allows for individual variation which relates to disposition (*qizhi* 氣質). Is the second component "loving the people," as is appropriate for a virtuous ruler who is beneficent and nurturing towards his populace, or is it to restore by one's own example the innate virtue in others to its original luminosity? Finally, what does coming to rest in the highest goodness entail? Is this simply to achieve the highest level of virtue and to establish oneself in this state like a mountain bird settling in the appropriate tree or is something else involved? The practical issues are found in the four components of the sorites which are set out in describing the process of self-cultivation: coming to or investigating things, extending (or perfecting) knowledge, making intentions *cheng* 誠 (pure, genuine and sincere), and rectifying the mind. Of these four, the two that are the more opaque are the first and the third.

The first of the four, coming to or investigating things (*ge wu* 格物), is clearly a critical step in the proposed sequence of self-cultivation. It is certainly recognised as foundational by Zhu Xi who postulated and partially recreated a lost section to elaborate on the process. But what is actually involved in *ge wu* 格物? The *Li ji* commentators offer a relatively simple explanation—*ge* 格 is equivalent to *lai* 來 (to come) and *wu* 物 is equivalent to *shi* 事 (matters, affairs)—so the phrase means, simply, "to come to matters"; this is Zheng Xuan's reading. Kong Yingda does elaborate somewhat, as follows: "knowledge is extended by study and practice; to come to good things is to extend one's knowledge of good and the more profound one's knowledge of good, the more good things one does in practice." Zhu Xi provides a more detailed analysis, which is hardly surprising given the importance he attaches to the process. In essence, he describes "investigating things" as the activity of the cognitive component of the mind engaging with all existing entities in the world and seeking to learn their "principle" (*li* 理) in each case. Only when this is done diligently and over a long period of time will knowledge approach the desired perfection or completion. However, when it comes down to the actual practice of such an activity, there remains something elusive in Zhu Xi's description.[12] This, no doubt, is why the phrase continued to be a matter of analysis and controversy in the centuries subsequent to Zhu Xi and is still a subject for discussion at the present time, as evidenced by Haiyu Wang's recent study.[13] It is clear, then, that there is no real consensus on the meaning of this phrase, its importance in the opening statement of the *Daxue* notwithstanding. From the standpoint of the translation, the views of the commentators have been followed in each case. From the standpoint of the reader, it must remain an unresolved issue, at least to some extent.

The third of the four, *cheng qi yi* 誠其意, involves issues as to what *cheng* 誠 means, whether in a nominal or verbal sense, and what is made *cheng* 誠 (i.e. *yi* 意)—is it intentions, the will, purposes, thoughts, ideas or

---

[12] Wang Yangming claimed, in fact, to have fallen ill in his unavailing search for principle in things—see, for example, Fung Yu-lan, *History of Chinese Philosophy*, trans. Derk Bodde (Princeton: Princeton University Press, 1952), 2:596–97.

[13] See Haiyu Wang, "On *Ge Wu*: Recovering the Way of the Great Learning," *Philosophy East and West* 57 (2007):204–26. See also Appendix 3.

meaning, or all of the above? *Cheng* 誠 is certainly a term that stubbornly resists a straightforward translation by a single English term. This was recognised early on by Legge who wrote in his original translation of the *Daxue* that " . . . we have no single term in English which can be considered as the complete equivalent of the character."[14] We shall return to the issue of translation of the key ethical terms later in this general introduction. The matter is also considered in Appendix 3 on terminology. In summary, as Zhu Xi's arrangement and commentary make clear, the remainder of the text is directed at the application and clarification of the matters raised in the opening section—the three elements of the highest/greater learning and the eight components of self-cultivation.

The second and fourth stages of the road to self-cultivation are more easily understood, although they too are not without aspects that are open to dispute. Thus the student needs to be clear what kind of knowledge it is that is to be extended or perfected—is it only knowledge of principle (or cohesion, *li* 理) in all things or is it the "intuitive knowledge" (*liang zhi* 良知) which constitutes the innate moral sense, as Wang Yangming 王陽明 (Wang Shouren 王守仁—1472–1529) suggests? Also, if the mind is to be rectified, this presupposes a non-rectified mind to begin with. How can this be satisfactorily correlated with the idea of original mind which is inherently correct and perfect? These are not issues that are addressed in the *Daxue* itself although, to some extent, they are considered in the *Zhongyong*. The three levels of the application of the cultivated self—to household/family, state/ country and world—are, in contrast, quite clear.

In the *Zhongyong* too, the opening section could be said to contain all the essential elements of the argument being advanced. However, it is an altogether more complex argument and critical components are introduced in later sections, most notably the pairing of *zhong* 中 (the centre, middle) and *yong* 庸 (to use, ordinary) and the consideration of *cheng* 誠 as a key factor in moral development. Further, the subsequent sections are less clearly focused on clarification of the issues of the opening section than in the *Daxue* and, in some cases, introduce apparently irrelevant material, such as matters to do with ghosts and spirits, a section in praise of Confucius and a section on the establishment of standards including the standardisation of cart tracks. These several factors have given rise to theories of a composite composition such as that of Wang Bo 王柏 (1197–1274) considered in the specific introduction

---

[14]   LCC, 1:414–15, n21.

to the *Zhongyong*. Be that as it may, the opening section does establish most of the major issues, as in the *Daxue*. First, there are the brief definitions of nature (i.e. human nature), the Way and teaching, the first of which involves the important and problematic concept of *tian* 天 or Heaven as the agent responsible for establishing this nature. Then, after mentioning some aspects of the conduct of the noble man, the two concepts *zhong* 中 and *he* 和 (harmony) are introduced although the latter is, in effect, replaced by *yong* 庸 in later sections. The concept of *cheng* 誠, critical to the work as a whole, is not given detailed consideration until the sections containing Confucius' response to Duke Ai's question on government although it is mentioned very briefly in an earlier section. In the sections containing Confucius' reply, *cheng* 誠 is further analysed and its relation to the other key virtues examined. The work ends with a series of sections which are something of a miscellany, although Zhu Xi describes the last section as Zisi's summarising statement.

The *Zhongyong* is, then, a more complex and philosophically interesting tract than the *Daxue*. While the *Daxue* offers a relatively straightforward account of the practical aspects of realising a programme of self-cultivation, the *Zhongyong* gives consideration to what might underlie such ethical development and make it possible. Moreover, it presents a rather more detailed examination of the distinguishing ethical features that characterise the sage and the noble man. These two texts, taken together with the material in the *Lunyu* and the *Mencius*, may be seen as providing all the teaching and instruction necessary for the person who wishes to pursue assiduously the path of self-cultivation with the goal of reaching the highest possible level of ethical development—a person who wishes to display this ethical excellence to the world in a way that is influential in the creation of goodness.

Finally, consideration must be given to the translation itself, both its form and its method. One of the major factors in determining how the translation is to be fashioned and presented is the concept of the ideal reader for whom it is intended. In the present case this is taken to be someone who intends to make a detailed study of these two tracts, and this applies not only to their actual content but also to how their interpretations may have changed with the passage of time, especially under the influence of important commentaries and analyses. As part of such considerations, the differences in the two most influential commentaries, those in the *Wujing zhengyi* version of the *Li ji* (preserved in the SSJZS) and Zhu Xi's own commentary in his SSZJ, reflecting decades of diligent personal study of these two texts and his engagement with other Neo-Confucian scholars, are of major interest. Of no less interest are the commentaries themselves, or at least Zhu Xi's, as philosophical statements in their own right. The envisaged reader would, then, be someone whose main language is English but who has also at least a working knowledge of Classical Chinese, and who wishes to study these texts in considerable detail. Readers of this kind may be uncommon, it must be admitted, but Legge's comment—to write for the "hundredth man"—is an encouragement as to the worth of such detailed editions, as is the endurance of his own exemplary works, presumably written with this dictum in mind.[15] In addition, the present work would be suitable for someone who wishes to read these texts in one or other of the two languages only as it is the first to present both versions of both texts side by side with their full commentaries.

In deciding on a format with these considerations in mind, the guiding principle has been to create a clear display of each of the main components of the two texts as they have been available in standard editions over the centuries. Thus, the *Li ji zhengyi* 禮記正義 text and the SSZJ text have been presented separately, the former being that found in the most recent edition of the SSJZS. The commentaries, those of Zheng Xuan and Kong Yingda in the first instance, and that of Zhu Xi in the second, are presented as numbered notes in the manner of the modern versions of the Zhu Xi commentary rather than being interlinear as in the SSJZS. Further, a brief English comment has been added to each section with a focus chiefly on contentious issues, either textual or interpretative, and the differences between the Han/Tang and Song commentaries. On the question of division into sections, the Zhu Xi text makes this clear with numbered sections and this, almost invariably, is the numbering that Western translators have followed. For the sake of comparison, we have divided the *Li ji* text into numbered sections also. For the *Zhongyong* this was done on the basis of the placement of Kong Yingda's commentary, resulting in divisions closely similar to those found in a recent, modern edition of the *Li ji*.[16] In the case of the *Daxue*, where Kong Yingda's commentary is gathered into two large blocks at the end of each of the two parts of the chapter, the numbered divisions are somewhat arbitrary and are based on a comparison with Zhu Xi's text, the arrangement in the modern version of the *Li ji*, the subject matter, and the aim of facilitating comparison with Zhu Xi's text. Finally, the Chinese text and the English translation are on alternate, facing pages with the numbered notes following each section

15   On Legge's idea, see Norman J. Girardot, *The Victorian Translation of China* (Berkeley: University of California Press, 2002), 62.
16   The *Xinyi Li ji duben* 新譯禮記讀本, ed. Jiang Yihua 姜義華 (Taipei: Sanmin Publishing Co., 2000).

to permit easy reading of the several components either separately or in any desired combination.

On the matter of the translation itself, dictated by the foregoing considerations three key objectives have been defined as follows:

1. To prepare a translation that retains the economy of expression of the original and closely adheres to it in structure.
2. To base the translation on the accompanying commentary in each of the four instances, i.e. the two versions of the *Daxue* and the two versions of the *Zhongyong*.
3. To transliterate the four ethical terms *cheng* 誠, *ren* 仁, *yi* 義 and *li* 禮 previously mentioned rather than translate them with an unsatisfactory English word.

On the first point, alternative strategies have been employed by others and obviously have their particular merits, being directed at an ideal reader differently envisaged. Two recent examples might be mentioned. The first is the translation of the *Zhongyong* by Ames and Hall (1997) who seek to provide what they call a "philosophical translation" drawing on the philosophy of process developed by A. N. Whitehead. One particular result of this is their idiosyncratic rendering of *cheng* 誠 as "creativity." The second example is the translation of both texts by Plaks (2003) which aims at displaying the conceptual and philosophical complexity of the works more completely to Western readers by an "expanded" translation of some of the key terms and a more discursive translation generally. These matters are considered more fully in Appendix 3.

The reasoning behind the second point is twofold: first, it is an attempt to bring out the differences between the two main commentarial traditions and second, it is an attempt to reflect how the tracts themselves might have been read by those using the particular edition. A more detailed study of the commentarial tradition and its influence on the readings of these texts would involve consideration of the many commentaries and analyses that arose after Zhu Xi's pivotal edition of 1190. In particular, the writings of men who opposed Zhu Xi's views—men such as Wang Yangming, Chen Que 陳 確 (1604–1677) and Luo Zhongfan 羅仲藩 (died c. 1850)—should be taken into account. A brief outline of these and other commentators and their works is given in Appendix 2.

On the third point, the four ethical terms chosen for transliteration are *cheng* 誠, *ren* 仁, *yi* 義 and *li* 禮. Associated ethical terms for which there is a satisfactory English equivalent (*xin* 信, *yong* 勇 and *zhi* 知/智) are also given in their transliterated form when they appear in a list with the non-translated terms but the English translation is included in parentheses. A brief modern comment on each of the four terms that are transliterated only is given to emphasise their range of meaning and the difficulty of finding a suitable English equivalent. All four terms have a scope and depth of meaning which carry them beyond a satisfactory rendering by any single English (or French, or German etc.) word. To study these two texts profoundly, one must come to grips with the profundity of these terms whose definition depends, at least in part, on these texts themselves.

1. *Cheng* 誠: Tu Wei-ming writes: " . . . I will often keep in its romanised form the term *ch'eng*, which has been somewhat unjustifiably translated as 'sincerity.' The complexities of this key concept, however, may be better appreciated if, through both textual and philosophical analysis, I am able to show that *ch'eng* connotes meanings such as 'genuineness,' 'truthfulness' and 'reality' as well as the commonly used notion of 'sincerity.'"[17]

2. *Ren* 仁: Chong writes: "For Confucius, *ren* connotes an ideal ethical orientation from which one sees the ethical life as a never-ending task. In different contexts, being a *ren* person connotes having emotions, attitudes, and values such as affection and reverence for elders, earnestness or the doing of one's best for others, sincerity, genuine feeling, cautiousness in speech and action. In this regard, I refer to the internal relation between *ren* and *li*. There are two aspects to this relation. First, learning to be a *ren* person involves the institutional and educational structures of *li*. Second, the emotions, attitudes, and values that *ren* encompasses are more or less similar to those that have been spelled out independently as the spirit of *li* . . . "[18]

3. *Yi* 義: Chong writes: "According to Lau, *yi* has the following more specific meanings: (1) 'right' as a moral quality of an act; (2) 'duty' as an act one ought to perform; (3) 'righteous' or 'dutiful' as descriptive of an agent. Lau takes it as distinctive of *yi*, however, that it is

---

[17] See Tu Wei-ming, *Centrality and Commonality: An Essay on Confucian Religiousness* (Albany, NY: State University of New York Press, 1989), 16. Tu adds another possibility in a note—"full realization." His detailed analysis of the term may be found on pp. 70–84.

[18] See Kim-chong Chong, *Early Confucian Ethics* (Chicago: Open Court, 2007), introduction, xiii.

act-based, i.e. the rightness of an action depends on its 'being morally fitting in the circumstances and has little to do with the disposition or motive of the agent.' An agent is described as 'righteous' or 'dutiful' derivatively in this regard: 'rightness is basically a character of acts and its application to agents is derivative.' . . . *Yi*, according to Lau, is the underpinning of Confucius' moral system."[19]

4. *Li* 禮: Nylan writes: " . . . the single term 'rites' or 'ritual' (*li* 禮) denoted the full panoply of appropriate and thus mutually satisfying behaviors built upon emotional insights. These behaviors, expressed in dress, countenance, bodily posture, and verbal phrasing, were designed to strengthen communal bonds among the living and the dead, and with the gods. In addition to decorous ceremonies performed in specific settings, there was everyday *li*, encompassing circumspect behavior, considerate acts, and exquisite courtesy. . . . One Ru master spoke of *li* as an all-embracing system whereby 'to join heaven and earth in harmony, . . . to moderate [human] likes and dislikes and to adjust joy and anger, as is proper.'"[20]

Detailed analysis of each of these four terms can be found in the original commentaries themselves and further views, arranged in chronological order, are provided in Appendix 3 where other important terms are also given consideration.

What we hope we have achieved are straightforward, accurate translations of the *Daxue* and the *Zhongyong* as they appear both in the *Li ji* (using the SSJZS) and in the SSZJ of Zhu Xi, together with the full commentaries in these two versions, all set out in such a manner as to make each component clearly identifiable and discrete so that it can be read independently if one wishes to do so. Our approach is intended to correspond to the first of the three "identities" listed by Wang Hui in his recent study of Legge's two translations of the *Zhongyong* for an "outsider undertak[ing] to translate a sacred Oriental text."[21]

> He can be a pilgrim and learner, who would listen attentively to the text unfolding itself through insider interpretations and figure out what he and his community can learn from it.

---

[19] See Chong, *Early Confucian Ethics*, 3.

[20] Michael Nylan, *The Five "Confucian" Classics* (New Haven: Yale University Press, 2001), 168–69.

[21] Wang Hui, *Translating Chinese Classics in a Colonial Context: James Legge and His Two Translations of the Zhongyong* (Bern: Peter Lang, 2008), 15.

大學

Introduction: The *Daxue*

The *Taixue* or *Daxue* 大學 is the shorter and simpler of the two texts taken from the *Li ji* 禮記 by the Song Neo-Confucian, Zhu Xi 朱熹 (1130–1200) to complete the Four Books. In their original, extant form in the *Li ji*, the *Taixue/Daxue* follows the *Zhongyong* 中庸; they are chapters 42 and 31 respectively. Zhu Xi reversed this order, placing the *Taixue/Daxue* as the first and the *Zhongyong* as the last, to form the two "bookends" of the Four Books. As Cheng Yi's 程頤 (1033–1107) introductory note to the work in the *Sishu zhangju* 四書章句 (SSZJ) makes clear, he viewed the *Taixue/Daxue* as the portal of entry into the study of these four seminal texts, a view obviously endorsed by Zhu Xi himself. Thus, the *Taixue/Daxue* was first accorded the high level of importance that was associated with the work from that time on.[1] Although this elevation of status did not go unchallenged, as exemplified in the evaluation offered by the late Ming scholar Chen Que 陳確 (1604–1677),[2] the short treatise nevertheless retained its elevated status until the end of the Imperial period. It remains a key element in Confucianism up to the present time. But the question of the work's merits and significance as an ethical treatise is not at issue here. In this brief introduction to the translations of the two versions of the work that follow, that is, of the *Li ji* text with Zheng Xuan's 鄭玄 (127–200) notes and Kong Yingda's 孔穎達 (574–648) commentary and of Zhu Xi's text and notes from the SSZJ, the matters addressed will be the title itself, the dating and authorship of the treatise, its content and arrangement, the ideas contained within it, and in particular, the differences in interpretation due to the different commentaries.

---

[1]   The Four Books became the basis of the official civil service examinations when they were re-established by the Yuan emperor in the early part of the 14th century (1315).

[2]   Chen Que's *Daxue bian* 大學辯 comprises *juan* 14–17 of the *Chen Que ji* 陳確集, 2:552–624.

The Title: This, the 大學, romanised as *Taixue* or *Daxue* and rendered in English as the "Highest Learning" or the "Greater Learning" ("Learning for Adults"), is taken, in the traditional manner, from the initial characters in the text and should not necessarily be expected to bear the weight of a title which summarises the content or indicates the aim of the tract as a whole. Nonetheless, the issues regarding the translation of the title must be addressed, not only as a title but also where it occurs as a term within the work. First, there is *da* 大. Accepting this as adjectival, the question becomes whether it should be read as positive, comparative or superlative. Whilst the first option is the simplest and is adopted by many, it is not altogether satisfactory for the use of the composite term in the body of the work unless it is read as simply referring to the work itself. Zhu Xi's analysis, in which he contrasts *daxue* 大學 with *xiaoxue* 小學, relating to the age of the learner and the subject matter of his studies, favours the use of the comparative, and this has been used in the translation of his text.[3] Zheng Xuan, responsible for the earliest extant commentary, suggests in a note that *da* is to be pronounced *tai*, giving it the reading of *tai* 太. Subsequently, both Lu Deming 陸德明 (556–625) and Kong Yingda refer to Zheng Xuan as the authority for taking *da* 大 to apply to the breadth or extent of the learning under consideration. That is, "taixue" is the highest level of learning and is applicable to ruling or governing. On these grounds, the use of the superlative is justified, and certainly seems appropriate in the context of the work as a whole, hence the use of the "highest learning" in the translation of the *Li ji* text. Second, there is *xue* 學. The translation of this as "learning" would seem unexceptionable and, indeed, virtually all English versions use "learning." The odd man out is Plaks who, in his recent translation, renders the title *The Highest Order of Cultivation*, arguing that "learning" fails to do justice to the magnitude and scope of what is described by the term, both in the title and in the body of the work.[4]

In accord with the avowed aim of keeping the translation as close to the original as possible and, with regard to the two versions, reflecting the views of the respective commentaries, "The Highest Learning," romanised as *Taixue*,

---

[3] For Zhu Xi's views on what constituted *daxue* 大學, see his preface to the work included in the translation that follows. He also interprets *Daxue* as "learning for adults"—see Legge's comment to follow.

[4] See Andrew Plaks, *Ta Hsüeh and Chung Yung (The Highest Order of Cultivation and On the Practice of the Mean)* (London: Penguin Books, 2003), 3–4. His observation is, indeed, valid. Whether it warrants the change which he makes in the usual translation is another question.

has been used for the *Li ji* text and "The Greater Learning," romanised as *Daxue*, for the Zhu Xi text. Legge has the following statement on this issue:

> I believe that the Book (i.e. the *Daxue*) should be styled *Taixue* 太學, and not *Daxue* 大學, and that it was so named as setting forth the higher and more extensive principles of moral science, which come into use and manifestation in the conduct of government. When Zhu Xi endeavours to make the title mean "the principles of Learning which were taught in the higher schools of antiquity," and tells us how at the age of fifteen, all the sons of the sovereign, with the legitimate sons of the nobles, and high officers, down to the more promising scions of the common people, all entered these seminaries, and were taught the difficult lessons here inculcated, we pity the ancient youth of China. Such "strong meat" is not adapted for the nourishment of youthful minds. But the evidence adduced for such educational institutions in ancient times is unsatisfactory, and from the older interpretations of the title we advance more easily to contemplate the object and method of the Work.[5]

Authorship and Date: Zhu Xi, in what became the definitive edition of the *Taixue/Daxue*, was quite unequivocal on the question of authorship. In his view the initial section, that is, the statement of the three basic aims or principles of the highest or greater learning and the eight stages along the way to their realisation, or particulars, was the work of Confucius himself, whilst the remainder, termed by Zhu Xi the commentary, was the work of the first generation Confucian disciple, Zeng Shen 曾參 (Zengzi 曾子—505–436 BCE), although possibly set down by the latter's own disciples. Legge's comment on this claim—"What he (i.e. Zhu Xi) says, however, as it is destitute of external support, is also contrary to the internal evidence"[6]—remains as apposite today as when it was written over a century ago. Another candidate for the authorship is Kong Ji 孔伋 (Zisi 子思—483–402 BCE), the grandson of Confucius and also the putative author of the *Zhongyong*. This view is expressed, for example, in Mao Qiling's 毛奇齡 (1623–1716) *Daxue zhengwen* 大學證文 as follows:

> Jia Kui 賈逵[7] of the Han said that Kong Ji, when he was living in poor circumstances in Song, feared lest the learning of the former sages would no longer be clear and the Way of emperors and kings would fall away. Therefore, he made the *Daxue* as the warp of these, and the *Zhongyong* as the woof.[8]

---

5   LCC, prolegomena, 1:28 (romanisations have been changed to *pinyin*).
6   LCC, prolegomena, 1:26.
7   Jia Kui 賈逵 (30–101) was a prominent scholar of the Eastern Han period.
8   Mao Qiling 毛奇齡, *Daxue zhengwen* 大學證文, CSJC, n.s., 17:415.

There is also no support of substance for this view.

What can be said with assurance is that the earliest available text is that of the Han dynasty compilation, the *Li ji*, and so dates from that time, as discussed in Appendix I. If we reflect on the possible sources of information on the issue of dating—evidence from extant material (actual mention of the work and/or textual parallels), stylistic pointers, internal evidence (reference to other works, mention of historically verified events), and new findings such as the Guodian material[9]—the best that can be said is that the present text of the *Taixue/Daxue* dates from some time between the late Warring States period and the later part of the Western (Former) Han dynasty. Whether it is the work of one hand and, if so, whose hand, is entirely a matter of conjecture at the present time.

The Components of the Text: There are, in essence, four distinct components discernible within the text of the *Taixue/Daxue*, although their arrangement and interpretation vary, as will be discussed in subsequent sections. The four are as follows:

1.   The basic statement of the key elements or principles of the highest learning, particulars of its practice and, to some extent, its beneficial consequences.
2.   Clarification and elaboration of some of these principles and particulars.
3.   Quotations from Zhou texts to support and illuminate the key elements.
4.   Additional statements on certain aspects of the text—specifically, clarification of certain key ethical concepts and their interrelationships.

1. The Basic Statement: This, which Zhu Xi takes as Confucius' contribution to the work, opens the work and itself begins with a statement of the

---

[9]   Whilst the remarkable discovery of a collection of ancient texts on bamboo slips in a tomb from at least as early as the first part of the 3rd century BCE at Guodian village near Jingmen City in Hubei (in 1993) has no direct bearing on either of these two texts, it certainly has relevance to the *Li ji* as a whole and to Zisi as an author. Of course, it also raises hopes of further such discoveries—for a brief account and relevant references, see, for example, Liu Xiaogan's article in the *Encyclopedia of Chinese Philosophy*, ed. Anthony S. Cua (New York: Routledge, 2003), and for more detailed consideration, Holloway, *Guodian: The Newly Discovered Seeds of Chinese Religious and Political Philosophy*.

fundamental principles or objectives which are: to perfect one's own virtue, to make it manifest, to extend this endeavour to others, and to "come to rest" or "abide" in the highest level of goodness. This "coming to rest" affords the noble man mental stability, calmness and tranquility, paving the way for contemplation and correct conduct. Thus, the central objective or first principle is to display perfect and enlightened virtue. This is achieved by assiduous application to the process of self-cultivation. Self-cultivation, in turn, involves a set of further processes (i.e. the particulars) which are, in order of their prosecution, extending knowledge to perfection by the examination (investigation) of the things and events in the world, making the will or intentions pure, genuine and sincere (*cheng* 誠), untainted by desire, self-interest and other adverse emotional factors, and finally, rectifying the mind such that the mind-heart expresses itself in the world essentially through the perfected performance of *ren* 仁, *yi* 義 and *li* 禮.[10] The noble man, when he achieves this self-cultivation, is, as a result, able to regulate his own household and, to the extent that his position allows, bring good order to the state and peace to the world. So there are, in fact, three processes on the path of self-cultivation—extending knowledge through one's interaction with the world (i.e. the investigation of things), making one's intentions *cheng* 誠 by bringing the knowledge acquired by the investigation of "things" to perfection, and rectifying the mind by making intentions *cheng* 誠 under all circumstances. It is on the basis of these activities that the self becomes cultivated, and on the basis of the cultivated self that good order is brought to the increasingly complex levels of social organisation of household, state and world. Self-cultivation is, then, the pivot, as it were, and is identified as the "root" (or "trunk") in this opening section. Clearly, the processes so tersely expressed need to be clarified, elaborated on and exemplified, which is the role of the remaining components, deemed commentary by Zhu Xi.

2. Clarification of the Particulars: There are five such sections. The first, which is about making intentions *cheng* 誠, differs slightly in form from the other four. The process is seen as enabling the noble man to give an immediate, spontaneous and genuine response to all situations regardless of whether he is under scrutiny by others or not. This response emanates from his

---

10   On the meaning of these essentially untranslatable terms (at least in our view) see the General Introduction, pp. 14–15. Common English translations that have been used are as follows: *ren* as benevolence or humanity; *yi* as righteousness or right action; *li* as propriety or rites.

perfected virtue. The other four sections take the form of "what is meant by X lies in Y" although in one of the four "it is necessary to" is found in place of "lies in." In these four sections X is, respectively, cultivating the self, regulating the household, bringing good order to the state and bringing peace to all under Heaven, whilst Y is, respectively, rectifying the mind, cultivating the self, regulating the household and bringing good order to the state. One notable difference between the two versions that follow is Zhu Xi's identification of a postulated sixth such section, now lost, on extending and perfecting knowledge being dependent on the investigation of things. This issue will be considered further below.

3. The Quotations: There are, in all, twenty-five quotations: twelve from the *Odes*, seven from the *Documents*, one from the *Lunyu* (*Analects*), three from unknown, presumably no longer extant, sources, one attributed to Zengzi and one described as an old adage. These quotations are scattered throughout the text and are used to illustrate, exemplify or reiterate various points in the basic teaching. That their placement varies between the two versions indicates that their interpretation and relation to the text itself is not necessarily agreed upon.

4. Additional Statements: There are, at least in the *Li ji* arrangement, three additional statements: one on the meaning of *ren* 仁, one on the relationship between *ren* 仁 and *yi* 義, and one on the relationship between *yi* 義 and *li* 利. *Ren* 仁 and *yi* 義, along with *li* 禮 and *cheng* 誠, are the key ethical concepts of the text as a whole and are left untranslated, as previously mentioned.

Arrangement (Table 1): There are significant differences between the *Li ji* text and that of Zhu Xi's SSZJ in the arrangement of the components listed above. These differences clearly impact on interpretation. To facilitate comparison, section numbers have been added to the *Li ji* text with the divisions being determined by the placement of Zheng Xuan's notes. In the standard version (i.e. the SSJZS version) of the *Li ji*, Kong Yingda's commentary is collected in two large sections following what are TX6 and TX15 below respectively. These notes have been rearranged to follow the sections to which they apply. The arrangements of the listed components in the two texts are, then, as follows.

(i) *Li ji*: The basic statement of principles and particulars comprises the first two sections (TX1 & TX2) with the division falling between the statement

Table 1: Comparison of the *Taixue/Daxue* in the *Li ji* and *Sishu zhangju* Texts

Li ji 禮記	*Sishu zhangju* 四書章句
TX1: The 3 Principles; the sequence from "coming to rest" to "attainment"; the distinctions between root and branch, end and beginning.	DX Text: Same as for TX1 plus TX2: i.e. the 3 Principles, the sequence, the distinctions, and the 8 Particulars.
TX2: The 8 Particulars.	DX Comm. 1: Quotations from the *Documents* (3) on the first Principle: "displaying luminous virtue."
TX3: Explication of "making intentions *cheng* 誠 (pure and true)."	DX Comm. 2: Quotations from the *Odes* (1), *Documents* (1) and an unknown source (1) on the second Principle: "renewing the people."
TX4: Quotations from the *Odes* (2) on "making intentions *cheng* 誠."	DX Comm. 3: Quotations from the *Odes* (5) on the third Principle: "coming to rest in perfect goodness."
TX5: Quotations from the *Documents* (3) on the Principles.	DX Comm. 4: A quotation from the *Lunyu* on "knowing the root."
TX6: Quotations from the *Odes* (4), *Documents* (1), Confucius (1) and an unknown source (1) on the Principles.	DX Comm. 5: Fragment of the presumed lost section on "investigating things (*ge wu* 格物)."
TX7: A quotation from the *Lunyu* on making intentions *cheng* 誠 as "knowing the root."	DX Comm. 6: Explication of "making intentions *cheng* 誠."
TX8: Explication of "cultivating the self lies in rectifying the mind-heart."	DX Comm. 7: Explication of "cultivating the self lies in rectifying the mind-heart."
TX9: Explication of "regulating the household lies in cultivating the self."	DX Comm. 8: Explication of "regulating the household lies in cultivating the self."
TX10: Explication of "bringing good order to the state lies in regulating the household" with 4 quotations (*Odes* 3, and *Documents* 1).	DX Comm. 9: Explication of "bringing good order to the state lies in regulating the household" with 4 quotations (*Odes* 3, *Documents* 1).
TX11: Explication of "bringing peace to all under Heaven lies in bringing good order to the state" with 2 quotations from the *Odes*.	DX Comm. 10.1–10.5: Explication of "bringing peace to all under Heaven lies in bringing good order to the state" with 6 quotations (*Odes* 3, *Documents* 1, unknown 2).
TX12: On virtue, goodness and *ren* 仁. Four quotations (*Documents* 2, *Odes* 1, unknown 1).	
TX13: On *ren* 仁 with one quotation from the *Documents*.	
TX14: On wealth and the relationship between *ren* 仁 and *yi* 義.	
TX15: On the relationship between *yi* 義 and *li* 利 with one quotation from an unknown source.	

on the three principles and their consequences, and that on the particulars or components of the programme of self-cultivation. The second section ends with the statement: "This is called knowing the root; this is called the perfection of knowledge." Then follows the section on making intentions *cheng* 誠, or pure, genuine and sincere, which includes the quotation attributed to Zengzi (TX3). This, in turn, is followed by four sections of quotations (TX4–TX7) which contain, in all, thirteen of the overall total of twenty-five quotations. The first such section (TX4) includes two quotations from the *Odes* seen as illustrating the process of making intentions *cheng* 誠.

TX5 contains three quotations from the *Documents* whilst TX6 contains four quotations from the *Odes*, a further quotation from the *Documents*, a quotation attributed to Confucius and a quotation from an unknown source. These are used to enlarge on the primary components, or principles of the highest learning, whilst the next section (TX7) has a single quotation from the *Lunyu* which is taken as supporting the identification of making intentions *cheng* 誠 with "knowing the root." The next four sections (TX8–TX11) complete the series of explications of the "particulars" or components of the processes and consequences of self-cultivation, with support from six quotations; five from the *Odes* and one from the *Documents* together with the previously mentioned old adage. The final four sections (TX12–TX15) give consideration to some of the key terms or components of the ethical view advanced in the text as a whole: *ren* 仁, *shan* 善 (goodness) and *de* 德 (virtue), the relationship between *ren* 仁 and *yi* 義, and that between *yi* 義 and *li* 禮. There are, in all, six quotations in these four sections—three from the *Documents*, one from the *Odes* and two from unknown sources, added to illustrate the points being made.

(ii) *Sishu zhangju* (SSZJ): Greatly expanding on the ideas of the Cheng brothers, particularly Cheng Yi, Zhu Xi made substantial changes in the *Taixue/Daxue* text which came to have a significant bearing on how the work was interpreted. The most fundamental change was to divide the text into a single opening section, identified as the Classic (this comprising the first two sections of the *Li ji* text, i.e. TX1 & TX2, apart from the omission of the final sentence of TX2), and the Commentary, itself subdivided into ten sections, enlarging on and illustrating the components of the Classic; that is, the three "principles" (*gangling* 綱領) and the eight "particulars" (*tiaomu* 條目). As discussed earlier, Zhu Xi attributed the Classic to Confucius, the assumption being that, even if it was not actually written by Confucius, it was nevertheless his direct teaching recorded by his disciples. He attributed the commentary to one specific disciple, Zeng Shen 曾參, and rearranged it to conform to a more systematic analysis of the "principles" and "particulars." To achieve this, Zhu Xi placed twelve of the twenty-five quotations to follow immediately after the Classic (his DX Comm. 1–4), taking all twelve quotations to refer to the three principles in order. The remaining six sections of commentary (DX Comm. 5–10) were then seen as dealing with the "particulars." A major problem with this proposal is that there is no section dealing with what, for Zhu Xi, is the foundational component of the particulars—that the extension or perfection of knowledge lies in the investigation of things. To solve this problem, he postulated a largely lost section of which only the ten characters which conclude section TX2 in the *Li ji* text remain. With suitable expressions of humility and unworthiness,[11] he added his own commentary on this "particular," ending with these ten characters. Finally, he grouped all the material following "what is meant by bringing peace to all under Heaven lies in bringing good order to the state" as a single section of commentary whereas we have taken it, following the *Li ji* text, as an explanation of this "particular" (TX11) followed by four additional statements on key ethical terms and concepts.

The essential differences in arrangement between the two versions may be summarised as follows:

(i) Grouping of the 3 Principles and 8 Particulars of the programme (and immediately related material) into a single opening section attributed to Confucius himself in the Zhu Xi version, compared to the division of this material into two sections without specific attribution in the *Li ji* version.

(ii) Treatment of all the remaining material as commentary attributable to Zeng Shen by Zhu Xi.

(iii) Transfer of a major part of the quoted material to follow the opening section by Zhu Xi. The grouped quotations constitute sections TX4–7 in the *Li ji* text.

(iv) Identification of a largely lost explicatory section represented by a remaining fragment of 10 characters (此謂知本，此謂知之至也) by Zhu Xi, which constitutes his DX Comm. 5. These 10 characters occur at the end of the listing of the eight "particulars" in the *Li ji* (TX2).

(v) Grouping of all the explicatory sections together by Zhu Xi; i.e. DX Comm. 6–10 plus the presumed lost section (DX Comm. 5). In the *Li*

---

[11] See Zhu Xi's Preface to the *Daxue* in the *Sishu zhangju.*

ji the first explicatory section (on making intentions *cheng* 誠) is TX3 which immediately follows the listing of the eight "particulars" and precedes the four sections of quotations.

(vi) The collection by Zhu Xi of all the material following the explicatory statement on "bringing peace to all under Heaven lies in bringing good order to the state" into a single long section (his DX Comm. 10). This corresponds to TX10–15 in the *Li ji* arrangement given. Sections TX12–15 do seem like a series of statements on ethical issues supplementary to those covered in the opening section and so somewhat divorced from the explication of the eight "particulars."

Zhu Xi's rearrangement, which became enshrined in the standard edition of the Four Books from the early Yuan period to the end of the Imperial period and, of course, is still present in modern editions of the SSZJ did, then, effect a significant change in how the *Taixue/Daxue* was viewed and how it was interpreted. On the first point, by identifying the opening section as "the Classic," directly attributed to Confucius, the work acquired much greater cachet. This considerably enhanced authority was very important in establishing the place of the *Taixue/Daxue* in the Confucian canon as the first of the Four Books and the gateway of entry into Confucian learning for the aspiring scholar. The issues of interpretation will be considered in the next section.

There can be no doubting the enduring impact of Zhu Xi's rearrangement. Not only did the Four Books, as defined by him, become the official version of the Confucian Classics but also translators almost invariably follow his arrangement in presenting the work to non-Chinese readers thus more or less obscuring the variations and controversy that existed in Chinese versions of the work. His rearrangement undoubtedly has a certain logic, and is conceptually attractive, especially for the scholar who intends to make a detailed and repeated study of the work so as to become fully imbued with its teaching, which was, of course, as Zhu Xi intended. What it lacks, as many later students of the work have pointed out, is any support from external historical and internal textual evidence.

Interpretation: In addition to the distinctive arrangements of the two versions, there are clear differences of interpretation reflected in the respective commentaries. In general terms, Zheng Xuan, whose commentary is the shortest, focuses primarily on explication of the meanings of specific characters and phrases, the assumption presumably being that once the difficulties presented by problematic characters are resolved, the meaning of the text itself will become clear. That is to say, Zheng Xuan takes a predominantly philological approach. Kong Yingda, whose commentary is the longest, echoes for the most part Zheng Xuan's views, but with considerable expansion, adding paraphrastic explanations of the text to the clarification of characters. He also includes a wealth of literary and historical detail as an aid to the understanding of the various references to people and events—that is, his is a literary-historical approach. Zhu Xi, whose commentary is midway in length between those of the two *Li ji* commentators, gives particular attention to the philosophical explanation of important passages, although by no means does he neglect the clarification of problematic characters. His is, however, primarily a philosophical approach. In examining these two main commentarial traditions, a significant difference in the interpretation of the text clearly emerges. This will be shown by a brief consideration of the two interpretations for each of the components of the text listed above.

(i) Principles & Particulars: The first component of the opening section is the statement of the three "principles." For the *Li ji* commentators, the first principle is to display enlightened virtue in one's own conduct. Although it is not made absolutely explicit, the clear implication is that this enlightened virtue is progressively acquired by assiduous attention to the programme of self-cultivation outlined in the remainder of the text and summarised in the eight "particulars." The second "principle" is to love or cherish the people, which obviously includes being attentive to both their moral well-being and their material needs, acting on the basis of the foundational ethical components—that is, *ren* 仁, *yi* 義 and *li* 禮. The third "principle," coming to rest in the utmost goodness, consists of attaining the attributes listed in the following sequence—in short, a stability and tranquility of mind which allows calm contemplation of the matters of day to day living, which in turn results in doing things in the proper way. The five components of the sequence listed are understood as follows by the *Li ji* commentators: *ding* 定 equates with having no doubt and being free from error; *jing* 靜 equates with not pursuing one's desires; *an* 安 equates with not being disturbed by one's emotions; *lü* 慮 equates with being able to give careful thought to matters; and *de* 得 equates with doing things in the right way, which may be taken to correspond to *yi* 義.

Zhu Xi's understanding of the three "principles" is fundamentally different. This is due primarily to a different concept of mind-heart and a different reading of *qin* 親 (i.e. as *xin* 新), following the Cheng brothers. For Zhu Xi, the original mind-heart of all people has a pure and unsullied innate virtue which, under normal circumstances, becomes obscured by the accretions of ordinary life (emotions, desires, matters of self-interest, etc.). *Ming ming de* 明明德 is to employ the programme of self-cultivation outlined in the following text to remove the stains of these impurities and allow the original brightness of the innate goodness of mind-heart to be revealed unblemished to the world. The process of restoring the original brightness, later exemplified by the polishing and cutting, and bathing metaphors, is then extended to other people, presumably by example. If this process is effectively carried out in oneself and effectively extended to others, one "abides" in the utmost goodness. In terms of the five components of the following sequence, this means that a person's intentions or thoughts have a stability of direction (*ding* 定) and the mind-heart does not take foolish action (*jing* 靜). It is, then, at rest and peaceful (*an* 安), so close attention can be given to managing affairs (*lü* 慮) and thus one attains (*de* 得) the proper place to rest, like the hill bird coming to rest in the foliage of the mountain trees. One particular difference that emerges from the two readings is that the *Li ji* version seems to be a programme for a ruler or prince, or at least for someone who assumes the pastoral care of others on a relatively large scale, whereas Zhu Xi's version suggests a programme applicable to any individual. The former may, then, be seen as "top down" in operation and the latter as "laterally diffusing."

The eight "particulars"—bringing peace to all under Heaven (*ping tianxia* 平天下), bringing good order to the state/country (*zhi guo* 治國), regulating the household/family (*qi jia* 齊家), cultivating the self (*xiu shen* 脩身), rectifying the mind-heart (*zheng xin* 正心), making intentions *cheng* (*cheng yi* 誠意), extending knowledge (*zhi zhi* 致知) and coming to/investigating things (*ge wu* 格物)—are set out as a sorites of eight components which is given both forwards and backwards. It is, however, explicitly stated in the text that cultivation of the self is fundamental. Indeed, it is obviously pivotal, since four of the particulars are aimed at bringing it about whilst the remaining three are dependent on it. The household can be regulated, the state brought to good order and all under Heaven pacified only by those who have achieved self-cultivation, as here defined. The *Li ji* commentators have relatively little to say about the sequence; more is given in the individual sections devoted to each particular. Zheng Xuan understands knowledge (*zhi* 知) in this context as " . . . knowing what the ends and beginnings of good and evil, good fortune and bad fortune, are." He equates the components of the problematic phrase *ge wu* 格物 with *lai* 來 and *shi* 事 respectively giving a meaning of "coming to things"—"if your knowledge of good is profound," he says, "then you come to good things; if your knowledge of evil is deep, then you come to bad things." Simply stated, knowledge of what is good, perhaps of goodness itself, results in good actions and the same with evil. Kong Yingda concurs on both points. A person bent on self-cultivation will then study and practise goodness, presumably using paradigms from the ancient literature and from direct experience.

Zhu Xi presents a clear, but somewhat different interpretation of the "particulars" and their sequence in his notes [4] & [5] on the Classic. The self is ruled by the mind-heart. *Yi* 意 (intentions, thoughts) are what the mind-heart sends forth. They are the outward manifestations of the inner state of the mind-heart—its "signature" as it were. *Cheng* 誠 is equivalent to *shi* 實 (real, true, genuine). That is, the intentions or thoughts are made or become real, true, genuine and sincere. The purpose of making intentions *cheng* 誠 is to become one with goodness and not to be deceptive in oneself—i.e. not to deceive either oneself or others. *Zhi* 知 is equivalent to *shi* 識 (to know, be acquainted with). In the phrase *ge wu* 格物, Zhu Xi equates *ge* 格 with *zhi* 至 (to reach, arrive at) rather than *lai* 來 (to come to), but is one with the *Li ji* commentators on taking *wu* 物 as *shi* 事. The important difference philosophically is the introduction of principle (*li* 理). What one must strive to know, whether in the events or in the things of the world, is, for Zhu Xi, principle. Further consideration on the interpretation of the "particulars" will be given in relation to the individual sections devoted to them.

On the final part of the section, which again involves a root/branch analogy, Zheng Xuan offers no comment. Kong Yingda identifies the root (or trunk) with the self and its cultivation. The branches are taken to represent intercourse with others. If the root is well ordered (i.e. the self is properly cultivated) then one treats others with respect, love and generosity. The converse applies if the root is in disorder. In the final sentence, which Zhu Xi transfers to his DX Comm. 5, Kong reiterates the earlier statement that the root is the self and, by extension, its cultivation, so knowing the root is to know the self which is the perfection or ultimate goal of knowledge.

(ii) Clarification of Particulars: The components of the sorites dealing with the interdependence of the eight "particulars" are not presented in an entirely systematic way. Thus, the first, relating extending or perfecting knowledge to the coming to, or investigating of, things/events, is not considered in the extant text but is "supplied" by Zhu Xi to fill a presumed lacuna as his DX Comm. 5. The second and third, the dependence of making intentions *cheng* 誠 on extending/perfecting knowledge and, in turn, the dependence of rectifying the mind-heart on making intentions *cheng* 誠, are not considered as such. Instead, there is specific consideration of making intentions *cheng* 誠 in other terms, this section being differently placed in the two versions. The remaining four components are each considered in separate sections following a similar opening statement—what is meant by X lies in Y—and these are placed consecutively in both texts.

Turning to the difference in interpretation between the two commentarial traditions, obviously the *Li ji* commentators have nothing to add to their comments to the initial statement (TX2) on the *ge wu* 格物/*zhi zhi* 致知 nexus. For Zhu Xi, however, it is important to elaborate on this foundational process which is the initial step in the process of self-cultivation. His statement, appended to the fragment moved from the end of TX2 to his DX Comm. 5, presents his ideas on this step. All people have knowledge; all things/events in the world have principle (*li* 理). The extension (*zhi* 致) of knowledge involves "approaching" these things/events and investigating principle in each of them. Perfecting or completing (*zhi* 至) knowledge lies in making this investigation exhaustive and complete. That is, if this process is extended over a sufficient time and carried out with sufficient diligence, a person will " . . . suddenly . . . come to understand how things are and will have a thoroughgoing comprehension of them." He concludes his comment on the presumed missing section as follows: " . . . for the multitude of things, what is manifest or hidden, what is fine or coarse, will, in all cases, be reached, and our minds in their whole substance and great workings will be entirely illuminated. This is what is meant by investigating things. This is what is meant by the perfecting of knowledge."

Zheng Xuan has little to say on the section about making intentions *cheng* 誠, offering only clarification of the three characters/phrases, *qian* 謙, *yan* 厭 and *yan hu* 嚴乎, which, he suggests, are to be read, respectively, as feeling justified or content (having an easy conscience), closing up or concealing, and being awe-inspiring. As usual, Kong Yingda provides more detail: " . . . with respect to making one's intentions *cheng* 誠, if one sees another person doing something good or bad, it is right that one must genuinely like or dislike it and not dissemble. It is not possible for the outward appearance to falsely display love or hate when the mind within does not truly love or hate. In both instances, one must be true and genuine (*cheng* 誠 and *shi* 實)."

Zhu Xi gives particular consideration to two other characters/phrases which present some difficulty in interpretation and, as a result, to translators: *zi qi* 自欺 and *du* 獨. On the first, the deception involves knowing that achieving goodness depends on eliminating evil and yet not being genuine or sincere in one's actions. As the section proceeds, it is clear that this is not self-deception in the usual sense. It is at least as much about deceiving others. In fact, being *cheng* 誠 is essentially about inner goodness, knowledge and truth being what is expressed and evident externally under all circumstances. On the second, *du* 獨, the issue is whether this refers simply to being alone physically, and therefore unobserved (as Kong Yingda takes it to be—Zheng Xuan makes no comment), or to some core element of the self, unknown and unknowable to others. Zhu Xi's two specific comments on this point are, first, "*du* 獨 is a place that others do not know but only the self knows" and, second, "nevertheless, his being true or not true is something others cannot get to know; it is something only he knows"—the latter, particularly, affords grounds for taking this to be the "inner self." As with the issue of deception, however, there is, in the development of the argument, the element of concealing what is bad in oneself. The person who is not *cheng* 誠 may allow bad conduct to be displayed if there is nobody to observe it or may feign good conduct in the presence of others to conceal his own inner badness. The fourth component, the dependence of self-cultivation on rectifying the mind-heart, elicits little comment from any of the three commentators. The key element in maintaining a rectified mind-heart is to avoid the disturbing effects of the emotions of whatever sort—happiness, sadness, anger, fear, etc. One possible minor point of difference between the two commentaries involves the reading of the character *zai* 在 in the phrase *xin bu zai yan* 心不在焉, although this is not the subject of specific comment. Kong Yingda appears to take the meaning of *zai* 在 as that of being engaged or involved in the activities subsequently listed whereas Zhu Xi clearly equates *zai* 在 with *cun* 存, presumably in the sense of "preserve" or "maintain."

On the fifth component, the dependence of regulation of the household on cultivation of the self, the difference between the commentaries depends on the different readings of the two characters *zhi* 之 and *pi* 辟. For both *Li ji* commentators, the reading of *zhi* 之 as *shi* 適 and *pi* 辟 as *pi* 譬 or *yu* 喻 makes the section about the role of comparison with others in the process of evaluating one's own self-cultivation, to which Kong Yingda adds an element of reciprocity. If one person compares himself to another and finds the latter lacks worth, and so dislikes him, he may expect the same response from another if he himself is not virtuous. On Zhu Xi's reading, which takes *zhi* 之 as *yu* 於 and *pi* 辟 as *pian* 偏, this is about the dangers of prejudice, whether positive or negative, in evaluating others or oneself. It is not about using others as yardsticks by which to evaluate one's own degree of self-cultivation. Examples of clouded judgement due to prejudice are a father's assessment of the goodness of his own son and a farmer's assessment of the size of his own grain.

On the sixth component, the dependence of bringing good order to the state on regulation of the household, both *Li ji* commentators place particular emphasis on the household under consideration being that of the ruler, in keeping with the overall impression that this is a tract about the training of those who will rule. Zhu Xi sets out the key elements of self-cultivation and regulation of the household as filial piety, fraternal respect and parental compassion, as in the text. These virtues are related, in the state, to the people, elders and the ruler and are manifest in the key virtues of *ren* 仁 (loving kindness) and *rang* 讓 (complaisance). On the final component, the dependence of bringing peace to all under Heaven on bringing good order to the state, there is no significant difference in interpretation between the two commentary traditions. Kong Yingda gives emphasis to the practical aspects of the ruler manifesting his self-cultivation in giving expression to the principle of reciprocity (here termed "the Way of measuring and modelling/squaring") in distributing materials to others and using worthy people, presumably in administrative roles. Zhu Xi again focusses on filial piety, fraternal respect and parental compassion, relating them to dealings with elders and those who are at a disadvantage.

(iii) Quotations: Of the twenty-five quotations, twelve are from the *Odes*, seven from the *Documents*, one from the *Lunyu*, and five from now-unknown sources. In considering the interpretation of these quotations, and particularly the differences between the two commentarial traditions, they may be divided into three groups. The first group comprises thirteen quotations (6 from the *Odes*, 4 from the *Documents*, 1 from the *Lunyu*, 1 attributed to Confucius but not from the *Lunyu* and 1 from an unknown source). In the *Li ji* version these quotations follow the section on making intentions *cheng* 誠 (TX 3) whereas, in Zhu Xi's version, they follow the opening statement of the "principles" and "particulars" that he attributes to Confucius. This different placement reflects the difference in interpretation. Zheng Xuan has relatively little to say about the quotations apart from the clarification of meaning of several characters. What he does have to say, and what Kong Yingda offers more extensively, suggests they should be read as examples of the beneficial effects of making intentions *cheng* 誠. Thus, in the long quotation from the "Qi ao" ode referring to King Wu, Kong finds, " . . . verification of the Way of making intentions *cheng* 誠" whilst on the three quotations from the *Documents* about manifesting virtue, he makes the following observation:

If you look within the winding bays of the Qi waters, they grow this striking green bamboo, which is luxuriant and abundant because of what it is imbued with by the Qi waters. It says that if you look within the Wei court, above there is Duke Wu himself, whose Way and virtue are glorious and abundant, which is also because of Kang Shu's abundance of merit. In quoting this, there is verification of the Way of making intentions *cheng* 誠. (TX4, Kong Yingda's commentary, 1.2)

Zhu Xi, however, clearly links these quotations with the opening statement of the three "principles." Furthermore, he divides all but the *Lunyu* quotation into three sections (DX Comm. 1–3), each section corresponding to one of the principles. The bathing metaphor in DX Comm. 2 is particularly apt for Zhu Xi's understanding of the process of wiping away the daily accretion of impurities which obscures the brightness of innate virtue, whether in oneself or, as a result of one's endeavours, in others. The quotation from the "Announcement to Kang" is also supportive of the reading of *qin* 親 (as in the *Li ji*) as *xin* 新 (as in the SSZJ). The final quotation in this group, that from the *Lunyu* on lawsuits, is taken by Zhu Xi as applying to the matter of root and branch, as the text itself indicates. The *Li ji* commentators, however, explicitly identify the root with making intentions *cheng* 誠.

The second group, comprising four quotations, pertains in both texts to the section on the dependence of bringing good order to the state on regulating the household (TX10, DX Comm. 9). The text identifies the key elements of the process as filial piety, fraternal respect and parental compassion, and the important ethical components as *ren* 仁 and *rang* 讓. Zheng Xuan offers only brief observations on the readings of characters in the quotations. Kong Yingda, as well as providing additional historical detail for the single *Documents* and the third *Odes* quotations, makes explicit the idea of the examples given in the quotations illustrating and exemplifying the process of people positively influencing the household or state through their own conduct—the young bride influencing the household, proper relations between brothers extending to the people more generally, and the ruler, by being exemplary in all his personal relationships, acting as a model and, as it were, a parent to the people of his state. Zhu Xi's reading is essentially similar. He makes the observation that the quotations support the idea of the importance of *ren* 仁 and *rang* 讓 and that, if there is good in oneself, one can seek good in others whilst, if one is free of evil, one can correct it in others.

The third group of eight quotations (3 *Odes*, 3 *Documents*, 2 unknown) follows the final section in explication of the dependence of bringing peace to all under Heaven on bringing good order to the state. In the *Li ji* version, the first two quotations are directly connected with this section (TX11). On these first two *Odes* quotations, Zheng Xuan offers only comments on the reading of certain characters and the observation that the rocky precipitous cliff is a metaphor for the imposing Grand Master Yin, a leading official under King You. Kong Yingda relates the first quotation, on the ruler as parent to the people, to the Way of measuring and modelling/squaring (i.e. the principle of reciprocity). By being in accord with, even determining, what the people desire, if this is an influence for good, it is an expression of the ruler's parental compassion for the people. Kong suggests that concrete examples of this are " . . . making issue from the public granaries, making bestowals on the poor and impoverished, and offering relief to those who are isolated and in want." This calls to mind the second of the three "principles"—the ruler loving and cherishing the people in the *Li ji* reading. Zhu Xi's interpretation of the first two *Odes* quotations is similar. The ruler, as parent to the people, must evaluate what is in their hearts and make it like the goodness in his own heart. This carries the responsibility of being especially careful about what is in his own heart so he can be a good example. He cannot allow himself to indulge in private dislikes and prejudices.

The next four quotations are taken, in the *Li ji* interpretation (TX12), to relate particularly to the conduct of the ruler. The way of bringing good order to the state is for the ruler to value virtue and despise wealth *per se*. If the ruler is virtuous, the material well-being of his people will automatically follow his virtuous conduct. If, on the other hand, he indulges in the greedy pursuit of wealth, this will result in contention among the people and will ultimately lead to the ruler's own downfall in the more extreme cases—hence the quotations on gaining and maintaining, or losing, Heaven's mandate. What is precious is goodness and *ren* 仁, not wealth, as the two quotations from unknown sources affirm. Both *Li ji* commentators, but particularly Kong Yingda, devote their attention primarily to the historical background of the quoted material. Of the last two of the eight quotations in the third group, the first is a long quotation from the *Documents*—"The Declaration of Qin" (TX13). Again, Zheng Xuan gives detailed consideration to several of the characters as well as some historical background. Kong Yingda expands on the historical background and relates the quotation to other early texts. Basically, the quotation is seen as being illustrative of the Great Way which is implemented through filial piety, fraternal respect and parental compassion, and by devotion to *ren* 仁 and *yi* 義. On the final quotation, from an unknown source referring to Master Meng Xian (TX15), both *Li ji* commentators focus particularly on the social and historical background.

Zhu Xi has little to say on the first two *Odes* quotations (DX Comm. 10.1). He observes that they are about those who are superiors or rulers having a mind-heart that it is in accord with the minds and hearts of the people. Such rulers and superiors can then be a model for the people—they are men who can be respected and revered. They cannot follow their own prejudices—either likes or dislikes. If they love the people like their own children the people, in turn, will love them like their own parents. On the four quotations in TX12 (his DX Comm. 10.2), Zhu Xi, in contrast to the *Li ji* commentators, pays little attention to the historical details referred to. He does, however, provide sources and some considerations on the reading of several characters. His main focus is on the meaning of the passages: the superior or ruler must be able to "measure and square" properly and avoid prejudice due to his own likes and dislikes. On the two quotations from unknown sources, he suggests they are to be taken as clarifying the meaning of not making the root external or secondary and the branches internal or primary. With respect to the final two quotations, for the first (from the *Documents*) his concern is about the reading of several characters. In this, he is similar to Zheng Xuan, and his readings are similar too. His comments on the final quotation, attributed to Master Meng Xian, are aimed entirely at the clarification of meaning.

(iv) Additional Statements: In the arrangement of the *Li ji* text that follows, these are the four final sections. Zhu Xi includes them all in his DX Comm. 10, which deals with the relationship between bringing good order to the state and peace to all under Heaven.[12] The first of these statements comprises four quotations (one from the *Odes*, two from the *Documents* and one from an unknown source) dealing, respectively, with virtue (*de* 德), goodness (*shan* 善) and *ren* 仁. Zheng Xuan focuses particularly on the meaning of certain characters but does make brief statements about the no longer extant work, the *Documents of Chu* and about Jiu Fan, the subject of the third quotation. Kong Yingda gives consideration to the meaning of each statement and adds historical, literary and biographical information on the second and third quotations. The second statement follows a quotation from the *Documents* and focuses on *ren* 仁. Zheng Xuan again concerns himself primarily with the clarification of characters but also restates the basic message: a man who

---

12   We have subdivided this section (DX Comm. 10.1–DX Comm. 10.5) to facilitate comparison with the *Li ji* text.

is *ren* 仁 can embrace those who are good and able, and reject those who are the opposite. Kong Yingda, in considering particularly the matter of the ruler advancing those who are worthy, provides historical detail related to the quotation. He, too, reiterates the central theme: the man who is *ren* 仁 loves the good person and abhors the bad person. Zhu Xi gives consideration to the readings of certain characters, in particular *zhong* 忠 (to manifest and exert oneself to the utmost) and *xin* 信 (to comply with things and not oppose them). His interpretation of the overall meaning is essentially the same as that of the *Li ji* commentators—to be a true man of *ren* 仁 a person must " . . . fully commit himself to the path of love and hate." That is, he must love the good and worthy and he must abhor the bad and unworthy.

The third statement concerns the relationship between *ren* 仁 and *yi* 義, as seen in terms of wealth. The right way to amass material wealth is to be diligent in production but restrained in use. The man (particularly the ruler) who builds up wealth in this way is exemplifying *ren* 仁, the display of which will elicit *yi* 義 (right action) from his subordinates. Again, there are no significant differences between the three commentators, although there is some variation in the chief point of focus. As Zhu Xi makes clear, the man/ruler who is *ren* 仁 disperses wealth and gains the people whereas the man/ruler who is not *ren* 仁 harms himself in the pursuit of material possessions. The superior or ruler loves and embraces *ren* 仁 and cherishes his inferiors and subordinates. In return, his inferiors love and are loyal to their superior, so affairs come to fulfilment.

The fourth and final additional statement is about the relationship between *yi* 義 (right action, righteousness) and *li* 利 (benefit, profit) beginning with a quotation from an unknown source attributed to the Lu grandee, Master Meng Xian. Both *Li ji* commentators give some attention to the identity of Meng Xian and, in Kong Yingda's case, provide other historical information. The point of the example for Kong is that someone who wishes to be a good ruler for a state must concentrate on *ren* 仁 and *yi* 義 and not on material wealth. Zhu Xi expands on this. What is fundamental lies in unifying the likes and dislikes of the people and not having individuals pursue a path of self-interest. What is of benefit (*li* 利) is *yi* 義 (right action) and not *li* 利 as profit.

Concluding Remarks: In summary, then, from the time of compilation of the *Li ji* (presumed to be sometime during the Eastern Han period) until the early Tang, the *Li ji* version of the *Taixue/Daxue* was the only version of this short text. During this time, the understanding of the text was aided predominantly by the interlinear commentary of Zheng Xuan, which focused particularly on the meaning of certain characters, although there is evidence of other studies no longer extant. In the early Tang, Zheng Xuan's commentary was supplemented by the much more extensive commentary attributed to Kong Yingda,[13] which added further philological detail, paraphrastic explanation of virtually every sentence, and a wealth of literary and historical information, especially in relation to the quotations. It is this version, with Zheng Xuan's interlinear commentary and Kong Yingda's subcommentary, preserved in the *Li ji zhengyi* 禮記正義 which is contained in the *Shisanjing zhushu* 十三經注疏 (SSJZS), first compiled in 1816 and most recently published in 46 volumes with punctuation and additional notes in 2001.[14] This is the text used for the *Li ji* version in the present translation.

Beginning with the writings of Han Yu 韓愈 (768–824) and Li Ao 李翱 (774–836) in the Tang and continuing with the work of the Song Neo-Confucians, a major change occurred in both the degree of focus on, and the interpretation of, the *Taixue/Daxue*. This change culminated in Zhu Xi's SSZJ version which included a major rearrangement of the text, a substantial increase in its authority brought about by identifying the central statement of principles and particulars as being due to Confucius himself, and the replacement of the earlier commentaries with his own detailed and heavily philosophical commentary. The elevated status of the work was signalled by its inclusion in the Four Books that shortly thereafter became the foundation of the Civil Service examinations,[15] and so they remained until the end of the Imperial period. Apart from the issues of attribution and arrangement, among other key points of difference, brought out by presentation of the two versions side-by-side, are the concepts of virtue and goodness—that is, whether these qualities are innate or acquired—the introduction of "principle" (*li* 理) into the analysis, and the particular emphasis on the "investigation of things" (*ge wu* 格物). These and other issues remained controversial during the centuries that followed, stimulated by the greatly increased focus on the work itself. In this regard, mention may be made of men such as Wang Yangming 王陽明 (Wang

---

[13]   This was as part of the project initiated by Tai Zong 太宗 in 638 under the overall direction of Yan Shigu 顏師古 (581–645) to prepare new commentaries on the Classics—the *Wujing zhengyi* 五經正義. It was a collective undertaking although it is Kong Yingda's name that appears associated with the commentary on the *Li ji*.

[14]   The *Shisanjing zhushu* 十三經注疏 was compiled under the direction of Ruan Yuan 阮元 (1764–1849) using the Song editions of the Thirteen Classics. It was first published in the 21st year of the *Jiaqing* 嘉慶 reign period (i.e. 1816).

[15]   See note 1 above.

Shouren 王守仁—1472–1529), Wang Fuzhi 王夫之 (1619–1692), Chen Que 陳確 (1604–1677) and Mao Qiling 毛奇齡 (1623–1716) among others.

Whilst there is no question that Zhu Xi's revision gave a new significance to the text and provided readings and interpretations that were different to the traditional *Li ji* version, the fundamental ethical teaching of the work is the same in the two versions. The differences, then, lie in the details. In essence, this teaching is that the primary aim (or aims) of ethical education, to be realised by the noble man (*junzi* 君子), is to become a paragon of virtue. Such a man will manifest enlightened or luminous virtue, whether this is by developing an inherent capacity for virtue to the maximum or by continously and assiduously removing obscuring factors from an innate, unblemished virtue. By doing this he can influence others to model themselves on him. The consequence, eminently desirable, will be peace and order at all levels of society.

The final words may be left to Legge, who produced the first detailed bilingual version of this treatise, a work which still remains one of the best versions, the somewhat archaic phraseology, the passage of time, and the barbs of criticism notwithstanding.

> The Treatise has undoubtedly great merits, but they are not to be sought in the severity of its logical processes, or the large-minded prosecution of any course of thought. We shall find them in the announcement of certain seminal principles, which, if recognised in government and the regulation of conduct, would conduce greatly to the happiness and virtue of mankind. . . . The Work which contains those principles cannot be thought meanly of. They are "commonplace" as the writer in the Chinese Repository[16] calls them, but at the same time they are eternal verities.[17]

---

[16] *The Chinese Repository*, 20 vols., Canton, China, 1832–1851.
[17] LCC, 1:33–34.

Taixue 太學: The Highest Learning

Notes 注: Zheng Xuan 鄭玄

Commentary 疏: Kong Yingda 孔穎達

大學：禮記 42

陸曰：「<u>鄭</u>云：『《大學》者，以其記博學，可以為政也。』」

疏(<u>孔穎達</u>)：《正義》曰：案鄭《目錄》云：「名曰《大學》者，以其記博學，可以為政也。此於《別錄》屬〈通論〉。」此《大學》之篇，論學成之事，能治其國，章明其德於天下，卻本明德所由，先從誠意為始。

The Highest Learning: *Taixue*

Lu [Deming] states: "Zheng [Xuan] says, 'In regard to the *Taixue*, with this record of wide learning it is possible to carry out government.'"

Commentary (Kong Yingda): The *Zhengyi* states that Zheng's *Mulu* says: "What is called the *Taixue*, through its recording of wide learning, can be used to conduct government. In the *Bielu*, this is included in the 'Tonglun.'"[1] This work, the *Taixue*, discusses the matters of bringing learning to completion, of being able to bring good order to one's state, of clearly displaying one's virtue in the world, and further, that the way of enlightened virtue starts from making intentions *cheng* 誠 (pure, genuine and sincere) as the beginning.

---

[1] The work in question is Zheng Xuan's *San Li mulu* 三禮目錄—see, for example the *Xinyi Li ji duben*, 869. The second work referred to is Liu Xiang's 劉向 *Bielu* 別綠, unfortunately no longer extant.

TX1: 大學之道，在明明德，在親民，在止於至善。知止而后有定，定而后能靜，靜而后能安，安而后能慮，慮而后能得。物有本末，事有終始。知所先後，則近道矣。**[1]**

Comment: This opening section is a concise statement of the three fundamental aims (the principles) in the programme of self-cultivation advocated in this text: allow one's natural and perfect virtue to shine forth clear and unclouded by emotions and desires, love the people, and settle oneself in a state of perfect (or the highest or utmost) goodness. These three components of the Way of the highest learning allow calm contemplation of the nature of the external world, both the things and the events within it, and therefore give rise to appropriate conduct. No position is taken, in either text or commentary, on whether the *ming de* 明德 (enlightened virtue) is innate or acquired. The other point of note is Zheng Xuan's comment on the pronunciation of 大 as *tai* and thus the reading as *tai* 太 indicating the superlative—see the introductory discussion on the title.

注 TX1 (鄭玄)

[1]「明明德」，謂顯明其至德也。止，猶自處也。得，謂得事之宜也。大，舊音泰，{劉直帶反。}近，附近之近。

疏 TX1 (孔穎達)

1.1　《正義》曰：此經大學之道，在於明明德，在於親民，在止於至善。積德而行，則近於道也。

1.2　「在明明德」者，言「大學之道」，在於章明己之光明之德。謂身有明德，而更章顯之，此其一也。

1.3　「在親民」者，言大學之道，在於親愛於民，是其二也。

1.4　「在止於至善」者，言大學之道，在止處於至善之行，此其三也。言大學之道，在於此三事矣。

1.5　「知止而后有定」者，更覆說「止於至善」之事。既知「止於至善」，而后心能有定，不有差貳也。

1.6　「定而后能靜」者，心定無欲，故能靜不躁求也。「靜而后能安」者，以靜故情性安和也。

---

*　Text from the classical commentaries in { } brackets primarily contains pronunciation guides for certain Chinese characters; this has been omitted in the English translation.

TX1: The Way of highest learning lies in displaying enlightened virtue; it lies in loving the people; it lies in coming to rest in the utmost goodness. Know [where] to come to rest, and afterwards there is stability; be stable, and afterwards there can be calmness; be calm, and afterwards there can be tranquility; be tranquil, and afterwards there can be contemplation; be contemplative, and afterwards things can be done in the proper way. Things have roots and branches; matters have ends and beginnings. Know what is first and what follows; then you come near to the Way. **[1]**

Notes TX1 (Zheng Xuan)

[1] *Ming ming de* 明明德 speaks of clearly displaying one's perfect virtue. *Zhi* 止 is like *zi chu* 自處 (being naturally at rest in, accepting one's position). *De* 得 refers to doing things in the proper way. The old pronunciation of *da* 大 was *tai* 泰 . . . *Jin* 近 is the *jin* of *fujin* 附近 (come near to, approach).

Commentary TX1 (Kong Yingda)

1.1   The *Zhengyi* says: "This classic's Way of highest learning lies in displaying enlightened virtue, in loving the people, and in coming to rest in the utmost goodness. If you accumulate virtue and put it into practice, then you come near to the Way.

1.2   *Lies in displaying enlightened virtue*: This says that the Way of highest learning lies in clearly displaying the radiance of one's virtue. This refers to having enlightened virtue oneself, and, moreover, displaying and manifesting it. This is its (i.e. the Way's) first component.

1.3   *Lies in loving the people*: This says that the Way of highest learning lies in being loving towards the people. This is its second component.

1.4   *Lies in coming to rest in the utmost goodness*: This says that the Way of highest learning lies in stopping and coming to rest in the the practice of the utmost goodness. This is its third component. That is to say, the Way of highest learning lies in these three things.

1.5   *Know [where] to come to rest, and afterwards there is stability* repeats the statement of the matter of *coming to rest in the utmost goodness*. When you know to come to rest in perfect goodness, and afterwards the mind can have stability, there is neither error nor doubt.

1.6   *Be stable, and afterwards there can be calmness*: If the mind is stable and without desires, there can be calmness without the press of seeking. *Be calm, and afterwards there can be tranquility*: By being calm, the emotions and nature are tranquil and harmonious.

1.7 「安而后能慮」者，情既安和，能思慮於事也。

1.8 「慮而后能得」者，既能思慮，然後於事得宜也。

1.9 「物有本末，事有終始」者，若於事得宜，而天下萬物有本有末，經營百事有終有始也。

1.10 「知所先後」者，既能如此，天下百事萬物，皆識知其先後也。

1.11 「則近道矣」者，若能行此諸事，則附近於大道矣。

TX2: 古之欲明明德於天下者，先治其國。欲治其國者，先齊其家。欲齊其家者，先脩其身。欲脩其身者，先正其心。欲正其心者，先誠其意。欲誠其意者，先致其知。**[1]**致知在格物。**[2]**物格而后知至，知至而后意誠，意誠而后心正，心正而后身脩，身脩而后家齊，家齊而后國治，國治而后天下平。自天子以至於庶人，壹是皆以脩身為本。其本亂而末治者否矣。其所厚者薄，而其所薄者厚，未之有也。此謂知本，此謂知之至也。**[3]**

Comment: These are the eight steps (the particulars) on the path to the primary objective for the noble man—"displaying enlightened virtue"—set out as "descending" and "ascending" sequences pivoting around *ge wu* 格物 (coming to things). By following the sequences through assiduous practice, the noble man (*junzi* 君子) not only manifests enlightened virtue but also brings about (or contributes to, depending on his position) peace in the world. The root of this process is cultivation of the self, which should be the aim of all people. The understanding of the brief statement "perfecting knowledge lies in coming to things" is something of a problem and became a matter of increasing importance in later analyses of this work. Zheng Xuan is clear about the reading of the two key words, *ge* 格 and *wu* 物. Based on this, Kong Yingda makes his interpretation quite explicit, this being, essentially, that good results follow good actions and the converse. The other point of note is the position of the final sentence, which may be appropriately placed here as a summarising statement or may, indeed, be misplaced, as Zhu Xi has argued.

1.7 *Be tranquil, and afterwards there can be contemplation*: When the emotions are tranquil and harmonious, you are able to give thought and contemplation to matters.

1.8 *Be contemplative, and afterwards things can be done in the proper way*: When you are able to think and contemplate, afterwards you attain appropriateness in matters (i.e. you do things in the proper way).

1.9 *Things have roots and branches; matters have ends and beginnings*: If you attain appropriateness in matters and the ten thousand things of the world have roots and branches, there are ends and beginnings in carrying out the hundred matters.

1.10 *Know what is first and what follows*: If you can be like this, then you recognise and know in all cases what is first and what follows in the hundred matters and the ten thousand things of the world.

1.11 *Then you come near to the Way*: If you are able to do these several things, then you come near to the Great Way.

TX2: The ancients, in wishing to display enlightened virtue in the world, first brought good order to their states. Wishing to bring good order to their states, they first regulated their households. Wishing to regulate their households, they first cultivated themselves. Wishing to cultivate themselves, they first rectified their minds. Wishing to rectify their minds, they first made their intentions *cheng* 誠 (sincere, genuine, pure). Wishing to make their intentions *cheng* 誠, they first perfected their knowledge. [1] Perfecting knowledge lies in coming to things. [2] Come to things, and subsequently knowledge is perfected. Make knowledge perfect, and subsequently intentions are made *cheng* 誠. Make intentions *cheng* 誠, and subsequently the mind is rectified. Rectify the mind, and subsequently the self is cultivated. Cultivate the self, and subsequently the household is regulated. Regulate the household, and subsequently the state is brought to good order. Bring good order to the state, and subsequently the world is at peace. From the Son of Heaven down to the ordinary people everyone without exception should take cultivation of the self as the root. It is not possible for this root to be in disorder but the branches to be well ordered. It should never be the case that what is important is trivialised or what is trivial is given importance. This is called knowing the root; this is called the perfection of knowledge. [3]

注 TX2 (鄭玄)

[1] 知，謂知善惡吉凶之所終始也。{其知如字，徐音智，下「致知」同。}

[2] 格，來也。物，猶事也。其知於善深則來善物，其知於惡深則來惡物，言事緣人所好來也。此「致」或為「至」。{格，古百反。好，呼報反。}

[3] 壹是，專行是也。{治，國治，並直吏反，下同。}

疏 TX2 (孔穎達)

1.1　「古之欲明明德於天下」者，前章言大學之道在明德、親民、止善，覆説止善之事既畢，故此經明明德之理。

1.2　「先治其國」者，此以積學能為明德盛極之事，以漸到。今本其初，故言欲章明己之明德，使偏於天下者，先須能治其國。

1.3　「欲治其國者，先齊其家」也。「欲齊其家者，先脩其身」，言若欲齊家，先須脩身也。

1.4　「欲脩其身者，先正其心」，言若欲脩身，必先正其心也。

1.5　「欲正其心者，先誠其意」者，揔包萬慮謂之為心，情所意念謂之意。若欲正其心使無傾邪，必須先至誠，在於憶念也。若能誠實其意，則心不傾邪也。

1.6　「欲誠其意者，先致其知」者，言欲精誠其己意，先須招致其所知之事，言初始必須學習，然後乃能有所知曉其成敗，故云「先致其知」也。

Notes TX2 (Zheng Xuan)

[1] *Zhi* 知 refers to knowing what the ends and beginnings of good and evil, good fortune and bad fortune are. . . .

[2] *Ge* 格 is equivalent to *lai* 來 (to come, arrive). *Wu* 物 is like *shi* 事 (matters, things, affairs). If one's knowledge of good is profound, then one comes to good things. If one's knowledge of evil is deep, then one comes to bad things, which is to say that matters (things) come about as a result of what people love. This *zhi* 致 is probably to be taken as *zhi* 至. . . .

[3] *Yi shi* 壹是 is to act only in this way. . . .

Commentary TX2 (Kong Yingda)

1.1   *The ancients, in wishing to display enlightened virtue in the world*: The previous chapter states that the Way of highest learning lies in displaying virtue, loving the people, and coming to rest in goodness. The reiteration of the matter of coming to rest in goodness stops here. Therefore, this is the classic's principle of displaying enlightened virtue.

1.2   *First brought good order to their states*: This takes the matter of the accumulation of learning being able to achieve the highest degree of enlightened virtue as something that is gradually reached. Now the root is its beginning, therefore it says that, in wishing to display and manifest one's enlightened virtue and allow it to spread throughout the world, one must first be able to bring order to one's state.

1.3   *Wishing to bring good order to their states, they first regulated their households* [and] *wishing to regulate their households, they first cultivated themselves*: This says that, if someone wishes to regulate his household, he must first cultivate himself.

1.4   *Wishing to cultivate themselves, they first rectified their minds*: This says that, if someone wishes to cultivate himself, he must first rectify his mind.

1.5   *Wishing to rectify their minds, they first made their intentions cheng* 誠: What combines and includes the ten thousand thoughts is called "mind" whilst what the emotions bring to thought are called "intentions." If someone wishes to rectify his mind so that it is without deviation and depravity, he must first reach perfect *cheng* 誠, which lies in reflection and thought. If he is truly able to make his intentions *cheng* 誠, then his mind will not deviate and be depraved.

1.6   *Wishing to make their intentions cheng* 誠, *they first perfected their knowledge*: This says that someone who wishes to make his intentions pure (*jing* 精), genuine and sincere (*cheng* 誠), must first attend to the matter of knowledge. That is to say, he must start with study and practice. Subsequently he can have a clear understanding of his successes and failures. Therefore, it says: *They first perfected their knowledge*.

2.1　「致知在格物」，此經明初以致知，積漸而大至明德。前經從盛以本初，此經從初以至盛，上下相結也。「致知在格物」者，言若能學習招致所知。格，來也。己有所知，則能在於來物。若知善深則來善物，知惡深則來惡物。言善事隨人行善而來應之，惡事隨人行惡亦來應之。言善惡之來緣人所好也。

3.1　「物格而后知至」者，物既來，則知其善惡所至。善事來，則知其至於善；若惡事來，則知其至於惡。既能知至，則行善不行惡也。

3.2　「知至而后意誠」，既能知至，則意念精誠也。

3.3　「意誠而后心正」者，意能精誠，故能心正也。

3.4　「國治而后天下平」者，則上「明明德於天下」，是以自天子至庶人皆然也。

3.5　「壹是皆以脩身為本」者，言上從天子，下至庶人，貴賤雖異，所行此者專一，以脩身為本。上言誠意、正心、齊家、治國，今皆獨云「脩身為本」者，細則雖異，其大略皆是脩身也。

3.6　「其本亂而末治者否矣」，本亂，謂身不脩也。末治，謂國家治也。言己身既不脩，而望家國治者否矣。否，不也。言不有此事也。

2.1 *Perfecting knowledge lies in coming to things*: This section makes it clear that in beginning to perfect knowledge there is a gradual accumulation, and, when knowledge is substantial, it reaches enlightened virtue. The previous section goes from great to taking the root as the beginning; this section goes from the beginning to reaching what is great, the former and the latter being interrelated. *Perfecting knowledge lies in coming to things*: This says that, if you are able to study and practise, this brings about perfection in what you know. *Ge* 格 is equivalent to *lai* 來 (to come, arrive). On the basis of what you know, you are able to be involved in coming to things. If you know good profoundly, then you come to good things; if you know evil profoundly, then you come to bad things. That is to say, good things follow a person doing good and come as a response to this whilst bad things follow a person acting badly and also come as a response to this. This says that good and bad come about as a result of what people love.

3.1 *Come to things, and subsequently knowledge is perfected*: When you already come to things, then knowledge of their being good or bad is what is perfected. If good things come, then you know that they come from goodness; if bad things come, you know they come from badness. If you are able to perfect knowledge, then you do good things and not bad things.

3.2 *Make knowledge perfect, and subsequently intentions are cheng* 誠: When you are able to perfect your knowledge, then intentions and thoughts are pure and sincere.

3.3 *Make intentions cheng* 誠, *and subsequently the mind is rectified*: If intentions can be pure and sincere, then you can rectify your mind.

3.4 *Bring good order to the state, and subsequently the world is at peace*: Then above [there is] *displayed enlightened virtue in the world*:[2] This applies uniformly from the Son of Heaven down to the ordinary people.

3.5 *Everyone without exception should take cultivation of the self as the root*: This says that from the Son of Heaven above to the common people below, although there are differences of nobility and baseness, in their doing this they should be as one—that is, in taking cultivation of the self to be the root. Before, it says make intentions *cheng* 誠, rectify the mind, regulate the household, and bring good order to the state. Now all these come down to saying that *cultivation of the self is the root*. Although there are differences in the finer points, the overall position is that all affirm cultivation of the self.

3.6 *It is not possible for the root to be in disorder but the branches to be well ordered*: The root being disordered refers to the self not being cultivated. The branches being well ordered refers to state and household being well ordered. That is to say, if your own self is not cultivated, you cannot expect the household and state to be well ordered. *Fou* 否 is equivalent to *bu* 不. That is to say, this state of affairs cannot be.

---

2 Kong Yingda offers no comment on the three intervening stages—rectifying the mind, cultivating the self and regulating the household.

3.7 「其所厚者薄,而其所薄者厚,未之有也」者,此覆説「本亂而末治否矣」
     之事也。譬若與人交接,應須敦厚以加於人。今所厚之處,乃以輕薄,
     謂以輕薄待彼人也。「其所薄者厚」,謂己既與彼輕薄,欲望所薄之處以
     厚重報己,未有此事也。言己以厚施人,人亦厚以報己也。若己輕薄施
     人,人亦輕薄報己,言事厚之與薄皆以身為本也。

3.8 「此謂知本,此謂知之至也」者,本,謂身也。既以身為本,若能自知其
     身,是「知本」也,是知之至極也。

TX3: 所謂誠其意者,毋自欺也,如惡惡臭,如好好色,此之謂自謙。
故君子必慎其獨也。小人閒居為不善,無所不至,見君子而后厭然,揜
其不善,而著其善。人之視己,如見其肺肝,然則何益矣?此謂誠於中
形於外,故君子必慎其獨也。[1]曾子曰:「十目所視,十手所指,其嚴
乎?」富潤屋,德潤身,心廣體胖,故君子必誠其意。[2]

Comment: This section is about the clarification of what is meant by *cheng* 誠 and what
being *cheng* 誠 entails. It is a process applied to, or a quality predicated of *yi* 意. Both
terms, *cheng* 誠 and *yi* 意, are somewhat contentious and variously rendered in English.
We have taken *yi* 意 to indicate intentions taken as the "output" of the mental faculty
responsible for initiating the volitional component of conduct. That is, the actions of
the will have external perceptible consequences, which is not necessarily the case with
thoughts. To *cheng* 誠 one's intentions is, then, to make them pure, genuine and sincere.
A further point of contention is the meaning of *du* 獨 in this context—whether it simply
means being alone and unobserved, as the early commentators clearly thought, or
whether it refers to some essential and idiosyncratic component of the self (one's selfhood,
uniqueness). Zengzi is, by tradition, the author of the *Taixue* (*Daxue*).

3.7 *It should never be the case that what is important is trivialised or what is trivial is given importance* reiterates the statement of the fact that, *if the root is in disorder, the branches cannot be well ordered.* For example, in intercourse with others you must be more sincere and honest than other people. Now if instead of being generous, you are disrespectful and mean, this is referred to as being disrespectful and mean in the treatment of others. *What is trivial is given importance* refers to you being disrespectful and mean towards others but wishing and expecting, in place of this disrespect and meanness, to be treated generously in return—such things never happen. That is to say, if you treat others generously and well, then others will, in return, treat you generously and well. If you are disrespectful and mean in treating others, then others will also be disrespectful and mean to you in return. That is to say, the matters of generosity (importance) and meanness (triviality) are both due to the self as the root.

3.8 *This is called knowing the root; this is called the perfection of knowledge*: The root refers to the self. Now taking the self to be the root, if you are able to have self-knowledge, this is *knowing the root*. This is the very perfection of knowledge.

TX3: What is called making one's intentions *cheng* 誠 (pure, genuine, sincere) is not to be deceptive in oneself—it is like hating a bad smell or loving a beautiful sight. This is called being content in oneself. Therefore, the noble man must be cautious when he is alone. The lesser man, when living alone, acts in ways that are not good; there are no lengths to which he will not go. When he sees a noble man, he dissembles, concealing his bad points and revealing his good points. But if, when others look at him, it is as though they see his very lungs and liver, then how is this of benefit? This is called *cheng* 誠 within being manifest without. Therefore, the noble man must be cautious when he is alone. [1] Zengzi said: "It is what ten eyes see; it is what ten hands point to—this is awe-inspiring!" Wealth enriches a house; virtue enriches the self. When the mind is broad, the body flourishes. Therefore, the noble man must make his intentions *cheng* 誠. [2]

注 TX3 (鄭玄)

[1] 謙，讀為慊，慊之言厭也。厭，讀為黶，黶，閉藏貌也。{毋音無。惡惡，上烏路反，下如字。臭，昌救反。好好，上呼報反，下如字。謙，依注讀為慊，徐苦簟反。閒音閑。厭，讀為黶，烏斬反，又烏簟反。揜，於檢反。著，張慮反，注同。肺，芳廢反。肝音干。言厭，於琰反，一音於涉反。}

[2] 嚴乎，言可畏敬也。胖，猶大也。三者，言有實於內，顯見於外。{胖，步丹反，注及下同。見，賢遍反。}

疏 TX3 (孔穎達)

1.1 「所謂誠其意」者，自此以下，至「此謂知本」，³ 廣明誠意之事。此一節明誠意之本，先須慎其獨也。

1.2 「毋自欺也」，言欲精誠其意，無自欺誑於身，言於身必須誠實也。

1.3 「如惡惡臭」者，謂臭穢之氣，謂見此惡事人嫌惡之，如人嫌臭穢之氣，心實嫌之，口不可道矣。

1.4 「如好好色」者，謂見此善事而愛好之，如以人好色，心實好之，口不可道矣。言誠其意者，見彼好事、惡事，當須實好、惡之，不言而自見，不可外貌詐作好、惡，而內心實不好、惡也。皆須誠實矣。

1.5 「此之謂自謙」者，謙，讀如慊，慊然安靜之貌。心雖好、惡而口不言，應自然安靜也。「見君子而后厭然，揜其不善，而著其善」者，謂小人獨居，無所不為，見君子而後乃厭然閉藏其不善之事，宣著所行善事也。

---

3   The final sentence of TX7.

Notes TX3 (Zheng Xuan)

[1] *Qian* 謙 is read as *qie* 慊, which is to say *yan* 厭 (to feel justified and content, have an easy conscience). *Yan* 厭 is read as *yan* 厭. *Yan* 厭 is the appearance of closing up and concealing (*bi cang* 閉藏). . . .

[2] *Yan hu* 嚴乎 says he can be awe-inspiring (*weijing* 畏敬). *Pan* 胖 is like *da* 大 (i.e. big). The three things speak of the truth (genuineness, reality) that is within being manifest outwardly. . . .

Commentary TX3 (Kong Yingda)

1.1   *What is called making one's intentions cheng* 誠 *(pure, genuine, sincere)*: From this point down to this is called knowing the root, expands and clarifies the matter of making intentions *cheng* 誠. This particular section makes it clear that the foundation of making one's intentions *cheng* 誠 is that one must first be careful when one is alone.

1.2   *Is not to be deceptive in oneself* says that, in wishing to make one's intentions pure and *cheng* 誠, one should not cheat and deceive oneself; that is to say, in oneself, one must be true and genuine (*cheng* 誠 and *shi* 實).

1.3   *Like hating a bad smell* refers to a foul odour which is to say that, if you see this person who does something evil, dislike and hate him like a person would hate the odour of a foul smell—[that is], the mind truly dislikes it and the mouth cannot express it.

1.4   *[Like] loving a beautiful sight* says that, if you see something good and you like it, it is like a person loves a beautiful sight—the mind truly loves it, and the mouth cannot express it. That is to say, with respect to making one's intentions *cheng* 誠, if one sees another person doing something good or bad, it is right that one must genuinely like or dislike it and not dissemble, for it is not possible for the outward appearance to falsely display love or hate when the mind within does not truly love or hate. In both instances, one must be true and genuine (*cheng* 誠 and *shi* 實).

1.5   *This is called being content in oneself*: *Qian* 謙 is read as *qie* 慊 (contented, happy). *Qieran* 慊然 is the appearance of peace and tranquility. Although the mind loves or hates, nevertheless the mouth does not give expression to this. Therefore, the self is at peace and tranquil. *When he sees a noble man, he dissembles, concealing his bad points and revealing his good points*: This says that when the lesser man dwells alone, there is nothing which he does not do. But if he sees a noble man then, in a dissembling manner, he conceals and covers up his bad actions and makes a display of the good things he has done.

1.6　「人之視己,如見其肺肝然,則何益矣」者,言小人為惡,外人視之,昭然明察矣,如見肺肝然。「則何益矣」者,言小人為惡,外人視之,昭然明察矣,如見肺肝,雖暫時揜藏,言何益矣。

1.7　「此謂誠於中形於外」者,言此小人既懷誠實惡事於中心,必形見於外,不可揜藏。

1.8　注「謙讀為慊」。

1.9　《正義》曰:以經義之理,言作謙退之字。既無謙退之事,故讀為慊,慊,不滿之貌,故又讀為厭,厭,自安靜也。云「厭讀為黶」,黶為黑色,如為閉藏貌也。

2.1　「曾子曰:十目所視」者,此經明君子脩身,外人所視,不可不誠其意。作《記》之人,引曾子之言以證之。「十目所視,十手所指」者,言所指、視者眾也。十目,謂十人之目,十手,謂十人之手也。

2.2　「其嚴乎」者,既視者及指者皆眾,其所畏敬,可嚴憚乎。

2.3　「富潤屋,德潤身」者,言此二句為喻也。言家若富,則能潤其屋,有金玉又華飾見於外也。

2.4　「德潤身」者,謂德能霑潤其身,使身有光榮見於外也。

2.5　「心廣體胖」者,言內心寬廣,則外體胖大,言為之於中,必形見於外也。「故君子必誠其意」者,以有內見於外,必須精誠其意,在內心不可虛也。

1.6 *But if, when others look at him, it is as though they see his very lungs and liver, then how is this of benefit*: This says that, if the lesser man does what is bad and others see this, he is very clearly observed; it is like seeing his lungs and liver. *Then how is this of benefit*: This says that when the lesser man does something bad and others see it, it is very clearly observed, like seeing his lungs and liver, so although there may be temporary concealment, how is this of benefit?

1.7 *This is called cheng* 誠 *within being manifest without*: This says that, if the lesser man harbours a true and genuine devotion to bad things in his mind-heart, it must be apparent on the outside—it cannot be hidden and concealed.

1.8 The note has that *qian* 謙 is read as *qie* 慊 (contented, happy).

1.9 The *Zhengyi* says that, on the principles of interpreting the [*Li*] *ji*, it speaks of writing the characters for self-deprecation (*qian tui* 謙退). Since it is not a matter of being self-deprecating, it is only *qie* 慊. *Qie* 慊 is the appearance of being dissatisfied. Therefore, it is also read as *yan* 厭. *Yan* is the self being *an jing* 安靜 (quiet and peaceful). It says that *yan* 厭 is read as *yan* 黶 which is a black colour, like the appearance of being concealed.

2.1 *Zengzi said: "It is what ten eyes see"*: This is the [*Li*] *ji* making clear the noble man's cultivation of the self and that what other people see cannot be otherwise than *cheng* 誠 in terms of intentions. The one writing the [*Li*] *ji* quotes Zengzi's words to verify this. *What ten eyes see, what ten hands point to* refers to the numerous people who point or see. "Ten eyes" refers to the eyes of ten people, and "ten hands" to the hands of ten people.

2.2 *This is awe-inspiring*: This means that those looking and pointing are many, and what they fear and respect can be awe-inspiring.

2.3 *Wealth enriches a house; virtue enriches the self*: These two sentences are taken as metaphors, saying that, if a household is wealthy, then it is able to adorn its buildings; if it has gold and jade it also presents a splendid appearance to the outside world.

2.4 *Virtue enriches the self* refers to virtue being able to permeate through one's self causing it to have a glorious external appearance.

2.5 *When the mind is broad, the body flourishes*: This says that, if within, the mind-heart is liberal and broad, then without, the body is at ease and substantial, which is to say that what exists within is inevitably displayed to the outside world. *Therefore the noble man must make his intentions cheng* 誠 because, if what is within is manifest without, then there must be purity and truth in one's intentions—the mind-heart within cannot be false.

TX4:《詩》云:「瞻彼淇澳,菉竹猗猗。有斐君子,如切如磋,如琢如磨。瑟兮僩兮,赫兮喧兮。有斐君子,終不可諠兮。」⁴「如切如磋」者,道學也。「如琢如磨」者,自脩也。「瑟兮僩兮」者,恂慄也。「赫兮喧兮」者,威儀也。「有斐君子,終不可諠兮」者,道盛德至善,民之不能忘也。**[1]**

《詩》云:「於戲前王不忘。」⁵ 君子賢其賢而親其親,小人樂其樂而利其利,此以沒世不忘也。**[2]**

Comment: This section consists of two quotations from the *Odes*, each followed by a brief explanatory statement. The first quotation refers to King Wu and contains the simile also found in Book 1 of the *Lunyu*—"like cutting, like polishing; like carving, like grinding." The initial pair is taken as referring to learning and the subsequent pair to cultivation of the self. Overall, the description of the paradigmatic King as unforgettable is attributed to his virtue and goodness (*de* 德 and *shan* 善). The second quotation emphasises the unforgettable nature of former kings more generally, but particularly Wen and Wu in this context. The translation of the terse and somewhat enigmatic following statement is based on Kong Yingda's commentary.

注 TX4 (鄭玄)

[1] 此「心廣體胖」之詩也。澳,隈崖也。「菉竹猗猗」,喻美盛。斐,有文章貌也。諠,忘也。道猶言也。恂,字或作「峻」,讀如嚴峻之「峻」,言其容貌嚴栗也。民不能忘,以其意誠而德著也。{淇音其。澳,本亦作奧,於六反,本又作「隩」,一音烏報反。菉音綠。猗,於宜反。斐,芳尾反,一音匪,文章貌。磋,七何反。琢,丁角反。磨,本亦作磨,末何反。}《爾雅》云:「骨曰切,象曰瑳,玉曰琢,石曰磨。」僩,下板反,又胡板反。赫,許百反。喧,本亦作咺,況晚反。諠,許袁反。}《詩》作諼,或作喧,音同。{恂,依注音峻,思俊反,一音思旬反。慄,利悉反。澳,於六反。隈,烏回反。}

[2] 聖人既有親賢之德,其政又有樂利於民。君子小人,各有以思之。{於音烏,下「於緝熙」同。戲,好胡反,徐范音義。樂其樂,並音岳,又音洛,注同。}

---

4   This is the opening verse of the *Odes*, Mao 55, LCC, 4:91.
5   This is the final line of the *Odes*, Mao 269, LCC, 4:573 apart from a variation in the second character—*hu* 乎 for *hu* 戲.

TX4: The *Odes* says:

> See the bays in the banks of the Qi,
> the green bamboo, how fresh and luxuriant.
> There is the elegant and accomplished prince.
> Like cutting, like polishing;
> like carving, like grinding.
> How strict he is, how resolute,
> how commanding he is, how dignified.
> There is the elegant and accomplished prince.
> He can never be forgotten.

"Like cutting, like polishing" speaks of learning; "like carving, like grinding" is cultivating the self; "how strict he is, how resolute" is being cautiously reverent; "how commanding he is, how dignified" is being imposing in demeanour. "There is the elegant and accomplished prince. He can never be forgotten" speaks of great virtue and the utmost goodness, which the people cannot forget. **[1]**

The *Odes* says: "Ah, alas! The former kings are not forgotten." Noble men [praise them for] taking as worthy those who are worthy and for holding dear their family members. Lesser men find joy in what they find joy in and benefit from their benefits. This is why they are not forgotten after death. **[2]**

Notes TX4 (Zheng Xuan)

[1] This is a "when the mind is broad the body flourishes" poem. *Ao* 澳 is equivalent to *wei ya* 隈崖 (coves and cliffs). *The green bamboo, how fresh and luxuriant* is a metaphor for a beautiful and flourishing appearance. *Fei* 斐 is a figured or brilliant [appearance] (*wen zhang* 文章). *Xuan* 諼 is equivalent to *wang* 忘 (to forget). *Dao* 道 is like *yan* 言 (to say). *Xun* 恂 is sometimes written *jun* 峻 and is read like *jun* 峻 in *yanjun* 嚴峻 (stern, severe) and says his appearance is *yanli* 嚴栗 (majestic, dignified). "The people cannot forget" him because his intentions are *cheng* 誠 and his virtue is manifest. . . . The *Er ya* says: "For bone, one says *qie* 切 (to cut); for ivory, one says *cuo* 瑳 (to polish); for jade, one says *zhuo* 琢 (to carve); and for stone, one says *mo* 磨 (to grind)." . . . The *Odes* has 諼 or 喧— the pronunciation is the same (i.e. *xuan*). . . .

[2] Since the sage has the virtues of loving and worthiness, so his government also brings happiness and benefit to the people. The noble man and the lesser man each have their ways of thinking of this. . . .

疏 TX4 (孔穎達)

1.1　「《詩》云：瞻彼淇澳」者，此一經廣明誠意之事，故引《詩》言學問自新、顏色威儀之事，以證誠意之道也。

1.2　「瞻彼淇澳，菉竹猗猗」者，此《詩‧衛風‧淇澳》之篇，<u>衛</u>人美<u>武公</u>之德也。澳，隈也。菉，王芻也。竹，萹竹也。⁶ 視彼<u>淇</u>水之隈曲之內，生此菉之與竹，猗猗然而茂盛，以<u>淇</u>水浸潤故也。言視彼<u>衛</u>朝之內，上有<u>武公</u>之身，道德茂盛，亦蒙<u>康叔</u>之餘烈故也。⁷ 引之者，證誠意之道。

1.3　「有斐君子」者，有斐然文章之君子，學問之益矣。

1.4　「如切如磋」者，如骨之切，如象之磋，又能自脩也。

1.5　「如琢如磨」者，如玉之琢，如石之磨也。

1.6　「瑟兮僩兮，赫兮喧兮。有斐君子，終不可喧兮」者，又瑟然顏色矜莊，僩然性行寬大，赫然顏色盛美，喧然威儀宣美，斐然文章之君子，民皆愛念之，終久不可忘也。諠，忘也。自此以上，《詩》之本文也。自此以下，記者引《爾雅》而釋之。「如切如磋者，道學也」者，論道其學矣。

1.7　「如琢如磨者，自脩也」者，謂自脩飾矣，言初習謂之學，重習謂之脩，亦謂《詩》本文互而相通也。

1.8　「瑟兮僩兮者，恂慄也」者，恂，讀為「峻」，言顏色嚴峻戰慄也。

1.9　「道盛德至善，民之不能忘也」，謂善稱也。「有斐君子，終不可諠兮」，論道<u>武公</u>盛德至極美善，人之愛念不能忘也。

{注「此心」至「著也」。}

6　It is probable that *wang* 王 should be emended to *yu* 玉 and *bian* 萹 emended to *bian* 篇, see SSJZS, 28:1864nn1–2.

7　The reference here is to Kang Shu, taken to be the first ruler of the state of Wei. The character *meng* 蒙 is contentious (see SSJZS, 28:1864) and has been omitted from the translation.

Commentary TX4 (Kong Yingda)

1.1 *The Odes says: "See the bays in the banks of the Qi"*: This section expands on and clarifies the matter of making intentions *cheng* 誠. Therefore, it quotes the words of the *Odes* on the subjects of study, self-renewal, appearance and dignity of demeanour as evidence of the Way of making intentions *cheng* 誠.

1.2 *See the bays in the banks of the Qi, the green bamboo, how fresh and luxuriant*: This is the "Qi Ao" ode from the "Wei feng." It is the Wei people praising the virtue of Duke Wu. *Ao* 澳 is the equivalent of *wei* 隈 (cove, bay); *lu* 菉 is the equivalent of *yu chu* 玉芻 (jade grasses); *zhu* 竹 is the equivalent of *pian zhu* 萹竹 (tablets of bamboo). If you look within the winding bays of the Qi waters, this striking green bamboo is growing luxuriantly and abundantly because it is imbued with the Qi waters. [The ode] is saying that, if you look within the Wei court, above there is Duke Wu himself, whose Way and virtue are glorious and abundant, and this is also because of Kang Shu's abundant merit. In quoting this, there is verification of the Way of making intentions *cheng* 誠.

1.3 *There is the elegant and accomplished prince*: The elegance and accomplishment of the prince (noble man) is the benefit of study.

1.4 *"Like cutting, like polishing"*: Cultivation of the self is like the cutting of bone and like the polishing of ivory.

1.5 *"Like carving, like grinding"*: Like the carving of jade, like the grinding of stone.

1.6 *How strict he is, how resolute, how commanding he is, how dignified. There is the elegant and accomplished prince. He can never be forgotten*: Also his grave countenance is stern and strong, his dignified conduct is liberal and expansive, his awe-inspiring countenance is grand and handsome, his dignified demeanour is widely displayed—this is the elegance and accomplishment of the prince (noble man). The people all love him and think of him, and finally can never forget [him]. *Xuan* 諼 is equivalent to *wang* 忘 (to forget). From this point above is the *Odes'* original text. From this point down, the [*Li*] *ji* quotes the *Er ya* to explain it. *"Like cutting, like polishing" speaks of learning* discusses and speaks of his learning.

1.7 *"Like carving, like grinding" is cultivating the self* refers to the "adornment" of self-cultivation. It says that when it is first practised it is termed study. When it is constantly practised, it is called cultivation, both referring to the original text from the *Odes* and combining it with explanation.

1.8 *"How strict he is, how resolute" is being imposing in demeanour*: *Xun* 恂 is read as *jun* 峻 (lofty, great) and says his appearance is severe and intimidating.

1.9 *Speaks of great virtue and the utmost goodness, which the people cannot forget* refers to the praise of his goodness. *There is the elegant and accomplished prince. He can never be forgotten* discusses Duke Wu's abundant virtue, his extreme excellence and goodness; people thought of him with love and could not forget him.

1.10 《正義》曰：「誼，忘也」，《釋訓》文也。云「道猶言也」，謂經中「道」盛
　　　德至善，恐為道德之「道」，故云「道猶言也」。云「恂，字或作峻，讀如
　　　嚴峻之峻」者，以經之「恂」字，他本或作「峻」字，故讀為嚴峻之「峻」。
　　　《詩》箋云：「還為恂也。」此《記》為「赫兮喧兮」，《詩經》云「赫兮喧兮」，
　　　本不同也。云「以其意誠而德著也」，以<u>武公</u>用意精誠德著於人，人不忘
　　　也。以經廣明誠意之事，故<u>鄭</u>云「意誠而德著也」。

2.1 「《詩》云：於戲前王不忘」者，此一經廣明誠意之事。此〈周頌・烈文〉
　　　之篇也，美<u>武王</u>之詩。於戲，猶言嗚呼矣。以<u>文王</u>、<u>武王</u>意誠於天下，
　　　故詩人歎美之云：此前世之王，其德不可忘也。

2.2 「君子賢其賢而親其親」者，言後世貴重之，言君子皆美此前王能賢其賢
　　　人而親其族親也。

2.3 「小人樂其樂而利其利」者，言後世卑賤小人，美此前王能愛樂其所樂，
　　　謂民之所樂者，前王亦愛樂之。「利其利」者，能利益其人之所利，民為
　　　利者，前王亦利益之。言前王施為政教，下順人情，不奪人之所樂、利
　　　之事故云「小人樂其樂而利其利」也。

2.4 「此以沒世不忘也」，由前王意能精誠，垂於後世，故君子小人皆所美念。
　　　以此之故，終沒於世，其德不忘也。

1.10 The *Zhengyi* says: "*Xuan* 諠 is equivalent to *wang* 忘 (to forget)" which is from the *Shi xun*. It says: "*Dao* 道 is like *yan* 言 (to say), which says that within the classic, "*dao* 道" in "道盛德至善" is probably the "*dao* 道" of "*daode* 道德." Therefore it says, "*dao* 道 is like *yan* 言." It says: "The character *xun* 恂 is sometimes written as *jun* 峻, and is read as *jun* 峻 in *yanjun* 嚴峻. The character written *xun* 恂 in the classic was originally written in other situations as *jun* 峻, therefore it is read as the *jun* 峻 of *yanjun* 嚴峻 (stern, severe). A note on the *Odes* says: "Again it is *xun* 恂." This, in the [*Li*] *ji*, is "赫兮喧兮." The *Odes* says "赫兮喧兮," but originally it was not the same. It says: "Because his intentions are *cheng* 誠 and his virtue is manifest," which takes Duke Wu to use intentions that are refined and sincere, and virtue that is manifest towards others, so the people did not forget him. This is to take the classic to be elaborating on and clarifying the matter of making intentions *cheng* 誠, therefore Zheng [Xuan] says: "Intentions were *cheng* 誠 and virtue was manifest."

2.1 *The Odes says: "Ah, alas! The former kings are not forgotten":* This is this section expanding on and clarifying the matter of making intentions *cheng* 誠. This is the "Lie Wen" ode from the "Zhou song." It is a poem praising King Wu. *Wu hu* 於戲 is like saying *wu hu* 嗚呼 (i.e. an exclamation of regret). Because the intentions of Kings Wen and Wu were *cheng* 誠 towards all under Heaven the poet praises them, saying: "With these kings of former ages, their virtue can never be forgotten."

2.2 *Noble men [praise them for] taking as worthy those who are worthy and holding dear their family members:* This says that later generations valued them highly. It says that noble men all praise the ability of these former kings to treat as worthy those who are worthy and to hold dear their family members.

2.3 *Lesser men find joy in what they find joy in and benefit from their benefits* says that lowly, base and lesser men of later generations praised these former kings' ability to love and find joy in what they find joy in, and says that what the people took pleasure in, the former kings also loved and took pleasure in. *Benefit from their benefits* means being able to provide benefit increases that from which their people are benefited; that is, what the people took to be benefit the former kings also brought benefit by increasing this. This says that, when former kings issued official exhortations, below they were in accord with people's feelings, and did not snatch away what people found joy in and benefited from. Therefore, it is said, *lesser men find joy in what they find joy in and benefit from their benefits.*

2.4 *This is why they are not forgotten after death* is that, because the intentions of former kings could be refined and *cheng* 誠 and handed down to later generations, they are something which both noble and lesser men all praise and think about. It is for this reason that they are never lost to the world, and their virtue is never forgotten.

TX5:〈康誥〉曰「克明德」。[8]
〈大甲〉曰「顧諟天之明命」。[9]
〈帝典〉曰「克明峻德」。[10]
皆自明也。**[1]**

Comment: These examples of manifesting great virtue are all taken from the *Shang shu* (*Documents*). Some background information on all three brief quotations is provided by Kong Yingda. The rationale for placing this section here is expressed in his note 1.4. It is notable that Zheng Xuan's readings of *gu* 顧 and *shi* 諟 (with which Kong Yingda concurs) are somewhat different from those later proposed by Zhu Xi.

注 TX5 (鄭玄)

[1] 皆自明明德也。克,能也。顧,念也。諟,猶正也。〈帝典〉、〈堯典〉,亦《尚書》篇名也。峻,大也。諟,或為「題」。{誥,古報反。大音泰。顧諟,上音故,本又作顧,同,下音是。峻,徐音俊,又私俊反。題,徐徒兮反。}

疏 TX5 (孔穎達)

1.1　「〈康誥〉曰:克明德」者,此一經廣明意誠則能明己之德。周公封康叔而作〈康誥〉,戒康叔能明用有德。此《記》之意,言周公戒康叔以自明其德,與《尚書》異也。「〈大甲〉曰:顧諟天之明命」者,顧,念也。諟,正也。伊尹戒大甲云:爾為君,當顧念奉正天之顯明之命,不邪僻也。

1.2　「〈帝典〉曰:克明峻德」者,〈帝典〉,謂〈堯典〉之篇。峻,大也。《尚書》之意,言堯能明用賢俊之德,此《記》之意,言堯能自明大德也。「皆自明也」,此經所云〈康誥〉、〈大甲〉、〈帝典〉等之文,皆是人君自明其德也,故云「皆自明也」。

1.3　注「皆自明明德也」。

1.4　《正義》口:明明德必先誠其意,此經誠意之章,由初誠意也,故人先能明己之明德也。

8　From the *Shang shu* 尚書 (*Book of Documents*)—see LCC, 3:383. The reference is to King Wen 文王. The full statement reads: 「惟乃丕顯考文王克明德慎罰。」

9　Also from the *Shang shu*—see LCC, 3:199. The subject is the former king, Tang 湯.

10　Also from the *Shang shu*—see LCC, 3:17. It is from the "Canon of Yao" 堯典. Legge's version reads: "He was able to make the able and virtuous distinguished"—see his note on p. 17.

TX5: The "Announcement to Kang" says: "He was able to display virtue."
The "Tai Jia" says: "He truly reflected on the enlightened decree of Heaven."
The "Di dian" says: "He was able to display great virtue."
These are all instances of the self displaying [enlightened virtue]. **[1]**

Notes TX5 (Zheng Xuan)

[1] All are examples of the self displaying enlightened virtue. *Ke* 克 is equivalent to *neng* 能 (to be able). *Gu* 顧 is equivalent to *nian* 念 (to think of, reflect on, consider). *Shi* 諟 is like *zheng* 正 (true, correct). The "Di dian" and "Yao dian" are also names of chapters of the *Shang shu* 尚書. *Jun* 峻 equates with *da* 大 (great). *Shi* 諟 is sometimes written as *ti* 題. . . .

Commentary TX5 (Kong Yingda)

1.1   *The "Announcement to Kang" says: "He was able to display virtue"*: This section enlarges on and clarifies [the point] that, if one's intentions are *cheng* 誠, then one can display one's own virtue. The Duke of Zhou ennobled Kang Shu and wrote the "Announcement to Kang" to warn Kang Shu to display and use the virtue he had. The [*Li*] *ji's* intention is to say that the Duke of Zhou provided a precept for Kang Shu to manifest his own virtue. It is different from the *Shang shu*. *The "Tai Jia" says: "He truly reflected on the enlightened decree of Heaven"*: [Here] *gu* 顧 equates with *nian* 念 (to think of, reflect on, consider) and *shi* 諟 with *zheng* 正 (correct, true). Yi Yin warned Tai Jia, saying: "You are the ruler and should reflect on and correctly receive the manifestation of Heaven's decree; you should not be depraved and prejudiced."

1.2   *The "Di dian" says: "He was able to display great virtue"*: The "Di dian" refers to the "Yao dian." *Jun* 峻 is equivalent to *da* 大 (great, large). The *Shang Shu's* intention is to say that Yao was able to display and use the virtue of one who was worthy and superior. The [*Li*] *ji's* intention is to say that Yao was himself able to display great virtue. *These are all instances of the self displaying [enlightened virtue]*: These quotations from the "Announcement to Kang," the "Tai Jia," the "Di dian," and other such writings are all instances of the ruler himself displaying his virtue. Therefore, it says: *These are all instances the self displaying [enlightened virtue]*.

1.3   According to the note: "All [are instances of] the self displaying [enlightened virtue]."

1.4   The *Zhengyi* states: To display enlightened virtue one must first make one's intentions *cheng* 誠. This is a chapter on making intentions *cheng* 誠. It is by making his intentions *cheng* 誠 at the start that a man is first able to display his own enlightened virtue.

TX6: 湯之〈盤銘〉曰:「苟日新,日日新,又日新。」

〈康誥〉曰:「作新民。」[11]

《詩》曰:「周雖舊邦,其命惟新。」[12] 是故君子無所不用其極。**[1]**

《詩》云:「邦畿千里,惟民所止。」[13]

《詩》云:「緡蠻黃鳥,止于丘隅。」[14] 子曰:「於止,知其所止,可以人
而不如鳥乎!」**[2]**

《詩》云:「穆穆文王,於緝熙敬止。」[15] 為人君止於仁,為人臣止於敬,
為人子止於孝,為人父止於慈,與國人交止於信。**[3]**

Comment: Of the six quotations in this section, one is from an unknown source (the inscription on Tang's bathing tub), one is from the *Documents* (*Shang shu* 尚書) and the remaining four are from the *Odes* (*Shi jing* 詩經). The first three are about "renewing" (*xin* 新), thus favouring Cheng Yi's later emendation of *qin* 親 to *xin* 新 in the opening statement of TX1. What both Zheng Xuan and Kong Yingda take to be the object of renewal is virtue (*de* 德). The fourth and fifth quotations are about *zhi* 止 (coming to rest), the examples being the people and the golden oriole, whilst the final quotation is about the recurring exemplar, King Wen, and his "coming to rest" in the various components of virtue, notably, *ren* 仁, *jing* 敬 (respect), *xiao* 孝 (filial piety), *ci* 慈 (compassion) and *xin* 信 (trustworthiness).

注 TX6 (鄭玄)

[1] 盤銘,刻戒於盤也。極,猶盡也。君子日新其德,常盡心力不有餘也。
{盤,步干反。銘,徐音冥,亡丁反。}

[2] 於止,於鳥之所止也。就而觀之,知其所止,知鳥擇岑蔚安閒而止處之耳。
言人亦當擇禮義樂土而自止處也。《論語》曰:「里仁為美,擇不處仁,焉得
知?」[16] {畿音祈,又作幾,音同。緡蠻,音緜,一音亡巾反,}《毛詩》作「緜」,
傳云:「緜蠻,小鳥貌。」

[3] 緝熙,光明也。此美文王之德光明,敬其所以自止處。{緝,七入反。熙,
許其反。}

11　See LCC, 3:388. Legge has, for the whole statement, referring to the people of Yin: "Thus also
　　shall you assist the king, consolidating the appointment of Heaven, and renovating this people."
12　The ode in question is Mao 235, LCC, 4:427. The first lines read:「文王在上,於昭于
　　天,周雖舊邦,其命維新。」
13　From the fourth verse of the *Odes*, Mao 303, LCC, 4:637.
14　From the second verse of the *Odes*, Mao 230, LCC, 4:419.
15　These are the opening lines of verse 4 of the *Odes,* Mao 235, LCC, 4:429.
16　*Lunyu* IV.1, LCC, 1:165.

TX6: The inscription engraved on Tang's bathing tub stated: "Truly renew [yourself] each day; day after day renew [yourself], and again, each day, renew [yourself]."

The "Announcement to Kang" states: "Stir the people to renewal."

The *Odes* says: "Although Zhou is an old country, its decree is new." This is why there is nothing in which the noble man does not use his utmost [endeavour]. **[1]**

The *Odes* says: "The royal domain is a thousand *li*. It is where the people come to rest."

The *Odes* says: "The little yellow bird comes to rest in the hill foliage." The Master said: "As for coming to rest, the bird knows where to do this. Can we take a man to be less than a bird?" **[2]**

The *Odes* says: "Profound indeed was King Wen. In continuing splendour, he gave honour [to his place of] coming to rest." As a ruler, he came to rest in loving kindness and devotion to others (*ren* 仁); as an official, he came to rest in respect (*jing* 敬); as a son, he came to rest in filial piety (*xiao* 孝); as a father, he came to rest in compassion (*ci* 慈); in his dealings with the people of the state, he came to rest in trustworthiness (*xin* 信). **[3]**

Notes TX6 (Zheng Xuan)

[1] *Pan ming* 盤銘 is to carve precepts on a bathing tub. *Ji* 極 is like *jin* 盡 (the utmost). The noble man, each day renewing his virtue, constantly exhausts the strength of his mind, leaving nothing in reserve. . . .

[2] *Yu zhi* 於止 (in coming to rest) is where the bird comes to rest. If you go and look at it, you will know where it comes to rest, and know that the bird chooses the peace and tranquility of isolated peaks and luxuriant foliage as its place to come to rest. This says that a man too should choose a place of proper conduct (*li* 禮), right action (*yi* 義) and happiness (*le* 樂), and himself come to rest in that place. The *Lunyu* says: "It is *ren* 仁 that makes a village excellent. If people choose not to abide in a place of *ren* 仁, how do they acquire wisdom?" . . . The *Mao Shi* has *mian* 緜; it is traditionally said that *mian man* is the appearance of a small bird.

[3] *Qixi* 緝熙 is equivalent to *guangming* 光明 (bright, brilliant). This praises the brilliance of King Wen's virtue and his honouring the place where he came to rest. . . .

疏 TX6 (孔穎達)

1.1 「<u>湯</u>之〈盤銘〉」，此一經廣明誠意之事。「<u>湯</u>之〈盤銘〉」者，<u>湯</u>沐浴之盤，而刻銘為戒。必於沐浴之盤者，戒之甚也。

1.2 「苟日新」者，此〈盤銘〉辭也。非唯洗沐自新。苟，誠也。誠使道德日益新也。

1.3 「日日新」者，言非唯一日之新，當使日日益新。

1.4 「又日新」者，言非唯日日益新，又須恒常日新，皆是丁寧之辭也。此謂精誠其意，脩德無已也。

1.5 「〈康誥〉曰：作新民」者，<u>成王</u>既伐<u>管叔</u>、<u>蔡叔</u>，以<u>殷</u>餘民封<u>康叔</u>，〈誥〉言<u>殷</u>人化<u>紂</u>惡俗，使之變改為新人。此《記》之意，自念其德為新民也。

1.6 「《詩》曰：<u>周</u>雖舊邦，其命惟新」者，此〈大雅•文王〉之篇。其詩之本意，言<u>周</u>雖舊是諸侯之邦，其受天之命，唯為天子而更新也。此《記》之意，其所施教命，唯能念德而自新也。「是故君子無所不用其極」者，極，盡也。言君子欲日新其德，無處不用其心盡力也。言自新之道，唯在盡其心力，更無餘行也。

2.1 「《詩》云：邦畿千里，惟民所止」，此一經廣明誠意之事，言誠意在於所止，故上云：「大學之道在止於至善。」此〈商頌•玄鳥〉之篇，言<u>殷</u>之邦畿方千里，為人所居止。此《記》斷章，喻其民人而擇所止，言人君賢則來也。

Commentary TX6 (Kong Yingda)

1.1 *The inscription engraved on Tang's bathing tub*: This particular section enlarges on and clarifies the matter of making intentions *cheng* 誠. *The inscription engraved on Tang's bathing tub* refers to the vessel in which Tang bathed, which was engraved with a precept. Certainly, that the precept was on the bathing tub is a measure of its great importance.

1.2 *Truly renew [yourself] each day*: These are the words engraved on the bathing tub. It is not only washing that renews the self. *Gou* 苟 is equivalent to *cheng* 誠 (truly). Truly cause the Way and virtue to be increased and renewed each day.

1.3 *Day after day renew [yourself]* says that there is not just the renewal of one day; what is right is to cause increasing renewal day after day.

1.4 *And again, each day renew [yourself]* says that there is not only renewal over a series of days. There must also be constant daily renewal. All these are words of repeated injunction. This says [you should] refine and make your intentions true and cultivate virtue unceasingly.

1.5 *The "Announcement to Kang" states: "Stir the people to renewal"*: When King Cheng cut down Guan Shu and Cai Shu, he enfeoffed Kang Shu on behalf of the remaining people of Yin. The "Announcement [to Kang]" says that the Yin people should change the evil customs of Zhou, so causing them to change and become a renewed people. The [*Li*] *ji's* meaning is that one should reflect on one's own virtue to effect renewal of the people.

1.6 *The Odes says: "Although Zhou is an old country, its decree is new"*: This is from the [*Odes*,] "Wen Wang" of the "Da ya" section. The basic intention of this poem is to say that, although Zhou was old, it was a state of the feudal lords and King Wen received Heaven's mandate. Being the Son of Heaven, he brought about change and renewal. The [*Li*] *ji's* meaning is that, in what he did in implementing the mandate, he was able to reflect on virtue and renew himself. *This is why there is nothing in which the noble man does not use his utmost [endeavour]*: [In this], *ji* 極 is equivalent to *jin* 盡 (the utmost, exhaust). This says that, if the noble man wishes to renew his virtue every day, there is no situation in which he does not use the utmost strength of his mind-heart. That is to say, the Way of daily renewal lies solely in exhausting the strength of the mind-heart and leaving nothing else to do.

2.1 *The Odes says: "The royal domain is a thousand li. It is where the people come to rest"*: This particular section expands on and clarifies the matter of making intentions *cheng* 誠. It says that making intentions *cheng* 誠 lies in where one comes to rest. Therefore, earlier it says: *The way of the highest learning lies in coming to rest in the utmost goodness.* The verse is the "Xuan niao" 玄鳥 from the "Shang song." It says that the country of Yin was one thousand *li* square and was where the people dwelt and came to rest. This excerpt from the [*Li*] *ji* gives the example of his people and where they chose to come to rest. It says that, if the ruler is worthy, then [the people] will come.

2.2 「《詩》云：緡蠻黃鳥，止于丘隅」者，此《詩•小雅•緡蠻》之篇，刺幽王之詩。言緡蠻然微小之黃鳥，止在於岑蔚丘隅之處，得其所止，以言微小之臣依託大臣，亦得其所也。

2.3 「子曰：於止，知其所止」者，孔子見其《詩》文而論之，云是觀於鳥之所止，則人亦知其所止。鳥之知在岑蔚安閒之處，則知人亦擇禮義樂土之處而居止也。

2.4 「可以人而不如鳥乎」者，豈可以人不擇止處，不如鳥乎？言不可不如鳥也。故《論語》云「里仁為美，擇不處仁，焉得知」是也。

3.1 「《詩》云：穆穆文王，於緝熙敬止」者，此〈大雅•文王〉之篇，美文王之詩。緝熙，謂光明也。止，辭也。《詩》之本意，云文王見此光明之人，則恭敬之。此《記》之意，「於緝熙」，言嗚呼文王之德緝熙光明，又能敬其所止，以自居處也。
{注「鳥擇」至「止處」。}

2.5 《正義》曰：岑，謂巖險。蔚，謂草木蓊蔚。言鳥之所止，必擇靜密之處也。

TX7: 子曰：「聽訟，吾猶人也。必也使無訟乎。」[17] 無情者不得盡其辭，大畏民志。[1] 此謂知本。[2]

---

17   *Lunyu* XII.13, LCC, 1:257.

2.2   *The Odes says: "The little yellow bird comes to rest in the hill foliage":* This poem is the "Min man" from the "Xiao ya" in the *Odes*, a poem criticising King You. It speaks of the small yellow bird (golden oriole) which comes to rest in the high and leafy hills. [Speaking of it] attaining its place to come to rest is a way of referring to small officials depending on great officials in also attaining their place [to come to rest].

2.3   *The Master said: "As for coming to rest, the bird knows where to do this":* Confucius considers this verse from the *Odes* and discusses it. He says that, if a man looks at where the bird comes to rest, then he too knows where to come to rest. If the bird knows [to come to rest in] a high and leafy place which is tranquil and quiet, then a man knows that he too should choose a place of *li* 禮, *yi* 義 and *le* 樂 (proper conduct, right action and happiness), and dwell and come to rest there.

2.4   *Can we take a man to be less than a bird?* How can a man not choose a place to come to rest like a bird can? That is to say, it is not possible [for a man] to be less than a bird. Therefore, the *Lunyu* saying: "It is *ren* 仁 that makes a village excellent. If one does not choose to dwell in a place of *ren* 仁, how can one attain wisdom?" is this.

3.1   *The Odes says: "Profound indeed was King Wen. In continuing splendour, he gave honour [to his place of] coming to rest":* This is from the "Wen Wang" of the "Da ya" section, a poem praising King Wen. *Qixi* 緝熙 is equivalent to *guangming* 光明 (bright, splendid). *Zhi* 止 is equivalent to *ci* 辭 (withdraw, retire, depart). The poem's basic intention is to say that because King Wen was this splendid person, he was honoured and respected. The [*Li*] *ji's* meaning is that *in continuing splendour* is an exclamation about the splendour and brightness of King Wen's virtue, and also that he was able to show respect for the place where he came to rest by his own choice of a place to dwell (come to rest).

2.5   The *Zhengyi* says: *Cen* 岑 refers to *yan xian* 巖險 (a cliff and narrow pass, a high and dangerous place). *Wei* 蔚 refers to *caomu wengwei* 草木翁蔚 (a place where grass and trees grow luxuriantly). That is to say, a bird, in choosing a place to come to rest, inevitably selects one that is tranquil and secluded.

TX7: The Master said: "In hearing lawsuits, I am like other men. What is necessary is to ensure that there are no lawsuits." Those who are without truth will not get to complete their statements [because of] the great awe [affecting] people's wills. **[1]** This is called knowing the root. **[2]**

Comment: This section takes a short quotation from the *Lunyu* and adds a comment, also short, to indicate that this is a reference to "knowing the root." There is, however, a difference between the *Li ji* commentators and Zhu Xi on what the root is in this context. Both Zheng Xuan and Kong Yingda take it to be making intentions *jing* 精 and *cheng* 誠 (i.e. pure and true). This will obviate false statements and hence reduce litigation. Zhu Xi, however, takes it to be "manifesting enlightened virtue" and "renovating the people."[18] It may be that the statement, "I am like other men" should read instead, "I put myself in the place of others"—that is, of each of the litigants, as Plaks has suggested.[19] This seems to be Kong Yingda's interpretation in 1.4 below.

注 TX7 (鄭玄)

[1] 情，猶實也。無實者多虛誕之辭。聖人之聽訟，與人同耳。必使民無實者不敢盡其辭，大畏其心志，使誠其意不敢訟。{吾聽訟，似用反。}「猶人也」，《論語》作「聽訟吾猶人也」。{毋訟音無。誕音但。}

[2] 本，謂「誠其意」也。

疏 TX7 (孔穎達)

1.1 《正義》曰：此一經廣明誠意之事，言聖人不惟自誠己意，亦服民使誠意也。孔子稱斷獄，猶如常人無以異也，言吾與常人同也。

1.2 「必也使無訟乎」者，必也使無理之人不敢爭訟也。

1.3 「無情者不得盡其辭」者，情，猶實也。言無實情虛誕之人，無道理者，不得盡竭其虛偽之辭也。

1.4 「大畏民志」者，大能畏脅民人之志，言人有虛誕之志者，皆畏懼不敢訟，言民亦誠實其意也。「聽訟吾猶人也，必也使無訟乎」，是夫子之辭。「無情者不得盡其辭，大畏民志」，是記者釋夫子「無訟」之事。然能「使無訟」，則是異於人也，而云「吾猶人」者，謂聽訟之時，備兩造，吾聽與人無殊，故云「吾猶人也」。但能用意精誠，求其情偽，所以「使無訟」也。

2.1 「此謂知本」者，此從上所謂「誠意」，以卜言此「大畏民志」。以上皆是「誠意」之事，意為行本，既精誠其意，是曉知其本，故云「此謂知本」也。

---

18 See his section DX Comm. 4 and also Legge's note, LCC, 1:165.
19 See Plaks, *Ta Hsüeh and Chung Yung (The Highest Order of Cultivation and On the Practice of the Mean)*, 67n1.

Notes TX7 (Zheng Xuan)

[1] *Qing* 情 is like *shi* 實 (true, real). *Wushi (qing) zhe* 無實 (情) 者 are statements containing much that is false. The sage is the same as other men in hearing lawsuits. It is necessary to ensure that people who are untruthful do not dare to complete their statements because the great awe affecting their minds and wills causes them to make their intentions *cheng* 誠 (genuine, true, sincere) so they dare not bring lawsuits. . . . [In regard to] "like others," the *Lunyu* has: "In hearing lawsuits, I am like other men." . . .
[2] *Ben* 本 refers to making one's intentions *cheng* 誠.

Commentary TX7 (Kong Yingda)

1.1   The *Zhengyi* says that this particular section elaborates on and clarifies the matter of making intentions *cheng* 誠. It says that the sage not only makes his own intentions *cheng* 誠 but also compels the people to make their intentions *cheng* 誠. Confucius, in hearing lawsuits, was no different from an ordinary person, saying that he and the ordinary person were the same.

1.2   *What is necessary is to ensure that there are no lawsuits.* What is necessary is to bring it about that unprincipled people dare not have recourse to the law.

1.3   *Those who are without truth will not get to complete their statements:* *Qing* 情 is like *shi* 實 (true, real). This speaks about people who do not tell the truth, people who lie, unprincipled people, not getting the chance to give full expression to their false statements.

1.4   *[Because of] the great awe [affecting] people's wills:* This means having a great ability to inspire awe and coerce the wills of the people. That is to say, if people have a will that is false, they will all be over-awed and fearful and will not dare to bring lawsuits, which is to say that people will also make their intentions *cheng* 誠. *In hearing lawsuits, I am like other men. What is necessary is to ensure there to be no lawsuits.* These are the Master's words. *Those who are without truth will not get to complete their statements [because of] the great awe [affecting] people's wills:* This is the [*Li*] *ji* explaining the Master's position on "no lawsuits." Nevertheless, if he were able "to cause there to be no lawsuits," then he would be different from others. In saying "I am like other men," he is referring to [the fact that], when he hears lawsuits and calls for the two parties in a suit, he listens to both without discrimination. Therefore, he said, "I am like other men." But being able to use intentions that are pure and true to search out feelings that are false is the way *to ensure that there are no lawsuits.*

2.1   *This is called knowing the root:* This refers to what is said from *making intentions cheng* 誠 above to *[because of] the great awe [affecting] people's wills* below. What is over-riding in all this is the matter of making intentions *cheng* 誠. Intentions are the basis of conduct so, when you make intentions pure and true, this is to understand and know this root. Therefore, it says: *This is called knowing the root.*

TX8: 所謂脩身在正其心者，身有所忿懥，則不得其正。有所恐懼，則不得其正。有所好樂，則不得其正。有所憂患，則不得其正。心不在焉，視而不見，聽而不聞，食而不知其味。此謂脩身在正其心。**[1]**

Comment: In this brief explication of cultivation of the self, only two points are made in regard to the dependency on rectifying the mind. First, if the mind is swayed by emotions, regardless of whether they are "positive" (joy, happiness) or "negative" (anger, resentment, fear, grief), then it does not attain rectitude (or correction or balance) and the self will remain "uncultivated." Second, for cultivation of the self, the mind must be "engaged." What this means is not elaborated on by the commentators. Presumably, it indicates that there must always be a mental or analytic component in the interaction with things or events in the world and not just an emotional or visceral response. The paucity of comment may, perhaps, be taken as a measure of the commentators' view of the clarity of the section itself. In Zhu Xi's version, *shen* 身 is read as *xin* 心. A certain liberty is taken in translating the recurring *you suo* 有所.

注 TX8 (鄭玄)

[1] 懥，怒貌也，或作懫，或為疐。{忿，弗粉反。懥，勑值反，范音稚，徐丁四反，又音勤。恐，丘勇反。好，呼報反，下「故好而知」同。樂，徐五孝反，一音岳。懫音致。疐音致，又得計反。}

疏 TX8 (孔穎達)

1.1 「所謂脩身」者，此覆說前脩身正心之事。

1.2 「身有所忿懥，則不得其正」者，懥，謂怒也。身若有所怒，「則不得其正」，言因怒而違於正也。所以然者，若遇忿怒，則違於理，則失於正也。

1.3 「有所恐懼，則不得其正」者，言因恐懼而違於正也。

1.4 「心不在焉，視而不見，聽而不聞，食而不知其味」者，此言脩身之本，必在正心。若心之不正，身亦不脩。若心之不在，視聽與食，不覺知也。是心為身本，脩身必在於正心也。

TX8: What is spoken of as "cultivating the self lies in rectifying one's mind" is this: If the self harbours anger and resentment, then [the mind] does not attain rectitude; if it is gripped by fear and terror, then [the mind] does not attain rectitude; if it gives itself to joy and happiness, then [the mind] does not attain rectitude; if it is beset by sorrow and grief, then [the mind] does not attain rectitude. If the mind is not "present" (engaged), one looks, but does not see; one listens, but does not hear; one eats, but does not know the taste. This is to say that "cultivating the self lies in rectifying one's mind." **[1]**

Notes TX8 (Zheng Xuan)

[1] *Zhi* 懥 is the appearance of anger. It is sometimes written as *zhi* 懫 and sometimes as *zhi* 疐....

Commentary TX8 (Kong Yingda)

1.1   *What is spoken of as "cultivating the self"*: This reiterates what was previously said about the matters of cultivating the self and rectifying the mind.

1.2   *If the self harbours anger and resentment, then [the mind] does not attain rectitude*: *Zhi* 懥 refers to *nu* 怒 (anger). If the self has that which angers it, *then [the mind] does not attain rectitude* says that this is because anger runs counter to rectitude. The reason why this is so is that, if indignation and anger occur, then there is opposition to principle and hence loss of rectitude.

1.3   *If it is gripped by fear and terror, then [the mind] does not attain rectitude* says that, because of the fear and terror, there is opposition to rectitude.

1.4   *If the mind is not "present" (engaged), one looks, but does not see; one listens, but does not hear; one eats, but does not know the taste*: This says the root (foundation) of cultivating the self must lie in rectifying the mind-heart. If the mind-heart is not rectified, the self is also not cultivated. If the mind-heart is not "present" (engaged), seeing, hearing and tasting are without awareness. This is the mind-heart being the root (foundation) of the self, and cultivation of the self necessarily lying in rectifying the mind-heart.

TX9: 所謂齊其家在脩其身者，人之其所親愛而辟焉，之其所賤惡而辟焉，之其所畏敬而辟焉，之其所哀矜而辟焉，之其所敖惰而辟焉。故好而知其惡，惡而知其美者，天下鮮矣。故諺有之曰：「人莫知其子之惡，莫知其苗之碩。」此謂身不脩，不可以齊其家。**[1]**

Comment: The key element in cultivating the self is to bring *zheng* 正, in the sense of rectitude, correctness or balance, to the mind-heart (*xin* 心). This is clearly identified as preventing the adverse effects of the emotions or feelings; it is achieved by comparison with others. The particular points of note in the interpretation by the *Li ji* commentators are the reading of the recurring *zhi* 之 as *shi* 適 (to go to) and *pi* 辟 or *pi* 譬 as *yu* 喻. Thus, the noble man, bent on the cultivation of the self, uses others as yardsticks against whom he can evaluate himself.

注 TX9 (鄭玄)

[1] 之，適也。譬，猶喻也。言適彼而以心度之，曰：吾何以親愛此人，非以其有德美與？吾何以敖惰此人，非以其志行薄與？反以喻己，則身脩與否可自知也。鮮，罕也。人莫知其子之惡，猶愛而不察。碩，大也。辟音譬，下及注同，謂譬喻也。{賤惡，烏路反，下「惡而知」同。敖，五報反。惰，徒臥反。其惡惡，上如字，下烏路反。鮮，仙善反，注同。諺，魚變反，俗語也。度，徒洛反。與音余，下「薄與」同。行，下孟反。}

疏 TX9 (孔穎達)

1.1 「所謂齊其家在脩其身」者，此經重明前經齊家、脩身之事。

1.2 「人之其所親愛而辟焉」者，之，猶適也。此言脩身之譬也，設我適彼人，見彼有德，則為我所親愛，當反自譬喻於我也。以彼有德，故為我所親愛，則我若自脩身有德，必然亦能使眾人親愛於我也。

1.3 「之其所賤惡而譬焉」者，又言我往之彼，而賤惡彼人者，必是彼人無德故也，亦當迴以譬我。我若無德，則人亦賤惡我也。

TX9: What is spoken of as "regulating one's household lies in cultivating one's self" is this: A man goes to someone he loves and holds dear and compares himself to him; he goes to someone he regards as worthless and dislikes and compares himself to him; he goes to someone he regards with awe and reverence and compares himself to him; he goes to someone he feels sympathy and pity for and compares himself to him; he goes to someone he is scornful and dismissive of and compares himself to him. So it is that there are few in the world who love someone and yet recognise his badness, or who hate someone and yet recognise his goodness. The old adage has this to say: "A man recognises neither the badness of his son nor the largeness of his grain." That is to say, if the self is not cultivated it is not possible to regulate one's household. **[1]**

Notes TX9 (Zheng Xuan)

[1] *Zhi* 之 is equivalent to *shi* 適 (to go to). *Pi* 譬 is like *yu* 喻 (to know, illustrate). This says that I go to another and evaluate him with my mind-heart, and ask how it is I cherish and love this man if not for his virtue and beauty. How is it that I feel superior and indifferent to another if not because his will and conduct are petty. If I compare myself with another, then I can determine whether I have achieved cultivation of the self. *Xian* 鮮 is equivalent to *han* 罕 (few). A man not knowing the badness of his son is like loving without examination. *Shuo* 碩 is equivalent to *da* 大 (large, great). *Pi* 辟 is pronounced as *pi* 譬 and the same in the notes. It refers to comparing. . . .

Commentary TX9 (Kong Yingda)

1.1   *What is spoken of as "regulating one's household lies in cultivating one's self"*: This section repeats and clarifies the matters of regulating the household and cultivating the self from the earlier section.

1.2   *A man goes to someone he loves and holds dear and compares himself to him*: *Zhi* 之 is like *shi* 適 (to go towards). This speaks of comparison in relation to cultivating the self. If I go towards that man and see that he is virtuous, then he is what I love and hold dear. It is proper to turn around and compare him to myself. Because the other is virtuous, he is what I love and hold dear. Then, if I cultivate myself and am virtuous, this will necessarily also cause the multitude of people to have love and kindness towards me.

1.3   *He goes to someone he regards as worthless and dislikes and compares himself to him*: This again speaks of my going towards another, and regarding him as worthless and disliking him. The reason must be that the other is not virtuous. It is also appropriate to turn around and compare myself [to him]. If I am without virtue, then others will also regard me as worthless and dislike me.

1.4 「之其所畏敬而譬焉」者，又我往之彼而畏敬彼人，必是彼人莊嚴故也，
　　　亦迴其譬我，我亦當莊敬，則人亦必畏敬我。

1.5 「之其所哀矜而辟焉」者，又我往之彼，而哀矜彼人，必是彼人有慈善柔
　　　弱之德故也，亦迴譬我，我有慈善而或柔弱，則亦為人所哀矜也。

1.6 「之其所敖惰而辟焉」者，又我往之彼，而敖惰彼人，必是彼人邪僻故
　　　也，亦迴譬我，我若邪僻，則人亦敖惰於我也。

1.7 「故好而知其惡，惡而知其美者，天下鮮矣」者，知，識也；鮮，少也。
　　　人心多偏，若心愛好之，而多不知其惡。若嫌惡之，而多不知其美。今
　　　雖愛好，知彼有惡事；雖憎惡，知彼有美善，天下之內，如此者少矣。

1.8 「故諺有之曰：人莫知其子之惡，莫知其苗之碩」者，碩，猶大也。言人
　　　之愛子其意至甚，子雖有惡不自覺知，猶好而不知其惡也。農夫種田，
　　　恆欲其盛，苗雖碩大，猶嫌其惡，以貪心過甚，故不知其苗之碩。若能
　　　以己子而方他子，己苗而匹他苗，則好惡可知，皆以己而待他物也。

1.9 「此謂身不脩，不可以齊其家」者，此不知子惡、不知苗碩之人，不脩其
　　　身，身既不脩，不能以己譬人，故不可以齊整其家。
　　　{注「之適」至「大也」。}

1.4 *He goes to someone he regards with awe and reverence and compares himself to him*: This is also about my going towards another and regarding him with awe and reverence. The reason must be that the other is stern and imposing. If I also turn around and compare myself and I, too, am properly stern and imposing, then others will, of necessity, regard me with awe and respect.

1.5 *He goes to someone he feels sympathy and pity for and compares himself to him*: This is also about my going towards another and feeling pity and sympathy for the other. The reason is certainly that this other has the virtues of compassion, goodness, compliance and gentleness. If I also turn around and compare myself to him, and if I have compassion and goodness, and am sometimes also compliant and gentle, then I too will receive sympathy and pity from others.

1.6 *He goes to someone he is scornful and dismissive of and compares himself to him*: This is also about my going towards another and being scornful and dismissive towards the other. The reason for this must be that the other is heterodox and prejudiced. If I also turn around and compare myself [to him] and find I am heterodox and prejudiced, then others will also be scornful and dismissive towards me.

1.7 *So it is that there are few in the world who love someone and yet recognise his badness, or who hate someone and yet recognise his goodness*: *Zhi* 知 is equivalent to *shi* 識 (to recognise, know). *Xian* 鮮 is equivalent to *shao* 少 (few). In men's minds there are many prejudices. If the mind loves or likes someone, it is very often unaware of his defects. If the mind hates or dislikes someone, it is very often unaware of his merits. Now, although one loves or likes, one should recognise that the other has bad aspects; although one hates or dislikes, one should recognise that the other has merits. Within the world, few are like this.

1.8 *The old adage has this to say: "A man recognises neither the badness of his son nor the largeness of his grain"*: *Shuo* 碩 is like *da* 大 (large, great). This says that when a person loves his son, his thoughts are quite extreme so, although his son has bad points, he himself does not perceive and recognise them, which is like loving and not knowing the bad aspects. If a farmer cultivates his fields, he constantly wishes them to flourish so, although the sprouts are very large, he still dislikes their bad aspects because his avaricious mind is greatly at fault. Therefore, he does not recognise his sprouts' largeness. If one is able to compare one's own son to another's son, or one's own sprouts (grain) to another's sprouts (grain), then what is good or bad can be recognised, and in all cases one can treat another's things like one's own things.

1.9 *That is to say, if the self is not cultivated it is not possible to regulate one's household*: This is the case of a man not knowing his son's badness or his grain's largeness. If you do not cultivate yourself, then the self is not cultivated, and you are not able to compare yourself to others. Therefore, it is not possible to regulate and arrange your household.

1.10 《正義》曰:「之,適也」,《釋詁》文。[20] 云「反以喻己」者,謂見他人所親
      愛,被賤惡,以人類己,他人之事反來自譬己身也。云「則身脩與否可自
      知也」者,謂彼人不脩,則被賤惡敖惰,己若不以脩身,事亦然也。若
      彼脩身,則被親愛敬畏,己若脩身亦當然也。故云「脩身與否,可自知
      也」。云「碩,大也」,《釋詁》文。[21]「此謂」至「其家」,此一節覆明前經
      治國齊家之事。

TX10: 所謂治國必先齊其家者,其家不可教,而能教人者無之,故君子
不出家而成教於國。孝者,所以事君也;弟者,所以事長也;慈者,所
以使眾也。

〈康誥〉曰:「如保赤子。」[22] 心誠求之,雖不中不遠矣。未有學養子而後
嫁者也。**[1]**

一家仁,一國興仁;一家讓,一國興讓;一人貪戾,一國作亂。其機如
此。此謂一言僨事,一人定國。**[2]**

堯、舜率天下以仁,而民從之;桀、紂率天下以暴,而民從之。其所令
反其所好,而民不從。**[3]**

---

20 *Er ya* 1, SSJZS, 8:7.
21 We cannot locate this statement in the *Er ya shigu*. The *Shuowen jiezi* has "碩頭大也."
    See Duan Yucai 段玉裁, *Shuowen jiezi zhu* (Taipei: Yiwen yinshuguan, 2005), 422.
22 See the *Documents*, LCC, 3:389.

1.10   The *Zhengyi* says: "*Zhi* 之 is equivalent to *shi* 適 (to go towards)." This is from the *Shigu*. "Turn around and compare yourself" refers to looking at other people whom one loves and holds dear, or regards as worthless and hates. By drawing an analogy between others and oneself, the affairs of others reflect back and offer a comparison to oneself. It (i.e. the *Zhengyi*) says: "Then I can myself know whether or not I have achieved cultivation of the self." That is to say, if another is not cultivated, then he will be regarded as worthless and disliked, he will be scorned and dismissed, and the same will apply to me if I have not cultivated myself. If the other has cultivated himself, then he will be loved and held dear, he will be revered and held in awe, and if I have cultivated the self the same will properly apply to me. Therefore, it says: "Then I can myself know whether or not I have achieved cultivation of the self." *Shuo* 碩 is equivalent to *da* 大 (large, great). This is from the *Shigu*. From "this is to say" to "one's household" is this particular section repeating and clarifying the matters in the earlier section of bringing good order to the state and regulating the household.

TX10: What is meant by saying, "to bring good order to a state it is first necessary to regulate one's household" is this: nobody can teach others if he cannot teach his own household. Therefore, the noble man does not go beyond his household and yet he completes his teaching in the state. Filial piety is the way to serve the ruler. Fraternal respect is the way to serve elders. Parental compassion is the way to act towards the multitude.
The "Announcement to Kang" states: "It is like protecting an infant." If the mind-heart truly seeks it, even if you do not hit the mark, you will not be far away. There has never been a girl who would only marry after learning how to rear a child. **[1]**
If one household (i.e. the ruler) is *ren* 仁 (shows loving kindness), the whole state is moved to *ren* 仁. If one household (i.e. the ruler) is *rang* 讓 (complaisant), the whole state is moved to *rang* 讓 (complaisance). If one man (the ruler) is greedy and violent, the whole state acts in a disorderly way. The origins of action are like this. This is what is meant by "one word can ruin affairs; one man can stabilise a kingdom." **[2]**
Yao and Shun led the world by *ren* 仁 and the people followed them. Jie and Zhou led the world by cruelty and the people followed them. If what is ordered is contrary to what is loved, the people will not follow. **[3]**

是故君子有諸己而后求諸人，無諸己而后非諸人。所藏乎身不恕而能喻
諸人者，未之有也。故治國在齊其家。**[4]**

《詩》云：「桃之夭夭，其葉蓁蓁。之子于歸，宜其家人。」²³「宜其家
人」，而后可以教國人。

《詩》云：「宜兄宜弟。」²⁴「宜兄宜弟」，而后可以教國人。

《詩》云：「其儀不忒，正是四國。」²⁵ 其為父子，兄弟足法，而后民法之
也。此謂治國在齊其家。**[5]**

Comment: This section, on the penultimate stage in the sequence of passing from the
coming to (or investigating) things to bringing peace to all under Heaven is, unlike the
three previous sections, supported by several examples from the classical literature (one
from the *Documents* and three from the *Odes*) as well as reference to the oft-mentioned paradigms of moral excellence, Yao and Shun, and their negative counterparts, Jie and Zhou.
The key elements identified in the noble man's teaching are *xiao* 孝 (filial piety), which is
the appropriate attitude to the ruler, *di* 弟 (fraternal respect), which is the appropriate attitude to elders generally, and *ci* 慈 (parental compassion), which is the appropriate attitude
to the masses. Two terms introduced for the first time in this section are *rang* 讓 (complaisance) paired with *ren* 仁 (loving kindness), and *shu* 恕 or the principle of reciprocity.

注 TX10 (鄭玄)

[1] 養子者，推心為之而中於赤子之嗜欲也。{弟音悌。長，丁丈反，下「長長」
并注同。中，丁仲反，注同。嗜欲，時志反。}

[2]「一家」、「一人」，謂人君也。戾之言利也。機，發動所由也。僨，猶覆敗
也。《春秋傳》曰：「登戾之。」又曰：「鄭伯之車僨於濟。」戾，或為畜；僨，或
為犇。{戾，力計反。賁，徐音奮，本又作「僨」，注同。覆，芳福反。濟，子禮
反。犇音奔。}

[3] 言民化君行也。君若好貨而禁民淫於財利，不能止也。{好，呼報反，注
同。行，下孟反，或如字。}

[4]「有於己」，謂有仁讓也。「無於己」，謂無貪戾也。

[5]「夭夭」、「蓁蓁」，美盛貌。「之子」者，是子也。{夭，於驕反。蓁音臻。
忒，他得反。}

---

²³ *Odes*, Mao 6, LCC, 4:13.
²⁴ *Odes*, Mao 173, LCC, 4:275.
²⁵ *Odes*, Mao 152, LCC, 4:223.

This is why the noble man should have these qualities (i.e. *ren* 仁 and *rang* 讓) in himself and afterwards seek them in others; it is why he should not have [greed and violence] in himself and afterwards condemn these qualities in others. There has never been a man who did not have the principle of reciprocity (*shu* 恕) in himself and still was able to instruct others. Therefore, bringing good order to a state lies in regulating one's household. [4]

The *Odes* says: "The peach tree—how fresh and young, how green and luxuriant its leaves. A young girl goes off to be married, and is fitting for her household." Be "fitting for your household" and afterwards you can teach the people of the state.

The *Odes* says: "Let the relationships between older and younger brothers be as they should be." "Let the relationships between older and younger brothers be as they should be" and afterwards there can be teaching of the people of the state.

The *Odes* says: "His demeanour is without blemish. He brings rectitude to the whole state." Let him be an adequate model as a father, son, older and younger brother, and subsequently the people will model themselves on him. That is to say, bringing good order to the state lies in regulating one's household. [5]

Notes TX10 (Zheng Xuan)

[1] *Yang zi* 養子 is to devote one's mind to doing this—giving central importance to the desires and wishes of the infant. . . .

[2] "One household" and "one person" refer to the ruler. 戾 is pronounced as 利 (*li*). *Ji* 機 is what the beginnings of action come from. *Fen* 僨 is like *fu bai* 覆敗 (utterly overturn, defeat). The *Chunqiu Commentary* says: "Ascending, he did violence to it." It also says: "Zheng Bo's carriage was completely overturned at the Ji waters. *Li* 戾 is sometimes written as *lin* 吝. *Fen* 僨 is sometimes written as *ben* 犇. . . .

[3] This says that the people change from the ruler's conduct. If the ruler loves material possessions and yet prohibits the people going to excess in wealth and profit, he cannot stop them. . . .

[4] "Have in himself" refers to there being loving kindness (*ren* 仁) and complaisance (*rang* 讓). "Not have in himself" refers to there not being greed and violence.

[5] *Yao yao* 夭夭 and *zhen zhen* 蓁蓁 are the appearances of beauty. *Zhi zi* 之子 is "this young person (girl)" (*shi zi* 是子). . . .

疏 TX10 (孔穎達)

1.1 「〈康誥〉曰：如保赤子」者，此成王命康叔之辭。赤子，謂心所愛之子。言治民之時，如保愛赤子，愛之甚也。

1.2 「心誠求之，雖不中不遠矣」者，言愛此赤子，內心精誠，求赤子之嗜欲，雖不能正中其所欲，去其所嗜欲，其不甚遠。言近其赤子之嗜欲，謂治人之道亦當如此也。

1.3 「未有學養子而后嫁者也」，言母之養子，自然而愛，中當赤子之嗜欲，非由學習而來，故云「未有學養子而后嫁者」。此皆本心而為之，言皆喻人君也。

2.1 「一家仁，一國興仁。一家讓，一國興讓」者，言人君行善於家，則外人化之，故一家、一國，皆仁讓也。

2.2 「一人貪戾，一國作亂」者，謂人君一人貪戾惡事，則一國學之作亂。

2.3 「其機如此」者，機，謂關機也。動於近，成於遠，善惡之事，亦發於身而及於一國也。

2.4 「此謂一言僨事，一人定國」者，僨，猶覆敗也。謂人君一言覆敗其事，謂惡言也。「一人定國」，謂由人君一人能定其國，謂善政也。古有此言，今《記》者引所為之事以結之。上云「一人貪戾，一國作亂」，是「一言僨事」也。又云一家仁讓，則一國仁讓，是知「一人定國」也。一家則一人也，皆謂人君，是一人之身，先治一家，乃後治一國。

Commentary TX10 (Kong Yingda)

1.1   The *"Announcement to Kang" states: "It is like protecting an infant"*: These are the
      words of King Cheng's directive to Kang Shu. *Chi zi* 赤子 refers to a child whom
      the heart loves. This says that a time of bringing good order to the people is like
      protecting and loving an infant; the love for the infant is very great.

1.2   *If the mind-heart truly seeks it, even if you do not hit the mark, you will not be far
      away*: This says that in loving this infant, the mind within is pure and sincere,
      seeking what the infant desires and wishes. Although one may not be able to
      determine exactly what it does wish, one is not very far away from what it desires
      and wishes. That is to say, being close to what one's infant desires speaks of the
      Way of bringing good order to people also being just like this.

1.3   *There has never been a girl who would only marry after learning how to rear a child*:
      This says that a mother, in nurturing a child, naturally loves it and determines
      exactly what the infant desires and wishes. This does not come about through
      study. Therefore, it says: *There has never been a girl who would only marry after
      learning how to rear a child*. These are things that are done innately and are all
      used to illustrate [how] the ruler should behave.

2.1   *If one household (i.e. the ruler) is ren* 仁 *(shows loving kindness), the whole state
      is moved to ren* 仁. *If one household (i.e. the ruler) is rang* 讓 *(complaisant), the
      whole state is moved to rang* 讓 *(complaisance)*: This says that, if the ruler acts with
      goodness in his own household, then those beyond [the household] are changed
      by this. Therefore, both household and state are *ren* 仁 and *rang* 讓.

2.2   *If one man (the ruler) is greedy and violent, the whole state acts in a disorderly way*:
      This says that, if the ruler himself is greedy and violent and does evil things, then
      the whole state learns this, creating disorder.

2.3   *The origins of action are like this*: *Ji* 機 refers to *guanji* 關機 (instrument, mechanism).
      Action in the near comes to completion in the distant. The goodness and badness of
      things also arise in the self and extend to the whole state.

2.4   *This is what is meant by "one word can ruin affairs; one man can stabilise a
      kingdom"*: *Fen* 僨 is like *fubai* 覆敗 (to overturn, ruin, defeat). This refers to the
      ruler uttering one word that can ruin his affairs, referring to bad words. *One man
      can stabilise a kingdom* refers to the fact that through one person (the ruler) his
      kingdom can be stabilised, referring to good government. Anciently, there were
      these words and now the [*Li*] *ji* quotes what gives a practical expression to them.
      First, it says: *If one man (the ruler) is greedy and violent, the whole state acts in a
      disorderly way*, which is equivalent to *one word can ruin affairs*. It also says, *if one
      household is ren* 仁 *and rang* 讓, then the whole state is moved to *ren* 仁 and *rang* 讓,
      which is to know that *one man can stabilise a state*. One household, then, is one
      person, and both refer to the ruler. That is, one person individually first brings
      good order to one household and then afterwards brings good order to the whole
      state.

3.1 「其所令反其所好,而民不從」者,令,謂君所號令之事。若各隨其行之所好,則人從之。其所好者是惡,所令者是善,則所令之事反其所好,雖欲以令禁人,人不從也。

4.1 「是故君子有諸己而后求諸人」者,諸,於也。謂君子有善行於己,而后可以求於人,使行善行也。謂於己有仁讓,而后可求於人之仁讓也。「無諸己而后非諸人」者,謂無惡行於己,而后可以非責於人為惡行也。謂無貪利之事於己,而後非責於人也。

4.2 「所藏乎身不恕而能喻諸人者,未之有也」者,謂所藏積於身既不恕實,而能曉喻於人,使從己者,未之有也。言無善行於身,欲曉喻於人為善行,不可得也。

5.1 「《詩》云:桃之夭夭,其葉蓁蓁」者,此〈周南 • 桃夭〉之篇,論昏姻及時之事。言「桃之夭夭」少壯,其葉蓁蓁茂盛,喻婦人形體少壯、顏色茂盛之時,似「桃之夭夭」也。

5.2 「之子于歸,宜其家人」者,「之子」者,是子也;歸,嫁也;宜,可以為夫家之人。引之者,取「宜其家人」之事,「宜其家人,而后可以教國人」者,言人既家得宜,則可以教國人也。

3.1   *If what is ordered is contrary to what is loved, the people will not follow*: Ling 令
      refers to the matter of what the ruler commands. If each [ruler] follows what he
      loves in his actions, then others will follow him. If what he loves is bad but what
      he orders is good, then the matters which he orders are contrary to what he loves
      and, although he may wish to prohibit people by his orders, they will not follow
      him.

4.1   *This is why the noble man should have these qualities in himself and afterwards seek
      them in others*: Zhu 諸 is equivalent to *yu* 於 (in). This says that, if the noble
      man has good conduct in himself, then subsequently he can seek it in others,
      causing [their] conduct to be good conduct. That is to say, if in himself there
      is *ren* 仁 (loving kindness) and *rang* 讓 (complaisance), afterwards he can seek
      these qualities in others. *It is why he should not have [greed and violence] in himself
      and afterwards condemn these qualities in others*: This says that, if there is not
      bad conduct in himself, then afterwards he can demand that there not be bad
      conduct in others. It says that, if there are not matters of greed and profit in
      himself, afterwards he can demand that they not be in others.

4.2   *There has never been a man who did not have the principle of reciprocity* (shu 恕)
      in himself and still was able to instruct others: This says that, if what is stored and
      accumulated in the self is not true reciprocity, it is never possible to be a clear
      example to others and cause them to follow you. That is to say, if there is not
      good conduct in the self, the wish to be a clear example to others in doing good
      cannot be realised.

5.1   *The Odes says: "The peach tree—how fresh and young, how green and luxuriant its
      leaves"*: This is from the "Tao yao" ode in the "Zhou nan." It discusses matters
      pertaining to the time of marriage. Saying, *the peach tree–how fresh and young* [is
      to refer to the time] when it is young and vigorous, and its foliage is green and
      flourishing. This is a metaphor for the young and vigorous appearance of the
      bride at the time when her beauty is in full bloom. She is herself like the peach
      tree when it is fresh and young.

5.2   *A young girl goes off to be married, and is fitting for her household*: Zhi zi 之子 is
      equivalent to *shi zi* 是子 (this young girl). *Gui* 歸 is equivalent to *jia* 嫁 (to go
      to be married). *Yi* 宜 is that she can be an appropriate person in her husband's
      household. This quotation picks out the matter of being *fitting for her household*.
      Be "fitting for your household" and afterwards you can teach the people of the state
      says that, if the person in the household is the right one, then he can teach the
      people of the state.

5.3 「《詩》云：宜兄宜弟」者，此〈小雅・蓼蕭〉之篇，美<u>成王</u>之詩。《詩》之
      本文，言<u>成王</u>有德，宜為人兄，宜為人弟。此《記》之意，「宜兄宜弟」，
      謂自與兄弟相善相宜也。既為兄弟相宜，而可兄弟之意，而后可以教國
      人也。

5.4 「《詩》云：其儀不忒，正是四國」者，此〈曹風・鳲鳩〉之篇。忒，差也；
      正，長也。言在位之君子，威儀不有差忒，可以正長是四方之國，言可
      法則也。

5.5 「其為父子兄弟足法，而后民法之也」者，「此謂治國在齊其家」，謂其脩
      身於家，在室家之內，使父子兄弟足可方法，而後民皆法之也。是先齊
      其家，而後能治其國也。

{注「一家」至「於濟」。}

5.6 《正義》曰：「一家一人，謂人君也」者，以經言「治家」，故知是人君也，
      若<u>文王</u>「刑于寡妻，至于兄弟，以御于家邦」是也。[26] 云「《春秋傳》曰：
      登戾之」者，此<u>隱</u>五年《公羊傳》文。案彼傳：「<u>文公</u>觀魚于<u>棠</u>，何以書？
      譏。何譏爾？遠也。公曷為遠而觀魚？登來之也。」彼注意謂以思得而來
      之，<u>齊</u>人語，謂「登來」為「得來」也。聲有緩急，得為登。謂<u>隱公</u>觀魚
      於<u>棠</u>，得此百金之魚，而來觀之。《公羊傳》為「登來」，<u>鄭</u>所引《公羊》本
      為「登戾之」，以「來」為「戾」，與《公羊》本不同也。<u>鄭</u>意以戾為「貪戾」，
      故引以證經之「貪戾」也。云「又曰<u>鄭伯</u>之車，僨於<u>濟</u>」者，<u>隱</u>三年《左傳》
      文。[27]

---

26 See the *Odes*, Mao 240, LCC, 4:447.
27 See the *Zuo zhuan* for the third and fifth years of Yin (LCC, 5:11, 17). In regard to the
     fifth year, Legge has: "The text, 'The duke reviewed a display of the fishermen at Tang'
     intimates the impropriety of the affair, and tells, moreover, how far off the place was."
     For the *Gongyang zhuan* quotation see SSJZS, 7:34.

5.3   *The Odes says: "Let the relationships between older and younger brothers be as they should be"*: This is from the "Liao xiao" in the "Xiao ya," a poem praising King Cheng. The original text of the *Odes* says that King Cheng was virtuous and acted correctly both as an older and younger brother. The [*Li*] *ji's* purpose in quoting *let the relationships between older and younger brothers be as they should be* is to say that he himself and his older and younger brothers were mutually good and mutually correct. When, in older and younger brothers, there is mutual correctness, and this can inform the intentions of older and younger brothers, then afterwards it is possible to teach the people of the state.

5.4   *The Odes says: "His demeanour is without blemish. He brings rectitude to the whole state"*: This is from the "Shi jiu" in the "Cao feng." *Te* 忒 is equivalent to *cha* 差 (error, fault); *zheng* 正 is equivalent to *zhang* 長 (to be a leader). This says that, when the ruler occupies his position and the dignity of his demeanour has no fault or blemish, he can be a true leader of the state in all four directions. It says he can be a model and standard.

5.5   *Let him be an adequate model as a father, son, older and younger brother, and subsequently the people will model themselves on him. That is to say, bringing good order to the state lies in regulating one's household*: This refers to his cultivating the self in the household. That is, within the household, if he causes fathers, sons, and older and younger brothers to be sufficient such that they can be standards, afterwards the people will take them as standards. This is "first regulating one's household and afterwards being able to bring good order to the state."

5.6   The *Zhengyi* says: "One household and one person refer to the ruler." Therefore one knows the section saying "bring good order to the household" refers to the ruler. For example, King Wen's "he was a model to his wife and this extended to older and younger brothers, and was a way to bring supervision to household and country" is a case in point. The *Chunqiu* commentary says, "He ascended to do violence to it." This is for the 5th year of Duke Yin in the *Gongyang zhuan*. According to the other commentary, "The Duke went to see the fishermen at Tang. How is this recorded? By inspecting. How did he inspect? From afar. Why did the Duke look at the fishermen from a distance? He ascended to come to them." The meaning of the commentary's note is that he gave consideration to the question of *de* 得 and *lai* 來. A phrase of the Qi people says, "*deng lai* 登 來." The sound is opposite and *de* 得 becomes *deng* 登. This says that Duke Yin went to see the fishermen at Tang, got this 100 *catties* of fish and came to see it. The *Gongyang zhuan* has *deng lai* 登來. What Zheng quotes is that the *Gongyang zhuan* originally had "*deng li zhi* 登戾之" taking *lai* 來 to be *li* 戾 and so the *Gongyang* was not originally the same. Zheng took the meaning of *li* 戾 to be *tan li* 貪戾 (greedy and violent), therefore he quotes this to verify the classic's *tan li* 貪戾. He says, "It also states that Zheng Bo's carriage was overturned at the Ji waters," which is from the 3rd year of Duke Yin in the *Zuo zhuan*.

TX11: 所謂平天下在治其國者，上老老而民興孝，上長長而民興弟，上恤孤而民不倍，是以君子有絜矩之道也。**[1]**所惡於上，毋以使下；所惡於下，毋以事上；所惡於前，毋以先後；所惡於後，毋以從前；所惡於右，毋以交於左；所惡於左，毋以交於右。此之謂「絜矩之道」。**[2]**《詩》云：「樂只君子，民之父母。」[28] 民之所好好之，民之所惡惡之，此之謂「民之父母」。**[3]**
《詩》云：「節彼南山，維石巖巖。赫赫<u>師尹</u>，民具爾瞻。」[29] 有國者不可以不慎，辟則為天下僇矣。**[4]**

Comment: This section, which considers the final stage of the sequence, i.e. bringing good order to the state being the foundation of bringing peace to all under Heaven, comprises an extended statement of the principle of reciprocity, followed by two examples, one positive and one negative. The principle is couched in negative terms and expressed with reference to those who rule, but it remains a general principle nonetheless. The opening sequence, on treating the aged as they should be treated etc, is similar to *Mencius* IA.7. The term used for the principle of reciprocity here is *xie ju zhi dao* 絜矩之道 which is rather unusual as Kong Yingda's comment indicates (2.5). Both examples are from the *Odes*, the first possibly referring to King Cheng as a positive exemplar and the second clearly to Grand Master Yin, an officer at the time of Emperor You (781–770 BCE), a black period for the Zhou dynasty. There is some question about the correct reading for *lu* 僇 in the final sentences. Does it signify disgrace and contempt, or being punished or slain? We have followed Kong Yingda in taking it to be the latter.

注 TX11 (鄭玄)

[1] 老老、長長，謂尊老敬長也。恤，憂也。「民不倍」，不相倍棄也。絜，猶結也，挈也。矩，法也。君子有挈法之道，謂當執而行之，動作不失之。倍，或作偝。矩，或作巨。{弟音悌。倍音佩，注同。絜音結。拒之音矩，本亦作「矩」。偝棄音佩，本亦作「倍」，下同。挈也，苦結反。巨音拒，本亦作矩，其呂反。}

[2]「絜矩之道」，善持其所有，以恕於人耳。治國之要盡於此。{惡，烏路反，下皆同。毋音無，下同。}

[3] 言治民之道無他，取於己而已。{只音紙。好好，皆呼報反。}

---

28   *Odes*, Mao 172, LCC, 4:273.
29   *Odes*, Mao 191, LCC, 4:309.

TX11: What is spoken of as "bringing peace to all under Heaven lies in bringing good order to one's state" is this: The ruler treats the aged as they should be treated and the people are stirred to filial piety; the ruler treats elders as they should be treated and the people are stirred to fraternal respect; the ruler has sympathy for those who are alone and the people are not refractory. This [all] comes about through the noble man having the Way of "measuring and modelling" (reciprocity). **[1]** What is hated in superiors, do not use in employing inferiors. What is hated in inferiors, do not use in serving superiors. What is hated in those in front, do not use in leading those behind. What is hated in those behind, do not use in following those in front. What is hated in those on the right, do not use in dealings with those on the left. What is hated in those on the left, do not use in dealings with those on the right. This is called the Way of "measuring and modelling." **[2]**

The *Odes* says: "Happy, indeed, is the prince; he is father and mother to the people." What the people love, he loves; what the people hate, he hates. This is called "being father and mother to the people." **[3]**

The *Odes* says: "How lofty is that southern mountain, with its precipitous rocky cliffs. Awe-inspiring are you, Grand Master Yin; the people all look up to you."[30] One who possesses a state cannot but be careful. If he is prejudiced, then he bears the punishment of the world. **[4]**

Notes TX11 (Zheng Xuan)

[1] *Lao lao* 老老 and *zhang zhang* 長長 refer, respectively, to venerating those who are old and having respect for one's elders. *Xu* 恤 is equivalent to *you* 憂 (sorrow, to sympathise with). *Min bu bei* 民不倍 is not to mutually oppose and reject. *Xie* 絜 is like *jie* 結 or *qie* 挈. *Ju* 矩 is like *fa* 法 (i.e. rule, pattern). *The noble man having the Way of "measuring and modelling" (reciprocity)* means that he properly grasps and implements it, and in his actions does not lose it. *Bei* 倍 is sometimes written as *bei* 偣; *ju* 矩 is sometimes written as *ju* 巨. . . .

[2] The Way of "measuring and modelling" (*xie ju zhi dao* 絜矩之道) is to skillfully maintain that which you have in order to show reciprocity towards others. The essential element of bringing good order to a state lies entirely in this. . . .

[3] This says that the Way of bringing good order to the people is nothing other than taking what is in oneself. . . .

---

30   Legge has the following introductory comment on this ode: "A lamentation over the miserable state of the kingdom, denouncing the injustice and carelessness of the Grand-Master Yin as the cause of it, and blaming also the conduct of the King."

[4] 巖巖，喻師尹之高嚴也。師尹，天子之大臣，為政者也。言民皆視其所行而則之，可不慎其德乎？邪辟失道，則有大刑。{節，前切反，又音如字。巖，五銜反。辟，匹亦反，又必益反，與僻同。僇，力竹反，與戮同，注同。}

疏 TX11 (孔穎達)

1.1　「所謂平天下，在治其國者」，《正義》曰：自此以下至終篇，覆明上文「平天下在治其國」之事。但欲平天下，先須治國，治國事多，天下理廣，非一義可了，故廣而明之。言欲平天下，先須脩身，然後及物。自近至遠，自內至外，故初明「絜矩之道」，次明散財於人之事，次明用善人、遠惡人。此皆治國、治天下之綱，故揔而詳說也。今各隨文解之。

1.2　「上恤孤而民不倍」者，孤弱之人，人所遺棄，在上君長若能憂恤孤弱不遺，則下民學之，不相棄倍此人。「是以君子有絜矩之道也」者，絜，猶結也；矩，法也。言君子有執結持矩法之道，動而無失，以此加物，物皆從之也。

2.1　「所惡於上，毋以使下」者，此以下皆是「絜矩之道」也。譬諸侯有天子在於上，有不善之事加己，己惡之，則不可迴持此惡事，使己下者為之也。

[4] "Rocky precipice" is a metaphor for the great dignity of Grand Master Yin, who was one of the Son of Heaven's high officials involved in the conduct of government. This says that the people all looked at what he did and modelled themselves on him. How could he not be careful about his virtue? If there was heterodox and perverse conduct such as to lose the Way, heavy punishment resulted. . . .

Commentary TX11 (Kong Yingda)

1.1   *What is spoken of as "bringing peace to all under Heaven lies in bringing good order to one's state" is this*: The *Zhengyi* says that from this down to the end of the chapter, there is repetition and clarification of the matter of the previous statement, *bringing peace to all under Heaven lies in bringing good order to one's state.* But if one desires to bring peace to all under Heaven, one must first bring good order to the state. Bringing good order to a state involves many things. The world's principles are broad and cannot be encompassed in a single interpretation, hence the need to expand and clarify this. This says that, if one wishes to bring peace to all under Heaven, one must first cultivate the self and afterwards extend this to things. [The process goes] from what is near at hand to what is distant, from what is within to what is without. Therefore, the first thing is to clarify the Way of "measuring and modelling" (reciprocity). The next thing is to clarify the matter of distributing materials to others, and the next is to make clear [the importance of] using good people and keeping distant from bad people. These are all [principles of] bringing good order to a state and good order to the network of the world. Therefore, they must be gathered together and carefully explained. Now each of the following statements elucidates this.

1.2   *The ruler has sympathy for those who are alone and the people are not refractory*: People who are alone and weak are those that others neglect and abandon. Those in high positions, rulers and elders, if they can be anxious about and sympathetic towards those who are alone and weak and, if they do not neglect them, then the people below learn from them and [also] do not abandon and reject these people. [In the statement], *this [all] comes about through the noble man having the Way of "measuring and modelling" (reciprocity)*, *xie* 絜 is read as *jie* 結 (measuring) and *ju* 矩 as *fa* 法 (model, standard). This says that the noble man maintains a firm grasp on the Way of "measuring and modelling," puts it into action, and does not lose it. By this, he adds to "things" and "things" all follow him.

2.1   *What is hated in superiors, do not use in employing inferiors*: From here onward, everything is about the Way of "measuring and modelling." For example, feudal lords have the Son of Heaven above them and, if there are bad things inflicted on them which they themselves abhor, then it is possible, in turn, to take these bad things and do them to those below.

2.2 「所惡於下,毋以事上」者,言臣下不善事己,己所有惡,則己不可持此
     惡事,迴以事己之君上也。

2.3 「所惡於前,毋以先後」者,前,謂在己之前,不以善事施己,己所憎
     惡,則無以持此惡事施於後人也。「所惡於後,毋以從前」者,後,謂在
     己之後,不以善事施己,己則無以惡事施於前行之人也。

2.4 「所惡於右,毋以交於左」者,謂與己平敵,或在己右,或在己左,以惡
     加己,己所憎惡,則無以此惡事施於左人。舉此一隅,餘可知也。

2.5 「此之謂絜矩之道」者,上經云「君子有絜矩之道也」,其「絜矩」之義未
     明,故此經申説。能持其所有,以待於人,恕己接物,即「絜矩之道」也。

3.1 「《詩》云:樂只君子,民之父母」,此記者引之,又申明「絜矩之道」。若
     能以己化,從民所欲,則可謂民之父母。此〈小雅・南山有臺〉之篇,美
     成王之詩也。只,辭也。言能以己化民,從民所欲,則可為民父母矣。

3.2 「民之所好好之」者,謂善政恩惠,是民之願好,己亦好之,以施於民,
     若發倉廩、賜貧窮、賑乏絕是也。

3.3 「民之所惡惡之」者,謂苛政重賦,是人之所惡,己亦惡之而不行也。

4.1 「《詩》云:節彼南山」者,上經説恕己待民,此經明己須戒慎也。「《詩》
     云:節彼南山,維石巖巖」,此〈小雅・節南山〉之篇,刺幽王之詩。言幽
     王所任大臣,非其賢人也。節然高峻者,是彼南山,維積累其石,巖巖
     然高大,喻幽王大臣師尹之尊嚴。

2.2   *What is hated in inferiors, do not use in serving superiors*: This says that, if officials below are bad in serving oneself, and one dislikes it, then one cannot take these bad things and turn around and use them in relation to the ruler above.

2.3   *What is hated in those in front, do not use in leading those behind*: Qian 前 refers to those in front of oneself and their acting badly in relation to oneself. What one hates and dislikes then should not be maintained and done to the people behind. *What is hated in those behind, do not use in following those in front*: Hou 後 refers to those behind oneself. If they do bad things to oneself, then one should not do bad things to the people in front.

2.4   *What is hated in those on the right, do not use in dealings with those on the left*: This refers to the self pacifying enemies, some being on one's right and some being on one's left. If they do harmful things to oneself which one hates and dislikes, then one should not do these bad things to people on the left. By raising this one corner, it is possible to know the rest.

2.5   *This is called the Way of "measuring and modelling" (reciprocity)*: The section above states: "The noble man has the 'Way of measuring and modelling (reciprocity).'" The meaning of *xie ju* 絜矩 is not clear, therefore this section extends the explanation. One is able to grasp what it is in terms of the treatment of others and the reciprocal relationship one has with things—this is the Way of "measuring and modelling" (reciprocity).

3.1   *The Odes says: "Happy, indeed, is the prince; he is father and mother to the people"*: The [*Li*] *ji* quotes this also to extend and clarify [the meaning of] the Way of "measuring and modelling" (reciprocity). If one can change oneself and follow what the people desire, then one can be spoken of as being father and mother to the people. This is from the "Nanshan you tai" in the "Xiao ya," a poem praising King Cheng. *Zhi* 只 is a particle. This says that, if one is able through oneself to change the people and follow what the people desire, then one can be a parent of the people.

3.2   *What the people love, he loves*: This says that good government with grace and kindness affirms the good desires of the people and that he himself [as the ruler] also loves them, and implements them for the people. Examples of this are: making issue from public granaries, making bestowals on the poor and impoverished, and offering relief to those who are in want and isolated.

3.3   *What the people hate, he hates*: This refers to harsh government and heavy taxes being what the people hate, and he himself also hating this and not doing it.

4.1   *The Odes says: "How lofty is that southern mountain"*: The earlier section speaks of the reciprocity of his treatment of the people. This section makes it clear that he himself must be careful and cautious. *The Odes says: "How lofty that southern mountain, with its precipitous rocky cliffs"*: This is from the "Jie nanshan" of the "Xiao ya," a poem criticizing King You. It says that the one put into office as a great minister by King You was not a worthy man. Lofty, high and great is the southern mountain's piling up and amassing of its stones. "Rocky, precipitous cliffs" is a metaphor for King You's great official, Grand Master Yin and his stern and imposing appearance.

4.2 「赫赫<u>師尹</u>，民具爾瞻」者，赫赫，顯盛貌。是太師與人為則者。具，俱也。爾，汝也。在下之民，俱於汝而瞻視之，言皆視<u>師尹</u>而為法。此《記》之意，以喻人君在上，民皆則之，不可不慎。

4.3 「有國者不可以不慎」者，有國，謂天子、諸侯。言民皆視上所行而則之，不可不慎其德乎，宜慎之也。

4.4 「辟則為天下僇矣」者，僇，謂刑僇也。君若邪辟，則為天下之民共所誅討，若<u>桀</u>、<u>紂</u>是也。

TX12:《詩》云：「<u>殷</u>之未喪師，克配<u>上帝</u>。儀監于<u>殷</u>，峻命不易。」[31] 道得眾則得國，失眾則失國。是故君子先慎乎德。有德此有人，有人此有土，有土此有財，有財此有用。德者本也，財者末也。外本內末，爭民施奪。是故財聚則民散，財散則民聚。是故言悖而出者，亦悖而入，貨悖而入者，亦悖而出。**[1]**

〈康誥〉曰：「惟命不于常。」道善則得之，不善則失之矣。[32] **[2]**

《楚書》曰：「楚國無以為寶，惟善以為寶。」**[3]**

<u>舅犯</u>曰：「亡人無以為寶，仁親以為寶。」**[4]**

Comment: This section comprises four further quotations, the first two from extant sources but the second two not now traceable. The historical background of the latter two is provided in part in Kong Yingda's commentary 3–4.1–2 below. The general theme continues to be bringing peace to all under Heaven. The important elements here identified are virtue (*de* 德), goodness (*shan* 善) and *ren* 仁. Virtue, ultimately, is the root. With this, the ruler might expect to retain the mandate; without it, the mandate will be lost.

---

31 *Odes*, Mao 235, verse 6, LCC, 4:431.
32 *Documents*, LCC, 3:397.

4.2   *Awe-inspiring are you, Grand Master Yin, the people all look up to you*: *He he* 赫赫 is to display an illustrious and glorious appearance. This is the Grand Master acting as a model for the people. *Ju* 具 is equivalent to *ju* 俱 (all); *er* 爾 is equivalent to *ru* 汝 (you). The people below all look to you with reverence, which is to say that all look at Grand Master Yin and take him as a model. The [*Li*] *ji*'s intention is to indicate by metaphor that by taking the ruler above as an example, the people all model themselves on him, so he must be careful.

4.3   *One who possesses a state cannot but be careful*: Possessing the state refers to the Son of Heaven and the feudal lords. This says that the people all look at what the ruler does and take this as a model, so he must be careful about his virtue, and act with caution.

4.4   *If he is prejudiced, then he bears the punishment of the world*: *Lu* 僇 refers to *xing lu* 刑僇 (capital punishment). If the ruler is depraved, then he is put to death by the people of the world collectively—Jie and Zhou were thus.

TX12: The *Odes* says: "When the Yin had not yet lost the people, they could be regarded as equal to Shangdi. Take warning from the Yin. The great mandate is not easy [to retain]." This says that to gain the multitude is to gain the state; to lose the multitude is to lose the state. This is why the noble man gives priority to the care of his own virtue. To have virtue is to have the people; to have the people is to have the land; to have the land is to have wealth; to have wealth is to have resources. Virtue is the root; wealth is the branch. [If the ruler] distances himself from the root and draws near to the branch, he will contend with the people and teach them to plunder. This is why the people disperse when wealth is gathered but gather when wealth is dispersed. This is also why contrary words come back when contrary words go forth and why ill-gotten goods go out when ill-gotten goods come in.[1]

The "Announcement to Kang" states: "The mandate of Heaven is not everlasting." If the Way is good then it is attained; if the Way is not good then it is lost. [2]

The *Documents of Chu* state: "The state of Chu takes nothing to be precious other than goodness." [3]

Jiu Fan said: "The lost person (exiled prince) took nothing to be precious other than loving and cherishing the Way of *ren* 仁." [4]

注 TX12 (鄭玄)

[1] 師，眾也。克，能也。峻，大也。言殷王帝乙以上，未失其民之時，德亦有能配天者，謂天享其祭祀也。及紂為惡，而民怨神怒，以失天下。監視殷時之事，天之大命，得之誠不易也。道，猶言也。用，謂國用也。施奪，施其劫奪之情也。悖，猶逆也。言君有逆命，則民有逆辭也。上貪於利，則下人侵畔。《老子》曰：「多藏必厚亡。」[33]{喪，息浪反。峻，恤俊反。易，以豉反，注同。爭，爭鬭之爭。施如字。悖，布內反，下同。上，時掌反。藏，才浪反。}

[2] 于，於也。天命不於常，言不專祐一家也。{專佑音又。}

[3] 《楚書》，楚昭王時書也。言以善人為寶。時謂觀射父，昭奚恤也。{射父，食亦反，又食夜反。父音甫。}

[4] 舅犯，晉文公之舅狐偃也。亡人，謂文公也。時辟驪姬之讒，亡在翟。而獻公薨，秦穆公使子顯弔，因勸之復國，舅犯為之對此辭也。仁親，猶言親愛仁道也。明不因喪規利也。{辟音避。驪，力宜反，本又作麗，亦作孋，同。翟音狄。顯，許遍反。為之，于偽反。}

疏 TX12 (孔穎達)

1.1　「《詩》云：殷之未喪師，克配上帝」，此一經明治國之道在貴德賤財。此〈大雅·文王〉之篇，美文王之詩，因以戒成王也。克，能也；師，眾也。言殷自紂父帝乙之前，未喪師眾之時，所行政教，皆能配上天而行也。

1.2　「儀監于殷，峻命不易」者，儀，宜也；監，視也。今成王宜監視于殷之存亡。峻，大也。奉此天之大命，誠為不易，言其難也。

1.3　「道得眾則得國，失眾則失國」者，道，猶言也。《詩》所云者，言帝乙以上「得眾則得國」，言殷紂「失眾則失國」也。

33　See D. C. Lau, *Tao Te Ching: A Bilingual Edition* (Hong Kong: The Chinese University Press, 2001), 64–66.

Notes TX12 (Zheng Xuan)

[1] *Shi* 師 is equivalent to *zhong* 眾 (the multitude, masses). *Ke* 克 is equivalent to *neng* 能 (to be able). *Jun* 峻 is equivalent to *da* 大 (great, large). This says that Yin kings, from Emperor Yi and before, at a time when they had not yet lost the people, had virtue that could match Heaven, meaning that Heaven received their sacrifices. When it came to Zhou, he was evil. The people grew angry and the spirits grew resentful, causing him to lose all under Heaven. If you look into the affairs of the time of Yin, then gaining the great mandate of Heaven is truly not easy. *Dao* 道 is like *yan* 言 (to say). *Yong* 用 refers to the state's resources. *Shi duo* 施奪 is to stir up feelings of robbery and plunder. *Bei* 悖 is like *ni* 逆 (contrary, refractory). This says that, if the ruler acts in opposition to Heaven's mandate, then the people will make rebellious statements. If the ruler is covetous of goods for profit, then those below invade and transgress. The *Laozi* says: "Storing up much inevitably brings heavy loss." . . .

[2] *Yu* 于 is equivalent to *yu* 於 (in, on). "The mandate of Heaven is not everlasting" says that it does not only protect one house. . . .

[3] The *Chu Documents* is a book from the time of King Zhao of Chu. This speaks of taking the good person as precious, which at the time referred to Guan Shefu and Zhao Xixu. . . .

[4] Jiu Fan was Duke Wen of Jin's maternal uncle, Hu Yan. The "lost person" refers to Duke Wen. At the time, he suffered Li Ji's slander and was banished to Di. When Duke Xian died, Duke Mu of Qin sent Zi Xian to condole with [Duke Wen, then Chong'er,] and took the opportunity to persuade him to return to the kingdom. Jiu Fan responded to it with this line. *Ren qin* 仁親 is like saying loving and cherishing the Way of *ren* 仁. Clearly, he did not contrive to benefit from the decease [of his father]. . . .

Commentary TX12 (Kong Yingda)

1.1 *The Odes says: "When the Yin had not yet lost the people, they could be regarded as equal to Shangdi"*: This section makes it clear that the Way of bringing good order to the state lies in valuing virtue and despising wealth. This is the "Wen Wang" ode from the "Da ya," a poem praising King Wen by way of a warning to King Cheng. *Ke* 克 is equivalent to *neng* 能 (to be able); *shi* 師 is equivalent to *zhong* 眾 (the multitude, masses). This says that what Yin did in terms of government before Zhou's father Emperor Yi, at a time when it had not yet lost the people, was in all instances able to match Heaven above and be implemented.

1.2 *Take warning from the Yin. The great mandate is not easy [to retain]*: *Yi* 儀 is equivalent to *yi* 宜 (right, fitting); *jian* 監 is equivalent to *shi* 視 (to look at). Now it was fitting for King Cheng to look at the preservation and loss of Yin. *Jun* 峻 is equivalent to *da* 大 (great, large). Receiving this great mandate of Heaven is truly not easy refers to its difficulty.

1.3 *This says that to gain the multitude is to gain the state; to lose the multitude is to lose the state*: *Dao* 道 is like *yan* 言 (to say). What the *Odes* says is that from Emperor Yi and before *they gained the multitude and then gained the state*, but that Zhou of Yin *lost the multitude and then lost the state*.

1.4 「有德此有人」者,有德之人,人之所附從,故「有德此有人」也。「有人此有土」者,有人則境土寬大,故「有土」也。

1.5 「有土此有財」,言有土則生植萬物,故「有財」也。

1.6 「有財此有用」者,為國用有財豐,以此而有供國用也。

1.7 「德者本也,財者末也」者,德能致財,財由德有,故德為本,財為末也。

1.8 「外本內末,爭民施奪」者,外,疏也;內,親也;施奪,謂施其劫奪之情也。君若親財而疏德,則爭利之人皆施劫奪之情也。

1.9 「是故財聚則民散,財散則民聚」者,事不兩興,財由民立。君若重財而輕民,則民散也。若散財而賙恤於民,則民咸歸聚也。

1.10 「是故言悖而出者,亦悖而入」者,悖,逆也。若人君政教之言悖逆人心而出行者,則民悖逆君上而入以報荅也,謂拒違君命也。

1.11 「貨悖而入者,亦悖而出」者,若人君厚斂財貨,悖逆民心而入積聚者,不能久如財,人畔於上,財亦悖逆君心而散出也。言眾畔親離,財散非君有也。

{注「師眾」至「厚亡」。}

1.4   *To have virtue is to have the people*: Those who have virtue are those whom others adhere to and follow. Therefore, *to have virtue is to have the people*. In the case of *to have the people is to have the land*, if he (the ruler) has the people, then boundaries and lands are wide and great. Thus it is "to have the land."

1.5   *To have the land is to have wealth* says that, if one has land, then one can grow very many things and therefore "have wealth."

1.6   *To have wealth is to have resources*: For the state's use there is wealth and abundance and, through this, there is supply for the state's use.

1.7   *Virtue is the root; wealth is the branch*: Virtue enables one to achieve wealth so wealth is dependent on virtue. Therefore, virtue is the root and wealth the branch.

1.8   *[If the ruler] distances himself from the root and draws near to the branch, he will contend with the people and teach them to plunder*: *Wai* 外 is equivalent to *shu* 疏 (distant); *nei* 內 is equivalent to *qin* 親 (near). *Shi duo* 施奪 refers to stirring up a spirit of plunder. If the ruler holds wealth dear and distances himself from virtue, then people who contend for profit all bring about a spirit of plunder.

1.9   *This is why the people disperse when wealth is gathered but gather when wealth is dispersed*: The two matters do not arise separately; wealth is established through the people. If the ruler attaches great importance to wealth and treats the people lightly, then the people disperse. If there is distribution of wealth and generosity towards the people, then the people all return and gather.

1.10 *This is also why contrary words come back when contrary words go forth*: *Bei* 悖 is equivalent to *ni* 逆 (contrary, opposing). If the words of the ruler's official exhortations are contrary to the people's hearts and come forth, then the people are refractory towards the ruler above so what comes back by way of response is opposition to the ruler's decree.

1.11 *And why ill-gotten goods go out when ill-gotten goods come in*: If the ruler attaches importance to gathering wealth and goods in opposition to the people's hearts, and embarks on a course of accumulating and amassing, he will not be able to retain the wealth for long. People will be in opposition to him above and the wealth also will be contrary to the ruler's heart and will be dispersed and go forth. That is to say, if the multitudes are rebellious and want to leave, the wealth is dispersed and the ruler does not have it.

1.12　《正義》曰：「師，眾也」，「峻，大也」，皆〈釋詁〉文。[34]《爾雅》「峻」字馬旁為之，與此同也。「克，能也」，〈釋言〉文也。[35] 云「君有逆命，則民有逆辭也」者，「君有逆命」，解經「言悖而出」也。「民有逆辭」，解經「亦悖而入」，謂人有逆命之辭以拒君也。云「《老子》曰：多藏必厚亡」[36] 者，言積聚藏之既多，必厚重而散亡也。引之者，證「貨悖而入，亦悖而出」。

2.1　「〈康誥〉曰：惟命不于常」者，謂天之命，不於是常住在一家也。「道善則得之，不善則失之矣」，《書》之本意，言道為善則得之，不善則失之，是不常在一家也。

3–4.1　「<u>舅犯</u>曰：亡人無以為寶，仁親以為寶」者，此<u>舅犯</u>勸<u>重耳</u>之辭。於時<u>重耳</u>逃亡在<u>翟</u>，<u>秦穆公</u>欲納之反國，而勸<u>重耳</u>不受<u>秦</u>命，對<u>秦</u>使云：奔亡之人，無以貨財為寶，唯親愛仁道以為寶也。

{注「楚書」至「奚恤」。}

3–4.2　《正義》曰：<u>鄭</u>知是「<u>楚昭王</u>時書」者，案〈楚語〉云：「<u>楚昭王</u>使<u>王孫圉</u>聘於<u>晉</u>，<u>定公</u>饗之。<u>趙簡子</u>鳴玉以相問於<u>王孫圉</u>，曰：『<u>楚</u>之白珩猶在乎？其為寶幾何矣？』<u>王孫圉</u>對曰：『未嘗為寶。<u>楚</u>之所寶者，曰<u>觀射父</u>，能作訓辭，以行事於諸侯，使無以寡君為口實。』」[37] 又《新序》云：「<u>秦</u>欲伐<u>楚</u>，使者觀<u>楚</u>之寶器。<u>楚</u>王召<u>昭奚恤</u>而問焉，對曰：『寶器在賢臣。』王遂使<u>昭奚恤</u>應之。<u>昭奚恤</u>發精兵三百人，陳於西門之內，為東面之壇一，南面之壇四，西面之壇一。<u>秦</u>使者至，<u>昭奚恤</u>曰：『君客也，請就上居東面之壇。』<u>令尹子西</u>南面，<u>太宗子牧</u>次之，<u>葉公子高</u>次之，<u>司馬子發</u>

34　*Er ya* 1, SSJZS, 8:21, 7.

35　*Er ya* 2, SSJZS, 8:44.

36　Lau, *Tao Te Ching: A Bilingual Edition*, 44, 64–66.

37　See the *Guoyu* ("Chuyu xia"), SBCK, 14:134.

1.12 The *Zhengyi* says: "*Shi* 師 is equivalent to *zhong* 眾 (the multitude, masses); *jun* 峻 is equivalent to *da* 大 (great, large)." Both are from the *Shigu* 釋詁. In the *Er ya*, the character *jun* is written with *ma* 馬 beside it (i.e. 駿), and is the same. *Ke* 克 is equivalent to *neng* 能 (to be able) which is from the *Shiyan*. In the statement: "If the ruler acts in opposition to [Heaven's] decree, then the people will make opposing statements," "If the ruler acts in opposition to [Heaven's] decree" explains the section's *contrary words go forth*. "The people will make opposing statements" explains the section's *it is also contrary words that come back*, which is to say that the people's contrary statements are in opposition to the ruler. In the *Laozi* it says: "Storing up much inevitably brings heavy loss." This says that, when much is amassed, collected and stored, there is certainly a substantial amount that will be lost as well. In quoting it, there is verification of *ill-gotten goods go out when ill-gotten goods come in*.

2.1 The *"Announcement to Kang"* states: *"The mandate of Heaven is not everlasting"*: This says that the decree of Heaven does not remain everlastingly with one house. *If the Way is good then it is attained; if the Way is not good then it is lost* is the original meaning from the *Documents* and says that, if the Way is good then one gets it (i.e. the mandate) and if it is not good then one loses it, which is being not everlastingly with one house.

3–4.1 *Jiu Fan said: "The lost person (exiled prince) took nothing to be precious other than loving and cherishing the Way of ren* 仁*"*: These are Jiu Fan's words of exhortation to Chong'er. At the time, Chong'er fled and was exiled in Di. Duke Mu of Qin wished to receive him back in the state and [Jiu Fan] exhorted Chong'er not to receive the Qin decree. To the Qin envoy, he said: "I am a man who has fled into exile and do not take wealth and material goods to be precious. I take only the love of the Way of *ren* 仁 to be precious."

3–4.2 The *Zhengyi* says that Zheng knew this "*Documents* from the time of King Zhao of Chu." According to the "Chuyu," it is said: "King Zhao of Chu sent Wangsun Yu with gifts to Jin, offering them to Duke Ding. Zhao Jianzi struck the jade and questioned Wangsun Yu, saying: "What is Chu's white gem like? How precious is it?" Wangsun Yu replied: "It is not precious at all. What Chu has is precious— I speak of Guan Shefu. He is able to write instructions for the conduct of affairs with the feudal lords and make it so that the ruler is not the cause for talk." Also, the *Xinxu* says: "Qin wished to invade Chu and sent an envoy to look at Chu's precious instrument. The Chu king summoned Zhao Xixu and asked him about it. He replied: 'Precious treasures lie in worthy officials.' The king subsequently sent Zhao Xixu to respond to this. Zhao Xixu raised picked troops to the number of three hundred men and positioned them within the Western gate. He made one altar facing east, four altars facing south, and one altar facing west. When the Qin envoy arrived, Zhao Xixu said: 'You, sir, are a guest. I ask that you ascend to the east-facing altar.' The Lingyin Zixi faced the south, the Taizong Zimu came after him, the Ye duke, Zigao came after him, and Sima Zifa came after him.

次之。<u>昭奚恤</u>自居西面之壇,稱曰:『客欲觀楚之寶器乎?<u>楚</u>之所寶者,既賢臣也。唯大國之所觀!』<u>秦</u>使無以對也。使歸,告<u>秦王</u>曰:『<u>楚</u>多賢臣,無可以圖之。』」[38] 何知有<u>觀射父</u>,<u>昭奚恤</u>者?案《戰國義》云:「<u>楚王</u>築壇,<u>昭奚恤</u>等立於壇上。<u>楚王</u>指之,謂<u>秦</u>使曰:『此寡人之寶。』」[39] 故知有<u>昭奚恤</u>等也。謂賢為寶者,案《史記》云:「理百姓,實府庫,使黎甿得所者,有<u>令尹子西</u>而能也。執法令,奉圭璋,使諸侯不怨,兵車不起者,有<u>大宗子牧</u>能也。守封疆,固城郭,使鄰國不侵,亦不侵鄰國者,有<u>葉公子高</u>能也。整師旅,治兵戈,使蹈白刃,赴湯蹈火,萬死不顧一生者,有<u>司馬子發</u>能也。坐籌帷幄之中,決勝千里之外,懷霸王之業,撥理亂之風,有大夫<u>昭奚恤</u>能也。是皆為寶也。」[40] 引之者,證為君長能保愛善人為寶也。

{注「舅犯」至「利也」。}

3–4.3 《正義》曰:「<u>舅犯</u>,<u>晉文公</u>之舅<u>狐偃</u>」者,《左傳》文也。[41] 云「時避<u>驪姬</u>之讒,亡在<u>翟</u>而獻公薨。<u>秦穆公</u>使<u>子顯</u>弔之,因勸之復國。<u>舅犯</u>為之對此辭也」,〈檀弓〉篇文。[42]

---

38 See the *Xinxu* 新序, CSJC, n.s, 18:664.
39 There is no record of a work of this name in either the SKQS Index or the ZWDCD.
40 This could not be located in the *Shiji* but see the *Guoyu* ("Chuyu xia"), note 37 above.
41 Not located in the *Zuo zhuan*.
42 *Li ji* 4 ("Tan Gong xia"), SSJZS, 5:166–67.

Zhao Xixu himself took his position at the west-facing altar and declared: 'Does the guest wish to see Chu's precious instrument? What Chu has that is precious is just worthy officials. These are what a great state sees.' The Qin envoy had no way of replying. He returned and informed the Qin king, saying: 'Chu has many worthy officials—not something we would want.'" How do we know there were Guan Shefu and Zhao Xixu? According to the *Zhanguo yi*, which says: "The Chu king built altars. Zhao Xixu and others were positioned at the altars. The Chu king pointed to them and spoke to the Qin envoy, saying: 'These are my treasures.'" Therefore we know that there was Zhao Xixu and the others. In speaking of worthiness being a treasure, the *Shiji* states: "To manage the ordinary people, fill the treasuries and storehouses, and cause the ordinary people to find a place, there is the Lingyin Zixi and he is able. To manage law and order, to receive the jade tally, to cause the feudal lords to be without resentment, and armed forces not to be raised, there is the Taizong Zimu and he is able. To defend and block-ade the borders, to establish walls and fortifications, to cause neighbouring states not to invade and also not to invade neighbouring states, there is Yegong Zigao and he is able. To marshal the *shilü* (body of 2,500 troops), to put weapons in order, to face down naked blades, to brave fire and water, and to risk a thousand deaths in one life without a backward glance, there is Sima Zifa and he is able. To sit and calculate behind curtains and screens, to decide victory a thousand *li* away, to look after the matter of hegemons and kings, and to dissipate the atmo-sphere of rebellion, there is the grandee Zhao Xixu and he is able. All these men are treasures." The quotation verifies the fact that princes and rulers are able to protect and love good men as treasures.

3–4.3 The *Zhengyi* saying that Jiu Fan was Hu Yan, Duke Wen of Jin's maternal uncle, is from the *Zuo zhuan*. The statement, "At the time he suffered Li Ji's slander and was banished to Di. When Duke Xian died, Duke Mu of Qin sent his son Xian Diao to persuade him to return to the kingdom. Jiu Fan took exception to this statement" is based on the "Tan Gong."

TX13:〈秦誓〉曰：「若有一介臣，斷斷兮，無他技，其心休休焉，其如有容焉。人之有技，若己有之。人之彥聖，其心好之，不啻若自其口出，寔能容之，以能保我子孫黎民，尚亦有利哉！人之有技，媢嫉以惡之。人之彥聖，而違之，俾不通，寔不能容，以不能保我子孫黎民，亦曰殆哉！」[43] **[1]**唯仁人放流之，迸諸四夷，不與同中國。此謂唯仁人，為能愛人，能惡人。**[2]**見賢而不能舉，舉而不能先，命也。見不善而不能退，退而不能遠，過也。**[3]**好人之所惡，惡人之所好，是謂拂人之性，菑必逮夫身。**[4]**是故君子有大道，必忠信以得之，驕泰以失之。**[5]**

Comment: The first half of this section consists of a quotation from the *Documents* on the qualities required in a good minister contrasted with those displayed by a bad minister. On this quotation, Legge has: "The declaration of the duke of Ch'in is the last book of the Shu-ching. It was made by one of the dukes of Ch'in to his officers, after he had sustained a great disaster, in consequence of neglecting the advice of his most faithful minister. Between the text here, and that which we find in the Shu, there are some differences, but they are unimportant."[44] The second half of the section comprises four statements about the proper conduct for a noble man.

注 TX13 (鄭玄)

[1]〈秦誓〉，《尚書》篇名也。秦穆公伐鄭，為晉所敗於殽，還誓其羣臣，而作此篇也。斷斷，誠一之貌也。他技，異端之技也。有技，才藝之技也。「若己有之」，「不啻若自其口出」，皆樂人有善之甚也。美士為「彥」。黎，眾也。尚，庶幾也。媢，妬也。違，猶戾也。俾，使也。佛戾賢人所為，使功不通於君也。殆，危也。彥，或作「盤」。{一个，古賀反，一讀作「介」，音界。}「臣」，此所引與《尚書》文小異。{斷，丁亂反。無它音他。技，其綺反，下及注同。}休休，{許虯反。}《尚書傳》曰：「樂善也。」鄭注《尚書》云：「寬容貌。」[45] 何休注《公羊》云：「美大之貌。」[46] {好，呼報反。啻音試，詩豉反。媢，莫報反。《尚書》作冒，音同，謂覆蔽也。惡，烏路反，下「能惡人」同。俾，本又作卑，必爾反。敗，必邁反。殽，戶交反。樂音岳，又音洛。妬，丁路反。佛戾，上扶弗反，下力計反。}

---

43 The *Documents*, "Qin shi," LCC, 3:629. For the circumstances underlying the writing of this Declaration, see Legge's note on pp. 626–27.

44 See LCC, 1:378.

45 See *Shang shu*, in SSJZS, 1:315 and for Zheng Xuan's 鄭玄 comment, LCC, 3:629 (Legge's note).

46 He Xiu's 何休 notes to the *Gongyang zhuan* 公羊傳 are to be found in the SSJZS, vol. 7.

TX13: The "Declaration of Qin" states: "Suppose there is one resolute minister, a decisive and unswerving man without unusual skills, but with a mind at ease and well-disposed, and a demeanour in keeping. When others have skills, it is as if he himself has them; when others are accomplished and sage-like, he loves them in his heart more than his words express and is truly able to accept them. Because he would be able to preserve my descendants and the masses, it may be that he too would be of benefit. Suppose, however, there is a man who is jealous and envious when others have skills such that he hates them, and when others are accomplished and sage-like, he opposes them, obstructs their advancement and is truly unable to accept them. Because he would not be able to protect my descendants and the masses, I would say he was dangerous." **[1]** Only a man who is imbued with *ren* 仁 will send away and banish such a person, driving him off to the four barbarians, and will not allow him to dwell with him in the Central Kingdom. That is to say, only a man who is imbued with *ren* 仁 is able to love others and to hate others. **[2]** To see one who is worthy and yet not be able to bring him forward, or to bring him forward but not be able to put him first, is to be disrespectful. To see one who is bad and not be able to send him away, or to send him away but not be able to send him far away, is a fault. **[3]** To love what others hate, or to hate what others love—this is called going against human nature and invites certain disaster. **[4]** This is why the noble man has the great Way. Certainly, loyalty and trust are the ways to attain it, whereas arrogance and pride are the ways to lose it. **[5]**

Notes TX13 (Zheng Xuan)

[1] The "Declaration of Qin" is the name of a chapter of the *Shang shu*. Duke Mu of Qin attacked Zheng and was defeated by Jin at Xiao. On returning, he made the declaration to his many officials and wrote this chapter. *Duan duan* 斷斷 indicates the appearance of one who is sincere and single-minded (devoted). *Ta ji* 他技 are skills that are unusual; *you ji* 有技 are the attributes of talent and ability. *It is as if he himself has them* and *more than his words express* both indicate his great happiness at others being good. An excellent officer is *yan* 彥 (accomplished). *Li* 黎 is equivalent to *zhong* 眾 (the multitude, masses). *Shang* 尚 is equivalent to *shuji* 庶幾 (it may be). *Mao* 媢 is equivalent to *du* 妒 (to be jealous, envy). *Wei* 違 is like *li* 戾 (perverse, unreasonable). *Bi* 俾 is equivalent to *shi* 使 (to let, allow). If you go against what a worthy person does, this causes the achievement not to extend to the ruler. *Dai* 殆 is equivalent to *wei* 危 (dangerous). *Yan* 彥 is sometimes written *pan* 盤. . . . On *chen* 臣, what is quoted is a little different from the *Shang shu* text. . . . On *xiu xiu* 休休 . . . the *Shang shu Commentary* says: "Liking to be good." Zheng's notes on the *Shang shu* speak of "a tolerant appearance." He Xiu's notes on the *Gongyang* speak of "an admirable and imposing appearance." . . .

[2] 放去惡人媚嫉之類者，獨仁人能之，如舜放四罪而天下咸服。[47]{迸，比孟反，又逼諍反。諍音爭鬭之爭。皇云：「迸猶屏也。」去，丘呂反。}

[3] 命，讀為「慢」，聲之誤也。舉賢而不能使君以先己，是輕慢於舉人也。{命，依注音慢，武諫反。遠，于萬反。}

[4] 拂，猶佹也。逮，及也。{好，呼報反，下皆同。惡，烏路反，下同。拂，扶弗反，注同。菑音哉，下同。逮音代，一音大計反。夫音扶。佹，九委反。}

[5] 道行所由。

疏 TX13 (孔穎達)

1.1　「〈秦誓〉曰」者，此一經明君臣進賢詘惡之事。〈秦誓〉，《尚書》篇名。<u>秦穆公</u>伐<u>鄭</u>，為<u>晉</u>敗於<u>殽</u>，還歸誓羣臣而作此篇，是<u>秦穆公</u>悔過自誓之辭。記者引之，以明好賢去惡也。

1.2　「若有一介臣，斷斷兮」者，此<u>秦穆公</u>誓辭云，羣臣若有一耿介之臣，斷斷然誠實專一謹愨。兮是語辭。《古文尚書》「兮」為「猗」。言有一介之臣，其心斷斷，猗猗然專一，與此本異。

1.3　「無他技，其心休休焉，其如有容焉」者，言此專一之臣，無他奇異之技，惟其心休休然寬容，形貌似有包容，如此之人，我當任用也。

1.4　「人之有技，若己有之」者，謂見人有技藝，欲得親愛之，如己自有也。

1.5　「人之彥聖，其心好之，不啻若自其口出」者，謂見人有才彥美通聖，其心中愛樂，不啻如自其口出。心愛此彥聖之美，多於口說，言其愛樂之甚也。

---

[47]　"Shun dian," *Documents*, LCC, 3:39–40.

[2] To send away evil men of the sort who are jealous and envious is something only a man who is *ren* 仁 is able to do. For example, Shun sent away the "four criminals" and the world became compliant. . . .

[3] *Ming* 命 is read as *man* 慢 (to be disrespectful, dilatory)—the sound is wrong. To bring forward worthy men and yet be unable to get the ruler to give them primacy is to be disrespectful to those brought forward. . . .

[4] *Fu* 拂 is like *gui* 佪 (read as *gui* 詭—to oppose, offend). *Kang* 康 is like *ji* 及 (to come to, reach to). . . .

[5] The method of implementing the Way.

Commentary TX13 (Kong Yingda)

1.1   *The "Declaration of Qin" states*: This section clarifies the matter of ruler and minister advancing worthiness and reducing evil. The "Declaration of Qin" is a chapter of the *Shang shu* (*Documents*). When Duke Mu of Qin attacked Zheng, he was defeated by Jin at Xiao. On returning, he made a declaration to the many officials and wrote this chapter. This is Duke Mu of Qin's statement acknowledging his failure and making a declaration. The [*Li*] *ji* quotes this to clarify loving worthiness and getting rid of evil.

1.2   *Suppose there is one resolute minister, a decisive and unswerving man*: This is what the words of Duke Mu of Qin's declaration say—that if, among the many officials, there is one resolute man who is absolutely sincere, single-minded and completely honest. *Xi* 兮 is a particle. In the *Guwen Shang Shu*, *xi* 兮 is *yi* 猗. To say "suppose there is one resolute official whose mind is straightforward and honest, and who is fiercely single-minded in his devotion" differs from this version.

1.3   *Without unusual skills but with a mind at ease and well-disposed, and a demeanour in keeping* says that this is a wholly devoted official who is without unusual or different skills. His mind is just, tolerant and liberal; his demeanour is one of patience. A man like this would be proper for me to employ.

1.4   *When others have skills, it is as if he himself has them*: This says that, if he sees a man who has skills, he wishes to cherish and love him as if he himself had the skills.

1.5   *When others are accomplished and sage-like, he loves them in his heart more than his words express*: This refers to seeing a person who is talented, accomplished, elegant, perceptive and sagacious, and, in his heart, feeling love and happiness more than he himself can express in his words. If, in his heart, he loves this elegant and sage-like excellence more than words can say, it speaks of the magnitude of his love and happiness.

1.6 「寔能容之，以能保我子孫黎民，尚亦有利哉」者，實，是也。若能好賢如此，是能有所包容，則我國家得安，保我後世子孫。黎，眾也。尚，庶幾也。非直子孫安，其下眾人皆庶幾亦望有利益哉也。

1.7 「人之有技，媢疾以惡之」者，上明進賢之善，此論蔽賢之惡也。媢，妒也。見人有技藝，則掩藏媢妒，疾以憎惡之也。

1.8 「人之彥聖，而違之，俾不通」者，見他人之彥聖，而違戾抑退之。俾，使也，使其善功不通達於君。《尚書》「通」為「達」字也。

1.9 「寔不能容，以不能保我子孫黎民，亦曰殆哉」者，若此蔽賢之人，是不能容納，家國將亡，不能保我子孫。非唯如此，眾人亦曰殆危哉。
   {注「秦誓」至「危也」。}

1.10 《正義》曰：「秦穆公伐鄭，為晉所敗於殽，還誓其羣臣，而作此篇也」者，案《尚書•序》秦穆公伐鄭，晉襄公帥師敗諸殽，還歸，作〈秦誓〉。[48] 又《左傳》僖三十二年秦穆公興師伐鄭，蹇叔等諫之，公不從，為晉人與姜戎要而擊之，敗諸殽，是其事也。[49] 云「美士為彥」者，《爾雅•釋訓》文。[50]「黎，眾也」，「俾，使也」，皆《釋詁》文。[51]「尚，庶幾」者，《釋言》文。《爾雅》「庶幾，尚也」，是「尚」為「庶幾」矣。[52] 云「媢，妒也」者，《說文》云「媢，夫妒婦」，是「媢」為「妒」也。[53]

48 See the preface to the *Documents*, LCC, 3:14.
49 See the *Zuo zhuan* for the 32nd year of Duke Xi, LCC, 5: 220–21.
50 *Er ya* 4, SSJZS, 8:60.
51 *Er ya* 2, SSJZS, 8: 21, 28.
52 *Er ya* 3, SSJZS, 8:37.
53 See Xu, *Shuowen jiezi zhu*, 628.

1.6   *Is truly able to accept them. Because he would be able to preserve my descendants and the masses, it may be that he too would be of benefit*: *Shi* 實 is equivalent to *shi* 是 (this). If I am able to love a worthy person like this, this is being able to be patient, so then my state and household will attain peace and there will be protection for my descendants of later generations. *Li* 黎 is equivalent to *zhong* 眾 (the multitude, masses); *shang* 尚 is equivalent to *shuji* 庶幾 (it may be, so that). Not only would my descendants be peaceful but it may be that the masses below could also all expect to have benefits and advantages.

1.7   *Suppose, however, there is a man who is jealous and envious when others have skills such that he hates them*: Above, there is clarification of the good of advancing worthiness; this considers the evil of concealing worthiness. *Mao* 媢 is equivalent to *du* 妬 (to be jealous, to envy). If he sees another with skills and abilities then, concealing and hiding his own jealousy, he hates and dislikes him.

1.8   *And when others are accomplished and sage-like, he opposes them and obstructs their advancement*: He sees others who are accomplished and sage-like and he himself is refractory and perverse, curbing them and sending them away. *Bi* 俾 is equivalent to *shi* 使 in the sense of not allowing their goodness and merit to get through to the ruler. In the *Shang shu*, *tong* 通 is written as *da* 達.

1.9   *Is truly unable to accept them. Because he would not be able to protect my descendants and the masses, I would say he was dangerous*: If this man concealed worthiness and could not truly tolerate it, the household and state would be lost and he would not be able to protect my descendants. Not only this, but the ordinary people could also be said to be in danger.

1.10   The *Zhengyi* says: "Duke Mu of Qin attacked Zheng but was defeated by Jin at Xiao. On his return, he made a declaration to his numerous officials and wrote this chapter." According to the preface to the *Shang shu*, Duke Mu of Qin attacked Zheng. Duke Xiang of Jin led an army which defeated him at Xiao. On his return, he wrote the "Declaration of Qin." Also, in the *Zuo zhuan* for the 32nd year of Duke Xi it has that Duke Mu of Qin raised an army to attack Zheng. Jian Shu and others pleaded with him but the Duke did not follow their advice. So it was that the Jin people made an agreement with Jiang Rong and he was attacked and defeated at Xiao. This is the matter in question. The statement, "fine officers are accomplished" is from "Shixun" of the *Er ya*. *Li* 黎 being equivalent to *zhong* 眾 (the multitude, masses) and *bi* 俾 being equivalent to *shi* 使 (to let, allow) are both from the *Shigu*. *Shang* 尚 being equivalent to *shuji* 庶幾 (it may be, so that) is from the *Shiyan*. The *Er ya* has "*shuji* 庶幾 is equivalent to *shang* 尚," which is *shang* 尚 being *shuji* 庶幾. On saying, "*mao* 媢 is equivalent to *du* 妬," the *Shuowen* says that "*mao* 媢 is *dufu* 妬婦," which is *mao* 媢 being *du* 妬.

2.1　「唯仁人放流之，迸諸四夷，不與同中國」者，言唯仁人之君，能放流此蔽善之人，使迸遠在四夷，不與同在中國。若舜流四凶，而天下咸服是也。

2.2　「此謂唯仁人，為能愛人，能惡人」者，既放此蔽賢之人遠在四夷，是仁人能愛善人，惡不善之人。

3.1　「見賢而不能舉，舉而不能先，命也」者，此謂凡庸小人，見此賢人而不能舉進於君。假設舉之，又不能使在其己之先，是為慢也。謂輕慢於舉人也。

3.2　「見不善而不能退，退而不能遠，過也」者，此謂小人見不善之人而不能抑退之。假令抑退之，而不能使遠退之。過者，言是愆過之人也。

4.1　「好人之所惡」者，人謂君子，君子所惡者，凶惡之事，今乃愛好凶惡，是好人之所惡也。

4.2　「惡人之所好」者，君子所好仁義善道。今乃惡此仁義善道，是「惡人之所好」也。

4.3　「是謂拂人之性」者，若如此者，是謂拂戾善人之性。

4.4　「菑必逮夫身」者，逮，及也。如此，菑必及夫身矣。

5.1　「是故君子有大道」者，大道，謂所由行孝悌仁義之大道也。

5.2　「必忠信以得之，驕泰以失之」者，言此孝悌仁義，必由行忠信以得之，由身驕泰以失之也。

2.1   *Only a man who is imbued with ren* 仁 *will send away and banish such a person, driving him off to the four barbarians, and will not allow him to dwell with him in the Central Kingdom*: This says that only a ruler who is a man of *ren* 仁 is able to banish this person who conceals goodness, sending him far away among the four barbarians, and not letting him dwell together with him in the Central Kingdom. For example, Shun banishing the "four criminals" and the world all becoming compliant was this.

2.2   *That is to say, only a man who is ren* 仁 *is able to love others and to hate others*: When one sends away and banishes far distant among the four barbarians those people who conceal worthiness, this is the man who is *ren* 仁 being able to love the good person and hate the bad person.

3.1   *To see one who is worthy and yet not be able to bring him forward, or to bring him forward but not be able to put him first, is to be disrespectful*: This refers to ordinary lesser men seeing this worthy man and not being able to advance him and present him to the ruler; or advancing him but not being able to put him above themselves. This is to be disrespectful. This speaks of being disrespectful in advancing others.

3.2   *To see one who is bad and yet not be able to send him away, or to send him away but not be able to send him far away, is a fault*: This refers to a lesser man seeing someone who is not good but not being able to curb him and send him away or, if he does curb him and send him away, not being able to send him far away. *Guozhe* 過者 says this is a person at fault.

4.1   *To love what others hate*: *Ren* 人 refers to the noble man. What a noble man hates are the matters of misfortune and evil. Now, in fact, to love misfortune and evil is to love what a good person hates.

4.2   *To hate what others love*: What the noble man loves are *ren* 仁 (loving kindness), *yi* 義 (right action) and goodness and the Way. Now, in fact, to hate this *ren* 仁 and *yi* 義 and goodness and the Way is "to hate what others love."

4.3   *This is called going against human nature*: This is like speaking of being contrary to the nature of a good person.

4.4   *And invites certain disaster*: *Dai* 逮 is equivalent to *ji* 及 (to come to, to reach). Like this, disaster will certainly befall oneself.

5.1   *This is why the noble man has the great Way*: The Great Way (*da dao* 大道) refers to the great Way that is implemented through filial piety (*xiao* 孝), fraternal respect (*ti* 悌), loving kindness (*ren* 仁) and right action (*yi* 義).

5.2   *Certainly, loyalty and trust are the ways to attain it, whereas arrogance and pride are the ways to lose it*: That is to say, filial piety (*xiao* 孝), fraternal respect (*ti* 悌), loving kindness (*ren* 仁) and right action (*yi* 義) must be achieved by acting with loyalty and trust. It is by being arrogant and proud that this is lost.

TX14: 生財有大道，生之者眾，食之者寡，為之者疾，用之者舒，則財恒足矣。**[1]**仁者以財發身，不仁者以身發財。**[2]**未有上好仁而下不好義者也，未有好義其事不終者也，未有府庫財非其財者也。**[3]**

Comment: In this and the following section the matter of the accumulation of wealth and resources, and the need to set this in the appropriate ethical context, is addressed. That is, there must be diligence in production coupled with restraint in use. Then material wealth can be put to its proper use and, in the case of the ruler, expresses his *ren* 仁. The responses of the beneficiaries will then be by *yi* 義 so this may be seen as an extension of the principle of reciprocity. The sequence is: if the superior loves *ren* 仁, his inferiors will respond with *yi* 義 and so affairs will invariably come to a satisfactory conclusion. The converse is considered in the next and final section.

注 TX14 (鄭玄)

[1] 是不務祿不肖，而勉民以農也。{肖音笑。}

[2] 發，起也。言仁人有財，則務於施與，以起身成其令名。不仁之人，有身貪於聚斂，以起財務成富。{施，始豉反。予，由汝反。}

[3] 言君行仁道，則其臣必義。以義舉事無不成者。其為誠然，如己府庫之時為己有也。

疏 TX14 (孔穎達)

1.1　「生財有大道」者，此一經明人君當先行仁義，愛省國用，以豐足財物。上文「大道」，謂孝悌仁義之道，此言人君生殖其財，有大道之理，則下之所云者是也。

1.2　「生之者眾」者，謂為農桑多也。

1.3　「食之者寡」者，謂減省無用之費也。

1.4　「為之者疾」者，謂百姓急營農桑事業也。

1.5　「用之者舒」者，謂君上緩於營造費用也。

TX14: There is a great Way for the creation of wealth. Let those who create wealth be many; let those who consume it be few. Let those who create wealth do so with urgency; let those who use it do so with restraint. Then wealth will always be sufficient. **[1]** The man of *ren* 仁 uses wealth to raise himself. The man without *ren* 仁 uses himself to raise wealth. **[2]** There has never been a case of a superior (ruler) loving *ren* 仁 and inferiors not loving *yi* 義. There has never been a case of [inferiors] loving *yi* 義 and affairs not reaching fulfilment. There has never been a case of the wealth stored in the treasuries and storehouses not being his (i.e. the ruler's) wealth. **[3]**

Notes TX14 (Zheng Xuan)

[1] This is to emphasise that salary is of little importance and to encourage people towards agriculture. . . .

[2] *Fa* 發 is equivalent to *qi* 起 (to raise). This says that, if the man of *ren* 仁 has wealth, then he places importance in largesse to raise himself and establish his reputation. A man without *ren* 仁 has a self that is greedy in amassing wealth and takes raising wealth as important in becoming rich. . . .

[3] This says that, if the noble man (ruler) implements the Way of *ren* 仁, then his officials are necessarily *yi* 義. By conducting affairs with *yi* 義, there is nothing that is not brought to fulfilment. His being *cheng* 誠 is exemplified by his treasuries and storehouses at the time being what he has.

Commentary TX14 (Kong Yingda)

1.1　*There is a great Way for the creation of wealth*: This section makes it clear that the ruler should first practice *ren* 仁 and *yi* 義, and should love frugality in using the state's resources so as to have an adequate abundance of materials. The "great Way" of the above text refers to the Way of filial piety, fraternal love, loving kindness (*ren* 仁) and right action (*yi* 義). That is to say, if the ruler creates wealth and has the principles of the "great Way," then what is said in the following passage is true.

1.2　*Let those who create wealth be many* says that there should be many who carry out agriculture and sericulture.

1.3　*Let those who consume it be few* says that there should be reduction of wasteful expenditure.

1.4　*Let those who create wealth do so with urgency* says that the ordinary people should manage the occupations of agriculture and sericulture with urgency.

1.5　*Let those who use it do so with restraint* refers to the ruler being measured in regulating the costs of building.

1.6 「則財恒足矣」者,言人君能如此,則國用恒足。

2.1 「仁者以財發身」者,謂仁德之君,以財散施發起身之令名也。

2.2 「不仁者以身發財」者,言不仁之人,唯在吝嗇,務於積聚,勞役其身,發起其財。此在治家、治國天下之科,皆謂人君也。

3.1 「未有上好仁而下不好義者也」,言在上人君好以仁道接下,其下感君仁恩,無有不愛好於義,使事皆得其宜也。

3.2 「未有好義其事不終者也」,言臣下悉皆好義,百事盡能終成,故云「未有好義其事不終者」,言皆能終成也。

3.3 「未有府庫財非其財者也」,又為人君作譬也。君若行仁,民必報義,義必終事。譬如人君有府庫之財,必還為所用也,故云「未有府庫財非其財者也」。

   {注「其為」至「有也」。}

3.4 《正義》曰:言君行仁道,則臣必為義。臣既行義,事必終成。以至誠相感,必有實報,如己有府庫之財,為己所有也。其為誠實而然,言不虛也。

1.6   *Then wealth will always be sufficient* says that, if the ruler is able to act in this way, then there is always enough for the state's use.

2.1   *The man of ren* 仁 *uses wealth to raise himself* says that the ruler who is *ren* 仁 (imbued with loving kindness) and *de* 德 (virtuous) uses the distribution of wealth to develop and raise his own good name.

2.2   *The man without ren* 仁 *uses himself to raise wealth* says that the man who is without *ren* 仁 only exists in a state of parsimony, giving importance to amassing and accumulating, wearing out his body to increase his own wealth. When this exists at the level of bringing order to the household and of bringing order to the state and the world, in all instances it relates to the ruler.

3.1   *There has never been a case of a superior (ruler) loving ren* 仁 *and inferiors not loving yi* 義: This says that, if above the ruler loves to follow the Way of *ren* 仁, he connects with those below, his inferiors are moved by the ruler's *ren* 仁 and kindness, and invariably have a love of *yi* 義, causing affairs all to achieve their proper completion.

3.2   *There has never been a case of [inferiors] loving yi* 義 *and affairs not reaching fulfilment*: This says that, if officials and subordinates all love *yi* 義, then the hundred matters can be brought entirely to completion. Therefore, it says *there has never been a case of [inferiors] loving yi* 義 *and affairs not reaching fulfilment*, which is to say that all things can ultimately be completed.

3.3   *There has never been a case of the wealth stored in treasuries and storehouses not being his wealth* also takes the ruler as the example. If the ruler acts with *ren* 仁, then the people inevitably repay him with *yi* 義, and *yi* 義 necessarily brings affairs to completion. For example, if the ruler has materials stored in his treasuries and storehouses, this must always be what is used. Therefore, it says, *there has never been a case of the wealth stored in treasuries and storehouses not being his (i.e. the ruler's) wealth*.

3.4   The *Zhengyi* states that this says, if the ruler practises the way of *ren* 仁, then the ministers will necessarily be *yi* 義. When officials practise *yi* 義, matters are necessarily and finally brought to completion. If there is the influence of mutual perfect *cheng* 誠, there is certainly true recompense, like the wealth that is in treasuries and storehouse being what he himself has. This is absolutely true and states nothing false.

TX15: <u>孟獻子</u>曰：「畜馬乘，不察於雞豚。伐冰之家，不畜牛羊。百乘之家，不畜聚斂之臣。與其有聚斂之臣，寧有盜臣。」此謂國不以利為利，以義為利也。**[1]**長國家而務財用者，必自小人矣。**[2]**彼為善之，小人之使為國家，菑害並至，雖有善者，亦無如之何矣？**[3]**此謂國不以利為利，以義為利也。

Comment: There is no traceable extant source for the opening quotation, attributed to Meng Xianzi, who is identified by both Zheng Xuan and Kong Yingda as a grandee from the state of Lu. The quotation itself directs attention to the important relationship between *yi* 義 (right action, doing what is right) and *li* 利 (seeking profit, benefit). If the ruler falls under the adverse influence of lesser men such that he puts *li* 利 in the sense of profit ahead of *yi* 義, that is, if he makes his focus the accumulation of wealth and commodities, then misfortune will follow.

注 TX15 (鄭玄)

[1] <u>孟獻子</u>，魯大夫<u>仲孫蔑</u>也。「畜馬乘」，謂以士初試為大夫也。「伐冰之家」，卿大夫以上，喪祭用冰。「百乘之家」，有采地者也。雞豚、牛羊，民之所畜養以為財利者也。國家利義不利財，盜臣損財耳，聚斂之臣乃損義。《論語》曰：「<u>季氏</u>富於<u>周公</u>，而<u>求</u>也為之聚斂，非吾徒也，小子鳴鼓而攻之可也。」[54]{畜，許六反，下同。乘，徐繩證反，下及注同。蔑，莫結反。以上，時掌反。采，七代反，本亦作菜。為之，于偽反。}

[2] 言務聚財為己用者，必忘義，是小人所為也。{長，丁丈反。}

[3] 彼，君也。君將欲以仁義善其政，而使小人治其國家之事，患難猥至，雖云有善，不能救之，以其惡之已著也。{難，乃旦反。猥，烏罪反。捄音救，本亦作救。著，張慮反。}

疏 TX15 (孔穎達)

1.1 「<u>孟獻子</u>曰：畜馬乘，不察於雞豚」者，此一經明治國家不可務於積財，若務於積財，即是小人之行，非君上之道。言察於雞豚之所利，為畜養馬乘。士初試為大夫，不闚察於雞豚之小利。

---

[54] *Lunyu* XI.16 (1–2), LCC, 1:242–3. "而附益之," present in the *Lunyu* text, is omitted here.

TX15: Meng Xianzi said: "A man who keeps horses and a carriage does not give thought to chickens and pigs. A household that cuts (i.e. uses) ice does not keep oxen and sheep. A household with a hundred chariots should not retain an officer who collects [wealth from tax levies]. Rather than having an officer who collects [wealth from tax levies], it would be better to have an officer who is a robber." That is to say, a state should not take profit to be a benefit; it should take *yi* 義 to be a benefit. **[1]** If the man who heads a state or household devotes attention to wealth and consumption, this must come from the conduct of a lesser man. **[2]** If the ruler considers lesser men to be good and uses them for the affairs of state or household, both calamity and harm will follow. Even if there is one who is good, of what use will he be? That is to say, a state should not take profit to be of benefit; it should take *yi* 義 to be of benefit. **[3]**

Notes TX15 (Zheng Xuan)

[1] Meng Xianzi was the Lu grandee, Zhongsun Mie. *A man who keeps horses and a carriage* refers to an officer first attempting to become a grandee. *A household that cuts (i.e. uses) ice* indicates ranks above grandee who use ice at funerals. *A household with a hundred chariots* is one with wealth and land. Chickens and pigs, and oxen and sheep are what the ordinary people nurture and raise for wealth and profit. A state or household is benefited by *yi* 義 (right action) and not by profit and wealth. Robber officials harm wealth, but those officers who amass wealth harm *yi* 義. The *Lunyu* says: "The head of the Ji clan is richer than the Duke of Zhou and yet there is Qiu to collect wealth from tax levies. He is no disciple of mine. My children, you may strike the drum and assail him." . . .

[2] This says that to give importance to accumulating wealth for one's own use is a sure way of neglecting *yi* 義. This is what a lesser man does. . . .

[3] *Bi* 彼 is the ruler. If the ruler desires to make his government good through *ren* 仁 and *yi* 義, but lets lesser men attend to the affairs of his state and household, then calamities and difficulties will be many, and, even though he says there is goodness, he is not able to save the situation because this evil is already manifest. . . .

Commentary TX15 (Kong Yingda)

1.1   *Meng Xianzi said: "A man who keeps horses and a carriage does not give thought to chickens and pigs"*: This section makes it clear that in bringing good order to a state or household, it is not possible to devote attention to amassing wealth. If attention is devoted to amassing wealth, then this is the action of a lesser man. It is not the Way of a ruler. This speaks of looking at what the benefits of chickens and pigs are and what the benefits of the nurture and maintenance of horses and carriages are. When an officer first attempts to become a grandee, he does not look to the small profit from chickens and pigs.

1.2 「伐冰之家，不畜牛羊」者，謂卿大夫喪祭用冰，從固陰之處伐擊其冰，以供喪祭，故云「伐冰」也。謂卿大夫為伐冰之家，不畜牛羊為財利，以食祿不與人爭利也。

1.3 「百乘之家，不畜聚斂之臣」者，百乘，謂卿大夫有采地者也。以地方百里，故云「百乘之家」。言卿大夫之家，不畜聚斂之臣，使賦稅什一之外徵求采邑之物也，故《論語》云「百乘之家」[55]是也。

1.4 「與其有聚斂之臣，寧有盜臣」者，覆解「不畜聚斂之臣」之本意。若其有聚斂之臣，寧可有盜竊之臣，以盜臣但善財，聚斂之臣則害義也。

1.5 「此謂國不以利為利，以義為利也」者，言若能如上所謂，是國家之利，但以義事為國家利也。

1.6 《正義》曰：「孟獻子，魯大夫仲孫蔑」者，此據《左傳》文也。[56]「畜馬乘，謂以士初試為大夫」者，案《書》傳「上飾車騑馬」，[57]《詩》云「四牡騑騑」。[58]大夫以上，乃得乘四馬。今下云「伐冰之家」，「百乘之家」，家是卿大夫。今別云「畜馬乘者，不察雞豚」，故知「士初試為大夫」也。伐冰之家，卿大夫者，案昭四年《左傳》云：「大夫命婦，喪浴用冰。」[59]〈喪大記〉注云：士不用冰。[60]故知卿大夫也。士若恩賜及食，而得用，亦有冰也。但非其常，故〈士喪禮〉「賜冰則夷槃」[61]可也，《左傳》又云「食肉之祿，冰皆與焉」[62]是也。云「百乘之家，有采地者也」，此謂卿也。故《論語》云「百乘之家」，鄭云「采地，一同之廣輪」是也。

{「彼為」至「利也」。}

---

[55] *Lunyu* V.7(3), LCC, 1:175 (the quotation is repeated in 1.6).
[56] See the *Chunqiu* and *Zuo zhuan* for the 9th year of Duke Xuan, LCC, 5: 303–5 and particularly Legge's note on par. 3, 304.
[57] Not located.
[58] *Odes*, Mao 162, verse 1, LCC, 4:247.
[59] *Zuo zhuan* for the 4th year of Duke Zhao, LCC, 5:592ff.
[60] On the use of ice see the *Li ji* 22 ("Sang da ji"), SSJZS, 5:769.
[61] *Yi li* 36, SSJZS, 4:420.
[62] See the *Zuo zhuan* for the 4th year of Duke Zhao, LCC, 5:592.

1.2 *A household that cuts (i.e. uses) ice does not keep oxen and sheep* refers to the fact that grandees use ice for funeral sacrifices. From very cold places, they cut and break this ice for their offerings at the funeral sacrifices. Therefore, it says "cut ice." This refers to the households of grandees being those that cut ice, not those that nurture oxen and sheep for wealth and profit. By living on their salaries, they do not contend with other people for profit.

1.3 *A household with a hundred chariots should not retain an officer who collects [wealth from tax levies]*: "A hundred chariots" refers to a grandee having allotted land. The term "a household of a hundred chariots" is used because the land is a hundred *li* square. This says that the household of a grandee should not retain a wealth-amassing officer. It should not retain a wealth-amassing officer and let him collect materials from his fief other than taking one-tenth as tax revenue. This is what is referred to in the *Lunyu* as "a household of a hundred chariots."

1.4 *Rather than having an officer who collects [wealth from tax levies] it would be better to have an officer who is a robber* is a reiteration and explanation of the basic meaning of "should not retain a wealth-amassing officer." Rather than having a wealth-amassing officer, it would be better to have an officer that is a robber, in that an officer who is a robber is good for wealth whereas a wealth-amassing officer is harmful to *yi* 義.

1.5 *That is to say, a state should not take profit to be a benefit; it should take yi* 義 *to be a benefit*: This says that, if one is able to act as outlined above, this is of benefit to a state or household, but it is only through matters of *yi* 義 that a state or household is [truly] benefited.

1.6 The *Zhengyi* says: "Meng Xianzi was the Lu grandee, Zhongsun Mie." This is based on the *Zuo zhuan*. "*One who keeps horses and a carriage refers to an officer's first attempt at becoming a grandee*" is according to the commentary on the *Documents* [as follows]: "Those above have ornamented carriages and pairs of horses." The *Odes* says: "A team of four stallions." Those of the rank of grandee and above acquire four-horse carriages. Now the following statements, *a household that cuts ice* and *a household with a hundred chariots* are the households of grandees. Elsewhere it says: *one who keeps horses and a carriage does not give thought to chickens and pigs* so we know these are "officers who are first trying to become grandees." [With regard to] households that cut ice being those of grandees, according to the *Zuo zhuan* for the 4th year of Duke Zhao, "grandees and their principal wives used ice for washing at funerals." The notes to the "Sangda ji" say that officers did not use ice. Therefore, we know that these are grandees. If officers receive gifts of grace extending to food that they can use, there is also ice. But this was not constant. Thus, the "Shi sangli" saying, "ice was for the ice tray" is possible. Also the *Zuo zhuan* saying that "salaries which allowed the eating of meat all included ice" is this. To say "a household of a hundred chariots had allotted land" is to refer to grandees. Therefore, the *Lunyu* speaks of "a hundred chariot household." Zheng says that *cai di* 采地 is one area together, which is right.

1.7 前經明遠財重義，是「不以利為利，以義為利」，此經明為君治國，棄遠
小人，亦是「不以利為利，以義為利」也。

2.1 「長國家而務財用者，必自小人矣」者，言為人君長於國家而務積聚財以
為己用者，必自為小人之行也。

{注「孟獻」至「可也」。}

3.1 「彼為善之」，彼，謂君也。君欲為仁義之道，善其政教之語辭，故云「彼
為善之」。「小人之使為國家，菑害並至」者，言君欲為善，反令小人使為
治國家之事，毒害於下，故菑害患難，則並皆來至。

3.2 「雖有善者，亦無如之何矣」者，既使小人治國，其君雖有善政亦無能奈
此患難之何。言不能止之，以其惡之已著故也。

1.7   The earlier section clarified [the concept of] distancing oneself from wealth and giving importance to *yi* 義. This is "not taking profit (*li* 利) to be of benefit but taking right action (*yi* 義) to be of benefit." This section makes it clear that to be a ruler who brings good order to a state one must get rid of, and distance oneself from, lesser men. This is also "not taking profit to be of benefit but taking *yi* 義 to be of benefit."

2.1   *If the man who heads a state or household devotes attention to wealth and consumption, this must come from the conduct of a lesser man*: This says that, if the one who heads a state or household gives primary importance to amassing wealth which he takes for his own use, this must be because he himself acts like a lesser man.

3.1   *The other may be good*: The "other" refers to the ruler. If the ruler wishes to implement the Way of *ren* 仁 and *yi* 義, it speaks of his government being good (skillful). *If the ruler considers lesser men to be good and uses them for the affairs of state or household, both calamity and harm will follow* says that, if the ruler desires to be good but, on the contrary, allows lesser men to manage the affairs of state or household, this will have poisonous and harmful effects on those below, therefore calamity, harm, misfortune and difficulty will all come together.

3.2   *Even if there is one who is good, of what use will he be?* When you let lesser men administer the state, even if their ruler is a good administrator, how will he be able to avoid suffering and difficulties? This says that he will not be able to stop them because their badness has already become manifest.

Daxue 大學: The Greater Learning

Notes 注: Zhu Xi 朱熹

大學章句序

《大學》之書，古之大學所以教人之法也。蓋自天降生民，則既莫不與之以仁義禮智之性矣。然其氣質之稟或不能齊，是以不能皆有以知其性之所有而全之也。一有聰明睿智能盡其性者出於其閒，則天必命之以為億兆之君師，使之治而教之，以復其性。此伏羲、神農、黃帝、堯、舜，所以繼天立極，而司徒之職 ，[1] 典樂之官 [2] 所由設也。

三代之隆，其法寖備，然後王宮、國都以及閭巷，莫不有學。人生八歲，則自王公以下，至於庶人之子弟，皆入小學，而教之以灑掃、應對、進退之節 ，[3] 禮樂、射御、書數之文；及其十有五年，則自天子之元子、眾子，以至公、卿、大夫、元士之適子，與凡民之俊秀，皆入大學，而教之以窮理、正心、修己、治人之道。此又學校之教、大小之節所以分也。

---

[1] See the *Documents*, LCC, 3:44, 529 and also Hucker #5801 where he describes the position as " . . . one of great prestige from high antiquity." See Charles O. Hucker, *A Dictionary of Official Titles in Imperial China* (Stanford: Stanford University Press, 1985).

[2] See the *Documents*, LCC, 3: 47–48. The title seems to have had a different significance in the Tang/Song period—see Hucker #6684.

[3] For the first three accomplishments, attributed to the followers of Zixia 子夏, see the *Lunyu* XIX.12, LCC, 1:343.

Preface to the *Daxue zhangju*

The book, the *Daxue*, was the method by which men were instructed in the greater learning in ancient times. Now, from the time Heaven first created people, there was nobody to whom it did not give a nature of *ren* 仁, *yi* 義, *li* 禮, and *zhi* 智.[4] Nevertheless, the endowment of temperament in individuals could not always be equal, which meant that not everyone could have the wherewithal to know what his nature was and perfect it. If someone who was intelligent, perspicacious, astute and wise, someone who could complete his nature, were to come forth from their midst, then Heaven would certainly ordain him as the ruler and teacher of the myriad people, causing him to bring order to them and instruct them so that they might restore their natures. This was how Fu Xi, Shen Nong, Huang Di, Yao and Shun carried on Heaven's establishment of the highest point [of excellence].[5] This is why the position of Minister of Education and the office of Manager of Music were set up.

During the glory of the Three Dynasties,[6] these methods were gradually perfected. Subsequently, from the imperial palace and state capital on down to the villages, there was nowhere without a school. At the age of eight years, from kings and dukes down to the common people, sons and younger brothers all entered on the "lesser learning" (*xiaoxue* 小學) and were instructed in sprinkling and sweeping, answering questions, the etiquette of advancing and retiring, and the accomplishments of ritual, music, archery, charioteering, writing, and mathematics. When they reached the age of 15, the Son of Heaven's eldest son, and other sons down to the legitimate sons of dukes, ministers, great officers, and senior officials, along with outstanding sons of the people in general, all entered the "greater learning" and received instruction in the Way of thorough investigation of principle, rectifying the mind, cultivating the self, and bringing order to the people. This was how the teaching of the schools was divided into "greater" and "lesser."

---

[4]   These four key terms are considered in detail in Appendix 3. There we argue that there is no satisfactory English equivalent for the first three whilst the fourth, *zhi* 智 (also written 知) might be rendered as "wisdom" or "knowledge."

[5]   Fu Xi, Shen Nong and Huang Di were the first three rulers of the legendary period whose reigns, according to tradition, covered the period from 2858 to 2597 BCE. Yao and Shun were the final two emperors of the period prior to the establishment of the Xia dynasty in 2205 BCE under its first emperor, Da Yu 大禹.

[6]   The Xia (2205–1766 BCE), the Shang (1766–1122 BCE) and the Zhou (1122–255 BCE).

夫以學校之設，其廣如此，教之之術，其次第節目之詳又如此，而其所
以為教，則又皆本之人君躬行心得之餘，不待求之民生日用彝倫之外，
是以當世之人無不學。其學焉者，無不有以知其性分之所固有，職分之
所當為，而各俛焉以盡其力。此古昔盛時所以治隆於上，俗美於下，而
非後世之所能及也！

及周之衰，賢聖之君不作，學校之政不修，教化陵夷，風俗頹敗，時則
有若孔子之聖，而不得君師之位以行其政教，於是獨取先王之法，誦而
傳之以詔後世。若〈曲禮〉、〈少儀〉、〈內則〉、〈弟子職〉諸篇，固小學 [7]
之支流餘裔，而此篇者，則因小學之成功，以著大學之明法，外有以極
其規模之大，而內有以盡其節目之詳者也。三千之徒，蓋莫不聞其説，
而曾氏之傳獨得其宗，於是作為傳義，以發其意。及孟子沒而其傳泯
焉，則其書雖存，而知者鮮矣！

---

[7]   Gardner has the following note on "lesser learning" (*xiao xue* 小學): "Chu Hsi suspected
      that historically there had existed a whole text concerning 'lesser learning' but that it had
      become fragmented with the passage of time . . . " See Daniel K. Gardner, *Chu Hsi and
      the Ta-hsueh* (Cambridge: Harvard University Press, 1986), 82n30.

In the setting up of schools, their range was like this and so too were their methods of instruction and the details of their sequence and programme. What they took to be teaching was also based, in all cases, on the superabundance of the noble man's personal practice and acquisition of knowledge from study. But they did not seek to go beyond the cardinal human relationships which the ordinary people followed every day of their lives. This is why, at that time, there was nobody who did not learn. And in this learning, there was nobody without the means of knowing what constituted his individual nature and what was appropriate for his situation, and each made diligent efforts in this to his utmost capacity. This was how, in those splendid times of old, government was glorious in those above and customs were admirable in those below. This is something no later age has been able to achieve.

When it came to the decline of Zhou, worthy and sage-like rulers did not arise, the organisation of schools was not maintained, teaching deteriorated and customs degenerated. At that time, even a sage like Confucius did not attain a position from which he could put into practice his teachings on government. And so it happened that he alone chose the methods of former kings, sung their praises and, through his proclamations, transmitted these methods to later ages. Chapters like the "Quli," "Shaoyi," "Neize" and "Dizi zhi" were surely just the remnants of the arts of "lesser learning."[8] But this chapter sets out the enlightened method of the "greater learning" for the sake of those who had completed the "lesser learning." Outwardly, there was the great magnitude of its scope; inwardly, there was the completeness of the considerations of its sections. Of the three thousand disciples, there was none who did not hear its words, and yet it was Zengzi[9] alone who grasped its essence. As a consequence, he wrote this as a transmission of the meaning to bring out its ideas. However, when Mencius died its transmission came to an end.[10] Then, although the book itself was preserved, those who understood it were few.

---

8   The "Quli" comprises chapters 1 and 2 of the *Li ji*, the "Shaoyi" chapter 17, and the "Neize" chapter 12. The "Dizi zhi" is chapter 59 of the *Guanzi* 管子.

9   Zengzi (Zeng Shen 曾參, 505–437 BC), the putative author of both the *Daxue* 大學 and the *Xiaojing* 孝經, was a first generation disciple of Confucius.

10   The usual date given for Mencius' death is 289 BC.

自是以來，俗儒記誦詞章之習，其功倍於小學而無用；異端虛無寂滅[11]
之教，其高過於大學而無實。其他權謀術數，一切以就功名之説，與夫
百家眾技之流，所以惑世誣民、充塞仁義者，又紛然雜出乎其間。使
其君子不幸而不得聞大道之要，其小人不幸而不得蒙至治之澤，晦盲否
塞，反覆沈痼，以及五季之衰，而壞亂極矣！

天運循環，無往不復。宋德隆盛，治教休明。於是<u>河南程氏</u>兩夫子出，
而有以接乎<u>孟氏</u>之傳。實始尊信此篇而表章之，既又為之次其簡編，發
其歸趣，然後古者大學教人之法、聖經賢傳之指，粲然復明於世。雖以
<u>熹</u>之不敏，亦幸私淑而與有聞焉。顧其為書猶頗放失，是以忘其固陋，
采而輯之，間亦竊附己意，補其闕略，以俟後之君子。極知僭踰，無所
逃罪，然於國家化民成俗之意、學者修己治人之方，則未必無小補云。

(淳熙己酉二月甲子，<u>新安朱熹</u>序)

---

11 On *xuwu* 虛無, the LSCQ 17/5 has: "用虛無為本" to which is added the following
    note:「虛無，無所愛惡也。」In the ZWDCD there is also reference to the *Shiji* which
    has:「道家無為……其術以虛無為本，以因循為用」—see 10:3292. On *jimie* 寂滅, the
    ZWDCD quotes the *Wuliang shoujing* 無量壽經 as follows:「超出世間，深樂。」The
    term may be taken as equivalent to *nirvana*—see Lin Yutang's dictionary and Gardner,
    Chu Hsi and the Ta-hsueh, 84n37.

From this time forth, vulgar Confucians practised memorising, reciting and fashioning ornate phrases, redoubling their efforts in the "lesser learning," but all to no avail. The teachings of heterodox doctrines—*xuwu* (nothingness) and *jimie* (nirvana)[12]—they regarded as higher than the "greater learning," but they were without substance. Other political intrigues and arcane practices, all for the purpose of going on to success and fame, along with the sects of the hundred schools and the many arts, were how doubt was brought to the age and deception to the people. The obstruction to *ren* 仁 and *yi* 義 also occurred in the midst of all this confusion. This brought misfortune to the ruler and he did not get to hear the principles of the Great Way. It brought misfortune to lesser men and they did not get the benefits of perfect order. Instead, there was darkness and despair like a chronic disease, going on to the decay of the Five Dynasties[13] and the extremes of ruin and disorder.

Heaven revolves, ever rotating; nothing departs that does not return. The virtue of the Song period flourished; good order and teaching prospered again. From this, the two Henan Masters, the Cheng brothers, emerged to continue the transmission of Mencius. In fact, they were the first to honour and have faith in this chapter (i.e. the *Daxue*) and reveal [its merits].[14] Also, they put the text in its proper sequence and brought out its restored relevance. Subsequently, the method of teaching men the greater learning in ancient times, that is, the Sage's classic and the worthy's commentary,[15] shone brilliantly in the world once more. Although I am aware of my own foolishness, I have been fortunate enough to have learned indirectly from them and have heard about it. Considering it to be a book which still has errors, I have set aside my own lack of sophistication to collate and edit it, as well as adding my own thoughts and filling in its lacunae. Thus it awaits the noble men who will come after me. I know full well that I have overstepped the mark and have no way to escape censure. Nevertheless, for the purpose of the state transforming the people and perfecting customs, and as a device for the student to cultivate himself and bring good order to others, it is not, certainly, without some small benefit.

Preface by Zhu Xi of Xin'an—the day *jiazi*, in the second month of the year *jiyou*, in the *Chunxi* reign period—i.e. February 20, 1189.

---

12   Reference, respectively, to Daoism and Buddhism.

13   The five short-lived dynasties that followed the Tang from 907 to 959.

14   The studies of the Cheng brothers and Zhu Xi himself saw the separation of both the *Daxue* and the *Zhongyong* from the body of the *Li ji* and their treatment as individual texts. Sima Guang 司馬光, whose own commentary has been lost, also played a role here.

15   Confucius and Zeng Shen 曾參 respectively.

大學

<u>子程子</u>[16] 曰:「《大學》,<u>孔氏</u>之遺書,而初學入德之門也。」於今可見
古人為學次第者,獨賴此篇之存,而《論》、《孟》次之。學者必由是而
學焉,則庶乎其不差矣。

---

[16] Reference here is to both Cheng brothers, Cheng Hao 程顥 and Cheng Yi 程頤—for
further details, see Gardner, *Chu Hsi and the Ta-hsueh*, 87n50.

The *Daxue*

The Masters Cheng said: "The *Daxue* (*The Greater Learning*) is a work handed down by Confucius. It is the gateway of entry to virtue for those setting out on their studies." That we today can see what the ancients took to be the sequence of study relies solely on the preservation of this work. The *Analects* and the *Mencius* come after it. The student must follow this [sequence] in his studies. Then, perhaps, he will not fall into error.

DX: 大學之道，在明明德，在親民，在止於至善。[1]知止而后有定，定而后能靜，靜而后能安，安而后能慮，慮而后能得。[2]物有本末，事有終始，知所先後，則近道矣。[3]

古之欲明明德於天下者，先治其國；欲治其國者，先齊其家；欲齊其家者，先脩其身；欲脩其身者，先正其心；欲正其心者，先誠其意；欲誠其意者，先致其知；致知在格物。[4]物格而后知至，知至而后意誠，意誠而后心正，心正而后身脩，身脩而后家齊，家齊而后國治，國治而后天下平。[5]自天子以至於庶人，壹是皆以脩身為本。[6]其本亂而末治者否矣，其所厚者薄而其所薄者厚，未之有也。[7]

DX: The Way of greater learning lies in manifesting the original brightness of innate virtue; it lies in restoring the original brightness of that virtue in the people generally; it lies in coming to rest in the utmost goodness. **[1]** Know where to rest, and afterwards there is stability; be stable, and afterwards there can be calmness; be calm, and afterwards there can be tranquility; be tranquil, and afterwards there can be contemplation; be contemplative, and afterwards there can be attainment. **[2]** In things there is root (the brightness of innate virtue) and branch (restoring the original brightness of innate virtue in the people). In activities there is a beginning (finding a place to rest) and an end (attaining completion of the sequence). Know what is first and what follows. Then you come near to the Way. **[3]**

The ancients, in wishing to manifest luminous virtue in the world, first brought good order to their states. In wishing to bring good order to their states, they first regulated their households. In wishing to regulate their households, they first cultivated themselves. In wishing to cultivate themselves, they first rectified their minds. In wishing to rectify their minds, they first made their intentions *cheng* 誠 (true, genuine, sincere). In wishing to make their intentions *cheng* 誠, they first extended their knowledge to the limit. Extending knowledge to the limit lies in investigating things. **[4]** Investigate things and then knowledge is perfected. When knowledge is perfected, then intentions become *cheng* 誠. When intentions are *cheng* 誠, then the mind is rectified. Rectify the mind and the self is cultivated. Cultivate the self and the household is regulated. Only after the household is regulated is the state well ordered. Only after the state is well ordered is the world at peace. **[5]** From the Son of Heaven down to the common people, all without exception should take self-cultivation as the root. **[6]** For the root to be in disorder and yet the branches to be well ordered is not possible. For what is important to be trivialised or what is trivial to be given importance should never be the case. **[7]**

右經一章，蓋<u>孔子</u>之言，而<u>曾子</u>述之。（凡二百五字。）其傳十章，則<u>曾子</u>之意而門人記之也。舊本頗有錯簡，今因<u>程子</u>所定，而更考經文，別為序次如<u>左</u>。（凡千五百四十六字。凡傳文，雜引經傳，若無統紀，然文理接續，血脈貫通，深淺始終，至為精密。熟讀詳味，久當見之，今不盡釋也。）

Comment: Zhu Xi makes several important changes to the *Li ji* text in fashioning his initial chapter: (i) he combines what are sections 1 and 2 in the *Li ji* version; (ii) he transfers the final sentence of TX2 in the *Li ji* to his DX Comm. 5 which he regards as a largely lost chapter; (iii) he attributes this first chapter to Confucius himself and takes the remaining ten chapters in his version to be commentary by Zengzi 曾子. As Legge pointed out over a century ago, there is no conclusive evidence to support this supposition, nor indeed the assumption that chapter 5 of the commentary is the remaining part of a largely lost chapter on "investigating things." Legge's comment remains apposite today. In addition, Zhu Xi follows Cheng Yi in reading *qin* 親 as *xin* 新, in the sense of "renew" rather than *qin'ai* 親愛 in the sense of "to love," so significantly altering the meaning of the opening statement. Several other important points of difference are discussed in the Introduction and Appendix 3 on terminology.

注 DX (朱熹)

[1] <u>程子</u>曰：「親，當作新。」[17] 大學者，大人之學也。明，明之也。明德者，人之所得乎天，而虛靈不昧，以具眾理而應萬事者也。但為氣稟所拘，人欲所蔽，則有時而昏；然其本體之明，則有未嘗息者。故學者當因其所發而遂明之，以復其初也。新者，革其舊之謂也，言既自明其明德，又當推以及人，使之亦有以去其舊染之污也。止者，必至於是而不遷之意。至善，則事理當然之極也。言明明德、新民，皆當至於至善之地而不遷。蓋必其有以盡夫天理之極，而無一毫人欲之私也。此三者，大學之綱領也。

[2] 后，與後同，後放此。止者，所當止之地，即至善之所在也。知之，則志有定向。靜，謂心不妄動。安，謂所處而安。慮，謂處事精詳。得，謂得其所止。

Cheng Yi in the *Yichuan xiansheng gaizheng daxue* 伊川先生改正大學, *Er Cheng quanshu* 二程全書 (Taipei: Zhongwen chubanshe, 1969), 2:1750.

To the right (above) is the first chapter of the classic comprising the words of Confucius and transmitted by Zengzi. (Altogether, there are 205 characters.) Its commentary in ten chapters consists, then, of the thoughts of Zengzi recorded by his disciples. The old original version (of the Daxue) has, to some degree, disordered writing slips. Now, because of what Master Cheng has established, as well as [my own] further study of the Classic, it has been rearranged to give the sequence which follows to the left (below). (Altogether, there are 1,546 characters. In general, the commentary variously quotes the classics as if there is no governing principle. Nevertheless, the style is coherent, and one argument pervades the whole. This argument is both profound and simple. It has a beginning and an end and it achieves precision. If one reads it closely and examines its essence carefully, then after a long time one ought to see it. When this happens, no exhaustive explanation [is needed].)

Notes DX (Zhu Xi)

[1] Cheng Zi says: "*Qin* should be made *xin* 新 (to renew)." *Da xue* 大學 is learning for adults. *Ming* 明 is to make something clear (display or manifest it). *Ming de* 明德 is what a person gets from Heaven and is pure spirit unobscured. It is the instrument of the myriad principles and is what responds to the ten thousand matters. But if there is the endowment of *qi* 氣 (disposition) which restrains it and human desires which conceal it, then there are times when it is obscured. Nevertheless, the brightness of its original substance will never die away. Therefore, the learner ought to rely on what it gives out and subsequently let it shine forth, so restoring it to what it was at the beginning. *Xin* 新 (to renew) refers to getting rid of the old. This says that once one has let one's own innate virtue shine forth, one also ought to extend it to others, letting them also find a way to rid themselves of the stains of old impurities. *Zhi* 止 (to come to rest) has the meaning of certainly reaching to this and not changing position. *Zhi shan* 至善 (perfect or utmost goodness) is, then, the proper end-point for matters and principles. That is to say, manifesting the original brightness of innate virtue and restoring the original brightness of that virtue in the people should, in both cases, come to rest in a place of perfect goodness and not shift. This must be seen as the highest point of the Heavenly principle and must not be tainted by one iota of private desire. These three things are the essential points of the greater learning (learning for adults).

[2] *Hou* 后 is the same as *hou* 後, i.e. *hou* 後 is like this. "To come to rest" (*zhi* 止) refers to the place where one ought to come to rest (abide); that is, the place where perfect goodness exists. Know this, then the will has stability of direction. *Jing* 靜 (calmness) refers to the mind not acting foolishly. *An* 安 (tranquility) refers to what is at rest and peaceful. *Lü* 慮 (contemplation) refers to managing matters with close attention to detail. *De* 得 (to attain) refers to attaining this place of rest.

[3] 明德為本，新民為末。知止為始，能得為終。本始所先，末終所後。此結上文兩節之意。

[4] {治，平聲，後放此}明明德於天下者，使天下之人皆有以明其明德也。心者，身之所主也。誠，實也。意者，心之所發也。實其心之所發，欲其一於善而無自欺也。致，推極也。知，猶識也。推極吾之知識，欲其所知無不盡也。格，至也。物，猶事也。窮至事物之理，欲其極處無不到也。此八者，大學之條目也。

[5] {治，去聲，後放此}物格者，物理之極處無不到也。知至者，吾心之所知無不盡也。知既盡，則意可得而實矣，意既實，則心可得而正矣。脩身以上，明明德之事也。齊家以下，新民之事也。物格知至，則知所止矣。意誠以下，則皆得所止之序也。

[6] 壹是，一切也。正心以上，皆所以脩身也。齊家以下，則舉此而措之耳。

[7] 本，謂身也。所厚，謂家也。此兩節結上文兩節之意。

DX Comm. 1: 〈康誥〉曰：[18]「克明德。」**[1]**

〈大甲〉曰：[19]「顧諟天之明命。」**[2]**

〈帝典〉曰：[20]「克明峻德。」**[3]**

皆自明也。**[4]**

---

[18]   From the *Shang shu* 尚書 (*Book of Documents*)—see LCC, 3:383. The reference is to King Wen 文王. The full statement reads: 「惟乃丕顯考文王克明德慎罰。」

[19]   Also from the *Shang shu*—see LCC, 3:199. The subject is King Tang 湯.

[20]   Also from the *Shang shu*—see LCC, 3:17. It is from the "Canon of Yao" 堯典. Legge's version reads: "He was able to make the able and virtuous distinguished."—see his note on p. 17.

[3] Manifesting the original brightness of innate virtue is the root; restoring the original brightness of that virtue in the people generally is the branch. "Know where to rest" is the beginning; "being able to attain" is the end. Root and beginning are what come first; branch and end are what come afterwards. This brings together the meanings of the previous two sections.

[4] . . . Manifesting the original brightness of innate virtue in the world is to cause the people of the world all to have the means to manifest the original brightness of their own innate virtue. *Xin* 心 (heart, mind) is what rules the self. *Cheng* 誠 is equivalent to *shi* 實 (to make true, real, genuine). *Yi* 意 (thoughts, intentions) are what the mind sends forth. In making genuine (true) what the mind sends forth, one wishes to become one with goodness and not deceive oneself. *Zhi* 致 is equivalent to *tui ji* 推極 (extend to the limit). *Zhi* 知 is like *shi* 識 (to know, be acquainted with). Extending to the limit what I know is to wish what I know to be without limit (absolutely exhaustive). *Ge* 格 is equivalent to *zhi* 至 (to reach, arrive at, extend). *Wu* 物 is like *shi* 事 (matters, affairs). To investigate thoroughly the principles of matters and things is to wish to reach this extreme point definitively. These eight things are the specifics of the greater learning (*Daxue*).

[5] . . . "Investigating things" is unfailingly to reach the extreme point in the principle of things. Knowledge being perfected is what my mind knows being without limit. When knowledge is without limit (exhaustive), then intentions can, indeed, be made genuine (true). When intentions are genuine (true), then the mind can, indeed, be rectified. Down to *xiu shen* 脩身 (cultivating the self) is about the matter of manifesting the original brightness of innate virtue. From *qi jia* 齊家 (regulating the household) on is about the matter of renewing the people. If one investigates (gets to the core of) things, and knowledge is perfected, then one knows where to rest. From *yi cheng* 意誠 (intentions are made *cheng* 誠) down is, then, all about the sequence of attaining a place to come to rest.

[6] *Yi shi* 壹是 equates with *yiqie* 一切 (all, the whole, uniformity). Prior to and including *zheng xin* 正心 is all on how to cultivate the self. Including and following *qi jia* 齊家 (regulating the household) is about raising this and putting it into place.

[7] *Ben* 本 (the root) refers to *shen* 身 (the self). *Suo hou* 所厚 (what is important) refers to the household. These two sections unite the two preceding sections in meaning.

DX Comm. 1: The "Announcement to Kang" states: "He was able to manifest virtue." [1]
The "Tai Jia" states: "He gave constant attention to this enlightened decree of Heaven." [2]
The "Di dian" states: "He was able to manifest great virtue." [3]
These are all instances of the self manifesting [innate virtue]. [4]

---

* Text from the classical commentaries in { } brackets primarily contains pronunciation guides for certain Chinese characters; this has been omitted in the English translation.

右傳之首章。釋明明德。(此通下三章至「止於信」，舊本誤在「沒世不忘」之下。)

Comment: These three brief quotations from the *Shang shu* 尚書 (*Documents*) all pertain to the opening statement of the supposed Confucian text, giving examples of "manifesting the original brightness of innate virtue," as the short summarising statement indicates. The exemplars, three ancient rulers and paradigmatic noble men (*junzi* 君子), are King Wen, King Tang, and Emperor Yao. This section occurs later in the *Li ji* text—TX5 in the present arrangement. If its purpose is to expand on the opening sentence of the opening statement, Zhu Xi's placement has an obvious logic.

注 DX Comm. 1 (朱熹)

[1]〈康誥〉，〈周書〉。克，能也。

[2] 大，讀作泰。諟，古是字。〈大甲〉，〈商書〉。顧，謂常目在之也。諟，猶此也，或曰審也。天之明命，即天之所以與我，而我之所以為德者也。常目在之，則無時不明矣。

[3] 峻，《書》作俊。〈帝典〉，〈堯典〉，〈虞書〉。峻，大也。

[4] 結所引《書》，皆言自明己德之意。

DX Comm. 2: 湯之盤銘曰：「苟日新，日日新，又日新。」**[1]**

〈康誥〉曰：「作新民。」[21] **[2]**

《詩》曰：「周雖舊邦，其命惟新。」[22] **[3]**

是故君子無所不用其極。**[4]**

右傳之二章。釋新民。

---

21 See LCC, 3:388. Legge has, for the whole statement, which refers to the people of Yin: "Thus also shall you assist the king, consolidating the appointment of Heaven, and renovating this people."

22 The ode in question is Mao 235 (LCC, 4:427). The first lines read:「文王在上，於昭于天，周雖舊邦，其命維新。」

Above (to the right) is the commentary on the first chapter. It explains manifesting the original brightness of innate virtue. (This connects with the following three sections to "止於信." In the old text it was mistakenly placed after "沒世不忘.")

Notes DX Comm. 1 (Zhu Xi)

[1] The "Announcement to Kang" is from the "Zhou shu" 周書. *Ke* 克 equates with *neng* 能 (to be able).

[2] *Da* 大 is read as *tai* 泰 (greatest, extreme). *Shi* 諟 is an old form of *shi* 是. The "Tai jia" is from the "Shang shu" 商書. *Gu* 顧 means "constantly direct attention to it." *Shi* 諟 is like *ci* 此 (this) although some say [it is like] *shen* 審 (to investigate, examine). "Heaven's enlightened decree" is what Heaven gives to me and what I take to be virtue. If there is constant focus on this, then at no time will it not be manifest.

[3] In the *Documents jun* 峻 is written as *jun* 俊. The "Di dian" 帝典 refers to the "Yao dian" 堯典 which is from the "Yu shu" 虞書. *Jun* 峻 equates with *da* 大 (great, large).

[4] This summarises what is quoted from the *Documents*: The intention of all [the quotations] is to say that the self manifests its own virtue.

DX Comm. 2: The inscription engraved on Tang's bathing tub said: "Truly renew [yourself] each day. Day after day renew [yourself], and again, each day, renew [yourself]. [1]

The "Announcement to Kang" states: "Stir the people to renewal." [2]

The *Odes* says: "Although Zhou is an old country, its decree is new." [3]

This is why, for the noble man, there is nothing in which he does not use his utmost endeavour. [4]

Above (to the right) is the commentary on the second chapter. It explains renewing the people.

Comment: In his rearrangement, Zhu Xi takes the second set of quotations (chapter 2 of the commentary) to relate to the second of the three essential points (principles), i.e. "to renew the people" (accepting Cheng Yi's reading of *xin* 新 for *qin* 親). There is no apparent source for the first quotation, as Legge remarks (see LCC, 1:361, note 2). The second statement, from the *Shang shu* 尚書, was made by King Cheng to Kang Shu and refers to the people of Yin. The quotation from the *Odes* refers to King Wen. These examples are to encourage both renewal of the self and renewal of the people. The "renewal" may, perhaps, be understood as a rededication to the programme outlined in the second part of the initial chapter.

注 DX Comm. 2 (朱熹)

[1] 盤，沐浴之盤也。銘，名其器以自警之辭也。苟，誠也。湯以人之洗濯其心以去惡，如沐浴其身以去垢。故銘其盤，言誠能一日有以滌其舊染之污而自新，則當因其已新者，而日日新之，又日新之，不可略有間斷也。

[2] 鼓之舞之之謂作。言振起其自新之民也。

[3]《詩・大雅・文王》之篇。言周國雖舊，至於文王，能新其德以及於民，而始受天命也。

[4] 自新新民，皆欲止於至善也。

DX Comm. 3:《詩》云：「邦畿千里，惟民所止。」[23] **[1]**

《詩》云：「緡蠻黃鳥，止於丘隅。」[24] 子曰：「於止，知其所止，可以人而不如鳥乎！」**[2]**

《詩》云:「穆穆文王，於緝熙敬止！」[25] 為人君，止於仁；為人臣，止於敬；為人子，止於孝；為人父，止於慈；與國人交，止於信。**[3]**

---

[23] From the fourth verse of the *Odes*, Mao 303, LCC, 4:637.
[24] From the second verse of the *Odes*, Mao 230, LCC, 4:419.
[25] These are the opening lines of verse 4 of the *Odes,* Mao 235, LCC, 4:429.

DX Comm. 2 Notes (Zhu Xi)

[1] *Pan* 盤 is a bathing tub. *Ming* 銘 is to name one's utensils using words of self-admonition. *Gou* 苟 is read as *cheng* 誠 (sincerely, truly). Tang took a man "washing" his mind to get rid of evil to be like a man washing his body to get rid of dirt. Therefore, he engraved his bathing tub with words saying that, if for one day you are truly able to wash away the dirt of old stains and renew yourself, then you ought to take what has already been renewed and every day renew it, and again, each day renew it. There cannot be the slightest interruption (in this process).

[2] To rouse them (*gu zhi* 鼓之) and to encourage them (*wu zhi* 舞之) is what is meant by *zuo* 作. This speaks of exciting and stirring up the self-renewal of the people.

[3] This is from the *Odes*, "Da ya," "Wen Wang." It says that, although Zhou was an old kingdom, when it came to King Wen, he was able to renew his virtue and extend it to the people, and he began by receiving Heaven's mandate.

[4] In both self-renewal and renewing the people, [the noble man] desires to come to rest in the utmost goodness.

DX Comm. 3: The *Odes* says: "The royal domain is a thousand *li*. It is where the people come to rest (abide)." [1]

The *Odes* says: "*Min-man* sings the golden oriole. It comes to rest in the hill foliage." The Master said: "Ah, abiding: it knows where to abide. Can we take a man to be less than a bird?" [2]

The *Odes* says: "Profound indeed was King Wen. In continuing splendour and complete seriousness[26] he came to rest." In being a ruler, he came to rest in loving kindness (*ren* 仁); in being an official, he came to rest in respect (*jing* 敬); in being a son, he came to rest in filial piety (*xiao* 孝); in being a father, he came to rest in compassion (*ci* 慈); in his dealings with the people of the state, he came to rest in trustworthiness (*xin* 信). [3]

---

[26] See Gardner's detailed note on this quotation, and especially on the reading of *jing* 敬, in *Chu Hsi and the Ta-hsueh*, 98–99n87.

《詩》云:「瞻彼淇澳,菉竹猗猗。有斐君子,如切如磋,如琢如磨;
瑟兮僩兮,赫兮喧兮。有斐君子,終不可諠兮!」[27] 如切如磋者,道學
也;如琢如磨者,自脩也;瑟兮僩兮者,恂慄也;赫兮喧兮者,威儀
也;有斐君子,終不可諠兮者,道盛德至善,民之不能忘也。[4]

《詩》云:「於戲前王不忘。」[28] 君子賢其賢而親其親,小人樂其樂而利其
利,此以沒世不忘也。[5]

右傳之三章。釋止於至善。(此章內自引〈淇澳〉詩以下,舊本誤在誠意章下。)

Comment: In this section, Zhu Xi groups together five quotations from the *Odes*. It corresponds to the last three of the six quotations in TX6 of the *Li ji* version, followed by the
two quotations from the *Odes* that constitute all of TX4 of the *Li ji* version. In the section
above, the first three quotations are about *zhi* 止 (coming to rest), physically in the case
of the people and the golden oriole (although more is implied) and ethically in the case of
King Wen. The penultimate quotation refers to King Wu[29] as an example of "great virtue
and the utmost goodness" and the last to both King Wen and King Wu, unforgettable by
virtue of their "coming to rest in the utmost goodness" and the effect this had on their
subjects, whether noble or lesser men. There is some uncertainty in the interpretation of
the terse and rather enigmatic sentence which immediately follows the final quotation. In
attempting to clarify this, Zhu Xi writes (in the *Daxue zuanshu* 大學纂疏): "As for *qin* 親,
xian 賢, *le* 樂, and *li* 利, the first appearance of each is spoken of from the point of view
of the men of later generations, while the second appearance of each refers in some cases
to the former kings' persons and in some cases to their benignities."[30]

注 DX Comm. 3 (朱熹)

[1]《詩‧商頌‧玄鳥》之篇。邦畿,王者之都也。止,居也,言物各有所當止之
處也。

[2] 緡,詩作綿。《詩‧小雅‧綿蠻》之篇。緡蠻,鳥聲。丘隅,岑蔚之處。子曰
以下,孔子說《詩》之辭。言人當知所當止之處也。

---

[27] This is the opening verse of the *Odes*, Mao 55 (LCC, 4:91), other than having *fei* 匪
instead of *fei* 斐.
[28] This is the final line of the *Odes*, Mao 269 (LCC, 4:573), other than having *hu* 乎
instead of *hu* 戲.
[29] See Legge's note on this in the *Odes*, LCC, 4:91.
[30] Translation after Gardner, *Chu Hsi and the Ta-hsueh*, 102.

The *Odes* says:

> See the bays in the banks of the Qi,
> the green bamboo, how fresh and luxuriant.
> There is the elegant and accomplished prince.
> Like cutting, like filing,
> like chiselling, like polishing.
> How strict he is, how resolute.
> How commanding he is, how dignified.
> There is the elegant and accomplished prince.
> He can never be forgotten.

"Like cutting, like filing" speaks of learning; "like chiselling, like polishing" is cultivating the self; "how strict he is, how resolute" is being cautiously reverent; "how commanding he is, how dignified" is being imposing in manner. "There is the elegant and accomplished prince. He can never be forgotten" speaks of his great virtue and utmost goodness, which the people cannot forget. **[4]**
The *Odes* says: "Ah, indeed! The former kings are not forgotten." Noble men take as worthy their worthiness and hold dear what they hold dear. Lesser men delight in their delights and benefit from their benefits. This is why they are not forgotten after death. **[5]**

Above (to the right) is the third chapter of the commentary. It explains coming to rest in the highest goodness. (Within this chapter, [the material] from the quotation from the "Qi'ao" poem onwards is, in the old text, mistakenly placed after the chapter on making intentions *cheng* 誠.)

Notes DX Comm. 3 (Zhu Xi)

[1] The verse is from the "Xuan niao" in the "Zhou song." *Bang ji* 邦畿 is the king's capital. *Zhi* 止 is equivalent to *ju* 居 (to abide). It says that for all things each has a proper place to abide.
[2] In the *Odes, min* 緡 is written as *mian* 緜. This is from the *Odes*, "Xiao ya," "Min-man." *Min-man* 緡蠻 is the sound of the bird. *Qiu yu* 丘隅 is a place of luxuriant foliage on a hill (or peak). From "the Master says" (*zi yue* 子曰) on down are the words of Confucius explaining the poem. He says a man ought to know the place in which it is proper to abide.

[3] {於緝之於，音烏。}《詩•文王》之篇。穆穆，深遠之意。於，歎美辭。緝，
繼續也。熙，光明也。敬止，言其無不敬而安所止也。引此而言聖人之止，
無非至善。五者乃其目之大者也。學者於此，究其精微之蘊，而又推類以盡其
餘，則於天下之事，皆有以知其所止而無疑矣。

[4] {澳，於六反。}菉，詩作綠。{猗，叶韻音阿。僩，下版反。}喧，詩作咺，
諠，詩作諼；{並況晚反。}恂，<u>鄭</u>氏讀作峻。《詩•衛風•淇澳》之篇。<u>淇</u>，水
名。澳，隈也。猗猗，美盛貌。興也。斐，文貌。切以刀鋸，琢以椎鑿，皆
裁物使成形質也。磋以鑢鍚，磨以沙石，皆治物使其滑澤也。治骨角者，既切
而復磋之。治玉石者，既琢而復磨之。皆言其治之有緒，而益致其精也。瑟，
嚴密之貌。僩，武毅之貌。赫喧，宣著盛大之貌。諠，忘也。道，言也。學，
謂講習討論之事。自脩者，省察克治之功。恂慄，戰懼也。威，可畏也。儀，
可象也。引詩而釋之，以明明明德者之止於至善。道學自脩，言其所以得之之
由。恂慄、威儀，言其德容表裏之盛。卒乃指其實而歎美之也。

[5] {於戲，音嗚呼。樂，音洛。}《詩•周頌•烈文》之篇。於戲，歎辭。前王，
謂<u>文</u>、<u>武</u>也。君子，謂其後賢後王。小人，謂後民也。此言前王所以新民者止
於至善，能使天下後世無一物不得其所，所以既沒世而人思慕之，愈久而不忘
也。此兩節詠歎淫泆，其味深長，當熟玩之。

[3] . . . The verse is from the "Wen Wang" ode. *Mu mu* 穆穆 means "deep and distant" (i.e. "profound"). *Yu* 於 is an exclamation of admiration. *Ji* 緝 equates with *jixu* 繼續 (to continue, carry on). *Xi* 熙 equates with *guangming* 光明 (bright, light). *Jing zhi* 敬止 speaks of his always being reverent and at peace where he abides. Quoting this and speaking of the sage's abiding, it is invariably in the utmost goodness. The five things, then, are his great objectives. If those who study them look into their collective subtlety, and also, for completeness, infer the remainder, then, in the affairs of the world, all have the means to know where to abide and be free of doubt.

[4] . . . In the *Odes*, *lü* 菉 is written as *lü* 綠 . . . *xuan* 喧 is written as *xuan* 咺 and *xuan* 誼 is written as *xuan* 諼. . . . *Xun* 恂 was read by Zheng Xuan as *jun* 峻. The verse is from the "Qi'ao" in the "Wei feng." *Qi* 淇 is the name of a water. *Ao* 澳 equates with *wei* 隈 (a cove or bay). *Yi yi* 猗猗 is an appearance of beauty abounding. It is flourishing. *Fei* 斐 is an elegant appearance. Cutting is with a knife or saw; chiselling is with a mallet or chisel. Both cut something to make it take a particular shape. Filing is with a file or plane; polishing is with sand or stone. Both treat something to make it smooth. In crafting bone and horn, one cuts and then repeatedly files them. In treating jade and stone, one chisels and then repeatedly polishes them. Both of these say that in bringing order to something there is a sequence which increasingly brings it to a refined state. *Se* 瑟 is a strict appearance. *Xian* 僩 is a resolute appearance. *He xuan* 赫喧 is to display a majestic appearance. *Xuan* 諼 is equivalent to *wang* 忘 (to forget). *Dao* 道 is equivalent to *yan* 言 (to say). *Xue* 學 refers to expounding and practising the matters under discussion. Self-cultivation is looking into the achievement of being able to bring order to things. *Xun li* 恂慄 is equivalent to *zhan ju* 戰懼 (to be fearful). *Wei* 威 is being able to intimidate. *Yi* 儀 is to be able to resemble. Quoting this poem and explaining it is a way of making it clear that "manifesting the original brightness of innate virtue consists of abiding in the utmost goodness." To speak about learning and self-cultivation is to speak about how to attain this. *Xun li* 恂慄 and *wei yi* 威儀 speak of the greatness of displaying a virtuous appearance. Finally, it indicates its genuineness and the great admiration for it.

[5] . . . The verse is from the "Lie wen" 烈文 in the "Zhou song" 周頌. *Wuhu* 於戲 is an exclamation. "Former kings" refers to Wen and Wu. *Junzi* 君子 (noble men) refers to later worthies and kings. *Xiaoren* 小人 (lesser men) refers to later people generally. This tells how the former kings renewed the people by abiding in the utmost goodness and were able to let the later generations of the world find this place. This is why, after they were dead, people still thought of them and invariably yearned for them. They were not forgotten for a very long time. These two sections should be gone over repeatedly in that their "flavour" is deep and profound, so it is right to be well acquainted with them.

DX Comm. 4: 子曰：「聽訟，吾猶人也。必也使無訟乎！」[31] 無情者不得盡其辭。大畏民志，此謂知本。[1]

右傳之四章。釋本末。（此章舊本誤在「止於信」下。）

Comment: This occurs as a discrete section in the arrangement of the *Li ji* (TX7). It follows not only the various quotations, as in the *Sishu zhangju* text, but also what is Zhu Xi's DX Comm. 6. The quotation is from the *Lunyu*. There is some question about the reading of the statement immediately following the quotation, evidenced by the differing punctuation in modern versions. Zhu Xi makes his own understanding of the statement clear. The noble man, by manifesting his enlightened virtue, will so overawe the minds and wills of people generally that he will inhibit them entirely from initiating litigation.

注 DX Comm. 4 (朱熹)

[1] 猶人，不異於人也。情，實也。引夫子之言，而言聖人能使無實之人不敢盡其虛誕之辭。蓋我之明德既明，自然有以畏服民之心志，故訟不待聽而自無也。觀於此言，可以知本末之先後矣。

---

[31]   *Lunyu* XII, 13, LCC, 1:257.

DX Comm. 4: The Master said: "In hearing lawsuits I am like other men. What is necessary is to cause there to be no lawsuits." Those without anything true [to say] will not get to complete their statements. Great awe [will affect] people's wills. This is called knowing the root. **[1]**

Above (to the right) is the fourth chapter of the commentary. It explains root and branch. (In old editions this chapter was mistakenly placed after "止於信.")

Notes DX Comm. 4 (Zhu Xi)

[1] *You ren* 猶人 is to be no different from others. *Qing* 情 equates with *shi* 實 (true, real, substantial). This quotes the Master's words and says that the sage is able to bring it about that those with nothing true [to say] dare not spend themselves on false statements. Once my own enlightened virtue is already manifest, I then have the means of bringing awe and submission to the minds and wills of the people. Thus lawsuits will not be heard and will spontaneously disappear. If you consider these words, you can know that the root is first and the branches subsequent.

DX Comm. 5: 此謂知本，[1]此謂知之至也。[2]

右傳之五章，蓋釋格物、致知之義，而今亡矣。（此章舊本通下章，誤在經
文之下。）閒嘗竊取<u>程子</u>之意以補之曰：「所謂致知在格物者，言欲致吾
之知，在即物而窮其理也。蓋人心之靈莫不有知，而天下之物莫不有
理，惟於理有未窮，故其知有不盡也。是以大學始教，必使學者即凡天
下之物，莫不因其已知之理而益窮之，以求至乎其極。至於用力之久，
而一旦豁然貫通焉，則眾物之表裏精粗無不到，而吾心之全體大用無不
明矣。此謂物格，此謂知之至也。」

Comment: This is, perhaps, the most significant part of Zhu Xi's rearrangement. He takes the ten characters of this statement from what is TX2 of the *Li ji* text and isolates them as the concluding remarks to a presumed lost section on *ge wu* 格物 (coming to things, investigating things). Then, in an expanded comment of his own, he clarifies what this is, citing the views of the Cheng brothers. This matter is considered in greater detail in the introductory section on terminology.

注 DX Comm. 5 (朱熹)

[1] <u>程子</u>曰：「衍文也。」[32]
[2] 此句之上別有闕文，此特其結語耳。

---

[32] The reference is to Cheng Yi: In the *Yichuan xiansheng gaizheng daxue* there is "四字衍." See *Er Cheng quanshu*, 2:1751.

DX Comm. 5: This is called knowing the root. **[1]** This is called the perfecting of knowledge. **[2]**

To the right (above) is the fifth chapter of the Commentary possibly explaining the meaning of investigating things and extending knowledge to the limit, but now lost. (This chapter in old editions connects with the chapter below, being mistakenly placed after the text of the classic.) I have presumed to take the ideas of Master Cheng to supplement it. He says: "What is meant by 'extending knowledge to the limit lies in investigating things' is that, if we wish to extend our knowledge to the limit, this involves approaching things and thoroughly investigating their principle [in each case]. In all probability the intelligence of men's minds is such that there is none without knowledge and, in the case of the world's things, there is none without principle so, to the extent that these principles are not thoroughly investigated, then a man's knowledge is incomplete. This is why the initial teaching of the greater learning must be to cause the person learning to approach all the things in the world and, on the basis of the principles which he already knows, to increase his thorough investigation of them in order to seek to reach this limit. If he exerts his strength on this over a long time, he will suddenly come to understand how things are and will have a thoroughgoing comprehension of them. Then, for the multitude of things, what is manifest or hidden, what is fine or coarse, will in all cases be reached, and his mind in its whole substance and great workings will be entirely illuminated. This is what is meant by investigating things. This is what is meant by the perfecting of knowledge."

Notes DX Comm. 5 (Zhu Xi)

[1] Master Cheng said: "This is corrupt text."
[2] Before this sentence, there is a hiatus. These are only its (i.e. the section's) concluding words.

DX Comm. 6: 所謂誠其意者：毋自欺也，如惡惡臭，如好好色，此之謂自謙，故君子必慎其獨也！**[1]**小人閒居為不善，無所不至，見君子而后厭然，揜其不善，而著其善。人之視己，如見其肺肝然，則何益矣。此謂誠於中，形於外，故君子必慎其獨也。**[2]**曾子曰：「十目所視，十手所指，其嚴乎。」**[3]**富潤屋，德潤身，心廣體胖，故君子必誠其意。**[4]**

右傳之六章。釋誠意。（經曰：「欲誠其意，先致其知。」又曰：「知至而后意誠。」蓋心體之明有所未盡，則其所發必有不能實用其力，而苟焉以自欺者。然或已明而不謹乎此，則其所明又非己有，而無以為進德之基。故此章之指，必承上章而通考之，然後有以見其用力之始終，其序不可亂而功不可闕如此云。）

Comment: The remaining five chapters of commentary (DX Comm. 6–10) advance in order through five of the components of the programme of self-cultivation, proceeding from the personal (making intentions *cheng* 誠) to the general (bringing peace to all under Heaven). In the first three instances there are no supporting quotations from the literature, whilst the last two (and in particular the final one) are heavily buttressed by quotations from the *Odes*. Specific issues in the present section are the interpretations of *cheng* 誠, *yi* 意, *zi qi* 自欺, and *du* 獨. These have been addressed in the introduction and in Appendix 3 on terminology, but the position taken by the present authors may be summarised as follows:

(i)   *Cheng* 誠, which serves both verbal and nominal use, is most commonly rendered as "sincerity." This is unquestionably inadequate in giving the term its proper weight, as are the several other English terms used. Therefore, we have chosen to romanise it.

(ii)   *Yi* 意 is most commonly rendered as "thoughts" but we would argue that "intentions" (or even "will") is more satisfactory in that what are referred to are the outward manifestations of volition.

(iii)   *Du* 獨 is contentious insofar as some translators take it to mean simply the individual being alone and therefore unobserved whereas others see it as the uniqueness, as it were, of the individual, the central core of the self. The *Li ji* commentators are unequivocal in taking it to indicate the former whereas Zhu Xi's notes would seem to allow, if not actually support, the latter reading.

(iv)   *Zi qi* 自欺 is commonly rendered "self-deception" by English translators but seems, in the context and according to the commentators, to indicate the self being deceptive generally. That is to say, the outward manifestations of the inner workings should be spontaneously pure, genuine and true—there must be no dissembling.

There is no identifiable source for the apparent quotation from Zengzi.

DX Comm. 6: What is called making your intentions *cheng* 誠 (genuine, true, sincere) is to forbid deception in yourself—it is like hating a bad smell or loving a beautiful sight. This is called being content in yourself. Therefore, the noble man must act with care when he is alone. **[1]** The lesser man, when dwelling alone, does what is not good; there are no lengths to which he will not go. When he sees a noble man he dissembles, concealing his bad points and revealing his good points. But if, when others look at him, it is as though they see his very lungs and liver, then how is this of benefit? This is called *cheng* 誠 within being manifest without. Therefore, the noble man must act with care when he is alone. **[2]** Zengzi said: "It is what ten eyes see; it is what ten hands point to—this is awe-inspiring!" **[3]** Wealth enriches a house; virtue enriches the self. When the mind is broad, the body is at ease. Therefore, the noble man must make his intentions *cheng* 誠. **[4]**

Above (to the right) is the sixth chapter of the commentary. It explains making intentions *cheng* 誠. (The classic says: "Wishing to make his intentions *cheng* 誠, he first extends his knowledge to the limit." It also says: "Extend knowledge to the limit and afterwards intentions are *cheng* 誠." In fact, when the enlightenment of mind and body has that which is not yet complete, then in what it brings forth, there must be an inability to truly use its strength and an acceptance that there is deception in oneself. Nevertheless, there are some who are already enlightened and yet are not careful about this. Then that which is enlightenment is not what one has and there will be no way of making progress towards the foundations of virtue. Therefore, what this chapter points out certainly carries on from the previous chapter and thoroughly examines it. Afterwards there can be, by seeing the beginning and end of using one's strength, no possibility of confusion regarding its sequence and no possibility of deficiency regarding its achievement, as this says.)

注 DX Comm. 6 (朱熹)

[1] {惡、好上字,皆去聲。}謙讀為慊,{苦劫反。}誠其意者,自脩之首也。毋者,禁止之辭。自欺云者,知為善以去惡,而心之所發有未實也。謙,快也,足也。獨者,人所不知而己所獨知之地也。言欲自脩者知為善以去其惡,則當實用其力,而禁止其自欺。使其惡惡則如惡惡臭,好善則如好好色,皆務決去,而求必得之,以自快足於己,不可徒苟且以殉外而為人也。然其實與不實,蓋有他人所不及知而己獨知之者,故必謹之於此以審其幾焉。

[2] {閒,音閑。}厭,鄭氏讀為厭。閒居,猶處也。厭然,消沮閉藏之貌。此言小人陰為不善,而陽欲揜之,則是非不知善之當為與惡之當去也;但不能實用其力以至此耳。然欲揜其惡而卒不可揜,欲詐為善而卒不可詐,則亦何益之有哉!此君子所以重以為戒,而必謹其獨也。

[3] 引此以明上文之意。言雖幽獨之中,而其善惡之不可揜如此。可畏之甚也。

[4] {胖,步丹反。}胖,安舒也。言富則能潤屋矣,德則能潤身矣,故心無愧怍,則廣大寬平,而體常舒泰,德之潤身者然也。蓋善之實於中而形於外者如此,故又言此以結之。

Notes DX Comm. 6 (Zhu Xi)

[1] . . . *Qian* 謙 is read as *qie* 慊 (contented, happy). . . . Making your intentions *cheng* 誠 is the chief aspect of cultivating of the self. *Wu* 毋 is a word meaning prohibit or forbid. What "deception in yourself" 自欺 means is to know that being good involves getting rid of evil, and yet what the mind gives forth is not true. *Qian* 謙 equates with *kuai* 快 (happy, pleased, gratified) or *zu* 足 (satisfied). *Du* 獨 is a place that others do not know but only the self knows. That is to say, if one who wishes to cultivate the self knows to become good by getting rid of his evil, then he ought truly to make use of his strength and forbid deception in himself. This causes his hatred of evil to be like the hatred of a bad smell and his love of goodness to be like the love of a beautiful sight. Both take getting rid [of one] and seeking certain attainment [of the other] as fundamental. In this way, you are happy and satisfied in yourself and cannot, simply without thought, follow what is external and dependent on others. Nevertheless, your being true or not true is something others cannot get to know; it is something only you know. Therefore, you must be very vigilant in this matter by carefully examining your motivation.

[2] . . . Zheng [Xuan] read *yan* 厭 as *yan* 厭 (the appearance of closing up and concealing).[33] *Xian ju* 閒居 is like *chu* 處 (to dwell, be at rest in). *Yan ran* 厭然 is the appearance of drawing back and concealing. This is to say that the lesser man secretly does what is not good and wishes to conceal it outwardly. It is not, then, that he is unaware of the fact that it is right to practise good and cast out evil, but that he is unable truly to use his strength to achieve this. Nevertheless, he wishes to hide his evil, but in the end he cannot hide it; he wishes to feign being good, but in the end he cannot feign it. How is there any advantage in this! This is what the noble man takes as important, what he regards as a precept, and what he must be vigilant about when he is alone.

[3] This is quoted to clarify the meaning of what precedes it. It says that, even if you are hidden and alone, your goodness and evil still cannot be concealed in this way. This can inspire great awe!

[4] . . . *Pan* 胖 equates with *an shu* 安舒 (contented). This says that, if you have wealth, you can enrich the house; if you have virtue, you can enrich the self. Therefore, if the mind-heart is without shame, then it is extensive, great, broad, and has equanimity, and the body is at all times at ease and prosperous. Virtue enriching the self is like this. In fact, the reality of goodness being internal and its form being external is like this. Therefore, it also says this by way of conclusion.

---

[33]　See *Li ji*, "Taixue" TX3, Zheng Xuan, note [1].

DX Comm. 7: 所謂脩身在正其心者，身有所忿懥，則不得其正；有所恐懼，則不得其正；有所好樂，則不得其正；有所憂患，則不得其正。**[1]** 心不在焉，視而不見，聽而不聞，食而不知其味。**[2]** 此謂脩身在正其心。

右傳之七章。釋正心脩身。(此亦承上章以起下章。蓋意誠則真無惡而實有善矣，所以能存是心以檢其身。然或但知誠意，而不能密察此心之存否，則又無以直內而脩身也。自此以下，並以舊文為正。)

Comment: This section, dealing with the next stage in the progression—rectifying the mind to cultivate the self—is clear and clearly expressed without supporting quotations. The important point here is the identification of emotions and feelings as factors preventing rectitude or correctness of the mind-heart and therefore obstacles on the path to the cultivation of the self. This idea is important also in the *Zhongyong*. One textual variant is the reading of the second *shen* 身 in the opening statement as *xin* 心 (due to Cheng Yi). *Shen* 身 is accepted by the *Li ji* commentators. Finally, it is noted that the textual rearrangement ends with this section.

注 DX Comm. 7 (朱熹)

[1] 程子曰：「身有之身當作心。」[34] {忿，弗粉反。懥，勑值反。好、樂，並去聲。} 忿懥，怒也。蓋是四者，皆心之用，而人所不能無者。然一有之而不能察，則欲動情勝，而其用之所行，或不能不失其正矣。

[2] 心有不存，則無以檢其身，是以君子必察乎此而敬以直之，然後此心常存而身無不脩也。

---

[34]　See Cheng Yi, *Yichuan xiansheng gaizheng daxue*, in *Er Cheng quanshu*, 2:1752.

DX Comm. 7: What is spoken of as "cultivating the self lies in rectifying one's mind" is this: If the mind harbours anger and resentment, it does not attain this rectitude; if the mind harbours fear and terror, it does not attain this rectitude; if the mind harbours joy and happiness, it does not attain this rectitude; if the mind harbours sorrow and grief, it does not attain this rectitude. [1] If the mind is not "present" (engaged), one looks, but does not see; one listens, but does not hear; one eats, but does not know the taste. [2] This is what is meant by "cultivating the self lies in rectifying one's mind."

Above (to the right) is the seventh chapter of commentary. It explains rectifying the mind and cultivating the self. (This both continues the previous chapter and introduces the following one. In fact, if intentions were *cheng* 誠 then truly there would be no evil and, in reality, there would be good. In this way one would be able to preserve one's mind as a way of regulating one's self. Nevertheless, there are some who know only about making intentions *cheng* 誠 but are unable to keep close watch over whether their mind is preserved or not. Then they too have no way to correct what is within and cultivate the self. From this [chapter] onward, the old text becomes correct.)

Notes DX Comm. 7 (Zhu Xi)

[1] Cheng Zi said: "The *shen* 身 of *shen you* 身有 should be written *xin* 心 (mind, heart)." . . . *Fen* 忿 and *zhi* 懥 equate with *nu* 怒 (anger, indignation). These four things (listed) are all activities of the mind-heart and are what people cannot be without. Nevertheless, if one person has them but cannot closely monitor them, then desires will be aroused and emotions will triumph. And if these emotions proceed, in some cases you cannot avoid losing your rectitude.
[2] If the mind is not preserved, then there is no way of regulating your self. This is why the noble man must carefully examine this matter and with reverent attention correct it. Afterwards, his mind is constantly maintained and the self is inevitably cultivated.

DX Comm. 8: 所謂齊其家在脩其身者：人之其所親愛而辟焉，之其所賤惡而辟焉，之其所畏敬而辟焉，之其所哀矜而辟焉，之其所敖惰而辟焉。故好而知其惡，惡而知其美者，天下鮮矣！**[1]**故諺有之曰：「人莫知其子之惡，莫知其苗之碩。」**[2]** 此謂身不脩不可以齊其家。

右傳之八章。釋脩身齊家。

Comment: Zhu Xi's interpretation of this section differs somewhat from that of the *Li ji* commentators. The difference hinges on the different readings of the recurring characters *zhi* 之 (read as *yu* 於 by Zhu Xi rather than as *shi* 適 by the *Li ji* commentators) and *pi* 辟 (read as *pian* 偏 by Zhu Xi rather than as *pi* 譬 or *yu* 喻 by the *Li ji* commentators). Despite these variations, the basic argument is the same—bringing rectitude or balance to the mind-heart depends on restraining the emotions. With the desired balance or rectitude attained, the household can be effectively regulated. Zhu Xi's DX Comm. 8 corresponds to the *Li ji* TX9.

注 DX Comm. 8 (朱熹)

[1] {辟，讀為僻。惡而之惡、敖、好，並去聲。鮮，上聲。}人，謂眾人。之，猶於也。辟，猶偏也。五者，在人本有當然之則；然常人之情惟其所向而不加審焉，則必陷於一偏而身不脩矣。

[2] {諺，音彥。碩，叶韻，時若反。}諺，俗語也。溺愛者不明，貪得者無厭，是則偏之為害，而家之所以不齊也。

DX Comm. 9: 所謂治國必先齊其家者，其家不可教而能教人者，無之。故君子不出家而成教於國：孝者，所以事君也；弟者，所以事長也；慈者，所以使眾也。**[1]**
〈康誥〉曰：「如保赤子」。[35] 心誠求之，雖不中不遠矣。未有學養子而后嫁者也！**[2]**

---

35   The *Documents*, LCC, 3:389.

DX Comm. 8: What is spoken of as "regulating the household lies in cultivating the self" is this: People are partial towards what they love and hold dear; they are prejudiced against what they regard as worthless and detest; they are partial towards what they regard with awe and reverence; they are partial towards what they feel sympathy and pity for; they are prejudiced against what they are scornful and dismissive towards. Therefore, there are few [people] in the world who love something and yet know its evil, or who hate something and yet know its goodness. **[1]** The old adage has this to say: "A man knows neither his son's badness nor the sturdiness of his young crop." **[2]** That is to say, if the self is not cultivated, it is not possible to regulate one's household.

Above (to the right) is the eighth chapter of commentary. It explains cultivating the self and regulating the household.

Notes DX Comm. 8 (Zhu Xi)

[1] . . . *Ren* 人 refers to *zhongren* 眾人 (people generally, the multitude). *Zhi* 之 is like *yu* 於 (in reference to, towards). *Pi* 辟 is like *pian* 偏 (partial, prejudiced). These five things are proper elements of a person's nature. Nevertheless, an ordinary person's feelings, if there is something they are directed towards without careful consideration, will sink inevitably into prejudice, and the self will not be cultivated.

[2] . . . *Yan* 諺 is a common saying or proverb (*suyu* 俗語). One who is immersed in love is not clear thinking; one who is greedy to attain is insatiable. These, then, are prejudices being harmful, and reasons why a family is not regulated.

DX Comm. 9: What is meant by saying, "to bring good order to a state it is first necessary to regulate the household" is this: Nobody can teach others if he cannot teach his own household. Therefore, the noble man does not leave his household and yet he accomplishes his teaching in the state. Filial piety is the way to serve the prince. Fraternal respect is the way to serve elders. Parental compassion is the way to act towards the multitude. **[1]**

The "Announcement to Kang" states: "It is like protecting an infant." If your mind-heart truly seeks it, even if you do not hit the mark, you will not be far away. There has never been a girl who would marry only after learning how to rear a child. **[2]**

一家仁，一國興仁；一家讓，一國興讓；一人貪戾，一國作亂；其機如此。此謂一言僨事，一人定國。**[3]**

堯舜帥天下以仁，而民從之；桀紂帥天下以暴，而民從之；其所令反其所好，而民不從。是故君子有諸己而后求諸人，無諸己而后非諸人。所藏乎身不恕，而能喻諸人者，未之有也。**[4]**故治國在齊其家。**[5]**

《詩》云：「桃之夭夭，其葉蓁蓁；之子于歸，宜其家人。」[36] 宜其家人，而后可以教國人。**[6]**

《詩》云：「宜兄宜弟。」[37] 宜兄宜弟，而后可以教國人。**[7]**

《詩》云：「其儀不忒，正是四國。」[38] 其為父子兄弟足法，而后民法之也。**[8]**

此謂治國在齊其家。**[9]**

右傳之九章。釋齊家治國。

Comment: This section, on the penultimate stage in the sequence, corresponds to TX10 of the *Li ji* text above. There are only minor, and insignificant differences in Zhu Xi's reading compared to that of the *Li ji* commentators.[39] There is, however, some variation among translators as to how the sentence indicated by note 41 is understood. In particular, such variation depends on whether it is taken as a general statement applicable to both kinds of rulers (as above) or whether it is taken to apply only to Jie and Zhou. Legge, who takes the latter position, offers a translation in which the sentence appears to contradict what precedes it.[40]

---

[36] The *Odes*, Mao 6, LCC, 4:13.

[37] The *Odes*, Mao 173, LCC, 4:275.

[38] The *Odes*, Mao 152, LCC, 4:223.

[39] An example is Gardner's note 124, p. 111 which reads as follows: "Zhu Xi says: '一人 (*yi ren*; 'the One Man') refers to the ruler.' Zheng Xuan and Kong Yingda both gloss . . . both 一家 and 一人 as 'the ruler'; that Zhu, by contrast, glosses only the 一人 would seem to indicate that his understanding of 一家 differs from theirs. Hence I have translated it as 'one household.'"

[40] See also Legge, LCC, 1:371, Plaks, *Ta Hsüeh and Chung Yung (The Highest Order of Cultivation and On the Practice of the Mean)*, 70n5 and Gardner, *Chu Hsi and the Ta-hsueh*, 111n128.

If one household is *ren* 仁, the whole state is moved to *ren* 仁. If one household is complaisant (*rang* 讓), the whole state is moved to complaisance (*rang* 讓). If one man (the ruler) is greedy and violent, the whole state acts in a disorderly way. The origins of action are like this. This is what is meant by "one word can ruin affairs; one man can settle a kingdom." **[3]**

Yao and Shun led the world by *ren* 仁 and the people followed them. Jie and Zhou led the world by violence and the people followed them. If what one orders is contrary to what one loves, the people will not follow.[41] This is why the noble man only seeks in others what he has within himself, and rejects in others what he does not have within himself. There has never been a man who did not embody the principle of reciprocity (*shu* 恕) in himself and yet could expect others to follow him. **[4]** Therefore, bringing good order to a state lies in regulating the household. **[5]**

The *Odes* says: "The peach tree—how fresh and young, how green and luxuriant its leaves. The young girl goes off to get married, and brings goodness to her household." If one brings goodness to the people of one's household, one can subsequently teach the people of the state. **[6]**

The *Odes* says: "Let the relations between older and younger brothers be as they should be." Let the relations between older and younger brothers be as they should be and subsequently there can be teaching of the people of the state. **[7]**

The *Odes* says: "His demeanour is without blemish; he sets the right example for states on all sides." Let him be an adequate model as a father, son, older and younger brother, and subsequently the people will model themselves on him. **[8]**

This says that bringing good order to the state lies in regulating the household. **[9]**

Above (to the right) is the ninth chapter of the Commentary. It explains regulating the household and bringing good order to the state.

---

[41] On the meaning of this statement, see the Comment on the previous page.

注 DX Comm. 9 (朱熹)

[1]｛弟，去聲。長，上聲。｝身脩，則家可教矣；孝、弟、慈，所以脩身而教於家者也；然而國之所以事君事長使眾之道不外乎此。此所以家齊於上，而教成於下也。

[2]｛中，去聲。｝此引《書》而釋之，又明立教之本不假強為，在識其端而推廣之耳。

[3]｛僨，音奮。｝一人，為君也。機，發動所由也。僨，覆敗也。此言教成於國之效。

[4]｛好，去聲。｝此又承上文一人定國而言。有善於己，然後可以責人之善；無惡於己，然後可以正人之惡。皆推己以及人，所謂恕也，不如是，則所令反其所好，而民不從矣。喻，曉也。

[5] 通結上文。

[6]｛夭，平聲。蓁，音臻。｝《詩・周南・桃夭》之篇。夭夭，少好貌。蓁蓁，美盛貌。興也。之子，猶言是子，此指女子之嫁者而言也。婦人謂嫁曰歸。宜，猶善也。

[7]《詩・小雅・蓼蕭》篇。

[8]《詩・曹風・鳲鳩》篇。忒，差也。

[9] 此三引詩，皆以詠歎上文之事，而又結之如此。其味深長，最宜潛玩。

Notes DX Comm. 9 (Zhu Xi)

[1] . . . Cultivate the self and then you can teach the household. Filial piety, fraternal respect, and parental compassion are ways of cultivating the self and teaching the household. However, for a state, the way to serve the ruler, serve elders, and act towards the multitude does not lie outside these things. This is why, when the household is regulated above, teaching is completed below.

[2] . . . This quotes the *Documents* and explains it, as well as clearly establishing that the foundation of the teaching does not lie in compulsion. It lies in recognising its origin and extending and broadening it.

[3] . . . "One man" is the ruler. *Ji* 機 is the source of action. *Fen* 僨 equates with *fubai* 覆敗 (to overturn completely). This speaks of the efficacy of the teaching being accomplished in the state.

[4] . . . This also continues the preceding statement and speaks about one man (the ruler) stabilising the state. If there is good in yourself, then subsequently you can demand goodness of others. If there is no evil in yourself, then subsequently you can correct the evil in others. Both of these things extend from the self to reach out to others. They are what are termed "reciprocity" (*shu* 恕). If you are not like this, then what you order is contrary to what you love and the people will not follow. *Yu* 喻 equates with *xiao* 曉 (to understand, know).

[5] This continues the previous section.

[6] . . . The ode is the "Tao yao" in the "Zhou nan." *Yao yao* 夭夭 is a young and beautiful appearance. *Zhen zhen* 蓁蓁 is a beautiful and excellent appearance. It is "flourishing." *Zhi zi* 之子 is like saying *shi zi* 是子 (this child). This indicates and speaks of a young woman getting married. A woman going to get married is referred to as *gui* 歸. *Yi* 宜 is like *shan* 善 (good, goodness).

[7] The ode is the "Liao bian" from the "Xiao ya."

[8] The ode is the "Shi jiu" from the "Cao feng." *Te* 忒 equates with *cha* 差 (fault, error).

[9] The three odes quoted all refer to (sing of) the affairs of the preceding text and so also bring it together in this way. Their flavour is deep and extensive; it is very appropriate to ponder them deeply.

DX Comm. 10.1: 所謂平天下在治其國者：上老老而民興孝，上長長而民興弟，上恤孤而民不倍，是以君子有絜矩之道也。[1]所惡於上，毋以使下；所惡於下，毋以事上；所惡於前，毋以先後；所惡於後，毋以從前；所惡於右，毋以交於左；所惡於左，毋以交於右：此之謂絜矩之道。[2]

《詩》云：「樂只君子，民之父母。」[42] 民之所好好之，民之所惡惡之，此之謂民之父母。[3]

《詩》云：「節彼南山，維石巖巖。赫赫師尹，民具爾瞻。」[43] 有國者不可以不慎，辟則為天下僇矣。[4]

Comment: The one continuous section 10 of the commentary in Zhu Xi's arrangement has been divided here into five subsections corresponding to sections TX11–15 inclusive in the *Li ji* text. The whole section is about the final stage in the sequence—bringing good order to the state as a basis for bringing peace to all under Heaven. In the first subsection above (DX Comm. 10.1) there is an expanded and clarified version of the principle of reciprocity followed by two quotations from the *Odes*, the first positive and possibly referring to King Cheng and the second negative, referring to the Grand Master Yin.[44] Subsection 10.2 continues the theme with further examples from the classic texts, focussing on the need for virtue and its preservation in a ruler. Subsection 10.3 begins with a long quotation from the final book of the *Documents*. The historical details are supplied in Kong Yingda's commentary to the *Li ji* version.[45] This leads to a statement about what constitutes *ren* 仁 which is continued in the following subsection (10.4). Here the focus is on the specific connection between *ren* 仁 and *yi* 義. In the final subsection, 10.5, again beginning with a long quotation, attributed to Meng Xian but from an unknown source, the focus is on the nature of *yi* 義, including its relationship to *li* 利 (right action as against profit or benefit).

注 DX Comm. 10.1 (朱熹)

[1] {長，上聲。弟，去聲。倍，與背同。絜，胡結反。}老老，所謂老吾老也。興，謂有所感發而興起也。孤者，幼而無父之稱。絜，度也。矩，所以為方也。言此三者，上行下效，捷於影響，所謂家齊而國治也。亦可以見人心之所同，而不可使有一夫之不獲矣。是以君子必當因其所同，推以度物，使彼我之間各得分願，則上下四旁均齊方正，而天下平矣。

---

[42] The *Odes*, Mao 172, verse 3, LCC, 4:273.
[43] The *Odes*, Mao 191, verse 1, LCC, 4:309.
[44] See Legge's note on the historical context, LCC, 4:310.
[45] See also Legge's introductory comments to the book in question—LCC, 4: 626–27.

DX Comm. 10.1: What is meant by "bringing peace to all under Heaven lies in bringing good order to the state" is this: The ruler treats the aged as they should be treated, and the people are moved to filial piety; the ruler treats elders as they should be treated, and the people are moved to fraternal respect; the ruler has sympathy for those who are young and without a father, and the people are not rebellious. This comes about through the noble man following the Way of "measuring and squaring" (reciprocity). **[1]** What is hated in superiors, do not use in employing inferiors. What is hated in inferiors, do not use in serving superiors. What is hated in those in front, do not use in leading those behind. What is hated in those behind, do not use in following those in front. What is hated in those on the right, do not use in dealings with those on the left. What is hated in those on the left, do not use in dealings with those on the right. This is called the Way of "measuring and squaring" (reciprocity). **[2]**

The *Odes* says: "Happy indeed is the prince; he is a parent to the people." What the people love, he loves; what the people hate, he hates. This is called being a parent to the people. **[3]**

The *Odes* says: "How lofty is the southern mountain, with its precipitous rocky cliffs. Awe-inspiring are you, Grand Master Yin. All the people look up to you." He who possesses a state cannot but be careful. If he is prejudiced, then he becomes an object of the world's contempt. **[4]**

Notes DX Comm. 10.1 (Zhu Xi)

[1] . . . *Lao lao* 老老 is what refers to *lao wu lao* 老吾老, i.e. "treat the aged of your own family in a manner befitting their venerable age."[46] *Xing* 興 refers to what moves and gives rise to (stirs). *Gu* 孤 is a name for someone who is young and without a father. *Xie* 絜 is equivalent to *du* 度 (rule, measure, estimate). *Ju* 矩 is what makes a square. It is said of these three things, when superiors do them, inferiors follow, quick as a shadow or echo. This is what is meant by "regulate the household and the state will be well ordered." Also, if you can see what is the same in the hearts (minds) of others, there cannot be a single person who is not positively influenced. This is why the noble man must make what is the same in himself right, judging this by the Way of "measuring and squaring" so causing others each to attain their wishes by what he has in himself. Then, above and below, and on the four sides, all will be regular and correct, and all under Heaven will be at peace.

---

[46] *Mencius* IA.7, D. C. Lau, *Mencius: A Bilingual Edition* (Hong Kong: Chinese University Press, 2003), 36.

[2] {惡、先，並去聲。}此覆解上文絜矩二字之義。如不欲上之無禮於我，則必以此度下之心，而亦不敢以此無禮使之。不欲下之不忠於我，則必以此度上之心，而亦不敢以此不忠事之。至於前後左右，無不皆然，則身之所處，上下、四旁、長短、廣狹，彼此如一，而無不方矣。彼同有是心而興起焉者，又豈有一夫之不獲哉。所操者約，而所及者廣。此平天下之要道也。故章內之意，皆自此而推之。

[3] {樂，音洛。只，音紙。好、惡，並去聲，下並同。}《詩•小雅•南山有臺》之篇。只，語助辭。言能絜矩而以民心為己心，則是愛民如子，而民愛之如父母矣。

[4] 節，讀為截。辟，讀為僻。僇，與戮同。《詩•小雅•節南山》之篇。節，截然高大貌。<u>師尹</u>，<u>周</u>太師<u>尹氏</u>也。具，俱也。辟，偏也。言在上者人所瞻仰，不可不謹。若不能絜矩而好惡殉於一己之偏，則身弒國亡，為天下之大戮矣。

[2] . . . This repeats the explanation of the meaning of the two characters *xie ju* 絜矩 from the previous section. If I do not wish superiors to be disrespectful towards me, then I must use this to measure the hearts (minds) of inferiors, and also on this basis I dare not treat them disrespectfully. If I do not wish inferiors to be disloyal towards me, then I must use this to measure the hearts (minds) of superiors, and also on this basis I dare not serve them disloyally. When it comes to front and behind, and left and right, everything is like this, so then, in terms of where the self is placed, whether above or below, to the four sides, long or short, broad or narrow, that or this are like one, and there is nothing that is not "squared." If the other's mind-heart is the same as this mind-heart and is moved and stirred up with it, then how will there be a single person whose mind-heart is not "captured"? Those in control are few and yet their influence is far-reaching. This is the key element in bringing peace to all under Heaven. Thus, the meaning within this chapter all starts from this and extends it.

[3] . . . The verse is the "Nanshan you tai" from the *Odes*, "Xiao ya." *Zhi* 只 is an interjection or auxiliary word. This (i.e. the quotation) says that, if he is able to measure and take the people's hearts (minds) as his own heart (mind), then this constitutes his loving the people like his children and the people loving him like a parent.

[4] *Jie* 節 is read as *jie* 截. *Pi* 辟 is read as *pi* 僻. *Lu* 僇 (to despise, humiliate) and *lu* 戮 (to disgrace, to slay) are the same. The ode is the "Jie nanshan" from the "Xiao ya." *Jie* 節 is *jieran* 截然 (completely, an eminent appearance). Grand Master Yin refers to the great Zhou official, Yin Shi. *Ju* 具 equates with *ju* 俱 (all). *Pi* 辟 equates with *pian* 偏 (partial, prejudiced). This says that the one who occupies a superior position is someone others look up to and respect; he cannot be other than careful. If he is unable to "measure and square" properly and follows the prejudices of his own individual likes and dislikes, then he himself will be killed and his country lost, making him one of the great disgraces of the world.

DX Comm. 10.2:《詩》云：「殷之未喪師，克配上帝；儀監于殷，峻命不
易。」[47] 道得眾則得國，失眾則失國。**[5]**是故君子先慎乎德。有德此有
人，有人此有土，有土此有財，有財此有用。**[6]**德者本也，財者末也。**[7]**
外本內末，爭民施奪。**[8]**是故財聚則民散，財散則民聚。**[9]**是故言悖
而出者，亦悖而入；貨悖而入者，亦悖而出。**[10]**

〈康誥〉曰：「惟命不于常！」道善則得之，不善則失之矣。**[11]**

《楚書》曰：「楚國無以為寶，惟善以為寶。」**[12]**

舅犯曰：「亡人無以為寶，仁親以為寶。」**[13]**

注 DX Comm. 10.2 (朱熹)

[5] {喪，去聲。}儀，詩作宜。峻，詩作駿。{易，去聲。}《詩‧文王》篇。師，
眾也。配，對也。配上帝，言其為天下君，而對乎上帝也。監，視也。峻，大
也。不易，言難保也。道，言也。引詩而言此，以結上文兩節之意。有天下
者，能存此心而不失，則所以絜矩而與民同欲者，自不能已矣。

[6] 先慎乎德，承上文不可不慎而言。德，即所謂明德。有人，謂得眾。有土，
謂得國。有國則不患無財用矣。

[7] 本上文而言。

[8] 人君以德為外，以財為內，則是爭鬥其民，而施之以劫奪之教也。蓋財者人
之所同欲，不能絜矩而欲專之，則民亦起而爭奪矣。

---

47   The *Odes*, Mao 235, verse 7, LCC, 4:431.

DX Comm. 10.2: The *Odes* says: "When the Yin [rulers] had not yet lost the people, they could be taken as equal to Shang Di. Take warning from the Yin; the great mandate is not easy [to hold on to]." This says that to gain the multitude is to gain the state; to lose the multitude is to lose the state. **[5]** This is why the noble man gives priority to the care of his own virtue. To have virtue is to have the people; to have the people is to have the land; to have the land is to have wealth; to have wealth is to have resources. **[6]** Virtue is the root; wealth is the branch. **[7]** [If the ruler] makes the root external and the branch internal, he causes contention among the people and teaches them to plunder. **[8]** This is why, when wealth is gathered the people scatter, and when wealth is distributed the people gather. **[9]** This is why it is that, if contrary words go forth, it is also contrary words that come back. If it is ill-gotten goods that come in, it is ill-gotten goods that go out. **[10]**
The "Announcement to Kang" states: "The mandate of Heaven is not ever-lasting." That is to say, goodness gets it and lack of goodness loses it. **[11]**
The *Documents of Chu* says: "The state of Chu takes nothing to be precious other than goodness." **[12]**
Jiu Fan said: "The lost person (fugitive prince) takes nothing to be precious other than love for his parents." **[13]**

Notes DX Comm. 10.2 (Zhu Xi)

[5] . . . *Yi* 儀 in the *Odes* is written *yi* 宜. *Jun* 峻 in the *Odes* is written 駿. . . . This is from the *Odes*, "Wen Wang." *Shi* 師 equates with *zhong* 眾 (the multitude). *Pei* 配 equates with *dui* 對 (comparable to). *Pei Shang Di* 配上帝 refers to his being ruler of the world and comparable to Shang Di. *Jian* 監 equates with *shi* 視 (to observe). *Jun* 峻 equates with *da* 大 (great, large). *Bu yi* 不易 means *nan bao* 難保 (difficult to protect, maintain). *Dao* 道 equates with *yan* 言 (to say). Quoting the *Odes* and saying this is a way of connecting the meaning of the previous two sections. If the one who possesses all under Heaven is able to preserve this mind-heart and not lose it, then by his "measuring and squaring" and joining the people in the same desires, he himself cannot come to an end.
[6] "Gives priority to the care of his own virtue" continues the discussion of the previous text about not being able to be otherwise than cautious. *De* 德 is, then, what has been spoken of as "the original brightness of innate virtue" (*ming de* 明德). "Having the people" speaks of gaining the multitude. "Having land" speaks of gaining the state. If there is "having the state," then there is not the calamity of being without wealth and resources.
[7] *Ben* 本 (root) refers to the previous text.
[8] If the ruler takes virtue (*de* 德) to be external (secondary) and wealth (*cai* 財) to be internal (primary), then this makes his people contentious and teaches them to plunder. In fact, wealth is something people all desire and [if he] is unable to follow [the Way of] "measuring and squaring" (i.e. reciprocity, proper conduct), and desires to monopolise the wealth, then the people will also rise up in strife and plunder.

[9] 外本內末故財聚，爭民施奪故民散，反是則有德而有人矣。

[10] {悖，布內反。}悖，逆也。此以言之出入，明貨之出入也。自先慎乎德以下至此，又因財貨以明能絜矩與不能者之得失也。

[11] 道，言也。因上文引<u>文王</u>詩之意而申言之，其丁寧反覆之意益深切矣。

[12]《楚書》，楚語。言不寶金玉而寶善人也。

[13] <u>舅犯</u>，<u>晉文公</u>舅<u>狐偃</u>，字<u>子犯</u>。亡人。<u>文公</u>時為公子，出亡在外也。仁，愛也。事見〈檀弓〉。此兩節又明不外本而內末之意。

DX Comm. 10.3:〈秦誓〉曰：「若有一个臣，**斷斷**兮無他技，其心休休焉，其如有容焉。人之有技，若己有之，人之彥聖，其心好之，不啻若自其口出，寔能容之，以能保我子孫黎民，尚亦有利哉。人之有技，媢疾以惡之，人之彥聖，而違之俾不通，寔不能容，以不能保我子孫黎民，亦曰殆哉。」**[14]**唯仁人放流之，迸諸四夷，不與同中國。此謂唯仁人為能愛人，能惡人。**[15]**

[9] If the root is made external (secondary) and the branches are made internal (primary), then wealth is gathered and the people, driven to contention and plunder, are scattered. If there is the converse of this, then virtue prevails and he has possession of the people.

[10] . . . *Bei* 悖 equates with *ni* 逆 (rebellious, refractory, contrary). This usage of "going out (forth)" and "coming in (back)" clarifies the going out and coming in of goods. From "giving priority to the care of his own virtue" down to this, there is also the use of wealth and goods to make clear the equating of being able to "measure and square" and not being able to "measure and square" with gaining and losing respectively.

[11] *Dao* 道 equates with *yan* 言 (to say). Because the above text quotes the meaning of the "Wen Wang" ode and speaks further on it, by giving repeated examples of its meaning, it increases its profundity.

[12] The *Chu shu* 楚書 is the "Chu yu" 楚語 (Sayings of Chu). This says, do not treasure gold and jade; treasure good men.

[13] Uncle Fan is Hu Yan, the maternal uncle of Duke Wen of Jin, whose style name was Zifan. He is the "lost person." At the time when Duke Wen was still a duke's son, he fled into exile and was "lost." *Ren* 仁 equates with *ai* 愛 (to love). For this matter see the "Tan Gong." These two sections also clarify the meaning of not making the root external (secondary) and the branch internal (primary).

DX Comm. 10.3: The "Declaration of Qin" states: "Suppose there is one resolute minister who is loyal and honest but without other skills, who is broadminded and magnanimous, a man at ease with a demeanour in keeping. If others have skills, it is as if he himself has them; if others are fine officers and perspicacious, he loves them in his heart more than his words express and he is truly able to accept them. Such a man would be able to preserve my descendants and all the ordinary people, so that there may also be benefit indeed! But if, when others have skills, he is jealous and hates them, or when others are fine officers and perspicacious, he opposes them and prevents them advancing and is truly unable to accept them, he would not be able to protect my descendants and all the ordinary people, and I would also say he was dangerous." **[14]** Only a man who is *ren* 仁 will send away and banish such a person, driving him off to the four barbarians, and will not allow him to dwell with him in the Middle Kingdom. This is to say that only a man who is *ren* 仁 is able to love others and able to hate others. **[15]**

見賢而不能舉，舉而不能先，命也；見不善而不能退，退而不能遠，過也。[16]好人之所惡，惡人之所好，是謂拂人之性，菑必逮夫身。[17]是故君子有大道，必忠信以得之，驕泰以失之。[18]

注 DX Comm. 10.3 (朱熹)

[14] {个，古賀反，書作介。斷，丁亂反。媢，音冒。}〈秦誓〉，《周書》。斷斷，誠一之貌。彥，美士也。聖，通明也。尚，庶幾也。媢，忌也。違，拂戾也。殆，危也。

[15] 迸，讀為屏，古字通用。迸，猶逐也。言有此媢疾之人，妨賢而病國，則仁人必深惡而痛絕之。以其至公無私，故能得好惡之正如此也。

[16] 命，鄭氏云：「當作慢。」程子云：「當作怠。」[48]未詳孰是。{遠，去聲。}若此者，知所愛惡矣，而未能盡愛惡之道，蓋君子而未仁者也。

[17] 菑，古災字。{夫，音扶。}拂，逆也。好善而惡惡，人之性也；至於拂人之性，則不仁之甚者也。自〈秦誓〉至此，又皆以申言好惡公私之極，以明上文所引〈南山有臺〉、〈節南山〉之意。

[18] 君子，以位言之。道，謂居其位而修己治人之術。發己自盡為忠，循物無違謂信。驕者矜高，泰者侈肆。此因上所引<u>文王</u>、〈康誥〉之意而言。章內三言得失，而語益加切，蓋至此而天理存亡之幾決矣。

---

48   In the *Yichuan Xiansheng gaizheng daxue* there is "作怠之誤也." See *Er Cheng quanshu*, 2:1757.

To see one who is worthy and yet not be able to advance him, or to advance him but not be able to give him priority, is to be remiss. To see someone who is not good and yet not be able to send him away, or to send him away but not be able to send him far enough, is a fault. **[16]** To love what other people hate, or to hate what other people love is called going against human nature and will inevitably bring disaster upon oneself. **[17]** This is why the noble man has the great Way. Certainly, loyalty and trust are the ways to attain it, whereas arrogance and pride are the ways to lose it. **[18]**

Notes DX Comm. 10.3 (Zhu Xi)

[14] . . . The "Declaration of Qin" is in the "Zhou shu" (section of the *Shang shu*). *Duan duan* 斷斷 is the appearance of being loyal and honest. *Yan* 彥 equates with a fine officer. *Sheng* 聖 indicates clear understanding. *Shang* 尚 equates with *shu ji* 庶幾 (so that, it may be). *Mao* 媢 equates with *ji* 忌 (jealous, to hate, fear). *Wei* 違 equates with *fu li* 拂戾 (to oppose, be contrary to). *Dai* 殆 equates with *wei* 危 (danger).

[15] *Ping* 迸 is read as *bing* 屏, the ancient character having the same use. *Ping* 迸 is like *zhu* 逐 (to expel, pursue). This says that, if there are such jealous men who hinder the worthy and injure the state, then the man of *ren* 仁 must deeply dislike and thoroughly reject them. Because he is extremely public-spirited and without self-interest, he is therefore able to achieve correctness in what he loves and hates like this.

[16] On *ming* 命, Zheng Shi (Zheng Xuan) says: "This ought to be *man* 慢 (slow, dilatory, to treat rudely)." Master Cheng (Yi) says: "This ought to be *dai* 怠 (idle, remiss, disrespectful, insolent). It is not clear who is right. . . . If someone like this knows what to love and what to hate and yet is never able to fully commit himself to the path of love and hatred, although he may be a noble man, he will never be *ren* 仁.

[17] *Zi* 菑 is an ancient form of *zai* 災. . . . *Fu* 拂 equates with *ni* 逆 (to oppose, go against). Loving good and hating evil is part of human nature. When it comes to going against human nature, then this is the very antithesis of *ren* 仁. From the "Declaration of Qin" to this, all is again used to extend the discussion of the extremes of good and evil, both public and private, in order to make clear the meaning of what, in the preceding text, was quoted from the "Nan shan you tai" and the "Jie nanshan."

[18] *Jun zi* 君子 is used to speak of position. *Dao* 道 speaks of the method of [a man] occupying his position whilst cultivating himself and bringing order to others. To manifest and exert oneself to the utmost is *zhong* 忠 (loyalty). To comply with things and not oppose them is called *xin* 信 (trustworthiness). *Jiaozhe* 驕者 is one who is arrogant and *taizhe* 泰者 is one who is wilful. This accords with the ideas of the "Wen Wang" ode and the "Announcement to Kang" quoted above. Within this chapter, the issue of gain (*de* 得) and loss (*shi* 失) is raised three times, each instance being stronger than the last, reaching a climax on the question of whether Heaven's principle is preserved or lost.

DX Comm. 10.4: 生財有大道，生之者眾，食之者寡，為之者疾，用之者舒，則財恆足矣。**[19]**仁者以財發身，不仁者以身發財。**[20]**未有上好仁而下不好義者也，未有好義其事不終者也，未有府庫財非其財者也。**[21]**

注 DX Comm. 10.4 (朱熹)

[19] {恆，胡登反。} 呂氏曰：「國無遊民，則生者眾矣；朝無幸位，則食者寡矣；不奪農時，則為之疾矣；量入為出，則用之舒矣。」[49]愚按：此因有土有財而言，以明足國之道在乎務本而節用，非必外本內末而後財可聚也。自此以至終篇，皆一意也。

[20] 發，猶起也。仁者散財以得民，不仁者亡身以殖貨。

[21] 上好仁以愛其下，則下好義以忠其上；所以事必有終，而府庫之財無悖出之患也。

---

[49]   Lü Dalin 呂大臨 (1044–1093) was a disciple of the Cheng brothers. A brief biography is given in the *Song shi* 宋史, 31: 340.10848. See also the *Song Yuan xue'an* 宋元學案 30. The source of the quotation was not located.

DX Comm. 10.4: For the creation of wealth there is the great Way. Let those who create wealth be many and those who consume it be few. Let those who create wealth do so with urgency and those who consume it do so with restraint. Then wealth will always be sufficient. **[19]** The man of *ren* 仁 uses wealth to raise himself. The man without *ren* 仁 uses himself to raise wealth. **[20]** There has never been a case of a superior (ruler) loving *ren* 仁 and inferiors not loving *yi* 義. There has never been a case of [inferiors] loving *yi* 義 and affairs not reaching fulfillment. There has never been a case of the wealth stored in the storehouses not being his (i.e. the ruler's) wealth. **[21]**

Notes DX Comm. 10.4 (Zhu Xi)

[19] . . . Lü Shi said: "When the country is without vagrants, then those who produce will be many. When the court is without favourites, then those who consume will be few. When the time for farming is not snatched away, then it will be done expeditiously. When expenditure is related to income, then its use will be extended." Simply put, this says that because there is land, there is wealth, to make clear that the road to sufficiency for the state lies in giving priority to the root and being frugal in use. One must not take the root as external (secondary) and the branches as internal (primary) and think that subsequently wealth can be gathered. From this to the final section, there is all the one meaning.

[20] *Fa* 發 is like *qi* 起 (to raise). The man of *ren* 仁 disperses his wealth as a way of gaining the people; the man without *ren* 仁 ruins himself to gain material possessions.

[21] When a superior (ruler) loves *ren* 仁 and so cherishes his inferiors, then the inferiors will love *yi* 義 and so be loyal to their superior. Thus will they inevitably bring affairs to fulfillment and the wealth of the granaries and storehouses will not suffer the calamity of being dissipated improperly.

DX Comm. 10.5: <u>孟獻子</u>曰：「畜馬乘不察於雞豚，伐冰之家不畜牛羊，百乘之家不畜聚斂之臣，與其有聚斂之臣，寧有盜臣。」此謂國不以利為利，以義為利也。**[22]** 長國家而務財用者，必自小人矣。彼為善之，[50] 小人之使為國家，菑害並至。雖有善者，亦無如之何矣！此謂國不以利為利，以義為利也。**[23]**

右傳之十章。釋治國平天下。（此章之義，務在與民同好惡而不專其利，皆推廣絜矩之意也。能如是，則親賢樂利各得其所，而天下平矣。）凡傳十章：前四章統論綱領指趣，後六章細論條目功夫。其第五章乃明善之要，第六章乃誠身之本，在初學尤為當務之急，讀者不可以其近而忽之也。

注 DX Comm. 10.5 (朱熹)

[22] {畜，許六反。乘、斂，並去聲。} <u>孟獻子</u>，<u>魯</u>之賢大夫<u>仲孫蔑</u>也。畜馬乘，士初試為大夫者也。伐冰之家，卿大夫以上，喪祭用冰者也。百乘之家，有采地者也。君子寧亡己之財，而不忍傷民之力；故寧有盜臣，而不畜聚斂之臣。此謂以下，釋<u>獻子</u>之言也。

[23] {長，上聲。}「彼為善之」，此句上下，疑有闕文誤字。自，由也，言由小人導之也。此一節，深明以利為利之害，而重言以結之，其丁寧之意切矣。

DX Comm. 10.5: Master Meng Xian said: "A man who keeps horses and a carriage does not think about chickens and pigs. A household that cuts ice does not keep oxen and sheep. A household with a hundred chariots should not retain an official who accumulates [wealth]. Rather than having an officer who accumulates [wealth], it would be better to have an officer who is a robber." That is to say, a state should not take profit to be a benefit; it should take *yi* 義 (right action) to be a benefit. [22] If the one who leads a state or household devotes himself to wealth and consumption, it must be because he is influenced by lesser men. He may be a good man but, if a lesser man is used to manage the affairs of a state or household, calamity and harm will both come. Even if there are those who are good, of what use will they be! That is to say, a state should not take profit to be of benefit; it should take *yi* 義 to be of benefit. [23]

Above (to the right) is the tenth chapter of the commentary explaining "bringing good order to the state" and "peace to all under Heaven." (This chapter's meaning is that what is fundamental lies in unifying the likes and dislikes of the people and not having individuals seeking their own benefit, in all cases amplifying the meaning of *xie ju* 絜矩 [measuring and squaring]. If things can be like this, then cleaving to worthiness and delighting in benefit each obtains its place and the world is at peace.) Altogether, there are ten chapters of commentary. The first four chapters discuss the essential principles in general. The last six chapters discuss the work involved in the particular aspects in detail. The fifth chapter makes clear the essential elements of goodness, and the sixth chapter deals with the fundamental element of making the self *cheng* 誠 (genuine, true, sincere). At the outset of one's studies, [these two chapters] especially should be accorded the proper recognition of their pressing importance. The reader cannot neglect them just because of their simplicity.

Notes DX Comm. 10.5 (Zhu Xi)

[22] . . . Master Meng Xian was a worthy grandee (great officer) from Lu, Zhongsun Mie. "Keeping horses and a carriage" refers to an officer's first experience of being a grandee. "A household that cuts ice" refers to officers from grandee up who use ice at funerals and sacrifices. "A household of a hundred chariots" refers to those who have received lands. The noble man would rather lose his own wealth than allow himself to harm the strength of the people. Therefore, he would rather have officials who are robbers (i.e. rob him) than those who amass and accumulate [wealth from the people]. From *ci wei* 此謂 ("that is to say") on is an explanation of Master Xian's words.

[23] . . . With respect to the sentence "彼為善之," both before and after, I suspect there are omissions and mistakes. *Zi* 自 is to be equated with *you* 由 (by, because of), saying that it is because of lesser men guiding him. This particular section clarifies at a deep level the harms of taking profit to be beneficial, and reiterates the point to emphasise it with the urgency of repeated injunction.

中庸

Introduction: The *Zhongyong*

The *Zhongyong* 中庸 is the longer and more complex of the two chapters taken from the *Li ji* 禮記 to join with the *Lunyu* 論語 of Confucius and the *Mencius* 孟子 in the Four Books. It constitutes the end point for scholars embracing the Confucian canon as defined by Zhu Xi. Wing-tsit Chan has described it as " . . . a philosophical work, perhaps the most philosophical in the whole body of ancient Confucian literature."[1] As befits such a work of acknowledged complexity and significance, the *Zhongyong* has attracted a considerable amount of attention and analysis over the many centuries of its existence. Some idea of the extent of this attention may be gained from the section on commentaries in Appendix 2. Moreover, issues do not only involve the understanding of its content. They also concern the title of the work, its authorship and date of composition, its arrangement, and the terminology used to express the teaching it contains. These matters will be briefly addressed in what follows.

The Title: Of the titles of the two works, the *Zhongyong* and the *Daxue*, the former is by far the more problematic, not only for translators, as evidenced by the much greater variety of renderings, but also for Chinese commentators. There are two aspects to the problem: what the term *zhong yong* actually means and why it does not occur at the start of the work as might be expected. On the question of meaning the difficulty is primarily with *yong* 庸 but also involves, to a lesser extent, the relationship between the two characters. There is also the subordinate question of the relationship between *zhong he* 中和, used in the first section (ZY1) but not subsequently, and *zhong yong* 中庸, used from the second section (ZY2) onward. We shall consider each of these three issues in turn. First, on the meaning of *yong* 庸 the possibilities are as follows:

---

1   Wing-tsit Chan, *A Source Book in Chinese Philosophy* (Princeton: Princeton University Press, 1963), 96.

1. That *yong* 庸 is to be understood as its homophone *yong* 用. This is what is given in the ancient dictionary, the *Shuowen* 説文[2] and is the position taken by the *Li ji* commentators in their introductory remarks.

2. That *yong* 庸 is to be equated with *chang* 常 in the sense of "constant" (i.e. like *heng* 恆) which is the position taken by Cheng Yi 程頤 (1033–1107) in particular.

3. That *yong* 庸 is to be understood as *pingchang* 平常 in the sense of "ordinary," "commonplace" or "quotidian," which is probably Zhu Xi's final position, although he does quote Cheng Yi's view in his opening statement to the tract in the *Sishu zhangju* 四書章句 (SSZJ—The Four Books in Chapters and Sentences).[3]

There is also variation in the reading of *zhong* 中—as "centre/central" or "middle" most obviously, but also as "moderation" or (commonly) "Mean," extending to "balance" or "equilibrium," and as "inner" referring to the inner attributes of the individual person.[4]

Second, on the relationship between the two characters, there are again several possibilities:

1. That *zhong* 中 is nominal and *yong* 庸 is verbal with an anteposed object—for example, "Using the Centre," "Using the Middle [Way]," "Application of the Inner" or "The Mean in Action" (Hughes).

2. That *zhong* 中 is verbal and *yong* 庸 is nominal in the sense of either "ordinary" or "commonplace"—for example, "Centering on the Commonplace" or "Focusing the Familiar" (Ames & Hall).

---

2   See Xu, *Shuowen jiezi zhu*, 129.

3   Wing-tsit Chan, in his translation of Chen Chun's 陳淳 (1159–1223) *Beixi ziyi* 北溪 字義 (*Neo-Confucian Terms Explained*), has: "Master Cheng (Cheng Yi) said, 'By *yong* 庸 is meant what is unchangeable.' What he said was of course good but does not fully express the meaning. It is not as clear and complete as Wen Gong's (Zhu Xi's) interpretation of it as 'ordinary.' The idea of ordinary includes that of unchangeability but unchangeability does not include the idea of the ordinary. In reality, they are but one principle. You Dingfu 游定夫 (i.e. You Zuo) said that *zhong he* 中和 refers to nature and feelings, thus making the distinction between substance and function and between action and tranquility, while *zhong yong* 中庸 refers to moral activity, combining both activity and affairs." See Chan, *Neo-Confucian Terms Explained (The Pei-hsi tzu-i)* (New York: Columbia University Press), 126.

4   Riegel renders the title "Application of the Inner" where "inner" indicates "one's own, individual, inborn character." See Jeffrey Riegel, "The Four 'Tzu Ssu' Chapters of the 'Li Chi': An Analysis and Translation of the *Fang Chi, Chung Yung, Piao Chi*, and *Tzu I*" (PhD diss., Stanford University, 1978), 85–86.

3. That *zhong* 中 is nominal and *yong* 庸 is adjectival—for example, "L'invariable Milieu" (Rémusat), "De Medio Sempiterno" (Intorcetta et al.) or "The Unwobbling Pivot" (Pound).

4. That *zhong* 中 and *yong* 庸 are coordinate terms—for example, "[The State of] Equilibrium and Harmony" (Legge), [The Way of] Central and Constant/Commonplace," "Centrality and Commonality" (Tu Wei-ming) or "Undeviating and Unchanging" (following Cheng Yi).

Finally, there is the question of the relationship between *zhong yong* 中庸 and *zhong he* 中和 referred to above. This is examined in some detail in Appendix 3 on terminology but the distinction made by You Zuo 游酢 (1053–1123), which Zhu Xi includes in his commentary and is given in note 3 above, is illuminating on this point.

Legge, who must be held in large part responsible for the enduring, albeit somewhat misleading, title "The Doctrine of the Mean," judiciously addressed these several issues in the opening note to the work, to be found in the 1960 reprint of *The Chinese Classics* in which he explains his oft-criticised but much used choice. As the note gives a balanced appraisal of other early views on the matter and ends with a consideration of why he changed to "The State of Equilibrium and Harmony" in his later translation of the *Li ji*, it is given below *in extenso*.

[In the] title of the work, "The Doctrine of the Mean," I have not attempted to translate the Chinese character 庸, as to the exact force of which there is considerable difference of opinion, both among native commentators, and among previous translators. Zheng Xuan said: "The work is named *Zhongyong* 中庸 because it records the practice of the non-deviating mind and of harmony." He takes *yong* 庸 in the sense of *yong* 用, "to use," "to employ," which is the first given to it in the dictionary, and is found in the *Shu jing* 書經. . . . This appears to have been the accepted meaning of *yong* 庸 in this combination (i.e. 中庸), till Cheng Yi introduced that of *bu yi* 不易, "unchanging," as in the introductory note, which, however, the dictionary does not acknowledge. Zhu Xi himself says: "*Zhong* 中 is the name for what is without inclination or deflection, which neither exceeds nor comes short. *Yong* 庸 means ordinary, constant." The dictionary gives another meaning of *yong* 庸, with special reference to the point before us. It is said, 又和也 "it also means harmony"; and then reference is made to [Zheng Xuan's] words given above, the compilers not having observed that he immediately subjoins, 庸，用也, showing that he takes *yong* 庸 in the sense of "to employ" and not of "harmony." Many, however, adopt this meaning of the term in ZY2, and my own opinion is decidedly in favour of it, here in the title.

The work then treats of the human mind in its state of *zhong* 中, absolutely correct, as it is in itself; and in its state of *he* 和, or harmony, acting *ad extra*, according to its correct nature. In the version of the work, given in the collection of *Memoires concernant l'histoire les sciences etc des Chinois* (vol. 1), it is styled "*Juste Milieu.*" Rémusat calls it: *L'invariable Milieu* after Cheng Yi. Intorcetta and his co-adjutors call it *Medium constans vel sempiternum.* The book treats, they say, "De medio sempiterno, sive de aurea mediocrate illa, quae est, ut ait Cicero, inter nimium et parum, constanter et omnibus in rebus tenenda." Morrison, character *yong* 庸, says, "*Zhongyong*, the constant (golden) Medium." Collie calls it "The golden Medium." The objection which I have to all these names is that from them it would appear as if *zhong* 中 were a noun, and *yong* 庸 a qualifying adjective, whereas they are co-ordinate terms. My own version of the title in translation published in the Sacred Books of the East is *The State of Equilibrium and Harmony.*[5]

What may we conclude from all this? First, in keeping with our intention of following the commentators of each version, for the *Li ji* 禮記 version, we must take *yong* 庸 as *yong* 用, making it verbal to give the meaning of "using the centre" or "using the middle Way." This means that in practice the noble man in his conduct maintains a position midway between "going beyond" (*guo* 過) and "not reaching" (*bu ji* 不及), Wang Fuzhi's 王夫之 (1619–1692) objection notwithstanding.[6] For the SSZJ version, we have followed Cheng Yi's reading since Zhu Xi quotes this at the outset, giving a rendering of "central and constant" ("undeviating and unchanging"). This could be taken to mean that the noble man maintains a central position between going beyond and falling short and does not deviate from this regardless of circumstances. If the reading of *yong* 庸 as *pingchang* 平常 in the sense of "ordinary," "commonplace" or "quotidian" is thought preferable, for example on the basis of other comments by Zhu Xi, *zhong yong* could be rendered

---

5   LCC, 1:382–83 (minor changes have been made in the inclusion or otherwise of characters and in romanization).

6   On this distinction, Wang Fuzhi has: "The phrase with the two characters *zhong* 中 and *yong* 庸 most certainly cannot be compared with exceeding and falling short. . . . Wickedness will always be a matter of falling short. How can it be to go beyond? The sagely Way is the peak of majesty, the best, what is so lofty it is like Heaven. How can one go beyond it? . . . One must take *zhong* 中 as the utmost, be a partner to Heaven and Earth, praise transformation and generation and there can be nothing that can be exceeded. Do not want to let people say that the Way has limits and boundaries and thus take refuge in the vale of wrong." Originally from *The Great and Comprehensive Reading of the Four Books*, quoted by E. Ryden in his translation of Zhang Dainian's *Key Concepts in Chinese Philosophy* (Beijing: Foreign Languages Press, 2002), 336.

"centred on the commonplace" meaning, as the following quotation from Chen Chun's *Beixi ziyi* sets out, holding a central path, a path of moderation in the conduct of everyday affairs:

> Wen Gong (Zhu Xi) interpreted *zhongyong* 中庸 as being ordinary. It is not that outside of *zhong* 中 there is another *yong* 庸. It simply means that when what is central is manifested externally, without any excess or deficiency, that is the ordinary daily principle. The ordinary and the strange are opposed to each other. The ordinary is what people are used to, while the strange is what people are not used to. When they suddenly see it they feel strange. And in the cases of affection between father and son, righteousness between ruler and minister, attention to their separate functions between husband and wife, proper order between old and young, and faithfulness between friends, they are daily matters and ordinary principles without anything extraordinary or special.[7]

As a result of these various considerations, we have settled on a rendering of the title *Zhongyong* as "Using the Centre" for the *Li ji* version and as "Central and Constant" for the SSZJ version.

Authorship and Date: There are two separate components to the traditional view regarding the authorship (and hence the date, broadly) of the *Zhongyong*. The first is that the work was compiled by Kong Ji 孔伋 (c. 483–422 BCE), the grandson of Confucius, who prepared a tract from the words of the Sage, quotations from the *Odes* and his own explanatory remarks. The second is that Kong Ji was the same person as Zisi 子思 to whom a work is attributed in the *Han shu*, "Yiwenzhi." The early evidence on both components is certainly scanty but what there is does seem to favour the traditional view. Thus, Sima Qian 司馬遷 (c. 145–86 BCE) in the *Shiji* 史記 wrote as follows: "Boyu 伯魚 engendered Ji whose style was Zisi. He lived to 62. When he was in difficult circumstances in Song, he wrote the *Zhongyong* 中庸."[8] A similar position is taken by Ban Gu 班固 (32–92) in the *Han shu* 漢書.[9] What written evidence there is suggests that Confucius' son, Boyu died before his father, hence it must be concluded that Kong Ji (Zisi) was born before Confucius died. One date suggested is 483 BCE which puts his death at 422 BCE, thereby creating

---

[7]   Chan, *Neo-Confucian Terms Explained (The Pei-hsi tzu-i)*, 125.

[8]   *Shiji*, 47.1946.

[9]   *Han shu*, 30.1724. There is also reference to a *Zhongyong shuo* 中庸説 in 2 *pian* with no author identified (p. 1710).

some difficulty with the anecdotes linking Zisi with Duke Miu 繆 of Lu.[10]
Both *Li ji* commentators accept Zisi's role in composition without elaboration, whilst Zhu Xi actively supports the view and specifically identifies what
he takes to be Zisi's own contributions as distinct from statements by Confucius and quotations from the *Odes* in his SSZJ text. A relatively detailed account of the early evidence, flimsy though it may be, is provided by Legge in
his introduction to the *Zhongyong*.[11]

Dissenting voices have been raised against both components of the traditional view right from the time it was first fully articulated by Zhu Xi. For
example, there was the opposition voiced by the Song scholar, Wang Bo 王柏
(1197–1274), which is expressed in two essays preserved in the *Lu Zhai Wang
Wenxian Gong wenji* 魯齋王文憲公文集: the *Zhongyong lun* 中庸論 and the
Gu Zhongyong ba 古中庸跋. Two quotations from these which will serve to illustrate his views are as follows:[12]

> In my view I seem to sense the slight existence of discontinuities in the argument
> and that the *kong* and *shang* notes do not sound in the right order. . . . There are real
> discontinuities that Master Zhu never notes. At first, *zhi* 知, *ren* 仁, and *yong* 勇 are
> referred to separately. But then they are all called "the far-reaching virtues." This is
> out of place. After seven or eight sections, the analogy of journeying far and climb-
> ing high is followed with "surely the power of ghosts and spirits is replete." The two
> are so different they do not fit. The altogether three sections beginning with "Great
> indeed is the Way of the sage" are not of the same kind as "complete *cheng* 誠 never
> ceases," "Duke Ai asked about government" and "Zhongni took as his ancestors and
> succeeded to" are especially far apart. These all represent my view of the text and af-
> ter swimming about and researching them completely, I have been unable to resolve
> them.

> The *Zhongyong* was a document written by Master Zisi to open the great source,
> establish the great root, and continue the thread of the sage. The subtlety of its
> meaning is difficult to fathom, the breadth of its scope difficult to encompass, and
> the complexity of its doctrines difficult to unravel. Master Zhu Zi having shoul-
> dered the responsibility for these, his disciples can now, as in a prolonged spring,

---

10   Duke Mu reigned from 407 to 376 BCE. In the *Han shu* entry (see note 9 above),
     Kong Ji is identified as Duke Mu's teacher.
11   LCC, 1:36–42.
12   CSJC, 132:294–96, 316. The translations follow Riegel with minor modifications. See
     Riegel, "The Four 'Tzu Ssu' Chapters of the 'Li Chi': An Analysis and Translation of
     the *Fang Chi, Chung Yung, Piao Chi*, and *Tzu I*," 77–79.

enjoy eternal release. In my humble view, however, I often sense discontinuities in its argument as well as contradictions. I did not dare give expression to my thoughts nor formulate my doubts into questions. One day I happened to notice that a work entitled *Zhongyong shuo* in two fascicles is listed in the *Treatise on Arts and Letters* of the Western Han. Yan Shigu's 顏師古 (581–645) note reads, "Now in the *Li ji* there is the *Zhongyong* in one fascicle . . . " He does not say that it lost one. In a flash of inspiration I realised that in Ban Gu's time there were still two fascicles. Were they perhaps mixed together by the hand of Small Dai 小戴 (Dai Sheng 戴聖, 1ˢᵗ century BCE)? He did not know that the ancients never entitled their own fascicles and that titles are the divisions of later men. He merely saw that the meaning of the passages in the two fascicles was not the same and so he accordingly mixed them to form a general overall theme.

It would seem that during the period of prolonged pre-eminence enjoyed by Zhu Xi's SSZJ as the authoritative text, the dissident views of Wang Bo made little impact. With the development of the text-critical movement of the Qing, and more particularly in the twentieth century, some support did emerge for Wang Bo's ideas, or at least for his basic thesis. One example of this is Feng Youlan (Fung Yu-lan) who wrote in his *History of Chinese Philosophy*:[13]

> Wang Bo is very suggestive here, though he has not pushed the problem to its conclusion. If we examine the ideas in the *Zhongyong* closely, we find that the first section, beginning with the first sentence and extending to the words: "Heaven and Earth would have their proper positions, and all things would be nourished"; together with the closing section, beginning with the words: "When those in inferior positions do not obtain confidence from their superiors," to the end of the work, discuss for the most part the relation of man to the universe, and seem to be a development of Mencius's mystical ideas, while the style is that of a formal essay. The intervening section, on the other hand, discusses human affairs, and seems to be a development of the doctrines of Confucius, while its style is that of recorded conversations. Thus this central section would seem to constitute the original *Zhongyong* of Zisi, as listed under his name in the "Yiwen zhi." The opening and closing sections, on the other hand, have been added by a later Confucian and so probably constitute the *Zhongyong shuo* in two sections spoken of in the "Yiwenzhi." This assumption is strengthened by the fact that all the references to the standard cart-wheel gauge used throughout the empire, etc., occur in this latter section. The fact that the author of these opening and concluding sections named them *Zhongyong shuo* shows that he must have been a follower of Zisi; yet at the same time they contain ideas derived

---

[13] Fung Yu-lan, *A History of Chinese Philosophy*, trans. D. Bodde, 2 vols. (Princeton: Princeton University Press, 1952), 370–71, translation after Bodde with minor modifications.

from Mencius, from which it would seem that their author was a follower of the latter as well. The probable explanation is that the two groups of Confucians headed by Zisi and Mencius were originally similar to each other, which would also explain why the *Xunzi* (chapter 6) has grouped the two men together.

More recent still are the views expressed by some Western scholars. First, for example, is the position advanced by Riegel.[14] Following an excellent account of the existing views on the compilation and structure of the *Zhongyong*, he presents his own theory. His analysis of the structure of the work is as below (using Zhu Xi's numbering):

ZY1: " . . . a series of definitions of technical terms . . . " which " . . . should be read together as an aphoristic and elliptical summary of passages from a text on self-cultivation philosophy."

ZY2–11: a series of *logia* in the style of the *Lunyu*.

ZY12: no specific comment other than that it contains two quotes from the *Odes*.

ZY13–15: a collection of passages which " . . . resembles in general a series of proverbs, some originally perhaps *scholia* on the *Book of Songs* . . . "

ZY16: "a panegyric to ghosts and spirits . . . " which " . . . serves as another *scholium* on a poem in the *Book of Songs*."

ZY17–19: further *scholia* on the *Odes* and also the *Documents* with added passages.

ZY20: the dialogue between Confucius and Duke Ai in a somewhat abbreviated form compared to the *Kongzi jiayu* 17.

ZY21–26: " . . . a series of extremely prolix and flowery passages" which detail how one who maintains his natural *cheng* 誠 will become a force equal to Heaven and Earth.

ZY27–28: [ZY27 is] " . . . a remarkably eclectic section which resumes phrases found earlier in the chapter" which is elaborated on in ZY28.

ZY29: " . . . details the procedures an individual should follow to verify he is suited to be 'king of all the world' . . . "

ZY30–32: a series of statements in praise of Confucius.

ZY33: quotations of eight couplets from the *Odes* "interspersed with interpretation."

Riegel, then, rejects the traditional view of the *Zhongyong* as the work of Zisi, and rejects also the multiple author/multiple strata theory advocated initially by Wang Bo. Instead, he postulates that the work is a record of a Han debate and concludes that there is " . . . no 'internal' unity to the *Zhongyong*

---

14   For the chapter on the structure of the *Zhongyong*, see Riegel, "The Four 'Tzu Ssu' Chapters of the 'Li Chi': An Analysis and Translation of the *Fang Chi, Chung Yung, Piao Chi, and Tzu I*," 74–109.

but only one that appears ephemeral and contrived."[15] On the second component of the traditional theory, Csikszentmihalyi has given detailed consideration to what he calls the "Zisi myth," questioning particularly the identification of a single Zisi with Kong Ji.[16]

In summary, then, there is the traditional view, supported by very flimsy early evidence but accepted and established by the more or less tacit agreement of the *Li ji* commentators and particularly by the quite explicit formulations of Zhu Xi. This is that Kong Ji, styled Zisi and the grandson of Confucius, was the author of the work. Opponents of this position question the identification of Zisi with Kong Ji and, in some cases, favour the idea that the *Zhongyong* is a composite work from the hands of Han dynasty scholars—perhaps even a record of a debate during that period. Although the recent discoveries at Mawangdui and Guodian, referred to in the "General Introduction," have shed light on some writings of Zisi they have not, as yet, contributed in any way to clarification of the issue of authorship of the *Zhongyong*. However, in one way at least, questions of authorship are irrelevant in the present work insofar as its aim is to present the tract in the two forms in which it was influential over almost two millennia, during which time it must be presumed that the traditional view of composition was, in effect, universally accepted by readers.

Components of the Text: Taking the *Li ji* version as the basis, five distinct components of the text may be identified.[17] These are as follows:

1. The basic statement listing and in part defining three key concepts: nature (i.e. human nature), the Way and teaching. There is also some consideration of the conduct of the noble man and the introduction of the terms *zhong* 中 (the centre) and *he* 和 (harmony) (ZY1).

2. Quotations from Confucius elaborating on the key concepts and introducing other issues including *cheng* 誠 and *li* 禮 (ZY2–13).

3. Confucius' reply to Duke Ai of Lu's question on government which involves a consideration of the key virtues, in particular, *cheng* 誠 (ZY14–19).

4. Elaboration of the concept of *cheng* 誠 (ZY20–26).

5. Concluding sections (ZY27–33).

---

15 Riegel, "The Four 'Tzu Ssu' Chapters of the 'Li Chi': An Analysis and Translation of the *Fang Chi, Chung Yung, Piao Chi,* and *Tzu I,*" 99.

16 Csikszentmihalyi, *Material Virtue: Ethics and the Body in Early China,* 86–100.

17 Other more complex divisions have been made including those of Riegel and Haloun.

190 Daxue and Zhongyong

Each of these components will be considered in greater detail before discussing and comparing their arrangement in the two texts and then examining their interpretation with a particular focus on the differences between the three commentators.

1. The Basic Statement: This opens with three axioms/claims which include the four important terms—*tian* 天 (Heaven), *xing* 性 (nature), *dao* 道 (the Way) and *jiao* 教 (teaching). Rephrased, these axioms/claims are:

- Nature, i.e. human nature, is determined by Heaven. That is, it is innate. Left unanswered are important questions about the nature of Heaven and about the nature of nature itself, in particular whether the nature decreed by Heaven is the same for all people and, if so, wherein the differences between individuals lie. As much of the rest of the work is about how to improve this Heaven-decreed nature by the process of self-cultivation, this is clearly a critical issue.
- The Way is the path of following the presumably foundational, Heaven-decreed nature. It is, then similar to "manifesting luminous (enlightened) virtue" in that the true nature, which is inherently good, is allowed to shine forth.
- Teaching is the means of expressing this nature through self-cultivation and extending the concept and its practice to others.

There is then an admonition that in following the Way one must never deviate, not even for an instant, and that the correct practice of the Way must be maintained whether one is under scrutiny or not, although it must be recognised that doubt surrounds the reading of these sentences. The claim that the Way cannot be left, even for an instant, is unexceptionable in theory. Practice, of course, is another matter altogether. The problem arises in the subsequent sentences. The simplest (and quite possibly the correct) reading is that in following the Way, the noble man must maintain his constant adherence to the Way even when he is unobserved. The alternative (which appears to be supported by Zhu Xi's note 3 to the ZY1) is that what the noble man must be careful about is what he alone has (or is), his inner being or self, and the source of his conduct, which is inscrutable to others.[18]

---

[18] On the phrase 慎其獨, Riegel has: "[This] does not mean 'when one is alone'—a famous Legge mistranslation thoughtlessly repeated by later scholars even though Henri Maspero, *Le Chine Antique*, corrected it: 'The superior man must cultivate what is unique to him,'

The remainder of this first section introduces two terms *zhong* 中 and *he* 和 which, whilst not again used in direct conjunction within the work, represent two of the basic concepts, being more or less equated with *zhong* 中 and *yong* 庸. On this point, Zhu Xi quotes You Zuo as follows: "When it is spoken of in terms of emotions and feeling, then it is called *zhong he* 中和; when it is spoken of in terms of virtue and conduct, then it is called *zhong yong* 中庸." *Zhong* 中, the centre, is clearly defined as the state (presumably of the mind-heart) unclouded by emotions. *He* 和 is the state of the mind-heart when emotions are in play but are in balance or equilibrium.

2. Quotations from Confucius: In the *Li ji* version there are 17 of these, the first beginning "Zhongni said" and the remainder beginning "The Master said." Zhu Xi arranges these quotations somewhat differently, as discussed below. Only two of the quotations are from an identifiable source (the *Lunyu*) whilst in four instances they include, in Confucius' statement, a quotation from the *Odes*. The first 13 of the 17 quotations are about aspects of the basic statement: that is, about using the centre, the Way and the conduct of the noble man. One uses Shun as an example and one is a discussion with Zilu on strength, also found in the *Lunyu*, used here to elaborate on the Way and the noble man. Of the last four of the 17 quotations, all of which are relatively long, one is about ghosts and spirits, this including the introduction of the concept of *cheng* 誠 in this text, one is about Shun, in particular his virtues and filial piety, and two are about the rites (*li* 禮) considering the sequence from Tai Wang to Wu Wang and also the Duke of Zhou.

3. Confucius' Reply to Duke Ai: Although the Duke's question is about government, Confucius' reply is quite wide-ranging. First, he deals with the Way and virtue generally, proceeding then to several specific virtues, notably *ren* 仁 (benevolence, humanity, loving kindness), *yi* 義 (right action, righteousness, justice), *zhi* 知 (wisdom, knowledge), *yong* 勇 (courage, particularly moral courage) and *li* 禮 (proper conduct in relationships, rites, ceremonies). He then outlines the "nine canons" before re-introducing the concept of *cheng* 誠. These sections correspond in part to material in both the *Kongzi jiayu* 孔子家 語 (*The Family Sayings of Confucius*) and the *Mencius*.

---

that is to say that which was given to him by Heaven, his selfness" (Riegel, "The Four 'Tzu Ssu' Chapters of the 'Li Chi': An Analysis and Translation of the *Fang Chi, Chung Yung, Piao Chi,* and *Tzu I,*" 87 and 209n9). In our view, this is a harsh and unwarranted criticism, especially given what the *Li ji* commentators have to say on the matter.

<u>4. On *Cheng* 誠:</u> There are seven sections on the matter of *cheng*, beginning with an exhortation to diligently pursue its study and practice. A distinction is made between two ways of coming to be *cheng*: one is through innate enlightenment which characterises the sage and the other is through acquired enlightenment which characterises the worthy man. Being perfectly or completely *cheng* is the way of perfecting or completing one's nature. This can then be extended to others. *Cheng* has the capacity to change and transform the world. It carries the possibility of foreknowledge. The last of these sections gives a detailed account of *cheng* as a virtue and what it can achieve through its embodiment in the noble man. It also links *cheng* with two of the other virtues, *ren* 仁 and *zhi* 知.

<u>5. Concluding Sections:</u> These are something of a miscellany; seven sections comprising three on ritual (*li* 禮) in relation to both the sage and the noble man, two consisting of further quotations from Confucius on the establishment of standards and on *li*, one long section in praise of Confucius which includes six quotations from the *Odes* and a brief final section including two quotations from the *Odes* (also brief) and relating to virtue.

Arrangement (Table 2): The differences between the *Li ji* text and that of Zhu Xi's SSZJ version are less marked in the case of the *Zhongyong* than in the case of the *Daxue*. Nevertheless, they are present and do have some significance in terms of interpretation, as will be detailed in the next section. Divisions in the *Li ji* text are based on the placement of Kong Yingda's commentary. Zhu Xi's text is clearly divided into numbered sections by the comment following each one. Numbers have been added to the start of each section in both texts to facilitate comparison.

<u>1. *Li ji*:</u> The first section (ZY1) is the basic statement in its entirety. Then follow 12 sections (ZY2–13), each consisting of one or more quotations from Confucius; in four instances these include a quotation from the *Odes*. Confucius' response to Duke Ai's question on government, material which closely corresponds to part of the *Kongzi jiayu* 17 and contains material very similar to that found in the *Mencius* IVA.12, comprises the six sections ZY14–19. All this is taken to be Confucius' reply apart from the initial question by Duke Ai and two instances of "The Master said." The next seven sections (ZY20–26) consist of statements elaborating on *cheng*, a subject raised in the final part of Confucius' reply. The last of these sections (ZY26) gives a series of examples of how the large arises from an accumulation of the small. Although *cheng*

is not mentioned specifically, this is taken by the commentators to refer to it, and perhaps to virtue more generally. ZY27 considers the Way of the sage and how it relates to virtue. Sections ZY28 and 29 consider the conduct of the noble man—how he uses the centre and implements *li*, and how he reacts when the state has or does not have the Way. ZY30 is about the establishment of standards with particular attention being given to rites (*li* 禮) and music (*yue* 樂). This has been considered an important section in relation to the dating of the tract as a whole. ZY31 is again on *li*, this time through a quotation from Confucius. ZY32 is an encomium for Confucius as a transmitter of the ancient Way and an example of perfect *sheng* 聖 (sagehood, sagacity) and perfect *cheng* (purity, genuineness, sincerity). It contains a further six *Odes* quotations pertaining to these matters. The final section (ZY33) is a quotation from Confucius, who borrows from the *Odes* in making the claim that virtue is as light as a feather but still has substance.

Table 2: Comparison of the *Zhongyong* in the *Li ji* and *Sishu zhangju* Texts

Li ji	*Sishu zhangju*
ZY1: The basic statement.	ZY1: The basic statement.
ZY2–6: 9 quotations from Confucius (2 corresponding to the *Lunyu*).	ZY2–10: 9 quotations from Confucius (2 corresponding to the *Lunyu*).
ZY7: One quotation from Confucius including a quotation from the *Odes*.	ZY11–12: One quotation from Confucius (ZY11) plus a statement from Zisi (ZY12).
ZY8–13: 7 quotations from Confucius including 4 quotations from the *Odes*.	ZY13–19: 7 quotations from Confucius including 4 quotations from the *Odes* plus 2 statements by Zisi.
ZY14–19: Confucius' reply to Duke Ai's question on government.	ZY20.1–20.6: Confucius' reply to Duke Ai's question on government.
ZY20–26: Clarification of *cheng*.	ZY21–26: Clarification of *cheng*.
ZY27–29: On the sage and the noble man in relation to *li*.	ZY27: On the Way of mankind as exemplified by the sage and the noble man.
ZY30–31: On standards and the establishment of rites; 2 quotations from Confucius.	ZY28–29: On the same topics but with a major part attributed to Zisi.
ZY32: Encomium for Confucius followed by 6 *Odes* quotations plus comments.	ZY30–32: Encomium for Confucius.
ZY33: Final statement by Confucius on virtue including an *Odes* quotation.	ZY33: 6 quotations from the *Odes* plus the final statement from Confucius including a further *Odes* quotation.

2. <u>SSZJ</u>: As in the *Li ji* text, the basic statement is the first section (ZY1) in its
entirety. However, Zhu Xi arranges the following 17 quotations from Confucius differently. Each of the first 10 quotations is given as a separate section
(ZY2–11). These are described as being chosen by Zisi to clarify and amplify
the meaning of the opening statement. The following section (ZY12) is identified by Zhu Xi as a statement by Zisi, directed at explaining the meaning of
"the Way cannot be departed from" in the opening section (ZY1). In the *Li ji*
arrangement, Zhu Xi's ZY12 is treated as part of a quotation from Confucius.
This, then, is the first significant difference in arrangement between the two
texts. The next section (ZY13) is a long quotation from Confucius on the
Way. It is followed by a section (ZY14) largely attributed to Zisi and concluding with a brief quotation from Confucius. ZY15 is similar but also includes
a quotation from the *Odes*. The next four sections (ZY16–19) are all relatively
long quotations from Confucius, the first two including quotations from the
Odes. They are essentially about conduct. The next section (ZY20) is the
response by Confucius to Duke Ai's question on government. In our text it
has been divided into six subsections (ZY20.1–20.6) to facilitate comparison
with the *Li ji* (ZY14–19). There is variation in punctuation relating to what
is, or is not, part of Confucius' reply. In Zhu Xi's text there is a variation from
the *Li ji* in the sections on *cheng* which follow Confucius' reply to Duke Ai's
question. Zhu Xi takes the first seven sentences of what is ZY25 in the *Li ji* as
his ZY25 and relates them to the Way of mankind. The remaining sentences
he makes part of his ZY26 to which he attaches all of the *Li ji* ZY26, taking
this to be about perfect *cheng* as the Way of Heaven. Following this, Zhu Xi
groups the three short sections ZY27–29 in the *Li ji* into a single section (his
ZY27) which he takes to be about the Way of mankind. His ZY28 is equivalent to the *Li ji* ZY30 and the opening statement of ZY31, thus combining
the two quotations from Confucius on *li* as rites into a single section, again
taken to be about the Way of mankind. The rest of the *Li ji* ZY31 is then
equivalent to all of Zhu Xi's ZY29 which continues the consideration of the
Way of mankind. Zhu Xi does not take this to be a continuation of Confucius' statement as in the *Li ji* 31. The very long section in the *Li ji* in praise
of Confucius (ZY32) is broken up in Zhu Xi's text into three sections (his
ZY30–32) all relating to the Way of Heaven. Zhu Xi's final section, ZY33
then comprises the series of *Odes* quotations (eight in his arrangement), each
with an explanatory comment. He takes this section to be a summarising
statement by Zisi on the whole work. This corresponds to the second part of
ZY32 and all of ZY33 in the *Li ji* arrangement.

A summarised comparison of the two texts, focusing on the differences, is as follows:

- The opening statement is the same.
- Zhu Xi breaks the sequence of 17 quotations from Confucius clarifying the opening statement with a statement attributed to Zisi after the tenth quotation.
- Among the final seven of the 17 initial Confucian quotations there are two sections that also include statements by Zisi.
- Zhu Xi extends Confucius' reply to Duke Ai by including his section 20.6 (ZY20 in the *Li ji*), recognising that this is not in accord with the arrangement of the dialogue in the *Kongzi jiayu*.
- Zhu Xi makes minor changes in the arrangement of the final seven sections (ZY27–33).

It can be seen that the changes made in the *Zhongyong* text by Zhu Xi are relatively slight compared with those he made in the *Daxue* text.

Interpretation: Issues of interpretation are more complex in the *Zhongyong* than in the *Daxue*. Not only is the critical opening section in the former less clear in expression than the relatively straightforward exposition of the components and benefits of the programme of self-cultivation in the latter, but the key propositions themselves contain philosophical issues that are not fully addressed. In addition, later sections in the *Zhongyong* introduce other key concepts (particularly the sections on *cheng*) rather than simply elaborate on those in the opening statement. Matters of interpretation will be considered under the headings already used for the components of the text and their arrangement, with the focus on a comparison of the views of the three commentators.

1. The Basic Statement: In explication of the opening three claims Zheng Xuan quotes the *Classic of Filial Piety* as follows: "Nature is the decreed disposition of what is born. It is what a person receives as a natural endowment." He lists the following five virtues as components of this nature: *ren* 仁 (benevolence, loving kindness, humanity), *yi* 義 (right action, righteousness, a sense of justice), *li* 禮 (observation of the rules and methods of proper conduct in interpersonal relationships and formal ceremonial practices), *xin* 信 (trustworthiness, adherence to one's word, good faith) and *zhi* 知 (wisdom, knowledge and its application). To act in accord with this Heaven-decreed

nature, that is to express these virtues in action, is to follow the Way. To maintain and build on this Way and to cause others to emulate the "Way-following
self" is teaching. Kong Yingda adds a comment about Heaven to the effect
that it is " . . . fundamentally without substance and its decree is without
verbal expression." He also recognises that there are variations in the Heaven-
decreed nature: " . . . people have feelings which naturally arise and are worthy or foolish, fortunate or unfortunate." He explicitly allows that there are
variations in the endowment of the five virtues listed by Zheng Xuan, and
that the individual nature may be good or evil. The Way is a road which
" . . . opens a path for the decreed nature like a road opens a way through for
people." If people go off the road they enter " . . . wild, difficult and obstructed places." Kong gives very detailed consideration to this statement in terms
of the Five Phases (*wu xing* 五行) and the Five Constant Virtues (*wu chang* 五
常) as listed above. He quotes a number of early texts and the commentary
of He Yang 賀瑒 (fl. early 6th century) and also speaks of the *qi* 氣 (spirit) of
Heaven as descending to give rise to the Five Phases.

Zhu Xi offers a somewhat different interpretation. Heaven acts through
yin and *yang* and the Five Phases or Elements—metal, wood, earth, water,
fire—to give rise to the ten thousand things. *Qi* then completes their forms
and *li* 理 (principle) is bestowed on them like a decree. In this formulation,
li 理 (principle) corresponds to *xing* 性 (nature), as Zhu Xi explicity states.
In his view, then, " . . . each person acquires the *li* 理 that is bestowed on him
[which] may be taken as an unvarying compliance with the Five Constant Virtues. The path to follow, which is designated as the Way, is the spontaneous
functioning of this nature in everyday activities. Zhu Xi also acknowledges
that "although nature and the Way are constant, natural endowment may
vary and this is what constitutes the faults of 'going beyond' and 'not reaching.'" The sage is someone who acts in a way (Way) that is right for a person,
regulating this, and serving as a model for other people. This is teaching, and
incorporates rites, music, government, punishments, etc.

Following this initial statement there are two further statements relating
to the practice of the Way. First, there is the claim that the Way cannot and
must not be departed from, even for an instant—all very well in theory but another matter altogether when it comes to practice. Little is made of this statement by the *Li ji* commentators who simply confirm that it is bad (and even
dangerous, presumably in a moral sense) to depart from the Way. Zhu Xi takes
a somewhat different view. Having further defined the Way as " . . . the daily
use of the principles of proper action in relation to matters and things" and as
the " . . . virtue of all natures and in all cases in the mind-heart," he states that

it cannot (rather than should not) be departed from. The second of the claims
is more contentious. To both *Li ji* commentators it is a statement about the
noble man acting in a proper manner even when he is alone and unobserved.
Thus, Zheng Xuan says: "The lesser man, when living alone, does things that
are not good; there is nothing he does not do. The noble man is not like this.
Although there are no others to see or hear him, he is still on guard and cautious, fearful and apprehensive, and is naturally well-ordered and correct."
This is what constitutes following the Way even when unobserved, and not departing from it for an instant. Kong Yingda's rather long clarification is entirely
in accord with this and is quite clear. Zhu Xi's explanation is less clear and has
allowed the interpretation that a number of Western scholars have followed,
which is that what is being referrred to here is not being physically alone but
some part of the self, perhaps an inner core of being, which is not accessible
to others.[19] Zhu Xi has these glosses on the key characters: *yin* 隱 is a hidden
place; *wei* 微 equates with trifling affairs; *du* 獨 refers to a place that others do
not know—a place that only the self knows. His concluding comment is that
the noble man is " . . . able to nip his desires in the bud, not letting them grow
larger in the midst of the hidden and the trifling so that he reaches the point of
becoming distant from the Way." We could well conclude that all three commentators are taking essentially the same position on this point although the
possibility remains that Zhu Xi has in mind some core inner self unknowable
by others.

The final part of the opening statement introduces two further key terms,
zhong 中 and *he* 和 —there is no mention of *yong* 庸. The definitions are quite
clear from the text itself. Zhu Xi remarks that the "centre" is " . . . the great
foundation because it restrains joy, anger, sorrow and happiness; it is the source
of *li* 禮. Government and teaching come out of this." He makes no comment on *he* 和. Kong Yingda takes the same position on the centre being the
foundation. He says that in the centre (i.e. when emotions have not yet arisen)
" . . . there is tranquility and abstraction, the mind has nothing to think about
and is properly in accord with principle (*li* 理)." Harmony is when the emotions have arisen but are regulated and restrained—that is, "nature and conduct are in harmonious concert." Zhu Xi takes essentially the same position.
When the emotions have not yet arisen, this is nature which does not deviate
to one side or the other and is in the "centre." When emotions have arisen
but are regulated and correct " . . . there is nothing which is unreasonable

---

[19]   See note 18 above.

or perverse," which is harmony. In his concluding remarks on the section Zhu Xi does, however, go beyond the *Li ji* commentators. He says, in part, " . . . because Heaven and Earth, the ten thousand things and myself are all one substance, if my mind-heart is rectified, then the mind-heart of Heaven and Earth are also rectified; if my *qi* 氣 (spirit, vital force) is propitious, then the *qi* of Heaven and Earth is also propitious. Therefore, in this way, its fulfil-ment is complete. Thus it is that the extreme efficacy of learning and enquir-ing and the sage's ability in affairs from the first do not depend on what is external and the teaching which regulates the Way also lies in what is within."

2. Quotations from Confucius: In the *Li ji* there are 17 quotations in suc-cession comprising sections ZY2–13 (four quotations are included in ZY2 and two in both ZY5 and ZY9). In Zhu Xi's arrangement there is a series of ten quotations, each given a separate section (ZY2–11), a statement by Zisi (ZY12), and then the remaining seven quotations attributed to Confucius. The first ten quotations are all clearly about the Way of "using the centre" (*Li ji*) or the Way of "central and constant" (Zhu Xi)—what it is, that it is char-acteristic of the noble man (examples are Shun and Yan Hui) as opposed to the lesser man, and that it is so hard to follow that few are able to follow it for long. All these quotations are, then, about clarification and elaboration of the opening section (ZY1). Two important issues as far as the commentators are concerned are the introduction of *yong* 庸, particularly how this relates to *he* 和, and what is meant by "going beyond" and "failing to reach."

On the first issue, Zheng Xuan equates *yong* 庸 with *chang* 常 which can, of course, mean either constant or commonplace. Kong Yingda agrees with this equivalence. We have taken the meaning of *chang* 常 here to be "constant" or "a constant principle," thus reading Zheng Xuan's comment as "using the centre and being constant is the Way." It should be noted that this reading of *chang* 常 is at odds with the statement of the equivalence of *yong* 庸 with *yong* 用 in the introductory comment attributed to Lu Deming and reflecting the *Shuowen* 説文 definition. Zhu Xi also seems to read *yong* 庸 as "constant" in line with Cheng Yi's reading as *bu yi* 不易. On the relationship between *he* 和 and *yong* 庸, Zhu Xi refers to You Zuo.[20] On the matters of "not reaching" and "going beyond," both *Li ji* commentators rather shirk the issue. They identify "not reaching" with the "foolish and unworthy" and "going beyond" with the "wise and worthy" but do not really attempt to make clear what

---

20   See Chan, *Neo-Confucian Terms Explained (The Pei-hsi tzu-i)*, 126.

those two failings involve. Zhu Xi takes "going beyond" as reaching the centre but losing it, and "not reaching" as never achieving the centre. All agree that achieving and maintaining the centre is a difficult matter and is difficult to sustain even if achieved. Other differences between the *Li ji* commentators and Zhu Xi on these ten quotations involve minor issues only—issues such as the readings of certain characters as detailed in the Comments to the various sections.

The next issue concerns what is the major part of ZY7 in the *Li ji* arrangement and the separate section ZY12 in Zhu Xi's text. In the *Li ji* text, at least in modern editions, this is taken to be a continuation of the quotation from Confucius on being unable to stop in his diligent pursuit of the Way. Zhu Xi, however, takes these sentences, which include a quotation from the *Odes*, to be from Zisi and aimed at clarifying the matter of the Way being something that cannot be departed from. Zheng Xuan's comments on this section are brief and are largely glosses on a number of characters. In particular, the great matter is identified with the Way of former kings, while small matters are what ordinary men know and do. On the latter, Kong Yingda is at pains to point out that it is these small matters that the sage does not know and cannot do—it is not that sages cannot do great things. Nevertheless, he makes it clear that the Way of the sage has its origin in what ordinary men and women know and do. He also comments on the *Odes* quotation, claiming that it is taken out of context and therefore has a different meaning from that in the original ode. Zhu Xi, however, takes the quotation as being used by Zisi " . . . to clarify the presence of transforming and nourishing" which is clearly evident above and below, and that there is nothing apart from the functioning of principle, which is what is called "far-reaching in its use." On the matter of what the sage does not know, Zhu Xi takes this as being " . . . exemplified by things like Confucius asking about rites and office." As for what he cannot do, this is " . . . exemplified by things like Confucius not gaining a position and by Yao and Shun being deficient in their liberal gifts." Finally, on this section, Zhu Xi quotes Cheng Hao as follows: "This section is a critical point for Zisi, is very stimulating and vivid, and stirs thoughts in the reader's [mind]."

The remaining seven of the 17 quotations from Confucius following the opening section comprise sections ZY8–13 in the *Li ji* arrangement (there are two quotes in ZY9). The same material, arranged somewhat differently and including statements imputed to Zisi, comprises section ZY13–19 in Zhu Xi's text. The differences between the two commentarial traditions will be briefly considered for each section.

ZY8 in the *Li ji* is taken in its entirety to be a quotation from Confucius which includes a quotation from the *Odes*. It is about the Way being near at hand and accessible to all. Despite this, Zheng Xuan claims, people are unable to practise it. Most of his brief notes are glosses on individual characters, including the equating of *yong* 庸 with *chang* 常 in the sense of constant—he speaks of virtue being constantly practised and speech as being constantly cautious. He also makes the point that, when others have faults and transgress, the noble man uses the Way of mankind to bring order to them. Kong Yingda makes essentially the same points, expanding on the metaphor of cutting an axe handle, based on the *Odes* quotation. He also gives attention to the two virtues of *zhong* 忠 (loyalty) and *shu* 恕 (reciprocity)—a point of emphasis for Zhu Xi too. The last part of the quotation, which is not included in this section by Zhu Xi, is about the conduct of the noble man, the essential feature of which Kong Yingda sums up with a quotation from the *Lunyu*—"the noble man in his thoughts does not go beyond his position." In short, his actions are always appropriate to his circumstances. He does not make demands on others that he does not make on himself, he meets misfortune with equanimity, and accepts what Heaven dictates. Again Kong quotes from the *Lunyu*—"The Master said: 'I do not feel resentment towards Heaven, I do not blame others.'"

Zhu Xi takes the first ten sentences of the *Li ji* ZY8 as his ZY13 and accepts this as a quote from Confucius. Again the fact of the Way being near at hand and accessible is stressed—it is not far removed from people, and that means all people. He offers clear definitions of the two characters *zhong* 忠 (to exert one's mind-heart to the utmost) and *shu* 恕 (to extend oneself to reach out to others). He links these virtues and the virtue of *ren* 仁 (quoting Zhang Zai's definition of this as "loving others with a mind-heart that loves the self is, then, complete *ren* 仁") with the Way being near at hand. He ends with a further quote from Zhang Zai: "To have a mind-heart that demands of the self what one demands of others is, then, to be complete in the Way."

ZY9 in the *Li ji* arrangement is entirely a quotation from Confucius comparing the noble man to an archer accepting responsibility for his performance, and also comparing following the Way of the noble man to going on a journey. Zheng Xuan's notes are entirely devoted to the clarification of characters apart from a final statement that following the Way of the noble man will make the household compliant—one of the stages in the opening statement of the *Daxue*. Kong Yingda expands on this point, concluding that the Way of using the centre first causes the household to be harmonious and compliant and then is able to extend harmony and compliance beyond the family. Zhu Xi's arrangement is different hence his interpretation is somewhat different. He takes the last five sentences of ZY8 in the *Li ji* as the major part of his ZY14 (i.e. about the noble man acting according to his circumstances without resentment or ill-will) and attributes this statement to Zisi. He then concludes the section with the quotation from Confucius about the archer to emphasise the point. His notes on this section are very brief.

ZY10 in the *Li ji* arrangement is entirely a quotation from Confucius which contains a quotation from the *Odes*. As it concerns ghosts and spirits, there has been the suggestion that it is misplaced here, particularly given Confucius' position on this issue as expressed in the *Lunyu*. Neither of the *Li ji* commentators remarks on this. Apart from a series of glosses on individual characters, Zheng Xuan makes three points: (i) that every one of the ten thousand things is born of the *qi* 氣 of ghosts and spirits; (ii) that the form and appearance of ghosts and spirits cannot be known; (iii) that although ghosts and spirits are without form or words, they are nevertheless *cheng* 誠. Kong Yingda confirms this last point and adds *xin* 信 to *cheng* 誠. His comments are in agreement with those of Zheng Xuan and he makes the added point that the Way of using the centre and the Way of ghosts and spirits are very similar " . . . in that both go from the obscure to the manifest, are without words, and yet are naturally *cheng* 誠." It is clear from Kong Yingda's comments that ghosts and spirits are thought to really exist and to have a significant role in human affairs. Zhu Xi, whose ZY16 corresponds in content, likewise accepts the existence of ghosts and spirits, quoting in support both Cheng Yi ("ghosts and spirits are the effective agents of Heaven and Earth and the traces of creation and transformation") and Zhang Zai ("in the case of ghosts and spirits, they represent the natural capacities of the two ethereal vapours"). Zhu Xi also offers a definition of *cheng* 誠 as " . . . being true and genuine and not false."

ZY11 in the *Li ji* arrangement is an exact equivalent of Zhu Xi's ZY17 and is again a quote from Confucius which contains a quotation from the *Odes*. It is a statement in praise of Emperor Shun—his filial piety and virtue generally are seen as being the reasons why he was rewarded by Heaven. Thus, for the *Li ji* commentators, Heaven is capable of rewarding the good and punishing the bad. Kong Yingda does, however, raise the paradox of why Confucius did not receive any tangible reward, given his sage-like virtue. Zhu Xi's notes on this section are very brief consisting only of short statements clarifying terms and recording the sources of the *Odes* quotations. Sections ZY12 and 13 in the *Li ji* correspond exactly to ZY18 and 19 in Zhu Xi's text. Both are relatively long quotations attributed to Confucius and are about three ancient exemplars of virtue and filial piety, Kings Wen and Wu and the Duke of Zhou.

In particular, there is consideration of rites and ceremonies associated with burial, mourning and subsequent sacrifices. The *Li ji* commentators concern themselves with the clarification of characters, and in Kong Yingda's case, with further detail on ceremonial practices and additional historical information. Zhu Xi is also primarily concerned with the meanings of certain characters and with providing further detail on these practices. The contributions of all three commentators are, to some extent, complementary, although there is also a degree of repetition. There are no significant points of divergence—rather there is agreement, especially in regard to the lessons to be drawn from the conduct of these three universally acknowledged noble or exemplary men.

3. Confucius' reply to Duke Ai's question: This long passage occupies sections ZY14 to 19 in the *Li ji* arrangement and section ZY20 (which is subdivided into ZY20.1 to ZY20.6) in Zhu Xi's text. As mentioned earlier, there is some doubt as to whether Zhu Xi's ZY20.6 (corresponding to the *Li ji* ZY20) is part of Confucius' response or not. It is not found in the *Kongzi jiayu* version of the dialogue. There is also a close, but not exact, correspondence between ZY18 and 19 (Zhu Xi's ZY20.5) and *Mencius* IVA.12. This is one of the key sections of the whole work. Not only is there a relatively detailed consideration of four of the five constant virtues (*ren* 仁, *yi* 義, *li* 禮 and *zhi* 知) and also *xin* 信 and *zhong* 忠 as well as *yong* 勇, but there is the formal introduction of *cheng* 誠, a term not used in the sense of a virtue in the *Lunyu* and only briefly so introduced in the *Mencius* in the passage duplicated in the present sections. Zhu Xi, in the conclusion to his ZY20, writes: "Within this chapter, the word *cheng* 誠 is first examined. What is termed *cheng* 誠 is truly the pivotal point of this work."

Zheng Xuan's notes for the four sections ZY14–17 are largely concerned with the meanings of characters and phrases. He does, however, make two general statements. The first is as follows: " . . . if one cultivates the self, then one knows filial piety; if one knows filial piety, then one knows others; if one knows others, then one knows the worthy and the unworthy; if one knows the worthy and the unworthy, then one knows the decree of Heaven and what it protects and helps." The second is to the effect that cultivating the self through *zhi* 知 (wisdom, knowledge), *ren* 仁 (loving kindness) and *yong* 勇 (moral courage) is the foundation. On the issue of *cheng* 誠, he makes two points: if one has the goodness that comes from knowing goodness, then one can act with *cheng* 誠 (ZY18), and that being *cheng* 誠 is the nature of Heaven, whilst becoming *cheng* 誠 is achieved through study (ZY19).

Kong Yingda summarises the opening statement as expressing Confucius' view that the essential elements of government are cultivating the self and choosing men, and that the all-pervading Way has five components (i.e. the five relationships) and three methods of implementation (i.e. the virtues listed—*ren* 仁, *yi* 義 and *zhi* 知). He expands on these virtues thus: *Ren* 仁 refers to being beneficent and loving in relationships with relatives and then extending comparable attitudes to others. *Yi* 義 involves honouring worthiness. *Zhi* 知 is about loving learning. *Yong* 勇 is about knowing shame and having the courage to practise good deeds regardless of any danger that may be involved. Kong also elaborates on the specifics of treating officials properly, referring to the *Zhou li*. In relation to ZY17, he expands on the idea of prior preparation in respect to both words and deeds.

Zhu Xi's position on these four sections (his ZY20.1–20.4) is very similar to that of the *Li ji* commentators. He too emphasizes the importance of cultivating the self and choosing the right men in conducting government. He does give a more elaborate definition of *ren* 仁: "*Ren* 仁 is the mind-heart of Heaven and Earth that gives birth to things; it is what people acquire by being born and is what is spoken of as the growth of goodness." On the constantly practised (all-pervading) Way, he says, " . . . the means by which it is known is *zhi* 知; the means by which it is practised is *ren* 仁; the means by which it comes to the successful realisation of knowledge and is one is *yong* 勇." In relation to these virtues, and quoting Lü Dalin, he adds, in opposition to Kong Yingda's remarks quoted above: "One who is foolish is self-satisfied and does not seek; one who is selfish is obsessed with human desires and forgets to reflect; one who is weak voluntarily places himself in an inferior position and does not resign. Therefore, to love to learn is not *zhi* 知 (wisdom, knowledge). Nevertheless, it is enough to get rid of foolishness. To practise with diligent effort is not *ren* 仁. Nevertheless, it is enough to forget selfishness. To know shame is not *yong* 勇 (courage, bravery). Nevertheless, it is enough to get rid of weakness."

In the remaining two sections of Confucius' response the issue of *cheng* 誠 comes to the forefront. He re-emphasises the importance of *cheng* 誠 in his comment to ZY20.4: "The one way is *cheng* 誠. If the one way is not *cheng* 誠 then the nine canons are all just empty words—this is the reality of the nine canons."

4. On *cheng* 誠: The central issue now becomes *cheng* 誠, beginning with the statement that closely resembles *Mencius* IVA.12 but is here attributed to Confucius rather than Mencius. Regardless of where the statement by Confucius actually ends, this material occupies sections ZY18 to ZY26 in the *Li ji*

arrangement and ZY20.5 to ZY26 in Zhu Xi's text. In addition to the glosses on various characters, Zheng Xuan makes a series of brief remarks about *cheng* 誠 in his notes to these sections. First, he reiterates that goodness which comes from knowing goodness allows the individual to act with *cheng* 誠. He then states that being *cheng* 誠 is the nature of Heaven whilst becoming *cheng* 誠 is achieved through study hence the section (ZY20) which encourages the study that can lead to *cheng* 誠. From *cheng* 誠 that is complete or perfect there comes enlightened virtue which characterises the sage. From enlightened virtue there comes perfect or complete *cheng* 誠 which characterises the worthy man who achieves such virtue through diligent study. Perfect *cheng* 誠 and enlightened virtue are mutually interdependent. "Completing nature" in ZY22 is described as following principle, so things do not lose that which makes them what they are. In ZY23 Zheng Xuan links *cheng* 誠 with *yi* 義 and in ZY24 with the capability of gaining foreknowledge through the methods of divination. In ZY25 he stresses the connection between complete or perfect *cheng* 誠 and the Way, and also the connection between *ren* 仁 and *zhi* 知. The point of the final section on *cheng* 誠 is that this virtue can grow from the very small to the very large in the way posited for the examples.

In Kong Yingda's more detailed analysis a number of additional points are made. These may be summarised as follows: (i) to be a successful and effective official one must have *cheng* 誠 and *xin* 信; (ii) without perfect *cheng* 誠 one cannot be properly compliant towards family members, which is the starting point for winning the trust of friends and gaining the confidence of superiors; (iii) on the distinction between being *cheng* 誠 and becoming *cheng* 誠, the former only applies to the sage who is spontaneously and effortlessly in accord with goodness and is centred in the Way (this is the Way of Heaven), whereas the latter is achieved through study and is the province of the worthy man (this is the Way of mankind). This involves choosing to do good deeds, practising them unceasingly and ultimately achieving perfect *cheng* 誠; (iv) on the matter of completing one's nature (ZY24), this requires perfection in both *cheng* 誠 and *xin* 信; (v) change and transformation are effected through *cheng* 誠 which is why those with perfect *cheng* 誠 form a triad with Heaven and Earth; (vi) on the matter of perfect *cheng* 誠 allowing foreknowledge, Kong Yingda offers examples from other texts.

Zhu Xi provides a more detailed account than the *Li ji* commentators of the distinction between being *cheng* 誠 and becoming *cheng* 誠, but it is essentially the same in substance. Being *cheng* 誠 is a term signifying "being true and genuine without falseness"—it is the foundation of heavenly principle and is the Way of Heaven. Becoming *cheng* 誠 refers to the person who is not yet true and genuine without falseness but wishes to be so. Such a person, if he chooses goodness, can become *cheng* 誠—this is the Way of mankind. In his note to ZY20.6, which he identifies as concluding Confucius' reply to Duke Ai, Zhu Xi states: "What is termed *cheng* 誠 is truly the pivotal point of this work." He concludes that studying, enquiring, thinking, distinguishing and sincerely planning are the five essential activities in the process of becoming *cheng* 誠, quoting Cheng Yi to this effect. He also provides a long quotation from Lü Dalin on the matter of study as the means of changing one's disposition (*qizhi* 氣質) for the good. Moreover, to be effective, the study must be assiduous and unremitting. What follows ZY20.6 are, in Zhu Xi's view, the words of Zisi "reflecting on, reiterating, enlarging on and clarifying the meaning of the whole section (i.e. ZY20.1 to 20.6). These activities focus initially on the distinction between the Way of Heaven (i.e. being *cheng* 誠) and the Way of mankind (i.e. becoming *cheng* 誠). The former is characteristic of the sage whose virtue is entirely genuine, who is without the selfishness of human desire, and in whom the decree of Heaven truly exists. The latter, which is the "next level," relates to those whose *cheng* 誠 has not yet reached completion or perfection. The capacity to have foreknowledge of events through divination depends on perfect *cheng* 誠. *Cheng* is the means of completing or perfecting the self and pertains to the mind-heart. The Way relates to principle and is the application of the mind-heart to the external world. This involves *ren* 仁 and *zhi* 知. ZY26, on the creation of the large from the small, is taken by Zhu Xi as completing the analysis of *cheng* 誠.

5. Concluding Sections: As mentioned earlier, the remaining sections are something of a miscellany and seem neither to add much to the main argument nor to bring this to a conclusion. Further, although there are differences between the two texts in terms of arrangement, these are minor, as are the differences in viewpoint between the three commentators. Sections ZY27–29 in the *Li ji* text are given as one section (ZY27) by Zhu Xi. The material relates to the Ways of the sage and the noble man with particular reference to *li* 禮. Zheng Xuan summarises the point of ZY27 as "government is through *li* 禮" and clarifies the significance of reviving the old and understanding the new in ZY28. Otherwise, his notes are all glosses on specific characters or expressions. Kong Yingda provides greater detail on the matter of "warming up" or reviving the old and also refers to the *Zhou li* and the *Yi li* on the rites mentioned. He does differentiate between ZY27 and ZY28 as pertaining to the innate perfect *cheng* 誠 of the sage and the acquired *cheng* 誠 of the noble man, achieved through study. He takes ZY29 as a further description of the worthy

man's study of the Way of perfect *cheng* 誠 and the practice of *li* 禮. Zhu Xi provides a more detailed consideration of the content of his composite section ZY27. "The path of enquiry and study" is the way of extending knowledge and thoroughly understanding the fine points of the Way's essence. "Honouring a virtuous nature" is the way of preserving the mind-heart and reaching to the greatness of the Way's essence. Progress is made through *li* 禮 and *yi* 義. He identifies this section as a detailed exposition on how to enter virtue as directed by the sage and the worthy man—it is the Way of mankind.

ZY30 in the *Li ji* arrangement consists of a single quotation from Confucius about establishing standards in rites and music, and in the more immediately practical matters of the written script and the width of cart tracks. Some commentators have suggested that this section may indicate a later time of composition of the work than the traditional account allows, having in mind the standardisations imposed by the first Qin emperor, but Zheng Xuan specifically states that Confucius is referring to his own time. Kong Yingda elaborates on this point, remarking that the rites were in disarray in Confucius' time, but because he did not hold an appropriate position, he did not himself dare to attempt to establish standards in rites or music. This is amplified in the following section (ZY31) which is taken to be entirely a further quotation from Confucius. The point is that to be worthy of following, the rites must have been proven in past usage. Kong Yingda adds a wealth of historical data with reference to other works, as well as providing a detailed analysis of the two included *Odes* quotations.

Zhu Xi takes a somewhat different position in terms of arrangement, his section comprising a brief quotation from Confucius (corresponding to the first part of ZY30 in the *Li ji*) followed by Zisi's comments on this relating to the issue of standards in his own time, and then a further brief quotation from Confucius on following the rites of Zhou. The two interpretative points he makes are first, that *li* 禮 is the essential element of the interaction between near and distant and between noble and base, and second, that the creation of rites and music is the province of the sage alone, who is also a Son of Heaven. Zhu Xi's section ZY29 corresponds to the major part of what is ZY31 in the *Li ji* arrangement, but he does not take this to be a quotation from Confucius, nor does he specifically attribute it to Zisi, although presumably this is the assumption. He identifies it as a continuation of the previous section about occupying a superior position without arrogance and as a further characterisation of the Way of mankind. He quotes Lü Dalin in identifying the "three important things" as determining *li* 禮 (rites), establishing standards and verifying the script. He states that knowing Heaven and knowing man is to know their principles, whereas Zheng Xuan speaks of this as knowing their respective Ways.

The remaining material, arranged slightly differently in the two texts (a long ZY32 and a brief ZY33 in the *Li ji* and ZY30–33 in the Zhu Xi text) consists, essentially of five components. The first is a statement about Confucius following the Way of Yao and Shun and of Kings Wen and Wu, and being in accord with Heaven and Earth, and so exemplifying the person who follows the Way. Thus he manifests perfect *sheng* 聖 and perfect *cheng* 誠, an elaboration of which comprises the next two sections. There then follows a series of six quotations from the *Odes*, each of which illustrates an aspect of the conduct of the noble man. There is then a final quotation from Confucius incorporating a further quotation from the *Odes* in which he characterises virtue as being as light as a feather, but as still having substance. Zheng Xuan, in elaborating on the matter of Confucius' virtue, quotes him as saying: "My will lies in the *Chunqiu* (*Spring and Autumn Annals*); my conduct lies in the *Xiaojing* (*The Classic of Filial Piety*)"—a point reiterated by Kong Yingda. The latter also remarks, apropos the section as a whole, that the " . . . *Zhengyi* says that this particular section clarifies Zisi's elucidation of the Master's virtue and its similarity to Heaven and Earth, that it is worthy of being paired with Heaven and Earth, and that it gives rise to the ten thousand things. It was grievous that such a sage virtue was without its position. Now each subsequent part explains this." In his very detailed notes Kong Yingda gives a wealth of historical data referring to ancient texts such as the *Documents* and the *Spring and Autumn Annals*. He also provides detailed analyses of the *Odes* quotations.

On the final quotation from Confucius (*Li ji* ZY33) Zheng Xuan has this to say: " . . . although a feather is light, if it has weight there is still that to which it can be compared. Above, when Heaven creates and gives rise to the ten thousand things, people do not hear its sound nor do they perceive its smell. The virtue that transforms people is pure and clear like a spirit, deep and still, great and magnificent, and in the end good." Zhu Xi, who also provides details and analysis of the *Odes* quotations, takes his final section (i.e. the six *Odes* quotations and the quotation from Confucius, which includes a further *Odes* quotation), as Zisi's summarising statement on the central argument of the whole work.

Concluding Remarks: The *Zhongyong*, which is the fourth of the Four Books in Zhu Xi's prescribed sequence of study, was, like the *Daxue,* which is the first of the four, taken from the *Li ji* to occupy this elevated position. It also has, like the *Daxue*, the original commentary by Zheng Xuan with the more elaborate sub-commentary by Kong Yingda characteristic of all the chapters of the *Li ji* in the *Li ji zhengyi* 禮記正義. Then there is the later, detailed commentary by Zhu Xi in his hugely influential SSZJ first published in 1190. The *Zhongyong* also shares with the *Daxue* controversies regarding authorship and date of composition, and to a greater extent, over the reading of the title. On the first issue, the traditional view, accepted and supported by the three commentators mentioned, is that it is the work of Confucius' grandson, Kong Ji (Zisi) whose dates are given provisionally as 483–422 BCE. That is, it is taken to consist of a series of statements by Zisi interspersed with quotations from Confucius himself (for the most part not to be found in extant texts although there is one from the *Lunyu*, and one found at greater length in the *Kongzi jiayu*), from the *Odes* and from the *Documents* together with parallels to other early texts including the *Mencius*, the *Xunzi* and even the *Mozi*. In the *Shiji*, the work is attributed to Kong Ji (Zisi) whilst in the bibliographic chapter of the *Han shu*, "Yiwenzhi," there is brief reference to a *Zisi* in 23 *pian* and a *Zhongyong shuo* 中庸説 in 2 *pian*.

It must be said, however, that solid evidence to support Zisi as the author is hard to find, and there has been an increasing tendency to ascribe a later date to the composition of the work, starting with Wang Bo in the Song period, gathering pace with the text-critical movement of the Qing period, and continuing into the modern era to include Western scholars. Alternative theories include a composite composition, part by Zisi and part added by a later Confucian(s), composition by a Qin or early Han Confucian, and as a record of a Han debate on an earlier text. No doubt the elevated, canonical status of the work is closely dependent on its being the product of an early Confucian sage such as Zisi, and in reading the text in its cultural context, such an authorship is best accepted. In Western readings of the text as an ethical tract of timeless relevance, issues of authorship are not particularly intrusive.

The structure of the work is less obvious than in the *Daxue* and there are discontinuities in the presentation of the central thesis which have contributed to the difficulty of interpretation as well as to theories of composite composition. However, as with the shorter text, there is a critically important opening section. In this, (human) nature is described as decreed by Heaven and as what is to be nurtured, developed and expressed by following the Way of self-cultivation. There are inherent difficulties in the terse opening statement which are not at all fully explored—the nature of nature and of Heaven, and how and in what respects nature can be changed for the better by striving for *zhong* 中 and *he* 和, the foundation and the all-pervading Way of the world respectively. There are other key sections, notably ZY12–15 and ZY21, interspersed with quotations, as alluded to above, and other apparent digressions. Overall, the *Zhongyong* may be seen as a description of the path of self-cultivation, the Way of the *junzi* 君子, which involves the development of the key virtues, already known from the *Lunyu* (*ren* 仁, *yi* 義, *li* 禮, *zhi* 知 and *yong* 勇), to which is added *cheng* 誠, a virtue given pride of place among those considered in the *Zhongyong*, and taken as the basis, essentially, of all the others. It is impossible to find a suitable single English word that can do justice to concept of *cheng* 誠—it is succinctly defined by Zhu Xi as "true and genuine without falseness" (*zhen shi wu wang* 真實無妄) which may be expanded as a genuineness, truth and purity that pervades one's entire being, which allows of no self-deception, and which is manifest in all dealings at all times with all other people and things in the world.

Finally, in the two texts of the *Zhongyong* presented, the commentaries are of critical importance, both in clarifying the meaning of particular characters and difficult passages and also, especially in Zhu Xi's case, considering the philosophical implications of the various sections. Indeed, it could be argued that with both the *Zhongyong* and the *Daxue*, but particularly with the former, the text itself cannot be read satisfactorily without these commentaries. At the very least, in both cases the significance of these works in Chinese social, cultural and intellectual history cannot be properly understood apart from them.

Zhongyong 中庸: Using the Centre

Notes 注: **Zheng Xuan** 鄭玄

Commentary 疏: **Kong Yingda** 孔穎達

中庸 *Zhongyong*:《禮記》*Li ji* 31

陸曰:「鄭云:『以其記中和之為用也。庸,用也。<u>孔子</u>之孫<u>子思</u>作之,以昭明聖祖之德也。』」¹

《正義》曰:案<u>鄭</u>《目錄》云:「名曰《中庸》者,以其記中和之為用也。庸,用也。<u>孔子</u>之孫<u>子思</u>伋作之,以昭明聖祖之德,此於《別錄》屬〈通論〉。」

Comment: Both early commentators here quoted endorse Zheng Xuan's initial reading of *yong* 庸 as *yong* 用 in the sense of "to use" or "to apply," which is the *Shuowen* definition. Appropriate English renderings could be "Using the Centre," "Using the Middle Way" or "Using the Mean."² We have chosen the first as being most in keeping with the comments of the *Li ji* commentators. As Haloun has pointed out, words such as "balance" and "equilibrium" are not entirely satisfactory. What seems to be indicated in the subsequent passages is the central point between "going beyond" and "not reaching." There is, however, the problem of the later equating of *yong* 庸 with *chang* 常.

---

¹ The reference is to Zheng Xuan's 鄭玄 *San Li mulu* 三禮目錄—see CSJC, 12:442. Lu Deming's 陸德明 (550–625) statement can be found in his *Jingdian shiwen* 經典釋文, CSJC, n.s., 39:70.

² This issue is discussed at some length in the introduction to the *Zhongyong* and in the "General Introduction."

Using the Centre

Lu [Deming] states: "Zheng [Xuan] said: 'In taking this to be a record of using the centre and harmony, *yong* 庸 is equivalent to *yong* 用 (to use, apply). Confucius' grandson, Zisi wrote it in order to display clearly the virtue of his sage ancestor.'"

The *Zhengyi* says that according to Zheng's *Mulu*: "The title *Zhongyong* 中庸 takes this to be a record of the use of the centre and harmony. *Yong* 庸 is equivalent to *yong* 用 (to use, apply). Confucius' grandson, Zisi [Kong] Ji 子思孔伋, wrote it to display clearly the virtue of his sage ancestor. In the *Bielu*, this is included in the "Tonglun."[3]

---

3   A work by Liu Xiang 劉向 (c. 79 BCE–c. 6 CE), no longer extant. A version of the
     revision of the *Bielu* by Liu Xiang's son, Liu Xin 劉歆 (50 BCE–23 CE), survives in the
     "Yiwenzhi" chapter of the *Han shu* 漢書.

ZY1: 天命之謂性，率性之謂道，脩道之謂教。[1]道也者，不可須臾離
也，可離非道也。[2]是故君子戒慎乎其所不睹，恐懼乎其所不聞。[3]
莫見乎隱，莫顯乎微，故君子慎其獨也。[4]喜怒哀樂之未發謂之中，
發而皆中節謂之和。中也者，天下之大本也。和也者，天下之達道
也。[5]致中和，天地位焉，萬物育焉。[6]

Comment: The first issue with this section is whether it is part of the original work or not. Doubt was raised in particular by Wang Bo 王柏 (1194–1274), primarily because the title *Zhongyong* does not occur in this section. Nonetheless, it is an important statement of one of the central components of the work—the thesis that nature is decreed by Heaven and that it is innate and inherently good. The true Way is to follow this nature, to put it into practice, and by putting it to effective use, displaying it to others, so teaching them. There are several specific issues in interpretation as follows: (i) How should *xiu* 脩 be read in the opening statement? Following the commentary, it is taken as *zhi* 治, but not in the sense of "regulate" which Legge, for example, uses (Haloun has pointed out the difficulties of this). We have taken *zhi* 治 in the sense of "administer" which we have rendered somewhat freely as "properly practising," whether in terms of the self or in administration more generally. (ii) Whether the verbs *du* 睹 and *wen* 聞 in the third sentence should be taken as active or passive. Following the commentary, they are taken as passive but the active form may be more appropriate on grammatical grounds, i.e. he is cautious about what he does not see or hear. (iii) The sentence "故君子慎其獨也," which also appears in the *Daxue* 大學: Does this mean when he is alone and unobserved, as the commentary suggests, or is it referring to some inner and hidden component of the self—"uniqueness" (Ames and Hall), "inner core" (Haloun)?

注 ZY1 (鄭玄)

[1] 天命，謂天所命生人者也，是謂性命。木神則仁，金神則義，火神則禮，水
神則信，土神則知。《孝經説》曰：「性者，生之質命，人所稟受度也。」率，循
也。循性行之，是謂道。脩，治也。治而廣之，人放傚之，是曰「教」。{率，
所律反。知音智，下「知者」、「大知」皆同。放，方往反。傚，胡教反。}

[2] 道，猶道路也，出入動作由之。離之惡乎從也？{離，力智反，下及注同。
惡音烏。}

[3] 小人閒居為不善，無所不至也。君子則不然，雖視之無人，聽之無聲，猶戒
慎恐懼自脩正，是其不須臾離道。{睹，丁古反。恐，匡勇反，注同。閒音閑，
下同。}

---

*   Text from the classical commentaries in { } brackets primarily contains pronunciation guides for certain Chinese characters; this has been omitted in the English translation.

ZY1: What Heaven decrees is called "nature." Complying with nature is called the "Way." Properly practising the Way is called "teaching." **[1]** The Way cannot be departed from even for an instant; if it can be departed from it is not the Way. **[2]** This is why the noble man is on guard and cautious where he is not seen; this is why he is fearful and apprehensive where he is not heard. **[3]** There is nothing more apparent than what is hidden; there is nothing more manifest than what is obscure. Therefore, the noble man is cautious when he is alone. **[4]** When joy, anger, sorrow and happiness have not yet arisen, we call this "the centre" (*zhong* 中). When they have arisen, but are all in the centre and regulated, we call this "harmony" (*he* 和). The centre is the great foundation of the world. Harmony is the all-pervading Way of the world. **[5]** Reach the "centre" and "harmony" and Heaven and Earth are in their proper positions and the ten thousand things will be born and grow. **[6]**

Notes ZY1 (Zheng Xuan)

[1] *Tian ming* 天命 refers to what Heaven decrees for mortals; this is called "the nature that is decreed." The spirit of wood is *ren* 仁; the spirit of metal is *yi* 義; the spirit of fire is *li* 禮; the spirit of water is *xin* 信 (trustworthiness, fidelity); the spirit of earth is *zhi* 知 (wisdom, knowledge). The *Explanation of the Classic of Filial Piety* says: "Nature is the decreed disposition of what is born; it is what a person receives as a natural endowment." *Shuai* 率 equates with *xun* 循 (to follow, comply with). To act in compliance with nature is called the Way (*dao* 道). *Xiu* 脩 equates with *zhi* 治 (to put in order, regulate). To regulate and expand it (i.e. the Way), and for others to imitate it, is called "teaching." . . .
[2] *Dao* 道 is like a road (*daolu* 道路). The actions of going out and entering are by it. What course can a person take if he departs from it (i.e. the Way)? . . .
[3] The lesser man living alone does things which are not good; there is nothing he does not do. The noble man is not like this. Although there are no others to see or hear him, he is still on guard and cautious, fearful and apprehensive, and is naturally well-ordered and correct. This is his "not departing from the Way even for an instant." . . .

[4] 慎獨者，慎其閒居之所為。小人於隱者，動作言語，自以為不見睹，不見聞，則必肆盡其情也。若有佔聽之者，是為顯見，甚於眾人之中為之。{見，賢遍反，注「顯見」同，一音如字。佔，勑廉反。}

[5] 中為大本者，以其含喜怒哀樂，禮之所由生，政教自此出也。{樂音洛，注同。中，丁仲反，下注「為之中」同。}

[6] 致，行之至也。位，猶正也。育，生也，長也。{長，丁丈反。}

疏 ZY1 (孔穎達)

{「天命」至「育焉」。}

1.1 《正義》曰：此節明中庸之德，必脩道而行；謂子思欲明中庸，先本於道。

1.2 「天命之謂性」者，天本無體，亦無言語之命，但人感自然而生，有賢愚吉凶，若天之付命遣使之然，故云「天命」。老子云：「道本無名，強名之曰道。」[4] 但人自然感生，有剛柔好惡，或仁、或義、或禮、或知、或信，是天性自然，故云「之謂性」。

1.3 「率性之謂道」，率，循也；道者，通物之名。言依循性之所感而行，不令違越，是之曰「道」。感仁行仁，感義行義之屬，不失其常，合於道理，使得通達，是「率性之謂道」。

1.4 「脩道之謂教」，謂人君在上脩行此道以教於下，是「脩道之謂教」也。

{注「天命」至「曰教」。}

---

4   This does not appear to be an exact quotation from the *Laozi*, either the Wang Bi text or the excavated text from Mawangdui. The concept is, however, expressed in several places, notably *Laozi* 25.

[4] Being "cautious when he is alone" is his being cautious in what he does when living alone. When the lesser man lives in seclusion, if he takes himself to be unseen and unheard in his actions and words, then he inevitably gives free rein to his feelings. If someone were to see him or hear him, this would be very apparent—even more so than if he were in the midst of a crowd. . . .

[5] "The centre" is the foundation because it restrains joy, anger, sorrow and happiness; it is the source of *li* 禮. Government and teaching naturally come out of this. . . .

[6] *Zhi* 致 is to achieve something through actions. *Wei* 位 is like *zheng* 正 (correct, true). *Yu* 育 equates with *sheng* 生 (to be born, arise) and *zhang* 長 (to grow). . . .

Commentary ZY1 (Kong Yingda)

1.1   The *Zhengyi* states that this section makes clear the virtue of using the centre and that one must regulate the Way and act. It refers to Zisi's wish to make it clear that "using the centre" first originates in the Way (*dao* 道).

1.2   *What Heaven decrees is called "nature"*: Heaven is fundamentally without substance and its decree is also without words, but people are born with natural endowments. They are worthy or foolish, fortunate or unfortunate; it is as if Heaven's decree is bestowed on them and causes them to be so. Therefore, it is called "Heaven's decree." Lao Zi said: "The Way originally had no name. If we are compelled to name it, it is called the Way." But if people are born with natural endowments, they can be resolute or yielding, and they have their likes and dislikes; some are *ren* 仁, some are *yi* 義, some are *li* 禮, some are *zhi* 知, and some are *xin* 信—these are natures that Heaven spontaneously [brings about]. Therefore it says it "is called 'nature.'"

1.3   *Complying with nature is called the "Way"*: *Shuai* 率 equates with *xun* 循 (to follow, comply with). *Dao* 道 is the term for understanding things. This says that if one performs actions complying with nature and does not allow opposition and overstepping, this is called the "Way." If, when moved by *ren* 仁, one acts with *ren* 仁, and when moved by *yi* 義, one acts with *yi* 義, and so on, and one does not lose this constancy, and conforms with the Way and principle, this allows one to acquire a thorough understanding. This is *complying with nature is called the "Way."*

1.4   *Properly practising the Way is called "teaching"*: This refers to the ruler above regulating and practising this Way in order to teach those below. This is *properly practising the Way is called "teaching."*

1.5　《正義》曰：云「天命，謂天所命生人者也，是謂性命」，案《易‧乾象》云「乾道變化，各正性命」是也。[5] 云「木神則仁」者，皇氏云「東方春，春主施生」，[6] 仁亦主施生。云「金神則義」者，秋為金，金主嚴殺，義亦果敢斷決也。云「火神則禮」者，夏為火，火主照物而有分別，禮亦主分別。云「水神則信」，冬主閉藏，充實不虛，水有內明，不欺於物，信亦不虛詐也。云「土神則知」者，金、木、水、火，土無所不載，土所含義者多，知亦所含者眾，故云「土神則知」。云「《孝經說》曰：性者，生之質命，人所稟受度也」，不云命者，鄭以通解性命為一，故不復言命。但性情之義，說者不通，亦略言之。[7] 賀瑒云：「性之與情，猶波之與水，靜時是水，動則是波；靜時是性，動則 是情。」[8]

案《左傳》云天有六氣，降而生五行。[9] 至於含生之類，皆感五行生矣。唯人獨稟秀氣，故〈禮運〉云：人者五行之秀氣，被色而生。[10] 既有五常仁、義、禮、智、信，因五常而有六情，則性之與情，似金與鐶印，鐶印之用非金，亦因金而有鐶印。情之所用非性，亦因性而有情，則性者靜，情者動。故〈樂記〉云：「人生而靜，天之性也。感於物而動，性之欲也。」[11] 故《詩‧序》云「情動於中」是也。[12]

5　*Yi jing,* "Gan 乾," SSJZS, 1:10.

6　Huang Kan 皇侃 (488–545) was a co-contributor with He Yan 何晏 (190–249) to the *Lunyu jijie yishu* 論語集解義疏 which can be found in the CSJC, n.s., 17:494–567. We have not located this particular quotation.

7　No work of this name is listed in the *Han shu,* "Yiwenzhi," the *Sui shu* bibliography, or the SKQS *Catalogue.*

8　He Yang 賀瑒 was a commentator on various classics (see the *Liang shu* 48, 3:672–73), but was particularly noted for his knowledge of the *San li* 三禮.

9　*Zuo zhuan,* Duke Zhao, 1st year, LCC, 5:573.

10　*Li ji,* "Li yun," SSJZS, 5:432 & 434.

11　*Li ji,* "Yue ji," SSJZS, 5:666.

12　*Odes* Preface ("Da xu") 2, LCC, 4:34.

1.5   The *Zhengyi* states that saying "Heaven's decree refers to what Heaven decrees for mortals; this is called the nature that is decreed" is based on the *Changes* (*qian tuan* 乾象) saying: "The Way of *qian* (Creation, Heaven) is change and transformation and each person has the right nature decreed," which is this. On saying: "The wood spirit is *ren* 仁," Huang [Kan] says: "The eastern direction is spring; spring is responsible for bestowing life." *Ren* 仁 is also responsible for bestowing life. On saying: "The metal spirit is *yi* 義," autumn is metal and metal is responsible for the decay of what is flourishing. *Yi* 義 also entails resolute action. On saying: "The fire spirit is *li* 禮," summer is fire; fire is responsible for illuminating things and making distinctions. *Li* 禮 is also responsible for making distinctions. On saying: "The spirit of water is *xin* 信," winter is responsible for storing up and being full rather than empty. Water is transparent and does not deceive in things; *xin* 信 also means not being false and deceptive. On saying: "The spirit of earth is *zhi* 知," metal, wood, water, fire and earth have nothing they do not contain. The meaning is that, just as earth contains a great deal, what knowledge contains is also all-embracing. Therefore, it says "the spirit of earth is *zhi* 知." It says that the *Explanation of the Classic of Filial Piety* states: "Nature is the decreed disposition one is born with and what people receive as a natural endowment." In not saying *ming* 命 (decreed), Zheng understands by this that *xing* 性 (nature) and *ming* 命 are one, therefore there is no repetition of the word *ming* 命. But "nature" and "emotions" have different connotations which commentators do not understand so they only mention them briefly. He Yang says: "Nature is joined with emotions like waves are joined with water; at a time when it is still, it is water; when in motion, it is waves. In times of stillness, this is nature; when there is movement, this is emotion."

According to the *Zuo zhuan*, Heaven has six spirits (*qi*) which descend to give rise to the Five Phases. When it comes to combining the classes of living things, all are born under the influence of the Five Phases. Only people alone are endowed with excellent spirit (*xiu qi* 秀氣). Therefore, the "Li yun" says that in the case of people [there is] "the excellent spirit of the Five Phases" [and] "is made to appear and come into being." Then there are the "Five Constant Virtues"—*ren* 仁, *yi* 義, *li* 禮, *zhi* 知, and *xin* 信. Because there are the "Five Constant Virtues" and there are the six emotions, nature is joined with emotions like metal is joined to a metal seal; but the metal seal's use is not metal; however, it is because of the metal that there is a metal seal. What the emotions use is not nature; however, it is because of nature that there are emotions. Then nature is stillness and the emotions are movement. Thus the "Yue ji" says: "If a man is born and is tranquil, it is Heaven's nature; if he is influenced by things and actions, it is the nature of desire." That is why the "Preface" to the *Odes* saying, "the emotions move in harmony (the centre)" is this.

但感五行，在人為五常，得其清氣備者則為聖人，得其濁氣簡者則為愚人。降聖以下，愚人以上，所稟或多或少，不可言一，故分為九等。<u>孔子</u>云：「唯上智與下愚不移。」[13] 二者之外，逐物移矣，故《論語》云：「性相近，習相遠也。」[14] 亦據中人七等也。「道也者，不可須臾離也」者，此謂聖人脩行仁、義、禮、知，信以為教化。道，猶道路也。道者，開通性命，猶如道路開通於人，人行於道路，不可須臾離也。若離道則礙難不通，猶善道須臾離棄則身有患害而生也。「可離非道也」者，若荒梗塞澀之處是可離棄，以非道路之所由。猶如凶惡邪僻之行是可離棄，以亦非善道之行，故云「可離非道也」。

3.1 「是故君子戒慎乎其所不睹」者，言君子行道，先慮其微。若微能先慮，則必合於道，故君子恒常戒於其所不睹之處。人雖目不睹之處猶戒慎，況其惡事睹見而肯犯乎？故君子恒常戒慎之。

3.2 「恐懼乎其所不聞」者，言君子恒恐迫畏懼於所不聞之處。言雖耳所不聞，恒懷恐懼之，不睹不聞猶須恐懼，況睹聞之處恐懼可知也。

4.1 「莫見乎隱，莫顯乎微」者，莫，無也。言凡在眾人之中，猶知所畏，及至幽隱之處，謂人不見，便即恣情，人皆佔聽，察見罪狀，甚於眾人之中，所以恒須慎懼如此。以罪過愆失無見於幽隱之處，無顯露於細微之所也。

---

13 *Lunyu* XVII.3, LCC, 1:318.
14 *Lunyu* XVII.2, LCC, 1:318.

But influencing the Five Phases lies in people having the "Five Constant Virtues," and the one who acquires a pure *qi* 氣 (spirit) and perfects it becomes a sage, whereas the one who acquires an impure *qi* 氣 (spirit) and treats it carelessly becomes a fool. Between the sage above and the fool below what is bestowed as a natural endowment can be more or less; it cannot constitute one class only. Therefore people are divided into nine grades. Confucius said: "Only the wise of the highest class and the fools of the lowest class cannot be changed." Apart from these two [extremes], they can be changed. Therefore, the *Lunyu* says: "By nature, people are close together; by practice, they are far apart." That also refers to the seven ranks between. *The Way cannot be departed from even for an instant*: This says that the sage cultivating himself and practising *ren* 仁, *yi* 義, *li* 禮, *zhi* 知, and *xin* 信 is taken to be teaching and transformation. The Way (道 *dao*) is like a road (*daolu* 道路). The Way opens a path for the decreed nature like a road opens a way through for people. People travel on the road and cannot, even for an instant, leave it. If they leave the road, they encounter difficulties and cannot pass. It is like a good road—if you leave it for a moment then you find misfortune and calamity arising. *If it can be departed from it is not the Way*: If it is a wild, difficult and obstructed place, this can be left because there is no road to travel by. It is like evil and heterodox actions can be left and abandoned because this too is not a good road to travel. Therefore it says, *if it can be departed from it is not the Way*.

3.1   *This is why the noble man is on guard and cautious where he is not seen*: This says that the noble man, in practising the Way, first gives thought to minor matters. If minor matters can be first given consideration, then there must be an accord with the Way. Therefore, the noble man is constantly cautious when he is in a place where he is not being observed. If a man is on guard and cautious even when he is not seen, how would he carry out evil actions if he were being observed? Therefore, the noble man is constantly on guard and cautious about this.

3.2   *Fearful and apprehensive where he is not heard*: This says that the noble man is constantly fearful and apprehensive when he is in a place where he is not heard. It says that he constantly carries fear in his heart, although he is in a place where ears do not hear. [That is,] when he is not seen or not heard, he must still be fearful and apprehensive. Thus, we can know how much more fearful and apprehensive he is when he is in a place where he is seen or heard.

4.1   *There is nothing more obvious than what is hidden; there is nothing more manifest than what is obscure*: Mo 莫 is equivalent to *wu* 無 (a negation). This says that, in general, in the midst of the throng, he still knows what is fearful. When he comes to a place of extreme seclusion, he assumes that others do not see, and thus gives free rein to his passions. Yet people all observe the circumstances of his transgression, even more so than when he is in the midst of the throng. Therefore, a noble man must constantly be careful and cautious like this so that no transgressions, faults, errors and failings will be displayed even in a place of seclusion and in what is obscure.

4.2 「故君子慎其獨也」者，以其隱微之處，恐其罪惡彰顯，故君子之人恒慎其獨居。言雖曰獨居，能謹慎守道也。

5.1 「喜怒哀樂之未發謂之中」者，言喜怒哀樂緣事而生，未發之時，澹然虛靜，心無所慮而當於理，故「謂之中」。

5.2 「發而皆中節謂之和」者，不能寂靜而有喜怒哀樂之情，雖復動發，皆中節限，猶如鹽梅相得，性行和諧，故云「謂之和」。

5.3 「中也者，天下之大本也」者，言情慾未發，是人性初本，故曰「天下之大本也」。

5.4 「和也者，天下之達道也」者，言情慾雖發而能和合，道理可通達流行，故曰「天下之達道也」。

6.1 「致中和，天地位焉，萬物育焉」，致，至也。位，正也。育，生長也。言人君所能至極中和，使陰陽不錯，則天地得其正位焉。生成得理，故萬物其養育焉。

ZY2: <u>仲尼</u>曰：「君子中庸，小人反中庸。君子之中庸也，君子而時中。小人之〔反〕中庸也，小人而無忌憚也。」[1]
子曰：「中庸其至矣乎！民鮮能久矣。」[2]

4.2   *Therefore, the noble man is cautious when he is alone*: Because, when he is in a
        secluded and obscure place, he fears that his transgressions and wrongdoing are
        apparent, so the noble man is a person who is constantly careful when dwelling
        alone. That is to say, although it is said he dwells alone, he is able to be cautious
        and careful in maintaining the Way.

5.1   *When joy, anger, sorrow and happiness have not yet arisen, we call this "the centre"*:
        This says that joy and anger, sorrow and happiness arise because of matters. At a
        time when they have not yet arisen, when there is tranquility and abstraction, the
        mind-heart has nothing to think about and is properly in accord with principle.
        Therefore, *we call this "the centre."*

5.2   *When they have arisen, but are all in the centre and regulated, we call this "harmony"*:
        If someone is unable to be still and tranquil and has the emotions of joy, anger,
        sorrow and happiness, even though they are repeatedly stirred and arise, if they
        are all in the centre, regulated and restrained, it is like the fitting accord between
        salt and plums, so nature and conduct are in harmonious concert. Therefore it is
        said, *we call this "harmony."*

5.3   *The centre is the great foundation of the world*: This says that when emotions and
        desires have not yet arisen, this is the first foundation of a person's nature. There-
        fore, it is called *the world's great foundation.*

5.4   *Harmony is the all-pervading Way of the world*: This says that although emotions
        and desires have arisen, if they can be brought to harmonious union, the Way
        and principle can penetrate and extend everywhere. Therefore it is called the
        world's all-pervading Way.

6.1   *Reach the "centre" and "harmony" and Heaven and Earth are in their proper positions
        and the ten thousand things will be born and grow*: *Zhi* 致 is eqivalent to *zhi* 至 (to
        reach, arrive at). *Wei* 位 is equivalent to *zheng* 正 (right, correct). *Yu* 育 is equiva-
        lent to *sheng zhang* 生長 (to be born and to grow). This says that when the ruler is
        able to achieve the ultimate centre and harmony causing *yin* and *yang* to be alto-
        gether right, then Heaven and Earth attain their right positions. Birth and comple-
        tion attain principle, therefore the ten thousand things are reared and nurtured.

ZY2: Zhongni (Confucius) said: "The noble man uses the centre. The lesser
man does the opposite of using the centre. The noble man's using the centre is
his being a noble man and at all times in the centre. The lesser man's doing the
opposite of using the centre is his being a lesser man and without scruples." **[1]**
The Master said: "Using the centre—this is, indeed, perfection! The people
are seldom able [to practise it] for long." **[2]**

子曰：「道之不行也，我知之矣。知者過之，愚者不及也。道之不明
也，我知之矣。賢者過之，不肖者不及也。人莫不飲食也，鮮能知味
也。」[3]

子曰：「道其不行矣夫。」[4]

Comment: These four quotations from Confucius are grouped together here as ZY2. Zhu
Xi separates them as his ZY2–5. There is a difference between the first, where Confucius is
referred to as Zhongni (his cognomen), and the other three where the more common *zi* 子 (the
Master) is used. It is not clear whether any significance should be attached to this. There are
three issues in the first statement. First, there is the equating of *yong* 庸 with *chang* 常 which
is taken as "constant," as opposed to equating it with *yong* 用 (to use, apply) as earlier. The
second is how *shi* 時 should be understood—whether as "always" or "constantly," which is the
view of the majority and seems to be supported by Zhu Xi's commentary, or as "at the proper
time" which would accord with the statements of the *Li ji* commentators.[15] Third, there is the
question of whether *fan* 反 should be added in the third sentence following Wang Su.

注 ZY2 (鄭玄)

[1] 庸，常也。用中為常，道也。「反中庸」者，所行非中庸，然亦自以為中庸
也。「君子而時中」者，其容貌君子，而又時節其中也。「小人而無忌憚」，其容
貌小人，又以無畏難為常行，是其「反中庸」也。「小人之中庸也」，王肅本作「小
人之反中庸也」。{忌憚，徒旦反。}忌，畏也。憚，難也。{難，乃旦反。行，
下孟反。}

[2] 鮮，罕也。言中庸為道至美，顧人罕能久行。「中庸其至矣乎」，一本作「中
庸之為德，其至矣乎」。{鮮，息淺反，下及注同。罕，胡坦反，希也，少也。}

[3] 罕知其味，謂「愚者所以不及也」。過與不及，使道不行，唯禮能為之中。
{知音智，下文「大知也」、「予知」，注「有知」皆同。肖音笑，下同。}

[4] 閔無明君教之。{夫音扶。}

See, for example, Plaks, *Ta Hsüeh and Chung Yung (The Highest Order of Cultivation
and On the Practice of the Mean)*, 82n2.

The Master said: "I know why it is that the Way is not practised—the wise go beyond it; the foolish do not reach it. I know why it is that the Way is not clear—the worthy go beyond it; the unworthy do not reach it. All people drink and eat but few are able to know the flavours." **[3]**

The Master said: "Ah, alas, the Way!—it is not practised." **[4]**

Notes ZY2 (Zheng Xuan)

[1] *Yong* 庸 is equivalent to *chang* 常 (constant). Using the centre and being constant is the Way. *Doing the opposite of using the centre* is to negate *using the centre* in what he (i.e. the lesser man) does. Nonetheless, he also takes himself to be using the centre. *Being a noble man and at all times in the centre* is his demeanour being that of a noble man and also his being at all times in the centre. *Being a lesser man and without scruples* is his demeanour being that of a lesser man and also taking not having scruples to be constancy in conduct. This is his *doing the opposite of using the centre*. [On the phrase] *the lesser man's using the centre*, Wang Su originally wrote: "The lesser man's doing the opposite of using the centre."[16] . . . *Ji* 忌 is equivalent to *wei* 畏 (to fear, dread, be in awe). *Dan* 憚 is equivalent to *nan* 難 (difficulty). . . .

[2] *Xian* 鮮 is equivalent to *han* 罕 (few, seldom). This says that "using the centre" is the Way of perfect goodness, therefore few people are able to practise it for long. *Using the centre—this is, indeed, perfection* is in one original [source] written "using the centre is virtue—this is, indeed, perfection." . . .

[3] Few knowing the flavours refers to *the foolish do not reach it*. "Going beyond" and "not reaching" cause the Way not to be practised. Only *li* 禮 can make it central. . . .

[4] This expresses regret that there is no enlightened ruler to teach it. . . .

---

[16] Wang Su 王肅 (195–256) was the "discoverer" (putative author) of the *Kongzi jiayu* 孔子家語. The quotation is not from that work. The emendation is widely accepted.

疏 ZY2 (孔穎達)

{「仲尼」至「矣夫」}

1.1　《正義》曰：此一節是子思引仲尼之言，廣明中庸之行，賢者過之，不肖者不及也；中庸之道，鮮能行之。

1.2　「君子中庸」者，庸，常也。君子之人用中以為常，故云「君子中庸」。

1.3　「小人反中庸」者，小人則不用中[以]為常，是「反中庸」也。

1.4　「君子之中庸也，君子而時中」者，此覆説君子中庸之事，言君子之為中庸，容貌為君子，心行而時節其中，謂喜怒不過節也，故云君子而時中。

1.5　「小人之中庸也，小人而無忌憚也」者，此覆説小人反中庸之事，言小人為中庸，形貌為小人，而心行無所忌憚，故云「小人而無忌憚也」。小人將此以為常，亦以為中庸，故云「小人之[反]中庸也」。

2.1　「子曰中庸，其至矣乎」，前既言君子、小人不同，此又歎中庸之美，人寡能久行，其中庸之德至極美乎！

2.2　「民鮮能久矣」者，但寡能長久而行。鮮，罕也。言中庸為至美，故人罕能久行之。

3.1　「子曰：道之不行也，我知之矣」者，此覆説人寡能行中庸之事。道之所以不行者，言我知其道之不行所由，故云「我知之矣」。

3.2　「知者過之，愚者不及也」，以輕於道，故「過之」。以遠於道，故「不及」。

3.3　「道之不明也，我知之矣」者，言道之所以不顯明，我亦知其所由也。

Commentary ZY2 (Kong Yingda)

1.1 The *Zhengyi* says that this particular section comprises Zisi quoting the words of Zhongni to explicate the practice of "using the centre"; the worthy go beyond it and the foolish do not reach it. The Way of "using the centre" can rarely be practised.

1.2 *The noble man uses the centre*: *Yong* 庸 equates with *chang* 常 (constant). A noble man is one who uses the centre (*zhong* 中) as a constant principle. Therefore it is said, *the noble man uses the centre*.

1.3 *The lesser man does the opposite of using the centre*: The lesser man then does not use the centre by taking this to be a constant principle. This is *doing the opposite of using the centre*.

1.4 *The noble man's using the centre is his being a noble man and at all times in the centre*: This reiterates the explanation of the matter of the noble man's using the centre and says that in his embodying the use of the centre his demeanour is that of the noble man; his mind acts and at all times is in the centre. That is to say, neither in joy nor in anger does he go beyond moderation. Therefore, it says "he is a noble man and at all times in the centre."

1.5 *The lesser man's doing the opposite of using the centre is his being a lesser man and without scruples*: This reiterates the explanation of the matter of the lesser man doing the opposite of using the centre and says the lesser man, in doing the opposite of using the centre, has the demeanour of a lesser man and his mind-heart acts without scruples. Therefore it says he is *a lesser man and without scruples*. The lesser man will take this as being constant and also will take it as using the centre. Therefore it speaks of, *the lesser man does the opposite of using the centre*.

2.1 *The Master said: "Using the centre—this is, indeed, perfection"*: Previously, it has been said that the noble man and the lesser man are not the same. This also laments the fact that, despite the goodness of "using the centre," few men are able to practise it for long; how perfect and good the virtue of using the centre is.

2.2 *The people are seldom able [to practise it] for long*: Few only are able to practise it for long. *Xian* 鮮 equates with *han* 罕 (few, seldom). That is to say, using the centre is perfect goodness, therefore few people are able to practise it for long.

3.1 *The Master said: "I know why it is that the Way is not practised"*: This again explains the matter of few people being able to practise "using the centre." As to why the Way is not practised, this says, I (Confucius) know the reason why the Way is not put into practice. Therefore, it says, *I know it*.

3.2 *The wise go beyond it; the foolish do not reach it*: By being careless towards the Way, they *go beyond it*; by being distant from the Way, they *do not reach it*.

3.3 *I know why it is that the Way is not clear*: This says that I (Confucius) also know the reason why the Way is not clearly manifest.

3.4 「賢者過之，不肖者不及也」，言道之不行為易，故「知者過之，愚者不及」；道之不明為難，故云「賢者過之，不肖者不及」。是以變知稱賢，變愚稱不肖，是賢勝於智，不肖勝於愚也。

3.5 「人莫不飲食也，鮮能知味也」者，言飲食，易也；知味，難也。猶言人莫不行中庸，但鮮能久行之。言知之者易，行之者難，所謂愚者不能及中庸也。案《異義》云：張華辨鮮，師曠別薪，符朗[17]為青州刺史，善能知味，食雞知棲半露，食鵝知其黑白。此皆《晉書》文也。[18]

4.1 「子曰：道其不行久矣夫」者，夫子既傷道之不行，又哀閔傷之，云時無明君，其道不復行也。

{注「反中」至「庸也」。}

4.2 《正義》曰：「反中庸者，所行非中庸者」，言用非中以為常，是「反中庸」，故云「所行非中庸」。云「亦自以為中庸也」，解經「小人之中庸」，雖行惡事，亦自謂為中庸。云「其容貌君子，而又時節其中也」，解經「君子而時中」。云「其容貌小人，又以無畏難為常行」者，解經「小人而無忌憚」。既無忌憚，則不時節其中庸也。

---

[17] See SSJZS (2001 edition), "Zhongyong," 28:1665n1.

[18] Zhang Hua 張華 (232–300) was a prominent scholar and official of the Jin dynasty—see the *Jin shu* 36, 4:1068–79. Shi Kuang (師曠—Master Kuang) was a noted blind musician; see *Mencius* IVA.1, LCC, 2.288 and the *Sui Shu* 69, 3.1601. For Fu Lang 苻朗, see the *Jin Shu* 114, 9:2936–37.

3.4   *The worthy go beyond it; the unworthy do not reach it*: This says that it is easy for the Way not to be practised. Therefore, *the wise go beyond it: the foolish do not reach it*. The Way not being clear constitutes a difficulty. Therefore, it says: *the worthy go beyond it; the unworthy do not reach it*. This is to change "wise" to "worthy" and "foolish" to "unworthy" so that "worthy" is equivalent to "wise" and "unworthy" is equivalent to "foolish."

3.5   *All people drink and eat but few are able to know the flavours*: This says that it is easy to drink and eat but difficult to know the flavours. It is like saying that people all practise "using the centre" but few are able to do so for long. That is to say—knowing it is easy but practising it is hard; that is why it is said that the foolish are not able to reach using the centre. In the *Yiyi* it states: "Zhang Hua differentiated what was fresh. Shi Kuang could distinguish firewood. Fu Lang was made the regional inspector of Qingzhou. He was skilled at being able to recognise flavours. If he ate a chicken he knew whether it roosted partially exposed; if he ate a goose he knew whether it was black or white." This is all written in the *Jin shu*.

4.1   In respect to the Master saying, "Ah, alas, the Way!—has not been practiced for a long time," when the Master was distressed that the Way was not being practised, and also was sadly lamenting this, he said that the time had no enlightened ruler and the Way was not again being practised.

4.2   The *Zhengyi* saying that "doing the opposite of using the centre is to practise what is not using the centre" says that using what is not central and taking it to be constant is *doing the opposite of using the centre*. Therefore it says, "what is practised is not using the centre." Saying, "he (i.e. the lesser man) also takes himself to be using the centre" explains the section on "the lesser man's doing the opposite of using the centre"—that is, although he does bad things, he also takes himself to be using the centre. Saying that "his demeanour is that of a noble man and that he, too, is at all times in the centre" explains the statement on *his being a noble man and at all times in the centre*. Saying "his demeanour is that of a lesser man and he also takes being without scruples as being constant in conduct" explains the statement *being a lesser man and without scruples*. Since he is without scruples, then he is not at all times in the centre.

ZY3: 子曰:「舜其大知也與?舜好問而好察邇言,隱惡而揚善,執其兩端,用其中於民,其斯以為舜乎!」[1]

Comment: Both texts treat this as a discrete section. It is the first example of Shun as one of the ancient exemplars. Shun is said to have listened to what the people were saying and to have taken what was good from what he heard. *Er* 邇 is read as *jin* 近 (which is the *Shuowen* definition), that is, "near" in the sense of simple and familiar. Both Zheng Xuan and Kong Yingda take the two "ends" as being "going beyond" (*guo* 過) and "not reaching" (*bu ji* 不及) thereby defining the centre (*zhong* 中) as the midpoint or mean in conduct. Here "centre" seems the most appropriate translation of *zhong* 中. There is some uncertainty about the final statement. Zheng Xuan takes the view that because of the qualities identified, he was styled Shun. His words being "full" suggests *chong* 充 as a gloss for *shun* 舜. Riegel (213n26) suggests that *chong* 充 is a scribal error for *yun* 允 in the sense of "sincere" or "earnest."

注 ZY3 (鄭玄)

[1] 邇,近也。近言而善,易以進人,察而行之也。「兩端」,過與不及也。「用其中於民」,賢與不肖皆能行之也。斯,此也。其德如此,乃號為「舜」,舜之言「充」也。{與音餘,下「強與」皆同。好,呼報反,下同。易,以豉反。}

疏 ZY3 (孔穎達)

{「子曰」至「舜乎」。}

1.1   《正義》曰:此一經明舜能行中庸之行,先察近言而後至於中庸也。

1.2   「舜其大知也與」者,既能包於大道,又能察於近言,即是「大知」也。

1.3   「執其兩端,用其中於民」者,端謂頭緒,謂「知者過之,愚者不及」,言舜能執持愚、知兩端,用其中道於民,使愚、知俱能行之。

1.4   「其斯以為舜乎」者,斯,此也,以其德化如此,故號之為「舜」。

{注「舜之言充也」。}

1.5   《正義》曰:案《謚法》云:「受禪成功曰舜。」又云:「仁義盛明曰舜。」[19] 皆是道德充滿之意,故言舜為「充」也。

---

19   See the *Shifa*, p. 2, in CSJC, n.s., 31:40. In fact, the first statement there is about Yu and not Shun.

ZY3: The Master said: "Shun had great wisdom did he not? Shun loved to ask questions and he loved to examine 'near' (i.e. simple, familiar) words. Concealing the bad and revealing the good, he grasped these two ends and used their centre in relation to the people. This was what made him Shun!"

Notes ZY3 (Zheng Xuan)

[1] *Er* 邇 is equivalent to *jin* 近 (near). Words that are simple and good make it easy to approach others and are what he (Shun) examined and acted upon. *Liang duan* 兩端 are the two "ends" of "going beyond" and "not reaching." *Used their centre in relation to the people* means that the worthy and the unworthy were able to put this into practice. *Si* 斯 is equivalent to *ci* 此 (this). Since his virtue was like this, then he was styled Shun. Shun's words were *chong* 充 (ample, full, abundant). . . .

Commentary ZY3 (Kong Yingda)

1.1 The *Zhengyi* says that this particular section makes it clear that Shun was able to put into practice the conduct of using the centre. First, he examined "near" (familiar, simple) words and afterwards progressed to using the centre.

1.2 *Shun had great wisdom did he not?* Since he was able to embrace the great Way, he was also able to look at "near" (familiar, simple) words. This was "great wisdom."

1.3 *He grasped these two ends and used their centre in relation to the people*: *Duan* 端 (ends, extremes) refers to the starting points [and here] refers to *the wise go beyond it* and *the foolish do not reach it*. That is to say, Shun was able to take hold of the two "ends" of "foolish" and "wise" and to employ using the centre in relation to the people, making it possible for both the foolish and the wise to practise it.

1.4 *This was what made him Shun*: *Si* 斯 is equivalent to *ci* 此 (this). Because his virtue was transforming like this, so he was styled "Shun."

1.5 The *Zhengyi* says that in the *Shifa* it states that "he accepted the abdication [of Yao] and was successful, and was called Shun." It also says that his "*ren* 仁 and *yi* 義 were abundant and enlightened, and he was called Shun." Both these have the meaning of his Way and virtue being "full," therefore it says that Shun was *chong* 充 (full, abundant).

ZY4: 子曰：「人皆曰『予知』，驅而納諸罟擭陷阱之中，而莫之知辟也。人皆曰『予知』，擇乎中庸，而不能期月守也。」**[1]**

Comment: This corresponds to Zhu Xi's ZY7. The meaning is quite clear. Men are not, as they all claim to be, wise. They fall into the trap of their own selfish desires and cannot sustain the Way of "using the centre" for any length of time.

注 ZY4 (鄭玄)

[1] 予，我也。言凡人自謂有知，人使之入罟，不知辟也。自謂擇中庸而為之，亦不能久行，言其實愚又無恒。{罟音古，罔之揔名。擭，胡化反。}《尚書傳》云：「捕獸機檻。」陷，陷沒之陷。阱，才性反，本或作穽，同。阱，穿地陷獸也。《説文》云：「穽或為阱字也。」{辟音避，注「知辟」、「辟害」皆同。期音基。}

疏 ZY4 (孔穎達)

{「子曰」至「守也」。}

1.1   《正義》曰：此一經明無知之人行中庸之事。予，我也。世之愚人，皆自謂言我有知。

1.2   「驅而納諸罟擭陷阱之中，而莫之知辟也」者，此謂無知之人設譬也。罟，網也。擭，謂柞鄂 [20] 也。陷阱，謂坑也。穿地為坎，豎鋒刃於中以陷獸也。言禽獸被人所驅，納於罟網、擭陷阱之中，而不知違辟，似無知之人為嗜欲所驅，入罪禍之中而不知辟，即下文是也。

1.3   「擇乎中庸，而不能期月守也」者，鄭云：「自謂擇中庸而為之，亦不能久行，言其實愚又無恒也。」小人自謂選擇中庸，而心行亦非中庸。假令偶有中庸，亦不能期帀一月而守之，如入陷阱也。

---

[20]   The text has a variant writing for *e* 鄂—see ZWDCD, #15496, 5:356.

ZY4: The Master said: "All men say, 'I am wise,' but drive them on and catch them in various nets, traps or pits, and they do not know how to escape. All men say, 'I am wise,' yet if they choose the use of the centre they cannot sustain it for a whole month."[1]

Notes ZY4 (Zheng Xuan)

[1] *Yu* 予 is equivalent to *wo* 我 (I, we). This says that men in general speak of themselves as being wise, yet when others cause them to fall into traps, they do not know how to escape. They speak of themselves as choosing to use the centre and applying it, but they also cannot do this for long, which is to say that, in truth, they are foolish as well as inconstant. . . .

Commentary ZY4 (Kong Yingda)

1.1 The *Zhengyi* says that this particular section clarifies the matter of people without wisdom practising the use of the centre. *Yu* 予 is equivalent to *wo* 我 (I, we). Foolish people of the age all speak of themselves as being wise.

1.2 *Drive them on and catch them in various nets, traps or pits, and they do not know to escape*: This offers an example of people being without wisdom. *Gu* 罟 is equivalent to *wang* 網 (a net). *Huo* 擭 refers to *zuo e* 柞鄂 (a device for catching animals). *Xian jing* 陷阱 refers to a *keng* 坑 (pit, hole). [This involves] digging out earth to make a pit and setting up sharpened stakes within it to catch animals. That is to say, what birds and animals are driven into and caught in by people are nets and pits, and they do not know how to avoid or escape from them. This is like people without wisdom being driven by their lusts and desires, entering into wrongdoing and misfortune without knowing how to escape. The text that follows is about this.

1.3 *If they choose the use of the centre they cannot sustain it for a whole month*: Zheng says: "They speak of themselves as choosing the use of the centre and applying it, but they also cannot do this for long, which is to say that, in truth, they are foolish as well as inconstant." Lesser men speak of themselves as choosing the use of the centre, yet when their minds act, they too do not use the centre. If by chance they do use the centre, they are unable to maintain this for a whole month, which is like falling into a trap or a pit.

ZY5: 子曰：「<u>回</u>之為人也，擇乎中庸，得一善，則拳拳服膺而弗失之矣。」[1]

子曰：「天下國家可均也，爵祿可辭也，白刃可蹈也，中庸不可能也。」[2]

Comment: Yan Yuan/Hui, the exemplary disciple, is presented as someone who attempted to follow "using the centre." In the second sentence the difficulties inherent in maintaining such a course are stressed, although they are not specifically identified. Riegel has suggested that in view of the syntax, *zhong yong* 中庸 here and in the previous and following sections may refer to a body of teaching—see his note 29, pp. 213–14.

注 ZY5 (鄭玄)

[1] 拳拳，奉持之貌。{拳音權，又起阮反，徐羌權反。膺，徐音應，又於陵反。奉，芳勇反。}

[2] 言中庸難為之難。{蹈音悼，又徒報反。}

疏 ZY5 (孔穎達)

{「子曰」至「能也」。}

1.1 《正義》曰：此一節是夫子明<u>顏回</u>能行中庸，言中庸之難也。

1.2 「得一善，則拳拳服膺而弗失之矣」者，言<u>顏回</u>選擇中庸而行，得一善事，則形貌拳拳然奉持之。膺，謂胸膺，言奉持守於善道，弗敢棄失。

2.1 「子曰：天下國家可均也」，「天下」謂天子，「國」謂諸侯，「家」謂卿大夫也。

2.2 「白刃可蹈也」者，言白刃雖利，尚可履蹈而行之。

2.3 「中庸不可能」也，言在上諸事，雖難猶可為之，唯中庸之道不可能也。為知者過之，愚者不及，言中庸難為之難也。

ZY5: The Master said: "Hui was a man who chose to use the centre. If he acquired one virtue, then he took it in, held it fast within his breast, and did not lose it." **[1]**

The Master said: "All under Heaven, states and houses can be equal, rank and salary can be declined, and naked blades can be trampled underfoot, yet the use of the centre may not be possible. **[2]**

Notes ZY5 (Zheng Xuan)

[1] *Quan quan* 拳拳 is the appearance of *feng chi* 奉持 (receiving and holding fast). . . .

[2] This speaks of how the difficulties of using the centre make it hard [to maintain]. . . .

Commentary ZY5 (Kong Yingda)

1.1   The *Zhengyi* says that this particular section is the Master making it clear that Yan Hui was able to practise using the centre, and speaks of the difficulties of using the centre.

1.2   *If he acquired one virtue, then he took it in, held it fast within his breast, and did not lose it*: This says that Yan Hui chose the use of the centre and put it into practice. If he acquired one good thing (virtue), then he gave the appearance of taking it in and holding it as if clasping it. *Ying* 膺 refers to *xiongying* 胸膺 (breast) and says that he took in and held fast to the Way of goodness, not daring to abandon or lose [it].

2.1   *The Master said: "All under Heaven, states and houses can be equal"*: *Tianxia* 天下 refers to the Son of Heaven (*Tian zi* 天子), *guo* 國 refers to the feudal lords (*zhu hou* 諸侯), and *jia* 家 refers to ministers and grandees (*qing da fu* 卿大夫).

2.2   *Naked blades can be trampled underfoot*: This says that, although naked blades are sharp, it is still possible to tread and walk on them.

2.3   *The use of the centre may not be possible*: This speaks of the several matters considered above. Although difficult to achieve, they can still be done. Only the use of the centre may not be possible. Those who are wise go beyond it; those who are foolish do not reach it—which is to say that the difficulties of using the centre make it hard [to maintain].

ZY6: 子路問強。[1]子曰:「南方之強與?北方之強與?抑而強與? [2]寬柔以教,不報無道,南方之強也,君子居之。[3]衽金革,死而不厭,北方之強也,而強者居之。[4]故君子和而不流,強哉矯;中立而不倚,強哉矯;國有道,不變塞焉,強哉矯;國無道,至死不變,強哉矯。」[5]

Comment: Zilu was the disciple particularly noted for his love of courage and his propensity for impulsive action. There are many references to him in the *Lunyu*, but note especially V.7 and VII.10. Both commentators take "your strength" (*er* 而 equates with *ru* 汝, i.e. "you") to indicate Zilu himself as representing the Central States. Thus the "three" in Zheng Xuan's note 2 are the southern and northern regions and the Central States. The relationship between climate and *yin/yang* is made explicit by Kong Yingda.

注 ZY6 (鄭玄)

[1] 強,勇者所好也。{強,其良反,下同。好,呼報反。}

[2] 言三者所以為強者異也。抑,辭也。「而」之言「女」也,謂中國也。{女音汝,下「抑女」同。}

[3] 南方以舒緩為強。「不報無道」,謂犯而不校也。{校,交孝反,報也。}

[4] 衽猶席也。北方以剛猛為強。{衽,而忍反,又而鴆反。厭,於艷反。}

[5] 此抑女之強也。流,猶移也。塞,猶實也。國有道,不變以趨時。國無道,不變以辟害。有道、無道一也。矯,強貌。塞,或為「色」。{矯,居表反,下同。倚,依彼反,徐其蟻反。}

疏 ZY6 (孔穎達)

{「子路」至「哉矯」。}

1.1 《正義》曰:此一節明中庸之道,亦兼中國之強。子路聞孔子美顏回能「擇中庸」,言己有強,故問之,問強中亦兼有中庸否?庾氏云:問強中之中庸者。[21] 然此問之,亦如《論語》云「子謂顏淵曰:『用之則行,舍之則藏,唯我與爾有是夫?』子路曰:『子行三軍,則誰與』」[22] 之類是也。

---

[21] This is presumably the Yu Shi 庾氏 to whom a work, the *Li ji luejie* 禮記略解 is attributed. We have been unable to trace this work which would appear to be no longer extant—see *Sui shu* 32, 2:923.

[22] *Lunyu* VII.10, LCC, 1:197–98.

ZY6: Zilu asked about strength. **[1]** The Master said: "Do you mean the strength of the southern region? Do you mean the strength of the northern region? Or do you mean your own strength? **[2]** To be tolerant and mild in teaching [others] and not to exact retribution against those without the Way is the strength of the southern region. Noble men live by this. **[3]** To lie down to sleep with weapons and armour and to die without regret is the strength of the northern region. Strong men live by this. **[4]** Therefore, the noble man is in harmony and does not waver—how firm is his resolve! He establishes the centre and does not deviate—how firm is his resolve! If the state possesses the Way, he is unchanging in his genuineness—how firm is his resolve! If the state does not possess the Way, he is unchanging in the face of death—how firm is his resolve!" **[5]**

Notes ZY6 (Zheng Xuan)

[1] Strength is what the brave love. . . .

[2] This speaks of the differences between three ways of what is taken as strength. *Yi* 抑 is equivalent to *ci* 辭. *Er* 而 refers to *ru* 女 (i.e. used for *ru* 汝, "you") and refers to the Central States. . . .

[3] The southern region takes a relaxed approach to strength. *Not to exact retribution against those without the Way* refers to being opposed [to this] and yet not entering into altercation. . . .

[4] *Ren* 衽 is like *xi* 席 (a sleeping mat). The northern region takes an unyielding fierceness to be strength. . . .

[5] This asks about your (i.e. Zilu's) strength. *Liu* 流 is like *yi* 移 (shift, move across, change). *Se* 塞 is like *shi* 實 (genuine, real). If the state possesses the Way, he (i.e. the noble man) does not change to follow the trends of the times. If the state is without the Way, he does not change in order to avoid harm. With or without the Way, he is the same. *Jiao* 矯 is the appearance of strength. *Se* 塞 is sometimes taken as *se* 色. . . .

Commentary ZY6 (Kong Yingda)

1.1 The *Zhengyi* says that this particular section clarifies the Way of using the centre, and also links it with the strength of the Central States. Zilu asked Confucius about praising Yan Hui for being able to "choose the use of the centre," saying that he himself had strength and was therefore asking about it—that is, he was asking whether strength partakes of using the centre or not. Yu Shi said: "He asked whether strength being central is using the centre." Certainly, this questioning [of Confucius] is also like that in the *Lunyu*, where it says: "The Master spoke to Yan Yuan saying, 'when used, to act; when dismissed, to retire—are only you and I like this?' Zilu asked: 'If you were in command of the three armies who would you have with you?'" These statements are of this type.

2.1　「子曰：南方之強與，北方之強與，抑而強與」者，抑，語助也，「而」之言「女」也；女，子路也。夫子將荅子路之問，且先反問子路，言強有多種，女今所問，問何者之強，為南方，為北方，為中國，女所能之強也。子路之強，行中國之強也。

3.1　「寬柔以教，不報無道，南方之強也，君子居之」者，反問既竟，夫子遂為歷解之。南方，為苪陽之南，其地多陽。陽氣舒散，人情寬緩和柔，假令人有無道加己，己亦不報，和柔為君子之道，故云「君子居之」。

4.1　「衽金革，死而不厭，北方之強也，而強者居之」者，衽，臥席也。金革，謂軍戎器械也。北方沙漠之地，其地多陰。陰氣堅急，故人性剛猛，恒好鬥爭，故以甲鎧為席，寢宿於中，至死不厭，非君子所處，而強梁者居之。然唯云南北，不云東西者，鄭沖云：「是必南北互舉，蓋與東西俗同，故不言也。」[23]「故君子和而不流，強哉矯」，此以下，皆述中國之強也。流，移也。矯亦強貌也。不為南北之強，故性行和合而不流移，心行強哉，形貌矯然。

5.1　「中立而不倚，強哉矯」者，中正獨立而不偏倚，志意強哉，形貌矯然。

5.2　「國有道，不變塞焉，強哉矯」者，若國有道，守直不變，德行充實，志意強哉，形貌矯然。

23　Zheng Chong 鄭沖 (Zheng Wenhe 鄭文和), was a co-compiler with He Yan and others of the *Lunyu jijie* 論語集解—see the *Jin shu* 33, 4:991–93 and also John Makeham, *Transmitters and Creators* (Cambridge, MA: Harvard University Press, 2003), 26–29. The particular quotation has not been located.

2.1 *The Master said: "Do you mean the strength of the southern region? Do you mean the strength of the northern region? Or do you mean your own strength?"* Yi 抑 is an auxiliary word. *Er* 而 refers to *ru* 女 (you). *Ru* 女 is Zilu. The Master was about to reply to Zilu's question but first asked Zilu a question in return, saying that there are several kinds of strength and asking him what kind of strength he was presently referring to—that of the southern region, that of the northern region, or that of the Central States, i.e. the strength he himself was capable of. Zilu's strength was to put into practice the strength of the Central States.

3.1 *To be tolerant and mild in teaching [others] and not to exact retribution against those without the Way is the strength of the southern region. Noble men live by this:* Having formulated the return question, the Master then subsequently explains it. The southern region is the region to the south of Chu (Jing); this land has much *yang*. The *yang* spirit [makes people] relaxed and their emotional state is one of gentleness, harmony and mildness. If those without the Way approach such people, they do not attempt retribution [against them] because harmony and mildness are the Way of the noble man [there]. Therefore, it says, *noble men live by this.*

4.1 *To lie down to sleep with weapons and armour and to die without regret is the strength of the northern region. Strong men live by this:* Ren 衽 is a sleeping mat. *Jin ge* 金革 refers to the weapons and implements of war. The northern region is desert; this land has much *yin*. The *yin* spirit is determined and pressing, therefore the nature of the people is hard and fierce, and there is a constant love of conflict. Thus, they make armour and weapons their sleeping mats, taking their rest among them, and facing death without regret. This is not where noble men live; those who are violent and overbearing live there. Nevertheless, he (i.e. Confucius) only speaks of the southern and northern regions and not of the eastern and western regions. Zheng Chong says: "This must be that the south and north are both brought up because they are commonly taken together with the east and the west, therefore [the latter] are not spoken of." From *therefore, the noble man is in harmony and does not waver* onward, everything is about the strength of the Central States. *Liu* 流 is equivalent to *yi* 移 (to shift, move across, change). *Jiao* 矯 is also the appearance of strength. [The Central States' strength] is not the strength of the south and the north. Thus, nature and conduct are harmonious and unwavering, the actions of the mind-heart are strong, and the appearance is one of resolve.

5.1 *He establishes the centre and does not deviate—how firm is his resolve!* Once the centre is truly established and there is no inclining or deviating, will and purpose are strong and demeanour resolute.

5.2 *If the state possesses the Way, he is unchanging in his genuineness—how firm is his resolve!* If the state possesses the Way he maintains his straightforward [nature] and does not change. His virtuous conduct is abundant, his will and purpose are strong, and his appearance is resolute.

5.3 「國無道，至死不變，強哉矯」者，若國之無道，守善至死，性不改變，
志意強哉，形貌矯然。

{注「此抑」至「強貌」。}

5.4 《正義》曰：「此抑女之強也」，何以知之？上文既說三種之強，又見南方
之強，又見北方之強，唯「抑而之強」未見，故知此經所云者，是「抑女
之強也」。云「流，移也」者，以其性和同，必流移隨物，合和而不移，
亦中庸之德也。云「國有道，不變以趨時」者，國雖有道，不能隨逐物以
求榮利。今不改變己志，以趨會於時也。云「矯，強貌」者，矯是壯大之
形，故云「強貌」也。

ZY7: 子曰：「素隱行怪，後世有述焉，吾弗為之矣。[1]君子遵道而行，
半塗而廢，吾弗能已矣。[2]君子依乎中庸，遯世不見，知而不悔，唯
聖者能之。」[3]君子之道，費而隱。[4]夫婦之愚，可以與知焉。及其至
也，雖聖人亦有所不知焉。夫婦之不肖，可以能行焉。及其至也，雖聖
人亦有所不能焉。[5]天地之大也，人猶有所憾。[6]故君子語大，天下
莫能載焉；語小，天下莫能破焉。[7]《詩》云：『鳶飛戾天，魚躍于淵。』
言其上下察也。[8]君子之道，造端乎夫婦；及其至也，察乎天地。」[9]

Comment: What is here taken together in the *Li ji* is separated into two sections by Zhu
Xi, with the new section, beginning with 君子之道, marking a definite transition in the
work (see Comment for Zhu Xi, ZY12). As it stands above, the section is coherent and
about the Way of the noble man in contrast to the conduct of "ordinary men and women."
The noble man, exemplified at the outset by Confucius, follows the Way with absolute
resolve, regardless of the circumstances. If the times are not propitious, he is prepared to
withdraw to continue his pursuit of the Way. Nonetheless, the Way is open to all, although
both the sage and the ordinary person fall short, to a greater or lesser degree.

5.3 *If the state does not possess the Way, he is unchanging in the face of death—how firm is his resolve!* If the state does not possess the Way, he preserves his own goodness right to death. His nature does not change, his will and purpose are strong, and his demeanour resolute.

5.4 The *Zhengyi* says: "Could it be your own strength?" But how do we know? The preceding text has already spoken of three kinds of strength and has considered both the strength of the southern region and the strength of the northern region. It is only *yi er zhi qiang* 抑而之強 that has not been considered. Therefore, we know that what this section speaks of is this *yi ru zhi qiang ye* 抑女之強也 (i.e. "your strength"). In saying "*liu* 流 equates with *yi* 移 (to shift, change, waver)," he takes his nature to be harmonious and agreeable, and necessarily to flow along and be compliant with things, and to be harmonious and unwavering, which is also the virtue of using the centre. Saying, *if the state possesses the Way, he is unchanging in his genuineness* means that although the state possesses the Way, he is not able to follow and comply with things as a means of seeking glory and benefit. Now, he does not change his own will (purpose) in order to follow the trends of the times. In saying, *how firm is his resolve*, *jiao* 矯 is the appearance of *zhuang da* 壯大 (vigorous strength), therefore it says "the appearance of strength."

ZY7: The Master said: "[Some men] incline towards obscurity and behave in strange ways so there is something handed down to later generations— I do not do this. **[1]** [Some] noble men follow the Way and act, go halfway along the path, and stop—I am not able to stop. **[2]** A noble man relies on using the centre, withdraws from the world unseen, knows [this], and is without regret—only a sage is capable of this. **[3]** If the Way of the noble man is perverted, he withdraws to seclusion. **[4]** Ordinary men and women in their foolishness can share in knowing it, but in reaching its perfection, sages too have that which they do not know in it. Ordinary men and women in their unworthiness may be able to practise it, but in reaching its perfection, sages too have that which they are unable [to do] in it. **[5]** Despite the greatness of Heaven and Earth, people still have that which they dislike. **[6]** Therefore, what the noble man speaks of as great, the world is not able to contain; what he speaks of as small, the world is not able to divide. **[7]** The *Odes* says: 'The hawk flies up to reach the heavens; fish frolic in the deep pools.' This speaks of [the Way] being manifest above and below. **[8]** The Way of the noble man takes its origin from ordinary men and women; in reaching its perfection, it is manifest throughout Heaven and Earth." **[9]**

注 ZY7 (鄭玄)

[1]「素」讀如攻城攻其所傃之「傃」，傃，猶鄉也。言方鄉辟害隱身，而行詭譎以作後世名也。「弗為之矣」，恥之也。{傃音素。鄉，本又作「嚮」，許亮反，下皆同。佄，久委反，下同。譎音決。}

[2] 廢，猶罷止也。「弗能已矣」，汲汲行道，不為時人之隱行。{汲音急。隱行，下孟反。}

[3] 言隱者當如此也。唯舜為能如此。{遯，本又作「遁」，同徒頓反。}

[4] 言可隱之節也。費，猶佄也。道不費則仕。{費，本又作「拂」，同扶弗反，徐音弗，注同。}

[5]「與」讀為贊者皆與之「與」。言匹夫匹婦愚耳，亦可以其與有所知，可以其能有所行者。以其知行之極也，聖人有不能，如此舜好察邇言，由此故與。{以與音預，注「皆與之與」、「以其與」同。好，呼報反。故與音餘。}

[6] 憾，恨也。天地至大，無不覆載，人尚有所恨焉，況於聖人能盡備之乎。{憾，本又作「感」，胡暗反，注同。}

[7] 語猶説也。所説大事，謂先王之道也。所説小事，謂若愚、不肖夫婦之知行也。聖人盡兼行。

[8] 察，猶著也。言聖人之德至於天，則「鳶飛戾天」；至於地，則「魚躍于淵」，是其著明於天地也。{鳶，悦專反，字又作「鵏」。[24] 戾，力計、呂結二反。躍，羊灼反。著，張慮反，下同。}

[9] 夫婦，謂匹夫匹婦之所知、所行。{造，在老反。}

疏 ZY7 (孔穎達)

{「子曰」至「天地」}

1.1　《正義》曰：此一節論夫子雖隱遯之世，亦行中庸。又明中庸之道，初則起於匹夫匹婦，終則徧於天地。

1.2　「素隱行怪，後世有述焉」者，素，鄉也。謂無道之世，身鄉幽隱之處，應須靜默。若行怪異之事，求立功名，使後世有所述焉。

24　This character is ZWDCD #47810, 10:740.

Notes ZY7 (Zheng Xuan)

[1] *Su* 素 is read like the *su* 傃 in "攻城攻其所傃," i.e. *su* 傃 is like *xiang* 鄉 (inclining towards). This speaks of inclining towards concealment of the self to avoid harm and acting cunningly to create a reputation for later generations. *I do not do this* is to feel shame about it. . . .

[2] *Fei* 廢 is like *ba zhi* 罷止 (to stop). *I am not able to stop* is to practise the Way with untiring effort and not to carry out the obscure actions of people of the times. . . .

[3] This says that [even] recluses ought to be like this. However, only Shun was able to be like this. . . .

[4] This speaks of the possibility of a period of reclusiveness. *Fu* 費 is like *gui* 佹 (crafty, treacherous, perverse). If the Way is not perverted, then one takes office. . . .

[5] *Yu* 與 is read like the *yu* 與 in "為贊者皆與" (i.e. to join, share in). This says that, although ordinary men and women are foolish, they too can share in what is known and are able to do what is practised. But when it comes to the extremes of knowing and practising, even sages have that which they cannot do. This is why Shun loved to examine familiar words and by this shared in [them]. . . .

[6] *Han* 憾 is equivalent to *hen* 恨 (to hate, dislike). Heaven and Earth are very great and there is nothing they do not cover and support, yet people still have that which they dislike. How much more does a sage have the ability to completely perfect it. . . .

[7] *Yu* 語 is like *shuo* 説 (to speak). What is spoken of as the "great matter" refers to the Way of former kings. What are spoken of as "small matters" refer, for example, to the knowledge and conduct of foolish and unworthy men and women. The sage completely encompasses great and small matters in his conduct.

[8] *Cha* 察 is like *zhu* 著 (to manifest, set forth, display). This says that the sage's virtue reaches to Heaven; that is, *the hawk flies up to reach the heavens*. It extends to earth; that is, *fish frolic in the deep pools*. These are its manifestations in heaven and on earth. . . .

[9] *Fu fu* 夫婦 refers to what ordinary men and women know and do. . . .

Commentary ZY7 (Kong Yingda)

1.1   The *Zhengyi* says that this particular section discusses the fact that the Master, although withdrawing from the world, also practised using the centre. It also makes it clear that the Way of using the centre first arises in ordinary men and women. Then finally, it is everywhere in the world.

1.2   *[Some men] incline towards obscurity and behave in strange ways so there is something handed down to later generations*: *Su* 傃 is equivalent to *xiang* 鄉 (to incline towards). This speaks of the age being without the Way and oneself inclining towards a place of seclusion, expecting stillness and quiet. Something like the matter of behaving in strange and unusual ways, seeking to establish a meritorious name, causes later generations to have what is handed down.

1.3 「吾弗為之矣」者，恥之也。如此之事，我不能為之，以其身雖隱遯而名欲彰也。

{注「素讀如攻城攻其所傃之傃」。}

1.4 《正義》曰：《司馬法》文。言身隱而行佹譎，以作後世之名，若許由洗耳之屬是也。[25]

2.1 「君子遵道而行，半塗而廢」者，言君子之人，初既遵循道德而行，當須行之終竟。今不能終竟，猶如人行於道路，半塗而自休廢。廢，猶罷止也。

2.2 「吾弗能已矣」，已，猶止也。吾弗能如時人半塗而休止，言汲汲行道無休已也。

{注「不為時人之隱行」。}

2.3 《正義》曰：謂作佹譎求名是也。君子以隱終始，行道不能止也。

{「君子」至「能之」。}

3.1 言君子依行中庸之德，若值時無道隱遯於世，雖有才德，不為時人所知，而無悔恨之心，如此者非凡人所能，唯聖者能然。若不能依行中庸者，雖隱遯於世，不為人所知，則有悔恨之心也。

{注「唯舜為能如此」。}

3.2 《正義》曰：知者，《史記》云：「舜耕於歷山，漁於雷澤，陶於河濱。」[26]是不見知而不悔。

4.1 「君子之道，費而隱」，注云：「言可隱之節。費，猶佹也。」言君子之人，遭值亂世，道德違費則隱而不仕。若道之不費，則當仕也。

5.1 「夫婦之愚，可以與知焉」，言天下之事，千端萬緒，或細小之事，雖夫婦之愚，偶然與知其善惡，若蒭蕘之言有可聽用，故云「與知」。

---

25 The *Sima fa* 司馬法 is a short work attributed to Sima Rangju 司馬穰苴 of the Zhou period, apparently the first of the family line (see the *Shiji* 64, 7:2157–60). It can be found in the CSJC, n.s., 32:76–78. Xu You 許由 was one of the four legendary philosphers of Miaoguye 藐姑射 Mountain who, when offered the throne by the Emperor Yao, hurried off to wash his ears clean of the contamination of the offer.

26 See *Shiji*, 1:32.

1.3   *I do not do this*: This is to be ashamed about it. In matters like this, I am not able to do this, because for myself, although I dwell in obscurity, I still wish my name to become known.

1.4   The *Zhengyi* says that this is from the *Sima fa*. It speaks of a person living in seclusion but acting cunningly and falsely to create a reputation for later generations. Xu You's washing his ears is an example of this sort of thing.

2.1   *[Some] noble men follow the Way and act, go halfway along the path, and stop*: This speaks of a noble man who, when first he follows and complies with the Way and virtue and acts, judges it right that he must act in this way to the end. Now if he is not able to keep on to the end, he is like a person walking along a road, getting halfway, and spontaneously stopping. *Fei* 廢 is like *ba zhi* 罷止 (to stop).

2.2   *I am not able to stop*: Yi 已 is like *zhi* 止 (to stop). I am not able to travel halfway along the road and stop, as others of the age are. This speaks of the untiring effort to practise the Way without ceasing.

2.3   The *Zhengyi* says that this refers to acting in a cunning and false manner in seeking a reputation. The noble man, when in seclusion, follows the Way from beginning to end and is unable to stop.

3.1   This speaks of the noble man relying on the practice of the virtue of using the centre. For example, if it should happen to be a time without the Way, he withdraws from the world to seclusion. Although he has talent and virtue, if this is not known by others of the age, and yet he harbours no regret or enmity in his heart, this is not something an ordinary man can do; only a sage can be like this. For example, in the case of one who is not able to rely on the practice of using the centre, although he withdraws from the world to seclusion and is not known by others, he still harbours regret and enmity in his heart.

3.2   The *Zhengyi* says that on "the one who knows," the *Shiji* says: "Shun ploughed on Li Mountain, fished in Lei Marsh, and made pottery on the banks of the He." This is not to be known and yet to have no regrets.

4.1   *If the Way of the noble man is perverted, he withdraws to seclusion*: The notes say, "this speaks of the possibility of a time of withdrawal. *Fu* 費 is like *gui* 佹 (perverse, cunning, treacherous)." This says that, if the noble man as an individual should meet with disordered times, when the Way and virtue are abandoned and perverted, then he withdraws to seclusion and does not serve. If the Way is not perverted, then it is proper for him to serve.

5.1   *Ordinary men and women in their foolishness can share in knowing it*: This says that the affairs of the world are very complicated but some are small matters, so although ordinary men and women are foolish, it can happen that they share in knowing what is good and bad. For example, the words of grass and reed cutters can be listened to and put to use. Therefore it is said, *can share in knowing it*.

5.2　「及其至也，雖聖人亦有所不知焉」者，言道之至極，如造化之理，雖聖人不知其所由，故云「及其至也，雖聖人亦有所不知焉」。

5.3　「夫婦之不肖，可以能行焉」，以行之至極故也。前文據其知，此文據其行，以其知、行有異，故別起其文。但知之易，行之難。知之易，故上文云「夫婦之愚」。行之難，故此經云「夫婦之不肖」。不肖勝於愚也。

5.4　「及其至也，雖聖人亦有所不能焉」者，知之與行之皆是至極，既是至極，故聖人有不能也。

{注「與讀為贊者皆與之與」。}

5.5　《正義》曰：〈士冠禮〉云：「其饗冠者，贊者皆與」，[27] 謂于與也。云「舜好察邇言，由此故與」者，即愚夫愚婦有所識知故也。與，語助也。

6.1　「天地之大也，人猶有所憾」者，憾，恨也。言天地至大，無物不養，無物不覆載，如冬寒夏暑，人猶有怨恨之，猶如聖人之德，無善不包，人猶怨之，是不可備也。中庸之道，於理為難，大小兼包，始可以備也。

7.1　「故君子語大，天下莫能載焉」者，語，說也；大，謂先王之道。言君子語說先王之道，其事既大，天下之人無能勝載之者。

7.2　「語小，天下莫能破焉」者，若說細碎小事，謂愚不肖，事既纖細，天下之人無能分破之者。言事似秋毫，不可分破也。

{注「聖人盡兼行」。}

27　See the *Yi li*, "Shi guanli," SSJZS, 4:22.

5.2   *In reaching its perfection, sages too have that which they do not know in it:* This says
      that the extreme point of the Way is like a principle of creation—even sages do
      not know where it comes from. Therefore it is said, *In reaching its perfection sages
      too have that which they do not know.*

5.3   *Ordinary men and women in their unworthiness may be able to practise it:* The rea-
      son is the perfection of its practice. The previous statement is about their know-
      ing it; this statement is about their practising it. Because of their knowledge their
      actions are different, hence a difference arises in these statements. But knowing
      it is easy; practising it is hard. Knowing it is easy, therefore the prior statement
      speaks of "the foolishness of ordinary men and women." Practising it is hard,
      therefore this statement speaks of the "unworthiness of ordinary men and wom-
      en." Unworthiness is more significant than foolishness.

5.4   *In reaching its perfection, sages too have that which they are unable [to do] in it:*
      Knowing it and practising it are both this farthest extreme. Since they are this
      farthest extreme, the sage has that which he is not able [to do].

5.5   The *Zhengyi* says that the "Shi guanli" [chapter of the *Yi li,*] states: "In the cap-
      ping ceremony those assisting all participate." This refers to joining in. It says: "Shun
      loved to examine 'near' (familiar) words and for this reason he joined in." This,
      then, is the reason why foolish men and women have that which they know. *Yu*
      與 is an auxiliary word.

6.1   *Despite the greatness of Heaven and Earth, people still have that which they dislike:*
      Han 憾 is equivalent to *hen* 恨 (to dislike, hate). This says that, although Heaven
      and Earth are very great, there is nothing that is not nurtured, nothing that is not
      covered and supported. It is like winter cold and summer heat; there are still people
      who resent and dislike these. It is like the sage's virtue where what is not good is
      not embraced; people still resent this and it is not possible to make this perfect.
      The Way of using the centre is difficult in terms of principle. Only when the great
      and small are all included (or taken into consideration) can it begin to be perfect.

7.1   *Therefore, what the noble man speaks of as great, the world is not able to contain:* *Yu*
      語 is equivalent to *shuo* 説 (to speak, explain). *Da* 大 refers to the Way of former
      kings. This says that, when the noble man speaks about the Way of former kings,
      since its matters are great, they are what the people of the world are not able to
      bear and sustain.

7.2   *What he speaks of as small, the world is not able to divide:* For example, speaking of
      small and fragmented matters refers to the foolish and unworthy. Since the matters
      are small and trivial, they are what the people of the world are not able to divide.
      This says that matters are like autumn down which cannot be further divided.

7.3　《正義》曰：謂兼行大、小之事。小事則愚夫愚婦所知行，大事則先王之道。前文云雖聖人有所不知、不能，此云大事聖人兼行之者，前云有所「不知」、「不能」，謂於小事不勝匹夫匹婦耳，非謂大事不能也，故此云盡兼行之。

8.1　「《詩》云：鳶飛戾天，魚躍于淵，言其上下察也」者，《詩•大雅•旱麓》之篇，[28] 美文王之詩。引之者，言聖人之德上至於天，則「鳶飛戾天」，是翱翔得所。聖人之德下至於地，則「魚躍于淵」，是游泳得所。言聖人之德，上下明察。《詩》本文云「鳶飛戾天」，喻惡人遠去；「魚躍于淵」，喻善人得所。此引斷章，故與詩義有異也。

9.1　「君子之道，造端乎夫婦」者，言君子行道，初始造立端緒，起於匹夫匹婦之所知所行者。

9.2　「及其至也，察乎天地」者，言雖起於匹夫匹婦所知所行，及其至極之時，明察於上下天地也。

---

[28]　*Odes*, Mao 239, verse 3, LCC, 4:445.

7.3 The *Zhengyi* says that this refers jointly to the conduct of both great and small matters. Small matters, then, are what foolish ordinary men and women know and do; great matters are, then, the Way of former kings. The previous text says that, although a sage has that which he does not know and is not able [to do], this says that great matters are what sages all do. The previous statement that there is what [the sage] "does not know" and "is not able to do" refers to small matters in which the sage does not surpass ordinary men and women; it does not refer to the sage not being able [to do] great things. Therefore, this statement completely covers the matter of doing things. ·

8.1 *The Odes says: "The hawk flies up to reach the heavens; fish frolic in the deep pools." This speaks of [the Way] being manifest above and below:* This is from the *Odes,* "Da ya," "Han Lu" and is a poem in praise of King Wen. The quotation from it speaks of the sage's virtue reaching to Heaven above, which is "the hawk flies up to reach the heavens," that is, soaring to achieve that place. The sage's virtue extending below to the earth is then, "fish frolic in the deep pools," that is, their getting a place to swim to and fro in. This speaks of the sage's virtue being clearly manifest above and below. The original analysis of the *Odes* says the "the hawk flies up to reach the heavens" is a metaphor for the evil person straying afar whilst "fish frolic in the deep pools" is a metaphor for the good person attaining a place. This quotation is taken out of context so the meaning is different from that in the ode.

9.1 *The Way of the noble man takes its origin from ordinary men and women:* This says that the noble man, in practising the Way, at the beginning first creates a point of origin which arises out of what ordinary men and women know and do.

9.2 *In reaching its perfection, it is manifest throughout Heaven and Earth:* This says that, although it arises in what ordinary men and women know and do, in reaching to the time of its extreme perfection, it is manifest above and below in Heaven and on Earth.

ZY8: 子曰：「道不遠人，人之為道而遠人，不可以為道。[1]《詩》云：
『伐柯伐柯，其則不遠。』執柯以伐柯，睨而視之，猶以為遠。[2]故
君子以人治人，改而止。[3]忠恕違道不遠，施諸己而不願，亦勿施於
人。[4]君子之道四，<u>丘</u>未能一焉。所求乎子以事父，未能也。所求乎臣
以事君，未能也。所求乎弟以事兄，未能也。所求乎朋友先施之，未能
也。[5]庸德之行，庸言之謹，有所不足，不敢不勉，有餘不敢盡，言顧
行，行顧言。[6]君子胡不慥慥爾。[7]君子素其位而行，不願乎其外。
素富貴行乎富貴，素貧賤行乎貧賤，素夷狄行乎夷狄，素患難行乎患
難。君子無入而不自得焉。[8]在上位不陵下，在下位不援上。[9]正己
而不求於人，則無怨。上不怨天，下不尤人。[10]故君子居易以俟命，
小人行險以徼幸。」[11]

Comment: The opening statement is clear enough. The Way to follow is not something
remote or abstruse. It is near at hand and accessible to all. This view is supported by the
single example from the *Odes*; cutting a new axe handle is based on the model of an existing handle. The next statement, tersely expressed, is somewhat more opaque. The *Li ji*
commentators take the initial *ren* 人 to refer to the Way of mankind (*ren dao* 人道). Components of the Way are identified as *zhong* 忠 (loyalty) and *shu* 恕 (reciprocity). Confucius
then introduces a personal note, apparently admitting his own deficiencies in the several
aspects of the Way (of the noble man), as listed. As Legge points out, a more general statement of the Way resumes after the fourth and final *neng ye* 能也. The first sentence after
this resumption presents some difficulty. Riegel, for example, suggests emendation on the
basis of a similar passage in the *Zhou yi* 周易,[29] supported by other references. In translation, many take *yong* 庸 to be "ordinary" but the *Li ji* commentators gloss it as *chang* 常
in the sense of "constant," at least to judge by the juxtaposition of *chang* 常 and *heng* 恒 in
Kong Yingda's commentary. In the statement covered by note [8] above, there is some variation in the reading of *su* 素 which here, as elsewhere, the *Li ji* commentators equate with
su 傃—see Kong Yingda's comment in his note 8.1 for the version given in the translation.
To quote Legge again, "the meaning comes to much the same in all these interpretations"
(395n14). This comment might apply generally to the differing views expressed regarding
all the more or less contentious elements of the section as a whole.

---

29   See Riegel, "The Four 'Tzu Ssu' Chapters of the 'Li Chi': An Analysis and Translation
     of the *Fang Chi, Chung Yung, Piao Chi,* and *Tzu I*," 219n57.

ZY8: The Master said: "The Way is not far removed from men. If what a man takes to be the Way is far removed from men, then it cannot be regarded as the Way. **[1]** The *Odes* says: 'Cutting an axe handle, cutting an axe handle; its pattern is not far removed.' If you take hold of one axe handle to cut another axe handle, and look at them both obliquely, then it seems like they are far apart. **[2]** Thus the noble man uses [the Way of] man to bring order to others; he effects a change and stops. **[3]** Loyalty and reciprocity are not far removed from the Way. What you do not wish to be done to yourself, you also do not do to others. **[4]** The Way of the noble man has four [criteria]. I have not yet been able to achieve a single one of them. What is looked for in a son serving a father, I am not yet able to do. What is looked for in a subject serving a prince, I am not yet able to do. What is looked for in a younger brother serving an older brother, I am not yet able to do. What is looked for in a friend to do first, I am not yet able to do. **[5]** In the practice of constant virtue, in the attention to constant speech, if there are deficiencies, one dare not fail to strive [to make them good]; if there are excesses, one dare not fail to curb them. Words should have regard to actions and actions should have regard to words. **[6]** If this is so, then how is the noble man not honest! **[7]** The noble man occupies his position and acts [accordingly]; he does not wish to go beyond this. If he occupies a position of wealth and honour, his actions are appropriate to wealth and honour. If he occupies a position of poverty and lowliness, his actions are appropriate to poverty and lowliness. If he occupies a position among the eastern and northern tribes (Yi and Di), his actions are in accord with the Yi and Di. If he occupies a position of misfortune and hardship, his actions are appropriate to misfortune and hardship. The noble man does not enter and not be at ease [with himself]. **[8]** When he occupies a high position, he does not mistreat inferiors. When he occupies a lowly position, he does not cling to superiors. **[9]** He rectifies himself and asks nothing of others; then he is without resentment. Above, he does not find fault with Heaven; below, he does not blame others. **[10]** Therefore, the noble man dwells in equanimity and accepts his lot; the lesser man acts dangerously in pursuit of good fortune." **[11]**

注 ZY8 (鄭玄)

[1] 言道即不遠於人，人不能行也。

[2] 則，法也。言持柯以伐木，將以為柯近，以柯為尺寸之法，此法不遠人，人尚遠之，明為道不可以遠。{柯，古何反。睨，徐音詣，睥睨也。}

[3] 言人有罪過，君子以人道治之，其人改則止赦之，不責以人所不能。

[4] 違猶去也。

[5] 聖人而曰我未能，明人當勉之無已。

[6] 庸猶常也，言德常行也，言常謹也。聖人之行，實過於人，「有餘不敢盡」，常為人法，從禮也。{行行，皆下孟反，注「聖人之性」同，或一讀皆如字。}

[7] 君子，謂眾賢也。慥慥，守實言行相應之貌。{慥，七到反。行，下孟反。應，於陵反。舊音應對之應。}

[8] 素皆讀為傃。「不願乎其外」，謂思不出其位也。「自得」，謂所鄉不失其道。{難，乃旦反，下同。}

[9] 援，謂牽持之也。{援音園，注同。}

[10] 「無怨」，人無怨之者也。《論語》曰：「君子求諸己，小人求諸人。」[30]{己音紀。怨，於願反，又於元反，下及注並同。}

[11] 易，猶平安也。俟命，聽天任命也。險，謂傾危之道。{易，以豉反，注同。徼，古堯反。}

30   *Lunyu* XV.20, LCC, 1:300.

Notes ZY8 (Zheng Xuan)

[1] This says that, although the Way is not far removed from men, they are not able to practise it.

[2] *Ze* 則 is equivalent to *fa* 法 (pattern, model). This says that someone taking hold of an axe to cut wood will take the axe to be near and to be a model in terms of dimensions. This model is not far removed from men, but men still take it to be far removed. It is clear that what is taken as the Way cannot be far removed. . . .

[3] This says that when others have faults and transgressions, the noble man uses the Way of man to bring order to them. When these others change, then he stops and forgives them, and does not ask of others what they cannot [do].

[4] *Wei* 違 is like *qu* 去 (to go away from, abandon).

[5] To be a sage and say "I am not yet able to do [this]" makes it clear that people ought to exert themselves without stopping.

[6] *Yong* 庸 is like *chang* 常 (constant, unchanging) and speaks of virtue being constantly practised and speech being constantly cautious. The actions of a sage truly surpass those of others. *If there are deficiencies, one dare not fail to strive [to make them good]* is to constantly be a model for others and follow *li* 禮. . . .

[7] *Junzi* 君子 refers to many worthies. *Zaozao* 慥慥 is the appearance of maintaining a true correspondence between words and deeds. . . .

[8] *Su* 素 is in all instances read as *su* 傃 (towards, to). "不願乎其外" speaks of not considering anything outside one's position. *Zi de* 自得 speaks of not losing this Way. . . .

[9] *Yuan* 援 means to connect with and hold on to it. . . .

[10] *Wu yuan* 無怨 is a man being without resentment. The *Lunyu* says: "The noble man seeks it in himself; the lesser man seeks it in others." . . .

[11] *Yi* 易 is like *ping'an* 平安 (tranquility, equanimity). To "await fate" (*si ming* 俟命) means to listen to Heaven and accept its decree. *Xian* 險 refers to a dangerous path (course of action). . . .

疏 ZY8 (孔穎達)

{「子曰」至「徼幸」}

1.1 《正義》曰：此一節明中庸之道去人不遠，但行於己則外能及物。「道不遠人」者，言中庸之道不遠離於人身，但人能行之於己，則是中庸也。「人之為道而遠人，不可以為道」，言人為中庸之道，當附近於人，謂人所能行，則己所行可以為道。若違理離遠，則不可施於己，又不可行於人，則非道也，故云「人之為道而遠人，不可以為道也」。

2.1 「《詩》云『伐柯伐柯，其則不遠』。執柯以伐柯，睨而視之，猶以為遠」，此〈豳風・伐柯〉[31]之篇，美周公之詩。柯，斧柄也。《周禮》云：「柯長三尺，博三寸。」[32] 則，法也。言伐柯，斫也。柯柄長短，其法不遠也，但執柯睨而視之，猶以為遠。言欲行其道於人，其法亦不遠，但近取法於身，何異持柯以伐柯？人猶以為遠，明為道之法亦不可以遠。即所不願於上，無以交於下；所不願於下，無以事上。況是在身外，於他人之處，欲以為道，何可得乎？明行道在於身而求道也。

3.1 「故君子以人治人，改而止」者，以道去人不遠，言人有過，君子當以人道治此有過之人。「改而止」，若人自改而休止，不須更責不能之事。若人所不能，則己亦不能，是行道在於己身也。

---

31   *Odes*, Mao 158, verse 2, LCC, 4:240.
32   *Zhou li*, "Che ren," SSJZS, 3:656.

Commentary ZY8 (Kong Yingda)

1.1   The *Zhengyi* says that this particular section makes it clear that the Way of using the centre is not far removed from men, but by putting it into practice in oneself, one is then able to extend it externally to things. *The Way is not far removed from men* says that the Way of using the centre is not far removed from oneself and others, but if a man is able to implement it in himself, then this is "using the centre." *If what a man takes to be the Way is far removed from men, it cannot be regarded as the Way* saying that what men deem be the Way of using the centre should be close to people states that what others being able to practise what I practise can be taken to be the Way. If one abandons principle and leaves it far distant, then it is not possible to implement it in oneself, just as it is also not possible for others to implement it. This, then, is not the Way. Therefore, it says *if what a man takes to be the Way is far removed from men, then it cannot be regarded as the Way.*

2.1   *The Odes says: "Cutting an axe handle, cutting an axe handle; its pattern is not far removed." If you take hold of one axe handle to cut another axe handle and look at them both obliquely, then it seems like they are far apart.* This is the "Fa ke" ode from the "Bin feng" and is a poem in praise of the Duke of Zhou. *Ke* 柯 is an axe handle. The *Zhou li* says: "A handle is three *chi* long and three *cun* thick." *Ze* 則 is equivalent to *fa* 法 (model, pattern). Saying *fa ke* 伐柯 is equivalent to *zhuo* 斫 (to cut). In cutting the axe handle to size, its pattern is not remote, but if you take hold of the handle and look at it obliquely, it is as if it were distant. This says that, if one wishes to practise this Way among men, its pattern too is not far removed. But in approaching and choosing the pattern in oneself, how is it different from taking hold of a handle to cut a handle? Men still take it to be far removed, but it is clear that the pattern of the Way cannot be taken as far removed. Accordingly, what one does not wish for in superiors, one does not use in dealing with inferiors; what one does not wish for in inferiors, one does not use in serving superiors. Moreover, if this lies outside the self and is situated in other people, and one wishes it to be taken as the Way, how can this be done? Clearly practising the Way lies in oneself and in seeking the Way.

3.1   *Thus the noble man uses [the Way of] man to bring order to others; he effects a change and stops:* Because the Way is not far removed from men, this says that if others have faults, it is right for the noble man (ruler) to use the Way of man to bring good order to those people with faults. *He effects a change and stops:* If others change themselves, he stops; it is not necessary to go on demanding things they cannot do. If others have what they cannot do, then he himself is also not able to do it. That is [to say], putting the Way into practice lies in oneself.

4.1 「忠恕違道不遠」者，忠者，內盡於心，恕者，外不欺物。恕，忖也。忖度其義於人。違，去也。言身行忠恕，則去道不遠也。

4.2 「施諸己而不願，亦勿施於人」者，諸，於也。他人有一不善之事施之於己，己所不願，亦勿施於人，人亦不願故也。「所求乎子以事父，未能也」，言此四者，欲明求之於他人，必先行之於己。欲求其子以孝道事己，己須以孝道事父母，故云「所求乎子以事父，未能也」。恐人未能行之。夫子，聖人，聖人猶曰我未能行，凡人當勉之無已。

5.1 「所求乎臣以事君，未能也」，譬如己是諸侯，欲求於臣以忠事己，己當先行忠於天子及廟中事尸，是全臣道也。「所求乎朋友先施之，未能也」，欲求朋友以恩惠施己，則己當先施恩惠於朋友也。「庸德之行，庸言之謹」，庸，常也。謂自修己身，常以德而行，常以言而謹也。

6.1 「有所不足，不敢不勉」，謂己之才行有所不足之處，不敢不勉而行之。

6.2 「有餘不敢盡」，謂己之才行有餘，於人常持謙退，不敢盡其才行以過於人。「言顧行」者，使言不過行，恒顧視於行。

6.3 「行顧言」者，使行副於言，謂恒顧視於言也。

7.1 「君子胡不慥慥爾」，「慥慥，守實言行相應之貌」。胡，猶何也。既顧言行相副，君子何得不慥慥然守實言行相應之道也。

4.1　*Loyalty and reciprocity are not far removed from the Way.* Zhong 忠 (loyalty) is "within, to be fully committed in one's heart"; *shu* 恕 (reciprocity) is "without, not to cheat others." *Shu* 恕 is equivalent to *cun* 忖 (to consider, reflect)—to gauge and estimate its meaning for others. *Wei* 違 is equivalent to *qu* 去 (to be removed from). This says that, if one practises loyalty and reciprocity, then one is not far removed from the Way.

4.2　*What you do not wish to be done to yourself, you also do not do to others*: *Zhu* 諸 is equivalent to *yu* 於 (to, on). If another person does something to you that is not good, something that you do not wish for, you in turn do not do that to the other person for the reason that the other person also does not wish it. *What is looked for in a son serving a father, I am not yet able to do*: Speaking of these four [criteria] is to wish to make clear that one must first practise in oneself what one seeks in other people. If what you wish is for your son to serve you in a filial way, you must serve your father and mother in a filial way. Therefore, it says: *What is looked for in a son serving a father, I am not yet able to do.* I fear that others are not yet able to practise this. The Master was a sage and yet he said "I am not yet able to do this," so it is right that ordinary men should exert themselves without stopping.

5.1　*What is looked for in a subject serving a prince, I am not yet able to do*: For example, if you are a feudal lord, you would wish to seek loyalty in a minister serving you, in which case you should rightly first practise loyalty to the Son of Heaven extending to the service to the impersonator of the dead in the ancestral temple, this being the Way of the complete minister. *What is looked for in a friend to do first, I am not yet able to do*: If you wish to seek kindness and graciousness from a friend towards yourself, then you first ought to extend kindness and graciousness towards that friend. *In the practise of constant virtue and the attention to constant speech*: *Yong* 庸 is equivalent to *chang* 常. This means that in cultivating yourself there should be constancy in the practice of virtue and constancy in the attention to speech.

6.1　*If there are deficiencies, one dare not fail to strive [to make them good]*: This says that, if one's intended action has some deficiency in it, then one dares not fail to strive to [make it good].

6.2　*If there are excesses, one dare not fail to curb them*: This says that, if one's intended action is excessive, one should constantly maintain a humility towards others and not dare to fail to curb one's intended action to surpass others. *Words should have regard to actions*: Let words not exceed actions; constantly give attention to actions.

6.3　*Actions should have regard to words*: Let actions be supported by words; that is to say, be constant in giving attention to words.

7.1　*If this is so, then how is the noble man not honest*: "*Zao zao* 慥慥 is the appearance of maintaining a true correspondence between words and actions." *Hu* 胡 is like *he* 何 (interrogative). Since he has regard for the mutual correspondence between words and actions, how can the noble man fail to achieve honesty in the Way of maintaining a true correspondence between words and actions?

8.1 「君子素其位而行，不願乎其外」至「行乎患難」，素，鄉也。鄉其所居之
     位，而行其所行之事，不願行在位外之事。《論語》云：「君子思不出其位
     也。」[33] 鄉富貴之中，行道於富貴，謂不驕、不淫也。鄉貧賤之中，則行
     道於貧賤，謂不諂、不懾也。鄉夷狄之中，行道於夷狄，夷狄雖陋，雖
     隨其俗而守道不改。鄉患難之中，行道於患難，而臨危不傾，守死於善
     道也。

8.2 「君子無入而不自得焉」者，言君子所入之處，皆守善道。在上位不陵
     下，此「素富貴行富貴」也。若身處富貴，依我常正之性，不使富貴以陵
     人。若以富貴陵人，是不行富貴之道。

9.1 「在下位不援上」者，此「素貧賤行貧賤」也。援，牽持也。若身處貧賤則
     安之，宜令自樂，不得援牽富貴。若以援牽富貴，是不行貧賤之道。

10.1 「正己而不求於人，則無怨」，此「素夷狄行夷狄」也。若身入夷狄，夷狄
     無禮義，當自正己而行，不得求於彼人，則彼人無怨己者。《論語》云：
     「言忠信，行篤敬，雖之夷狄，不可棄。」[34]

10.2 「上不怨天，下不尤人」，此「素患難行患難」也。尤，過也，責也。苟皆
     應之患難，則亦甘為，不得上怨天下尤人，故《論語》云：「不怨天，不尤
     人」[35] 是也。

---

33   *Lunyu* XIV.28, LCC, 1:286. The statement is made by Zengzi 曾子.
34   This is not an exact quotation; see *Lunyu* XV.5, LCC, 1:296 and XIII.19, LCC, 1:271.
35   *Lunyu* XIV.37(2), LCC, 1:288.

8.1 *The noble man occupies his position and acts [accordingly]. He does not wish to go beyond this to his actions are appropriate to misfortune and hardship*: Su 素 is equivalent to *xiang* 鄉 (towards, to). *Xiang* is the position which he occupies and his actions in the matters in which he acts—he does not wish to act outside the matters pertaining to his position. The *Lunyu* says: "The noble man in his thoughts does not go beyond his position." When his position is in the midst of wealth and honour, he practises the Way pertaining to wealth and honour, which is to say that he is neither arrogant nor dissolute. When his position is in the midst of poverty and lowliness, he follows the Way pertaining to poverty and lowliness, which is to say he is neither obsequious nor faint-hearted. When his position is in the midst of the Yi and Di, he practises the Way pertaining to the Yi and Di; although the Yi and Di are rustic, he nevertheless follows their customs and maintains the Way without changing. When his position is in the midst of misfortune and hardship, he follows the Way pertaining to misfortune and hardship. He faces danger without flinching and accepts death in the goodness of the Way.

8.2 *The noble man does not enter and not be at ease [with himself]*: This says that, whatever place the noble man enters, in all cases he preserves the Way of goodness. In a superior position, he does not insult inferiors. This is *to occupy a position of wealth and honour and act appropriately to wealth and honour*. If he is in a position of wealth and honour, he relies on a nature of constancy and correctness and does not allow wealth and honour to be used to insult others. If he uses wealth and honour to insult others, this is not practising the Way of wealth and honour.

9.1 *When he occupies a lowly position, he does not cling to superiors*: This is *if he occupies a position of poverty and lowliness, his actions are appropriate to poverty and lowliness*. *Yuan* 援 is equivalent to *qianchi* 牽持 (to join with and hold onto). If he himself is in a position of poverty and lowliness, then he is at ease with it. He rightly allows himself to be happy and does not attempt to grasp and hold on to wealth and honour. If he grasps and holds on to wealth and honour, this is not to practise the Way of poverty and lowliness.

10.1 *He rectifies himself and asks nothing of others; then he is without resentment*: This is *if he occupies a position among the Yi and Di, his actions are in accord with the Yi and Di*. If he himself enters the Yi and Di [regions] and the Yi and Di are without *li* 禮 and *yi* 義, it is proper for him to correct himself and act, but not make demands on others. Then others will harbour no resentment towards him. The *Lunyu* says: "Let his words be loyal and trustworthy and his actions genuine and respectful; then, although he is among the Yi and Di, he cannot be cast aside."

10.2 *Above, he does not find fault with Heaven; below, he does not blame others*: That is, *if he occupies a position of misfortune and hardship, his actions are appropriate to misfortune and hardship*. *You* 尤 is equivalent to *guo* 過 and to *ze* 責 (to find fault, blame). In all cases, if one is responding to misfortune and hardship, then one should do so willingly and not be resentful towards Heaven above or blame other people below. Thus, the *Lunyu* saying: "[The Master said, I] do not feel resentment towards Heaven, I do not blame others" is this.

11.1 「故君子居易以俟命」者，易，謂平安也。言君子以道自處，恒居平安之中，以聽待天命也。

11.2 「小人行險以徼幸」，小人以惡自居，恒行險難傾危之事以徼求榮幸之道，《論語》曰「不仁者，不可以久處約」[36]是也。

ZY9: 子曰：「射有似乎君子，失諸正鵠，反求諸其身。**[1]**君子之道，辟如行遠必自邇，辟如登高必自卑。**[2]**《詩》曰：『妻子好合，如鼓瑟琴。兄弟既翕，和樂且耽。宜爾室家，樂爾妻帑。』」**[3]**
子曰：「父母其順矣乎！」**[4]**

Comment: This section begins with a statement of the Way of the noble man being like both archery and going on a journey, and continues with a quotation from the *Odes*. The meaning is clear—the individual is himself responsible for any failings in his pursuit of the Way which is something near at hand. The final statement, in Zheng Xuan's interpretation, is taken as a comment on the *Odes* quotation. Kong Yingda's observations on this appear to be missing (see his note 4.1). Zhu Xi's arrangement of this material is slightly different.

注 ZY9 (鄭玄)

[1] 反求於其身，不以怨人。畫曰正，[37]棲皮曰鵠。{正音征，注同。鵠，古毒反，注同。}正、鵠皆鳥名也。一曰正，正也。鵠，直也。大射則張皮侯而棲鵠，賓射張布侯而設正也。{棲，細兮反。}

[2] 自，從也。邇，近也。行之以近者、卑者，始以漸致之高遠。{辟音譬，下同。邇音爾。卑音婢，又如字，注同。}

[3] 琴瑟，聲相應和也。翕，合也。耽，亦樂也。古者謂子孫曰「帑」，此《詩》言和室家之道，自近者始。{好，呼報反。翕，許急反。樂音洛，下及注同。耽，丁南反。帑音奴，子孫也，本又作孥，同，《尚書傳》、《毛詩》箋並云「子」也，杜預注《左傳》云：「妻子也。」應，應對之應。和，胡臥反。}

[4] 謂其教令行，使室家順。

---

36   *Lunyu* IV.2, LCC, 1:165.
37   There is a question as to whether *bu* 布 should be included to follow *hua* 畫—see SSJZS (2001 edition), "Zhongyong," 28:1674n1.

11.1   *Therefore the noble man dwells in equanimity and accepts his lot*: *Yi* 易 refers to *ping'an* 平安 (peace, tranquility, equanimity). This says that the noble man situates himself in the Way and constantly dwells in the midst of equanimity by listening to and accepting Heaven's decree.

11.2   *The lesser man acts dangerously in the pursuit of good fortune*: The lesser man situates himself in what is bad and constantly does difficult and dangerous things in his pursuit of good fortune. The *Lunyu* saying, "Someone who is not *ren* 仁 cannot long abide poverty" is this.

ZY9: The Master said: "The archer is like the noble man—if he fails to hit the target, he turns and places the blame on himself. [1] The Way of the noble man may be compared to travelling a long distance—one must start from nearby. It may be compared to scaling a height—one must start from below. [2] The *Odes* says: 'Happy accord with one's wife and children is like the playing of zither and lute; in accord between older and younger brothers, there is harmonious joy and pleasure. Let all be as it should be in your household, and there will be joy among your wife and offspring.'" [3]
The Master said: "Surely this accords with the parents' wishes." [4]

Notes ZY9 (Zheng Xuan)

[1] *He turns and places the blame on himself* is not to be resentful of another. The cloth target is called the *zheng* 正; the skin target is called the *gu* 鵠. . . . *Zheng* 正 and *gu* 鵠 are both bird names. The one called *zheng* 正 is horizontal. The *gu* 鵠 is vertical. The *Dashe* (principal archer) draws his bow and shoots at a leather target and a roosting owl. The *Binshe* (guest archer) draws his bow and shoots at a cloth target and a *zheng* 正 that is set up. . . .
[2] *Zi* 自 is equivalent to *cong* 從 (from). *Er* 邇 is equivalent to *jin* 近 (near). In going from what is near and low, one starts gradually to advance to what is high and distant. . . .
[3] The *qin* 琴 and the *se* 瑟 have sounds that respond to each other harmoniously. *Xi* 翕 is equivalent to *he* 合 (harmony). *Dan* 耽 is also *le* 樂 (joy, pleasure). Ancients, in referring to descendants, said *nu* 帑. This is the *Odes* saying that the Way of bringing harmony to a household has its beginning from what is near. . . .
[4] This says that the teaching of the prescribed path causes the household to be compliant.

疏 ZY9 (孔穎達)

{「子曰」至「妻帑」。}

1.1   《正義》曰：以上言行道在於己身，故此一節覆明行道在身之事，以射譬之。

1.2   「射有似乎君子」者，言凡人之射，有似乎君子之道。

1.3   「失諸正鵠，反求諸其身」者，諸，於也；求，責也；正，謂賓射之侯；鵠，謂大射之侯。言射者失於正鵠，謂矢不中正鵠。不責他人，反鄉自責其身，言君子之人，失道於外，亦反自責於己。

2.1   「君子之道，譬如行遠必自邇，譬如登高必自卑」者，自，從也；邇，近也；卑，下也。行之以遠者近之始，升之以高者卑之始，言以漸至高遠。不云近者遠始，卑者高始，但勤行其道於身，然後能被於物，而可謂之高遠耳。

3.1   「《詩》云妻子好合，如鼓瑟琴。兄弟既翕，和樂且耽」，此〈小雅‧常棣〉之篇，美文王之詩。記人引此者，言行道之法自近始，猶如詩人之所云，欲和遠人，先和其妻子兄弟，故云妻子好合，情意相得，如似鼓彈瑟與琴，音聲相和也。兄弟盡皆翕合，情意和樂且復耽之。耽之者，是相好之甚也。「宜爾室家，樂爾妻帑」者，宜善爾之室家，愛樂爾之妻帑。帑，子也。古者謂子孫為帑，故〈甘誓〉云：「予則帑戮汝。」[38] 於人則妻子為帑，於鳥則鳥尾為帑。《左傳》云「以害鳥帑」[39] 是也。

---

[38]   See the *Documents*, LCC, 3:155.

[39]   See the *Zuo zhuan* for the 28th year of Duke Xiang, LCC, 5:537.

Commentary ZY9 (Kong Yingda)

1.1 The *Zhengyi* says that, because the earlier statement is that to practise the Way lies in oneself, so in this particular section it again clarifies the matter of the putting into practice the Way lying in the self, taking archery as an example.

1.2 *The archer is like the noble man*: This says that for ordinary men, archery is like the Way for noble men.

1.3 *If he fails to hit the target, he turns and places the blame on himself*: *Zhu* 諸 is equivalent to *yu* 於 (on). *Qiu* 求 is equivalent to *ze* 責 (to blame). *Zheng* 正 refers to the "guest" archer's target. *Gu* 鵠 refers to the "principal" archer's target. This speaks of the archer failing to hit the *zheng* 正 or the *gu* 鵠 and refers to the arrow not hitting the centre of the target. Not putting the blame on others, but turning towards and putting the blame on himself speaks of the noble man as a person who, when he misses the Way in what is external, also turns and places the blame on himself.

2.1 *The Way of the noble man may be compared to travelling a long distance—one must start from nearby. It may be compared to scaling a height—one must start from below*: *Zi* 自 is equivalent to *cong* 從 (from); *er* 邇 is equivalent to *jin* 近 (near); *bei* 卑 is equivalent to *xia* 下 (below). One who travels a long distance starts from nearby; one who scales a height starts from a low point. This speaks of gradually reaching what is high or distant. It does not say that what is near is the start of what is distant or that what is low is the start of what is high. Rather, one starts to practise this Way in oneself and afterwards one is able to extend it to things, and this can be referred to as high and distant.

3.1 *The Odes says: "Happy accord with one's wife and children is like the playing of zither and lute; in accord between older and younger brothers, there is harmonious joy and pleasure"*: This is from the *Odes*, "Xiao ya," "Chang di" which is a poem in praise of King Wen. The [*Li*] *ji* in recording and quoting this is saying that the method of practising the Way starts from near at hand. As the poet says, if you wish to have harmonious accord with those who are distant, you must first have harmonious accord with wives, older and younger brothers, so he speaks of "happy accord with wife." Emotions and intentions are in mutual agreement, which is like the playing of zither and lute where the sounds are in harmony. When older and younger brothers are all completely in accord, emotions and intentions are harmonious and, moreover, pleasureable. What is pleasureable is this great degree of mutual love. As regards, *let all be as it should be in your household, and there will be joy among your wife and offspring*, if there is the proper goodness in the household, there is love and happiness with wife and children. *Nu* 帑 is equivalent to *zi* 子 (children). The ancients referred to descendants as *nu* 帑. Thus, the "Gan shi" said: "I will then put your descendants to death." Among people, then, wives and children are *nu* 帑 (dependants) and among birds, then, *niao wei* 鳥尾 is *nu* 帑 (a star). The *Zuo zhuan* saying, "by harming the *niao wei*" is this.

4.1 「子曰父母其順矣乎」者。

4.2 《正義》曰：因上和於遠人，先和室家，故此一經次之。「父母其順矣乎」，謂父母能以教令行乎室家，其和順矣乎。言中庸之道，先使室家和順，乃能和順於外，即上云道不遠、施諸己。

ZY10: 子曰：「鬼神之為德，其盛矣乎！視之而弗見，聽之而弗聞，體物而不可遺。[1]使天下之人，齊明盛服，以承祭祀。洋洋乎如在其上，如在其左右。[2]《詩》曰：『神之格思，不可度思，矧可射思。』[3]夫微之顯，誠之不可揜，如此夫。」[4]

Comment: It has been suggested that this section is incorrectly placed here on the grounds that reference to ghosts and spirits is inconsistent with the Confucius of the *Analects*.[40] Both texts have it here, however, without further comment. The majority of translators render *de* 德 here as power or efficacy rather than virtue. We have preferred to retain the use of "virtue" on the grounds of consistency and because it includes the senses of moral excellence and efficacy. There is variation in whether *jian* 見 and *wen* 聞 are taken as active or passive in the opening sentence. Both seem possible—for example, "look for them and they are not to be seen etc." This difference is insignificant as regards meaning. *Cheng* 誠, which is the primary focus of the last part of the work, appears here. It is romanised on the grounds presented in the introduction. Purity, truth, genuineness, authenticity, sincerity and creativity are all possible as single English equivalents, but none is comprehensive enough alone to give the term its proper weight.

注 ZY10 (鄭玄)

[1] 體，猶生也。可，猶所也。不有所遺，言萬物無不以鬼神之氣生也。

[2] 明，猶潔也。洋洋，人想思其傍僾之貌。{齊，側皆反，本亦作齋。洋音羊。傍，皇薄剛反，謂左右也，徐方岡反。僾，徐於愷反，又音愛。}

---

40   By Takeuchi Yoshio (1979)—see Ames, T. Roger and David L. Hall, *Focusing the Familiar: A Translation and Philosophical Interpretation of the Zhongyong* (Honolulu: University of Hawai'i Press, 2001), 124n40.

4.1   *The Master said: "Surely this accords with the parents' wishes."* . . .

4.2   The *Zhengyi* says that because, above, there was accord with those who were distant, there was first harmony within the household. Therefore, this particular section places them in this order. *Surely this accords with the parents' wishes* refers to the parents being able, by teaching the prescribed conduct within the household, to bring about harmony and compliance. This says that the Way of using the centre first causes the household to be harmonious and compliant, and then is able to effect harmony and compliance beyond [the family]. This, then, is what was said earlier—that the Way is not distant and is brought about in the self.

ZY10: The Master said: "In their being virtuous, how great are ghosts and spirits! Look for them, and you do not see them; listen for them, and you do not hear them. Nevertheless, they give rise to things and neglect nothing. **[1]** They cause the people of the world to fast and purify themselves, and to put on fine clothes to attend to the sacrifices. They circulate and fill [the world]. It is as if they are above and to the left and right. **[2]** The *Odes* says: 'The coming of spirits cannot be determined. How much less can one weary of them.' **[3]** Moreover, the manifestation of the obscure and the impossibility of concealing *cheng* 誠 are like this!" **[4]**

Notes ZY10 (Zheng Xuan)

[1] *Ti* 體 is like *sheng* 生 (to give rise to, beget). *Ke* 可 is like *suo* 所 (what, that which). *They neglect nothing* says that, of the ten thousand things, there is not one that is not born of the *qi* 氣 (vital spirit) of ghosts and spirits.

[2] *Ming* 明 is like *jie* 潔 (clean, pure). *Yang yang* 洋洋 is the appearance of people imagining ghosts and spirits all around them . . .

[3] 格，來也。矧，況也。射，厭也。思，皆聲之助。言神之來，其形象不可億度而知，事之盡敬而已，況可厭倦乎。{格，古百反。度，待洛反，注同。矧，詩忍反，注同。射音亦。厭，於豔反，字又作「懕」，下同。盡，子忍反。}

[4] 言神無形而著，不言而誠。{揜音掩，於檢反。此夫音扶。著，張慮反。}

疏 ZY10 (孔穎達)

{「子曰」至「此夫」。}

1.1　《正義》曰：此一節明鬼神之道無形，而能顯著誠信。中庸之道與鬼神之道相似，亦從微至著，不言而自誠也。

1.2　「體物而不可遺」者，體，猶生也；可，猶所也。言萬物生而有形體，故云「體物而不可遺」者，言鬼神之道，生養萬物，無不周徧而不有所遺，言萬物無以鬼神之氣生也。

2.1　「使天下之人，齊明盛服，以承祭祀」者，明，猶絜也。言鬼神能生養萬物，故天下之人齊戒明絜，盛飾衣服以承祭祀。

2.2　「洋洋乎如在其上，如在其左右」者，言鬼神之形狀，人想像之，如在人之上，如在人之左右，想見其形也。

3.1　「《詩》曰：神之格思，不可度思，矧可射思」者，格，來也；思，辭也；矧，況也；射，厭也。此〈大雅・抑〉之篇，[41] 刺厲王之詩。詩人刺時人祭祀懈倦，故云神之來至，以其無形不可度知，恒須恭敬，況於祭祀之末可厭倦之乎？言不可厭倦也。記者引《詩》，明鬼神之所尊敬也。

41　*Odes*, Mao 256, verse 7, LCC, 4:515.

[3] *Ge* 格 is equivalent to *lai* 來 (to come). *Shen* 矧 is equivalent to *kuang* 況 (how much more/still less). *Yi* 射 is equivalent to *yan* 厭 (to weary of, dislike, resent). *Si* 思 in all cases is a particle. This says that when spirits come their form and appearance cannot be determined and known. Serve them with complete reverence and that is all. How much less can one weary of them. . . .

[4] This says that spirits have no form yet they are manifest; they are without words yet they are *cheng* 誠. . . .

Commentary ZY10 (Kong Yingda)

1.1 The *Zhengyi* says that this particular section makes it clear that the Way of ghosts and spirits is without form yet can manifest and display *cheng* 誠 and *xin* 信. The Way of using the centre and the Way of ghosts and spirits are very similar in that both go from the obscure to the manifest, are without words, and yet are naturally *cheng* 誠.

1.2 *They give rise to things and neglect nothing*: *Ti* 體 is like *sheng* 生 (to give rise, beget); *ke* 可 is like *suo* 所 (what, that which). This says that the ten thousand things arise and have form and substance. Therefore it says, *they give rise to things and neglect nothing*. That is to say, the Way of ghosts and spirits gives rise to and nurtures the ten thousand things, is everywhere, and there is nothing without it. It says that the ten thousand things without exception are born of the *qi* (vital spirit) of ghosts and spirits.

2.1 *They cause the people of the world to fast and purify themselves, and to put on fine clothes to attend to the sacrifices*: *Ming* 明 is like *jie* 絜 (pure, clean). This says that ghosts and spirits are able to give rise to and nurture the ten thousand things, therefore the people of the world fast and purify [themselves], and adorn [themselves] with garments in order to undertake the sacrifices.

2.2 *They circulate and fill the world as if they are above and to the left and right*: This says that the appearance of ghosts and spirits, as people imagine it, is like seeing the forms of people above and to the left and right.

3.1 *The Odes says: "The coming of spirits cannot be determined. How much less can one weary of them"*: *Ge* 格 is equivalent to *lai* 來 (to come); *si* 思 is a particle; *shen* 矧 is equivalent to *kuang* 況 (how much more/less); *yi* 射 is equivalent to *yan* 厭 (to weary of, dislike, resent). This is the ode "Yi" from the "Da ya" and is a poem criticising King Li. The poet criticises the people of the time as being remiss and lazy in their sacrifices. Therefore, he says that the spirits come, but because they are without form, they cannot be evaluated or known, so they must be constantly honoured and revered. How can one weary of them at the end of sacrifices? This says that it is not possible to weary [of them]. The [*Li*] *ji* quotes the *Odes* to make it clear that ghosts and spirits are to be respected and honoured.

4.1　「夫微之顯」者，言鬼神之狀微昧不見，而精靈與人為吉凶，是「從微之顯」也。

4.2　「誠之不可揜」者，言鬼神誠信，不可揜蔽。善者必降之以福，惡者必降之以禍。「如此夫」者，此詩人所云，何可厭倦？夫，語助也。此鬼神即與《易•繫辭》云「是故知鬼神之情狀，與天地相似」，[42] 以能生萬物也。案彼注：「木火之神生物，金水之鬼終物。」彼以春夏對秋冬，故以春夏生物，秋冬終物。其實鬼神皆能生物、終物也。故此云「體物而不可遺」。此雖說陰陽鬼神，人之鬼神亦附陰陽之鬼神，故此云「齊明盛服，以承祭祀」，是兼人之鬼神也。

ZY11：子曰：「舜其大孝也與？德為聖人，尊為天子，富有四海之內，宗廟饗之，子孫保之。[1]故大德必得其位，必得其祿，必得其名，必得其壽。[2]故天之生物，必因其材而篤焉。[3]故栽者培之，傾者覆之。[4]《詩》曰：『嘉樂君子，憲憲令德。宜民宜人，受祿于天。保佑命之，自天申之。』故大德者必受命。」[5]

42　*Yi jing*, "Ji ci," SSJZS, 1:147.

4.1   *Moreover, the manifestion of the obscure*: This says that the form of ghosts and
      spirits is subtle and obscure and not seen, and in an ethereal fashion they are
      linked with people and with good and bad fortune. This is *the manifestation of
      the obscure*.

4.2   *The impossibility of concealing cheng* 誠: This says that ghosts and spirits are *cheng* 誠
      and *xin* 信 and cannot be concealed. For those who are good, they inevitably send
      down good fortune; for those who are bad, they inevitably send down misfortune.
      Ru ci fu 如此夫 (are like this!) is what the poet says—how can one weary of them?
      Fu 夫 is an auxiliary word. This links ghosts and spirits with the "Commentary"
      of the *Yi* [*jing*] which says: "This is why we know that the circumstances of ghosts
      and spirits and Heaven and Earth are similar." It is because they are able to give
      rise to the ten thousand things. According to another note, "the spirits of wood and
      fire give rise to things; the spirits of metal and water bring things to an end." In
      that, spring and summer are taken to be opposite to autumn and winter. Therefore,
      spring and summer give rise to things and autumn and winter bring them to an
      end. In truth, ghosts and spirits can both give rise to things and bring things to an
      end. Therefore this says, *they give rise to things and neglect nothing*. Although this
      speaks of *yin* and *yang* ghosts and spirits, the ghosts and spirits of people are also
      dependent on the ghosts and spirits of *yin* and *yang*. Therefore, this says, *they fast
      and purify themselves, and put on fine clothes to attend to the sacrifices*. This connects
      the ghosts and spirits of people.

ZY11: The Master said: "Great, indeed, was Shun's filial piety. His virtue was
that of a sage; his honour was that of the Son of Heaven; he was rich in having
all within the four seas. There were sacrifices to him in the ancestral temple
and his descendants were content with them. **[1]** Thus, [being a man of] great
virtue, he necessarily gained his position, he necessarily attained his prosperity,
he necessarily acquired his reputation, and he necessarily achieved longevity. **[2]** Therefore Heaven, in its giving rise to things, invariably acts in accord
with their natural dispositions and is bountiful. Things that are growing, it
increases; things that are decaying, it brings down. **[3]** The *Odes* says:

> Blessed and happy is the prince,
> flourishing is his goodness and virtue.
> He acts properly towards the people and officers,
> he receives prosperity from Heaven.
> Heaven is content with him and helps him,
> Heaven grants him the mandate,
> And from Heaven this is repeated. **[4]**

Therefore, one with great virtue necessarily receives the mandate." **[5]**

Comment: In this statement of praise for one of the recurring paradigms, the Emperor Shun, the meaning is clear. Shun demonstrated great filial piety and great virtue. It was because of the latter that he gained the mandate from Heaven, and therefore his position, as well as his material well-being, his reputation and his famed longevity. Several issues in translation are as follows: (i) Whether Shun sacrificed or was sacrificed to in the ancestral temple and how *bao* 保 is to be understood in sentence 1. (ii) Whether *da de* 大德 is to be taken impersonally or specifically associated with Shun in sentence 2. (iii) The readings of *cai* 材 and *du* 篤 in sentence 3. (iv) The readings of *zai* 栽 and *pei* 培 in sentence 4. (v) The substitution of *jia* 嘉 for *jia* 假 and the reading of *bao* 保 again in the quotation from the *Odes*. In all instances, the views of the commentators, where they are clear, are followed. At a more general level, there is the issue of why, if great virtue brings position, wealth, reputation and longevity, it so spectacularly failed to do so in the case of Confucius himself. This question is addressed in part by Kong Yingda in his note 2.1 where he refers to two works now lost.

注 ZY11 (鄭玄)

[1] 保，安也。{與音餘。}

[2] 名，令聞也。{聞音問，下令聞同。}

[3] 材，謂其質性也。篤，厚也。言善者天厚其福，惡者天厚其毒，皆由其本而為之。

[4] 栽讀如「文王初載」之「載」。栽猶殖也。培，益也。今時人名草木之殖曰「栽」，築牆立板亦曰「栽」，栽或為「茲」。覆，敗也。{栽，依注音災，將才反，注同，植也。培，蒲回反。覆，芳伏反。載之載並音災，本或作哉，同。}

[5] 憲憲，興盛之貌。保，安也。佑，助也。{嘉，戶嫁反，《詩》本作「假」，音同。假，嘉也，皇音加，善也。憲音顯，注同，一音如字。佑音祐，下注同。}

疏 ZY11 (孔穎達)

{「子曰」至「受命」。}

1.1　《正義》曰：此一節明中庸之德，故能富有天下，受天之命也。

1.2　「子孫保之」者，師説云：[43] <u>舜</u>禪與<u>禹</u>，何言保者，此子孫承保祭祀，故云「保」。<u>周</u>時<u>陳國</u>是<u>舜</u>之後。

---

[43]　It is not clear whether this is a particular work or not. The term *shi shuo* 師説 is equivalent to *shi jiao* 師教, the *shi* 師 being an instructor in morals to the emperor—see *Odes*, Mao 2, verse 3, LCC, 4:7.

Notes ZY11 (Zheng Xuan)

[1] *Bao* 保 is equivalent to *an* 安 (to arrange, be content with). . . .

[2] *Ming* 名 is equivalent to *ling wen* 令聞 (fine reputation). . . .

[3] *Cai* 材 refers to their disposition and nature. *Du* 篤 is equivalent to *hou* 厚 (generous, bountiful). This says that, in the case of those who are good, Heaven is generous with its good fortune; in the case of those who are evil, it is substantial in its harm. In both cases it does this from its essential nature.

[4] *Zai* 栽 is read like *zai* 載 in "*Wen wang chu zai* 文王初載" (when King Wen was in his early years). *Zai* 栽 is like *zhi* 殖 (to plant, set up, prosper). *Pei* 培 is equivalent to *yi* 益 (to increase). People of the present time, in describing the planting of grass and trees, say *zai* 栽; in building walls and setting up planks, they also say *zai* 栽. *Zai* 栽 is sometimes written *zi* 茲. *Fu* 覆 is equivalent to *bai* 敗 (to overturn, defeat). . . .

[5] *Xian xian* 憲憲 is the appearance of increase and flourishing. *Bao* 保 is equivalent to *an* 安 (to arrange, be content with). *You* 佑 is equivalent to *zhu* 助 (to help). . . .

Commentary ZY11 (Kong Yingda)

1.1   The *Zhengyi* states that this particular section clarifies the virtue of "using the centre." Therefore, he (the ruler) can be rich, having all under Heaven and receiving the mandate of Heaven.

1.2   *His descendants were content with them*: The teacher of morals ("Teacher's Explanations") says that Shun abdicated to Yu so how can we say *bao* 保? This is that his descendants carried on and were content with the sacrifices, therefore *bao* 保 is used. In Zhou times, the state of Chen was the posterity of Shun.

2.1 「故大德必得其位」者，以其德大能覆養天下，故「必得其位」。如孔子有大德而無其位，以不應王錄，雖有大德，而無其位也。案《援神契》云：「丘為制法，主黑綠，不代蒼黃。」言孔子黑龍之精，不合代周家木德之蒼也。《孔演圖》又云「聖人不空生，必有所制以顯天心，丘為木鐸制天下法」是也。[44]「必得其壽」者，據舜言之，而夫子不長壽，以勤憂故也。

3.1 「故天之生物，必因其材而篤焉」，材謂質性也；篤，厚也。言天之所生，隨物質性而厚之。善者因厚其福，舜、禹是也；惡者因厚其毒，桀、紂是也。故四凶黜而舜受禪也。

3.2 「故栽者培之，傾者覆之」，栽，殖也；培，益也。言道德自能豐殖，則天因而培益之。

3.3 「傾者覆之」者，若無德自取傾危者，天亦因而覆敗之也。

{注「栽讀」至「曰栽」。}

3.4 《正義》曰：「栽讀如文王初載之載」者，案《詩•大明》云：「文王初載，天作之合。」[45] 彼注云：「載，識也。言文王生適有所識，天為之生配，謂生大姒。」此載為栽殖者，載容兩義，亦得為識，亦得為殖。此對傾者覆之，故以為殖。云「築牆立板亦曰栽」者，案莊二十九年《左傳》云：「水昏正而栽」，[46] 謂立板築也。

---

44 Both these works, the *Yuanshenqi* 援神契 and the *Kongyantu* 孔演圖 (or *Yankongtu*) are now lost. The former was an excursus on the *Xiao jing* and the latter on the *Chunqiu* 春秋.

45 *Odes*, Mao 236, verse 4, LCC, 4:434.

46 *Zuo zhuan*, Duke Zhang, 29th year, LCC, 5:116 (trans. after Legge).

2.1   *Thus, [being a man of] great virtue, he necessarily gained his position*: Because his
      virtue was great, he was able to again nurture all under Heaven. Therefore, *he*
      necessarily gained his position. Confucius equally had great virtue, yet he did not
      have this position because he was not chosen as a king, so although he had great
      virtue, he did not have his position. According to the *Yuanshenqi*, it says: "Confucius
      created and established laws, he made black and green primary, and he did not
      substitute azure and yellow." This says that Confucius' black dragon spirit did
      not accord with or replace the green of the wood virtue in the Zhou house. Also,
      the *Kongyantu* saying: "A sage is not born for nothing, but must have that which
      he establishes to manifest his heavenly mind. Confucius created the bell with the
      wooden clapper to establish the world's laws" is this. In the case of *he necessarily*
      achieved longevity, this can be said about Shun, but the Master did not reach old
      age, which is why he is diligently mourned.

3.1   *Therefore Heaven, in its giving rise to things, invariably acts in accord with their*
      natural dispositions and is bountiful: Cai 材 refers to disposition and nature (*zhi*
      質 and *xing* 性); *du* 篤 is equivalent to *hou* 厚 (generous, bountiful, substantial).
      This says that in giving rise to things, Heaven invariably follows their dispositions
      and natures and is bountiful towards them. In the case of those who are good, it
      is generous with its good fortune—Shun and Yu were such. In the case of those
      who are bad, it is substantial in being harmful—Jie and Zhou were such. There-
      fore, the "four evils"[47] were cast out and Shun received the crown.

3.2   *Things that are growing, it increases; things that are decaying, it brings down*: Zai 栽
      is equivalent to *zhi* 殖 (to plant); *pei* 培 is equivalent to *yi* 益 (to increase). This
      says that the Way and virtue are themselves able to prosper and flourish. Then
      Heaven responds and further increases them.

3.3   *Things that are decaying, it brings down*: If those without virtue spontaneously
      choose dangerous courses, Heaven also responds and brings them down.

3.4   The *Zhengyi* states that *zai* 栽 is read like *zai* 載 in "*Wen wang chu zai* 文王初
      載." According to the *Odes*, "Da ming" it says: "When King Wen was in his
      early years, Heaven created a match for him." The other notes say: "*Zai* 載 is
      equivalent to *shi* 識 (to know, recognise). This says that, when King Wen bore
      an heir and this was known, Heaven created for him a mate who was referred to
      as Tai Si 太姒." On *zai* 載 being *zaizhi* 栽植 (to plant, prosper), *zai* 載 contains
      two meanings: that of *shi* 識 (to know, recognize) and that of *zhi* 殖 (to plant,
      prosper). Because here this is opposite to *things that are decaying, it brings down*,
      it is taken to be *zhi* 殖 (to plant, prosper). In the case of saying "building a wall
      or setting up planks," it was also called *zai* 栽. In the *Zuo zhuan* for the 29th year
      of Duke Zhuang it says: "When Mercury culminates at dusk the work should be
      going on." This speaks of setting up planks and building.

---

[47]   See the *Documents*, "Canon of Shun," LCC, 3:39–40.

4.1   「《詩》曰：嘉樂君子，憲憲令德」，此〈大雅・嘉樂〉之篇，[48] 美成王之詩。
         嘉，善也。憲憲，興盛之貌，詩人言善樂君子，此成王憲憲然，有令善
         之德。案《詩》本文「憲憲」為「顯顯」，與此不同者，齊、魯、韓《詩》與
         《毛詩》不同故也。

5.1   「宜民宜人，受祿於天。保佑命之，自天申之。故大德者必受命」者，
         宜民，謂宜養萬民，宜人，謂宜官人。其德如此，故受福于天。佑，助
         也。保，安也。天乃保安作助，命之為天子，又申重福之。作《記》者，
         引證大德必受命之義，則舜之為也。

ZY12: 子曰：「無憂者，其唯文王乎？以王季為父，以武王為子，父作
之，子述之。[1]武王纘大王、王季、文王之緒。壹戎衣而有天下，身
不失天下之顯名，尊為天子，富有四海之內，宗廟饗之，子孫保之。[2]
武王末受命，周公成文、武之德，追王大王、王季，上祀先公以天子之
禮。斯禮也，達乎諸侯、大夫及士、庶人。父為大夫，子為士，葬以大
夫，祭以士。父為士，子為大夫，葬以士，祭以大夫。期之喪，達乎大
夫。三年之喪，達乎天子，父母之喪，無貴賤一也。」[3]

---

48   See the *Odes*, Mao 249, verse 1, LCC, 4:481 and Legge's note on *jia* 假 versus *jia* 嘉 in
        the opening line.

4.1   *The Odes says: "Blessed and happy is the prince, flourishing is his goodness and vir-*
        tue": This is the "Jia Le" ode from the "Da ya" and is a poem in praise of King
        Cheng. *Jia* 嘉 is equivalent to *shan* 善 (good). *Xian xian* 憲憲 is the appearance
        of increase and flourishing. The poet is speaking of the good and happy ruler,
        this being King Cheng in his prosperity, and of his having the virtue of manifest
        goodness. In the original text of the *Odes*, *xian xian* 憲憲 was written *xian xian*
        顯顯 and this is not the same. The Qi, Lu and Han *Odes* do not have the same
        source as the Mao *Odes*.

5.1   *He acts properly towards the people and officers, he receives prosperity from Heaven.*
        Heaven is content with him and helps him. Heaven grants him the mandate, and from
        Heaven this is repeated. Therefore, one with great virtue necessarily receives the man-
        date: *Yi min* 宜民 refers to appropriately nourishing the ten thousand people; *yi ren*
        宜人 refers to appropriately [nurturing] officers. Because his virtue was like this,
        he received good fortune from Heaven. *You* 佑 is equivalent to *zhu* 助 (to help,
        aid). *Bao* 保 is equivalent to *an* 安 (to arrange, be content with). Heaven then was
        content with and assisted him, decreeing that he be the Son of Heaven, and it also
        substantially extended his good fortune. The [*Li*] *ji* quotes it to prove the meaning
        of great virtue necessarily receiving the mandate, Shun being such a case.

ZY12: The Master said: "Why was King Wen the only one who had no grief?
Because King Ji was his father and King Wu was his son, [he had] a father
who created [the foundation] and a son who continued [his Way]. **[1]** King
Wu carried on the work of Tai Wang, King Ji and King Wen. As one man he
took up arms, overthrew Yin, and gained possession of all under Heaven without losing his distinguished reputation in the world. He was honoured as the
Son of Heaven and was enriched by having all within the Four Seas. Sacrifices
were offered to him in the ancestral temple and his descendants were content
with them. **[2]** King Wu was old when he received the mandate. The Duke
of Zhou completed the virtuous [course] of Wen and Wu. He retrospectively
honoured Tai Wang and King Ji as kings, and sacrificed to the former dukes
preceding them, using the rites of the Son of Heaven. These rites he extended
to feudal lords and great officers as well as to ordinary officers and the common people. If the father was a great officer and the son was an ordinary officer, the burial was that of a great officer and the sacrifice that of an ordinary
officer. If the father was an ordinary officer and the son was a great officer, the
burial was that of an ordinary officer and the sacrifice that of a great officer.
The mourning period of one year extended to great officers and that of three
years applied to the Son of Heaven. The mourning for parents, whether noble
or base, was the same." **[3]**

Comment: Further paradigmatic noble men/virtuous rulers are considered—Kings Wen and Wu in particular. The first sentence is framed as a question following the punctuation in the modern version of the SSJZS. Some licence has been taken in the translation of the response, following particularly Kong Yingda's commentary. On this opening section, Legge has: "King Ji was the duke, Ji Li 季歷, the most distinguished by his virtues, and prowess, of all the princes of his time. In 父作之，子述之, the *zhi* 之 is made to refer to *ji ye* 基業, 'the foundation of the kingdom' but it may as well be referred to Wen himself" (400n18). In the second statement of the section, attention turns to King Wu. There is variation in the reading of *yi rong yi* 壹戎衣; the notes of the two *Li ji* commentators are not entirely consistent in their readings—i.e. "as one man" or "once." The last eighteen characters of the sub-section (from *zun* 尊 to *zhi* 之) are repeated from the previous section. Here, there is no discussion of *bao* 保 which, accordingly, has been given its usual sense. The third and final sub-section on funeral and mourning practices receives detailed attention from Kong Yingda, and to a lesser extent from Zheng Xuan.

注 ZY12 (鄭玄)

[1] 聖人以立法度為大事，子能述成之，則何憂乎？堯、舜之父子則有凶頑，禹、湯之父子則寡令聞。父子相成，唯有文王。

[2] 纘，繼也。緒，業也。戎，兵也。衣讀如「殷」，聲之誤也。齊人言殷聲如「衣」，虞、夏、商、周氏者多矣。今姓有衣者，殷之冑與？「壹戎殷」者，壹用兵伐殷也。{纘，徐音纂，哉管反。大音泰，下及注「大王」皆同。「壹戎衣」，依注衣作殷，於巾反，謂一用兵伐殷也。《尚書》依字讀，謂一著戎衣而天下大定。冑與，直救反，下音餘。}

[3] 末，猶老也。「追王大王、王季」者，以王跡起焉，先公組紺以上至后稷也。「斯禮達於諸侯、大夫、士、庶人」者，謂葬之從死者之爵，祭之用生者之祿也。言大夫葬以大夫，士葬以士，則「追王」者，改葬之矣。「期之喪，達於大夫」者，謂旁親所降在大功者，其正統之期，天子諸侯猶不降也。大夫所降，天子諸侯絕之不為服，所不臣乃服之也。承葬、祭說期、三年之喪者，明子事父以孝，不用其尊卑變。{末，亡遏反。追王，于況反，注「追王」同。期音基，注同。組音祖。紺，古闇反。組紺，大王之父也，亦曰諸螫，螫音置留反。以上，時掌反。不為服，于偽反。}

Notes ZY12 (Zheng Xuan)

[1] If the sage takes the establishment of laws and measures to be a great matter and his son is able to continue and complete this, how will there be grief? But even in the father-son relationships of both Yao and Shun there was cruelty and waywardness; and even in the father-son relationships of both Yu and Tang there was a lack of good reputation. Only in the case of King Wen were father and son complementary. . . .

[2] *Zuan* 纘 is equivalent to *ji* 繼 (to succeed, carry on). *Xu* 緒 is equivalent to *ye* 業 (work). *Rong* 戎 is equivalent to *bing* 兵 (arms). *Yi* 衣 is read as *yin* 殷, there being an error in the sound. Qi people saying *yin* 殷 sounds like *yi* 衣 and the same with the Yu, Xia, Shang and Zhou clans in many instances. Now are those with the surname (*xing* 姓) of *yi* 衣 descendants of Yin 殷? *Yi rong Yin* 壹戎殷 [refers to him as] one man taking up arms to reduce Yin. . . .

[3] *Mo* 末 is like *lao* 老 (old). *He retrospectively honoured Tai Wang and King Ji as kings* is to take the traces of kingship to start from the former duke Zu Gan and go back to Hou Ji. *These rites he extended to feudal lords and great officers as well as to ordinary officers and the common people* says that in burial the rank of the deceased was followed, whereas in sacrificing the emolument of the living was used. That is to say, a grandee was buried as a grandee and an officer as an officer. Then *retrospectively honoured as kings* changes the burial. *The mourning period of one year extended to great officers* refers to what close relatives submitted to, i.e. the nine month mourning period (*da gong* 大功), this being the orthodox period which the Son of Heaven and the feudal lords still did not submit to. What great officers submitted to, the Son of Heaven and feudal lords broke off and did not accept, but those who were not ministers still accepted it. In carrying out funerals and sacrifices, to speak of the period, it was three years of mourning, making it clear that the son serves the father with filial piety and does not use his honour or lowliness to change this. . . .

疏 ZY12 (孔穎達)

{「子曰」至「一也」。}

1.1　《正義》曰：此一節明夫子論<u>文王</u>、<u>武王</u>聖德相承王有天下，上能追尊<u>大王</u>、<u>王季</u>，因明天子以下及士、庶人葬、祭祀之禮，各隨文解之。

1.2　「以<u>王季</u>為父，以<u>武王</u>為子，父作之，子述之」者，言<u>文王</u>以<u>王季</u>為父，則<u>王季</u>能制作禮樂，<u>文王</u>奉而行之。<u>文王</u>以<u>武王</u>為子，<u>武王</u>又能述成<u>文王</u>之道，故「無憂」也。

2.1　「<u>武王</u>纘<u>大王</u>、<u>王季</u>、<u>文王</u>之緒」者，纘，繼也；緒，業也。言<u>武王</u>能纘繼父祖之業，以王天下也。

2.2　「壹戎衣而有天下」者，戎，兵也。言一用兵伐<u>殷</u>而勝之也。

{注「衣讀為殷」。}

2.3　《正義》曰：案《尚書 • 武成》云「一戎衣」，[49] 謂一著戎衣而滅<u>殷</u>。此云「一」者，以經<u>武王</u>繼<u>大王</u>、<u>王季</u>、<u>文王</u>三人之業，一用滅<u>殷</u>，對三人之業為「一」耳。由三人之業，故一身滅之。<u>鄭</u>必以衣為「<u>殷</u>」者，以十一年觀兵于<u>孟津</u>，十三年滅<u>紂</u>，是再著戎服，不得稱「一戎衣」，故「以衣為<u>殷</u>」，故注云「<u>齊</u>人言殷聲如衣」。

3.1　「<u>武王</u>末受命」，此美<u>周公</u>之德也。末，猶老也，謂<u>武王</u>年老，而受命平定天下也。「斯禮也，達乎諸侯、大夫及士、庶人」者，斯，此也。言<u>周公</u>尊崇先公之禮，非直天子所行，乃下達於諸侯、大夫、士、庶人等，無問尊卑，皆得上尊祖父，以己之祿祭其先人，猶若<u>周公</u>以<u>成王</u>天子之禮祀其先公也。

49　See *Documents*, "Wu cheng," LCC, 3:315. See also p. 385 where the phrase "壹戎<u>殷</u>" appears.

Commentary ZY12 (Kong Yingda)

1.1   The *Zhengyi* says that this particular section makes clear the Master's discussion of the sage-like virtue of Kings Wen and Wu inheriting the rule of all under Heaven, and their being able to retrospectively honour Tai Wang and King Ji, and as a consequence makes it clear that from the Son of Heaven down to officers and ordinary people, the ceremonies for burial and sacrifice each followed the writings handed down.

1.2   *Because King Ji was his father and King Wu was his son, [he had] a father who created [the foundation] and a son who continued [his Way]*: This says that King Ji, by being King Wen's father, was able to regulate and create the rites and music which King Wen received and put into practice. King Wu, by being King Wen's son, was also able to transmit and complete the Way of King Wen. Therefore there was "no grief."

2.1   *King Wu carried on the work of Tai Wang, King Ji and King Wen*: Zuan 纘 is equivalent to *ji* 繼 (to succeed, carry on). *Xu* 緒 is equivalent to *ye* 業 (work). This says that King Wu was able to carry on and continue the work of his paternal ancestors in ruling all under Heaven.

2.2   *As one man he took up arms, overthrew Yin, and gained possession of all under Heaven*: Rong 戎 is equivalent to *bing* 兵 (arms, forces). This says that this one man took up arms to attack Yin and defeated it.

2.3   The *Zhengyi* says that according to the *Shang shu*, "Wu cheng," it states: "*Yi rong yi* 一戎衣" (As one man he donned his armour) which says that, as one person, he donned his armour and destroyed Yin. Saying *yi* 一 is to indicate that King Wu extended the work of Tai Wang, King Ji and King Wen and, as one person, used it to destroy Yin, reflecting that the work of three people was made one. Through the work of three people, therefore, one individual destroyed it (i.e. Yin). Zheng certainly takes *yi* 衣 to be Yin 殷 on the basis of "in the 11th year he inspected the army at Meng Ford" and "in the 13th year destroyed Jie," which is to twice don military garb so it is not to "once don armour." Therefore, "he takes *yi* 衣 to be Yin 殷" and so the notes say that "the Qi people saying Yin 殷 sounded like *yi* 衣."

3.1   *King Wu was old when he received the mandate*: This praises the virtue of the Duke of Zhou. Mo 末 is like *lao* 老 (old) and refers to King Wu being advanced in years when he received the mandate and brought peace and order to all under Heaven. *These rites he extended to the feudal lords and great officers as well as to ordinary officers and common people*: Si 斯 is equivalent to *ci* 此 (this). This refers to the Duke of Zhou's respect and veneration for the rites of the former dukes, so they were not only what the Son of Heaven carried out, but were then extended below to feudal lords, great officers, ordinary officers and common people, etc. There was no question of [whether a person was] honourable or base—all achieved veneration above for their paternal ancestors through their sacrifices to their progenitors on the basis of their own salary. For example, the Duke of Zhou used the ceremonies of King Cheng, the Son of Heaven, and sacrificed to these former dukes.

3.2 「父為大夫，子為士，葬以大夫，祭以士」者，謂父既為大夫，祭以士禮，貶其先人而云尊之者，欲明以己之祿祀其先人也。

3.3 「期之喪，達乎大夫」者，欲見大夫之尊，猶有期喪，謂旁親所降在大功者，得為期喪，還著大功之服，故云「達乎大夫」。若天子、諸侯旁期之喪，則不為服也。

3.4 「三年之喪，達乎天子」者，謂正統在三年之喪，父母及適子并妻也。「達乎天子」者，言天子皆服之。不云「父母」，而云「三年」者，包適子也。天子為后服期，以三年包之者，以后卒必待三年然後禫，所以達子之志，故通在三年之中。是以昭十五年《左傳》云：「穆后崩」，「大子壽卒」。[50] 叔向云：「王一歲而有三年之喪二焉。」[51] 是包后為三年也。直云「達乎天子」，不云「諸侯」者，諸侯旁親尊同則不降，故〈喪服・大功章〉云：「諸侯為姑姊妹嫁於國君者」是也。

3.5 「父母之喪，無貴賤一也」，唯父母之喪，無問天子及士、庶人，其服並同，故云「無貴賤一也」。

{注「末猶」至「卑變」。}

3.6 《正義》曰：「末猶老也」者，謂文王受命，十一年武王觀兵於孟津，白魚入王舟，是老而受命，受命後七年而崩。故鄭注〈洛誥〉，文王受赤雀，武王俯取白魚，皆七年是也。

50 See *Zuo zhuan*, Duke Zhao, 15th year, LCC, 5:657.
51 Shuxiang 叔向 was Yangshe Xi 羊舌肸—see, for example, *Zuo zhuan* for Duke Rang, 16th year (LCC, 5:471) and Duke Zhao, 5th year (LCC, 5:601) as well as the *Guoyu* for Zhou.

3.2   *If the father was a great officer and the son was an ordinary officer, the burial was that of a great officer and the sacrifice that of an ordinary officer* says that, when the father was a great officer, the sacrifice was by the ceremony for an officer in sending off his progenitor and publicly honouring him, the desire being to make clear one's own emolument in the sacrifice to one's progenitor.

3.3   *The mourning period of one year extended to great officers*: Wishing to see veneration for great officers, they stilll have a one year mourning period. Referring to close relatives and what was reduced to *da gong* 大功 (nine months), if they got the one-year mourning, they still wore the garments of *da gong* 大功 (nine months). Therefore it says, *extended to great officers*. If the mourning was for a near relative of the Son of Heaven or a feudal lord, then it was not worn.

3.4   *That of three years applied to the Son of Heaven*: This refers to the rightful ruler having a three year period of mourning which included parents (father and mother) and extended to the rightful heir and wife. *Extended to the Son of Heaven* says that Sons of Heaven all followed it. It does not say "father and mother" but says "three years" and this includes the rightful heir. The Son of Heaven took the mourning for an empress to be one year because the three years included it and, if the empress died, he must wait three years before taking a new wife, which is how it extends to the son's purpose. Therefore, the total time lies within the three years. This is from the 15th year of Duke Zhao where the *Zuo zhuan* says: "The Queen Mu died" and "the eldest son of the king died." Shuxiang says: "In a single year the king had three-year mourning periods for two people." This includes the queen as being three years. In only saying *extended to the Son of Heaven* and not saying "feudal lords," if the close relatives of feudal lords are honoured the same, then there is no reduction. Therefore, the "Sang fu," "Da gong," saying: "Feudal lords are regarded like paternal aunts, younger and older sisters and daughters to the ruler" is this.

3.5   *The mourning for parents, whether noble or base, was the same*: Only in mourning for parents (father and mother) was there no question of whether they were a Son of Heaven or officers or commoners—the mourning was in all cases the same. Therefore it says, *whether noble or base, was the same.*

3.6   The *Zhengyi* says that *mo* 末 is like *lao* 老 (old), referring to King Wen receiving the mandate. In the 11th year, King Wu was inspecting troops at Meng Ford when a white fish entered the royal boat. This is his being old and receiving the mandate. Seven years after receiving the mandate, he died. Therefore, Zheng Xuan's notes for the "Luo gao" say that King Wen received the red bird and King Wu bowed down and took the white fish, both being in the seventh year.

云「追王<u>大王</u>、<u>王季</u>者,以王跡起焉」,案《詩‧頌‧閟宮》云<u>大王</u>「居岐
之陽,實始翦<u>商</u>」,是王跡起也。云「先公<u>組紺</u>以上至<u>后稷</u>也」者,<u>組紺</u>,
<u>大王</u>之父,一名<u>諸盩</u>,〈周本紀〉云:「<u>亞圉</u>卒,子<u>太公叔穎</u>立。<u>太公</u>卒,
子<u>古公亶父</u>立。」又《世本》云:「<u>亞圉雲都</u>生<u>太公 組紺諸盩</u>」,則<u>叔穎</u>、
<u>組紺</u>、<u>諸盩</u>是一人也。此文云「追王<u>大王</u>、<u>王季</u>,上祀先公」,則先公之
中包<u>后稷</u>也,故云「<u>組紺</u>以上至<u>后稷</u>」也。案〈司服〉云:「享先王則袞
冕,先公則鷩冕。」以<u>后稷</u>為周之始祖,祫祭於廟,當同先王用袞,則先
公無<u>后稷</u>。故<u>鄭</u>注〈司服〉云,先公不窋[52]至<u>諸盩</u>。若四時常祀,唯<u>后
稷</u>及<u>大王</u>、<u>王季</u>之等,不得廣及先公。故《天保》云:「禴祠烝嘗于公。」
先王是四時常祀,但有<u>后稷 諸盩</u>以下,故<u>鄭</u>注《天保》云:「先公謂<u>后稷</u>
至<u>諸盩</u>。」此皆盡望經上下釋義,故不同,或有至字誤也。云「則追王
者,改葬之矣」者,以<u>大王</u>、<u>王季</u>身為諸侯,葬從死者之爵,則<u>大王</u>、<u>王
季</u>祗得為諸侯葬禮,不得言「追王」,從天子法。故知追王之時,而更改
葬,用天子禮。案《大傳》云:「<u>武王</u>追王<u>大王亶父</u>、<u>王季歷</u>。」此云<u>周公</u>
追王,不同者,<u>武王</u>既伐<u>紂</u>,「追王」布告天下,<u>周公</u>追而改葬,故不同
也。云「期之喪,達於大夫者,謂旁親所降在大功」者,<u>熊氏</u>云:「此對
天子、諸侯,故云

This character is taken as the name of Hou Ji's son—see ZWDCD #26047, 6:1737.

In relation to the statement, "he retrospectively honoured Tai Wang and King Ji as kings is to take the traces of kingship to start," the *Odes* ("Song," "Bi gong") has: "Tai Wang dwelt on the south of [Mount] Qi where the cutting off of Shang truly began." This is the traces of kingship arising. In saying, "from the former duke Zu Gan on back to Hou Ji," Zu Gan was Tai Wang's father. One of his names was Zhu Zhou. The "Zhou benji" says: "Yayu died and his son Taigong Shuying was established. Taigong died and his son Gugong Danfu was established." Also the *Shi ben* says: "Yayu Yundu gave birth to Taigong Zu Gan Zhu Zhou" so Shu Ying, Zu Gan and Zhu Zhou were all this one person. This is Wen Gong *retrospectively honouring Tai Wang and King Ji as kings and sacrificed to the former dukes preceding them.* Then the former dukes included among them Hou Ji. Therefore he (i.e. Zheng Xuan) says, "from Zu Gan on back to Hou Ji." According to the "Si fu," it says: "In presenting a sacrificial offering to former kings, there is the dragon-embroidered cap and gown (*gui mian*); for former dukes, there is the pheasant-embroidered cap and gown (*bi mian*)." Because Hou Ji was Zhou's first ancestor, he sacrificed at the ancestral temple in a lined garment which was properly equivalent to the use of robes by former kings, so then former dukes did not include Hou Ji. Therefore, Zheng's notes to the "Si fu" say that former dukes were not from Hou Ji's son to Zhu Zhuo. For example, in the regular sacrifices of the four seasons, it is only from Hou Ji to Tai Wang, King Ji etc and does not extend to former dukes. Therefore, the *Tian bao* says: "The spring sacrifices at the ancestral temple were to dukes." For the former kings these were the regular sacrifices of the four seasons but there were Hou Ji, Zhu Zhuo and on down, therefore Zheng's notes on the *Tian bao* say: "Former dukes refer to those from Hou Ji to Zhu Zhuo." These all completely overlook the classic's interpretation of the meaning of above and below, therefore they are not in agreement. Some even have mistaken characters. Saying, "then retrospectively honouring them as kings changes their burial," takes Tai Wang and King Ji themselves to be feudal lords and the burial to follow the rank of the deceased. Then Tai Wang and King Ji got what were only the burial rites of feudal lords, so it cannot be said [they were] *retrospectively honoured as kings* following the model of the Son of Heaven. Therefore, we know that at the time, "retrospectively honouring them as kings" meant a change in the burial to use the ceremonies for the Son of Heaven. According to the *Da zhuan*, it says: "King Wu retrospectively honoured as a king Tai Wang Danfu (progenitor of the Zhou house) and King Ji in succession." This says that the Duke of Zhou retrospectively honouring as a king was not the same. When King Wu cut down Zhou, "retrospectively honouring as a king" was proclaimed throughout the world, whereas when Zhou Gong "retrospectively honoured as a king" and changed the burial, then it was not the same. On saying "one year of mourning extends to great officers refers to near relatives having conferred on them the *da gong* (nine months mourning)," Xiong Shi says: "This is opposite to the Son of Heaven and the feudal lords. Therefore saying,

『期之喪達乎大夫』，其實大夫為大功之喪得降小功，小功之喪得降緦
麻。」是大功小功，皆達乎大夫。<u>熊氏</u>又云：「天子為正統之喪，適婦大
功，適孫之婦小功。」義或然，但無正文耳。云「所不臣乃服之也」者，
〈喪服傳〉云：「始封之君不臣諸父昆弟，封君之子不臣諸父而臣昆弟。」
但不臣者，皆以本服服也。

ZY13: 子曰：「<u>武王</u>、<u>周公</u>，其達孝矣乎！夫孝者，善繼人之志，善述
人之事者也。春秋脩其祖廟，陳其宗器，設其裳衣，薦其時食。[1]宗
廟之禮，所以序昭穆也。序爵，所以辨貴賤也；序事，所以辨賢也。旅
酬下為上，所以逮賤也。燕毛，所以序齒也。[2]踐其位，行其禮，奏
其樂，敬其所尊，愛其所親，事死如事生，事亡如事存，孝之至也。[3]
郊社之禮，所以事上帝也。宗廟之禮，所以祀乎其先也。[4]明乎郊社
之禮，禘嘗之義，治國其如示諸掌乎！」[5]

Comment: This section is without significant differences between the two commentaries
and continues the discussion of the conduct of the exemplary *junzi* 君子, here focussing
on the filial piety of King Wu and the Duke of Zhou. Down to the end of sub-section 3
where the final remark identifies the *xiao* 孝 of these two worthies as the "apogee of filial
piety," the description is of their deeds, particularly in ordering the sacrifices. The final two
sub-sections are generalised statements regarding the ceremonies of sacrifice, the final comment being also found elsewhere in the *Li ji* and in the *Lunyu*.[53]

---

53   See the *Lunyu* III.11 and the *Li ji*, "Zhongni yanju," 5:853.

'the one year mourning period extends to great officers' is really saying that the *da gong* mourning for great officers was reduced to *xiao gong* (five months) and *xiao gong* was reduced to *si ma* (coarse cloth, three months)." This is *da gong* and *xiao gong* both extending to great officers. Xiong Shi also says: "The Son of Heaven had the mourning for the rightful head of state, the legitimate wife had the *da gong*, and the legitimate descendants of the wife, the *xiao gong*." So it may be the meaning, but is not the correct text. On saying, "those who are not subjects still mourn him!" the "Sangfu zhuan" says: "Princes who are first enfeoffed are not subjects of their various fathers and older and younger brothers, whilst the sons of enfeoffed princes are not subjects of their fathers, but are subjects of their older and younger brothers." Yet those who are not subjects all mourn by using the original mourning garments.

ZY13: The Master said: "King Wu and the Duke of Zhou—how thorough-going was their filial piety! Now their being filial was to skillfully perpetuate their progenitors' purposes and to skillfully carry on their undertakings. In spring and autumn, it was to renovate their ancestral temples, to set out their ancestral utensils, to lay out their upper and lower garments, and to present offerings appropriate to the season. [1] The ceremonies of the ancestral temple were how the two rows of spirit tablets were ordered. Order of rank was how the noble and base were differentiated. Order of services was how worthiness was distinguished. The general pledging, where inferiors offered drinking cups to superiors, was the way of reaching down to those who were lowly. Hair colour was how seniority (age) was ordered. [2] Going up to their positions, carrying out their ceremonies, performing their music, having reverence for what they honoured and love for what they held dear, serving the dead like serving the living, and serving the departed like serving those who remained—this was the apogee of filial conduct. [3] The ceremonies of sacrifice to Heaven and Earth were the means of serving the Supreme Ruler. The ceremonies of the ancestral temples were the means of sacrificing to their ancestors. [4] If one is clear about the ceremonies of sacrifice to Heaven and Earth, and the meaning of the *Di* (summer) and *Chang* (autumn) sacrifices, bringing good order to the state is like placing something in the palm of one's hand. [5]

注 ZY13 (鄭玄)

[1] 脩，謂掃糞也。宗器，祭器也。裳衣，先祖之遺衣服也，設之當以授尸也。時食，四時祭也。{掃，悉報反。糞，弗運反，本亦作糞[54]，亦作拚，同。}

[2] 序，猶次也。爵，謂公、卿、大夫、士也。事，謂薦羞也。「以辨賢」者，以其事別所能也。若司徒「羞牛」，宗伯「共雞牲」矣。〈文王世子〉曰：「宗廟之中，以爵為位，崇德也。宗人授事以官，尊賢也。」[55]「旅酬下為上」者，謂若〈特牲饋食〉之禮賓，弟子、兄弟之子各舉觶於其長也。[56]「逮賤」者，宗廟之中，以有事為榮也。「燕」，謂既祭而燕也。燕以髮色為坐，祭時尊尊也，至燕親親也。齒，亦年也。{昭穆，常遙反。穆，又作繆，音同。逮，本又作逮，同音代。燕，於見反，注並同。別，彼列反。共音恭。饋，其位反。觶音至。長，丁丈反，下「謂長」同。}

[3] 踐，猶升也。「其」者，其先祖也。踐或為「纘」。

[4] 社，祭地神，不言后土者，省文。{省，色領反。}

[5] 示讀如「寘諸河干」之「寘」。寘，置也。物而在掌中，易為知力者也。序爵、辨賢、尊尊、親親，治國之要。{示，依注音寘，之豉反。易，以豉反。知力音智，本亦無力字。治之要也，治，直吏反，一本作「治國之要」，治則如字。}

疏 ZY13 (孔穎達)

{「子曰」至「掌乎」。}

1.1　《正義》曰：以前經論文王、武王聖德相承，此論武王、周公上成先祖，脩其宗廟，行郊社之禮，所以能治國如置物掌中也，各隨文解之。

1.2　「夫孝者，善繼人之志」者，人，謂先人。若文王有志伐紂，武王能繼而承之。《尚書・武成》曰：「予小子，其承厥志。」[57] 是「善繼人之志」也。

---

[54] *Fen* 糞 should be written with the *shou* 手 radical—see ZWDCD #13288, 4:838.

[55] See the *Li ji,* "Wen Wang shizi," SSJZS, 5:402. Although in the modern, punctuated version the quotation is given as ending with "德也," in fact it continues to "賢也" as above.

[56] See *Yi li,* "Te sheng kui shi," SSJZS, 4:529–42.

[57] See the *Documents,* "Wu cheng," LCC, 3:312.

Notes ZY13 (Zheng Xuan)

[1] *Xiu* 脩 refers to sweeping away dung. *Zong qi* 宗器 are utensils for sacrifice. *Chang yi* 裳衣 are clothes handed down by ancestors and are set up as appropriate to confer on the corpse (impersonator of the dead). *Shi shi* 時食 are the four seasonal sacrifices. . . .

[2] *Xu* 序 is like *ci* 次 (order, precedence). *Jue* 爵 refers to dukes, ministers, great officers and officers. *Shi* 事 refers to sacrifices of food. *Was how worthiness was distinguished* was to differentiate what they were able to do by means of their food offerings. For example, the person in charge of followers (*situ* 司徒) "brings forth the ox," and the senior ceremonialist (*zongbo* 宗伯) "holds the sacrificial chicken." The "Wen Wang shizi" says: "Within the ancestral temple, position is according to rank, honouring virtue. The Ancestral Intendant confers the food offerings on the basis of excellence, honouring worthiness." *The general pledging, where inferiors offered drinking cups to superiors* refers, for example, to the ceremonies for guests noted in "Tesheng kuishi," and the sons of older and younger brothers each raising a goblet to their elders. *Reaching down to those who were lowly* was to be honoured within the ancestral temple by there being food offerings. *Yan* 燕 refers to finishing the sacrifice and feasting. Seating for the feast was on the basis of hair colour (seniority). At the time of the sacrifice, there was veneration of the honourable. When it came to the feast, there was love for relatives. *Chi* 齒 is also years (of age). . . .

[3] *Jian* 踐 is like *sheng* 升 (to ascend, rise). The *qi* 其 is here former ancestors. *Jian* 踐 is sometimes [written] as *zuan* 纘.

[4] *She* 社, a sacrifice to the earth god, does not refer to Hou Tu [because it is] an abridged expression. . . .

[5] *Shi* 示 is read like *zhi* 寘 in "寘諸河干" (place it on the river bank). *Zhi* 寘 is equivalent to *zhi* 置 (to place, put). If something is in the palm of one's hand it is easy to know its strength. Giving order to rank, distinguishing worthiness, venerating the honourable, and loving relatives are elements of bringing good order to a state. . . .

Commentary ZY13 (Kong Yingda)

1.1   The *Zhengyi* says that, whilst the previous section discusses the continuation of the sage-like virtue of Kings Wen and Wu, this [section] discusses King Wu and the Duke of Zhou attending to their ancestors, renovating their ancestral temples, and carrying out the ceremonies of the state sacrifices, which is how they were able to bring good order to the state as easily as placing something in the palm of the hand. In each case what follows explains this.

1.2   *Now their being filial was to skillfully perpetuate their progenitors' purposes*: *Ren* 人 (others) refers to earlier people (predecessors, progenitors). For example, King Wen had the purpose of overthrowing Zhou and King Wu was able to continue and carry this on. The *Shang shu*, "Wu cheng" says: "I, a little child, continued and carried out his purpose" which is *to skillfully perpetuate their progenitors' purposes*.

1.3　「善述人之事者也」，言<u>文王</u>有文德為王基，而<u>周公</u>制禮以贊述之。故〈洛誥〉云「考朕昭之刑，乃單文祖德」，[58] 是善述人之事也。此是<u>武王</u>、<u>周公</u>繼孝之事。

2.1　「宗廟之禮，所以序昭穆也」者，若昭與昭齒，穆與穆齒是也。

2.2　「序爵，所以辨貴賤也」者，序，謂次序；爵，謂公、卿、大夫、士也。謂祭祀之時，公、卿、大夫各以其爵位齒列而助祭祀，是「辨貴賤」也。故〈文王世子〉云「宗廟之中，以爵為位，崇德也。宗人授事以官，尊賢也」[59] 是也。

2.3　「序事，所以辨賢也」者，事謂薦羞也，序謂次序，所共祭祀之事，若司徒奉牛，司馬奉羊，宗伯供雞，是分別賢能，堪任其官也。

2.4　「旅酬下為上，所以逮賤也」者，旅，眾也；逮，及也。謂祭末飲酒之時，使一人舉觶之後，至旅酬之時，使卑者二人各舉觶於其長者。卑下者先飲，是下者為上，賤人在先，是恩意先及於賤者，故云「所以逮賤也」。案〈特牲饋食〉之禮，[60] 主人洗爵，獻長兄弟，獻眾兄弟之後，眾賓弟子于西階，兄弟弟子于東階，各舉觶於其長也。弟子等皆是下賤而得舉觶，是有事於宗廟之中，是其榮也。又制受爵，是「逮賤」也。

2.5　「燕毛，所以序齒也」者，言祭末燕時，以毛髮為次序，是所以序年齒也。故注云：「燕謂既祭而燕也。燕以髮色為坐，祭時尊尊也，至燕親親也。」

58　*Documents,* "Luo gao," LCC, 3:448.
59　*Li ji,* "Wen Wang shizi," SSJZS, 5:402.
60　This does not appear to be an exact quotation—see *Yi li,* "Te sheng kui shi," SSJZS, 4:536.

1.3   *Skillfully carry on their undertakings*: This says King Wen had a refined virtue as the basis of his rule and the Duke of Zhou regulated ceremonies in order to assist and transmit this. Therefore, the "Luo gao" says: "I wish to complete the pattern to enlighten you, my son, then fully implement [the work] of your ancestor, Wen." This is *to skillfully carry on their undertakings*. This confirms that King Wu and the Duke of Zhou continued the matters pertaining to filial conduct.

2.1   *The ceremonies of the ancestral temple were how the two rows of spirit tablets were ordered*: For example, the *zhao* and the *zhao* order of seniority, and the *mu* and the *mu* order of seniority were this.

2.2   *Order of rank was how the noble and base were differentiated*: Xu 序 refers to *cixu* 次序 (order, precedence). *Jue* 爵 refers to dukes, ministers, great officers and officers. That is to say, at the time of sacrifice, dukes, ministers and great officers were each arranged according to their rank, position and seniority, and assisted at the sacrifice. This is *the noble and base were differentiated*. Thus, the "Wen Wang shizi" saying, "within the ancestral temple, position is taken according to rank, venerating virtue. The Ancestral Intendant confers food offerings on the basis of excellence, honouring worthiness" is this.

2.3   *Order of services was how worthiness was distinguished*: Shi 事 refers to *jianxiu* (offerings of food and wine to the gods for departed ancestors); *xu* 序 refers to the *cixu* 次序 (order, precedence, sequence) and what were common to the matters of the sacrifices. For example, the minister of education (*situ* 司徒) offered an ox, the minister of war (*sima*) offered a sheep, and the minister of rites (*zongbo* 宗伯) offered a fowl, this distinguishing worthiness, ability and fitness for the position of these officials.

2.4   *The general pledging, where inferiors offered drinking cups to superiors, was the way of reaching down to those who were lowly*: Lu 旅 is equivalent to *zhong* 眾 (general); *dai* 逮 is equivalent to *ji* 及 (to reach to). This refers to the time of drinking wine at the end of the sacrifice. After letting one person raise a drinking goblet, this went on to a time of general pledging, allowing two people who were lowly to each raise a drinking goblet to their elders. Those who were lowly drank first, which is "those below being above" or "the base being first." This is kindness and consideration being first extended to the lowly. Therefore, it says, *the way of reaching down to those who were lowly*. According to the ceremonies [described in the] "Tesheng guishi," the principal person rinsed the wine cup and offered it to the elders and older and younger brothers, and after offering it to the many older and younger brothers, the multitude of guests, younger brothers and sons at the western steps, and the older and younger brothers and sons at the eastern steps, each raised the drinking goblet to his elders. Juniors etc were all lowly and got to raise the drinking goblet, this being their service within the ancestral temple and their honour. They also organised the receiving of the goblet, this being *reaching down to the lowly*.

2.5   *Hair colour was how seniority (age) was ordered*: This says that, at the end of the sacrifice, at the time of feasting, order was established on the basis of hair colour, this being how age/seniority was ordered. Therefore, the note says: "*Yan* 燕 refers to the end of the sacrifice and the feasting. Seating at the feast was on the basis of hair colour. At the time of the sacrifice, there was veneration of the honourable; when it came to the feast, there was loving of relatives."

3.1　「踐其位，行其禮」者，踐，升也，謂孝子升其先祖之位，行祭祀之禮也。

5.1　「治國其如示諸掌乎」，注云「『示』，讀如『寘諸河干』之『寘』，寘，置也」者，若能明此序爵辨賢尊親，則治理其國，其事為易，猶如置物於掌中也。

ZY14: <u>哀公</u>問政。子曰：「<u>文武</u>之政，布在方策，其人存則其政舉，其人亡則其政息。[1]人道敏政，地道敏樹。[2]夫政也者，蒲盧也。[3]故為政在人，[4]取人以身，脩身以道，脩道以仁。[5]仁者，人也，親親為大。義者，宜也，尊賢為大。親親之殺，尊賢之等，禮所生也。[6]在下位不獲乎上，民不可得而治矣。[7]故君子不可以不脩身。思脩身，不可以不事親。思事親，不可以不知人。思知人，不可以不知天。[8]天下之達道五，所以行之者三：曰君臣也、父子也、夫婦也、昆弟也、朋友之交也。五者，天下之達道也。知、仁、勇三者，天下之達德也。所以行之者一也。[9]

3.1   *Going up to their positions, carrying out their ceremonies*: *Jian* 踐 is equivalent to
        sheng 升 (to ascend, rise). This refers to the filial son going up to his ancestor's
        position and carrying out the ceremonies of the sacrifice.

5.1   *Bringing good order to the state is like placing something in the palm of one's hand*:
        The note says: "*Shi* 示 should be read like *zhi* 寘 in '寘諸河干' (place it on the
        river bank). *Zhi* 寘 is equivalent to *zhi* 置 (to place, put)." If someone is able to
        make clear this order of rank, distinguish worthiness, and honour relatives, then
        bringing order to and regulating his state is an easy matter, like placing some-
        thing in the palm of one's hand.

ZY14: Duke Ai asked about government. The Master replied: "The government of Wen and Wu is recorded on wooden tablets and bamboo slips. When
those men lived, their government was implemented; when those men died,
their government was extinguished. **[1]** The Way of man is to strive for government; the Way of earth is to strive for the growth of plants. **[2]** Now government is like the silkworm wasp. **[3]** Therefore, the conduct of government
lies in men. **[4]** Choosing men is the purview of the ruler. [For the latter,]
cultivating the self is through the Way and cultivating the Way is through
ren 仁. **[5]** *Ren* 仁 is to be humane (concerned for the well-being of others)
and the key point is devotion to family members. *Yi* 義 is to be right [in
action] and the key point is honouring worthiness. In devotion to family
members, there is a hierarchy; in honouring worthiness, there are grades.
These are what give rise to *li* 禮. **[6]** (When those in inferior positions do
not have the support of their superiors, the people cannot be won over and
brought to good order.) **[7]** Therefore, the noble man (ruler) cannot do
otherwise than cultivate himself. If he wishes to cultivate himself, he cannot
do otherwise than serve his family members. If he wishes to serve his family
members, he cannot do otherwise than know men. If he wishes to know men,
he cannot do otherwise than know Heaven. **[8]** There are five [components]
to the world's constantly practised Way and three [components] to putting it
into practice. I say [the five are the relationships between] ruler and minister,
father and son, husband and wife, older and younger brother, and friend and
friend. The five [relationships] are the constantly practised Way of Heaven.
Three things—*zhi* 知 (knowledge, wisdom), *ren* 仁 and *yong* 勇 (courage, bravery)—are the world's constantly practised virtues. The way of putting them into
practice is one. **[9]**

或生而知之，或學而知之，或困而知之，及其知之，一也。[10]或安而
行之，或利而行之，或勉強而行之，及其成功，一也。」[11]

Comment: This section marks a distinct change in the work. The examples of the various
paradigmatic *junzi* 君子 (Yao, Shun, Kings Wen and Wu, the Duke of Zhou) come to an end
and there is now a series of expository statements attributed to Confucius about the conduct
of government specifically and conduct in general, given as a response to the question posed
by Duke Ai of Lu (5ᵗʰ century BCE). Within the discussion, key ethical terms are considered;
first *ren* 仁, *yi* 義 and *li* 禮 and then *zhi* 知, *ren* 仁 and *yong* 勇. In the *Li ji* version, these
considerations extend through sections 14–17 inclusive before passing on to a specific consideration of *cheng* 誠. At the end of the present section there is a statement of the tripartite
division of the means open to people to achieve the Way: through innate natural goodness
and ability (the sage), through diligent study (the worthy) and through difficulties, i.e. life's
vicissitudes, which relates to everybody else presumably. The concepts in the present section
are clear enough, but are also elaborated on in the notes and commentary. In terms of translation, there are three somewhat contentious points, although the divergent views have no real
bearing on the overall meaning. The first is the analogy given in sub-section 3, the alternative
being "reeds and rushes" (see, e.g. Haloun); the second is whether sub-section 7 is misplaced
here as suggested by Zheng Xuan, the general consensus being that it is; the third concerns *si*
思—whether it should be taken as a metrical word and left untranslated (e.g. Riegel, Ames &
Hall) or should be understood as "to think" or "to wish" (e.g. Legge, Chan, Haloun). Its use
in the usual sense in the notes of both Zheng Xuan and Kong Yingda favours the latter position. This chapter is found in a more extended form in the *Kongzi jiayu* 17.

注 ZY14 (鄭玄)

[1] 方，版也。策，簡也。息，猶滅也。{方筴，初革反。版音板，本亦作
「板」。}

[2] 敏，猶勉也。樹，謂殖草木也。人之無政，若地無草木矣。敏或為「謀」。

[3] 蒲盧，螺蠃，謂土蜂也。《詩》曰：「螟蛉有子，螺蠃負之。」⁶¹螟蛉，桑蟲
也。蒲盧取桑蟲之子，去而變化之，以成為己子。政之於百姓，若蒲盧之於桑
蟲然。{蒲盧，並如字，《爾雅》云「螺蠃，蒲盧」⁶²，即今之細腰蜂也，一名蠮螉。
螺音果。螺，力果反，本亦作蠃，音同。蜂，芳封反，字亦作蠭，同。螟，莫
瓶反。蛉音零。己音紀。}

[4] 在於得賢人也。

[5] 取人以身，言明君乃能得人。

---

⁶¹ *Odes*, Mao 196, verse 3, LCC, 4:334.
⁶² *Er ya*, SSJZS, 8:164.

Some are born and know these things, some study and know them, and some have difficulties and know them, but when it comes to their knowing them, it is one and the same thing. [10] Some practise them with a natural ease, some practise them for the benefits they bring, and some practise them through great effort, but when it comes to their succeeding, it is one and the same thing." [11]

Notes ZY14 (Zheng Xuan)

[1] *Fang* 方 is equivalent to *ban* 版 (wooden tablets); *ce* 策 is equivalent to *jian* 簡 (bamboo strips); *xi* 息 is like *mie* 滅 (to perish, destroy). . . .

[2] *Min* 敏 is like *mian* 勉 (to encourage, exert oneself). *Shu* 樹 refers to planting grasses and trees. Men being without government is like the earth being without grass and trees. *Min* 敏 is sometimes [written as] *mou* 謀.

[3] *Pu lu* 蒲盧 and *guo luo* 蜾蠃 refer to the *tufeng* 土蜂 (the silkworm wasp). The *Odes* has: "The mulberry insect has young and the solitary wasp (sphex) carries them away." *Mingling* 螟蛉 is the mulberry insect. The silkworm wasp (*pu lu* 蒲盧) takes the young of the mulberry insect, goes away and transforms them to complete their own young. The government being in the ordinary people is like the case of the silkworm wasp and the mulberry insect. . . .

[4] Lies in obtaining worthy men.

[5] Choosing men through the self refers to the enlightened ruler being able to obtain men.

[6] 人也，讀如相人偶之「人」。⁶³以人意相存問之言。{殺，色界反，徐所例反。}

[7] 此句其屬在下，著脫誤重在此。⁶⁴{治，直吏反，一音如字。脫音奪。重，直用反。}

[8] 言修身乃知孝，知孝乃知人，知人乃知賢、不肖，知賢、不肖乃知天命所保佑。

[9] 達者常行，百王所不變也。{知音智，下「近乎知」，注「言有知」皆同。}

[10] 「困而知之」，謂長而見禮義之事，己臨之而有不足，乃始學而知之，此「達道」也。{長，丁丈反。己音紀。}

[11] 利，謂貪榮名也。「勉強」，恥不若人。{強，其兩反。注同。}

疏 ZY14 (孔穎達)

{「哀公」至「一也」。}

1.1　《正義》曰：此一節明哀公問政於孔子，孔子荅以為政之道在於「取人」、「脩身」，并明「達道」有五，行之者三。今各隨文解之。

1.2　「文武之政，布在方策」者，言文王武王為政之道，皆布列在於方牘簡策。

1.3　「其人存則其政舉」者，雖在方策，其事久遠，此廣陳為政之道。「其人」，謂賢人。舉，猶行也。存，謂道德存在也。若得其人，道德存在，則能興行政教，故云「舉」也。

1.4　「其人亡則其政息」者，息，滅也。其人若亡，謂道德滅亡，不能興舉於政教。若位無賢臣，政所以滅絕也。

2.1　「人道敏政」者，敏，勉也。言為人君當勉力行政。

63　On the phrase given, see the *Yi li*, "Pin li," SSJZS, 4:242 including notes and commentary.

64　The opening sentence of ZY18 in the present arrangement.

[6] *Ren* 人 is like *ren* 人 in "*xiang ren ou* 相人偶." This takes the meaning of *ren* 人 to be a mutual concern for the well-being of others. . . .

[7] This sentence is included in what follows. It is mistakenly duplicated here. . . .

[8] This says that, if one cultivates the self, then one knows filial piety; if one knows filial piety, then one knows others; if one knows others, then one knows the worthy and the unworthy; if one knows the worthy and the unworthy, then one knows the decree of Heaven and what it protects and helps.

[9] *Da* 達 is to constantly practise, which is what the hundred kings did not change. . . .

[10] *Some have difficulties and know them* refers to growing up and observing matters of *li* 禮 and *yi* 義, coming to them oneself, and having a sense of insufficiency. Then one begins to study and know them—this is *da dao* 達道 (the constantly practised Way). . . .

[11] *Li* 利 refers to coveting a glorious reputation. *Mian qiang* 勉強 is to have shame that is not like [that of] others. . . .

Commentary ZY14 (Kong Yingda)

1.1   The *Zhengyi* says that this particular section makes clear Duke Ai's questioning of Confucius on government and Confucius' answering by taking the Way of government to lie in "choosing men" and "cultivating the self." It also makes it clear that in the "constantly practised Way there are five [components], whilst in implementing it there are three." Now each follows and the text explains them.

1.2   *The government of Wen and Wu is recorded on wooden tablets and bamboo slips*: This says that the Way of conducting government of Kings Wen and Wu was in both cases set out in detail on wooden tablets and bamboo slips.

1.3   *When those men lived, their government was implemented*: Although it is [preserved] on wooden tablets and bamboo slips, its affairs are remote in time. These [records] extensively set out the Way of conducting government. *Qi ren* 其人 refers to worthy men (*xian ren* 賢人). *Ju* 舉 is like *xing* 行 (to implement, put into practice). *Cun* 存 is the Way and virtue continuing to exist. If one obtains such men (i.e. worthy men), and the Way and virtue continue to exist, then government and teaching can flourish and be implemented. Therefore, it says "*ju* 舉."

1.4   *When those men died, their government was extinguished*: *Xi* 息 is equivalent to *mie* 滅 (to destroy, extinguish). If such men perish, it says that the Way and virtue are extinguished and perish, and cannot flourish in government. If positions are without worthy officials, government as a consequence is utterly destroyed.

2.1   *The Way of man is to strive for government*: *Min* 敏 is equivalent to *mian* 勉 (to urge, strive for, exert oneself). This says that, in being a ruler, it is right to strive to the utmost to implement government.

2.2 「地道敏樹」者,樹,殖草木也。言為地之道,亦勉力生殖也。人之無政,若地無草木。地既無心,云勉力者,以地之生物無倦,似若人勉力行政然也。

3.1 「夫政也者,蒲盧也」,蒲盧,取桑蟲之子以為己子。善為政者,化養他民以為己民,若蒲盧然也。

4.1 「故為政在人」,言君行善政,則民從之,故欲為善政者,在於得賢人也。

5.1 「取人以身」,明君欲取賢人,先以脩正己身,則賢人至也。

5.2 「脩身以道」,言欲脩正其身,先須行於道德也。

5.3 「脩道以仁」者,言欲脩道德,必須先脩仁義。

6.1 「仁者人也,親親為大」者,仁謂仁愛相親偶也。言行仁之法,在於親偶。欲親偶疏人,先親己親,然後比親及疏,故云「親親為大」。

6.2 「義者宜也,尊賢為大」,宜,謂於事得宜,即是其義,故云「義者宜也」。若欲於事得宜,莫過尊賢,故云「尊賢為大」。

6.3 「親親之殺,尊賢之等,禮所生也」者,五服之節,降殺不同,是親親之衰殺。公卿大夫,其爵各異,是「尊賢之等」。禮者所以辨明此上諸事,故云「禮所生也」。

7.1 「在下位不獲乎上」者,鄭謂此句應在下章,著脫誤重在此耳。

2.2   The *Way of earth is to strive for the growth of plants*: *Shu* 樹 is to plant grasses and trees. This says that the Way of earth is also to strive to the utmost for birth and growth. People being without government is like the earth being without grasses and trees. Although the earth lacks a mind, one speaks of it "striving to the utmost" because the earth gives rise to things without wearying in the same way that men strive to the utmost to implement government.

3.1   *Now government is like the silkworm wasp*: *Pu lu* 蒲盧 (silkworm wasps) take the offspring of silkworms to make their own offspring. The good conduct of government depends on transforming and nurturing other people to make them one's own people, which is what the silkworm wasp does.

4.1   *Therefore, the conduct of government lies in men*: This says that, if the ruler implements good government, then the people follow him. Therefore, the wish to carry out good government is based on obtaining worthy men.

5.1   *Choosing men is the purview of the ruler*: This makes it clear that, if the ruler wishes to choose worthy men, he must first rectify and cultivate himself. Then worthy men will come.

5.2   *[For the latter,] cultivating the self is through the Way*: This says that one who wishes to cultivate and rectify himself must first become practised in the Way and virtue.

5.3   *Cultivating the Way is through ren* 仁: This says that one who wishes to cultivate the Way and virtue must first cultivate *ren* 仁 and *yi* 義.

6.1   *Ren* 仁 *is to be humane and the key point is devotion to family members*: *Ren* 仁 refers to being beneficent and loving in relationships with relatives. It says that the model of acting beneficently lies in the relationships with family members. If one wishes to have close relationships with those who are distant, one must first have close relationships with one's own family members and afterwards extend comparable relationships to those who are distant. Therefore, it says, *the key point is devotion to family members*.

6.2   *Yi* 義 *is to be right [in action] and the key point is honouring worthiness*: *Yi* 宜 refers to achieving what is fitting in matters; then there is this *yi* 義 (right action). Therefore it says, *yi* 義 *is to be right [in action]*. If one wishes to achieve right action in matters, one cannot go beyond honouring worthiness. Therefore it says, *the key point is honouring worthiness*.

6.3   *In devotion to family members, there is a hierarchy; in honouring worthiness, there are grades*: In the divisions of the five grades of mourning the reductions are not the same. This represents the decreasing devotion to family members. Duke, minister and great officer each has a different rank; this is *in honouring worthiness, there are grades*. *Li* 禮 is how clear distinctions are made in the matters referred to above. Therefore it says, *these are what give rise to li* 禮.

7.1   *When those in inferior positions do not have the support of their superiors*: Zheng says that this sentence properly belongs in a later chapter and is erroneously duplicated here.

8.1　「故君子不可以不脩身。思脩身,不可以不事親」,言思念脩身之道,必先以孝為本,故云「不可以不事親」。

8.2　「思事親,不可以不知人」,既思事親,不可不先擇友取人也。

8.3　「思知人,不可以不知天」,欲思擇人,必先知天時所佑助也。謂人作善,降之百祥;作不善,降之百殃,當捨惡脩善也。「五者,天下之達道也」,五者,謂君臣、父子、夫婦、昆弟、朋夫之交,皆是人間常行道理,事得開通,故云「達道也」。

9.1　「知、仁、勇三者,天下之達德也」,言知、仁、勇,人所常行,在身為德,故云「天下之達德也」。

9.2　言百王用此三德以行五道。五事為本,故云「道」;三者為末,故云「德」。若行五道,必須三德。無知不能識其理,無仁不能安其事,無勇不能果其行,故必須三德也。

9.3　「所以行之者一也」,言百王以來,行此五道三德,其義一也,古今不變也。

10.1　「或生而知之」,謂天生自知也。

10.2　「或學而知之」,謂因學而知之。「或困而知之」,謂臨事有困,由學乃知。

10.3　「及其知之,一也」,言初知之時,其事雖別,既知之後,並皆是「知」,故云「及其知之,一也」。

8.1   *Therefore, the noble man (ruler) cannot do otherwise than cultivate himself. If he wishes to cultivate himself, he cannot do otherwise than serve his family members*: This says that, in giving thought to the Way of cultivating the self, he must first take filial piety to be fundamental. Therefore it says, *he cannot do otherwise than serve his family members.*

8.2   *If he wishes to serve his family members, he cannot do otherwise than know men*: Since he thinks to serve his family members, he cannot do otherwise than first select friends and choose men.

8.3   *If he wishes to know men, he cannot do otherwise than know Heaven*: If he wishes to give thought to choosing men, he must first know the seasons and what they aid and help. This refers to men who do good having a hundred good fortunes descend on them, and to those who do bad having a hundred evils descend on them, so it is right to forsake evil and cultivate good. *The five things are the world's constantly practised Way*: The "five" refers to [the relationships between] prince and minister, father and son, husband and wife, older and younger brother, and friends, all these being the constantly practised Way and principle of the relationships between people and the means of finding a path through (satisfactorily conducting affairs). Therefore it says, *the constantly practised Way.*

9.1   *Three things—zhi* 知 *(knowledge, wisdom), ren* 仁 *and yong* 勇 *(courage, bravery)— are the world's constantly practised virtues*: This says that, if *zhi* 知, *ren* 仁, and *yong* 勇 are what a man constantly puts into practice, it lies in the self to be virtuous. Therefore it says, *the world's constantly practised virtues.*

9.2   This says that the hundred kings used these three virtues in order to practise the five [components] of the Way. The "five matters" are the root, therefore one speaks of "the Way." The "three things" are the branches, therefore one speaks of "virtues." If one practises the five [components] of the Way, one necessarily has the three "virtues." Without *zhi* 知, one is not able to recognise one's principles; without *ren* 仁, one is not able to be at ease in one's affairs; without *yong* 勇, one is not able to be determined in one's actions. Therefore, one must have the three virtues.

9.3   *The way of putting them into practice is one*: This says that, from the hundred kings onward, in putting into practice these five [components] of the Way and three virtues, their significance/meaning was the same. Ancient or modern, it did not change.

10.1   *Some are born and know these things*: This refers to Heaven giving rise to natural (i.e. innate) knowledge.

10.2   *Some study and know them*: This says that it is through study that one knows them. *Some have difficulties and know them*: This refers to times of crisis when there are difficulties, and through study then knowing them.

10.3   *When it comes to their knowing them, it is one and the same thing*: This says that, at the time of first knowing them, although these matters are different, after they come to be known, they are all this "knowledge." Therefore it says, *when it comes to their knowing them, it is one and the same thing.*

11.1 「或安而行之」，謂無所求為，安靜而行之。

11.2 「或利而行之」，謂貪其利益而行之。行此五事，得其榮名，於己無害，則「利而行之」也。故《論語》云「知者利仁」[65]是也。

11.3 「或勉強而行之」，或畏懼罪惡，勉力自強而行之。「及其成功，一也」，雖行之有異，及其所行成功，是一也，言皆得成功矣。皇氏云：「所知、所行，謂上五道三德。」[66]今謂百行皆然，非唯三、五而已也。

ZY15: 子曰：「好學近乎知，力行近乎仁，知恥近乎勇。知斯三者，則知所以脩身。知所以脩身，則知所以治人。知所以治人，則知所以治天下國家矣。**[1]**凡為天下國家有九經，曰：脩身也，尊賢也，親親也，敬大臣也，體群臣也，子庶民也，來百工也，柔遠人也，懷諸侯也。**[2]**脩身則道立，尊賢則不惑，親親則諸父昆弟不怨，敬大臣則不眩，體群臣則士之報禮重，子庶民則百姓勸，來百工則財用足，柔遠人則四方歸之，懷諸侯則天下畏之。**[3]**

---

65   *Lunyu* IV.2, LCC, 1:165. There is some variation in how *li* 利 is rendered in this brief statement. Legge uses "desires" which he defends in a note. Others (e.g. Waley, Leys) have "benefit/profit."

66   Huang Kan 皇侃 (488–545)—see note 6 above.

11.1 *Some practise them with a natural ease*: This says there is nothing they seek to be—they are content and at peace in the practice of them.

11.2 *Some practise them for the benefits they bring*: This says that they desire their benefits and advantages and practise them. If they practise these five things to acquire their glorious reputation and in themselves are not good, then they *practise them for the benefits they bring*. Thus, the *Lunyu* saying, "The one who is wise benefits from *ren* 仁" is this.

11.3 *Some practise them through great effort*: Some who fear blame and evil exert themselves and with great effort practise them. *When it comes to their succeeding, it is one and the same thing*: Although there are differences in putting them into practice, when it comes to the success of what is done, this is one and the same thing. That is to say, all achieve success. Huang Shi said: "What is known and what is practised refer to the above five [components of] the Way and the three virtues." Now there is reference to the hundred actions all being so; there are not just the three and the five and that is all.

ZY15: The Master said: "To love learning comes close to *zhi* 知 (knowledge, wisdom); to practise with diligent effort comes close to *ren* 仁; to know shame comes close to *yong* 勇 (courage, bravery). To know these three things is, then, to know how to cultivate the self. To know how to cultivate the self is, then, to know how to bring good order to others. To know how to bring good order to others is, then, to know how to bring good order to the world, states and households. **[1]** In general, for the world, states and households, there are nine canons as follows: cultivate the self, honour worthiness, love one's family members, respect great officials, accept the mass of officials, love the ordinary people like one's children, encourage the hundred artisans, be kind to those from afar, and cherish the feudal lords. **[2]** If there is cultivation of the self, then the Way is established. If worthiness is honoured, then there is no doubt. If there is love for family members, then uncles and older and younger brothers will not be resentful. If there is respect for great officials, then there is no uncertainty. If there is acceptance of the mass of officials, then officers will repay the *li* 禮 many times over. If the ordinary people are loved like one's children, then the "hundred surnames" will be urged on. If there is encouragement for the hundred artisans, then the materials for use will be sufficient. If there is kindness towards those from afar, then the four regions will return to the fold. If the feudal lords are cherished, then the world will be in awe of him (i.e. the ruler). **[3]**

Comment: This continues Confucius' reply to Duke Ai of Lu on the art of government. In the *Kongzi jiayu* version, Confucius' initial statement (i.e. ZY14) is followed by Duke Ai's response: "Your words are fine, indeed perfect, but I am truly obstinate, and am not up to putting them into practice"[67] hence the repetition of *zi yue* 子曰. Here the three virtues selected for particular attention are *zhi* 知, *ren* 仁 and *yong* 勇 which are also considered together in *Lunyu* XIV.30(1) as the essential components of the Way of the noble man.[68] *Yong* 勇 is presumably to be understood in the particular sense defined in *Lunyu* II.24(2).[69] Here the three virtues are the objectives of self-cultivation which is the root of good government, as outlined in the nine canons which follow.

注 ZY15 (鄭玄)

[1] 言有知、有仁、有勇，乃知脩身，則脩身以此三者為基。{好，呼報反。} 近，附近之近，下同。{行，皇如字，徐下孟反。}

[2] 體，猶接納也。子，猶愛也。「遠人」，蕃國之諸侯也。{子，如字，徐將吏反，下句放此。蕃，方元反。}

[3] 「不惑」，謀者良也。不眩，所任明也。{眩，玄遍反。}

疏 ZY15 (孔穎達)

{「子曰」至「家矣」。}

1.1　《正義》曰：前文夫子荅哀公為政，須修身、知人、行五道三德之事，此以下夫子更為哀公廣說修身治天下之道，有九種常行之事。又明修身在於至誠，若能至誠，所以贊天地、動著龜也。博厚配地，高明配天，各隨文解之。此一節覆明上生而知之，學而知之，困而知之。

1.2　「好學近乎知」者，覆前文「或學而知之」，覆能好學，無事不知，故云「近乎知」也。

1.3　「力行近乎仁」者，此若前文「或利而行之」，以其勉力行善，故「近乎仁」也。

1.4　「知恥近乎勇」者，覆前文「困而知之」，及「勉強而行之」，以其知自羞恥，勤行善事，不避危難，故「近乎勇」也。前經「生而知之」不覆說者，以其生知自然合聖，故不須覆說也。

67　See the *Kongzi jiayu* 孔子家語 17:「公曰：『子之言美矣至矣，寡人實固，不足以成之也。』」

68　*Lunyu*, LCC, 1:286.

69　*Lunyu*, LCC, 1:154.

Notes ZY15 (Zheng Xuan)

[1] This says that, if there is 知 (wisdom, knowledge), *ren* 仁 and *yong* 勇 (courage, bravery), and if one knows to cultivate the self, then cultivating the self by means of these three things is the foundation. . . . *Jin* 近 is the *jin* 近 of *fujin* 附近 (near to). . . .

[2] *Ti* 體 is like *jiena* 接納 (to receive, accept). *Zi* 子 is like *ai* 愛 (love). *Yuan ren* 遠人 (distant people) are the feudal lords of foreign kingdoms. . . .

[3] *Bu huo* 不惑 (not to doubt, not to be uncertain) is when what is planned is good. *Bu xuan* 不眩 (no confusion, no error) is when what is undertaken is clear. . . .

Commentary ZY15 (Kong Yingda)

1.1   The *Zhengyi* says that in the previous text, the Master, replying to Duke Ai about conducting government, [stated] that there must be the matters of cultivating the self, knowing others, and practising the five [components] of the Way and the three virtues. In this which follows, the Master further expands his explanation for Duke Ai on the Way of cultivating the self and bringing good order to the world, and that there is the matter of constantly practising the nine canons. He also makes it clear that self-cultivation lies in perfect *cheng* 誠. If one is capable of perfect *cheng* 誠, it is how to assist Heaven and Earth, and activate the milfoil and tortoise. "Broad" and "deep" pair with Earth; "high" and "bright" pair with Heaven, each following the written explanation. This particular section again makes it clear that what is highest is to be born knowing these things, [next is] to study and know them; [and next is] to know them through difficulty.

1.2   *To love learning comes close to zhi* 知 *(knowledge, wisdom)*: This repeats the previous statement, *some study and know them* and reiterates that, if one is able to love learning, there is no matter that is not known. Therefore it says, *comes close to zhi* 知.

1.3   *To practise with diligent effort comes close to ren* 仁: This is like the previous statement, *some benefit and practise them*, which is to exert oneself strongly to practise good, therefore *it comes close to ren* 仁.

1.4   *To know shame comes close to yong* 勇 *(courage, bravery)*: This reiterates the previous statements, *some have difficulties and know them* and *some practise them through great effort*. Through knowing one's own sense of shame, one is encouraged to practise good deeds and not to avoid danger and difficulty. Therefore, it *comes close to yong* 勇. The earlier statement *some are born and know these things* is not again explained because to be born with innate wisdom is to be a sage, therefore there is no need for further reiteration.

2.1 「凡為天下國家有九經」者，此夫子為<u>哀公</u>說治天下國家之道有九種常行之事，論九經之次目也。

2.2 「體羣臣也」者，體，謂接納，言接納羣臣與之同體也。

2.3 「子庶民也」者，謂子愛庶民也。

2.4 「來百工也」者，謂招來百工也。

3.1 「脩身則道立」者，此一經覆說行「九經」，則致其功用也。「脩身則道立」者，謂脩正其身，不為邪惡，則道德興立也。

3.2 「尊賢則不惑」者，以賢人輔弼，故臨事不惑，所謀者善也。

3.3 「敬大臣則不眩」者，眩，亦惑也，以恭敬大臣，任使分明，故於事不惑。前文不惑，謂謀國家大事，此云「不眩」，謂謀國家眾事，但所謀之事，大小有殊，所以異其文。

3.4 「體羣臣則士之報禮重」者，群臣雖賤，而君厚接納之，則臣感君恩，故為君死於患難，是「報禮重」也。

3.5 「子庶民則百姓勸」，子，愛也，言愛民如子，則百姓勸勉以事上也。

3.6 「來百工則財用足」，百工興財用也，君若賞賚招來之，則百工皆自至，故國家財用豐足。

3.7 「柔遠人則四方歸之」，「遠」，謂蕃國之諸侯，「四方」，則蕃國也。「懷諸侯則天下畏之」。懷，安撫也。君若安撫懷之，則諸侯服從，兵強土廣，故「天下畏之」。

2.1 *In general, for the world, states and households, there are nine canons*: This is the Master explaining to Duke Ai that in the Way of bringing good order to the world and the states, there is the matter of constantly practising the nine important principles. He discusses these nine in succession.

2.2 *Accept the mass of officials*: Ti 體 refers to *jiena* 接納 (to accept, receive) and says to accept (receive) the mass of officials and join with them in one body.

2.3 *Love the ordinary people like one's children*: This refers to loving the ordinary people like one's own children.

2.4 *Encourage the hundred artisans*: This refers to calling for the hundred artisans.

3.1 *If there is cultivation of the self, then the Way is established*: This particular section repeats the practice of the "nine canons," then going on to their effective use. *If there is cultivation of the self, then the Way is established* refers to cultivating and rectifying oneself and not being depraved or evil. Then the Way and virtue flourish and are established.

3.2 *If worthiness is honoured, then there is no doubt*: By there being worthy men to assist, a crisis may be faced without uncertainty, and what is planned is good.

3.3 *If there is respect for great officials, then there is no uncertainty*: Xuan 眩 is also *huo* 惑 (doubt, uncertainty). By respecting and honouring great officials, their duties are clearly demarcated so there is no uncertainty in affairs. The "no doubt" of the earlier text refers to planning great matters for states and households. This saying "no confusion" refers to planning the multitude of affairs for states and households. But in the matters that are planned, there is a difference between great and small, which is why there is a difference in the statements.

3.4 *If there is acceptance of the mass of officials, then officers will repay the li* 禮 *many times over*: Although the mass of officials are lowly, if the prince magnanimously accepts them, then the officials are grateful for the prince's kindness. Therefore, if they would die for a prince in calamity and difficulty, this is *repaying the li* 禮 *many times over*.

3.5 *If the ordinary people are loved like one's children, then the "hundred surnames" will be urged on*: Zi 子 is equivalent to *ai* 愛 (to love). This speaks of loving the people like one's own children. Then the ordinary people are encouraged to serve their superiors.

3.6 *If there is encouragement for the hundred artisans, then the materials for use will be sufficient*: The hundred artisans produce materials for use. If the prince rewards them and summons them, then they will all come forward willingly. Therefore, the state's resources (materials for use) will be abundant and sufficient.

3.7 *If there is kindness towards those from afar, then the four regions will return to the fold*: Yuan 遠 refers to the feudal lords of foreign states. The "four regions" are, then, the foreign states. *If the feudal lords are cherished, then the world will be in awe of him*: Huai 懷 is equivalent to *anfu* 安撫 (to pacify). If the prince pacifies them and cherishes them, then the feudal lords will follow him obediently, the army will be strong, and the land will be extensive. Therefore, *the world will be in awe of him*.

ZY16:「齊明盛服,非禮不動,所以脩身也。去讒遠色,賤貨而貴德,所以勸賢也。尊其位,重其祿,同其好惡,所以勸親親也。官盛任使,所以勸大臣也。忠信重祿,所以勸士也。時使薄斂,所以勸百姓也。日省月試,既稟稱事,所以勸百工也。送往迎來,嘉善而矜不能,所以柔遠人也。繼絕世,舉廢國,治亂持危,朝聘以時,厚往而薄來,所以懷諸侯也。[1]

Comment: In the *Kongzi jiayu* version this section begins with a further question from Duke Ai—"how is this to be done?"—followed by "The Master said." What are listed are specific instructions, first on the matter of self-cultivation and worthiness, then on the relationships with the various groups considered in the previous paragraph (family members, great officers and officers, ordinary people, artisans and envoys), and then, finally, some specific instructions regarding foreign states and suggestions for them, directed at "cherishing" the feudal lords. The only notable points in the commentary are: (i) the readings of the opening four characters which differ somewhat in specifics (although not in content) from that given by Zhu Xi; (ii) the equating of *hao* 好 and *wu* 惡 in relation to family members with *qing shang* 慶賞 (congratulations and rewards) and *zhu fa* 誅罰 (punishments and penalties) respectively; and (iii) the reading of *ji* 既 as *xi* 餼 in the consideration of the hundred artisans.

注 ZY16 (鄭玄)

[1]「同其好惡」,不特有所好惡於同姓,雖恩不同,義必同也。尊重其祿位,所以貴之,不必授以官守,天官不可私也。「官盛任使」,大臣皆有屬官所任使,不親小事也。「忠信重祿」,有忠信者,重其祿也。「時使」,使之以時。「日省月試」,考校其成功也。「既」讀為「餼」,「餼稟」,稍食也。〈稾人職〉曰:「乘其事,考其弓弩,以下上其食。」[70] {齊,側皆反。去,起呂反。遠,于萬反。好惡,呼報反,下烏路反,又並如字,注同。斂,力驗反。既,依注音餼,許氣反。稟,彼錦反,一本又力錦反。稱,尺證反。朝,直遙反。稾,苦報反,一音古老反。上,時掌反。}

---

[70] See *Zhou li*, "Gao ren," SSJZS, 3:487–88. In the original "punishments and rewards" are added to "food ration."

ZY16: "Being well-ordered and well-disciplined, keeping one's garments and cap correct and not making movements contrary to *li* 禮 are ways to cultivate the self. Sending away flatterers and distancing oneself from beauties, despising worldly goods and valuing virtue are ways to encourage worthiness. Honouring their status, making their emolument substantial and making what they like and dislike (i.e. rewards and punishments) the same are ways to encourage devotion in family members. Providing them with numerous officers and letting them discharge their responsibilities are ways to encourage great ministers. Loyalty, trust, and a substantial salary are ways to encourage officers. Using them at appropriate times and making tax levies light are ways to encourage the ordinary people. Daily examinations and monthly trials, and making the grain allowance commensurate with work done are ways to encourage the hundred artisans. To give those departing a send-off and those arriving a welcome, to praise the good and be compassionate towards the incompetent are ways to be kind to those from afar. To restore continuity to lineages that have been broken and to raise states that have fallen, to bring order where there is disorder and give support where there is danger, to have proper times for court invitations, to be generous when sending them away, but requiring little when they come are ways to cherish the feudal lords. [1]

Notes ZY16 (Zheng Xuan)

[1] *Making what they like and dislike (i.e. rewards and punishments) the same*: This is to be even-handed in what is liked and disliked (i.e. rewards and punishments) by those with the same surname. Although the kindness (i.e. the closeness of the relationship) is not the same, right action must be the same. Respecting and giving weight to their salary and position is a way of honouring them. It is not necessary to confer office and the Ministry of State cannot be partial. *Providing them with numerous officers and letting them discharge their responsibilities*: Great officials all have many [lesser] officials to whom they can delegate responsibility, allowing [the former] not to devote themselves to minor matters. *Loyalty, trust and a substantial salary*: Where there are those who are loyal and trustworthy, make their salaries substantial. *Using them at appropriate times* is to use them according to the time. *Daily examinations and monthly trials* are to examine and compare their successful accomplishments. *Ji* 既 is read as *xi* 餼 (a monthly supply of grain); *xilin* 餼廩 is to reduce slightly their food ration. The "Gaoren zhi" says: "Evaluate their work and examine their bows and crossbows as a means of decreasing or increasing their food rations." . . .

疏 ZY16 (孔穎達)

{「齊明」至「侯也」。}

1.1　《正義》曰：此一節說行「九經」之法。

1.2　「齊明盛服」者，齊，謂整齊；明，謂嚴明；盛服，謂正其衣冠：是脩身之體也。此等「非禮不動」，是所以勸脩身。

1.3　「尊其位，重其祿，同其好惡，所以勸親親也」者，「尊其位」，謂授以大位；「重其祿」，謂重多其祿位。崇重而已，不可任以職事。「同其好惡」，好，謂慶賞，惡，謂誅罰。言於同姓既有親疏，恩親雖不同，義必須等，故不特有所好惡。

1.4　「勸親親也」者，尊位重祿以勉之，同其好惡以勵之，是「勸親親也」。

1.5　「官盛任使，所以勸大臣也。」官盛，謂官之盛大。「有屬臣」者，當令任使屬臣，不可以小事專勞大臣。大臣懷德，故云「所以勸大臣」也。「日省月試，既廩稱事，所以勸百工也」，既廩，謂飲食、糧廩也。言在上每日省視百工功程，每月試其所作之事，又飲食糧廩，稱當其事，功多則廩厚，功小則餼薄，是「所以勸百工也」。

1.6　「治亂持危」者，諸侯國內有亂，則治討之，危弱則扶持之。

Commentary ZY16 (Kong Yingda)

1.1 The *Zhengyi* says that this particular section explicates the method of practising the "nine canons."

1.2 *Being well-ordered and well-disciplined, keeping one's garments and cap correct*: Qi 齊 refers to *zhengqi* 整齊 (to be in good order, regular); *ming* 明 refers to *yanming* 嚴明 (being strict and impartial); *shengfu* 盛服 refers to correcting one's garments and cap. These are aspects of cultivating the self. They are equivalent to *not making movements contrary to li* 禮 and are ways of encouraging cultivation of the self.

1.3 *Honouring their status, making their salary substantial, and making what they like and dislike (i.e. rewards and punishments) the same are ways to encourage devotion in family members*: *Honouring their status* refers to conferring high status. *Making their salary substantial* refers to increasing considerably their salary and position. Just make the honour substantial; do not assign them official duties. In *making what they like and dislike the same*, hao 好 refers to *qingshang* 慶賞 (congratulations and rewards) and *wu* 惡 refers to *zhu fa* 誅罰 (punishments and penalties). This says that in those of the same surname, because some are close and some are distant, the kindness is not the same; nevertheless the *yi* 義 must be equivalent. Therefore, there is no partiality in terms of what is liked (rewards) and what is disliked (punishments).

1.4 *Encourage devotion in family members*: Honouring positions and making salaries substantial are ways to urge them on. Making what they like and dislike (i.e. rewards and punishments) the same (uniform) is a way to get them to put forth effort. This is *to encourage devotion in family members*.

1.5 *Providing them with numerous officers and letting them discharge their responsibilities are ways to encourage great ministers*: Guan sheng 官盛 refers to officials being very numerous. "There being subordinate officials" is that it is appropriate to allow the employment of subordinate officials because it is not possible to have only small matters burdening great officials. Great officials cherish virtue, therefore it says, *are ways to encourage great ministers*. *Daily examinations and monthly trials, and making the grain allowance commensurate with work done are ways to encourage the hundred artisans*: Ji lin 既廩 refers to drink and food, provisions and grain. This says that every day superiors examine and look at what the hundred artisans have achieved and every month test what they have made, and then they make their food and drink, provisions and grain commensurate with their work. If they have achieved much, then their grain ration is substantial; if they have achieved little, then their grain ration is slight. These are *the ways to encourage the hundred artisans*.

1.6 *To bring order where there is disorder and give support where there is danger*: If the feudal lords within the state are in disorder, then regulate and punish them. If there is danger and weakness, then help and support them.

1.7 「厚往而薄來，所以懷諸侯也」，「厚往」，謂諸侯還國，王者以其材賄厚重
往報之。「薄來」，謂諸侯貢獻，使輕薄而來。如此則諸侯歸服，故所以
懷諸侯也。

{注「尊重」至「其食」。}

1.8 《正義》曰：「尊重其祿位」者，言同姓之親，既非賢才，但尊重其祿位，
榮貴之而已，不必授以官守也。云「大臣皆有屬官所任，使不親小事也」
者，若《周禮》六卿其下，各有屬官，其細碎小事，皆屬官為之，是「不
親小事也」。云「既讀為餼，餼廩稍食也」者，以既與廩連文，又與餼字
聲同，故讀既為餼。「稍食」者，謂稍給之，故《周禮》「月終均其稍食」[71]
是也。引〈稾人職〉者，證其餼廩稱事。案《周禮‧夏官‧稾人》掌弓矢之
材，其職云「乘其事」，乘，謂計筭其所為之事。[72]「考其弓弩」，謂考校
弓弩之善惡多少。「以下上其食」，下，謂貶退；上，謂增益。善者則增
上其食，惡者則減其食故也。

ZY17:「凡為天下國家有九經，所以行之者一也。凡事豫則立，不豫則
廢。言前定則不跆，事前定則不困，行前定則不疚，道前定則不窮。[1]

---

[71] Presumably the reference is to *Zhou li*, "Guan zheng" and "Guan bo," which have: "幾
其出入均其稍食," "月終則會其稍食" and "月終則均秩"—see SSJZS, 3:51–53.
[72] See the *Zhou li*, "Gao ren," SSJZS, 3:487.

1.7   *To be generous when sending them away but requiring little when they come*:
      Hou wang 厚往 refers to the feudal lords returning to their kingdom. The king,
      through his materials and wealth, generously rewards those departing. *Bo lai* 薄來
      refers to the contribution from the feudal lords and that it should be slight when
      they come. In this way, then, the feudal lords submit. Therefore, it is the way to
      cherish the feudal lords.

1.8   The *Zhengyi* states that, "honouring and making substantial their salaries and
      positions" says that, with relatives of the same surname, for those who are not
      worthy and talented, one could nevertheless honour them and make their salaries
      and status substantial, glorify and respect them, and that is all. It is not necessary
      to confer official position [on them]. To say, "great officials all have many [lesser]
      officers for what they are responsible for, allowing them (i.e. the former) not to
      devote themselves to minor matters" is as in the *Zhou li* (Rites of Zhou) where
      the Six Ministers each had a group of officials below them, and their minor busi-
      ness, small things and odds and ends, were all done by this group of officials.
      This is "not being devoted to minor matters." It says, "*ji* 既 is read as *xi* 餼, i.e.
      the grain ration is slightly reduced" because *ji* 既 and *lin* 廩 are joined in the
      text, and also with the character *xi* 餼 the sound is the same, therefore *ji* 既 is
      then read as *xi* 餼. *Shao shi* 稍食 refers to reducing slightly what they gave them.
      Thus, the *Zhou li* saying: "At the end of the month equalise the *shao shi* 稍食" is
      this. Quoting the "Gaoren zhi" is proof that the grain ration was something that
      was estimated. According to the "Xia guan, Gaoren" of the *Zhou li*, grasping the
      materials of the bows and arrows, this assigned official says "assess his business."
      Cheng 乘 refers to calculating the business which he did. "Examine his bows and
      crossbows" refers to examining and comparing his bows and crossbows in terms
      of good and bad, many and few. "As a means of decreasing or increasing their
      food rations": *Xia* 下 refers to decreasing; *shang* 上 refers to increasing. If some-
      one is good, increase his food ration; if someone is bad, reduce his food ration.

ZY17: "All in all, for the world, states and households, there are nine canons,
[but] the means whereby they are implemented is one. In all matters, if there
is prior preparation, then they are established (i.e. succeed); if there is no
prior preparation, then they are destroyed (i.e. fail). If words are determined
beforehand, then there is no stumbling. If affairs are determined beforehand,
then nothing is lacking. If actions are determined beforehand, then there are
no faults. If the Way is determined beforehand, then there is no limit. **[1]**

Comment: This brief section acts as a concluding statement on the various aspects of the prescription for effective government offered by Confucius in response to Duke Ai's questioning. Both *Li ji* commentators take the one means of implementation to be prior preparation (*yu* 預), whereas Zhu Xi takes it to be *cheng* 誠 (see below). Glosses are offered for the three characters *jia* 跲 which is read as "to stumble," *kun* 困 which is read in the sense of *fa* 乏 (to lack, be in want), and *jiu* 疚 which is equated with *bing* 病 (fault, defect). These readings are incorporated into the translation.

注 ZY17 (鄭玄)

[1] 一，謂當豫也。跲，躓也。疚，病也。人不能病之。{跲，其劫反，皇音給。行，下孟反。疚音救。躓，徐音致。}

疏 ZY17 (孔穎達)

{「凡為」至「不窮」。}

1.1 《正義》曰：此一節明前「九經」之法，唯在豫前謀之，故云「所以行之者一也」。「一」，謂豫也。

1.2 「言前定則不跲」者，案《字林》云：「跲，躓也。」[73] 躓謂行倒躓也。將欲發言，能豫前思定，然後出口，則言得流行，不有躓躓也。

1.3 「事前定則不困」者，困，乏也。言欲為事之時，先須豫前思定，則臨事不困。

1.4 「行言[74]定則不疚」者，疚，病也。言欲為行之時，豫前思定，則行不疚病。

1.5 「道前定則不窮」者，言欲行道之時，豫前謀定，則道無窮也。

{注「人不能病之」。}

1.6 《正義》曰：解「經行前定則不疚」。人若行不豫前先定，人或不信病害之。既前定而後行，故人不能病害也。

---

[73]   This quotation was not located in either the *Zi lin* 字林 (CSJC, 69:21–32) or the *Zi lin jinghua* 字林精華 (CSJC, 73:395–584).

[74]   Read as *qian* 前 in conformity with the two preceding statements.

Notes ZY17 (Zheng Xuan)

[1] *Yi* 一 (one) refers to proper preparation. *Jia* 跲 is equivalent to *zhi* 躓 (to stumble). *Jiu* 疚 is equivalent to *bing* 病 (fault). Others are not able to fault him. . . .

Commentary ZY17 (Kong Yingda)

1.1   The *Zhengyi* says that this particular section clarifies the method of the previously mentioned "nine canons." It lies only in preparation and prior planning. Therefore it says, *the means whereby they are implemented is one. Yi* 一 (one) refers to preparation.

1.2   *If words are determined beforehand, then there is no stumbling:* According to the *Zi lin* 字林, *jia* 跲 is equivalent to *zhi* 躓 (to stumble). *Zhi* 躓 refers to falling down or stumbling when walking. If there is the intention to speak and one is able to prepare beforehand and establish one's thoughts, afterwards, when the words come forth, they achieve fluency and there is no stumbling or slipping.

1.3   *If affairs are determined beforehand, then nothing is lacking:* Kun 困 is equivalent to *fa* 乏 (to lack, be in want). This says that at the time one wishes to do things, one must prepare beforehand and establish one's thoughts, and then one can face a crisis without lacking anything (without difficulty).

1.4   *If actions are determined beforehand, then there are no faults:* Jiu 疚 is equivalent to *bing* 病 (fault, defect). This says that at the time one wishes to do something or act, if there is prior preparation and thoughts are established, then actions are free from faults and defects.

1.5   *If the Way is determined beforehand, then there is no limit:* This says that at the time one wishes to practise the Way, if there is prior preparation and plans are established, then the Way is without limit.

1.6   The *Zhengyi* says that this explains *if actions are determined beforehand, then there are no faults.* If men act without establishing things beforehand, they will be uncertain and lack confidence [and thereby] will be at fault and cause harm. When men establish things beforehand, and afterwards act, then they cannot be at fault or cause harm.

ZY18:「在下位不獲乎上，民不可得而治矣。**[1]**獲乎上有道，不信乎朋友，不獲乎上矣。信乎朋友有道，不順乎親，不信乎朋友矣。順乎親有道，反諸身不誠，不順乎親矣。誠身有道，不明乎善，不誠乎身矣。**[2]**

Comment: This is a problematic section. It is very similar to *Mencius* IVA.12 but there are several key differences as follows: (i) There the statement is attributed to Mencius. (ii) In the *Mencius* the preposition in the examples is *yu* 於 rather than *hu* 乎. (iii) Instead of "不順乎親," the *Mencius* has "事親弗悦" and the appropriate differences following this. (iv) The next two sentences in the *Mencius* IVA.12, which here are separated off as ZY19, show more substantial differences. The main problem of translation, accepting Zheng Xuan's reading of *huo* 獲 as *de* 得, is whether this and the corresponding verbs in the subsequent examples are to be taken as passive or active, and how *hu* 乎 is to be understood. As Haloun has argued, the passive form seems the more correct, but presents a particular problem in the third example. Here, as the construction is the same, the passive must be retained for consistency, and this is what we have done, albeit with reservations, particularly given the *Mencius* text. The overall argument, then, in reverse order to the text, is that to be *cheng* 誠 one has to be enlightened by goodness. If this is the case, then one can, successively, be obeyed by family members, trusted by friends, and apprehended by (i.e. gain the confidence of) superiors (the ruler) and therefore one can play an effective role in bringing about good order.

注 ZY18 (鄭玄)

[1] 獲，得也。言臣不得於君，則不得居位治民。

[2] 言知善之為善，乃能行誠。

疏 ZY18 (孔穎達)

{「在下」至「身矣」。}

1.1　《正義》曰：此明為臣為人，皆須誠信於身，然後可得之事。

1.2　「在下位不獲乎上」者，獲，得也。言人臣處在下位，不得於君上之意，則不得居位以治民，故云「民不可得而治矣」。

2.1　「獲乎上有道，不信乎朋友，不獲乎上矣」者，言臣欲得君上之意，先須有道德信著朋友。若道德無信著乎朋友，則不得君上之意矣。言欲得上意，先須信乎朋友也。

ZY18: "When those in inferior positions do not gain the confidence of supe-riors (the ruler), the people cannot be won over and brought to good order. **[1]** For gaining the confidence of superiors, there is the Way, but one who is not trusted by friends will not gain the confidence of superiors. For gaining the trust of friends, there is the Way, but one who is not compliant towards fam-ily members will not gain the trust of friends. For being compliant towards family members, there is the Way, but one who examines himself and finds he is not *cheng* 誠 will not be compliant towards family members. For becoming *cheng* 誠 in oneself, there is the Way, but one who is not enlightened by good-ness will not become *cheng* 誠 in himself. **[2]**

Notes ZY18 (Zheng Xuan)

[1] *Huo* 獲 is equivalent to *de* 得 (to get, apprehend, obtain). This says that, if ministers are not apprehended by (do not gain the confidence of) the prince, then they do not get to hold office and bring good order to the people.
[2] This says that, if one has the goodness that comes from knowing goodness, then one is able to act with *cheng* 誠.

Commentary ZY18 (Kong Yingda)

1.1   The *Zhengyi* says that this clarifies being an official and being a man. In both cases one must be *cheng* 誠 and *xin* 信 (trustworthy) in oneself. Afterwards, one can be successful in affairs.

1.2   *When those in inferior positions do not gain the confidence of superiors (the ruler)*: *Huo* 獲 is equivalent to *de* 得 (to get, apprehend, obtain). That is to say, if an of-ficial occupies an inferior position and does not gain the confidence of the ruler or superior in his purposes, then he will not get to hold office so as to bring good order to the people. Therefore it is said: *The people cannot be won over and brought to good order.*

2.1   *For gaining the confidence of superiors, there is the Way, but one who is not trusted by friends will not gain the confidence of superiors*: This says that, if officials wish to gain the confidence of a ruler or superior in his purposes, they must first have the Way and virtue and have the trust of their friends. If there is the Way and virtue, but no trust from their friends, then they will not gain the confidence of the ruler or superior. If they wish to gain the confidence of superiors, they must first be trusted by friends.

2.2　「信乎朋友有道，不順乎親，則不信乎朋友矣」者，言欲行信著於朋友，先須有道順乎其親。若不順乎其親，則不信乎朋友矣。

2.3　「順乎親有道，反諸身不誠，不順乎親矣」者，言順乎親，必須有道，反於己身，使有至誠。若身不能至誠，則不能「順乎親矣」。

2.4　「誠身有道，不明乎善，不誠乎身矣」者，言欲行至誠於身，先須有道明乎善行。若不明乎善行，則不能至誠乎身矣。言明乎善行，始能至誠乎身。能至誠乎身，始能順乎親。順乎親，始能信乎朋友。信乎朋友，始能得君上之意。得乎君上之意，始得居位治民也。

ZY19:「誠者，天之道也。誠之者，人之道也。誠者不勉而中，不思而得，從容中道，聖人也。誠之者，擇善而固執之者也。」[1]

2.2   *For gaining the trust of friends, there is the Way, but one who is not compliant towards family members will not gain the trust of friends*: That is to say, if one wishes to bring about trust in one's friends, one must first have the Way of compliance and obedience towards parents. If there is not compliance towards one's parents, then one will not be trusted by friends.

2.3   *For being compliant towards family members, there is the Way, but one who examines himself and finds he is not cheng* 誠 *will not be compliant towards family members*: This says that, if one wishes to be compliant towards family members, one must first have the Way. When one reflects on one's own self, let there be perfect *cheng* 誠. If one is not able to achieve perfect *cheng* 誠, then one cannot be *compliant towards family members.*

2.4   *For becoming cheng* 誠 *in oneself, there is the Way, but one who is not enlightened by goodness will not become cheng* 誠 *in himself*: That is to say, if one wishes to practise perfect *cheng* 誠 in oneself, one must first have the Way and manifest goodness in actions. If one does not manifest goodness in actions, then one is not able to have perfect *cheng* 誠 in oneself. That is to say, manifesting goodness in actions is the starting point of being able to be perfectly *cheng* 誠 in oneself. To be able to be perfectly *cheng* 誠 in oneself is the starting point of being able to be compliant towards family members. Being compliant towards family members is the starting point of being able to gain the trust of friends. Gaining the trust of friends is the starting point of being able to be apprehended by (gain the confidence of) the ruler or superior in his purposes. Being able to gain the confidence of the ruler or superior in his purposes is the starting point of getting an official position and bringing good order to the people.

ZY19: "Being *cheng* 誠 is the Way of Heaven. Becoming *cheng* 誠 is the Way of mankind. Being *cheng* 誠 is to exert no effort and yet be in the centre, not to think and yet to attain, to follow naturally the central Way and to be a sage. Becoming *cheng* 誠 is to choose goodness and hold fast to it." **[1]**

Comment: This corresponds to the antepenultimate and penultimate sentences of *Mencius* IVA.12(6) plus two further sentences not present in the *Mencius* but present in the *Kongzi jiayu*. *Mencius* concludes the section as follows: 「是故誠者，天之道也；思誠者，人之道也。至誠而不動者，未之有也；不誠，未有能動者也」 ("Hence being true is the Way of Heaven; to reflect on this is the Way of man. There has never been a man totally true to himself who fails to move others. On the other hand, there has never been one not true to himself who is capable of doing so."—trans. after Lau, 161). Primarily on the basis of the *Kongzi jiayu*, this is taken as being the end of Confucius' reply to Duke Ai. The section as a whole offers a definition of the two ways of being *cheng* 誠—the desired state of being true, genuine, absolutely sincere and without falseness. The first is the Way of Heaven in which the individual is innately *cheng* 誠 without effort, thought or study. He is naturally in the centre. This is for the sage. The second is the Way of mankind in which the individual becomes *cheng* 誠 through study and diligent effort with intense focus on goodness (*shan* 善). This is for others generally, or the worthy more specifically.

注 ZY19 (鄭玄)

[1] 言「誠者」，天性也。「誠之者」，學而誠之者也。因誠身説有大至誠。{中，丁仲反，又如字，下「中道」同。從，七容反。}

疏 ZY19 (孔穎達)

{「誠者」至「者也」。}

1.1 《正義》曰：前經欲明事君，先須身有至誠。此經明至誠之道，天之性也。則人當學其至誠之性，是上天之道不為而誠，不思而得。若天之性有生殺，信著四時，是天之道。「誠之者人之道也」者，言人能勉力學此至誠，是人之道也。不學則不得，故云人之道。

1.2 「誠者不勉而中，不思而得，從容中道，聖人也」者，此覆説上文「誠者，天之道也」。唯聖人能然，謂不勉勵而自中當於善，不思慮而自得於善，從容間暇而自中乎道，以聖人性合於天道自然，故云「聖人也」。

1.3 「誠之者，擇善而固執之者也」，此覆説上文「誠之者，人之道也」，謂由學而致此至誠，謂賢人也。言選擇善事，而堅固執之，行之不已，遂致至誠也。

{注「因誠身説有大至誠」。}

1.4 《正義》曰：以前經云欲事親事君，先須修身，有大至誠，故此説有大至誠。大至誠，則經云「誠者，天之道也」，聖人是矣。

Notes ZY19 (Zheng Xuan)

[1] That is to say, *being cheng* 誠 is the nature of Heaven. *Becoming cheng* 誠 is to study to become *cheng* 誠. For this reason, making oneself *cheng* 誠 speaks of there being great and perfect *cheng* 誠. . . .

Commentary ZY19 (Kong Yingda)

1.1   The *Zhengyi* says that the previous section was intended to make it clear that in serving the ruler, one must first have perfect *cheng* 誠 oneself. This section makes it clear that the Way of perfect *cheng* 誠 is the nature of Heaven. Then men ought to study the nature of its perfect *cheng* 誠. This is that the Way of Heaven above is not to act and yet to be *cheng* 誠, is not to think and yet to attain. This is like the nature of Heaven which creates and destroys, forever displaying the four seasons—this is the Way of Heaven. *Becoming cheng* 誠 *is the Way of mankind* says that people are able to devote diligent effort to study this perfect *cheng* 誠—this is the Way of mankind. If one does not study, then one does not attain [it]. Therefore, it speaks of "the Way of mankind."

1.2   *Being cheng* 誠 *is to exert no effort and yet be in the centre, not to think and yet to attain, to follow naturally the central Way and to be a sage.* This explicates the previous statement that *being cheng* 誠 *is the Way of Heaven.* Only a sage can be like this—referring to not putting forth effort and yet spontaneously being in proper accord with goodness, to not thinking or reflecting, and yet spontaneously achieving goodness, to following naturally and easily and being spontaneously centred in the Way because the nature of a sage is to be spontaneously in accord with the Way of Heaven. Therefore it says "to be a sage."

1.3   *Becoming cheng* 誠 *is to choose goodness and hold fast to it.* This explicates the previous statement that *becoming cheng* 誠 *is the Way of mankind*, referring to reaching this perfect *cheng* 誠 through study—a reference to worthy men. This speaks of choosing good deeds and firmly holding on to them, practising this unceasingly, and ultimately achieving perfect *cheng* 誠.

1.4   The *Zhengyi* states that, because the earlier section says that, if you wish to serve parents and the ruler, there must first be cultivation of the self and that this is great and perfect *cheng* 誠, this section explains what great and perfect *cheng* 誠 is. On great and perfect *cheng* 誠, then, the section says, *being cheng* 誠 *is the Way of Heaven*; the sage is this.

ZY20: 博學之，審問之，慎思之，明辨之，篤行之。有弗學，學之弗能，弗措也。有弗問，問之弗知，弗措也。有弗思，思之弗得，弗措也。有弗辨，辨之弗明，弗措也。有弗行，行之弗篤，弗措也。人一能之，己百之，人十能之，己千之。果能此道矣，雖愚必明，雖柔必強。[1]

Comment: This section, not included as part of Confucius' reply to Duke Ai, elaborates on the second of the two ways of attaining *cheng* 誠, i.e. the Way of mankind. In terms of translation, there are two issues: what *zhi* 之 refers to, and how *you* 有 is to be understood. On the first point, previous translators vary—e.g. "the way to be sincere" (Chan), "goodness" (Legge, Hughes, Haloun), "the way" (Ames and Hall), and unspecified (Riegel). Zheng Xuan's brief comment indicates that *cheng* 誠 is to be taken as an object of study. On the second point, most take *you* 有 to be non-specific—i.e. if there is something/anything not studied etc., but Kong Yingda's commentary indicates that this is to be taken as failure to study anything at all due to other demands.

注 ZY20 (鄭玄)

[1] 此勸人學誠其身也。果，猶決也。{措，七路反，下及注皆同，置也。強。其良反。}

疏 ZY20 (孔穎達)

{「博學」至「必強」。}

1.1　《正義》曰：此一經申明上經「誠之者，擇善而固執之」事。

1.2　「有弗學，學之弗能，弗措也」者，謂身有事，不能常學習，當須勤力學之。措，置也。言學不至於能，不措置休廢，必待能之乃已也。以下諸事皆然，此一句覆上「博學之」也。

1.3　「有弗問，問之弗知，弗措也」，覆上「審問之」也。「有弗思，思之弗得，弗措也」，覆上「慎思之」也。「有弗辨，辨之弗明，弗措也」，覆上「明辨之」也。「有弗行，行之弗篤，弗措也」，覆上「篤行之」也。

ZY20: Extensively study it (i.e. *cheng* 誠), judiciously enquire about it, carefully think about it, be clear about its distinctions, and sincerely practise it. If you have not studied, or have studied but not mastered it, do not put it aside. If you have not enquired, or have enquired but not understood it, do not put it aside. If you have not thought, or have thought but not grasped it, do not put it aside. If you have not distinguished, or have distinguished it but not clearly, do not put it aside. If you have not practised, or have practised it but not sincerely, do not put it aside. Even if others can do it after one attempt, you must make a hundred attempts. Even if others can do it after ten attempts, you must make a thousand attempts. If you are resolutely able to follow this Way, even if you are foolish, you will inevitably become enlightened; even if you are weak, you will inevitably become strong. **[1]**

Notes ZY20 (Zheng Xuan)

[1] This encourages men to study to make themselves *cheng* 誠. *Guo* 果 is like *jue* 決 (to resolve, decide). . . .

Commentary ZY20 (Kong Yingda)

1.1　The *Zhengyi* says that this particular section extends and clarifies the matter of the earlier section, i.e. *becoming cheng* 誠 *involves choosing goodness and holding fast to it.*

1.2　*If you have not studied, or have studied but not mastered it, do not put it aside*: This refers to the self having matters to attend to and not being able to study constantly. It is right that one must diligently study it. *Cuo* 措 is equivalent to *zhi* 置 (to put aside, dismiss). That is to say, if study does not come to be possible, you do not set it aside and stop. You must wait to be able to do it and complete it. The various matters following are all like this, with each sentence repeating the initial *extensively study it.*

1.3　*If you have not enquired, or have enquired but not understood it, do not put it aside* repeats the previous *judiciously enquire about it. If you have not thought, or have thought but not grasped it, do not put it aside* repeats the previous *carefully think about it. If you have not distinguished, or have distinguished it but not clearly, do not put it aside* repeats the previous *be clear about its distinctions. If you have not practised, or have practised it but not sincerely, do not put it aside* repeats the previous *sincerely practise it.*

1.4 「人一能之,己百之,人十能之,己千之」,謂他人性識聰敏,一學則能知之,己當百倍用功而學,使能知之。言己加心精勤之多,恒百倍於他人也。

1.5 「果能此道矣,雖愚必明,雖柔必強」,果,謂果決也。若決能為此百倍用功之道,識慮雖復愚弱,而必至明強。此勸人學誠其身也。

ZY21: 自誠明謂之性,自明誠謂之教。誠則明矣,明則誠矣。[1]

Comment: There are, then, two ways of being *cheng* 誠, an essentially untranslatable term which may be identified, with Rémusat, as "la perfection morale." One is through an innate enlightenment due to Heaven, which characterises the sage, and one is through a hard-won enlightenment gained through assiduous study, which characterises worthy men. Where there is enlightenment in the former instance, there is *cheng* 誠; where there is *cheng* 誠 in the second case, there is enlightenment.

注 ZY21 (鄭玄)

[1] 自,由也。由至誠而有明德,是聖人之性者也。由明德而有至誠,是賢人學以知之也。有至誠則必有明德,有明德則必有至誠。

疏 ZY21 (孔穎達)

{「自誠」至「誠矣」。}

1.1 《正義》曰:此一經顯天性至誠,或學而能。兩者雖異,功用則相通。

1.2 「自誠明謂之性」者,此說天性自誠者。自,由也,言由天性至誠,而身有明德,此乃自然天性如此,故「謂之性」。「自明誠謂之教」者,此說學而至誠,由身聰明,勉力學習,而致至誠,非由天性教習使然,故云「謂之教」。然則「自誠明謂之性」,聖人之德也。「自明誠謂之教」,賢人之德也。

1.4   *Even if others can do it after one attempt, you must make a hundred attempts. Even if others can do it after ten attempts, you must make a thousand attempts*: This refers to other men being, by nature, knowledgeable, intelligent and diligent, and being able to know it with a single study. It is right for you yourself to work a hundred times harder and study to allow you to be able to know it. That is to say, you must apply your mind and spirit unstintingly many times over, persevering a hundred times more than other men.

1.5   *If you are resolutely able to follow this Way, even if you are foolish, you will inevitably become enlightened; even if you are weak, you will inevitably become strong*: *Guo* 果 refers to *guojue* 果決 (firm, resolute). If you are resolutely able to carry out this way of a hundredfold diligence, although your knowledge and thought are repeatedly foolish and weak, you will inevitably reach enlightenment and strength. This encourages others to study to make themselves *cheng* 誠.

ZY21: *Ming* 明 (enlightenment, clarity, understanding) from *cheng* 誠 (purity, genuineness, sincerity) is referred to as nature. *Cheng* 誠 from *ming* 明 is referred to as teaching. If there is *cheng* 誠, there is *ming* 明. If there is *ming* 明, there is *cheng* 誠. **[1]**

Notes ZY21 (Zheng Xuan)

[1] *Zi* 自 is equivalent to *you* 由 (from). From perfect *cheng* 誠 there is enlightened virtue—this is the nature of the sage. From enlightened virtue there is perfect *cheng* 誠—this is the worthy man studying in order to know it. If there is perfect *cheng* 誠, then there must be enlightened virtue; if there is enlightened virtue, then there must be perfect *cheng* 誠.

Commentary ZY21 (Kong Yingda)

1.1   The *Zhengyi* says that this particular section displays heavenly nature either as perfect *cheng* 誠 or as studying and being able [to achieve it]. Although the two are different, the beneficial results are inter-related.

1.2   *Ming* 明 (enlightenment, clarity, understanding) from *cheng* 誠 (purity, genuineness, sincerity) is referred to as nature: This speaks of the *cheng* 誠 from heavenly nature. *Zi* 自 is equivalent to *you* 由 (from). That is to say, from the perfect *cheng* 誠 of heavenly nature, the self has enlightened virtue. This, then, is that heavenly nature is naturally like this, therefore it *is referred to as nature*. *Cheng* 誠 *from ming* 明 *is referred to as teaching*: This speaks of studying and [attaining] perfect *cheng* 誠. From one's own intelligence and diligent effort in studying, one reaches perfect *cheng* 誠. It is not from heavenly nature that teaching and practice cause it to be so. Therefore it is *referred to as teaching*. So then, *ming* 明 *from cheng* 誠 *is referred to as nature* is the virtue of the sage. *Cheng* 誠 *from ming* 明 *is referred to as teaching* is the virtue of the worthy man.

1.3 「誠則明矣」者,言聖人天性至誠,則能有明德,由至誠而致明也。

1.4 「明則誠矣」者,謂賢人由身聰明習學,乃致至誠,故云「明則誠矣」。是誠則能明,明則能誠,優劣雖異,二者皆通有至誠也。

ZY22: 唯天下至誠,為能盡其性。能盡其性,則能盡人之性。能盡人之性,則能盡物之性。能盡物之性,則可以贊天地之化育。可以贊天地之化育,則可以與天地參矣。[1]

Comment: Now the concept of perfect *cheng* 誠 is elaborated on. It comes about when the individual's nature, bestowed by Heaven, is *jin* 盡 (completed, fulfilled, fully realised, fully developed). Those who are able to complete or fully realise their Heaven-given natures are then able to beneficially affect other people and things to help their natures, and in so doing, join with Heaven and Earth. The readings of the three characters *jin* 盡, *zan* 贊 and *yu* 育 follow the glosses of Zheng Xuan.

注 ZY22 (鄭玄)

[1] 盡性者,謂順理之使不失其所也。贊,助也。育,生也。助天地之化生,謂聖人受命在王位致大平。{大音泰。}

疏 ZY22 (孔穎達)

{「唯天」至「參矣」。}

1.1 《正義》曰:此明天性至誠,聖人之道也。「唯天下至誠」者,謂一天下之內,至極誠信為聖人也。

1.3 *If there is cheng* 誠, *there is ming* 明: That is to say, if the sage has the perfect *cheng* 誠 of heavenly nature, then he is able to have enlightened virtue; from perfect *cheng* 誠, he reaches enlightenment.

1.4 *If there is ming* 明, *there is cheng* 誠: This refers to the worthy man, from his own intelligence and study, then coming to perfect *cheng* 誠. Therefore it says, *if there is ming* 明, *there is cheng* 誠. That is, if there is *cheng* 誠, then there can be enlightenment, and if there is enlightenment, then there can be *cheng* 誠. Although they are different in terms of superior and inferior, the two are both complete in being perfect *cheng* 誠.

ZY22: In the world only someone of perfect *cheng* 誠 is considered able to complete his nature. Someone who is able to complete his nature is then able to complete the natures of others. Someone who is able to complete the natures of others is then able to complete the natures of things. Someone who is able to complete the natures of things can then assist Heaven and Earth in their transforming and creating. Someone who can assist Heaven and Earth in their transforming and creating can then join with Heaven and Earth as a triad. **[1]**

Notes ZY22 (Zheng Xuan)

[1] "Completing nature" refers to [things] following principle, causing them not to lose their "whatness." *Zan* 贊 is equivalent to *zhu* 助 (to help, aid, assist). *Yu* 育 is equivalent to *sheng* 生 (to bring forth, give rise to). Aiding the transformations and creations of Heaven and Earth refers to the sage receiving the mandate and, in the position of king, bringing about great peace. . . .

Commentary ZY22 (Kong Yingda)

1.1 The *Zhengyi* says that this makes it clear that the perfect *cheng* 誠 of heavenly nature is the Way of the sage. *In the world only someone of perfect cheng* 誠 refers to someone who, within the world, reaches perfection in *cheng* 誠 and *xin* 信 being a sage.

1.2　「為能盡其性」者，以其至極誠信，與天地合，故能「盡其性」。既盡其
　　　性，則能盡其人與萬物之性，是以下云「能盡人之性」。既能盡人性，則
　　　能盡萬物之性，故能贊助天地之化育，功與天地相參。上云「誠者，天之
　　　道」，此兼云「地」者，上説至誠之理由神妙而來，故特云「天之道」。此
　　　據化育生物，故并云「地」也。

ZY23: 其次致曲，曲能有誠，誠則形，形則著，著則明，明則動，動則
變，變則化。唯天下至誠為能化。**[1]**

Comment: Two elements in this brief section are problematic—*qi ci* 其次 and *qu* 曲.
Zheng Xuan is quite clear as to his position in both. *Qi ci* 其次 refers to the second or next
level of *cheng* 誠, i.e. the *cheng* 誠 from enlightenment which is the Way of mankind followed by the worthy. It is next or second to the Way of Heaven, which is enlightenment
from *cheng* 誠 and is characterised by the sage. *Qu* 曲 refers to matters that are very small.
Whether these are the minutiae of everyday existence or something else—for example, the
essences (or "minutes" as Haloun calls them) of *jingqi* 精氣 theory—is unclear (see his
note, pp. 78–79).

注 ZY23 (鄭玄)

[1]「其次」，謂「自明誠」者也。致，至也。曲，猶小小之事也。不能盡性而有
至誠，於有義焉而已，形謂人見其功也。盡性之誠，人不能見也。著，形之大
者也。明，著之顯者也。動，動人心也。變，改惡為善也，變之久則化而性善
也。

疏 ZY23 (孔穎達)

{「其次」至「能化」。}

1.1　《正義》曰：此一經明賢人習學而致至誠，故云「其次致曲」。曲，謂細小
　　　之事。言其賢人致行細小之事不能盡性，於細小之事能有至誠也。

1.2   *Is considered able to complete his nature*: Because he reaches the ultimate perfection
        in *cheng* 誠 and *xin* 信, he joins in concert with Heaven and Earth. Therefore, he
        is able to "complete his nature." Since he is able to "complete his nature," then
        he is able to complete the natures of other people and of the ten thousand things.
        This is why it subsequently says "able to complete the natures of others." Since
        he is "able to complete the natures of others," then he is able to "complete the
        natures of the ten thousand things." Therefore, he is able to assist and help the
        transformations and creations of Heaven and Earth and in meritorious achieve-
        ment joins with Heaven and Earth as a triad. Previously it said *being cheng* 誠 *is
        the Way of Heaven*. This joining "Earth" in the statement above explains that the
        principle of perfect *cheng* 誠 comes from divine mystery. Here, particularly, it
        says *the Way of Heaven*. This is based on the transforming and creating of things.
        Therefore it also says "Earth."

ZY23: The next level pertains to minor matters. If there is *cheng* 誠 in minor
matters, then *cheng* 誠 has a form; if it has a form, then it is manifest; if it is
manifest, then it is clearly apparent; if it is clearly apparent, then it acts; if
it acts, then it effects change; if it effects change, then it transforms. In the
world, it is only perfect *cheng* 誠 that can transform. **[1]**

Notes ZY23 (Zheng Xuan)

[1] "The next level" (*qi ci* 其次) refers to *cheng* 誠 from *ming* 明 (enlightenment). *Zhi* 致 is
equivalent to *zhi* 至 (to reach to). *Qu* 曲 is like very small (trivial, minor) matters. Not being able to complete nature yet to have perfect *cheng* 誠 is in there being *yi* 義 and nothing
more. Form refers to others seeing its efficacy. The *cheng* 誠 of completing nature, others
cannot see. *Zhu* 著 is the largeness of the form. *Ming* 明 is the manifestation being
apparent. *Dong* 動 is to stir the human heart (mind). *Bian* 變 is changing evil to become
good. If the change is long-lasting, then there is transformation and nature is good.

Commentary ZY23 (Kong Yingda)

1.1   The *Zhengyi* says that this particular section makes it clear that the worthy man
        practises and studies, and so reaches perfect *cheng* 誠. Therefore it says, *the next
        level pertains to minor matters*. *Qu* 曲 refers to small (trivial) matters. That is to
        say, the worthy man who extends his actions to trivial matters is not able to com-
        plete nature, but in matters of little importance, he is able to have perfect *cheng* 誠.

1.2　「誠則形，形則著」者，謂不能自然至誠，由學而來，故誠則人見其功，是「誠則形」也。初有小形，後乃大而明著，故云「形則著」也。若天性至誠之人不能見，則不形不著也。

1.3　「著則明，明則動」者，由著故顯明，由明能感動於眾。

1.4　「動則變，變則化」者，既感動人心，漸變惡為善，變而既久，遂至於化。言惡人全化為善，人無復為惡也。

1.5　「唯天下至誠為能化」，言唯天下學致至誠之人，為能化惡為善，改移舊俗。不如前經天生至誠，能盡其次 [75] 性，與天地參矣。

{注「其次」至「善也」。}

1.6　《正義》曰：以前經云「自明誠謂之教」，是由明而致誠，是賢人，次於聖人，故云「其次，謂自明誠也」。云「不能盡性而有至誠，於有義焉而已」者，言此次誠不能如至誠盡物之性，但能有至誠於細小物焉而已。云「形謂人見其功也」者，由次誠彰露，人皆見其功也。云「盡性之誠，人不能見也」者，言天性至誠，神妙無體，人不見也。云「著，形之大者也」，解經「形則著」，初有微形，後則大而形著。云「變之久則化而性善也」者，解經「變則化」，初漸謂之變，變時新舊兩體俱有，變盡舊體而有新體謂之為「化」。如〈月令〉鳩化為鷹，[76] 是為鷹之時非復鳩也，猶如善人無復有惡也。

---

[75]　The character *ci* 次 here should probably be omitted—see SSJZS (2001 edition), "Zhongyong," 28:1692n1.

[76]　See *Li ji*, "Yue ling," SSJZS, 5:298. In the *Li ji* the 1st and 4th characters are transposed.

1.2   *Then cheng* 誠 *has a form; if it has a form, then it is manifest*: This refers to not
being able to have perfect *cheng* 誠 naturally [in that it] comes through study.
Therefore, if there is *cheng* 誠, then others see its efficacy. This is *then cheng* 誠
has a form. At first, there is a small form, but afterwards it becomes large and
clearly apparent. Therefore it is said *if it has a form, then it is manifest*. If the perfect *cheng* 誠 of heavenly nature is something others cannot see, then it has no
form and is not manifest.

1.3   *If it is manifest, then it is clearly apparent; if it is clearly apparent, then it acts*:
Through being manifest, it is clearly apparent, and through being clearly apparent, it can exert an influence on the multitude.

1.4   *If it acts, then it effects change; if it effects change, then it transforms*: Since it influences the human heart, it gradually changes bad to become good. If the change is
long-lasting, it subsequently reaches the level of a transformation. That is to say,
bad people completely change to become good and do not revert to being bad.

1.5   *In the world, it is only perfect cheng* 誠 *that can transform*: This says that, in the
world, only those men who study to reach perfect *cheng* 誠 are able to transform
the bad to become the good, are able to change and transform old habits. This is
not like the earlier section where the perfect *cheng* 誠 born of Heaven is able to
complete its nature and form a triad with Heaven and Earth.

1.6   The *Zhengyi* states that, when the earlier section says *cheng* 誠 *from ming* 明 *is
referred to as teaching*, this is to reach *cheng* 誠 through enlightenment. This is the
worthy man who is next in order to the sage. Therefore it says, "the next level
refers to *cheng* 誠 from enlightenment." Saying, "not able to complete nature and
yet having perfect *cheng* 誠 is in there being *yi* 義 and nothing more," means
that the next level of *cheng* 誠 is not, like perfect *cheng* 誠, able to complete the
nature of things, but is able to be perfect *cheng* 誠 in small things and that is
all. Saying, "having form refers to others seeing its efficacy," means that from
the next level of *cheng* 誠 being manifest and exposed, others all see its efficacy.
Saying, "the *cheng* 誠 of completing nature, others cannot see" means that the
perfect *cheng* 誠 of heavenly nature is a divine mystery without embodiment—
something which other people do not see. Saying, "being apparent is when the
form is large" explains the statement, *if it has a form, then it is manifest*. At first,
there is a minute form; afterwards, it is large and the form is manifest. Saying,
"if the change is long-lasting, then it is a transformation and the nature is good"
explains the statement *if it effects change, then it transforms*. At first, the change is
called gradual, but with change over time the new and the old, the two embodi-
ments are both present, but when there is complete change of the old embodiment and there is a new embodiment, this is referred to as "transformation." It
is like in the "Yue ling" where the turtle dove is transformed to become an eagle.
When it becomes an eagle, it does not return to being a turtle dove. In the same
way, the good person does not revert to being a bad person.

ZY24: 至誠之道，可以前知。國家將興，必有禎祥。國家將亡，必有妖孽。見乎蓍龜，動乎四體，禍福將至，善必先知之，不善必先知之，故至誠如神。[1]

Comment: It is clear from the commentary that the meaning here is that those with perfect *cheng* 誠, be they sages or worthies, have the ability to interpret the omens from divination, and such men will emerge even in dark times to give correct interpretations. Two minor points bearing on the translation are whether the omens or the events are the subject of the verbs *jian* 見 and *dong* 動 in the final sentence (Legge makes a point of suggesting the latter), and whether, in the last clause, *zhi cheng* 至誠 should be read as "the one with perfect *cheng* 誠."

注 ZY24 (鄭玄)

[1] 「可以前知」者，言天不欺至誠者也。前，亦先也。禎祥、妖孽，蓍龜之占，雖其時有小人、愚主，皆為至誠能知者出也。四體，謂龜之四足，春占後左，夏占前左，秋占前右，冬占後右。{禎音貞。妖，於驕反。《左傳》云：「地反物為妖。」《說文》作「䄏」，云「衣服、歌謠、草木之怪謂之䄏」。孽，魚列反，《說文》作「𡥂」，云「禽獸蟲蝗之怪謂之𡥂」。一本乎作於。蓍音尸。為，于偽反。}

疏 ZY24 (孔穎達)

{「至誠」至「如神」。}

1.1　《正義》曰：「至誠之道，可以前知」者，此由身有至誠，可以豫知前事。此至誠之內，是天生至誠，亦通學而至誠，故前經云「自明誠謂之教」，是賢人至誠同聖人也。言聖人、賢人俱有至誠之行，天所不欺，可知前事。「國家將興，必有禎祥」者，禎祥，吉之萌兆；祥，善也。言國家之將興，必先有嘉慶善祥也。《文說》：「禎祥者，言人有至誠，天地不能隱，如文王有至誠，招赤雀之瑞也。」[77] 國本有今異曰禎，本無今有曰祥。何為本有今異者？何胤云：「國本有雀，今有赤雀來，是禎也。國本無

---

[77]　See the *Li ji* (2001 edition), "Zhongyong," 28:1693n3 on this quotation.

ZY24: The Way of perfect *cheng* 誠 carries the possibility of foreknowledge. When a state is about to flourish, there are inevitably omens of good fortune. When a state is about to perish, there are inevitably omens of misfortune. These are seen in the milfoil and tortoise, and in the movements of the four limbs. When misfortune or good fortune is about to come, the good will certainly be known beforehand and the bad will certainly be known beforehand. Thus perfect *cheng* 誠 is like a spirit. **[1]**

Notes ZY24 (Zheng Xuan)

[1] *Carries the possibility of foreknowledge*: That is to say, Heaven does not deceive someone with perfect *cheng* 誠. *Qian* 前 is also *xian* 先 (first, beforehand). Auspicious omens and omens of misfortune are prognostications from the milfoil and tortoise. Although the times have lesser men and foolish rulers, all those who are perfectly *cheng* 誠 and are able to know come forth. The *si ti* 四體 refers to the four limbs of the tortoise. At the spring prognostication, it is the back left; at the summer prognostication it is the front left; at the autumn prognostication, it is the front right; and at the winter prognostication, it is back right. . . .

Commentary ZY24 (Kong Yingda)

1.1   The *Zhengyi* says, with respect to *the Way of perfect cheng* 誠 *carries the possibility of foreknowledge*, it is through the self being perfectly *cheng* 誠 that there can be knowledge before the event. This falls within perfect *cheng* 誠, both the perfect *cheng* 誠 born of Heaven and also the perfect *cheng* 誠 achieved through study. Therefore, the previous text says *cheng* 誠 *from ming* 明 *is referred to as teaching*, this being that the perfect *cheng* 誠 of the worthy man is the same as that of the sage. That is to say, the sage and the worthy man both have the actions of perfect *cheng* 誠 so Heaven is not deceptive and matters can be known beforehand. *When a state is about to flourish, there are inevitably omens of good fortune*: Good omens are indications of coming good fortune. *Xiang* 祥 is equivalent to *shan* 善 (good). This says that, if a state is going to prosper, it must first have good fortune and good omens. [According to] the *Wen shuo*, "Good omens refer to men who have perfect *cheng* 誠 which cannot be hidden from the world. For example, King Wen had perfect *cheng* 誠 and received the good omen of the red bird." What the state originally had but is now different is called *zhen* 禎 (auspicious); what it originally did not have but now has is called *xiang* 祥 (a good omen). How is it that what it originally had is now different? He Yin said: "The state originally had a bird (*qiao* 雀); now there is a red bird that comes and this is auspicious (*zhen* 禎). The state originally did not have a phoenix

鳳，今有鳳來，是祥也。」[78]《尚書》「祥桑、穀共生于朝」，[79] 是惡，此經云善，何？得入國者，以吉凶先見者皆曰「祥」，別無義也。「國家將亡，必有妖孽」者，妖孽，謂凶惡之萌兆也。妖猶傷也，傷甚曰孽，謂惡物來為妖傷之徵。若魯國鸜鵒來巢，以為國之傷徵。案《左傳》云：「地反物為妖。」[80]《說文》云：「衣服、歌謠、草木之怪為妖，禽獸、蟲蝗之怪為孽。」[81]

1.2　「見乎蓍龜，動乎四體」者，所以先知禎祥妖孽見乎蓍龜，卦兆發動於龜之四體也。

1.3　「禍福將至」者，禍謂妖孽，福謂禎祥。萌兆豫來，是「禍福將至」。

1.4　「善必先知之」者，善謂福也。

1.5　「不善必先知之」者，不善謂禍也。

1.6　「故至誠如神」者，言至誠之道，豫知前事，如神之微妙，故云「至誠如神」也。

1.7　注云「雖其時有小人、愚主，皆為至誠能知者出也」。

---

[78]　He Yin 何胤 was a scholar of the Liang dynasty. A work entitled the *Li ji yinyi* 禮記隱義 is attributed to him. It appears to be no longer extant—see the *Quan shanggu Sandai Qin Han Sanguo Liuchao wen* 全上古三代秦漢三國六朝文, *Liangwen* 梁文 7, 40:12.

[79]　This is from the *Shang shu*, "Da zhuan, Xia zhuan"—for the quote *in extenso* see ZWDCD, 6:1443.

[80]　See the *Zuo zhuan* for Xuan, 15th year, LCC, 5:326.

[81]　*Shuowen*—the entry for *yao* is given on p. 628. The quote above is not there.

(*feng* 鳳) but now there is a phoenix that comes and this is a good omen (*xiang* 祥)." The *Shang shu* says: "The mulberry trees and grain of good omen all arose in the morning." This was bad [yet] this classic says it was good. How so? Those who gained entry to the state, in first seeing it in terms of good and bad fortune, all said: "It was a good omen (*xiang* 祥) differentiating what was not *yi* 義." *When a state is about to perish, there are inevitably omens of misfortune*: Bad omens refer to warnings of impending misfortune or evil. *Yao* 妖 is like *shang* 傷 (to harm, wound) and when *shang* 傷 is extreme it is called *nie* 孽 and refers to bad things coming being evidence of what is strange and harmful. For example, the mynah bird coming to nest in Lu was taken as evidence of harm for the state. In the *Zuo zhuan* it says: "The land turning back things was strange." The *Shuowen* says: "Clothes, folk songs, and grasses and trees being strange is *yao* 妖; birds and beasts, insects and locusts being strange is *nie* 孽."

1.2   *These are seen in the milfoil and tortoise, and in the movements of the four limbs*: How there is foreknowledge of good or bad fortune is to look at the milfoil and tortoise and divine the omens in the movements of the four legs of the tortoise.

1.3   *When misfortune or good fortune is about to come*: *Huo* 禍 refers to *yao nie* 妖孽 (omens of misfortune); *fu* 福 refers to *zhen xiang* 禎祥 (omens of good fortune). Warnings of what is to come are *misfortune or good fortune is about to come*.

1.4   *The good will certainly be known beforehand*: *Shan* 善 refers to *fu* 福 (good fortune).

1.5   *The bad will certainly be known beforehand*: *Bu shan* 不善 refers to *huo* 禍 (misfortune).

1.6   *Thus perfect cheng* 誠 *is like a spirit*: That is to say, the Way of perfect *cheng* 誠 includes foreknowledge preceding events like the subtle mystery of the spirits. Therefore it says *perfect cheng* 誠 *is like a spirit*.

1.7   The note says: "Although at times there are lesser men and foolish rulers, all who are perfectly *cheng* 誠 and are able to know come forth."

1.8   《正義》曰：鄭以聖人君子將興之時，或聖人有至誠，或賢人有至誠，則
       國之將興，禎祥可知。而小人、愚主之世無至誠，又時無賢人，亦無至
       誠，所以得知國家之將亡而有妖孽者，雖小人、愚主，由至誠之人生在亂
       世，猶有至誠之德，此妖孽為有 至誠能知者出也。案〈周語〉云：「<u>幽王</u>
       三年，三川皆震，<u>伯陽父</u>曰：『<u>周</u>將亡矣。昔<u>伊</u>、<u>洛</u>竭而<u>夏</u>亡，<u>河</u>竭而<u>商</u>
       亡』。」時三川皆震，為<u>周</u>之惡瑞，是<u>伯陽父</u>有至誠能知<u>周</u>亡也。又<u>周惠</u>
       <u>王</u>十五年，有神降于<u>莘</u>。<u>莘</u>，<u>虢</u>國地名。<u>周惠王</u>問<u>內史過</u>，<u>史過</u>對曰：
       「<u>夏</u>之興也，<u>祝融</u>降于<u>崇山</u>，其亡也，<u>回祿</u>信于<u>聆隧</u>。<u>商</u>之興也，<u>檮杌</u>次
       於<u>丕山</u>，其亡也，<u>夷羊</u>在牧。<u>周</u>之興也，<u>鸑鷟</u>鳴於<u>岐山</u>，其衰也，<u>杜伯</u>
       射<u>宣王</u>於<u>鎬</u>。今<u>虢</u>多涼德，<u>虢</u>必亡也。」又<u>內史過</u>有至誠之德，神為之
       出。是愚主之世，以妖孽為至誠能知者出也。[82]

---

[82] This is an incomplete quotation from the *Guoyu*, "Zhou yu shang," SBCK, 14:8–9.

1.8   The *Zhengyi* states that according to Zheng, if the time was one when sages and
        noble men were going to flourish, or sages had perfect *cheng* 誠, or worthy men
        had perfect *cheng* 誠, then that the state would flourish could be known by good
        omens. But if the age was one of lesser men and foolish rulers without perfect
        cheng 誠, and the times were without worthy men, and also without perfect *cheng*
        誠, that was how to know that the state was about to perish and there would be
        bad omens. Although there were lesser men and foolish kings, because men of
        perfect *cheng* 誠 are born in a disordered age, there was still the virtue of perfect
        cheng 誠, and when these bad omens occurred, there would be those of perfect
        cheng 誠 and the ability to know who came forth. According to the "Zhou yu,"
        it says: "In the three years of King You the three rivers were all disturbed. Bo-
        yang Fu said: 'Zhou was about to be lost. Previously, the Yin and the Luo were
        exhausted and Xia was lost. The He was exhausted and Shang was lost.'" The
        time of the three rivers all being disturbed was Zhou's bad omen; this was a case
        of Boyang Fu having perfect *cheng* 誠, and being able to know that Zhou would
        perish. Also, in the 15th year of King Hui of Zhou, there was a spirit that came
        down in Xin. Xin was the name of a place in the state of Guo. The King [Hui
        of Zhou] asked the Royal Secretary [Guo who replied:] "When Xia was flourish-
        ing, the god of fire descended at Mount Chong; at its loss, Hui Lu (the god of
        fire) gave an indication at Ling Sui. In Shang's flourishing, the Tao Wu arrived at
        Pi Shan; at its loss, Yi Yang was at Mu. In Zhou's flourishing, the Yuezhuo bird
        called out at Mount Qi; at its decline, Du Bo shot at King Xuan at Hao. Now
        Gui has many with very little virtue so Gui must perish." Also, the Royal Secre-
        tary Guo had the virtue of perfect *cheng* 誠 and the spirits made him come forth.
        This was a time of foolish kings when, through bad omens, one who had perfect
        cheng 誠 and was able to know came forth.

ZY25: 誠者自成也，而道自道也。**[1]**誠者物之終始，不誠無物。**[2]**是故君子誠之為貴。**[3]**誠者非自成己而已也，所以成物也。成己，仁也。成物，知也。性之德也，合外內之道也。**[4]**故時措之宜也。**[5]**故至誠無息，不息則久，久則徵，徵則悠遠，悠遠則博厚，博厚則高明。**[6]**博厚所以載物也，高明所以覆物也，悠久所以成物也。博厚配地，高明配天，悠久無疆。**[7]**如此者，不見而章，不動而變，無為而成，天地之道，可壹言而盡也。**[8]**其為物不貳，則其生物不測。**[9]**天地之道博也，厚也，高也，明也，悠也，久也。**[10]**

Comment: The first part of this section, which Zhu Xi separates off (i.e. that ending with note [5] above) is somewhat problematical. To quote Legge: "I have had difficulty in translating this chapter, because it is difficult to understand it" (418n25). The difficulty hinges particularly on how *zi* 自 and *cheng* 成 in the first sentence are understood and the role of *zhe* 者 in the first clause. We have taken the Latin version of Intorcetta et al., with the direct translation of the two clauses being followed by an explanatory comment in each case, to capture the meaning as follows: "Vera solidaque perfectio est suimet ipsius perfecto. Id est, se ipsa perficatur: aut per se ipsam perfecta est et non per aliquid a se distinctum: Et regula est sui ipsius regula; ad quam sic exiguntur et diriguntur res aliae, ut ipsa per aliam non dirigatur."[83] This is reflected in the translation given above. *Cheng zhe* 誠者 is then in contrast to *cheng zhi zhe* 誠之者 in ZY19. A development of the argument here is that "*cheng*-ing" (perfecting, realising, completing) the self is equated with *ren* 仁, whilst "*cheng*-ing" things is equated with *zhi* 知 (knowledge, wisdom). There then follows an explanation of the qualities of *cheng* 誠 such that *cheng* 誠 (and therefore the person who is *cheng* 誠) is able to join with Heaven and Earth in the creating and transforming which make all things unique.

注 ZY25 (鄭玄)

[1] 言人能至誠，所以「自成」也。有道藝所以自道達。{自道音導，注「自道」同。}

[2] 物，萬物也，亦事也。人人無誠，萬物不生，小人無誠，則事不成。

[3] 言貴至誠。

[4] 以至誠成己，則仁道立。以至誠成物，則知彌博。此五性之所以為德也，外內所須而合也，外內猶上下。{知音智，注同。}

[5] 時措，言得其時而用也。

83 Prosperi Intorcetta et al., *Confucius Sinarum Philosophus* (Paris: Danielem Horthemels, 1687), "Scientiae Sinicae" (Book 2), 74.

ZY25: Being *cheng* 誠 is to be naturally complete and the Way is spontaneously directing. **[1]** Being *cheng* 誠 is the end and beginning of things; without *cheng* 誠 there are no things. **[2]** This is why the noble man regards *cheng* 誠 as prized. **[3]** But being *cheng* 誠 does not just naturally complete the self and nothing more—it is the way of completing things. Completing the self is *ren* 仁. Completing things is knowledge (*zhi* 知). The virtues of nature combine the external and internal [components] of the Way. **[4]** Therefore, to use them at the proper times is fitting. **[5]** Thus, perfect *cheng* 誠 is unceasing. Being unceasing, it is long-lasting. Being long-lasting, it is efficacious. Being efficacious, it is far-reaching. Being far-reaching, it is broad and thick. Being broad and thick, it is high and bright. **[6]** Being broad and thick is how it contains things. Being high and bright is how it spreads over things. Being far-reaching and long-lasting is how it completes things. In being broad and thick, it matches Earth. In being high and bright, it matches Heaven. In being far-reaching and long-lasting, it is without limit. **[7]** Being like this, it is not seen and yet it is displayed; it does not move and yet it effects change; it does not act and yet it brings about completion. The Ways of Heaven and Earth can be completely encapsulated in a single term. **[8]** Since the things they create are never duplicated, then their giving rise to things is unfathomable. **[9]** The Way of Heaven is broad; it is thick; it is high; it is bright; it is far-reaching; and it is long-lasting. **[10]**

Notes ZY25 (Zheng Xuan)

[1] This says that men can be perfectly *cheng* 誠 by being "naturally complete." There are moral principles and technical skills by which the self has access to the Way. . . .
[2] *Wu* 物 is equivalent to *wanwu* 萬物 (the ten thousand things) and also to *shi* 事 (matters, affairs, events). If great men are without *cheng* 誠, the ten thousand things do not arise. If small men are without *cheng* 誠, then matters are not brought to completion.
[3] This speaks of prizing perfect *cheng* 誠.
[4] If, through perfect *cheng* 誠, there is completion of the self, then *ren* 仁 and *dao* 道 (the Way) are established. If, through perfect *cheng* 誠, there is the completion of things, then *zhi* 知 (wisdom, knowledge) is full and extensive. This is how the five natures become virtuous; it is what external and internal must have and be in accord with. External (*wai* 外) and internal (*nei* 內) are like above (*shang* 上) and below (*xia* 下). . . .
[5] *Shi cuo* 時措 speaks of attaining its time and being put to use.

[6] 徵，猶效驗也。此言至誠之德既著於四方，其高厚日以廣大也。徵或為「徹」。

[7] 後言悠久者，言至誠之德，既至「博厚」、「高明」，配乎天地，又欲其長久行之。{疆，居良反。}

[8] 言其德化與天地相似，可一言而盡，要在至誠。

[9] 言至誠無貳，乃能生萬物多無數也。{不貳，本亦作貸，音二。}

[10] 此言其著見成功也。

疏 ZY25 (孔穎達)

1–3.1 「誠者自成也，而道自道也」者，言人能有至誠之德，則自成就其身，故云「誠者自成也」。若人有道藝，則能自道達於己，故云「而道自道也」。「誠者物之終始，不誠無物」者，言人有至誠，則能與萬物為終始。若無至誠，則不能成其物。若大人無至誠，則不能生萬物。若小人無至誠，則不能成其物。物，猶事也。小人無誠，則不能成事。

{「誠者」至「久也」。}

1–3.2 此經明己有至誠能成就物也。

4.1 「誠者非自成己而已也，所以成物也」者，言人有至誠，非但自成就己身而已，又能成就外物。

4.2 「成己，仁也。成物，知也」者，若能成就己身，則仁道興立，故云「成己，仁也」。若能成就外物，則知力廣遠，故云「成物，知也」。

4.3 「性之德也」者，言誠者是人五性之德，則仁、義、禮、知、信皆猶至誠而為德，故云「性之德也」。

[6] *Zheng* 徵 is like *xiaoyan* 效驗 (efficacious, verification). This says that, when the virtue of perfect *cheng* 誠 is already manifest in the four directions, each day its height and thickness are wider and greater. *Zheng* 徵 is sometimes written as *che* 徹 (discerning, intelligible).

[7] Subsequently, to say "far-reaching and long-standing" is to speak of the virtue of perfect *cheng* 誠. Since it is "broad and thick" and "high and bright," it pairs with Heaven and Earth and there is also the desire for its long-lasting action. . . .

[8] That is to say, this virtue transforms and is like Heaven and Earth. If there is one term that can completely express it, it must be "perfect *cheng* 誠."

[9] This says that perfect *cheng* 誠 is not duplicating and so is able to give rise to the ten thousand things that are numerous beyond number. . . .

[10] This speaks of its manifest efficacy.

Commentary ZY25 (Kong Yingda)

1–3.1 *Being cheng 誠 is to be naturally complete and the Way is spontaneously directing*: That is to say, if a man can have the virtue of perfect *cheng* 誠, then there is spontaneous completion as a consequence for himself. Therefore, it says *being cheng 誠 is to be naturally complete*. If a man has moral principles and technical skills, then he is spontaneously able to realise and attain the Way in himself. Therefore, it says, *the Way is spontaneously directing*. *Being cheng 誠 is the end and beginning of things; without cheng 誠 there are no things*: That is to say, if a man has perfect *cheng* 誠, then he is able to join with the ten thousand things in being ends and beginnings. If he is without perfect *cheng* 誠, then he is not able to complete these matters. *Wu* 物 is like *shi* 事 (matters, affairs). The lesser man is without *cheng* 誠 so he is not able to complete matters.

1–3.2 This section makes it clear that the self who has perfect *cheng* 誠 is able to complete matters.

4.1 *But being cheng 誠 does not just naturally complete the self and nothing more—it is the way of completing things*: That is to say, if a man has perfect *cheng* 誠, not only does he naturally complete the self and nothing more, but he is also able to complete external matters.

4.2 *Completing the self is ren 仁. Completing things is knowledge (zhi 知)*: If one is able to successfully complete oneself, then the Way of *ren* 仁 prospers and is established. Therefore, it says, *completing the self is ren 仁*. If one is able to successfully complete external matters, then intellectual power is broad and far-reaching. Therefore, it says, *completing things is knowledge (zhi 知)*.

4.3 *Virtues of nature* speaks of being *cheng* 誠 as the five virtues of a person's nature. Then *ren* 仁, *yi* 義, *li* 禮, *zhi* 知, and *xin* 信 are all like perfect *cheng* 誠 and are virtues. Therefore it says *virtues of nature*.

4.4　「合外內之道也」者，言至誠之行合於外內之道，無問外內，皆須至誠。於人事言之，有外有內，於萬物言之，外內猶上下。上謂天，下謂地。天體高明，故為外；地體博厚閉藏，故為內也。是至誠合天地之道也。

5.1　「故時措之宜也」，措，猶用也。言至誠者成萬物之性，合天地之道，故得時而用之，則無往而不宜，故注云「時措，言得其時而用也」。

6.1　「故至誠無息」，言至誠之德，所用皆宜，無有止息，故能久遠、博厚、高明以配天地也。

6.2　「不息則久」者，以其不息，故能長久也。

6.3　「久則徵」，徵，驗也。以其久行，故有徵驗。

6.4　「徵則悠遠」者，悠，長也。若事有徵驗，則可行長遠也。

6.5　「悠遠則博厚」，以其德既長遠，無所不周，故「博厚」也。養物博厚，則功業顯著，故「博厚則高明」也。

7.1　「博厚所以載物也」，以其德博厚，所以負載於物。

7.2　「高明所以覆物也」，以其功業高明，所以覆蓋於萬物也。

7.3　「悠久所以成物也」，以行之長久，能成就於物，此謂至誠之德也。

7.4　「博厚配地」，言聖人之德博厚配偶於地，與地同功，能載物也。

4.4   *Combine the external and internal [components] of the Way*: That is to say, the practice of perfect *cheng* 誠 conforms to the external and internal [components] of the Way and does not question external and internal, both necessarily being perfectly *cheng* 誠. In speaking of a man's affairs, there is external and there is internal; in speaking of the ten thousand things, external and internal are like above (*shang* 上) and below (*xia* 下). Above refers to Heaven; below refers to Earth. The substance of Heaven is high and bright, therefore it is external. The substance of Earth is broad and thick and is stored up, therefore it is internal. This is perfect *cheng* 誠 combining the Ways of Heaven and Earth.

5.1   *Therefore, to use them at the proper times is fitting*: *Cuo* 措 is like *yong* 用 (to use, employ). That is to say, perfect *cheng* 誠 completes the natures of the ten thousand things and combines the Ways of Heaven and Earth. Therefore, it uses the times that are right for it, so nothing goes forward that is not appropriate. Thus, the note states, "*shi cuo* 時措 says it gets its time and uses it."

6.1   *Thus perfect cheng* 誠 *is unceasing*: That is to say, the virtue of perfect *cheng* 誠 is in all cases fitting in what it is used for and does not come to rest or cease. Therefore, it can be long-lasting and far-reaching, broad and thick, and high and bright so as to match Heaven and Earth.

6.2   *Being unceasing, it is long-lasting*: By its being unceasing, it can therefore be long-lasting.

6.3   *Being long-lasting, it is efficacious*: *Zheng* 徵 is equivalent to *yan* 驗 (efficacious, fulfilling, verifying). Through its acting over a long time, it is therefore efficacious.

6.4   *Being efficacious, it is far-reaching*: *You* 悠 is equivalent to *chang* 長 (long). If matters are efficacious, then it is possible to implement them for a long time and over a distance.

6.5   *Being far-reaching, it is broad and thick*: By its virtue being long-lasting and far-reaching, there is nothing which it does not encompass. Therefore, it is *broad and thick*. If the nourishing of things is broad and thick, then efficacy is manifest and apparent. Therefore, *being broad and thick, it is high and bright*.

7.1   *Being broad and thick is how it contains things*: By its virtue being broad and thick is how it gives laborious service to things (how it bears the burden of things).

7.2   *Being high and bright is how it spreads over things*: By its efficacy being high and bright is how it spreads over and covers the ten thousand things.

7.3   *Being far-reaching and long-lasting is how it completes things*: Through acting over a long time it is able to successfully complete matters. This refers to the virtue of perfect *cheng* 誠.

7.4   *In being broad and thick, it matches Earth* says that the virtue of the sage, being broad and thick (extensive and substantial), pairs with Earth, joining Earth in the same efficacy, and is able to bear the burden of things.

7.5 「高明配天」，言聖人功業高明配偶於天，與天同功，能覆物也。

7.6 「悠久無疆」，疆，窮也。言聖人之德既能覆載，又能長久行之，所以無窮。「悠久」，則上經「悠遠」。「悠久」在「博厚高明」之上，此經「悠久」在「博厚高明」之下者，上經欲明積漸先悠久，後能博厚高明。此經既能博厚高明，又須行之悠久，故反覆言之。

8.1 「如此者，不見而章，不動而變，無為而成」者，言聖人之德如此博厚高明悠久，不見所為而功業章顯，不見動作而萬物改變，無所施為而道德成就。

8.2 「天地之道，可壹言而盡也」者，言聖人之德能同於天地之道，欲尋求所由，可一句之言而能盡其事理，正由於至誠，是「壹言而盡也」。

9.1 「其為物不貳，則其生物不測」者，言聖人行至誠，接待於物不有差貳，以此之故，能生殖眾物不可測量，故鄭云言「多無數也」。

7.5   *In being high and bright it matches Heaven* says that the sage's achievement being high and bright matches Heaven, joining Heaven in the same efficacy, and is able to cover things.

7.6   *In being far-reaching and long-lasting, it is without limit: Jiang* 疆 is equivalent to *qiong* 窮 (limit). That is to say, the sage's virtue, since it can be covering and containing, can also be practised for a long time, which is how it is without limit. *You jiu* 悠久 (far-reaching and long-lasting) is, then, the *you yuan* 悠遠 of the earlier text. *You jiu* 悠久 precedes *bohou gaoming* 博厚高明, [whereas] in this section, *you jiu* 悠久 follows *bohou gaoming* 博厚高明. In the first instance, the wish is to make it clear that the gradual build up that precedes is far-reaching and long-lasting and is subsequently able to be broad and thick, high and bright. In this section, since it is able to be broad and thick, high and bright, its practice must also be far-reaching and long-lasting, therefore it is reiterated.

8.1   *Being like this, it is not seen and yet is displayed; it does not move and yet it effects change; it does not act and yet it brings about completion* says that the sage's virtue is broad and thick, high and bright, and far-reaching and long-lasting like this. You do not see what is done and yet the effect is manifest; you do not see the actions and yet the ten thousand things undergo change. Nothing is done and yet the Way and virtue are successfully completed.

8.2   *The Ways of Heaven and Earth can be completely encapsulated in a single term:* That is to say, the virtue of the sage can combine with the Ways of Heaven and Earth. If you wish to seek out how this is so, it can be expressed in one sentence which is able to express completely its principles of action. Truly, it is through perfect *cheng* 誠—this is *can be completely encapsulated in a single term.*

9.1   *Since the things they create are never duplicated, then their giving rise to things is unfathomable* says that the sage's practice of perfect *cheng* 誠 admits of no error or duplication in things, and for this reason is able to give rise to and nurture an inestimable number of things. Therefore, Zheng says, "many beyond number."

ZY26: 今夫天，斯昭昭之多，及其無窮也，日月星辰繫焉，萬物覆焉。今夫地，一撮土之多，及其廣厚，載華嶽而不重，振河海而不洩，萬物載焉。今夫山，一卷石之多，及其廣大，草木生之，禽獸居之，寶藏興焉。今夫水，一勺之多，及其不測，黿鼉蛟龍魚鼈生焉，貨財殖焉。**[1]**《詩》曰：「惟天之命，於穆不已。」蓋曰天之所以為天也。「於乎不顯，文王之德之純。」蓋曰文王之所以為文也，純亦不已。**[2]**

Comment: The point of this section, simply stated and made with reference to Heaven, Earth, mountains and waters, is that whatever is large or great arises from small beginnings, and this applies also to virtues, specifically *cheng* 誠. Quotations from the *Yi jing* and from the *Odes* are adduced to support this claim. Interestingly, Kong Yingda takes issue with this analogy in his note 1.5.

注 ZY26 (鄭玄)

[1] 此言天之高明，本生「昭昭」；地之博厚，本由「撮土」；山之廣大，本起「卷石」；水之不測，本從「一勺」：皆合少成多，自小致大，為至誠者，亦如此乎！昭昭猶耿耿，小明也。振，猶收也。[84] 卷，猶區也。{夫音扶，下同。昭，章遙反，注同，本亦作「炤」，同。撮，七活反。華嶽，戶化、戶瓜二反，本亦作「山嶽」。洩，息列反。卷，李音權，又羌權反，范羌阮反，注同。藏，才浪反。勺，徐市若反。黿音元。鼉，徒河反，一音直丹反。蛟音交，本又作蛟。鼈，必列反。耿，公迥反，又公頂反，舊音孔頂反。區，羌俱反。}

[2] 天所以為天，文王所以為文，皆由行之無已，為之不止，如天地山川之云也。《易》曰「君子以順德，積小以成高大」[85]是與。{於穆，上音烏，下「於乎」亦同。乎，呼奴反。慎如字，一本又作「順」。與音餘。}

疏 ZY26 (孔穎達)

{「今夫」至「不已」。}

1.1 《正義》曰：此一節明至誠不已，則能從微至著，從小至大。

---

84   There is some question as to whether the previous nine characters should be included here—see SSJZS (2001 edition), "Zhongyong," 28:1697n4.

85   See the *Yi jing*, "Cui," SSJZS, 1:107.

ZY26: Now Heaven is this multiplicity of small points of light, yet such is its limitlessness that the sun, moon, planets and stars are suspended in it, and the ten thousand things are covered by it. Now the Earth is a multiplicity of handfuls of soil, yet such is its breadth and thickness that it supports the holy peak of Mount Hua and is not weighed down, collects the rivers and seas and they do not leak away, and the ten thousand things are contained in it. Now the mountains are a multiplicity of single small stones, yet such is their breadth and height that grasses and trees grow on them, birds and beasts dwell in them, and precious things are stored and flourish in them. Now the waters are a multiplicity of single scoops, yet such is their unfathomableness that salt-water turtles, water lizards, various dragons, fish and fresh-water turtles all arise in them, and goods and materials flourish in them. **[1]** The *Odes* says: "The decree of Heaven—Ah! how glorious and unending!" This tells why Heaven is Heaven. [The *Odes* also says:] "Ah! how brilliant it was, the purity of King Wen's virtue!" This tells why King Wen was *wen* (cultured) and that his purity too was unending. **[2]**

Notes ZY26 (Zheng Xuan)

[1] This says that Heaven's height and brightness originally arose from "small points of light"; that Earth's breadth and thickness was originally from "handfuls of earth"; that the mountains' greatness and width originally arose from "small stones"; that the waters' unfathomableness was originally from "single scoops." All these [are instances of] few combining to become many, of going from small to reach large. Becoming perfectly *cheng* 誠 is also like this! *Zhao zhao* 昭昭 is like *genggeng* 耿耿 and is a small light. *Zhen* 振 is like *shou* 收 (to receive, collect). *Juan* 卷 is like *qu* 區 (small). . . .

[2] How Heaven became Heaven, and how King Wen became *wen* 文 (cultured, refined) was, in both cases, from unceasing practice, from doing it and not stopping, as was said about Heaven, Earth, mountains and rivers. The *Changes* saying: "The noble man, by being obedient to virtue, accumulates the small to complete the high and great" is like this. . . .

Commentary ZY26 (Kong Yingda)

1.1 The *Zhengyi* says that this particular section makes it clear that, if perfecting *cheng* 誠 is a never-ending process, then it is able to reach the manifest from the minute, to reach the great from the small.

1.2 「今夫天，斯昭昭之多」者，斯，此也；昭昭，狹小之貌。言天初時唯有此昭昭之多小貌爾，故云「昭昭之多」。

1.3 「今夫地，一撮土之多」，言土之初時唯一撮土之多，言多少唯一撮土。

1.4 「振河海而不泄」者，振，收也。言地之廣大，載五嶽而不重，振收河海而不漏泄。

1.5 「今夫山，一卷石之多」，言山之初時唯一卷石之多，多少唯一卷石耳。故鄭注云：「卷猶區也。」「今夫水，一勺之多」，言水初時多少唯一勺耳。此以下皆言為之不已，從小至大。然天之與地，造化之初，清濁二氣為天地，分而成二體，元初作盤薄穹隆，非是以小至大。今云「昭昭」與「撮土」、「卷石」與「勺水」者何？但山或疊石為高，水或眾流而成大，是從微至著。因説聖人至誠之功亦是從小至大，以今天地體大，假言由小而來，以譬至誠，非實論也。

2.1 「《詩》曰：惟天之命，於穆不已」，此一經以上文至誠不已，已能從小至大，故此經引《詩》明不已之事。所引詩者，〈周頌・維天之命〉[86]文也。詩稱「維天之命」，謂四時運行所為教命。穆，美也。「於穆不已」者，美之不休已也，此詩之本文也。

2.2 「蓋曰天之所以為天也」，此是鄭子之言，記者載之。此詩所論，蓋説天之所以為天在乎不已。

---

86   The ode referred to here and in note 2.3 is Mao 267, LCC, 4:570–71.

1.2   *Now Heaven is this multiplicity of small points of light*: *Si* 斯 is equivalent to *ci* 此 (this); *zhao zhao* 昭昭 is the appearance of narrow and small. This says that at first Heaven was only this appearance of a multiplicity of small points of light. Therefore it says, *this multiplicity of small points of light.*

1.3   *Now the Earth is a multiplicity of handfuls of soil*: This says that the earth at first was only a multiplicity of single handfuls of soil, saying that the amounts were only single handfuls of soil.

1.4   *Collects the rivers and seas and they do not leak away*: *Zhen* 振 is equivalent to *shou* 收 (to receive, collect). This says that the Earth's breadth and largeness contains the five sacred peaks, and yet is not weighed down, receives the rivers and seas, and yet they do not leak away.

1.5   *Now the mountains are a multiplicity of single small stones*: This says that mountains were at first only a multiplicity of single small stones, that the amounts were only single small stones. Therefore, Zheng's note says, *juan* 卷 is like *qu* 區 (small). *Now the waters are a multiplicity of single scoops*: This says of waters that at first the amounts were only single scoops. This, and what follows, all say that by doing things unceasingly there will be progression from the small to reach to the large. Nevertheless, in Heaven's joining with Earth at the beginning of creation, the two *qi* 氣, clear and turbid, became Heaven and Earth, dividing to complete the two "bodies," and originally making an extensive vessel, lofty and arched; this was not a case of the small reaching to the large. Now it says "points of light" and "handfuls of soil," "small stones" and "scoops of water"—why? Only because a mountain is, perhaps, a piling up of stones to become high; waters are, perhaps, a multiplicity of streams becoming great—this is to reach to the manifest from the minute. As a consequence, it says that the merit of the sage's perfect *cheng* 誠 is also this, going from small to reach large. Because now Heaven and Earth are large bodies, it is false to say this came about from the small. As a way of comparing perfect *cheng* 誠, it is not a proper discussion.

2.1   *The Odes says: "The decree of Heaven—Ah! how glorious and unending"*: This particular section relates to the previous text's [observation on] perfect *cheng* 誠 not ending; ending can go from the small to reach the great. Therefore, this section quotes the *Odes* to clarify the matter of not ending. The ode that is quoted is the text of the "Zhou song," "Wei tian zhi ming." The ode called "Wei tian zhi ming" refers to the revolution of the four seasons as being what teaches the decree. *Mu* 穆 is equivalent to *mei* 美 (beautiful, glorious). *Ah! How glorious and unending* is that its gloriousness does not stop or end. This is this ode's basic meaning.

2.2   *This tells why Heaven is Heaven*: This affirms Confucius' words and the [*Li*] *ji's* recording them. What this ode discusses is the explanation of how Heaven became Heaven—it lies in its being unending.

2.3 「於乎不顯，<u>文王</u>之德之純」，此亦〈周頌•文王〉之詩。純，謂不已。顯，謂光明。詩人歎之云，於乎不光明乎，言光明矣。「<u>文王</u>之德之純」，謂不已也，言<u>文王</u>德教不有休已，與天同功。

2.4 「蓋曰<u>文王</u>之所以為文也」，此亦<u>孔子</u>之言，解《詩》之文也。

2.5 「純亦不已」者，言<u>文王</u>之德之純，亦如天之不休已，故云「純亦不已」。

2.6 注「《易》曰君子慎德，積小以高大」。

2.7 《正義》曰：此《易•升卦》之象辭。案〈升卦〉，巽下坤上，木生於地中，升進之義，故為「升」也。

ZY27: 大哉聖人之道。洋洋乎發育萬物，峻極于天。**[1]**優優大哉，禮儀三百，威儀三千，待其人然[而]⁸⁷後行，故曰：「苟不至德，至道不凝焉。」**[2]**

Comment: There are some minor issues regarding the readings of certain characters. These are dealt with in the notes and commentary. For example, Haloun argues for treating *fa yu* 發育 as a compound which he translates as "developing." The 300 and 3,000 forms of *li* 禮 are also referred to in the *Li ji,* "Li qi" 禮器 where the differentiation is between *jing li* 經禮 and *qu li* 曲禮 (see *Xinyi Li ji duben,* 353nn9–10 for clarification of these terms). *Qi* 其 in *qi ren* 其人 is read as *talis* (such, the following—see Haloun, 96). As mentioned in note 87 below, *er* 而 is used in the translation instead of *ran* 然, some texts having one character and some the other.

注 ZY27 (鄭玄)

[1] 育，生也。峻，高大也。{洋音羊。峻，思潤反。}

[2] 言為政在人，政由禮也。凝，猶成也。{優，於求反。}倡，優也。凝，本又作疑，{魚澄反}。

---

87   Some texts have *ran* 然 here and others *er* 而—see SSJZS (2001 edition), "Zhongyong," 28:1699n1. *Er* 而 is used in the translation.

2.3   *Ah! how brilliant it was, the purity of King Wen's virtue*: This, the poem "King Wen," is also from the "Zhou song." *Chun* 純 refers to not ending. *Xian* 顯 refers to *guangming* 光明 (bright, brilliant). The poet sighs and says: "Ah! How brilliant it was." This speaks of it being brilliant. *The purity of King Wen's virtue* refers to it not ending and says King Wen's virtue and teaching do not come to an end and are the same as Heaven in terms of efficacy.

2.4   *This tells why King Wen was wen* 文 *(cultured)*: These are also Confucius' words explaining the text of the *Odes*.

2.5   *And that his purity too was unending*: This speaks of the purity of King Wen's virtue which also, like Heaven's, does not cease or end. Therefore it says, *and that his purity too was unending*.

2.6   According to the notes, the *Changes* says the noble man's prudent virtue accumulates the small in order to become high and great.

2.7   The *Zhengyi* says that this is "Sheng gua" 升卦 from the figures of the diagrams in the *Changes*. According to the "Sheng gua" 升卦, *xun* 巽 below and *kun* 坤 above, wood arises from within the earth, *sheng* 升 has the meaning of *jin* 進 (to enter). Therefore it is "*sheng* 升."

ZY27: Great, indeed, is the Way of the sage! Vast and extensive, it brings forth and gives rise to the ten thousand things. Lofty and great, it reaches to Heaven. **[1]** Great, indeed, is its abundance. Its major forms of ceremony number three hundred and its minor forms of ritual number three thousand. They await such a man and afterwards can be put into practice. Therefore, it is said: "Without perfect virtue, the perfect Way is not realised." **[2]**

Notes ZY27 (Zheng Xuan)

[1] *Yu* 育 is equivalent to *sheng* 生 (to be born, give rise to). *Jun* 峻 is equivalent to *gaoda* 高大 (high and great). . . .

[2] This says that in conducting government among people, government is through *li* 禮. *Ning* 凝 is like *cheng* 成 (to complete, accomplish). . . .

疏 ZY27 (孔穎達)

{「大哉」至「凝焉」。}

1.1　《正義》曰：此一節明聖人之道高大，苟非至德，其道不成。洋洋，謂道
　　　德充滿之貌天下洋洋然。育，生也。峻，高也。言聖人之道，高大與山
　　　相似，上極于天。

2.1　「優優大哉」，優優，寬裕之貌。聖人優優然寬裕其道。「禮儀三百」者，
　　　《周禮》有三百六十官，言「三百」者，舉其成數耳。

2.2　「威儀三千」者，既《儀禮》行事之威儀。《儀禮》雖十七篇，其中事有
　　　三千。

2.3　「待其人然後行」者，言三百、三千之禮，必待賢人然後施行其事。

2.4　「故曰：苟不至德，至道不凝焉」，凝，成也。古語先有其文，今夫子既
　　　言三百、三千待其賢人始行，故引古語證之。苟，誠也。不，非也。苟
　　　誠非至德之人，則聖人至極之道不可成也。俗本「不」作「非」也。

ZY28: 故君子尊德性而道問學，致廣大而盡精微，極高明而道中庸。溫
故而知新，敦厚以崇禮。**[1]**

Comment: There are no significant issues in this short statement. The phrase, "revives the
old and understands the new" also appears in the *Lunyu* II.11 (LCC, 1:149).

注 ZY28 (鄭玄)

[1] 德性，謂性至誠者。道，猶由也。問學，學誠者也。廣大，猶博厚也。溫，
讀如「燖溫」之「溫」，謂故學之孰矣，後「時習之」謂之「溫」。{燖音尋。}

Commentary ZY27 (Kong Yingda)

1.1   The *Zhengyi* says that this particular section makes it clear that the Way of the
       sage is lofty and great, but if there is not perfect virtue, this Way is not realised.
       Yang yang 洋洋 refers to the appearance of the Way and virtue being full and
       abundant and extending as wide as the world. *Yu* 育 is equivalent to *sheng* 生
       (to be born, give rise to). *Jun* 峻 is equivalent to *gao* 高 (high, lofty). That is to
       say, the Way of the sage is high and great like a mountain, reaching upward to
       Heaven.

2.1   *Great, indeed, is its abundance*: *You you* 優優 is the appearance of abundance or
       plenty (*kuanyu* 寬裕). In the sage this Way is abundant in its plenitude. *Its major
       forms of ceremony number three hundred*: [In the] *Zhou li* there are 360 offices.
       Saying "300" rounds out the number.

2.2   *Its minor forms of ritual number three thousand*: The *Yi li* is about conducting af-
       fairs with a sense of decorum. Although the *Yi li* has [only] seventeen chapters,
       within them there are 3,000 matters.

2.3   *They await such a man and afterwards can be put into practice*: This says that the
       300 and the 3,000 forms of ritual must await worthy men before their matters
       are implemented.

2.4   *Therefore it is said: "Without perfect virtue, the perfect Way is not realised"*: *Ning* 凝
       is equivalent to *cheng* 成 (to complete, realise). The ancient phrase first had this
       form. Now the Master, since he speaks of the 300 and the 3,000 [forms of cer-
       emony] awaiting worthy men to first practise them, therefore quotes the ancient
       phrase to verify this. *Gou* 苟 is equivalent to *cheng* 誠 (truly, indeed). *Bu* 不 is
       equivalent to *fei* 非. Truly, if there are not men of perfect virtue, then reaching to
       the farthest extreme of the Way of the sage cannot be realised. By custom, *bu* 不
       was originally written as *fei* 非.

ZY28: Therefore, the noble man honours a virtuous nature, and follows the
path of enquiry and study. He reaches to the broad and great, and exhausts
the subtle and minute. He advances to the farthest point of the high and
bright, and fully understands using the centre. He revives the old and understands the new; he is honest and genuine through respecting *li* 禮. **[1]**

Notes ZY28 (Zheng Xuan)

[1] *De xing* 德性 refers to the nature of perfect *cheng* 誠. *Dao* 道 is like *you* 由 (to follow).
Wen xue 問學 is the study of *cheng* 誠. *Guangda* 廣大 is like *bohou* 博厚 (broad and great).
Wen 溫 is like the *wen* in *xunwen* 燖溫 (to warm up) and refers to the cause of study's
"ripeness." Subsequently, "constantly practising it" is spoken of as *wen* 溫. . . .

疏 ZY28 (孔穎達)

{「故君」至「崇禮」。}

1.1　《正義》曰：此一經明君子欲行聖人之道，當須勤學。前經明聖人性之至誠，此經明賢人學而至誠也。

1.2　「君子尊德性」者，謂君子賢人尊敬此聖人道德之性自然至誠也。

1.3　「而道問學」者，言賢人行道由於問學，謂勤學乃致至誠也。

1.4　「致廣大而盡精微」者，廣大謂地也，言賢人由學能致廣大，如地之生養之德也。「而盡精微」，謂致其生養之德既能致於廣大，盡育物之精微，言無微不盡也。

1.5　「極高明而道中庸」者，高明，謂天也，言賢人由學極盡天之高明之德。道，通也，又能通達於中庸之理也。

1.6　「溫故而知新」者，言賢人由學既能溫尋故事，又能知新事也。

1.7　「敦厚以崇禮」者，言以敦厚重行於學，故以尊崇三百、三千之禮也。

1.8　注「溫讀如燖溫之溫」。

1.9　《正義》曰：案《左傳》哀十二年，公會吳于橐皋，大宰嚭請尋盟。子貢對曰：「盟，若可尋也，亦可寒也。」賈逵注云：「尋，溫也。」[88] 又〈有司徹〉云「乃燅尸俎」，[89] 是燅為溫也。云「謂故學之孰矣，後時習之，謂之溫」者，謂賢人舊學已精熟，在後更習之，猶若溫尋故食也。

---

[88]　*Zuo zhuan*, Duke Ai, 12th year, LCC, 5:827 (this is a partial quotation only).
[89]　*Yi li*, "Yousi che," SSJZS, 4:580.

Commentary ZY28 (Kong Yingda)

1.1 The *Zhengyi* says that this particular section makes it clear that the noble man, in his desire to practise the Way of the sage, rightly must be diligent in study. The previous section clarifies the perfect *cheng* 誠 of the sage nature. This section makes it clear that the worthy man studies to reach *cheng* 誠.

1.2 *The noble man honours a virtuous nature*: This refers to the noble man and the worthy man honouring and respecting this nature of the sage's Way and virtue, one of spontaneous, perfect *cheng* 誠.

1.3 *And follows the path of enquiry and study*: This speaks of the worthy man practising the Way through enquiry and study. It refers to diligent study then going on to perfect *cheng* 誠.

1.4 *He reaches to the broad and great, and exhausts the subtle and minute*: *Broad and great* refers to the Earth and says that the worthy man, through study, is able to reach breadth and greatness, like the Earth's virtue of nurturing. *And exhausts the subtle and minute* refers to extending this virtue of giving rise to and nurturing being able to reach to the broad and great and to exhaust the subtle essence of nurturing (giving rise to) things. There is nothing subtle (minute) that is not exhausted.

1.5 *He advances to the farthest point of the high and bright, and fully understands using the centre*: *Gao ming* 高明 refers to *tian* 天 (Heaven). This says that the worthy man, through studying to the highest level, advances to the height and brightness of Heaven's virtue. *Dao* 道 is equivalent to *tong* 通 (to penetrate, go through). [That is,] he is also able to penetrate to the principle of using the centre.

1.6 *He revives the old and understands the new*: This says that the worthy man, through study, is able to "warm up" (i.e. revive) old matters and is also able to understand new matters.

1.7 *He is honest and genuine through respecting li* 禮: This says that by being honest and genuine, and repeatedly practising his studies, he is therefore reverential and respectful towards the 300 and 3,000 ceremonies.

1.8 According to the notes, *wen* 溫 is read as the *wen* 溫 of *xunwen* 燖溫 (to warm up, revive).

1.9 The *Zhengyi* says that, according to the *Zuo zhuan* for the 12th year of Duke Ai, the Duke had a meeting with Wu at Zhe Gao at which Chief Minister Pi requested a renewal of the covenant. Zigong replied, saying: "If a covenant can be made hot it can also be made cold." Jia Kui's note says, "*xun* 燖 is equivalent to *wen* 溫 (to warm up)." Also, the "Yousi che" says: "To heat up and arrange the meat dishes (for the sacrifice)." This is *xun* 燖 being equivalent to *wen* 溫 (to warm up). It says, "referring to the revival of ancient studies, and afterwards frequently practising them is called *wen* 溫 (warming up, reviving, renewing)." This refers to the worthy man already being thoroughly versed in old studies, so that subsequently their further practice is like warming up old food.

ZY29: 是故居上不驕，為下不倍。國有道，其言足以興。國無道，其默足以容。**[1]**《詩》曰：「既明且哲，以保其身。」，其此之謂與？**[2]**

Comment: There are, again, no significant issues in this brief statement. The second sentence is found in closely similar form (*guo jia* 國家 for *guo* 國 and *sheng* 生 for *xing* 興) in the *Da Dai Li ji* 大戴禮記 (CSJC, n.s., 34:473). This is taken as supporting a relatively late date for this section. One point of note is Zheng Xuan's reading of *bao* 保 as *an* 安 here and earlier.

注 ZY29 (鄭玄)

[1] 興謂起在位也。驕，本亦作「喬」，{音嬌。倍音佩。默，亡北反。}
[2] 保，安也。{哲，涉列反，徐本作知，音智。與音餘。}

疏 ZY29 (孔穎達)

{「是故」至「謂與」。}

1.1 《正義》曰：此一節明賢人學至誠之道，中庸之行，若國有道之時，盡竭知謀，其言足以興成其國。興，謂發謀出慮。

1.2 「國無道，其默足以容」，若無道之時，則韜光潛默，足以自容其身，免於禍害。

2.1 「《詩》云：既明且哲，以保其身」，此〈大雅 • 烝民〉[90] 之篇，美宣王之詩，言宣王任用仲山甫，能顯明其事任，且又哲知保安全其己身，言中庸之人亦能如此，故云「其此之謂與」。

---

[90]   See the *Odes*, Mao 260, verse 4, LCC, 4:543.

ZY29: For this reason, when occupying a superior position, he is not arrogant; when he is an inferior, he is not refractory. When the state has the Way, his words are sufficient for him to rise. When the state does not have the Way, his silence is enough for him to be tolerated. **[1]** The *Odes* says: "Since he is enlightened and wise, so he is at peace with himself." Surely this is what it refers to? **[2]**

Notes ZY29 (Zheng Xuan)

[1] *Xing* 興 refers to rising in position. *Jiao* 驕 originally was also written *qiao* 喬. . . .

[2] *Bao* 保 is equivalent to *an* 安 (to be content, to be at peace). . . .

Commentary ZY29 (Kong Yingda)

1.1 The *Zhengyi* says that this particular section makes clear the worthy man's study of the Way of perfect *cheng* 誠 and his practice of using the centre. If it is a time when the state possesses the Way, he gives of his utmost in terms of knowledge and planning, and his words are enough for the prosperity and success of his state. *Xing* 興 refers to issuing plans and displaying forethought.

1.2 *When the state does not have the Way, his silence is enough for him to be tolerated*: If it is a time without the Way, then he hides his light under a bushel, concealing himself in silence, and this is enough for he himself to be tolerated and avoid misfortune and harm.

2.1 *The Odes says: "Since he is enlightened and wise, so he is at peace with himself"*: This is from the "Da ya," "Zheng min," a poem in praise of King Xuan. It says that King Xuan employed Zhongshan Fu, who was able to manifest and display his serving in office. Moreover, he was also wise and knowledgeable, and completely content within himself, which is to say that the man who uses the centre can also be like this. Therefore it says, *surely this is what it refers to?*

ZY30: 子曰：「愚而好自用，賤而好自專，生乎今之世，反古之道，如此者，烖及其身者也。**[1]** 非天子不議禮，不制度，不考文。**[2]** 今天下車同軌，書同文，行同倫。**[3]** 雖有其位，苟無其德，不敢作禮樂焉。雖有其德，苟無其位，亦不敢作禮樂焉。」**[4]**

Comment: This is a problematic section and one which is cited as evidence for a post-Warring States date of composition for at least part of the *Zhongyong*. The first statement, attributed to Confucius, raises questions, especially concerning *fan* 反 in the third of the actions that invite disaster. Is the problem failure to act in a way appropriate to the time, rather looking back to ancient (and no longer applicable) methods, as Zheng Xuan's note suggests, or is it the converse—i.e. failing to heed the ways of the ancients as Kong Yingda's commentary indicates? Both appear to be possible interpretations. The second and third sentences are generally taken to refer to the unifying activities of the Qin, but both Zheng Xuan and Kong Yingda take the *jin* 今 to indicate Confucius' own time. Likewise, the final statement in the section is taken by Kong Yingda to relate to Confucius' own failure to hold a position commensurate with his virtue.

注 ZY30 (鄭玄)

[1] 「反古之道」，謂曉一孔之人，不知今王之新政可從。{好，呼報反，下同。烖音災。}

[2] 此天下所共行，天子乃能一之也。禮，謂人所服行也。度，國家宮室及車輿也。文，書名也。

[3] 今，孔子謂其時。{行，下孟反。}

[4] 言作禮樂者，必聖人在天子之位。

疏 ZY30 (孔穎達)

{「子曰」至「樂焉」。}

1.1　《正義》曰：上經論賢人學至誠，商量國之有道無道能或語或默，以保其身。若不能中庸者，皆不能量事制宜，必及禍患矣。因明己以此之故，不敢專輒制作禮樂也。

1.2　「生乎今之世，反古之道，如此者，烖及其身者也」，此謂尋常之人，不知大道。若賢人君子，雖生今時，能持古法，故〈儒行〉云「今人與居，古人與稽」[91] 是也。俗本「反」下有「行」字，又無「如此者」三字，非也。

91　See *Li ji*, "Ru xing," SSJZS, 5:977.

ZY30: The Master said: "To be foolish and yet like to rely on one's own opinions; to be lowly and yet like to act on one's own authority; to be born into the present age and yet to turn back to the ways of the past—things like these bring disaster down on oneself. **[1]** Nobody but the Son of Heaven determines the rites (*li* 禮), establishes standards, or verifies the written script. **[2]** Nowadays, in the world, carriages run in the same wheel-tracks, writings have the same script, and conduct has the same principles. **[3]** Although [a man] has this position [of ruler], if he does not have this virtue, he dare not create rites (*li* 禮) and music. Although he has this virtue, if he does not have this position [of ruler], he likewise does not dare to create rites and music." **[4]**

Notes ZY30 (Zheng Xuan)

[1] *To turn back to the ways of the past*: This refers to a man who understands one "hole" (principle) and does not know that the new government of the present king can be followed. . . .

[2] This is that what the world collectively practises is what the Son of Heaven is then able to unify. *Li* 禮 refers to what men submit to and practise. *Du* 度 are the palaces and houses, the carriages and chariots of the state. *Wen* 文 is a name for writing (a script).

[3] [By] "nowadays," Confucius refers to his own time. . . .

[4] This says that the one who creates rites and music must be a sage occupying the position of the Son of Heaven.

Commentary ZY30 (Kong Yingda)

1.1 The *Zhengyi* says that this section discusses worthy men studying [to achieve] perfect *cheng* 誠 and deliberates on their being able to either speak or remain silent depending on whether the state has the Way or not, by being content in their own persons. If a man cannot use the centre, in all instances he is unable to evaluate affairs and do what is proper, and must come to misfortune and calamity. Therefore, if he is clear on the reasons for this, he does not dare to regulate and create rites and music of his own accord and precipitately.

1.2 *To be born into the present age and yet turn back to the ways of the past—things like these bring disaster down on oneself:* This refers to ordinary men not knowing the great Way. In the case of worthy men and noble men, although they are born in the present time, they are able to grasp ancient methods. Therefore, the "Ruxing" saying, "to live among present men, to examine ancient men" is this. It was common originally to have *xing* 行 after *fan* 反 and also not to have the three characters *ru ci zhe* 如此者. This is wrong.

2.1 「非天子不議禮」者，此論禮由天子所行，既非天子，不得論議禮之是非。

2.2 「不制度」，謂不敢制造法度，及國家宮室大小高下及車輿也。

2.3 「不考文」，亦不得考成文章書籍之名也。

3.1 「今天下車同軌」者，今謂孔子時車同軌，覆上「不制度」。「書同文」，覆上「不考文」。「行同倫」，倫，道也，言人所行之行，皆同道理，覆上「不議禮」。當孔子時，禮壞樂崩，家殊國異，而云此者，欲明己雖有德，身無其位，不敢造作禮樂，故極行而虛己，先說以自謙也。

1.3 注「反古之道，謂曉一孔之人」。

1.4 《正義》曰：孔，謂孔穴，孔穴所出，事有多塗。今唯曉知一孔之人，不知餘孔通達，唯守此一處，故云「曉一孔之人」。

ZY31: 子曰：「吾說夏禮，杞不足徵也。吾學殷禮，有宋存焉。吾學周禮，今用之，吾從周。[1]王天下有三重焉，其寡過矣乎！[2]上焉者，雖善無徵，無徵不信，不信，民弗從。下焉者，雖善不尊，不尊不信，不信，民弗從。[3]

2.1   *Nobody but the Son of Heaven determines the rites* (*li* 禮): This discusses the fact
        that rites are implemented by the Son of Heaven. Without the Son of Heaven, it
        is not possible to discuss whether rites and ceremonies are right or wrong.

2.2   *Or establishes standards*: This refers to not daring to regulate and create laws and
        standards, and extends from the dimensions of palaces and houses of the state to
        those of carts and carriages.

2.3   *Or verifies the written script*: This is also not getting to examine and settle the
        names of essays and books.

3.1   *Nowadays, in the world, carriages run in the same wheel-tracks*: "Nowadays" refers
        to carts having the same wheel-tracks at the time of Confucius and repeats the
        previous *or establishes standards*. *Writings have the same script* repeats the previous
        or verifies the written script. In *run in the same wheel-tracks*, *lun* 倫 is equivalent to
        dao 道 (path, road) and speaks of the actions which men do all being the same
        in terms of principles and repeats the previous *not create rites* (*li* 禮). At the time
        of Confucius, the rites (*li* 禮) were spoiled and music had decayed, houses were
        dissimilar, and states were different. The one who is saying this wishes to make it
        clear that he himself (i.e. Confucius), although he had virtue, did not personally
        hold a position and did not dare to create rites (*li* 禮) and music. Therefore, he
        maintained the highest standard of conduct yet was humble, which is primarily
        to explain his own humility.

1.3   The notes [say], turning back to the ways of the past refers to a person who un-
        derstands one "hole."

1.4   The *Zhengyi* says that *kong* 孔 refers to a cave (or hole—*kongxue* 孔穴) and what
        comes forth from a cave (or hole). Affairs have many paths. Now a man who
        only knows and understands one "hole" and does not know where the remaining
        "holes" penetrate to, only maintains this one position. Therefore it says, "a man
        who understands one hole."

ZY31: The Master said: "I have spoken of the rites (*li* 禮) of Xia; Qi is not
enough to clarify them. I have studied the rites (*li* 禮) of Yin; there is Song
that has preserved them. I have studied the rites (*li* 禮) of Zhou and now use
them; I follow Zhou. **[1]** In ruling all under Heaven there are three important
things which will surely minimise errors. **[2]** Rulers, although they may be
good, may be unproven. If they are unproven, they are not trusted; if they are
not trusted, the people will not follow them. Ministers, although they may be
good, may not be honoured. If they are not honoured, they are not trusted; if
they are not trusted, the people will not follow them. **[3]**

故君子之道，本諸身，徵諸庶民，考諸三王而不繆，建諸天地而不悖，質諸鬼神而無疑，百世以俟聖人而不惑。『質諸鬼神而無疑』，知天也。『百世以俟聖人而不惑』，知人也。[4]是故君子動而世為天下道，行而世為天下法，言而世為天下則。遠之則有望，近之則不厭。[5]《詩》曰：『在彼無惡，在此無射，庶幾夙夜，以永終譽。』[92] 君子未有不如此而蚤有譽於天下者也。」[6]

Comment: On the several more or less contentious points in this section, Zheng Xuan makes his position quite clear and is supported by Kong Yingda. This is the interpretation followed in the translation. The particular issues are:

(i)   The incorporation of the initial statement (an alternative version of the *Lunyu* III.9 & 14) into this section as this is what the rest of the section relates to.

(ii)   Identification of the "three important things" as the rites (*li* 禮) of the exemplary kings of the Xia (King Yu), Yin (King Tang) and Zhou (King Wen) dynasties respectively.

(iii)   The reading of *shang* 上 and *xia* 下 as rulers and ministers respectively.

The interpretation is spelled out clearly in Kong Yingda's commentary 1.1–1.4. To be followed, the rites (*li* 禮) must be attested by their successful use in a current state, although there is the suggestion that Confucius was not entirely pure in restricting his use to the Zhou rites.

注 ZY31 (鄭玄)

[1] 徵，猶明也，吾能説夏禮，顧杞之君不足與明之也。「吾從周」，行今之道。{杞音起。}

[2] 「三重」，三王之禮。{王，于況反，又如字。}

[3] 上，謂君也。君雖善，善無明徵，則其善不信也。下，謂臣也。臣雖善，善而不尊君，則其善亦不信也。徵或為「證」。

[4] 知天、知人，謂知其道也。鬼神，從天地者也。《易》曰：「故知鬼神之情狀，與天地相似。」[93]聖人則之，百世同道。徵或為「證」。{繆音謬。悖，布內反，後同。}

[5] 用其法度，想思若其將來也。{遠如字，又于萬反。近如字，又附近之近。厭，於豔反，後皆同。}

[6] 射，厭也。永，長也。{射音亦，注同。蚤音早。}

---

92   See the *Odes*, Mao 278, verse 2, LCC, 4:585.

93   *Yi jing*, "Ji ci," SSJZS, 1:147.

Therefore, the Way of the noble man (ruler) has its foundation in his own person, is attested by the common people, and is verified in relation to the Three Kings, so there is no confusion. It is established in Heaven and on Earth, and is not contrary to what is right. It is rectified by the ghosts and spirits, and is without doubt. There is a preparedness to wait a hundred generations for a sage and yet be without misgivings. 'To be verified by ghosts and spirits and be without doubt' is to know Heaven. 'To be prepared to wait a hundred generations for a sage and yet be without misgivings' is to know man. **[4]** For this reason, the noble man (ruler) moves, and the age takes it to be the world's Way; he acts, and the age takes it to be world's laws; he speaks, and the age takes it to be the world's standards. Those who are distant are then hopeful; those who are near are then without dissatisfaction. **[5]** The *Odes* says: 'There, he is not disliked; here, he is not wearied of. Day after day, night after night, he is perpetually praised.' There has never been a noble man (ruler) like this who was not quick to find praise in the world." **[6]**

Notes ZY31 (Zheng Xuan)

[1] *Zheng* 徵 is like *ming* 明 (to make clear). I am able to speak of the Xia rites (*li* 禮) but looking back to the Qi ruler is not enough to make them clear. *I follow Zhou* is to implement the Way of the present time. . . .

[2] The *san zhong* 三重 are the rites (*li* 禮) of the Three Kings. . . .

[3] *Shang* 上 refers to the ruler (*jun* 君). Even though a ruler is good, if his goodness is not clearly evident, then this goodness is not trusted. *Xia* 下 refers to ministers (*chen* 臣). Even though ministers are good, if they are good but are not honoured by the ruler, then their goodness is also not trusted. *Zheng* 徵 is sometimes written *zheng* 證.

[4] "Knowing Heaven" and "knowing man" refer to knowing their Ways respectively. Ghosts and spirits follow Heaven and Earth. The *Changes* says: "Therefore, knowing the conditions of ghosts and spirits is to be like Heaven and Earth." The sage sets the standard, and for a hundred generations there is the same Way. *Zheng* 徵 is sometimes written as *zheng* 證. . . .

[5] Using his laws and standards and thinking as if he is going to come. . . .

[6] *Yi* 射 is equivalent to *yan* 厭 (to weary of, to detest). *Yong* 永 is equivalent to *chang* 長 (long). . . .

疏 ZY31 (孔穎達)

{「子曰」至「者也」。}

1.1　《正義》曰：以上文<u>孔子</u>身無其位，不敢制作二代之禮，<u>夏</u>、<u>殷</u>不足可
　　　從，所以獨從<u>周</u>禮之意，因明君子行道，須本於身，達諸天地，質諸鬼
　　　神，使動為天下之道，行則為後世之法，故能早有名譽於天下。蓋<u>孔子</u>
　　　微自明己之意。

1.2　「子曰：吾說<u>夏</u>禮，<u>杞</u>不足徵也」，徵，成也，明也。<u>孔子</u>言：我欲明說
　　　<u>夏代</u>之禮，須行<u>夏</u>禮之國贊而成之。<u>杞</u>雖行<u>夏</u>禮，其君暗弱，不足贊而
　　　成之。

1.3　「吾學<u>殷</u>禮，有<u>宋</u>存焉者」，<u>宋</u>行<u>殷</u>禮，故云「有<u>宋</u>存焉」。但<u>宋</u>君暗弱，
　　　欲其贊明<u>殷</u>禮，亦不足可成。故《論語》云：「<u>宋</u>不足徵也。」[94] 此云「<u>杞</u>
　　　不足徵」，即<u>宋</u>亦不足徵。此云「有<u>宋</u>存焉」，則<u>杞</u>亦存焉。互文見義。

1.4　「吾學<u>周</u>禮，今用之，吾從<u>周</u>」者，既<u>杞</u>、<u>宋</u>二國不足明，己當不復行前
　　　代之禮，故云「吾從<u>周</u>」。案<u>趙商</u>[95] 問：<u>孔子</u>稱「吾學<u>周</u>禮，今用之，吾
　　　從<u>周</u>」，〈檀弓〉云「今<u>丘</u>也，<u>殷</u>人也」，[96] 兩楹奠殯哭師之處，皆所法於<u>殷</u>
　　　禮，未必由<u>周</u>，而云「吾從<u>周</u>」者，何也？<u>鄭</u>荅曰：「今用之者，<u>魯</u>與諸侯
　　　皆用<u>周</u>之禮法，非專自施於己。在<u>宋</u>冠章甫之冠，在<u>魯</u>衣逢掖之衣，何
　　　必純用之。『吾從<u>周</u>』者，言<u>周</u>禮法最備，其為<u>殷</u>、<u>周</u>事豈一也。」如<u>鄭</u>此
　　　言，諸侯禮法則從<u>周</u>，身之所行雜用<u>殷</u>禮也。

---

[94]　See *Lunyu* III.9, LCC, 1:158.

[95]　Zhao Shang 趙商 was a pupil of Zheng Xuan—see the latter's biography in the *Hou
　　　Han shu* 35, 5:1207ff.

[96]　The "Tan gong" text actually has: 「而<u>丘</u>也，<u>殷</u>人也。」(SSJZS, 5:130) Earlier there is:
　　　"今<u>丘</u>也" in a different context (SSJZS, 5:112).

Commentary ZY31 (Kong Yingda)

1.1   The *Zhengyi* says that, according to the preceding text, Confucius himself did
       not have this position (i.e. of ruler) and did not dare to institute and implement
       the rites (*li* 禮) of the two dynasties. The Xia and Yin were not good enough
       to be able to follow, thus he intended to follow the Zhou rites (*li* 禮). Because
       it is clear that the noble man's practice of the Way must be based on the self,
       extended to Heaven and Earth, and verified by ghosts and spirits, this causes his
       movements to be the world's Way and his actions to be the model for later gen-
       erations. Therefore, he is early able to have fame and praise in the world. Now
       Confucius was briefly expressing his own intentions.

1.2.   *The Master said: "I have spoken of the rites (li 禮) of Xia; Qi is not enough to clarify
       them"*: *Zheng* 徵 is equivalent to *cheng* 成 (to complete) or *ming* 明 (to clarify).
       Confucius is saying: "If I want to make clear and explain the rites (*li* 禮) of the
       Xia dynasty, there must be a state practising the Xia rites (*li* 禮) which praises
       and completes them. Although Qi practised the Xia rites, its ruler was obscure
       and weak and was not adequate to praise and clarify (complete) them."

1.3   *I have studied the rites (li 禮) of Yin; there is Song that has preserved them*: Song
       practised the Yin rites (*li* 禮). Therefore, he says, *there is Song that has preserved
       them*. But the Song ruler was obscure and weak, and although he wished to praise
       and clarify the Yin rites (*li* 禮), he too was not adequate to do so. Therefore,
       the *Lunyu* says: "Song was not adequate to attest [them]." This saying *Qi is not
       enough to clarify them* [is to say that] Song was also not enough to clarify them.
       This saying *there is Song that has preserved them* [is to say that] Qi also preserved
       them. The two statements are interchangeable in meaning.

1.4   *I have studied the rites (li 禮) of Zhou and now use them; I follow Zhou*: Because
       the two states Qi and Song were not adequate to clarify [them], I rightly did not
       return to the practice of the rites (*li* 禮) of the earlier dynasties. Therefore, he
       says: *I follow Zhou*. According to Zhao Shang's question, Confucius declared: "I
       have studied the rites (*li* 禮) of Zhou; now I use them. I follow Zhou." The "Tan
       gong" says: "And Qiu is a Yin man." The acts of offering the libation between
       the two pillars and covering the coffin at the place of weeping for the Master are
       both modelled on the Yin rites (*li* 禮) and are not necessarily from Zhou. And
       yet he says, *I follow Zhou*. Why is this? Zheng says in response: "Of those who
       now use them, Lu and the feudal lords both use the model of the Zhou rites (*li* 禮)
       and they do not only employ them for themselves. In Song, there was capping
       with the ancient ceremonial cap; in Lu, there was the donning of the robes of the
       literati. Why must the use be pure? *I follow Zhou* is to say that the model of the
       Zhou rites (*li* 禮) was particularly perfect. How was it that he took Yin and Zhou
       matters to be one?" What Zheng means in saying this is that, as the model for
       the rites (*li* 禮) of the feudal lords, he followed Zhou. In what he himself did, he
       mixed in the use of the Yin rites (*li* 禮).

2.1 「王天下有三重焉,其寡過矣乎」,言為君王有天下者,有三種之重焉,謂<u>夏</u>、<u>殷</u>、<u>周</u>三王之禮,其事尊重,若能行之,寡少於過矣。

3.1 「上焉者,雖善無徵,無徵不信,不信,民弗從」,上,謂君也,言為君雖有善行,無分明徵驗,則不信著於下,既不信著,則民不從。「下焉者,雖善不尊,不尊不信,不信,民弗從」,下,謂臣也,言臣所行之事,雖有善行而不尊,不尊敬於君,則善不信著於下,既不信著,則民不從,故下云「徵諸庶民」,謂行善須有徵驗於庶民也。<u>皇氏</u>云「無徵,謂無符應之徵」,[97] 其義非也。

4.1 「故君子之道」者,言君臣為善,須有徵驗,民乃順從,故明之也。

4.2 「本諸身」者,言君子行道,先從身起,是「本諸身」也。

4.3 「徵諸庶民」者,徵,驗也;諸,於也。謂立身行善,使有徵驗於庶民。若<u>晉文公</u>出定<u>襄王</u>,示民尊上也;伐原,示民以信之類 [98] 也。

4.4 「考諸三王而不繆」者,繆,亂也。謂己所行之事,考校與三王合同,不有錯繆也。

4.5 「建諸天地而不悖」者,悖,逆也。言己所行之道,建達於天地,而不有悖逆,謂與天地合也。

---

[97] Huang Shi 皇氏 is Huang Kan 皇侃—see note 6 above.

[98] Read as *shi* 是—see SSJZS (2001 edition), "Zhongyong," 28:1703n1.

2.1   *In ruling all under Heaven, there are three important things which will surely min-imise errors*: This says that in being a ruler and having possession of all under Heaven, there are three important things, referring to the rites (*li* 禮) of the Three Kings of the Xia, Yin and Zhou. If, in one's affairs, their importance is respected, and if one is able to practise them, it will effect a reduction in errors.

3.1   *Rulers, although they may be good, may be unproven. If they are unproven, they are not trusted; if they are not trusted, the people will not follow them*: *Shang* 上 refers to the ruler. This says that one who is a ruler, although he practises what is good, if he is not clearly proven, then he is not trusted by those below, and when he is not trusted, then the people do not follow. *Ministers, although they may be good, may not be honoured. If they are not honoured, they are not trusted; if they are not trusted, the people will not follow them*: *Xia* 下 refers to ministers. This says that in the matters in which ministers act, if, although they act with goodness, they are not honoured, [that is,] if they are not honoured and respected by the ruler, then the goodness is not trusted by those below, and when it is not trusted, then the people do not follow. Therefore, below it says *attested by the common people* which is to say that good actions must have corroboration by the ordinary people. Huang Shi says: "*Wu zheng* 無徵 (not attested, unproven) refers to the *zheng* of no mutual correspondence." His interpretation is wrong.

4.1   *The Way of the noble man (ruler)*: This says that, if the prince and ministers are good, they must be proven. The people then comply and follow them, therefore completing (clarifying) it (i.e. the Way).

4.2   *Has its foundation in his own person*: This says that the noble man's (ruler's) practice of the Way first arises from within himself. This is, *has its foundation in his own person*.

4.3   *Is attested by the common people*: *Zheng* 徵 is equivalent to *yan* 驗 (to prove, attest, verify). *Zhu* 諸 is equivalent to *yu* 於 (for, by). This refers to establishing the self and practising goodness, causing there to be verification by the common people. For example, Duke Wen of Jin went forth and established King Xiang, displaying to the people respect for the ruler. Sending an expedition against Yuan to show the people the way to trust him is this sort of thing.

4.4   *It is verified in relation to the Three Kings, so there is no confusion*: *Miu* 繆 is equivalent to *luan* 亂 (confusion). This says that in the matters in which one acts, if there is examination and comparison so there is accord and agreement with the Three Kings, there are no errors or confusion.

4.5   *It is established in Heaven and on Earth, and is not contrary to what is right*: *Bei* 悖 is equivalent to *ni* 逆 (refractory, rebellious, contrary). This says that in the Way which one practises, if it is established and penetrates to Heaven and Earth and does not have what is perverse or refractory, it is said to be in accord with Heaven and Earth.

4.6　「質諸鬼神而無疑，知天也」者，質，正也。謂己所行之行，正諸鬼神不有疑惑，是識知天道也。此鬼神，是陰陽七八、九六之鬼神生成萬物者。此是天地所為，既能質正陰陽，不有疑惑，是識知天道也。

4.7　「百世以俟聖人而不惑，知人也」者，以聖人身有聖人之德，垂法於後，雖在後百世亦堪俟待。後世之聖人，其道不異，故云「知人也」。

{注「知天」至「同道」。}

4.8　《正義》曰：以經云知天、知人，故鄭引經總結之。云「知其道」者，以天地陰陽，生成萬物，今能正諸陰陽鬼神而不有疑惑，是知天道也。以聖人之道，雖相去百世，其歸一揆，今能百世以待聖人而不有疑惑，是知聖人之道也。云「鬼神從天地者也」，解所以質諸鬼神之德、知天道之意，引《易》曰「故知鬼神之情狀，與天地相似」者，證鬼神從天地之意。案《易·繫辭》云：「精氣為物，游魂為變。」[99] 鄭云：「木火之神生物，金水之鬼成物。」以七八之神生物，九六之鬼成物，是鬼神以生成為功，天地亦以生成為務，是鬼神之狀與天地相似。云「聖人則之，百世同道」者，解經知人之道，以前世聖人既能垂法以俟待後世聖人，是識知聖人之道百世不殊，故「聖人則之，百世同道」也。

---

[99]　*Yi jing*, "Xi ci," SSJZS, 1:147. The second sentence precedes the first.

4.6   *To be verified by ghosts and spirits and be without doubt is to know Heaven*: Zhi 質 is equivalent to *zheng* 正 (to correct, rectify). This refers to the actions that one practises. If they are correct in relation to ghosts and spirits, and there is no doubt or uncertainty, this is to recognise and know the Way of Heaven. These ghosts and spirits are the *yin* and *yang* seven and eight, nine and six ghosts and spirits which give rise to and complete the ten thousand things. This confirms what Heaven and Earth do, since they are able to correct the *yin* and *yang* and have no doubt or uncertainty. This is to recognise and know the Way of Heaven.

4.7   *To be prepared to wait a hundred generations for a sage and yet be without misgivings is to know man*: Because the sage himself has the virtue of a sage, if a method is left to posterity, although one hundred generations may pass, it is still applicable. The sage of later generations is not different in his Way. Therefore, it says, *to know man*.

4.8   The *Zhengyi* says that this section speaks of knowing Heaven and knowing man, therefore Zheng quotes the section to summarise it. It says, *know their Way*, because Heaven and Earth, *yin* and *yang* give rise to and complete the ten thousand things and now are able to verify the *yin* and *yang*, ghosts and spirits and not have doubt or uncertainty—this is to know the Way of Heaven. Taking the Way of the sage, although separated by a hundred generations, if his return is conjectured, now one is able to wait a hundred generations for a sage and not have doubt or uncertainty—this is to know the Way of the sage. To say, "ghosts and spirits follow Heaven and Earth" explains what it is to be rectified by the virtue of ghosts and spirits and is to know the purport of Heaven's Way. He (i.e. Zheng) quotes the *Changes* which says: "Therefore, knowing the conditions of ghosts and spirits is to be like Heaven and Earth" proving that ghosts and spirits follow the purport of Heaven and Earth. According to the *Changes*, "Xi ci," it says "*Jing* 精 and *qi* 氣 create things; the wandering soul creates change." Zheng says: "The spirits of wood and fire give rise to things; the ghosts of metal and wood complete things." Through the spirits of seven and eight, there is giving rise to things; through the ghosts of nine and six, there is completion of things—this is ghosts and spirits being efficacious by giving rise to and completing. Heaven and Earth also take giving rise to and completing to be their responsibility. This is the conditions of ghosts and spirits and Heaven and Earth being essentially the same. Saying, "the sage sets the standard and the hundred generations have the same Way" explains the classic's recognising the Way of man. To take the sages of former generations to be an example which awaits the sages of later generations is to recognise and know that the Way of the sage is not different over a hundred generations. Therefore he says, "the sage sets the standard, and for a hundred generations there is the same Way."

5.1 「遠之則有望，近之則不厭」者，言聖人之道，為世法則，若遠離之則有企望，思慕之深也。若附近之則不厭倦，言人愛之無已。

6.1 「《詩》云：在彼無惡，在此無射，庶幾夙夜，以永終譽」，此引〈周頌‧振鷺〉之篇，[100] 言微子來朝，身有美德，在彼宋國之內，民無惡之，在此來朝，人無厭倦。故庶幾夙夜，以長永終竟美善聲譽。言君子之德亦能如此，故引《詩》以結成之。

6.2 「君子未有不如此而蚤有譽於天下者也」，言欲蚤有名譽會須如此，未嘗有不行如此而蚤得有聲譽者也。

ZY32: 仲尼祖述堯舜，憲章文武，上律天時，下襲水土。[1]辟如天地之無不持載，無不覆幬。辟如四時之錯行，如日月之代明。萬物並育而不相害，道並行而不相悖，小德川流，大德敦化，此天地之所以為大也。[2]唯天下至聖為能，聰明睿知，足以有臨也。寬裕溫柔，足以有容也。發強剛毅，足以有執也。齊莊中正，足以有敬也。文理密察，足以有別也。[3] 溥博淵泉，而時出之。[4]

---

100 See note 92 above.

5.1 *Those who are distant are then hopeful; those who are near are then without dissatisfaction*: This says that the Way of the sage may be taken as a model and a standard for the age. If someone is distant and far removed from him (i.e. the sage), then that person has eager expectations and admiring thoughts that are deep. If someone is near to him, then that person does not feel dissatisfied or weary, which speaks to others' love for him and that is all.

6.1 *The Odes says: "There, he is not disliked; here, he is not wearied of. Day after day, night after night, he is perpetually praised"*: This is a quotation from the "Zhen Lu" in the "Zhou song" and says that when Weizi came to court, and he himself had admirable virtue, there, within the Song state, the people did not dislike him, whilst here, when he came to court, others were not dissatisfied and weary. Therefore, day after day and night and night there was perpetual praise for his beauty and goodness. This says that the noble man's (ruler's) virtue can also be like this. Therefore, quoting the *Odes* serves to sum it up.

6.2 *There has never been a noble man (ruler) like this who was not quick to find praise in the world*: This says that, if one wishes to find fame and praise quickly, one must be like this [in that] there has never been anyone who did not act like this yet gained fame and praise quickly.

ZY32: Zhongni (Confucius) began the transmission of [the Way of] Yao and Shun. He took as a model and made clear [the Way of] Wen and Wu. Above, he narrated the times of Heaven; below, he was in accord with water and land. **[1]** He may be compared to Heaven and Earth, [the latter] unfailing [in its] supporting and containing, [the former] unfailing [as a] cover and canopy. He may be compared to the four seasons in their alternating advance and was like the sun and moon in their alternating brightness. The ten thousand things are all nurtured together, and yet do not harm each other. Different paths are simultaneously traveled, and yet are not contrary to each other. Small virtue flows like a stream; large virtue is truly transforming. These things are what make Heaven and Earth great. **[2]** In the world, only [someone of] perfect sagacity is deemed able to be intelligent, enlightened, perceptive and knowledgeable enough to oversee [the world]; to be lenient, generous, kind and gentle enough to embrace [all things]; to be initiating, strong, upright and resolute enough to be decisive [in his judgement]; to be honourable, reverential, grave and correct enough to be respected [by others]; to be orderly, clear, careful and discerning enough to differentiate [between right and wrong]. **[3]** Wide-ranging and expansive, still and deep he is, and at the right time brings this forth. **[4]**

「溥博」如天,「淵泉」如淵。見而民莫不敬,言而民莫不信,行而民莫不説。是以聲名洋溢乎中國,施及蠻貊,舟車所至,人力所通,天之所覆,地之所載,日月所照,霜露所隊,凡有血氣者,莫不尊親,故曰「配天」。[5]

唯天下至誠,為能經綸天下之大經,立天下之大本,知天地之化育。[6]夫焉有所倚,肫肫其仁,淵淵其淵,浩浩其天。[7]苟不固聰明聖知達天德者,其孰能知之?[8]

《詩》曰:「衣錦尚絅」,惡其文之著也。故君子之道,闇然而日章;小人之道,的然而日亡。[9]君子之道,淡而不厭,簡而文,溫而理,知遠之近,知風之自,知微之顯,可與入德矣。[10]

《詩》云:「潛雖伏矣,亦孔之昭。」故君子內省不疚,無惡於志。[11]君子之所不可及者,其唯人之所不見乎?《詩》云:「相在爾室,尚不愧于屋漏。」[12]故君子不動而敬,不言而信。《詩》曰:「奏假無言,時靡有爭。」[13]

"Wide-ranging and expansive" he is, like Heaven; "still and deep" he is, like an abyss. He is seen, and the people cannot but respect [him]; he speaks, and the people cannot but trust [him]; he acts, and the people cannot but be pleased. This is why his great name spreads throughout the Central States and reaches to the Man and Mo [barbarians]. As far as boats and carriages travel, as far as human strength extends, whatever Heaven covers, whatever Earth contains, wherever sun and moon shine, wherever frost and dew fall, of all creatures that have blood and spirit, there is nobody that does not respect and love him. Therefore, he is said to match Heaven. [5]

In the world, only [one with] perfect _cheng_ 誠 is able to arrange and order the world's great classic (i.e. the _Spring and Autumn Annals_), establish the world's great basis (i.e. the _Classic of Filial Piety_), and comprehend the transformations and nurturings of Heaven and Earth. [6] Indeed, was there anything on which he depended? Honest and sincere was his _ren_ 仁; deep and still was his profundity; great and broad was his [understanding of] Heaven. [7] Indeed, other than a sage secure in intelligence and knowing the all-pervading virtue of Heaven, who can know him? [8]

The _Odes_ says: "Over her brocade garments she wore a plain, unlined coat"— she did not like to display her elegance. Thus, the Way of the noble man is hidden, and yet each day becomes more clearly apparent. The Way of the lesser man is clearly obvious, and yet each day becomes more deficient. [9] The Way of the noble man is plain and yet not tiresome, simple and yet refined, gentle and yet principled. He knows the nearness of the distant, the source of the wind, and the manifestations of the obscure. With these, it is possible to enter virtue. [10]

The _Odes_ says: "Although [the fish] lie on the bottom to hide, they are still highly visible." Thus the noble man, when he examines what is within, is not dissatisfied and finds nothing to dislike in his will. [11] Is what the noble man cannot reach to only that which others do not see? The _Odes_ says: "If you are seen alone in your own house, still be without shame even in the farthest corner." [12] Thus the noble man does not act and yet is revered, does not speak and yet is trusted. The _Odes_ says: "Entering and presiding without a word, at the time there is no contention." [13]

是故君子不賞而民勸，不怒而民威於鈇鉞。《詩》曰：「不顯惟德，百辟
其刑之。」[14] 是故君子篤恭而天下平。《詩》曰：「予懷明德，不大聲
以色。」[15]

Comment: This section is essentially the concluding section of the work—that is, apart
from a what is taken as a "footnote" in the form of a quotation from Confucius himself. It
is an encomium for Confucius in which he is identified as the possessor of perfect *sheng* 聖
and perfect *cheng* 誠. There are four sub-sections as follows:

(i)   Zhongni is recognised as the man who transmitted the Way of Yao and Shun,
        and advocated, as far as he was able, the Way of Wen and Wu. To the *Li ji*
        commentators, he did this particularly through the two classics, the *Chunqiu* 春秋
        (*Spring and Autumn Annals*) and the *Xiaojing* 孝經 (*Classic of Filial Piety*).
(ii)   Perfect *sheng* 聖 (sagacity) is described, and although the structure would lend itself
        to an impersonal reading, it is taken by the commentators to refer to Confucius and
        this is how it has been translated.
(iii)   Perfect *cheng* 誠 (purity, genuineness, sincerity) is described, and again imputed to
        Confucius.
(iv)   There are six quotations from the Odes, all exemplifying the characteristics of the
        noble man.

注 ZY32 (鄭玄)

[1] 此以《春秋》之義説孔子之德。孔子曰：「吾志在《春秋》，行在《孝經》。」[101]
二經固足以明之，孔子所述堯、舜之道而制《春秋》，而斷以文王、武王之法
度。《春秋傳》曰：「君子曷為為《春秋》？撥亂世，反諸正，莫近諸《春秋》。其
諸君子樂道堯舜之道與？末不亦樂乎？堯舜之知君子也。」又曰：「是子也，
繼文王之體，守文王之法度。文王之法無求而求，故譏之也。」又曰：「王者孰
謂，謂文王也。」[102] 此孔子兼包堯、舜、文、武之盛德而著之《春秋》，以俟後聖
也。律，述也。述天時，謂編年，四時具也。襲，因也。因水土，謂記諸夏之
事，山川之異。{行，下孟反。斷，丁亂反。曷為，于偽反。以，如字。撥，生
末反。近，附近之近，又如字。與音餘。編，必縣反，又甫連反。}

---

101 For the source of this quotation and further consideration of it, see the *Xiaojing yizhu* 孝
     經譯注, preface, p. 19.
102 The references are to the *Gongyang zhuan* 公羊傳 for Yin 1, Wen 9 and Ai 14
     respectively.

This is why the noble man does not give rewards, and yet the people are encouraged. This is why, without his showing anger, the people fear him more than blade or axe. The *Odes* says: "He makes no display of his virtue, yet the hundred princes take him as an exemplar." **[14]** This is why the noble man is genuine and reverential, and all under Heaven is at peace. The *Odes* says: "I return to enlightened virtue; it is not ostentatiously proclaimed by outward show." **[15]**

Notes ZY32 (Zheng Xuan)

[1] This uses the purport of the *Chunqiu* (*Spring and Autumn Annals*) to explain Confucius' virtue. Confucius said: "My will lies in the *Chunqiu*; my conduct lies in the *Xiaojing* (*Classic of Filial Piety*)." The two classics are certainly sufficient to make this clear. What Confucius transmitted was the Way of Yao and Shun and he created the *Chunqiu*, stopping with the laws and measures of Kings Wen and Wu. The commentary on the *Chunqiu* says: "Why did the noble man create the *Chunqiu*? In turning away from a confused age and returning to rectitude, nothing approaches the *Chunqiu*. In it, does the noble man find joy in the talk of the Way of Yao and Shun? Is it not also a source of joy? The wisdom of Yao and Shun was that of the noble man." It also says: "This Master gave judgement on the person of King Wen and preserved his laws and measures. King Wen's laws do not seek and yet seek, therefore he examined them." It also says: "Of kings, who is referred to? King Wen is referred to." This is Confucius including together Yao, Shun, Wen and Wu in their abundant virtue, and writing about this in the *Chunqiu* so as to await a later sage. *Lü* 律 is equivalent to *shu* 述 (to transmit, hand down). *He narrated the times of Heaven* refers to the annual registers and the seasons. *Xi* 襲 is equivalent to *yin* 因 (to follow, accord with). To accord with water and earth refers to recording the affairs of the summer and the differences of mountains and rivers. . . .

[2] 聖人制作，其德配天地，如此唯五始可以當焉。幬亦覆也。「小德川流」，浸潤萌芽，喻諸侯也。「大德敦化」，厚生萬物，喻天子也。幬或作「燾」。{辟音譬，下同。幬，徒報反。錯，七各反。當，丁浪反，又下郎反。浸，子鴆反。燾，徒報反。}

[3] 言德不如此，不可以君天下也。蓋傷孔子有其德而無其命。{叡音銳。知音智，下「聖知」同。齊，側皆反。別，彼列反。}

[4] 言其臨下普徧，思慮深重，非得其時不出政教。{溥音普。徧音遍。思，息嗣反，又如字。}

[5] 如天取其運照不已也，如淵取其清深不測也。「尊親」，尊而親之。{見，賢遍反。說音悅。施，以豉反。貉，本又作「貊」，武伯反。《說文》云：「北方人也。」隊，直類反。}

[6] 「至誠」，性至誠，謂孔子也。「大經」，謂六藝，而指《春秋》也。「大本」，《孝經》也。{論，本又作「綸」，同音倫。}

[7] 安有所倚，言無所偏倚也。故人人自以被德尤厚，似偏頗者。肫肫讀如「誨爾忳忳」之「忳」。忳忳，懇誠貌也。肫肫，或為「純純」。{焉，於虔反。倚，依綺、於寄二反，注同。肫，依注音之淳反。浩，胡老反。被，皮義反。頗，破河反。懇，苦狠反。純音淳，又之淳反。}

[8] 言唯聖人乃能知聖人也。《春秋傳》曰「末不亦樂乎，堯舜之知君子」，明凡人不知。

[9] 言君子深遠難知，小人淺近易知。人所以不知孔子，以其深遠。禪為絅。錦衣之美而君子以絅表之，為其文章露見，似小人也。絅，本又作「穎」，《詩》作「褧」，{同口迴反。徐口定反，一音口穎反。惡，烏路反。著，張慮反。闇，於感反，又如字。日，而一反，下同。的，丁歷反。易，以豉反，下「易舉」同。禪為音丹。為其，于偽反。見，賢遍反。}

[10] 淡其味似薄也，簡而文，溫而理，猶簡而辨，直而溫也。「自」，謂所從來也。「三知」者，皆言其睹末察本，探端知緒也。入德，入聖人之德。{淡，徒暫反，又大敢反，下注同。厭，於豔反。睹音覩。探音貪。}

[11] 孔，甚也。昭，明也。言聖人雖隱居，其德亦甚明矣。疢，病也。君子自省，身無愆病，雖不遇世，亦無損害於己志。昭，本又作炤，{同之召反，又章遙反。疢，九又反。遯，大困反，本又作「遁」，字亦同。愆，起虔反。}

[12] 言君子雖隱居，不失其君子之容德也。相，視也。室西北隅謂之「屋漏」。視女在室獨居者，猶不愧于屋漏。屋漏非有人也，況有人乎？{相，息亮反，注同。愧，本又作媿，同九位反。女音汝。}

[2] The sage establishes and creates; his virtue matches Heaven and Earth. Only in this way can the "five beginnings" be right. *Chou* 幬 is also *fu* 覆 (to cover). *Small virtue flows like a stream* is to be irrigated and to sprout and is a metaphor for the feudal lords. *Large virtue is truly transforming* is to be magnanimous and to give rise to the ten thousand things, and is a metaphor for the Son of Heaven. *Chou* 幬 is also written as *dao* 燾. . . .

[3] This says that, if his virtue is not like this, he cannot rule all under Heaven. Now what is distressing is that Confucius had this virtue, but did not have this decree. . . .

[4] This says that he looked down over everything and his thoughts and plans were deep and profound, but it was not his time so he did not come forth to govern. . . .

[5] Like Heaven has its revolutions and illumination and is unending, like an abyss has its clarity and depth and is unfathomable. *Zun qin* 尊親 is equivalent to *zun er qin zhi* 尊而親之 (to respect and love him). . . .

[6] "Perfect *cheng* 誠" is innate perfect *cheng* 誠 and refers to Confucius. *Da jing* 大經 refers to the six arts (*liu yi* 六藝) and indicates the *Chunqiu* (*Spring and Autumn Annals*). *Da ben* 大本 is the *Xiao jing* 孝經 (*Classic of Filial Piety*). . . .

[7] *Indeed, was there anything on which he depended* implies there is nothing on which he relied and depended. Therefore, everyone takes themselves to be the object of virtue that is particularly substantial, as if he were partial. *Zhun zhun* 肫肫 is read like *zhun* 忳 in *hui er zhun zhun* (誨爾忳忳). *Zhun zhun* 肫肫 is the appearance of *ken cheng* 懇誠 (sincerity). *Zhun zhun* 肫肫 is sometimes written for *zhun zhun* 純純. . . .

[8] This says that only a sage is able to know a sage. The *Chunqiu Commentary* says: "Is it not joyful, Yao and Shun's knowing a noble man?' This makes it clear that ordinary men do not know.

[9] This says the noble man is deep and distant, and hard to know, [whereas] the lesser man is lowly and limited, and easy to know. The reason why people did not know Confucius was because he was deep and distant. A *dan* 襌 is a *jiong* 絅 (a garment of one colour with no lining). Elegant clothes are beautiful yet the noble man, through a simple unlined garment, displays himself, making his outward display like that of the lesser man. *Jiong* 絅 was originally written as *jiong* 穎. The *Odes* has *jiong* 褧. . . .

[10] Weak is his flavour as if slight, simple and yet refined, gentle and yet principled, like being simple and yet discriminating, direct and yet gentle. *Zi* 自 refers to what is *conglai* 從來 (from the beginning). The "three wisdoms" all refer to his observing the "branches" and examining the "root," investigating the beginning and knowing the end. "Entering virtue" is to enter the sage's virtue. . . .

[11] *Kong* 孔 is equivalent to *shen* 甚 (very, extremely). *Zhao* 昭 is equivalent to *ming* 明 (bright). This says that, although the sage dwells in seclusion, his virtue nonetheless is very bright. *Jiu* 疚 is equivalent to *bing* 病 (defect, fault). The noble man examines himself and is without faults and defects in his person. Although he is not in tune with the times, he also does not damage or harm his own will. *Zhao* 昭 was originally also written as *zhao* 炤. . . .

[12] This says that, although the noble man dwells in seclusion, he does not lose the virtuous demeanour of the noble man. *Xiang* 相 is equivalent to *shi* 視 (to look at, regard). The north-west corner of the house refers to the *wu lou* 屋漏 (inner courtyard). If you are looked at while at home living alone, and are still not ashamed in the inner courtyard where there are no others, how much more will this be the case if there are others present? . . .

[13] 假，大也。此〈頌〉也。言奏大樂於宗廟之中，人皆肅敬。金聲玉色[振]，[103] 無有言者，以時太平，和合無所爭也。{奏如字，《詩》作奏，子公反。假，古雅反。爭，爭鬪之爭，注同。大平音泰。}

[14] 不顯，言顯也。辟，君也。此〈頌〉也。言不顯乎<u>文王</u>之德，百君盡刑之，謂諸侯法之也。{鈇，方于反，又音斧。鉞音越。辟音璧，注同。}

[15] 予，我也。懷，歸也。言我歸有明德者，以其不大聲為嚴厲之色以威我也。

疏 ZY32 (孔穎達)

{「<u>仲尼</u>」至「以色」。}

1.1　《正義》曰：此一節明<u>子思</u>申明夫子之德，與天地相似，堪以配天地而育萬物，傷有聖德無其位也。今各隨文解之。

1.2　「<u>仲尼</u>祖述<u>堯</u><u>舜</u>」者，祖，始也。言<u>仲尼</u>祖述始行<u>堯</u>、<u>舜</u>之道也。

1.3　「憲章<u>文</u><u>武</u>」者，憲，法也；章，明也。言夫子法明<u>文</u>、<u>武</u>之德。

1.4　「上律天時」者，律，述也。言夫子上則述行天時，以與言陰陽時候也。

1.5　「下襲水土」者，襲，因也。下則因襲諸侯之事，水土所在。此言<u>子思</u>贊揚聖祖之德，以<u>仲尼</u>修《春秋》而有此等之事也。

{注「吾志」至「之異」。}

1.6　《正義》曰：「吾志在《春秋》，行在《孝經》」者，《孝經緯》文，[104] 言褒貶諸侯善惡，志在於《春秋》，人倫尊卑之行在於《孝經》。云「二經固足以明之」者，此是<u>鄭</u>語，言《春秋》、《孝經》足以顯明先祖述憲章之事。

---

[103] *Se* 色 is emended to *zhen* 振, the two components of the term (*jin sheng* 金聲 and *yu zhen* 玉振) signalling the beginning and the end of the music—see, for example, *Mencius* VB.1(6), LCC, 2:372.

[104] The *Xiaojing wei* 孝經緯 is in the *Wei jun* 緯攟 9, CSJC 44, 59–67.

[13] *Jia* 假 is equivalent to *da* 大 (great, large). This is a *song* (hymn). It speaks of playing great music within the ancestral temple and people all being respectful and reverent. The metallic sound and the jade colour without any words make a time of great peace and harmony without anything that is contentious. . . .

[14] "No display" speaks of display (manifestation). *Pi* 辟 is equivalent to *jun* 君 (ruler, prince). This is a *song* (hymn). It says that, although there is no display of King Wen's virtue, the hundred princes all take him as exemplary, which refers to the feudal lords making him their model. . . .

[15] *Yu* 予 is equivalent to *wo* 我 (I, me). *Huai* 懷 is equivalent to *gui* 歸 (to return to). This says that my returning to the one who has enlightened virtue is because his being severe and strict without great display fills me with awe.

Commentary ZY32 (Kong Yingda)

1.1   The *Zhengyi* says that this particular section clarifies Zisi's elucidation of the Master's virtue and its similarity to Heaven and Earth, that it is worthy to be paired with Heaven and Earth, and that it gives rise to the ten thousand things. It was grievous that such sage virtue was without its position. Now each subsequent part explains this.

1.2   *Zhongni (Confucius) began the transmission [of the Way of] Yao and Shun*: *Zu* 祖 is equivalent to *shi* 始 (to start, begin). This says that Confucius was the beginning of the transmission of the practice of the Way of Yao and Shun.

1.3   *He took as a model and made clear [the Way of] Wen and Wu*: *Xian* 憲 is equivalent to *fa* 法 (model, pattern); *zhang* 章 is equivalent to *ming* 明 (to clarify, elucidate). This says that the Master took the virtue of Wen and Wu as a model and made it clear.

1.4   *Above, he narrated the times of Heaven*: *Lü* 律 is equivalent to *shu* 述 (to transmit, narrate). This says that, above, the Master then narrated and practised the times of Heaven by joining in with the discussion of the times of *yin* and *yang*.

1.5   *Below, he was in accord with water and land*: *Xi* 襲 is equivalent to *yin* 因 (to accord with, follow). Below, then, he followed and was in accord with the matters of the feudal lords where water and land were what existed. This says that Zisi praised the virtue of the sage ancestors through Confucius' arranging of the *Chunqiu* (*Spring and Autumn Annals*) and various other matters.

1.6   The *Zhengyi* says that in regard to "My will lies in the *Chunqiu* (*Spring and Autumn Annals*); my conduct lies in the *Xiaojing* (*Classic of Filial Piety*)," the text of the *Xiaojing wei* speaks of praising and criticising the good and bad feudal lords respectively, that his will lay in the *Chunqiu* and the practice of grading human relationships lay in the *Xiaojing*. Saying, "the two classics are certainly sufficient to make this clear" is to confirm Zheng's statement that the *Chunqiu* and the *Xiaojing* are sufficient to make clear the matters of "began the transmission" and "took as a model and made clear."

云「孔子祖述堯舜之道而制《春秋》」者，則下文所引《公羊傳》云「君子樂道，堯、舜之道與」是也。云「斷以文王 武王之法度」者，則下文引《公羊》云「王者孰謂？謂文王」是也。云「《春秋傳》曰」至「堯舜之知君子」也，哀十四年《公羊傳》文。引之者，證祖述堯、舜之事。「君子曷為為《春秋》」，曷，何也；「君子」，謂孔子。傳曰「孔子何為作《春秋》」，云「撥亂世，反諸正，莫近諸《春秋》」者，此傳之文，苔孔子為《春秋》之意。何休云：「撥猶治也。」[105] 言欲治於亂世，使反歸正道。莫近，莫過也。言餘書莫過於《春秋》，言治亂世者，《春秋》最近之也。云「其諸君子樂道堯舜之道與」者，上「道」，論道；下「道」，謂道德；「與」，語辭；言「君子」，孔子也。言孔子樂欲論道堯舜之道與也。云「末不亦樂乎，堯舜之知君子也」者，末謂終末，謂孔子末，聖漢之初，豈不亦愛樂堯、舜之知君子也。案何休云：「得麟之後，天下血書魯端門，曰『趨作法，孔聖沒，周姬亡，彗東出。秦政起，胡破術，書記散，孔不絕』。子夏明日往視之，血書飛為赤鳥，化為白書。」漢當秦大亂之後，故作撥亂之法，是其事也。云「又曰是子也，繼文王之體，守文王之法度，文王之法無求而求，故譏之也」者，此文九年《公羊傳》文。八年天王崩，謂周襄王也。

---

105 He Xiu 何休 (129–182): commentator on the *Gongyang zhuan* (春秋公羊傳註疏) in SSJZS 7.

Saying, "Confucius began the transmission of the Way of Yao and Shun and organized the *Chunqiu*" is, then, what the later text quotes from the *Gongyang zhuan* which says, "the noble man takes delight in the Way; that is the Way of Yao and Shun." Saying, "stopped at the laws and measures of King Wen and King Wu," the later text quotes the *Gongyang*, saying: "Who does 'king' refer to? It refers to King Wen" is this. In saying, "the *Chunqiu Commentary* says" to "Yao and Shun knowing the noble man" is from the 14th year of Duke Ai in the *Gongyang Commentary*. The quotation from it attests to his beginning the transmission of the matters of Yao and Shun. In "Why did the noble man create the *Chunqiu* (*Spring and Autumn Annals*)?" *he* 曷 is equivalent to *he* 何 (interrogative). *Junzi* 君子 (noble man) refers to Confucius. The commentary asks, "Why did Confucius create the *Spring and Autumn Annals*?" and replies, "For bringing order to a disordered age and turning back to correctness, nothing is more immediately relevant than the *Spring and Autumn Annals*." This is the text of the commentary and answers the question of Confucius' intention in creating the *Spring and Autumn Annals*. He Xiu says: "*Bo* 撥 is like *zhi* 治 (to bring good order)." This speaks of wishing to bring good order to a disordered age and cause a return to the path of rectitude. *Mo jin* 莫近 is equivalent to *mo guo* 莫過 (not going beyond). This says that none of the other books surpasses the *Spring and Autumn Annals*, and that in respect to bringing good order to a disordered age, the *Spring and Autumn Annals* comes closest. In saying, "Is this not the noble man taking joy in, and discussing, the Way of Yao and Shun?" the first *dao* 道 is *lundao* 論道 (to discuss) and the second *dao* 道 refers *daode* 道德 (the Way and virtue). *Yu* 語 is a particle. Saying *junzi* 君子 (noble man) is equivalent to Confucius. This says that Confucius took delight in, and wished to discuss, the Way of Yao and Shun. In saying "was it not in the end also pleasant, Yao and Shun knowing the noble man," *mo* 末 refers to *zhong mo* 終末 (in the end, finally) and refers to Confucius as the end and the sages of Han as the [new] beginning. That is, did they not also love and take joy in Yao and Shun knowing the noble man. Accordingly, He Xiu says: "After getting the unicorn, the world found a letter in blood at the south gate of Lu, saying 'there was haste to make laws, the Confucian sage passed away, Zhou Ji perished; a comet came forth from the east; Qin Shi Huangdi arose and Hu Hai ended the transmission. Books and records were scattered, but Confucius was not cut off.' The next day Zi Xia went to look at it and the writing in blood flew away as a red bird and changed to be white writing." Han put right the consequences of the great disorder of Qin, therefore creating methods to get rid of disorder was its business. The statement that, "it also says this son continued King Wen's substance and preserved King Wen's laws and measures, and that King Wen's laws did not seek and yet sought, therefore he examined them" was written for the 9th year of Wen in the *Gongyang Commentary*. In the 8th year, the Heavenly King died, referring to King Xiang of Zhou.

九年春，<u>毛伯</u>來求金，傳云：「是子繼<u>文王</u>之體，守<u>文王</u>之法度。<u>文王</u>之法無求而求，故譏之。」「是子」謂嗣位之王，在喪未合稱王，故稱「是子」。嗣位之王，守<u>文王</u>之法度。<u>文王</u>之法度無所求也。謂三分有二以服事<u>殷</u>。謂在喪之內，無合求金之法度，今遣<u>毛伯</u>來求金，是「無求而求」也，故書以譏之。彼傳云「是子」，俗本云「子是」，者，誤也。云「又曰王者孰謂，謂<u>文王</u>也」此<u>隱</u>元年《公羊傳》文。

案傳云：「元年，春，王，正月。王者孰謂？謂<u>文王</u>也。」<u>武王</u>道同，舉<u>文王</u>可知也。云「著之《春秋》，以俟後聖者也」，<u>哀</u>十四年《公羊傳》云「制《春秋》之義，以俟後聖」。<u>何休</u>云：「待聖<u>漢</u>之王，以為法也。」云「述天時，謂編年，四時具也」，案《合成圖》云：「皇帝立五始，制以天道。」《元命包》云：「諸侯不上奉王之正，則不得即位。[106] 正不由王出，不得為正。王不承於天以制號令，則無法。天不得正其元，則不能成其化也。」

---

[106] The *Yuanmingbao* is a lost excursus on the *Spring and Autumn Annals*. We have not been able to identify the *Hechengtu*.

In the spring of the 9th year, the Earl of Mao came seeking money. The *Commentary* says: "This son continued King Wen's substance and preserved King Wen's laws and measures. King Wen's laws sought without seeking, therefore he examined them." "This son" refers to the king's successor to the throne. At the funeral, he did not agree to be styled king, therefore he was styled "this son." The king's successor to the throne preserved King Wen's laws and measures. King Wen's laws and measures were not what were sought. In referring to the three divisions, two were for serving Yin. Speaking of matters at the funeral, there was not agreement on the method of seeking money. He sent the Earl of Mao away when he came seeking money.[107] This is "not seeking and yet seeking." Therefore, the *Documents* examined this. Another commentary says "this son" was customarily originally written "*zi shi* 子是." This is wrong. Saying "also saying in the case of the king who is being referred to, it is King Wen that is being referred to," is from the *Gongyang Commentary* for the 1st year of Duke Yin.

According to the commentary, it says: "First year, spring; the king, the first month of the year. To whom does 'king' refer? It refers to King Wen." Raising the matter of King Wen makes it known that King Wu's Way was the same. On saying, "he wrote it as the *Spring and Autumn Annals* in order to await a later sage" the *Gongyang Commentary* for the 14th year of Duke Ai says: "His purpose in arranging the *Spring and Autumn Annals* was to await a later sage." He Xiu says: "He awaited a sage Han king to create laws." On saying, "he narrated Heaven's times" refers to the arrangement according to years and the four seasons being written out," according to the *Hechengtu* it says: "The emperor set up the five beginnings and regulated them through the heavenly Way." The *Yuanmingbao* says: "If the feudal lords did not follow orders from the king above correctly, they did not obtain a position. If correctness does not come forth from the king, it is not correctness. If the king does not carry on from Heaven by regulating rewards, then there are no laws. If Heaven does not acquire correctness at its origin, then it is not able to complete its transformations."

---

[107] See the *Spring and Autumn Annals* for the 9th year of Duke Wen (LCC, 5:252 ff).

2.1 「五始」者，元年，一也；春，二也；王，三也；正月，四也；公即位，
五也。此《春秋》元年，即當〈堯典〉「欽若昊天」也。《春秋》四時，即當
〈堯典〉[108]「日中星鳥，日永星火，宵中星虛，日短星昴」之類是也。《春
秋》獲麟，則當〈益稷〉「百獸率舞，鳳凰來儀」是也。此皆祖述堯、舜之
事，言《春秋》四時皆具。桓四年及七年不書「秋七月」、「冬十月」，成十
年不書「冬十月」，桓十七年直云「五月」不云「夏」，昭十年直云「十二月」
不云「冬」，如此不具者，賈、服之義：若登臺而不視朔，則書「時」不
書「月」；若視朔而不登臺，則書「月」不書「時」；若雖無事視朔、登臺，
則空書時月。若杜元凱[109]之意，凡時月不具者，皆史闕文。其《公羊》、
《穀梁》之義，各為曲説，今略而不取也。云「襲，因也。因水土，謂記
諸夏之事，山川之異」者，「諸夏之事」，謂諸侯征伐、會盟所在之地。
「山川之異」，若僖十四年「沙鹿崩」，成五年「梁山崩」之屬是也。[110]

2.2 「譬如」至「大也」，此明孔子之德與天地日月相似，與天子、諸侯德化無
異。

2.3 「小德川流，大德敦化」者，言孔子所作《春秋》，若以諸侯「小德」言之，
如川水之流，浸潤萌芽。若以天子「大德」言之，則仁愛敦厚，化生萬物
也。

2.4 「此天地之所以為大也」，言夫子之德比並天地，所以為大不可測也。
{「唯天」至「別也」。}

---

[108] See the *Documents*, "Yao dian," LCC, 3:116 and Legge's note on this.

[109] Du Yuankai 杜元凱 (Du Yu 杜預, 222–284) rose to high office under the first Jin emperor. He was a noted student of the *Zuo zhuan*.

[110] For these two statements, see the *Spring and Autumn Annals* for Duke Xi, 14th year, LCC, 5:161 and for Duke Cheng, 5th year, LCC, 5:355 respectively.

2.1   With respect to the "five beginnings," the first year of a reign is one; spring is two; the king is three; the first month is four; a duke being already established is five. This "first year" in the *Chunqiu* (*Spring and Autumn Annals*) corresponds to "in reverent accord with the wide heavens" in the "Yao dian." The "four seasons" in the *Spring and Autumn Annals* corresponds to "the day is of medium length and the star is *niao*," "the day is at its longest and the star is *huo*," "the night is of medium length and the star is *xu*" and "the day is short and the star is *mao*"— this sort of thing. The *Spring and Autumn Annals'* "seizing the unicorn" then corresponding to "the hundred animals lead the dance" and "the male and female unicorn come with their deportment" in the "Yi Ji" is this. These are all beginnings of the transmission of the affairs of Yao and Shun and say the four seasons of the *Spring and Autumn Annals* were all written down. From the 4th year of King Huan to the 7th year it is not written "autumn, 7th month" and "winter, 10th month"; for the 10th year of Duke Cheng it is not written "winter, 10th month"; for the 17th year of Duke Huan it says directly "5th month" and does not say "summer"; for the 10th year of Duke Zhao it says directly "12th month" and does not say "winter." Things like this not being written have the meaning of *gu* 賈 and *fu* 服. If there is climbing the tower and not seeing the new moon, then there is written "time" and not "month." If there is seeing the new moon and not climbing the tower, then there is written "moon" and not "time." If there are not the matters of seeing the new moon and climbing the tower, then a blank is left in writing *shi* 時 or *yue* 月. For example, Du Yuankai's meaning is that, in general, if *shi* 時 or *yue* 月 is not written, these are all omissions of the scribe. The *Gongyang* and the *Guliang* each has its partial statement and their interpretations are now omitted and not accepted. It is said "*xi* 襲 is eqivalent to *yin* 因 (to accord with, unite). Being in accord with water and land refers to recording the affairs of the many states and the differences of mountains and streams"; "the affairs of the many states" refers to the feudal lords attacking or forming alliances of peace in the lands that existed. "The differences of mountains and rivers" is like [the statement for] the 14th year of Duke Xi, "Sha Lu hill fell down" and [the statement for] the 5th year of Duke Cheng, "Liang Mountain fell down"—this sort of thing.

2.2   From "*pi ru* 譬 如" to "*da ye* 大 也": This makes clear that Confucius' virtue was like Heaven and Earth, like the sun and moon, and was no different in terms of transforming from the virtue of the Son of Heaven and the feudal lords.

2.3   *Small virtue flows like a stream; large virtue is truly transforming*: This says that what Confucius created in the *Spring and Autumn Annals* was like taking the feudal lords' "small virtue" and speaking of it as the flow of river water irrigating new plants, or like taking the "great virtue" of the Son of Heaven and speaking of it, so then *ren* 仁 and *ai* 愛, generous and substantial, transform and give rise to the ten thousand things.

2.4   *These things are what make Heaven and Earth great*: This says that the Master's virtue was comparable to Heaven and Earth [in that] what made it great cannot be fathomed.

3.1 此又申明夫子之德聰明寬裕，足以容養天下，傷其有聖德而無位也。

3.2 「寬裕溫柔，足以有容也」，言夫子寬弘性善，溫克和柔，足以包容也。

3.3 「發強剛毅，足以有執也」，發，起也；執，猶斷也。言孔子發起志意，堅強剛毅，足以斷決事物也。

{「溥博」至「配天」。}

4.1 此節更申明夫子蘊蓄聖德，俟時而出，日月所照之處，無不尊仰。

4.2 「溥博淵泉」者，溥，謂無不周徧；博，謂所及廣遠。以其浸潤之澤，如似淵泉溥大也。既思慮深重，非得其時不出政教，必以俟時而出。

5.1 「溥博如天」者，言似天「無不覆幬」。

5.2 「淵泉如淵」，言潤澤深厚，如川水之流。

7.1 「夫焉有所倚」至「浩浩其天」，以前經贊明夫子之德，此又云夫子無所偏倚，而仁德自然盛大也。倚，謂偏有所倚近，言夫子之德，普被於人，何有獨倚近於一人，言不特有偏頗也。

7.2 「肫肫其仁」，肫肫，懇誠之貌。仁，謂施惠仁厚。言又能肫肫然懇誠行此仁厚爾。

7.3 「淵淵其淵」，淵水深之貌也，言夫子之德，淵淵然若水之深也。

7.4 「浩浩其天」，言夫子之德，浩浩盛大，其若如天也。

7.5 注「肫肫讀如誨爾忳忳之忳」。

3.1   This also explicates the Master's virtue being wise and abundant, and sufficient to nourish all under Heaven, and that there was distress at his having sage virtue but being without a position.

3.2   *Lenient, generous, kind and gentle enough to embrace [all things]*: This speaks of the Master's extensive and great nature for good, [how he was] mild and restrained, conciliatory and yielding, sufficient to be tolerant.

3.3   *Initiating, strong, upright and resolute enough to be decisive [in his judgement]*: *Fa* 發 is equivalent to *qi* 起 (to begin, initiate, rise); *zhi* 執 is equivalent to *duan* 斷 (to decide). This speaks of Confucius' initiating will and purpose and his strong resolve, sufficient to decide matters.

4.1   This section again explicates the Master's self-contained sage virtue, awaiting the [right] time and coming forth. In places illumined by sun and moon, there was none where he was not respected and looked up to.

4.2   *Wide-ranging and expansive, still and deep he is*: *Pu* 溥 refers to extending on all sides; *bo* 博 refers to what he reaches to being wide and distant. Through the enrichment of his imbuing (influence), he is like a source, extensive and great. Although his thoughts and plans were deep and weighty, he did not find his time and did not come forth to govern. It is necessary to await the [right] time to come forth.

5.1   *"Wide-ranging and expansive" he is, like Heaven*: This says that he was like Heaven—unfailing as cover and canopy.

5.2   *"Still and deep" he is, like an abyss*: This says that his kindness was deep and profound, like a stream of flowing water.

7.1   From *indeed, was there anything on which he depended* to *great and broad is his [understanding of] Heaven*: Where the earlier section praises and clarifies the Master's virtue, this also speaks of the Master not having anything he relied or depended on and yet his *ren* 仁 and *de* 德 were naturally abundant and great. *Yi* 倚 refers to being inclined to one side and having that which one depends on and is close to. It says that the Master's virtue was advanced to others. How was it only reliant on and advanced to one person? That is to say, it did not particularly have an inclination to one side.

7.2   *Honest and sincere was his ren* 仁: *Zhun zhun* 肫肫 is the appearance of sincerity. *Ren* 仁 refers to bestowing kindness, beneficence and generosity. This also says that he was able to be genuine and honest in his *cheng* 誠 and practised this *ren* 仁 generously.

7.3   *Deep and still was his profundity*: The water of an abyss has the appearance of depth. This says that the Master's virtue was deep and profound like the water's depths.

7.4   *Great and broad was his [understanding of] Heaven*: This says that the Master's virtue was great, wide and abundantly large, this being like Heaven.

7.5   The notes say that *zhun* 肫 is read like *zhun* 忳 in *hui er zhun zhun* 誨爾忳忳.

7.6　《正義》曰：此〈大雅‧抑〉之篇，刺厲王之詩。言詩人誨爾厲王忳忳然懇誠不已，厲王聽我藐藐然而不入也。

8.1　「苟不固聰明聖知達天德者，其孰能知之」者，上經論夫子之德大如天，此經論唯至聖乃知夫子之德。苟，誠也。固，堅固也。言帝誠不堅固聰明睿聖通知曉達天德者，其誰能識知夫子之德？故注引《公羊傳》云「堯舜之知君子」者，言有堯、舜之德乃知夫子，明凡人不知也。

9.1　「《詩》曰：衣錦尚絅，惡其文之著也」，[111] 以前經論夫子之德難知，故此經因明君子、小人隱顯不同之事。此《詩‧衛風‧碩人》之篇，美莊姜之詩。言莊姜初嫁在塗，衣著錦衣，為其文之大著，尚著襌絅加於錦衣之上。絅，襌也，以單縠為衣，尚以覆錦衣也。案《詩》本文云「衣錦褧衣」，此云「尚絅」者，斷截《詩》文也。又俗本云「衣錦褧裳」，又與定本不同者。記人欲明君子謙退，惡其文之彰著，故引《詩》以結之。

9.2　「故君子之道，闇然而日章」者，章，明也。言君子以其道德深遠謙退，初視未見，故曰「闇然」。其後明著，故曰日章明也。

9.3　「小人之道，的然而日亡」者，若小人好自矜大，故初視時「的然」。以其才藝淺近，後無所取，故曰日益亡。

{「君子」至「德矣」。}

111　See the *Odes*, Mao 57, verse 1, LCC, 4:94. For the revised verse, see Ames and Hall, *Focusing the Familiar: A Translation and Philosophical Interpretation of the Zhongyong*, 129n93.

7.6   The *Zhengyi* says that this is from the "Yi" ode in the "Da ya," a poem criticising King Li. It says that the poet was instructing King Li unceasingly and with genuine sincerity. King Li listened to me [it says] without paying attention and did not enter.

8.1   *Indeed, other than a sage secure in intelligence and knowing the all-pervading virtue of Heaven, who can know him?* The earlier text discusses the Master's virtue being great like Heaven. This section discusses [the fact that] only a perfect sage knows the Master's virtue. *Gou* 苟 is equivalent to *cheng* 誠 (indeed, actually). *Gu* 固 is equivalent to *jian gu* 堅固 (strong, secure). This says that, if the emperor was not one whose *cheng* 誠 was strong, whose intelligence and sage-like wisdom did not know and comprehend the all-pervading virtue of Heaven, then who would be able truly to know the Master's virtue? Therefore, the notes quote the *Gongyang Commentary* in saying, "Yao and Shun knew the noble man," which speaks of there being the virtue of Yao and Shun and then knowing the Master, making it clear that ordinary people did not know.

9.1   *The Odes says: "Over her brocade garments she wore a plain (unlined) coat," disliking to display her elegance*: The previous section discussed the fact that the Master's virtue is difficult to know, therefore this section, as a result, makes it clear that the noble man and the lesser man, in the matters of concealing and displaying, are not the same. This is from the ode "Shuo ren" in the "Wei feng," a verse in praise of Zhuang Jiang. It says that when Zhuang Jiang first went to marry and was on the road, her garments were brocade as a great display of her elegance, but she still wore a plain unlined coat over the top of the brocade garments. *Jiong* 絅 is equivalent to *dan* 襌, an unlined garment of thin silk which is still worn to cover embroidered garments. According to the original text of the *Odes*, it says "衣錦褧衣," whereas this has *shang jiong* 尚絅 which is an interruption of the text of the *Odes*. Also the common origin says "衣錦褧裳" and further establishes that the original was not the same. The [*Li*] *ji* records it, wishing to make clear that the noble man is humble and self-deprecating, and dislikes making a display of his elegance, and so quotes the *Odes* to affirm this.

9.2   *Thus, the Way of the noble man is hidden, and yet each day becomes more apparent*: *Zhang* 章 is equivalent to *ming* 明 (clear, apparent). This says that the noble man, in his Way and virtue, is deep and profound but humble and self-deprecating, and when first looked at, is not noticed. Therefore, it says "hidden." Afterwards it (i.e. his Way) becomes apparent, therefore it says that each day it is more clearly apparent.

9.3   *The Way of the lesser man is clearly obvious, and yet each day becomes more deficient*: For example, the lesser man is full of self-esteem and self-aggrandisement, therefore at the time of first looking, he is *de ran* 得然 (quite obvious). But his talents and abilities are shallow and slight and afterwards there are no grounds on which to choose him. Therefore, it is said that each day he is increasingly lost.

10.1 此一經明君子之道，察微知著，故能「入德」。

10.2 「淡而不厭」者，言不媚悅於人，初似淡薄，久而愈敬，無惡可厭也。

10.3 「簡而文」者，性無嗜慾，故簡靜，才藝明辨，故有文也。

10.4 「溫而理」，氣性和潤，故溫也。正直不違，故修理也。

10.5 「知遠之近」，言欲知遠處，必先之適於近，乃後及遠。「知風之自」，自，謂所從來處，言見目前之風則知之適所從來處，故鄭注云「睹末察本」。遠是近之末，風是所□□□□□從來之末也。「知微之顯」，此初時所微之事，久乃適於顯明，微是初端，顯是縱緒，故鄭注云「探端知緒」。

10.6 「可與入德矣」，言君子或探末以知本，或睹本而知末，察微知著，終始皆知，故可以入聖人之德矣。

11.1 「《詩》曰：潛雖伏矣，亦孔之昭」，此明君子其身雖隱，其德昭著。所引者〈小雅・正月〉之篇，[112] 刺幽王之詩。《詩》之本文以幽王無道，喻賢人君子雖隱其身，德亦甚明著，不能免禍害，猶如魚伏於水，亦甚著見，被人採捕。記者斷章取義，言賢人君子身雖藏隱，猶如魚伏於水，其道德亦甚彰矣。

11.2 「故君子內省不疚，無惡於志」者，疚，病也。言君子雖不遇世，內自省身，不有愆病，則亦不損害於己志。言守志彌堅固也。

---

[112] See the *Odes*, Mao 192, verse 11, LCC, 4:319.

10.1 This particular section makes clear the Way of the noble man, examining the subtle and knowing the manifest. Therefore he is able "to enter virtue."

10.2 *Plain and yet not tiresome*: This says he is not attractive and pleasing to others, and in the beginning is like something dull and slight. Over time, he is increasingly respected and not disliked; nor can he be wearied of.

10.3 *Simple and yet refined*: His nature is not addicted to desires, therefore it is simple and tranquil. Talents and accomplishments are clearly distinguished, therefore he is refined.

10.4 *Gentle and yet principled*: His disposition and nature are harmonious and enriching, therefore he is gentle. He is upright and non-refractory, therefore he cultivates principle.

10.5 *He knows the nearness of the distant*: This says that, if he desires to know a distant place, he must first go to the near and then afterwards advance to the distant. *He knows the source of the wind*: Zi 自 refers to the place from which it comes and says that, when he sees the wind in front of his eyes, he knows the place whence it came. Therefore, Zheng's notes say, "see the branches, examine the root." The distant is a terminus (branch) of the near. The wind . . . *He knows the manifestation of the obscure*: This is that matters which are at first obscure after a time go on to become apparent and clear. The obscure is the origin; the manifest is the end-point. Therefore, Zheng's notes say: "Enquire after the beginning to know the end."

10.6 *With these, it is possible to enter virtue*: This says that the noble man sometimes enquires into the branches in order to know the root, and sometimes looks at the root to know the branches. If he examines the obscure to know the manifest, the end and the beginning are both known. Therefore, it is possible to enter (i.e. reach) the virtue of the sage.

11.1 *The Odes says: "Although [the fish] lie on the bottom to hide, they are still highly visible"*: This makes it clear that, although the noble man's person may be hidden, his virtue is brightly manifest. What is quoted is the ode "Zheng yue" from the "Xiao ya," a poem criticising King You. The original text of the *Odes* takes King You to be without the Way and gives the illustration of a worthy or noble man who, although he is himself hidden, has virtue that is very brightly displayed. But he is not able to avoid misfortune and harm, so is just like a fish hiding in the water which is also very apparent and is caught by men. The [*Li*] *ji* "cutting short the writing to take out the meaning" (quoting out of context) is to say that the worthy or noble man is just like a fish hiding in the water. Although his body is hidden and concealed, his Way and virtue are very apparent.

11.2 *Thus the noble man, when he examines what is within, is not dissatisfied and finds nothing to dislike in his will*: Jiu 疚 is equivalent to *bing* 病 (fault, defect). This says that, although the noble man is not in tune with the times, if he has no faults or defects when he examines what is within, then this is also not harmful to his own will. It says that in the preservation of his will, he is entirely firm and resolute.

11.3　注「孔，甚也」。

11.4　《正義》曰：《爾雅‧釋言》文。

{「君子」至「室漏」。}

12.1　此明君子之閒居獨處，不敢為非，故云「君子所不可及者，其唯人之所不見乎」。

12.2　「《詩》云：相在爾室，尚不愧于屋漏」，此〈大雅‧抑〉之篇，[113] 刺厲王之詩。詩人意稱王朝小人不敬鬼神，瞻視女在廟堂之中，猶尚不愧畏於屋漏之神。記者引之斷章取義，言君子之人在室之中「屋漏」，雖無人之處不敢為非，猶愧懼于屋漏之神，況有人之處君子愧懼可知也。言君子雖獨居，常能恭敬。

{注「言君」至「人乎」。}

12.3　《正義》曰：言「君子雖隱居，不失其君子之容德也」者，隱居，謂在室獨居猶不愧畏，無人之處又常能恭敬，是「不失其君子之容德也」。云「西北隅謂之屋漏」者，《爾雅‧釋宮》文。[114] 以戶明漏照其處，故稱「屋漏」。「屋漏非有人」者，言人之所居，多近於戶，屋漏深邃之處，非人所居，故云無有人也。云「況有人乎」者，言無人之處尚不愧之，況有人之處不愧之可知也。言君子無問有人無人，恒能畏懼也。

---

[113] See the *Odes*, Mao 256, verse 7, LCC, 4:514–15.

[114] See the *Er ya*, SSJZS, 8:72.

11.3   The notes say that *kong* 孔 is equivalent to *shen* 甚 (very).

11.4   The *Zhengyi* says that this is the text of the *Er ya*, "Shi yan."

12.1   This makes it clear that, when the noble man is at ease and dwelling alone, he does not dare to do what is wrong. Therefore it says *is what the noble man cannot reach to only what others do not see?*

12.2   *The Odes says: "If you are seen in your own house, still be without shame even in the farthest corner".* This is the ode "Yi" from the "Da ya," a poem criticizing King Li. The poet's intention is to refer to the royal court and lesser men not respecting ghosts and spirits, so that when they look at you within the temple and hall, you still do not feel shame or fear towards the spirits in the farthest corner. The [*Li*] *ji*, in quoting this, "cuts short the writing to take out the meaning" (quotes out of context) to say that the noble man as a person within the farthest corner of his own house, although it is a place where there are no others, does not dare to do wrong, and is still ashamed and fearful of the spirits in the farthest corners of the house. How much more in places where there are other people, can the shame and fear of the noble man be known. This says that, although the noble man dwells alone, he is constantly able to be reverential and respectful.

12.3   The *Zhengyi* says this is saying that "although the noble man dwells in seclusion, he does not lose the virtuous demeanour of a noble man." *Yin ju* 隱居 (dwells in seclusion) refers to him being in his dwelling alone and still not being ashamed and fearful. In a place where there are no others, he is also constantly able to be reverential and respectful—this is "he does not lose the virtuous demeanour of the noble man." Saying "the north-west corner refers to the *shi lou* 室漏" is text from the *Er ya*, "Shi gong." By means of a door, brightness is disclosed and shines in this place, therefore it is called *shi lou* 室漏 (skylight, courtyard).[115] "The *shi lou* 室漏 does not have people" says that in a place where people dwell, many enter through the door; the *shi lou* 室漏 is a deep place and is not where people dwell. Therefore, it says there are no people. Saying "how much more so where there are people" says that, if there is still no feeling of shame in a place without people, how much more so, in places where there are people, can the noble man's not feeling shame be known. This says that the noble man does not question whether there are people or not; he is constantly able to be in awe and fearful.

---

115   In his note to the relevant ode, Legge has: "The open court in Chinese houses, to which several roofs converge, and which receives water from them and serves to admit the light to the rooms below, is called the *shi lou* 室漏 or 'dripping place' of a house. From the connection of the phrase here, however, I prefer to interpret it as the opening or window in the north-west wall through which the light was admitted" (LCC, 4:514–15).

13.1 「故君子不動而敬，不言而信」者，以君子敬懼如是，故不動而民敬之，不言而民信之。

13.2 「《詩》曰：奏假無言，時靡有爭」，此〈商頌•烈祖〉之篇，[116] 美成湯之詩。詩本文云「鬷假無言」，此云「奏假」者，與《詩》反異也。假，大也。言祭成湯之時，奏此大樂於宗廟之中，人皆肅敬，無有誼譁之言。所以然者，時既太平，無有爭訟之事，故「無言」也。引證君子不言而民信。

13.3 注「假，大也」。

13.4 《正義》曰：《爾雅•釋詁》文。

14.1 「《詩》曰：不顯惟德，百辟其刑之」，此〈周頌•烈文〉之篇[117]，美文王之德。不顯乎文王之德，言其顯矣。以道德顯著，故天下百辟諸侯皆刑法之。引之者，證君子之德猶若文王，其德顯明在外，明眾人皆刑法之。

14.2 注「辟，君也」。

14.3 《正義》曰：《爾雅•釋詁》文。

15.1 「《詩》云：予懷明德，不大聲以色」，此〈大雅•皇矣〉之篇[118]，美文王之詩。予，我也。懷，歸也。言天謂文王曰，我歸就爾之明德，所以歸之者，以文王不大作音聲以為嚴厲之色，故歸之。記者引之，證君子亦不作大音聲以為嚴厲之色，與文王同也。

---

[116] See the *Odes*, Mao 302, LCC, 4:634–35. The *Odes* has *zong* 鬷 instead of *zou* 奏—see Legge's note, p. 635.

[117] See the *Odes*, Mao 269, verse 2, LCC, 4:573.

[118] See the *Odes*, Mao 241, verse 7, LCC, 4:454.

13.1   *Thus the noble man does not act and yet is revered, does not speak and yet is trusted*: By the noble man being reverential and fearful like this, he does not act and yet the people respect him; he does not speak and yet the people trust him.

13.2   *The Odes says: "Entering and presiding without a word, at the time there is no contention"*: This is from the "Lie zu" in the "Shang song," a poem in praise of Cheng Tang. The original text of the poem says 鬷假無言." This says "*zou jia* 奏假" and is opposite and different to the *Odes. Jia* 假 is equivalent to *da* 大 (large, great). It says that at the time of sacrifice to Cheng Tang, they played this great music within the ancestral temple, people were all respectful and reverential, and there was no shouting or hubbub. Because this was so, the time was very peaceful and there were no contentious or disputed matters, therefore *there were no words.* The quotation attests to the fact that the noble man does not speak and yet the people trust [him].

13.3   The notes have "*jia* 假 is equivalent to *da* 大 (great, large)."

13.4   The *Zhengyi* says that the text is from the *Er ya*, "Shigu."

14.1   *The Odes says: "He makes no display of his virtue, yet the hundred princes take him as an exemplar"*: This is from the "Lie wen" in the "Zhou song," a poem in praise of King Wen's virtue. "King Wen's virtue is not displayed" speaks of its being apparent. Because the Way of virtue is displayed and made known, the hundred princes and feudal lords of the world all imitate it. Quoting this attests to the noble man's virtue being like that of King Wen; that is, manifest and apparent to the outside world, and makes it clear that the mass of people all take him as a model.

14.2   The notes have "*pi* 辟 is equivalent to *jun* 君 (prince, ruler)."

14.3   The *Zhengyi* says that this text is from the *Er ya*, "Shigu."

15.1   *The Odes says: "I return to enlightened virtue; it is not ostentatiously proclaimed by outward show"*: This is from the "Da ya," "Huang Yi" and is a poem in praise of King Wen. *Yu* 予 is equivalent to *wo* 我 (I). *Huai* 懷 is equivalent to *gui* 歸 (to return, revert). This speaks of Heaven addressing King Wen and saying, "I return to your enlightened virtue and the reason why I return to it is because you did not make a great outward display, adopting a severe and strict demeanour." Therefore, there was a return to it. The [*Li*] *ji* quotes this to prove that the noble man also does not make a great noise in order to create the appearance of a severe and strict demeanour, and King Wen was the same.

ZY33: 子曰：「聲色之於以化民，末也。《詩》曰：『德輶如毛。』[1] 毛猶有倫。『上天之載，無聲無臭』至矣。」[2]

Comment: This brief final section is identified here as a statement by Confucius, offering confirmation of Zisi's earlier statement to similar effect. The meaning is clear—virtue is insubstantial, as light as a feather or a hair, but it acts without outward manifestation to transform people, just as Heaven acts without outward display in its giving rise to things.

注 ZY33 (鄭玄)

[1] 輶，輕也。言化民常以德，德之易舉而用，其輕如毛耳。{末，下葛反。輶音酉，一音由，注同。易，以豉反。}

[2] 倫，猶比也。載讀曰「栽」，謂生物也。言毛雖輕，尚有所比，有所比，則有重。上天之造生萬物，人無聞其聲音，亦無知其臭氣者。化民之德，清明如神，淵淵浩浩然後善。載，依注讀曰栽，音災，生也，《詩》音再。{比，必覆反，下同；或音毗志反，又必利反，皆非也。重，直勇反，又直容反。}

疏 ZY33 (孔穎達)

{「子曰」至「至矣」。}

1.1　《正義》曰：此一節是夫子之言。子思既說君子之德不大聲以色，引夫子舊語聲色之事以接之，言化民之法當以德為本，不用聲色以化民也。若用聲色化民，是其末事，故云「化民末也」。

1.2　「《詩》曰：德輶如毛」者，此〈大雅・烝民〉之篇，[119] 美宣王之詩。輶，輕也。言用德化民，舉行甚易，其輕如毛也。

2.1　「毛猶有倫」，倫，比也。既引《詩》文「德輶如毛」，又言德之至極本自無體，何直如毛？毛雖細物，猶有形體可比，並故云「毛猶有倫」也。

---

[119] See the *Odes*, Mao 260, verse 6, LCC, 4:544.

ZY33: The Master said: "In transforming the people, sounds and sights are insignificant. The *Odes* says: 'Virtue is as light as a feather.' **[1]** But a feather can still be used as a comparison. [The *Odes* also says:] 'Above, Heaven's giving rise to things has neither sound nor smell'—how perfect!" **[2]**

Notes ZY33 (Zheng Xuan)

[1] *You* 輶 is equivalent to *qing* 輕 (light). This says that transforming the people is always through virtue. Virtue is easy to "raise" and use; its lightness is like a feather. . . .

[2] *Lun* 倫 is like *bi* 比 (to compare). *Zai* 載 is read as saying *zai* 栽 and refers to giving rise to things. This says that, although a feather is light, there is still that to which it can be compared; if there is, then it has weight. Above, when Heaven creates and gives rise to the ten thousand things, people do not hear its sound nor do they perceive its smell. The virtue that transforms people is pure and clear like a spirit, deep and still, great and grand, and in the end good. *Zai* 載, according to the notes, is read as saying *zai* 栽, pronounced as *zai* 災, and is equivalent to *sheng* 生 (to give rise to, give birth to). In the *Odes* it is pronounced as *zai* 再. . . .

Commentary ZY33 (Kong Yingda)

1.1 The *Zhengyi* says that in this particular section these are the Master's words. Zisi has already explained that the virtue of the noble man has no great sound or sight, quoting the Master's old statement on the matter of sounds and sights to catch [the meaning]. It says that, in the method of transforming the people, it is right to take virtue as the foundation and not use sounds and sights to transform the people. If there is the use of sounds and sights to transform the people, they are matters of no importance. Therefore it says, "in transforming the people they are insignificant."

1.2 *The Odes says: "Virtue is as light as a feather."* This is from the "Zheng min" in the "Da ya" and is a poem in praise of King Xuan. *You* 輶 is equivalent to *qing* 輕 (light). This says that in using virtue to transform the people, putting it into action is very easy. It is as light as a feather.

2.1 *But a feather can still be used as a comparison*: *Lun* 倫 is equivalent to *bi* 比 (to compare). When it quotes the text from the *Odes*, *virtue is as light as a feather*, it is also saying that virtue's extreme perfection originally comes from no substance, so how is it still like a feather? Although a feather is something fine, it still has form and substance and can be used as a comparison. Both, therefore, say *but a feather can still be used as a comparison*.

2.2　「上天之載，無聲無臭。至矣」，載，生也，言天之生物無音聲無臭氣，寂然無象而物自生。言聖人用德化民，亦無音聲，亦無臭氣而人自化。是聖人之德至極，與天地同。此二句是〈大雅•文王〉之詩，[120] 美<u>文王</u>之德。不言「《詩》云」者，<u>孔子</u>略而不言，直取《詩》之文爾。此亦斷章取義。

{注「載讀」至「後善」。}

2.3　《正義》曰：案文以「載」為事，此讀為「栽」者，言其生物，故讀「載」為「栽」也。云「毛雖輕，尚有所比，有所比，則有重」，言毛雖輕物，尚有形體，以他物來比，有可比之形，則是有重。毛在虛中猶得隊下，是有重也。云「化民之德，清明如神，淵淵浩浩」，則上文「淵淵其淵，浩浩其天」是也。

---

120 See the *Odes*, Mao 235, verse 7, LCC, 4:431.

2.2   *Above, Heaven's giving rise to things has neither sound nor smell*. *Zai* 載 is equivalent
        to *sheng* 生 (to give rise to). This says that Heaven's giving rise to things is with-
        out sound and without smell. Silently and without form, things spontaneously
        arise. It says that the sage's use of virtue to transform the people is also without
        sound or smell, and yet the people are spontaneously transformed. This is the ex-
        treme perfection of the sage's virtue and is the same as Heaven and Earth. These
        two sentences are from the ode "Wen wang" in the "Da ya" which is in praise of
        King Wen's virtue. With respect to not saying, "the *Odes* says," Confucius omit-
        ted this and did not say that the text was taken directly from the *Odes*. This also
        is "cutting the text to pick out the meaning" (taking it out of context).

2.3   The *Zhengyi* says that, according to the text, *zhai* 載 is to be taken as *shi* 事, this
        being read as *zai* 栽 and as speaking of its giving rise to things. Therefore, *zai* 載
        is read as *zai* 栽. It says, "although a feather is light, there is still that to which
        it can be compared, and if there is that to which it can be compared, then it has
        weight." This says that, although a feather is a light thing, it still has form and
        substance so it can come to be compared with other things, and if you can com-
        pare its form, then this confirms its weight. If a feather is in empty space, it still
        falls, which confirms it has weight. It says, "the virtue that transforms the people
        is clear and bright like a spirit, deep and still, great and grand," which is, then,
        the previous text's *deep and still is his profundity; great and wide is his [understanding
        of] Heaven.*

Zhongyong 中庸: Central and Constant

Notes 注: Zhu Xi 朱熹

中庸章句序

《中庸》何為而作也？子思子憂道學之失其傳而作也。蓋自上古聖神繼天立極，而道統之傳有自來矣。其見於經，則「允執厥中」者，堯之所以授舜也；「人心惟危，道心惟微，惟精惟一，允執厥中」者，舜之所以授禹也。[1] 堯之一言，至矣，盡矣！而舜復益之以三言者，則所以明夫堯之一言，必如是而後可庶幾也。

蓋嘗論之：心之虛靈知覺，一而已矣，而以為有人心、道心之異者，則以其或生於形氣之私，或原於性命之正，而所以為知覺者不同，是以或危殆而不安，或微妙而難見耳。然人莫不有是形，故雖上智不能無人心，亦莫不有是性，故雖下愚不能無道心。二者雜於方寸之間，而不知所以治之，則危者愈危，微者愈微，而天理之公卒無以勝夫人欲之私矣。精則察夫二者之間而不雜也，一則守其本心之正而不離也。從事於斯，無少間斷，必使道心常為一身之主，而人心每聽命焉，則危者安、微者著，而動靜云為自無過不及之差矣。

---

[1] See the *Documents,* "Da Yu mo" 大禹謨, LCC, 3:61–62. The translation largely follows Legge. "Sincerely hold fast to the centre" is also found in the *Lunyu* XX.1(1), LCC, 1:350.

Preface to the *Zhongyong zhangju*

Why was the *Zhongyong* written? Master Zisi, distressed lest the transmission of the learning of the Way be lost, wrote it. Now, from remote antiquity, sages and spiritual men continued the perfection established by Heaven and the transmission of the body of orthodox teachings came from this. What is seen in the classics, that is, "sincerely hold fast to the centre," is what Yao imparted to Shun. "The *ren xin* 人心 (mind-heart of man) is wavering; the *dao xin* 道心 (mind-heart of the Way) is subtle. Be discriminating, be undivided, and strongly hold fast to the centre" is what Shun imparted to Yu. Yao's single sentence is perfect; it is complete! And yet Shun's increasing it to three sentences was done in order to clarify Yao's single sentence. This was necessary so that subsequently it could be properly understood.

I shall now attempt to discuss this. The unobstructed and ingenious knowing and perceiving of the mind-heart are one thing only and yet there are those who would take there to be a difference between the *ren xin* 人心 (mind-heart of man) and the *dao xin* 道心 (mind-heart of the Way). [If this were so] then the one would be born of the individual existence of form and spirit whilst the other would originate in the correctness of the decreed nature, and that is why knowing and feeling would not be the same. In this way, the one (*ren xin* 人心) would be wavering, unstable and not at peace, whereas the other (*dao xin* 道心) would be subtle, mysterious and hard to see. However, there is nobody who does not have this bodily form, therefore even a person of the highest wisdom cannot exist without *ren xin* 人心 (mind-heart of man). Also, there is nobody who does not have this nature, therefore even a person of the most profound foolishness cannot exist without *dao xin* 道心 (mind-heart of the Way). The two are brought together in the single square inch of the human heart, and if one does not know how to bring good order to this, then the instability becomes increasingly unstable, the subtlety increasingly subtle and the impartiality of heavenly principle finally has no way of overcoming the partiality of human desire. It is essential, then, to look into what is between the two and not be confused. If they are one, then preserve the correctness of this original mind and do not depart from it. In pursuing matters with this without the slightest interruption, it is necessary to cause the *dao xin* 道心 (mind-heart of the Way) to be the master of the self and the *ren xin* 人心 (mind-heart of man) always to follow its commands. Then what is wavering will be stabilised and what is obscure will become manifest, and movement and stillness will be spoken of as being naturally without the faults of going beyond and not reaching.

夫堯、舜、禹,天下之大聖也。以天下相傳,天下之大事也。以天下之
大聖,行天下之大事,而其授受之際,丁寧告戒,不過如此。則天下之
理,豈有以加於此哉?自是以來,聖聖相承:若成湯、文、武之為君,
皋陶、伊、傅、周、召之為臣,既皆以此而接夫道統之傳,若吾夫子,
則雖不得其位,而所以繼往聖、開來學,其功反有賢於堯舜者。然當
是時,見而知之者,惟顏氏、曾氏之傳得其宗。及曾氏之再傳,而復得
夫子之孫子思,則去聖遠而異端起矣。子思懼夫愈久而愈失其真也,於
是推本堯舜以來相傳之意,質以平日所聞父師之言,更互演繹,作為此
書,以詔後之學者。蓋其憂之也深,故其言之也切;其慮之也遠,故其
說之也詳。其曰「天命率性」,則道心之謂也;其曰「擇善固執」,則精
一之謂也;其曰「君子時中」,則執中之謂也。世之相後,千有餘年,
而其言之不異,如合符節。歷選前聖之書,所以提挈綱維、開示蘊奧,
未有若是之明且盡者也。自是而又再傳以得孟氏,為能推明是書,以承

Now Yao, Shun and Yu were the great sages of the world. Each handing the world on to the other were the great affairs of the world. Through the great sages of the world, the world's great affairs were carried out and the occasions of their giving and receiving, and the recurring injunctions were nothing more than this. Then how was the world's principle anything more than this? From this time on, there was a continuing succession of sages: for example, Cheng Tang, Wen and Wu as rulers and Gao Yao, Yi, Fu, Zhou and Shao as ministers all took their turn in transmitting the orthodox teaching. In the case of our Master, although he did not attain his [proper] position, he was still the means of carrying on the tradition of past sages and opening up the path for future scholars. His achievement had the worthiness of a Yao or Shun. Nevertheless, at the time, of those who saw and knew this, only the transmissions of Yan and Zeng apprehended his teaching. When it came to Zeng's later transmission, and this was further taken up by the Master's grandson Zisi, then it was distant [in time] from the sages and different doctrines had arisen. Zisi feared that with the increasing passage of time, there would be increasing loss of this true [teaching]. Because of this, he investigated the concepts handed down since Yao and Shun, took into account the words he heard day by day from his father and teachers and, drawing his conclusions from each of these, wrote this book in order to instruct scholars who were to follow. Because his distress was profound, so his words were urgent; because his thoughts were far-reaching, so his explanations were detailed. His saying "Heaven decrees" and "complying with nature" refers, then, to the *dao xin* 道 心 (mind-heart of the Way). His saying "choose the good and hold fast to it" refers, then, to one principle. His saying, "the noble man is at all time central" refers, then, to grasping the centre. Generations have followed, one upon the other, and more than a thousand years have passed, yet his words still ring true, fitting together like the two halves of a tally. Among all the writings of the former sages, as guides to the main principles and revealing the details of the many mysteries, none has the clarity and the completeness of this one (the *Zhongyong*). From this, the transmission was again taken up by Mencius, who was able to elaborate on and clarify this book in order to continue the line of the former sages.

先聖之統，及其沒而遂失其傳焉。則吾道之所寄不越乎言語文字之閒，而異端之說日新月盛，以至於老佛之徒出，則彌近理而大亂真矣。然而尚幸此書之不泯，故程夫子兄弟者出，得有所考，以續夫千載不傳之緒；得有所據，以斥夫二家似是之非。蓋子思之功於是為大，而微程夫子，則亦莫能因其語而得其心也。惜乎！其所以為說者不傳，而凡石氏之所輯錄，僅出於其門人之所記，是以大義雖明，而微言未析。至其門人所自為說，則雖頗詳盡而多所發明，然倍其師說而淫於老佛者，亦有之矣。

熹自蚤歲即嘗受讀而竊疑之，沈潛反復，蓋亦有年，一旦恍然似有以得其要領者，然後乃敢會眾說而折其中，既為定著章句一篇，以竢後之君子。而一二同志復取石氏書，刪其繁亂，名以輯略，且記所嘗論辯取舍之意，別為或問，以附其後。然後此書之旨，支分節解、脈絡貫通、詳略相因、巨細畢舉，而凡諸說之同異得失，亦得以曲暢旁通，而各極其趣。雖於道統之傳，不敢妄議，然初學之士，或有取焉，則亦庶乎行遠升高之一助云爾。

淳熙己酉春三月戊申，新安朱熹序

But when he died, there was subsequently loss of this transmission. Then what our Way relied on was confined to the interpretations of words and writings. Heterodox doctrines increased by the day and month to the point where followers of Lao Zi and the Buddha came forth—men whose principles were very similar and greatly confused the true [teaching]. However, by good fortune, this book was not destroyed and the brothers Cheng, the elder and the younger, emerged and were able to get hold of it and examine it so as to continue the thread of what had not been transmitted for a thousand years. But by apprehending what they received, they used this to drive out the seemingly similar errors of the two schools. Now Zisi's achievement in this was great, and yet, were it not for the Masters Cheng, we would not be able, just through his statements, to reach his mind-heart—how unfortunate! What he took as explanations were not transmitted, and all that Shi compiled and edited came merely from what his disciples recorded. Although this made the general meaning clear, it left the subtle aspects unanalysed. When it came to what his disciples themselves gave as explanations, then although these were rather detailed and made much of the material clear, nevertheless they were at odds with their teacher's explanations, some even revealing Daoist and Buddhist influences.

I myself, from my early years, received and read [this work], and with due humility, harboured some doubts. Again and again, I gave deep thought to it over many years until suddenly it was as if I grasped its chief points. After this, I dared to understand the many explanations and form a judgement on its centre. Then I completed the *Zhangju* 章句 in one *pian* to await the noble men of later times. Along with one or two comrades, I again took up Shi's book, expunged its many confusions and called it a compilation. Moreover, I recorded the meanings of what had previously been discussed and analysed, selected and set aside, separating off doubts and questions and adding them as an afterword. Subsequently, this book's purpose was to support or divide the various explanations, understand the logical thread [of the work], carefully summarise what was complementary, completely raise [matters] great and small and, in general, what was the same or different, successful or otherwise in the various explanations. It was also to get to the twists and turns, the several by-ways, and in each case fully explore their interest. Although in the transmission of true and orthodox doctrines, one dare not make reckless claims, nevertheless, for some scholars beginning their studies who choose this, then it may, perhaps, be said to be one of the aids to travelling far and climbing high.

Preface by Zhu Xi of Xin'an—the day *wushen*, in the third month in the spring of the year *jiyou* of the Chunxi reign period—i.e. March 3, 1189.

《中庸章句》

子程子曰：「不偏之謂中，不易之謂庸。中者，天下之正道，庸者，天下之定理。」此篇乃孔門傳授心法，子思恐其久而差也，故筆之於書，以授孟子。其書始言一理，中散為萬事，末復合為一理，「放之則彌六合，卷之則退藏於密」，其味無窮，皆實學也。善讀者玩索而有得焉，則終身用之，有不能盡者矣。

ZY1: 天命之謂性，率性之謂道，脩道之謂教。[1]道也者，不可須臾離也，可離非道也。是故君子戒慎乎其所不睹，恐懼乎其所不聞。[2]莫見乎隱，莫顯乎微，故君子慎其獨也。[3]喜怒哀樂之未發，謂之中；發而皆中節，謂之和。中也者，天下之大本也；和也者，天下之達道也。[4]致中和，天地位焉，萬物育焉。[5]

Central and Constant in Chapters and Sentences

The philosopher, Master Cheng, said: "Not deviating to either side is called being 'central' (*zhong* 中). Not changing is called being 'constant' (*yong* 庸). Being 'central' is the true Way for all under Heaven. Being 'constant' is the established principle for all under Heaven." This tract is, then, the model of the mind-heart as handed down by Confucius' disciples. Zisi feared that over a long period mistakes would arise. Therefore, he wrote it down in a book in order to pass it on to Mencius. This book starts by speaking of one principle; the body of the work expands on this to cover the myriad things; the end returns to combine them under one principle. "Unroll it, and it fills the entire world; roll it up, and it withdraws, hidden in mystery." Its significance is without limit; it is all true learning. The good reader turns it over and over in his mind until he grasps it; then he uses it throughout his life. It is something that cannot be exhausted.

ZY1: What Heaven decrees is called "nature"; complying with nature is called "the Way"; regulating the Way is called "teaching." **[1]** The Way is something that cannot be deviated from, even for an instant; what can be deviated from is not the Way. This is why the noble man is on guard and cautious about what he does not see; it is why he is fearful and apprehensive about what he does not hear. **[2]** There is nothing more visible than what is hidden; there is nothing more apparent than what is obscure. Therefore, the noble man is careful about his inner self. **[3]** When joy and anger, sorrow and happiness have not yet arisen, call it "the centre." When they have arisen, and yet are all in perfect balance, call it "harmony." Being in "the centre" is the great foundation of the world; being in "harmony" is the all-pervading Way of the world. **[4]** Reach "the centre" and "harmony," and Heaven and earth are in their positions and the ten thousand things are brought forth. **[5]**

右第一章。<u>子思</u>述所傳之意以立言：首明道之本原出於天而不可易，其實體備於己而不可離，次言存養省察之要，終言聖神功化之極。蓋欲學者於此反求諸身而自得之，以去夫外誘之私，而充其本然之善，<u>楊氏</u>[2]所謂一篇之體要是也。其下十章，蓋<u>子思</u>引夫子之言，以終此章之義。

Comment: Although there are no textual or structural variations, the interpretation of this section by Zhu Xi differs in several important respects from that of the *Li ji* commentators. On the question of arrangement, Zhu Xi takes this to be the foundational statement about the Way (*dao* 道) which is then amplified and exemplified by the following ten sections. The essentials of the Way are recognizing that one's nature is decreed by Heaven, following this Heaven-decreed nature, and regulating it so as to be able to act as an example to others. This Way cannot be deviated from at any time, which is why the noble man must be ever vigilant about the secret workings of his inner self or soul. There are two states that are consistent with the Way: when emotions are absent, which is the "centre"; when emotions are present but regulated, which is "harmony." Three distinct points of difference between Zhu Xi and the *Li ji* commentators are as follows: (i) Zhu Xi takes the verbs *du* 睹 and *wen* 聞 as active—it is about what the noble man does not see or hear rather than when he is not seen or heard. (ii) Following on from this, *du* 獨 is read in the sense of what he has (or is)—his "uniqueness" (Ames & Hall), his "inner core" (Haloun), or his inner self. (iii) In the analysis there is the use of the terms *li* 理 and *qi* 氣, and in general a greater degree of philosophical sophistication.

注 ZY1 (朱熹)

[1] 命，猶令也。性，即理也。天以陰陽五行化生萬物，氣以成形，而理亦賦焉，猶命令也。於是人物之生，因各得其所賦之理，以為健順五常之德，[3]所謂性也。率，循也。道，猶路也。人物各循其性之自然，則其日用事物之間，莫不各有當行之路，是則所謂道也。脩，品節之也。性道雖同，而氣稟或異，故不能無過不及之差，聖人因人物之所當行者而品節之，以為法於天下，則謂之教，若禮、樂、刑、政之屬是也。蓋人之所以為人，道之所以為道，聖人之所以為教，原其所自，無一不本於天而備於我。學者知之，則其於學知所用力而自不能已矣。故<u>子思</u>於此首發明之，讀者所宜深體而默識也。

---

2   Yang Shi 楊時 (1053–1135) was a disciple, first, of Cheng Hao and, subsequently, after Cheng Hao's death, of Cheng Yi. He was a noted opponent of Wang Anshi 王安石 (1021–1086).

3   Taken to be the same as *wu chang zhi dao* 五常之道—i.e. *ren* 仁, *yi* 義, *li* 禮, *zhi* 智 and *xin* 信.

To the right (above) is the first chapter. Zisi transmitted the meaning of what was handed down to him by setting out these words. At the start, he makes it clear that in its foundation and origin, the Way comes from Heaven and cannot be changed, and that its true substance is complete in ourselves and cannot be departed from. Next, he speaks of the importance of preserving, nourishing, examining, and looking into it. Finally, he speaks of the highest levels of efficacy and transformation of sages and spirits. His wish is for the student to reflect on it and seek it in himself and so naturally acquire it by casting off the external enticements of self-interest, so satisfying his basic goodness. This first chapter is what Yang called the essential statement of this. In the subsequent ten sections, Zisi quotes the Master's words to complete the meaning of this chapter.

Notes ZY1 (Zhu Xi)

[1] *Ming* 命 is like *ling* 令 (to order, decree, command). *Xing* 性 (nature) is *li* 理 (principle). Heaven, through *yin* and *yang* and the Five Phases, transforms and gives rise to the ten thousand things; *qi* 氣 (spirit) completes their forms, and *li* 理 (principle) is also bestowed on them like a decree. As a result, in the creation of people, because each acquires the *li* (principle) that is bestowed on him, this may be taken as an unvarying compliance with the "five constants" of virtue, and is what is called nature. *Shuai* 率 equates with *xun* 循 (to follow, comply with). *Dao* 道 is like *lu* 路 (path, road). If people each follow the spontaneous functioning of their nature, then, in their daily engagement with matters and things, there is nobody who does not have a proper path to follow. This, then, is what is called the Way (*dao* 道). *Xiu* 脩 is to regulate this. Although nature and the Way are the same, natural endowment is sometimes different, so there cannot but be the faults of "going beyond" and "not reaching." The sage, because he acts in a way that is right for a person and regulates this, may be taken as a model in the world. This, then, is called teaching—for example, rites, music, punishments, government, and such-like. What men take to be a person, what the Way takes to be the Way, and what the sage takes to be teaching, originate from what they are naturally and there is not one thing that does not find its origin in Heaven and its completion in oneself. The scholar who knows this, then knows in his studies what to use his strength on and that he himself can never bring [his studies] to an end. Therefore Zisi, in this opening section, explains this clearly. This is what the reader ought to consider deeply, and silently comprehend.

[2] {離，去聲。}道者，日用事物當行之理，皆性之德而具於心，無物不有，無時不然，所以不可須臾離也。若其可離，則為外物而非道矣。是以君子之心常存敬畏，雖不見聞，亦不敢忽，所以存天理之本然，而不使離於須臾之頃也。

[3] {見，音現。}隱，暗處也。微，細事也。獨者，人所不知而己所獨知之地也。言幽暗之中，細微之事，跡雖未形而幾則已動，人雖不知而己獨知之，則是天下之事無有著見明顯而過於此者。是以君子既常戒懼，而於此尤加謹焉，所以遏人欲於將萌，而不使其滋長於隱微之中，以至離道之遠也。

[4] {樂，音洛。中節之中，去聲。}喜、怒、哀、樂，情也。其未發，則性也，無所偏倚，故謂之中。發皆中節，情之正也，無所乖戾，故謂之和。大本者，天命之性，天下之理皆由此出，道之體也。達道者，循性之謂，天下古今之所共由，道之用也。此言性情之德，以明道不可離之意。

[5] 致，推而極之也。位者，安其所也。育者，遂其生也。自戒懼而約之，以至於至靜之中，無少偏倚，而其守不失，則極其中而天地位矣。自謹獨而精之，以至於應物之處，無少差謬，而無適不然，則極其和而萬物育矣。蓋天地萬物本吾一體，吾之心正，則天地之心亦正矣，吾之氣順，則天地之氣亦順矣，故其效驗至於如此。此學問之極功、聖人之能事，初非有待於外，而修道之教亦在其中矣。是其一體一用雖有動靜之殊，然必其體立而後用有以行，則其實亦非有兩事也。故於此合而言之，以結上文之意。

---

*   Text from the classical commentaries in { } brackets primarily contains pronunciation guides for certain Chinese characters; this has been omitted in the English translation.

[2] . . . The Way is the daily use of the principles of proper action in relation to matters and things. It is the virtue of all natures, and in all cases is in the mind-heart. There is nothing that does not have it. There is no time when it is not so. Therefore, it cannot be left, even for an instant. If it could be left, then it would be something external and would not be the Way. This is why the mind-heart of the noble man constantly preserves [a state of] respect and awe. Even if he does not see or hear something, he also does not dare to be careless. Therefore, he preserves what is fundamental in heavenly principle and does not let it go, even for an instant.

[3] . . . *Yin* 隱 is a hidden place. *Wei* 微 equates with trifling affairs. *Du* 獨 refers to a place that others do not know—a place only the self knows. This says that in the midst of darkness and obscurity, or in small and trifling affairs, and even if the effects do not yet have form and are hidden, there is already action. If others do not know, and yet the self alone knows it, then this is the affairs of the world not having anything that is more clearly apparent than this. This is why the noble man is constantly on guard and apprehensive, and is especially attentive to this. This is how he is able to nip human desires in the bud, not letting them grow larger in the midst of the hidden and trifling so as to reach the point of becoming distant from the Way.

[4] . . . Joy, anger, sorrow and happiness are emotions. When they have not yet arisen, this is nature. It does not deviate to one side or the other, therefore it is called "the centre." When they arise and are all in "the centre" and regulated, the emotions are correct and there is nothing which is unreasonable or perverse. Therefore, this is called "harmony." The great foundation, which is the nature decreed by Heaven, is what the principles of the world all come forth from, and is the essence of the Way. The "all-pervading Way," which is the term given to following nature, is what the world in ancient and modern times has shared in following, and is the use of the Way. This speaks of the virtue of nature and emotions in order to make clear the meaning [of the statement], "the Way cannot be departed from."

[5] *Zhi* 致 is extending it to the utmost point. *Wei* 位 is to rest in its [proper] place. *Yu* 育 is to complete its creation (birth). From being cautious and apprehensive, and restraining it, right up to the centre of extreme tranquility, if there is not the slightest deviation and its preservation is not lost, then it reaches this centre and Heaven and Earth are in their [proper] places. From being attentive to the "inner self" and refining it, right up to things being in their proper places, if there is not the slightest error or fault and there are no unwonted occurrences, then it reaches the extreme point of this "harmony" and the ten thousand things are brought forth. Now because Heaven and Earth, the ten thousand things, and myself are all one substance, if my mind-heart is rectified, then the mind-hearts of Heaven and Earth are also rectified; if my *qi* (spirit, vital force) is propitious, then the *qi* of Heaven and Earth is also propitious. Therefore, in this way, its fulfilment is complete. Thus it is that the extreme efficacy of learning and enquiring, and the sage's ability in affairs, from the first does not depend on what is external, and the teaching which regulates the Way also lies in what is within. This is its one substance and its one use, although there are the differences in terms of movement and stillness (activity and inactivity). This being so, it is necessary for its substance to be established and afterwards to be used in conduct, although its substance is not two things. That is why I combine them and speak about them to complete the meaning of the preceding text.

ZY2: 仲尼曰：「君子中庸，小人反中庸。**[1]**君子之中庸也，君子而時中；小人之[反]⁴中庸也，小人而無忌憚也。」**[2]**

右第二章。(此下十章，皆論中庸以釋首章之義。文雖不屬，而意實相承也。變和言庸者，游氏⁵曰：「以性情言之，則曰中和，以德行言之，則曰中庸是也。」然中庸之中，實兼中和之義。)

Comment: Zhu Xi also accepts (and mentions specifically) Wang Su's proposed addition of *fan* 反 in the final sentence. He also attempts to reconcile the use of *yong* 庸 here with that of *he* 和 in the first section, both being in conjunction with *zhong* 中. He quotes You Zuo 游酢 who, like Yang Shi 楊時, was mentioned in the previous section, and was also a student of the Cheng brothers. Clearly, the equating of *yong* 庸 with *he* 和 is an argument against the former being read as "commonplace" or "quotidian." *Pingchang* 平常, used in both of Zhu Xi's notes above, allows of both meanings, i.e. "constant" and "commonplace." "Constant" is, of course, in keeping with Cheng Yi's equating of *zhong* 中 and *yong* 庸 with *bu pian* 不偏 and *buyi* 不易 respectively in the first section. Other points in the notes which bear on the issues discussed in relation to the opening sections in the *Li ji* version are, firstly, that Zhu Xi clearly takes *shi* 時 to indicate "at all times" rather than "in a timely way," and secondly, the grammar in the penultimate sentence of note [2] favours taking the caution of the noble man to be manifest when he is neither seen nor heard and not about what is not seen or heard, i.e. his inner self.

注 ZY2 (朱熹)

[1] 中庸者，不偏不倚、無過不及，而平常之理，乃天命所當然，精微之極致也。惟君子為能體之，小人反是。

[2] 王肅本作「小人之反中庸也」，程子亦以為然。今從之。君子之所以為中庸者，以其有君子之德，而又能隨時以處中也。小人之所以反中庸者，以其有小人之心，而又無所忌憚也。蓋中無定體，隨時而在，是乃平常之理也。君子知其在我，故能戒謹不睹、恐懼不聞，而無時不中。小人不知有此，則肆欲妄行，而無所忌憚矣。

---

⁴   *Fan* 反 was initially inserted by Wang Su and was accepted by Zhu Xi (and others)—see his note 2 above.

⁵   You Zuo 游酢 was, with Yang Shi 楊時 (see note 2), a disciple of the Cheng brothers.

ZY2: Zhongni (Confucius) said: "The noble man is central and constant. The lesser man is the opposite of central and constant. **[1]** The noble man's central and constant is his being a noble man and at all times central. The lesser man's being the opposite of central and constant is his being a lesser man and without scruples or fears." **[2]**

To the right (above) is the second chapter. (This and the ten chapters that follow all discuss "central and constant" in order to explain the meaning of the first chapter. Although the writing is not all of a kind, the meaning is truly interconnected. With regard to changing *he* 和 [harmony] and speaking of *yong* 庸 [constant], You [Zuo] says: "When it is spoken of in terms of nature and emotions, then it is called '*zhong he*' 中和; when it is spoken of in terms of virtue and conduct, then it is called '*zhong yong*' 中庸." Nevertheless, the *zhong* of *zhong yong* 中庸 [central and constant] is really equivalent to its meaning in *zhong he* 中和 [central and harmonious].)

Notes ZY2 (Zhu Xi)

[1] To be *zhong yong* is to be neither partial nor deviating, neither to go beyond nor fail to reach, and is the principle of constancy. It is, then, what Heaven decrees as being naturally right and the extreme perfection of subtle essence. It is only the noble man who can embody this; the lesser man is the opposite of this.
[2] Wang Su originally wrote: 「小人之反中庸也。」Master Cheng (Yi) also thought this was right. Now [I] follow it. The way in which the noble man is central and constant is through his having the virtue of the noble man and also being able to stay in the centre at all times. The way in which the lesser man is the opposite of central and constant is through his having the mind-heart of the lesser man and also not having anything he fears or dreads. Because the centre has no fixed substance, yet exists at all times, it is in fact the principle of constancy. The noble man knows that it exists within himself. Therefore, he can be cautious and attentive when he is not seen, fearful and apprehensive when he is not heard, and there is no time when he is not central. If the lesser man does not know this, then he is dissolute in his desires and reckless in his conduct, and has nothing he fears and dreads.

ZY3: 子曰：「中庸其至矣乎！民鮮能久矣!」**[1]**

右第三章。

注 ZY3 (朱熹)

[1] {鮮，上聲。下同。}過則失中，不及則未至，故惟中庸之德為至。然亦人所同得，初無難事，但世教衰，民不興行，故鮮能之，今已久矣。《論語》無「能」字。

ZY4: 子曰：「道之不行也，我知之矣，知者過之，愚者不及也；道之不明也，我知之矣，賢者過之，不肖者不及也。**[1]** 人莫不飲食也，鮮能知味也。」**[2]**

右第四章。

Comment: ZY3 & 4 are the first two of the seven successive statements beginning *zi yue* 子曰 (the Master said)—i.e. ZY3–9. As they are flanked by sections where the statements are clearly attributed to Confucius, it is generally assumed that all seven should also be attributed to Confucius. As Riegel remarks, apropos all these sections, "the debate (i.e. on the terms and concepts in ZY1) survives in the form of *logia* which in syntax and diction are identical with the *Lunyu*."[6] There are variations in how "民鮮能久矣" and "過之" are construed, although these are largely unimportant as far as the basic argument is concerned—the Way is not now (i.e. at the time of writing) practised by many people and this is because the wise and the worthy go beyond it (pass it by, overstep it, stray from it) whilst the foolish and unworthy are not up to practising it.

---

6   See Riegel, "The Four 'Tzu Ssu' Chapters of the 'Li Chi': An Analysis and Translation of the *Fang Chi, Chung Yung, Piao Chi, and Tzu I*," 211n16.

ZY3: The Master said: "Central and constant—surely this is perfection! Yet among the people, for a long time few have been able [to practise it]." **[1]**

To the right (above) is the third chapter.

Notes ZY3 (Zhu Xi)

[1] . . . "To go beyond" is to lose the centre; "not to reach" is never to reach [the centre]. Therefore, only the virtue of "central and constant" is perfection. Nevertheless, it was also what people in general attained and, at first, was not a difficult matter. But the world's teaching declined and people began not to practise [it], therefore few are capable of it; the situation has already been like this for a long time. In the *Lunyu* there is not the character *neng* 能.[7]

ZY4: The Master said: "I know why it is that the Way [of central and constant] is not practised—the wise go beyond it while the foolish do not reach it. I know why it is that the Way is not clear—the worthy go beyond it and the unworthy do not reach it. **[1]** Among men, there is no-one who does not drink and eat, but few are able to know the flavours." **[2]**

To the right (above) is the fourth chapter.

---

7   In the *Lunyu* 6.27 there is: 「子曰：『中庸之為德也，其至矣乎，民鮮久矣。』」 (LCC, 1:193–94)

注 ZY4 (朱熹)

[1] {知者之知，去聲。}道者，天理之當然，中而已矣。知愚賢不肖之過不及，則生稟之異而失其中也。知者知之過，既以道為不足行；愚者不及知，又不知所以行，此道之所以常不行也。賢者行之過，既以道為不足知；不肖者不及行，又不求所以知，此道之所以常不明也。

[2] 道不可離，人自不察，是以有過不及之弊。

ZY5: 子曰：「道其不行矣夫！」[1]

右第五章。(此章承上章而舉其不行之端，以起下章之意。)

注 ZY5 (朱熹)

[1] {夫，音扶。}由不明，故不行。

ZY6: 子曰：「舜其大知也與！舜好問而好察邇言，隱惡而揚善，執其兩端，用其中於民，其斯以為舜乎！」[1]

右第六章。

Comment: In ZY5, Zhu Xi treats this lamentation as a link between the preceding and succeeding sections. As his brief note indicates, he believes the Way is not practised because it is not *ming* 明, i.e. "clear." In ZY6, the difference between Zhu Xi and the *Li ji* commentators lies in the interpretation of the two "ends." Whilst the latter take them to be the two failings of "going beyond" and "not reaching" (*guo* 過 and *bu ji* 不及), Zhu Xi understands them as the limits of the range of opinions, possibly on what constitutes goodness (*shan* 善), or possibly more generally. Only by knowing the range can the centre be accurately identified.

Notes ZY4 (Zhu Xi)

[1] . . . The Way is the proper expression of heavenly principle; it is being central and nothing more. The wise and the foolish, the worthy and the unworthy, in their going beyond and not reaching are different in their endowment at birth and lose this centre. The wise know it but go beyond it because they think that it is not enough to practise the Way. The foolish do not attain knowledge [of it] and also do not know how to practise it. This is why the Way is so often not practised. The worthy practise it but go beyond it because they think knowing the Way it is not enough. The unworthy do not reach the point of practice and also do not seek out how to know [it]. This is why the Way is so often unclear.

[2] People do not naturally realise that the Way cannot be departed from. This is why there are the failings of going beyond and not reaching.

ZY5: The Master said: "Alas, the Way is not practised." [1]

To the right (above) is the fifth chapter. (This chapter continues on from the previous chapter and raises the reasons for it not being practised in order to introduce the meaning of the following chapter.)

Notes ZY5 (Zhu Xi)

[1] . . . Because [the Way] is not clear, so it is not practised.

ZY6: The Master said: "Shun had great wisdom did he not! Shun loved to ask questions and he loved to examine simple words. Concealing the bad and revealing the good, he grasped these two 'ends' and used their centre in relation to the people. This was what made him Shun!" [1]

To the right (above) is the sixth chapter.

注 ZY6 (朱熹)

[1] {知,去聲。與,平聲。好,去聲。}舜之所以為大知者,以其不自用而取諸人也。邇言者,淺近之言,猶必察焉,其無遺善可知。然於其言之未善者則隱而不宣,其善者則播而不匿,其廣大光明又如此,則人孰不樂告以善哉。兩端,謂眾論不同之極致。蓋凡物皆有兩端,如小大厚薄之類,於善之中又執其兩端,而量度以取中,然後用之,則其擇之審而行之至矣。然非在我之權度精切不差,何以與此。此知之所以無過不及,而道之所以行也。

ZY7: 子曰:「人皆曰予知,驅而納諸罟擭陷阱之中,而莫之知辟也。人皆曰予知,擇乎中庸而不能期月守也。」[1]

右第七章。(承上章大知而言,又舉不明之端,以起下章也。)

Comment: This is equivalent to ZY4 in the *Li ji* text. There are no variations in the interpretation. Men's claims to wisdom are invalidated by their inability to remain on the path of "central and constant."

注 ZY7 (朱熹)

[1] {予知之知,去聲。罟,音古。擭,胡化反。阱,才性反。辟,避同。期,居之反。}罟,網也;擭,機檻也;陷阱,坑坎也;皆所以掩取禽獸者也。擇乎中庸,辨別眾理,以求所謂中庸,即上章好問用中之事也。期月,匝一月也。言知禍而不知辟,以況能擇而不能守,皆不得為知也。

Notes ZY6 (Zhu Xi)

[1] . . . What made Shun very wise was that he did not rely on himself but sought [the opinions] of all people. "Near words" (*er yan* 邇言) are words that are simple and easy to understand. They still must be examined. This being the case, one can know that nothing good would have gone unnoticed (by him). If there was nothing good in these words, they were concealed and not made known. If there was good, they were made known and not hidden. If their breadth and clarity are also like this, who would not be happy to present their goodness? The two "ends" refer to the extremes of the many and varied viewpoints. In general, things all have two "ends" (i.e. extremes), such as small and great or thick and thin. If you also grasp the goodness of the centre between these two "ends," and after evaluation choose this centre and subsequently use it, then the judgement in choosing it and practising it is perfect. However, unless I can weigh and evaluate all this accurately and without error, how am I to proceed in this? This is how knowledge is achieved without going beyond or failing to reach and how the Way can be practised.

ZY7: The Master said: "All men say, 'I am wise,' but drive them into nets, traps or pits, and they do not know how to escape. All men say, 'I am wise,' [yet] they choose [the Way of] central and constant but cannot sustain it for one whole month." **[1]**

To the right (above) is the seventh chapter. (This continues the previous chapter's discussion of great wisdom and also raises points that are not clear in order to introduce the following chapter.)

Notes ZY7 (Zhu Xi)

[1] . . . *Gu* 罟 is equivalent to *wang* 網 (a net); *huo* 擭 is equivalent to *ji jian* 機檻 (a trap or snare); *xian jing* 陷阱 is equivalent to *keng kan* 坑坎 (a pit or hole); all are means of catching birds and animals by surprise. To choose "central and constant" is to discriminate between the many principles in order to seek what is called "central and constant"; this is the matter of "loving to ask questions" and "using the centre" in the previous chapter. *Qi yue* 期月 is one full revolution of the moon (a month). This says that to know misfortune and yet not know how to avoid it is comparable to being able to choose it but not being able to sustain it—in both cases this must not be taken as wisdom.

ZY8: 子曰:「回之為人也,擇乎中庸,得一善,則拳拳服膺而弗失之矣。」[1]

右第八章。

注 ZY8 (朱熹)

[1] 回,孔子弟子顏淵名。拳拳,奉持之貌。服,猶著也。膺,胷也。奉持而著之心胷之間,言能守也。顏子蓋真知之,故能擇能守如此,此行之所以無過不及,而道之所以明也。

ZY9: 子曰:「天下國家可均也,爵祿可辭也,白刃可蹈也,中庸不可能也。」[1]

右第九章。(亦承上章以起下章。)

Comment: These two sections, ZY8 & ZY9, correspond to ZY5 in the *Li ji* version. Zhu Xi offers a slightly expanded interpretation of the final clause in ZY8. Yan Hui 顏回 (Yan Yuan 顏淵) was the Master's favourite disciple and was particularly noted for his love of learning (*Lunyu* VI.2, XI.6). His questioning of Confucius on *ren* 仁 is recorded in XII.1. Confucius was greatly distressed by Yan's death (XI.8–10). In ZY9, Zhi Xi specifically equates *jun* 均 with *pingzhi* 平治, whereas the *Li ji* commentators make no mention of this word.

注 ZY9 (朱熹)

[1] 均,平治也。三者亦知仁勇之事,天下之至難也,然不必其合於中庸,則質之近似者皆能以力為之。若中庸,則雖不必皆如三者之難,然非義精仁熟,而無一毫人欲之私者,不能及也。三者難而易,中庸易而難,此民之所以鮮能也。

ZY8: The Master said: "Hui was a man who chose [the Way of] central and constant. If he acquired one [aspect of] goodness, then he held it close, wore it on his breast, and did not lose it." **[1]**

To the right (above) is the eighth chapter.

Notes ZY8 (Zhu Xi)

[1] Hui is the name of Confucius' disciple Yan Yuan 顔淵. *Quan quan* 拳拳 is the appearance of respectfully receiving or holding. *Fu* 服 is like *zhu* 著 (to manifest, wear, put on). *Ying* 膺 equates with *xiong* 胸 (the breast). Respectfully receiving it and wearing it within the heart or on the breast refers to being able to sustain it. Yan Zi, because he truly knew it, was therefore able to choose it and sustain it in this way. This is how he did not go beyond or fail to reach in his conduct, and how the Way was made manifest.

ZY9: The Master said: "All under Heaven, states and houses, can be peacefully ordered, rank and salary can be declined, and naked blades can be trampled underfoot, yet [the Way of] central and constant may not be able to be achieved." **[1]**

To the right (above) is the ninth chapter. (This also continues the previous chapter by way of introducing the following chapter.)

Notes ZY9 (Zhu Xi)

[1] *Jun* 均 is to peacefully order (govern equably—平治). The three things, which also are the matters of *zhi* 知 (wisdom, knowledge), *ren* 仁 and *yong* 勇 (courage, bravery) are the world's great difficulties. Nevertheless, this does not necessarily pertain to their inclusion in [the Way of] central and constant because, if they are near to it in substance, they can all be accomplished by effort. Something like [the Way of] central and constant, although it is not necessarily altogether like the three things in difficulty, nevertheless cannot be reached if one has not completely mastered *yi* 義 and *ren* 仁 and has not one iota of the selfishness of private desires. The three things are difficult yet easy; [the Way of] central and constant is easy yet difficult. This is why few people are capable of it.

ZY10: <u>子路</u>問強。[1]子曰：「南方之強與？北方之強與？抑而強與？[2]寬柔以教，不報無道，南方之強也，君子居之。[3]衽金革，死而不厭，北方之強也，而強者居之。[4]故君子和而不流，強哉矯！中立而不倚，強哉矯！國有道，不變塞焉，強哉矯！國無道，至死不變，強哉矯！」[5]

右第十章。

Comment: This corresponds to ZY6 in the *Li ji* version. There are only minor differences in interpretation. Zhu Xi does not specifically take Zilu's strength to be representative of the Central States and he equates *se* 塞 with *bu da* 不達 rather than *shi* 實. *Liu* 流 is generally accepted as meaning "to shift," "to waver" or "to drift," for example in the current of popular opinion.

注 ZY10 (朱熹)

[1] <u>子路</u>，<u>孔子</u>弟子<u>仲由</u>也。<u>子路</u>好勇，故問強。

[2] {與，平聲。}抑，語辭。而，汝也。

[3] 寬柔以教，謂含容巽順以誨人之不及也。不報無道，謂橫逆之來，直受之而不報也。南方風氣柔弱，故以含忍之力勝人為強，君子之道也。

[4] 衽，席也。金，戈兵之屬。革，甲胄之屬。北方風氣剛勁，故以果敢之力勝人為強，強者之事也。

[5] 此四者，汝之所當強也。矯，強貌。《詩》曰：「矯矯虎臣」是也。倚，偏著也。塞，未達也。國有道，不變未達之所守；國無道，不變平生之所守也。此則所謂中庸之不可能者，非有以自勝其人欲之私，不能擇而守也。君子之強，孰大於是。夫子以是告<u>子路</u>者，所以抑其血氣之剛，而進之以德義之勇也。

ZY10: Zilu asked about strength. **[1]** The Master said: "Do you mean the strength of the southern region? Do you mean the strength of the northern region? Or do you mean your own strength? **[2]** To be tolerant and mild in teaching [others], and not to exact retribution from those without the Way is the strength of the southern region. Noble men live by this. **[3]** To lie down to rest with weapons and armour, and to die without regret is the strength of the northern region. Strong men live by this. **[4]** Therefore, the noble man is in harmony and does not drift—how firm is his resolve! He establishes the centre and does not deviate—how firm is his resolve! If the state possesses the Way, he does not change how he was when he was unknown—how firm is his resolve. If the state does not possess the Way, he faces death without changing—how firm is his resolve!" **[5]**

To the right (above) is the tenth chapter.

Notes ZY10 (Zhu Xi)

[1] Zilu was the Confucian disciple Zhong You 仲由. Zilu loved courage, therefore he asked about strength.
[2] ... *Yi* 抑 is a particle. *Er* 而 equates with *ru* 汝 (you).
[3] *Tolerant and mild in teaching [others]* refers to the use of forbearance and mildness as a way of admonishing people who do not reach [it]. *Not to exact retribution from those without the Way* refers to accepting perverse behaviour should it come, and not retaliating. The ethos of the southern region is mild and gentle, therefore the power of restraint and forbearance in overcoming others is taken to be strength and the Way of the noble man.
[4] *Ren* 衽 is a mat. *Jin* 金 represents weapons generally. *Ge* 革 represents armour generally. The ethos of the northern region is one of hardness and vigour; therefore, the power of daring and determination in overcoming others is taken to be strength and is the business of those who are strong.
[5] These four things are what you equate with strength. *Jiao* 矯 is the appearance of strength. The *Odes* saying: "Warlike and strong are the tiger officials" is this. *Yi* 倚 equates with *pian zhu* 偏著 (partial, prejudiced). *Se* 塞 equates with *wei da* 未達 (to not be known, never reaching, never being successful). If a state possesses the Way, he (the noble man) does not change, even if unsuccessful in what he upholds. If a state does not possess the Way, he does not change what he upholds throughout his life. This, then, is saying that [the Way of] central and constant cannot be possible unless one can overcome the selfishness of human desires and is able to choose it (this Way) and sustain it. Of the strengths of the noble man, what is greater than this? The Master uses this to explain to Zilu why he should restrain his impetuous strength and direct himself towards the courage of *de* 德 (virtue) and *yi* 義 (right action).

ZY11: 子曰:「素隱行怪,後世有述焉,吾弗為之矣。[1]君子遵道而行,半塗而廢,吾弗能已矣。[2]君子依乎中庸,遯世不見知而不悔,唯聖者能之。」[3]

右第十一章。(子思所引夫子之言,以明首章之義者止此。蓋此篇大旨,以知仁勇三達德為入道之門。故於篇首,即以大舜、顏淵、子路之事明之。舜,知也;顏淵,仁也;子路,勇也:三者廢其一,則無以造道而成德矣。餘見第二十章。)

Comment: This corresponds to the first part of ZY7 in the *Li ji* version. Zhu Xi, however, takes it to signal the end of Zisi's quoting of the words of Confucius in clarification of the opening statement. In his note he identifies the primary purpose of the work as being to make it clear that the three cardinal virtues, *ren* 仁, *zhi* 知, and *yong* 勇, are essential for gaining entrance to the Way. In this and the preceding sections, these three virtues are exemplified by Yan Hui, Shun and Zilu respectively. Zhu Xi points out that attention is again given to these three virtues in ZY20 (of his arrangement), as indeed it is, but it should be noted that prior consideration is given there to two other important virtues. Also, Zhu Xi reads *su* 素 in the opening sentence as *suo* 索 rather than as *su* 傃 in the sense of *xiang* 鄉, as the *Li ji* commentators do; this is reflected in the slightly different translation.

注 ZY11 (朱熹)

[1] 素,按《漢書》當作索,蓋字之誤也。索隱行怪,言深求隱僻之理,而過為詭異之行也。然以其足以欺世而盜名,故後世或有稱述之者。此知之過而不擇乎善,行之過而不用其中,不當強而強者也,聖人豈為之哉!

[2] 遵道而行,則能擇乎善矣;半塗而廢,則力之不足也。此其知雖足以及之,而行有不逮,當強而不強者也。已,止也。聖人於此,非勉焉而不敢廢,蓋至誠無息,自有所不能止也。

[3] 不為索隱行怪,則依乎中庸而已。不能半塗而廢,是以遯世不見知而不悔也。此中庸之成德,知之盡、仁之至、不賴勇而裕如者,正吾夫子之事,而猶不自居也。故曰唯聖者能之而已。

ZY11: The Master said: "[Some men] seek out esoteric doctrines and behave in strange ways so they are remembered by later generations—I do not do this. **[1]** [Some] noble men follow the Way and act, go halfway along the path and abandon it—I am not able to stop. **[2]** A noble man relies on [the Way of] central and constant, withdraws from the world without being known, and has no regrets—only a sage is capable of this." **[3]**

To the right (above) is the eleventh chapter. (Zisi's quoting of the Master's words in order to make clear the meaning of the first chapter ends with this. The primary purpose of this work is to identify *zhi* 知 (wisdom, knowledge), *ren* 仁 and *yong* 勇 (courage, bravery) as the three great virtues which give entry through the portals of the Way. Therefore, at the start of the work, the affairs of the great Shun, Yan Yuan and Zilu are cited as examples to illustrate this. Shun was *zhi* 知 (wise); Yan Yuan was *ren* 仁; Zilu was *yong* 勇 (brave). If one is missing from the three, then there is no means of advancing along the Way and perfecting virtue. For the rest (i.e. more on this) see the twentieth chapter.)

Notes ZY11 (Zhu Xi)

[1] *Su* 素, according to the *Han shu*, ought to be written as *suo* 索, so there is a mistake in the character. *[Some men] seek out esoteric doctrines and behave in strange ways* speaks of looking deeply into esoteric and heterodox principles and carrying out strange and unusual practices. Nevertheless, this is sufficient to deceive the age and gain a false reputation, therefore later generations sometimes speak favourably of it. This is going too far in knowledge but not choosing what is good; this is going too far in actions but not using "the centre"; this is being strong but inappropriately so. How can a sage do these things?

[2] *Follow the Way and act* is, then, being able to choose the good. To *go halfway along the path and abandon it* is, then, to have insufficient strength. That is, although his knowledge is enough to reach it, yet in conduct, there is a falling short; it is to approve of strength and yet not be strong. *Yi* 已 equates with *zhi* 止 (to stop). The sage does not exert himself in this and yet does not dare to abandon it. Perfect *cheng* 誠 does not cease and is naturally something that cannot stop.

[3] If one does not *seek out esoteric doctrines and behave in strange ways,* this is to rely on [the Way] of central and constant and that is all. Not to be able to *go halfway along the path and abandon it* is to withdraw from the world's ken without regrets. This is the fully realized virtue of central and constant, the extreme of *zhi* 知 (knowledge, wisdom), the perfection of *ren* 仁, not relying on *yong* 勇 (courage, bravery), and being in good circumstances. These are truly the matters of my Master and what I have still not achieved. Therefore, it is said that *only a sage is capable of this* and that is all.

ZY12: 君子之道費而隱。[1]夫婦之愚，可以與知焉，及其至也，雖聖人
亦有所不知焉；夫婦之不肖，可以能行焉，及其至也，雖聖人亦有所不
能焉。天地之大也，人猶有所憾。故君子語大，天下莫能載焉；語小，
天下莫能破焉。[2]《詩》云：「鳶飛戾天，魚躍于淵。」言其上下察也。[3]
君子之道，造端乎夫婦；及其至也，察乎天地。[4]

右第十二章。子思之言，蓋以申明首章道不可離之意也。其下八章，雜
引孔子之言以明之。

Comment: This corresponds to the second part of ZY7 in the *Li ji*. To Zhu Xi it represents
the start of a new part of the text. To quote Riegel: "With XII the format of the text changes. The language is more discursive, quotes from 'the Master' are fewer, and quotes from
the *Shih Ching* (*Odes*) are introduced. This suggests that, at this point, the Han masters
of the *Odes* joined in." (n. 44, p. 217) There are important differences in interpretation,
notably the reading of the first sentence. The *Li ji* commentators equate *fei* 費 with *gui* 侊,
whereas Zhu Xu glosses it as "用之廣也" which is the reading most translators follow—e.g.
Legge, "reaches wide and far," Couvreur, "d'un usage très éntendus." Also, *yin* 隱 is taken
in the sense of *wei* 微 (subtle, secret) rather than as seeking seclusion. Next, Zhu Xi gives
an explicit account of what it is the sage cannot know or do, quoting Hou Zhongliang 侯
仲良. Also, "great" and "small" are differently understood in the two commentaries. For
Zhu Xi it is the Way. For the *Li ji* commentators what is great is the Way of former kings
in contrast to the small concerns of ordinary men and women.

注 ZY12 (朱熹)

[1] {費，符味反。} 費，用之廣也。隱，體之微也。

[2] {與，去聲。} 君子之道，近自夫婦居室之間，遠而至於聖人天地之所不能
盡，其大無外，其小無內，可謂費矣。然其理之所以然，則隱而莫之見也。蓋
可知可能者，道中之一事，及其至而聖人不知不能。則舉全體而言，聖人固有
所不能盡也。侯氏曰：「聖人所不知，如孔子問禮問官之類；所不能，如孔子不
得位、堯舜病博施之類。」[8] 愚謂人所憾於天地，如覆載生成之偏，及寒暑災祥
之不得其正者。

---

8   Hou Zhongliang 侯仲良 (fl. 1100) was a student of Cheng Yi. He is included in *The*
    Record of the Origins of the School of the Two Cheng 伊洛淵源錄—see SB, 222–23.

ZY12: The Way of the noble man is far-reaching in its use and yet it is hidden. **[1]** Ordinary men and women in their foolishness can join in knowing it, but when it comes to its perfection, there is also that which even sages do not know. Ordinary men and women in their unworthiness are also able to practise it, but when it comes to its perfection, there is also that which even sages cannot do. Despite the greatness of Heaven and Earth, people still have things they are dissatisfied with. Therefore, when the noble man speaks of its greatness, the world is not able to contain it; when he speaks of its smallness, the world is not able to further divide it. **[2]** The *Odes* says: "The hawk flies up to reach the heavens; fish frolic in the [water's] depths." This speaks of its being manifest above and below. **[3]** The Way of the noble man takes its origin from ordinary men and women; in reaching its perfection, it is seen in Heaven and Earth. **[4]**

To the right (above) is the twelfth chapter. Zisi's words are aimed at explicating the meaning of *the Way cannot be departed from* in the first section. In the eight chapters which follow, he variously quotes the words of Confucius in order to clarify this [further].

Notes ZY12 (Zhu Xi)

[1] . . . *Fei* 費 is to use it widely; *Yin* 隱 is to embody it minutely.

[2] . . . The Way of the noble man is near at hand, in the dwellings of ordinary men and women; it is distant and reaches to what sages, and Heaven and Earth cannot exhaust. Its greatness has nothing beyond it; its smallness has nothing within it; it can be spoken of as being "far-reaching in its use." Nevertheless, the principle by which it is what it is, is hidden and not seen. Because what can be known and done is only one matter of the Way that is central, it comes to its perfection and sages do not know [it] and cannot [practise it]. In terms of the whole, then, the sage certainly has that which he cannot exhaust. Hou Shi said: "What the sage does not know is exemplified by things like Confucius asking about rites and offices. What [the sage] cannot do is exemplified by things like Confucius not gaining a position and by Yao and Shun being deficient in their liberal gifts." I say, what people find distressing in Heaven and Earth are things like their partiality in the overseeing and supporting of life, as well as cold, heat, calamity, and misfortune, and these not being put right.

[3] ﹛鳶，余專反﹜。《詩•大雅•旱麓》之篇。⁹鳶，鴟類。戾，至也。察，著也。子思引此詩以明化育流行，上下昭著，莫非此理之用，所謂費也。然其所以然者，則非見聞所及，所謂隱也。故程子曰：「此一節，子思喫緊為人處，活潑潑地，讀者其致思焉。」

[4] 結上文。

ZY13: 子曰：「道不遠人。人之為道而遠人，不可以為道。[1]《詩》云：『伐柯伐柯，其則不遠。』執柯以伐柯，睨而視之，猶以為遠。故君子以人治人，改而止。[2]忠恕違道不遠，施諸己而不願，亦勿施於人。[3]君子之道四，丘未能一焉：所求乎子，以事父未能也；所求乎臣，以事君未能也；所求乎弟，以事兄未能也；所求乎朋友，先施之未能也。庸德之行，庸言之謹，有所不足，不敢不勉，有餘不敢盡；言顧行，行顧言，君子胡不慥慥爾！」[4]

右第十三章。(道不遠人者，夫婦所能，丘未能一者，聖人所不能，皆費也。而其所以然者，則至隱存焉。下章放此。)

Comment: This corresponds to the first part of ZY8 of the *Li ji* text. There are several differences in interpretation. The first, a minor one, is that we have rendered *ren* 人 as "people" rather than "men" since Zhu Xi's notes indicate the more general sense. Next, in the clause "故君子以人治人," Zhu Xi takes the first *ren* 人 to indicate the noble man (or ruler) himself, rather than the Way of man(kind) more generally. In the identification of loyalty and reciprocity (*zhong* 忠 and *shu* 恕) as important to the Way, and the statement of the "Golden Rule," there are no differences. Neither are there differences in the listing of the "four criteria" other than the reading of *qiu* 求 as *ze* 責 in Zhu Xi's case (reflected in the translation). In the somewhat obscure statement "庸德之行，庸言之謹," Zhu Xi clearly takes *yong* 庸 as "ordinary" or "commonplace," whereas the *Li ji* commentators appear to take it as "constant." Again, the difference is reflected in the translation. Finally, Zheng Xuan is more precise in his glossing of "慥慥"—"maintain a true correspondence between word and deed"—than Zhu Xi, who glosses it as *du shi* 篤實 (sincere and genuine). In terms of meaning, the difference is, of course, insignificant.

---

9   See the *Odes*, "Da ya," Mao 239, verse 3, LCC, 4:445.

[3] . . . The verse is the "Han lu" from the *Odes,* "Da ya." *Yuan* 鳶 is a form of kite. *Li* 戾 equates with *zhi* 至 (to reach). *Cha* 察 equates with *zhu* 著 (to manifest). Zisi quotes this ode to clarify the prevalence of transforming and nourishing, which is clearly evident above and below, and that there is nothing apart from the functioning of this principle which is what is called "far-reaching in its use." Nevertheless, by being what it is, it extends to what is neither seen nor heard, and is what is called hidden. Therefore, Master Cheng said: "This section is a critical point for Zisi; it is very stimulating and vivid, and stirs thoughts in the reader['s mind].

[4] This concludes the chapter above.

ZY13: The Master said: "The Way is not far removed from people. If what people take to be the Way is far removed from people, then it cannot be regarded as the Way. **[1]** The *Odes* says: 'Cutting an axe handle, cutting an axe handle, its pattern is not far removed.' If you take hold of one axe handle to cut another axe handle, and look at them both obliquely, it is as if [the patterns] are far apart. Thus the noble man (ruler) uses one person (i.e. himself) to bring good order to others, effects [the necessary] change and stops. **[2]** Loyalty and reciprocity are not far removed from the Way. What one does not wish to be done to oneself, one also does not do to others. **[3]** The Way of the noble man has four aspects. I have not yet been able to achieve a single one of them. What is demanded of a son in serving a father, I am not yet able to do. What is demanded of a subject in serving a prince, I am not yet able to do. What is demanded of a younger brother in serving an older brother, I am not yet able to do. What is demanded of a friend, I have not yet been able to do first. If [the noble man] has deficiencies in the practice of ordinary virtue and the respectfulness of ordinary speech, he dare not fail to strive to make them good; if there are excesses, he dare not fail to strive to curb them. Words should have regard to actions and actions should have regard to words. If this is so, then how is the noble man not honest!" **[4]**

To the right (above) is the thirteenth chapter. (With regard to the Way not being far removed from people, it is what ordinary men and women are able to do; with regard to myself not yet being able [to do] one of the things, these are what the sage is not able to do, and all are far-reaching. And what makes them so is that extreme subtlety exists in them. The following chapter is in accord with this.)

注 ZY13 (朱熹)

[1] 道者，率性而已，固眾人之所能知能行者也，故常不遠於人。若為道者，厭其卑近以為不足為，而反務為高遠難行之事，則非所以為道矣。

[2] {睨，研計反。}《詩•豳風•伐柯》之篇。[10] 柯，斧柄。則，法也。睨，邪視也。言人執柯伐木以為柯者，彼柯長短之法，在此柯耳。然猶有彼此之別，故伐者視之猶以為遠也。若以人治人，則所以為人之道，各在當人之身，初無彼此之別。故君子之治人也，即以其人之道，還治其人之身。其人能改，即止不治。蓋責之以其所能知能行，非欲其遠人以為道也。張子所謂「以眾人望人則易從」[11] 是也。

[3] 盡己之心為忠，推己及人為恕。違，去也，如《春秋傳》「齊師違穀七里」[12] 之違。言自此至彼，相去不遠，非背而去之之謂也。道，即其不遠人者是也。施諸己而不願亦勿施於人，忠恕之事也。以己之心度人之心，未嘗不同，則道之不遠於人者可見。故己之所不欲，則勿以施之於人，亦不遠人以為道之事。張子所謂「以愛己之心愛人則盡仁」是也。

---

10 See the *Odes*, Mao 158, verse 2, LCC, 4:240.

11 This and the following two quotations from Zhang Zai 張載 are to be found in his "Zhongzheng pian" 中正篇 in the *Zhang Zai ji* 張載集 (Taipei: Hanjing wenhua shiye, 2004), 26–32.

12 See the *Zuo zhuan*, Duke Ai, 27th year, LCC, 5:860–61.

Notes ZY13 (Zhu Xi)

[1] The Way is just following [one's] nature. It is certainly something that ordinary people can understand and practise. Therefore, it is commonplace and not far removed from people. If what is deemed to be the Way involves distaste for its being lowly and near at hand, and it is taken to be insignificant, such that there is a striving instead for what is lofty, remote and difficult to practise, then this is not what the Way is.

[2] . . . The ode is the "Fa ke" from the "Odes of Bin." *Ke* 柯 is an axe handle. *Ze* 則 equates with *fa* 法 (model, pattern). *Ni* 睨 is to look obliquely. This says that, when a man takes hold of an axe handle to cut wood to make [another] axe handle, the pattern of the length of the second handle is based on the first handle. Nevertheless, there is still a difference between the two, the reason being that the one doing the cutting looks at them as if they are far apart. It is the same with one person bringing good order to others in that what is taken to be the Way of man exists in its correct form in each person so, at first, there is no difference between this person and that person. Therefore, the noble man's (ruler's) bringing good order to others, since it is by his Way as a man, reflects his own good order as a person. If his people are able to change, then he stops and does not bring order [any further]. And so he demands of them only what they are able to know and do, not wishing what is far removed from people to be taken as the Way. What Master Zhang said—"If what is expected is based on the ordinary people, it is easy to follow"—is this.

[3] To exert one's own heart to the utmost is *zhong* 忠 (loyalty). To extend oneself to reach out to others is *shu* 恕 (reciprocity). *Wei* 違 equates with *qu* 去, as in the *Spring and Autumn Commentary* for example, which has: "The Qi leader was seven *li* from Gu." Here it means "this is not far away from that" and does not mean "to turn your back on and leave." This, then, is the Way not being far removed from people. "What one does not wish to be done to oneself, one also does not do to others" is a matter of loyalty and reciprocity. If one is completely consistent in using one's own heart to measure the hearts of others, then the fact that the Way is not far removed from people can be seen. Therefore, not doing to others what one does not wish done to oneself is also a matter of not being far removed from what people take to be the Way. This is what Master Zhang meant when he said: "Loving others with a heart that loves the self is, then, complete *ren* 仁."

[4] 子、臣、弟、友,四字絕句。求,猶責也。道不遠人,凡己之所以責人者,
皆道之所當然也,故反之以自責而自修焉。庸,平常也。行者,踐其實。謹
者,擇其可。德不足而勉、則行益力;言有餘而訒,則謹益至。謹之至則言顧
行矣;行之力則行顧言矣。慥慥,篤實貌。言君子之言行如此,豈不慥慥乎,
贊美之也。凡此皆不遠人以為道之事。張子所謂「以責人之心責己則盡道」是也。

ZY14: 君子素其位而行,不願乎其外。**[1]**素富貴,行乎富貴;素貧賤,
行乎貧賤;素夷狄,行乎夷狄;素患難,行乎患難;君子無入而不自得
焉。**[2]**在上位不陵下,在下位不援上,正己而不求於人則無怨。上不
怨天,下不尤人。**[3]**故君子居易以俟命,小人行險以徼幸。**[4]**子曰:
「射有似乎君子;失諸正鵠,反求諸其身。」**[5]**

右第十四章。(子思之言也。凡章首無「子曰」字者放此。)

Comment: This section corresponds to the last part of ZY8 and the opening line of ZY9 in the *Li ji* arrangement. Zhu Xi makes the point that where the words *zi yue* 子曰 are lacking at the opening of the chapter, it may be assumed that the words are those of Zisi. In the arrangement above, there is a statement attributed to Confucius to conclude the section, finding something in archery which is akin to being a noble man. In fact, in this final statement slight licence is taken; first, in rendering *she* 射 as "archer" rather than "archery," and second, in translating *zheng gu* 正鵠 as "target," both in the interests of more direct expression. Commentators are agreed that *zheng* 正 refers to the painting of a bird, possibly a buzzard, on the target, whilst *gu* 鵠 is also a bird, possibly a goose or swan (difficult for an archer to hit), a leather likeness of which was attached to the target. There are, then, no real issues in this chapter, as the brevity of Zhu Xi's notes attests.

[4] *Zi* 子 (son), *chen* 臣 (subject), *di* 弟 (younger brother), and *you* 友 (friend); these four characters are four sentences (lines). *Qiu* 求 is like *ze* 責 (to ask of, require, demand). In regard to the Way not being remote from people in general, what the self demands of others is, in all cases, what is proper for the Way. Then, on the other hand, there is requiring of oneself and cultivation of oneself in it. *Yong* 庸 equates with *pingchang* 平常 (ordinary, common). *Xing* 行 means to put into practice. *Jin* 謹 (being cautious, careful) means to choose what is possible. If virtue is not enough and yet there is exertion of effort, then actions become increasingly strong. If words that are excessive are held back, then caution becomes increasingly perfect. If caution reaches perfection, then speech has regard for action. If actions are strong, then actions have regard for words. *Zao zao* 慥慥 is an honest appearance. This says that, if the noble man's words and actions are like this, how is he not honest, which is to praise him. In general, this is all part of the matter of the Way not being far removed from people. This is what Master Zhang meant when he said: "To have a heart that demands of the self what one demands of others is, then, to be complete in the Way."

ZY14: The noble man occupies his position and acts [accordingly]. He does not wish to go beyond this. [1] If he occupies a position of wealth and honour, his actions are appropriate to wealth and honour. If he occupies a position of poverty and lowliness, his actions are appropriate to poverty and lowliness. If he occupies a position among the Yi and Di tribes, his actions are in accord with the Yi and Di. If he occupies a position of misfortune and hardship, his actions are appropriate to misfortune and hardship. The noble man does not enter and find himself discomposed. [2] When he occupies a high position, he does not maltreat inferiors. When he occupies a low position, he does not cling to superiors. He rectifies himself and asks nothing of others, so he is without resentment. Above, he does not find fault with Heaven; below, he does not blame others. [3] Therefore, the noble man dwells in equanimity and accepts his lot, whereas the inferior man acts recklessly in pursuit of good fortune. [4] The Master said: "The archer is like the noble man—if he fails to hit the target, he turns and places the blame on himself." [5]

To the right (above) is the fourteenth chapter. (These are Zisi's words. In general, where the chapter heading is without "the Master said," this is the case.)

注 ZY14 (朱熹)

[1] 素，猶見在也。言君子但因見在所居之位而為其所當為，無慕乎其外之心也。

[2]｛難，去聲。｝此言素其位而行也。

[3]｛援，平聲。｝此言不願乎其外也。

[4]｛易，去聲。｝易，平地也。居易，素位而行也。俟命，不願乎外也。徼，求也。幸，謂所不當得而得者。

[5]｛正，音征。鵠，工毒反。｝畫布曰正，棲皮曰鵠，皆侯之中，射之的也。子思引此孔子之言，以結上文之意。

ZY15: 君子之道，辟如行遠必自邇，辟如登高必自卑。[1]《詩》曰：「妻子好合，如鼓瑟琴；兄弟既翕，和樂且耽；宜爾室家，樂爾妻帑。」[2]子曰：「父母其順矣乎！」[3]

右第十五章。

Comment: This short chapter, again without a quotation from Confucius at the start in Zhu Xi's arrangement, corresponds to ZY9 in the *Li ji* text where it is connected to the quotation regarding archery. In content, it provides a further comment on the Way, supported by a quotation from the *Odes*. Zhu Xi's understanding of *shun* 順 in the sense of *an le* 安樂 is reflected in the translation.

注 ZY15 (朱熹)

[1] 辟，譬同。

[2]｛好，去聲。耽，《詩》作湛，亦音耽。樂，音洛。｝《詩‧小雅‧常棣》之篇。[13] 鼓瑟琴，和也。翕，亦合也。耽，亦樂也。帑，子孫也。

[3] 夫子誦此詩而贊之曰：人能和於妻子，宜於兄弟如此，則父母其安樂之矣。子思引詩及此語，以明行遠自邇、登高自卑之意。

----

[13]   See the *Odes*, Mao 164, verse 7, LCC, 4:252–53.

Notes ZY14 (Zhu Xi)

[1] *Su* 素 is like *xian zai* 見在 (現在—to be present). This says that the noble man simply occupies the position which he presently has and does whatever is appropriate for him to do. He does not have a mind which desires what is outside this.

[2] . . . This says that he occupies his position and acts [accordingly].

[3] . . . This says that he does not wish for what is outside [his position].

[4] . . . *Yi* 易 is equivalent to *ping di* 平地 (level ground). *Ju yi* 居易 is to occupy a position and act. *Si ming* 俟命 means not wishing for what is outside [this]. *Jiao* 徼 is equivalent to *qiu* 求 (to seek). *Xing* 幸 refers to getting what it is not appropriate to get.

[5] . . . A painting on cloth is called *zheng* 正; a placement on skin is called *gu* 鵠, both being the centre of the target and the point for aiming at. Zisi quotes these words of Confucius in order to summarise the meaning of the preceding text.

ZY15: The Way of the noble man may be compared to travelling a long distance—one must start from nearby. It may be compared to scaling a great height—one must start from below. [1] The *Odes* says: "Happy accord with one's wife and children is like the playing of zither and lute. In accord between older and younger brothers there is harmonious joy and pleasure. Let all be as it should be in your household, and there will be joy among your wife and offspring." [2]

The Master said: "How peaceful and happy your parents would be!" [3]

To the right (above) is the fifteenth chapter.

Notes ZY15 (Zhu Xi)

[1] *Pi* 辟 is the same as *pi* 譬 (to compare).

[2] . . . The ode is "Chang di" in the "Xiao ya." Playing zither and lute equates with harmony. *Xi* 翕 is also being in accord. *Dan* 耽 is also pleasure (*le* 樂). *Nu* 帑 are descendants.

[3] The Master recited this ode and praised it, saying that if a man can be in harmony with his wife and children, and act properly towards his older and younger brothers like this, then his parents are at peace and happy. Zisi quoted the *Odes* with reference to these words to make clear the meaning of "travelling a long distance involves starting from nearby" and "scaling a great height involves starting from below."

ZY16: 子曰:「鬼神之為德,其盛矣乎![1]視之而弗見,聽之而弗聞,
體物而不可遺。[2]使天下之人齊明盛服,以承祭祀。洋洋乎!如在其
上,如在其左右。[3]《詩》曰:『神之格思,不可度思!矧可射思!』[4]
夫微之顯,誠之不可揜如此夫。」[5]

右第十六章。(不見不聞,隱也。體物如在,則亦費矣。此前三章,以其費之
小者而言。此後三章,以其費之大者而言。此一章,兼費隱、包大小而言。)

Comment: This corresponds to ZY10 in the *Li ji* arrangement. As there, the translation of *wei de* 為德 as "being virtuous" is an attempt to make sense of *wei* 為 in this sentence, a problem Haloun, for example, acknowledges. Several translators render *de* 德 as "power" in this context—for example, "abundant is the power of ghosts and spirits" is a possible translation of the opening statement. Zhu Xi enlarges on the description of ghosts and spirits with reference to their presumed actions in the world, and in relation to *qi* 氣 and the merging and dispersal of *yin* and *yang*. Both Cheng Yi and Zhang Zai are cited on these points.

注 ZY16 (朱熹)

[1] 程子曰:「鬼神,天地之功用,而造化之跡也。」張子曰:「鬼神者,二氣之
良能也。」[14] 愚謂以二氣言,則鬼者陰之靈也,神者陽之靈也。以一氣言,則至
而伸者為神,反而歸者為鬼,其實一物而已。為德,猶言性情功效。

[2] 鬼神無形與聲,然物之終始,莫非陰陽合散之所為,是其為物之體,而物所
不能遺也。其言體物,猶易所謂幹事。

[3] {齊,側皆反。}齊之為言齊也,所以齊不齊而致其齊也。明,猶潔也。洋
洋,流動充滿之意。能使人畏敬奉承,而發見昭著如此,乃其體物而不可遺
之驗也。孔子曰:「其氣發揚于上,為昭明焄蒿悽愴。此百物之精也,神之著
也」,[15] 正謂此爾。

[4] {度,待洛反。射,音亦,《詩》作斁。}《詩·大雅·抑》之篇。[16] 格,來也。
矧,況也。射,厭也。言厭怠而不敬也。思,語辭。

[5] {夫,音扶。}誠者,真實無妄之謂。陰陽合散,無非實者。故其發見之不可
揜如此。

---

14 We have not been able to locate the Cheng Yi 程頤 reference. For the Zhang Zai 張載 reference, see *Zhang Zai ji*, 9.

15 See the *Li ji* 47, "Jiyi," SSJZS, 5:814.

16 See the *Odes*, Mao 256, verse 7, LCC, 4:515.

ZY16: The Master said: "In their being virtuous, how great are ghosts and spirits! **[1]** You may look for them, but they are not to be seen; you may listen for them, but they are not to be heard. Nevertheless, they are substantial things and cannot be neglected. **[2]** They cause the people of the world to fast and purify themselves, and put on fine clothes to attend to the sacrifices. How widespread they are; it is as if they are above and on all sides. **[3]** The *Odes* says: 'The coming of spirits cannot be determined. Still less can they be disrespected.' **[4]** Moreover, the manifestation of the subtle and the impossibility of concealing *cheng* 誠 are just like this." **[5]**

To the right (above) is the sixteenth chapter. (The unseen and the unheard are *yin* 隱. They are substantial things, as if they existed, and are also far-reaching. These first three sections speak of what is small in the far-reaching, whilst the subsequent three sections speak of what is great in the far-reaching. This one section connects the far-reaching and the subtle, embraces the great and the small, and speaks of them.)

Notes ZY16 (Zhu Xi)

[1] Master Cheng said: "Ghosts and spirits are the effective agents of Heaven and Earth and the traces of creation and transformation." Master Zhang said: "In the case of ghosts and spirits, they represent the natural capacities of the two 'ethereal vapours.'" I say that, if one speaks of two "ethereal vapours," then ghosts are spiritual agents of *yin* and spirits are spiritual agents of *yang*. If one speaks in terms of one spiritual force, then what extend and reach out are spirits, and what turn back and return are ghosts. But in fact they are one and the same. Both have to do with virtue, referring to disposition and efficacy.

[2] Ghosts and spirits have neither form nor sound. Nevertheless, the ends and the beginnings of things are nothing other than what are created by the merging and dispersing of *yin* and *yang*. This creates the substance of things and is what things cannot neglect. What is meant by substantial things is still different from what is referred to as managing affairs.

[3] ... To fast and purify is to make those who do not fast and are not pure, fast and become pure. *Ming* 明 is like *jie* 潔 (clear, pure). *Yang yang* 洋洋 has the meaning of flowing and being filled with. To be able to cause people to be fearful, respectful and attentive, and to be clearly manifest like this, is then verification of the fact that their embodiment in things cannot be neglected. Confucius said: "The vapours that rise up and spread above are the fumes from the sacrifice affecting those in attendance. These are the essence of all things and the manifestation of the spirits." This is what is really being spoken of.

[4] ... The ode is the "Yi" from the "Da ya." *Ge* 格 equates with *lai* 來. *Shen* 矧 equates with *kuang* 況 (how much more/still less). *Yi* 射 equates with *yan* 厭 and means to dislike, or be insolent or disrespectful. *Si* 思 is a particle.

[5] ... To be *cheng* 誠 refers to being true and genuine and not false. *Yin* and *yang* coming together and dispersing is always substantial. Therefore, its manifestations not being able to be concealed is like this.

ZY17: 子曰：「舜其大孝也與！德為聖人，尊為天子，富有四海之內。宗廟饗之，子孫保之。[1]故大德必得其位，必得其祿，必得其名，必得其壽。[2]故天之生物，必因其材而篤焉。故栽者培之，傾者覆之。[3]《詩》曰：『嘉樂君子，憲憲令德！宜民宜人，受祿于天；保佑命之，自天申之！』[4]故大德者必受命。」[5]

右第十七章。(此由庸行之常，推之以極其至，見道之用廣也。而其所以然者，則為體微矣。後二章亦此意。)

Comment: This corresponds to ZY11 in the *Li ji* arrangement. No significant differences emerge in Zhu Xi's reading of the section, to judge from his brief notes. Two of Shun's descendants, Yu Si 虞思 and Duke Chen Hu 陳胡公, are identified, specific reference is made to Shun's longevity (traditionally accepted as 110 years), and *zai* 栽 is read as *zhi* 植 rather than *zhi* 殖 (a very minor difference, clearly), although *qi* 氣 is invoked to elaborate on the statement *zai zhe pei zhi* "栽者培之."

注 ZY17 (朱熹)

[1] {與，平聲。}子孫，謂虞思、陳胡公之屬。
[2] 舜年百有十歲。
[3] 材，質也。篤，厚也。栽，植也。氣至而滋息為培，氣反而游散則覆。
[4] 《詩•大雅•假樂》之篇。[17] 假，當依此作嘉。憲，當依《詩》作顯。申，重也。
[5] 受命者，受天命為天子也。

---

[17] See the *Odes*, Mao 249, verse 1, LCC, 4:481.

ZY17: The Master said: "Great, indeed, was Shun's filial piety. His virtue was that of a sage; his honour was that of the Son of Heaven; he was rich in having all within the four seas. There were sacrifices to him in the ancestral temple and his descendants preserved them. [1] Thus, [being a man of] great virtue, he inevitably gained his position, he inevitably attained his prosperity, he inevitably acquired his reputation, and he inevitably achieved longevity. [2] Thus Heaven, in its giving rise to things, invariably acts in accord with their capacities and is bountiful. So things that are growing, it increases, whilst things that are decaying, it brings down. [3] The *Odes* says:

> Blessed and happy is the prince,
> manifest is his goodness and virtue.
> He acts properly towards his people and others,
> he receives prosperity from Heaven.
> Heaven protects him and helps him,
> and it grants him the mandate.
> And from Heaven this is redoubled. [4]

Therefore, one with great virtue inevitably receives the mandate." [5]

To the right (above) is the seventeenth chapter. (This makes use of the principle of constancy in conduct and extends it to reach to the highest point, displaying the wide application of the Way. And that by which it is so, is, then, both substantial and subtle. The two following chapters also have this meaning.)

Notes ZY17 (Zhu Xi)

[1] ... "Descendants" refer to men such as Yu Si 虞思 and Duke Chen Hu 陳胡公.[18]

[2] Shun lived to the age of 110 years.

[3] *Cai* 材 is equivalent to *zhi* 質 (disposition). *Du* 篤 is equivalent to *hou* 厚 (substantial, bountiful). *Zai* 栽 is equivalent to *zhi* 植 (plant, to plant). The *qi* 氣 (vital spirit) reaching perfection and being nourished and growing is *pei* 培, whereas the *qi* 氣 (vital spirit) being dissipated and dispersed is *fu* 覆.

[4] The ode is the "Jia le" in the "Da ya." *Jia* 假, according to this, is properly *jia* 嘉. *Xian* 憲 is properly written as *xian* 顯. According to the *Odes*, *Shen* 申 is equivalent to *chong* 重 (to double).

[5] "Receiving the mandate" refers to receiving Heaven's mandate and becoming the Son of Heaven.

---

18 Yu Si 虞思 was a prince during the Xia dynasty (see *Zuo zhuan* for the 1st year of Duke Ai—LCC, 5:792–95). Duke Chen Hu 陳胡公, from the Zhou dynasty, was a descendant of Shun who was enfeoffed with Chen (see *Shiji* 36, 5:1575–87).

ZY18: 子曰：「無憂者其惟<u>文王</u>乎！以<u>王季</u>為父，以<u>武王</u>為子，父作之，子述之。**[1]**<u>武王</u>纘<u>大王</u>、<u>王季</u>、<u>文王</u>之緒。壹戎衣而有天下，身不失天下之顯名。尊為天子，富有四海之內。宗廟饗之，子孫保之。**[2]**<u>武王</u>末受命，<u>周公</u>成<u>文</u><u>武</u>之德，追王<u>大王</u>、<u>王季</u>，上祀先公以天子之禮。斯禮也，達乎諸侯大夫，及士庶人。父為大夫，子為士；葬以大夫，祭以士。父為士，子為大夫；葬以士，祭以大夫。期之喪達乎大夫，三年之喪達乎天子，父母之喪無貴賤一也。」**[3]**

右第十八章。

Comment: This corresponds to ZY12 in the *Li ji* arrangement and refers to the paradigms of virtuous conduct, Kings Wen and Wu and the Duke of Zhou, particularly in relation to their lineage and ceremonial practices. Zhu Xi's interpretation is essentially the same as that of the *Li ji* commentators; questionable characters are given the same reading. The only variation of note is in the phrase "壹戎衣" where Zhu Xi does not read *yi* 壹 as *yin* 殷, but takes *rong yi* 戎衣 as a kind of armour.

注 ZY18 (朱熹)

[1] 此言<u>文王</u>之事。《書》言：「<u>王季</u>其勤王家」，[19] 蓋其所作，亦積功累仁之事也。

[2] {大，音泰，下同。}此言<u>武王</u>之事。纘，繼也。<u>大王</u>，<u>王季</u>之父也。《書》云：「<u>大王</u>肇基王跡。」[20]《詩》云：「至于<u>大王</u>，實始翦<u>商</u>。」[21] 緒，業也。戎衣，甲冑之屬。壹戎衣，<u>武成</u>文，言一著戎衣以伐<u>紂</u>也。

[3] {追王之王，去聲。}此言<u>周公</u>之事。末，猶老也。追王，蓋推<u>文</u><u>武</u>之意，以及乎王跡之所起也。先公，<u>組紺</u>以上至<u>后稷</u>也。上祀先公以天子之禮，又推<u>大王</u>、<u>王季</u>之意，以及於無窮也。制為禮法，以及天下，使葬用死者之爵，祭用生者之祿。喪服自期以下，諸侯絕；大夫降；而父母之喪，上下同之，推己以及人也。

---

19   *Documents*, "Wu Cheng" 武成, LCC, 3:311.
20   *Documents*, "Wu Cheng," LCC, 3:311.
21   *Odes*, Mao 300, verse 2, LCC, 4:622.

ZY18: The Master said: "It was only King Wen who was without grief. Because King Ji was his father and King Wu his son, [he had] a father who created [the foundation] and a son who continued [his Way]. **[1]** King Wu continued the work of Tai Wang, King Ji and King Wen. Once he donned his armour and held all under Heaven, he did not lose his distinguished reputation in the world. He was honoured as the Son of Heaven and was rich in having all within the Four Seas. Sacrifices were offered to him in the ancestral temple and his descendants maintained them. **[2]** King Wu was old when he received the mandate. The Duke of Zhou completed the virtuous [course] of Wen and Wu. He retrospectively honoured Tai Wang and King Ji as kings, and offered sacrifices above to the former dukes using the rites of the Son of Heaven. These rites he extended to feudal lords and great officers as well as to ordinary officers and the common people. If the father was a great officer and the son was an ordinary officer, the burial was that of a great officer and the sacrifice that of an ordinary officer. If the father was an ordinary officer and the son was a great officer, the burial was that of an ordinary officer and the sacrifice that of a great officer. The mourning period of one year applied to great officers and that of three years applied to the Son of Heaven. The mourning for parents, whether noble or base, was the same." **[3]**

To the right (above) is the eighteenth chapter.

Notes ZY18 (Zhu Xi)

[1] This speaks of the affairs of King Wen, The *Documents* says: "King Ji was diligent with respect to the royal house." The things he did were such that he amassed merit and accumulated *ren* 仁.

[2] . . . This speaks of the affairs of King Wu. *Zuan* 纘 equates with *ji* 繼 (to continue). Tai Wang was King Ji's father. The *Documents* says: "Tai Wang established the foundation of the royal path." The *Odes* says: "When it came to Tai Wang, he truly began the 'clipping' of Shang." *Xu* 緒 equates with *ye* 業. *Rong yi* 戎衣 is a kind of armour. *Yi rong yi* is written with regard to Wu's success, referring to his donning his armour to cut down Zhou 紂.

[3] . . . This speaks of the affairs of the Duke of Zhou. *Mo* 末 is like *lao* 老 (i.e. "old"). *Zhui wang* is to extend the purpose of Wen and Wu, going back to those who gave rise to the royal path. The "former dukes" refers to Zu Gan extending back to Hou Ji. Offering sacrifices above to "former dukes" using the rites of the Son of Heaven also extended the purpose of Tai Wang and King Ji without limit. What were established as ceremonial methods were extended throughout the world, so that in burial the rank of the one dying was used, whilst in sacrificing the rank of the one living was used. The wearing of mourning garments for one year stopped at feudal lords. For great officers it was less. And yet, in the mourning for parents, high and low were the same, and this applied to oneself and extended to others.

ZY19: 子曰：「<u>武王</u>、<u>周公</u>，其達孝矣乎！[1]夫孝者：善繼人之志，善
述人之事者也。[2]春秋脩其祖廟，陳其宗器，設其裳衣，薦其時食。[3]
宗廟之禮，所以序昭穆也；序爵，所以辨貴賤也；序事，所以辨賢也；
旅酬下為上，所以逮賤也；燕毛，所以序齒也。[4]踐其位，行其禮，奏
其樂，敬其所尊，愛其所親，事死如事生，事亡如事存，孝之至也。[5]
郊社之禮，所以事上帝也，宗廟之禮，所以祀乎其先也。明乎郊社之
禮、禘嘗之義，治國其如示諸掌乎。」[6]

右第十九章。

Comment: This corresponds to ZY13 in the *Li ji* arrangement. Zhu Xi's notes are largely
explanatory of certain terms and practices. Apart from very minor variations (e.g. in the
final sentence) the interpretations in the two texts are the same. Zhu Xi points out that
down to the end of sub-section 5 is all about the example set by King Wu and the Duke
of Zhou. The final statement is a comment, presumably attributable to Confucius on the
basis of the other instances referred to in note 22.

注 ZY19 (朱熹)

[1] 達，通也。承上章而言<u>武王</u>、<u>周公</u>之孝，乃天下之人通謂之孝，猶<u>孟子</u>之言
「達尊」也。[22]
[2] 上章言<u>武王</u>纘<u>大王</u>、<u>王季</u>、<u>文王</u>之緒以有天下，而<u>周公</u>成<u>文武</u>之德以追崇其
先祖，此繼志述事之大者也。下文又以其所制祭祀之禮，通於上下者言之。

---

22   The full statement, in *Mencius* IIB.2(6), is:「天下有達尊三；爵一，齒一，德一。」
     Lau's translation reads: "There are three things which are acknowledged by the world to
     be exalted: rank, age and virtue." See Lau, *Mencius: A Bilingual Edition*, 80 and 83.

ZY19: The Master said: "King Wu and the Duke of Zhou—how thorough-going was their filial conduct! **[1]** Now their being filial was to skillfully perpetuate the purposes of others (i.e. their ancestors) and to skillfully carry on their undertakings. **[2]** In spring and autumn, it was to renovate their ancestral temples, to set out their ancestral utensils, to lay out their upper and lower garments, and to present offerings appropriate to the season. **[3]** The ceremonies of the ancestral temple were how the *zhao* and *mu* (the left and right spirit tablets) were ordered. Order of rank was how the noble and the base were differentiated. Order of services was how worthiness was distinguished. The general pledging, where inferiors offered drinking cups to superiors, was the way of reaching down to those who were lowly. Hair colour was how seniority (age) was ordered. **[4]** To take up their positions, to practise their ceremonies, to perform their music, to have reverence for what they honoured and love for what they held dear, to serve the dead like serving the living, to serve the departed like serving those who remained—this was the apogee of filial conduct. **[5]** The ceremonies of sacrifice to Heaven and Earth were the means of serving the Supreme Lord. The ceremonies of the ancestral temples were the means of sacrificing to their ancestors. If one is clear about the ceremonies of sacrifice to Heaven and Earth, and the meaning of the *Di* and *Chang* sacrifices, then bringing good order to the kingdom is just like looking at something in the palm of one's hand." **[6]**

To the right (above) is the nineteenth chapter.

Notes ZY19 (Zhu Xi)

[1] *Da* 達 is equivalent to *tong* 通 (thoroughly, universal). This continues on from the previous chapter and speaks of the filial conduct of King Wu and the Duke of Zhou which is, then, the filial conduct that people of the world understand and speak of—like Mencius speaks of being "thoroughly honourable."

[2] The previous chapter speaks of how King Wu succeeded to the throne held first by Tai Wang, then by King Ji, and then by King Wen. It speaks of how the Duke of Zhou completed the virtue of Wen and Wu by retrospectively honouring their former ancestors, this being the greatness of perpetuating their purposes and carrying on their undertakings. The subsequent text, by also being about regulating the ceremonies of the sacrifices, forms the link between what has gone before and what comes after, and speaks of this.

[3] 祖廟：天子七，諸侯五，大夫三，適士二，官師一。宗器，先世所藏之重器；若周之赤刀、大訓、天球、河圖之屬也。裳衣，先祖之遺衣服，祭則設之以授尸也。時食，四時之食，各有其物，如春行羔、豚、膳、膏、香之類是也。

[4] {昭，如字。為，去聲。}宗廟之次：左為昭，右為穆，而子孫亦以為序。有事於太廟，則子姓、兄弟、羣昭、羣穆咸在而不失其倫焉。爵、公、侯、卿、大夫也。事，宗祝有司之職事也。旅，眾也。酬，導飲也。旅酬之禮，賓弟子、兄弟之子各舉觶於其長而眾相酬。蓋宗廟之中以有事為榮，故逮及賤者，使亦得以申其敬也。燕毛，祭畢而燕，則以毛髮之色別長幼，為坐次也。齒，年數也。

[5] 踐，猶履也。其，指先王也。所尊所親，先王之祖考、子孫、臣庶也。始死謂之死，既葬則曰反而亡焉，皆指先王也。此結上文兩節，皆繼志述事之意也。

[6] 郊，祀天。社，祭地。不言后土者，省文也。禘，天子宗廟之大祭，追祭太祖之所自出於太廟，而以太祖配之也。嘗，秋祭也。四時皆祭，舉其一耳。禮必有義，對舉之，互文也。示，與視同。視諸掌，言易見也。此與《論語》文意大同小異，《記》有詳略耳。[23]

23 The *Lunyu* reference is III.1 (LCC, 1:158–59); the *Li ji* reference is *Li ji*, "Zhongni yanju," SSJZS, 5:853.

[3] With regard to ancestral temples, there were seven for the Son of Heaven, five for the feudal lords, three for great officers, two for leading officers, and one for ordinary officers. Temple vessels were important utensils stored away by former ages—for example, such things as the *chi dao* 赤刀 (a treasured sword) the *da xun* 大訓 (the great precepts), the *tian qiu* 天球 (the celestial globe), and the *He tu* 河圖 (river map) of Zhou times. The garments were clothes left behind by former ancestors which, at the sacrifices, were then set out to present to the impersonator of the dead. The appropriate foods were the foods of the four seasons, each season having its specific things—for example, spring had such things as lambs, suckling pigs, delicacies, fat and incense.

[4] . . . The order in the ancestral temple is the left being *zhao* 昭 (bright), the right being *mu* 穆 (dark), and the descendants also being taken in sequence. In the matters of the imperial ancestral temple, descendants, older and younger brothers, and the masses to the left and right were all present without losing their sequence. Ranks were *gong* (duke), *hou* (earl), *qing* (noble) and *daifu* (great officer). The matters, which were the prayers to ancestors, had an officer to manage them. *Lü* 旅 is equivalent to *zhong* 眾 (the whole of), which here equates with "general." *Chou* 酬 is to lead the drinking (pledge with wine). In the ceremony of general pledging, the guest younger brothers and sons, and the sons of older and younger brothers each raised his cup to their elders and all pledged each other. Now, within the ancestral temple, by there being that which was glorious, they extend this to those who are lowly and this also causes an extension of reverence. On the matter of hair colour and feasting, when the sacrifice is finished and there is feasting, then a distinction is made between old and young by the hair colour, and the seating is arranged accordingly. *Chi* 齒 is equivalent to age.

[5] *Jian* 踐 is like *lü* 履 (actions, conduct). *Qi* 其 indicates former kings. "Those who are honoured" and "those who are held dear" are the ancestors of former kings, descendants and subjects. *Shi si* 始死 refers to being dead; *ji zang* 既葬 speaks, on the contrary, of being lost (i.e. the former from the point of view of the dead and the latter from the point of view of the living). Both indicate former kings. This concludes the two sections above which are both on the meaning of perpetuating their purposes and carrying on their undertakings.

[6] *Jiao* 郊 is the sacrifice to Heaven. *She* 社 is the sacrifice to Earth. Not saying *hou tu* 后土 is just an abbreviation. *Di* 禘 is the great sacrifice in the Son of Heaven's ancestral temple and looks back to sacrifices which the first emperor (Taizu) himself brought forth in the ancestral temple and so matches what the first emperor did. *Chang* 嘗 is the autumn sacrifice. The four seasons all have sacrifices, but only one is mentioned here as an example. Ceremonies must have meanings, and with respect to raising them, there are reciprocal meanings. *Shi* 示 is the same as *shi* 視. *Shi zhu zhang* 視諸掌 means easy to see. This and the *Lunyu* are broadly the same in meaning, although there are small differences, the [*Li*] *ji* having the more detailed account.

ZY20.1: 哀公問政。[1]子曰：「文 武之政，布在方策。其人存，則其政舉；其人亡，則其政息。[2]人道敏政，地道敏樹。夫政也者，蒲盧也。[3]故為政在人，取人以身，脩身以道，脩道以仁。[4]仁者人也，親親為大；義者宜也，尊賢為大；親親之殺，尊賢之等，禮所生也。[5]在下位不獲乎上，民不可得而治矣！[6]故君子不可以不脩身；思脩身，不可以不事親；思事親，不可以不知人；思知人，不可以不知天。」[7]

天下之達道五，所以行之者三：曰君臣也，父子也，夫婦也，昆弟也，朋友之交也：五者天下之達道也。知、仁、勇三者，天下之達德也，所以行之者，一也。[8]或生而知之，或學而知之，或困而知之，及其知之，一也；或安而行之，或利而行之，或勉强而行之，及其成功，一也。[9]

Comment: This chapter, which we have divided into six subsections in the Zhu Xi version, marks a transition in the work. The examples of the various ethical paradigms are replaced by statements attributed to Confucius himself, initially in response to questioning by Duke Ai of Lu. The opening sub-section, ZY20.1 above, corresponds to ZY14 in the *Li ji* arrangement. In the initial paragraph (notes [1] to [7]), Confucius considers the nature of government, likening the Way of man in striving for government to the Way of earth in striving for the growth of plants; i.e. a fundamental impulse. Successful government depends on the ruler choosing the right men. He will be able to do this if he commits himself to self-cultivation, developing the qualities associated with the basic triad, *ren* 仁, *yi* 義 and *li* 禮, three terms succinctly defined here. Two relatively minor issues in this opening paragraph are the simile for government (note [3]), which Zhu Xi takes to be "rushes and reeds," and the sentence covered by note [6], which he follows Zheng Xuan in considering to be misplaced. In relation to the end of the paragraph (notes [8] & [9]), Zhu Xi is at pains to clarify exactly what is involved in *zhi* 知, *ren* 仁 and *yong* 勇 in terms of putting into practice the "thoroughgoing Way" (*da dao* 達道). In doing so, he invokes the "Wu dian" 五典, mentioned in several places in the *Documents* and also by Mencius, as well as providing a quotation from Lü Dalin (1044–1093), a noted Song scholar (one of the *si xiansheng* 四先生) who studied under Cheng Yi. Lü was particularly noted for his knowledge of the *Li ji*.

注 ZY20.1 (朱熹)

[1] 哀公，魯君，名蔣。

[2] 方，版也。策，簡也。息，猶滅也。有是君，有是臣，則有是政矣。

ZY20.1: Duke Ai asked about government. The Master replied: "The government of Wen and Wu is recorded on wooden tablets and bamboo slips. When those men lived, their government was implemented; when those men died, their government was extinguished. **[1]** The Way of man is to strive for government; the Way of earth is to strive for the growth of plants. **[2]** Now government is like rushes and reeds. **[3]** Therefore, the conduct of government lies in men. Choosing men is the purview of the ruler. [For the latter,] cultivating the self is through the Way and cultivating the Way is through *ren* 仁. **[4]** *Ren* 仁 is to be human(e); the key point is devotion to one's family members. *Yi* 義 is to be right [in action] and the key point is honouring worthiness. In devotion to family members, there is a hierarchy; in honouring worthiness, there are grades. These are what give rise to *li* 禮. **[5]** (When those in inferior positions do not have the support of their superiors, the people cannot be won over and brought to good order.) **[6]** Therefore, the noble man (ruler) cannot do otherwise than cultivate himself. If he intends to cultivate himself, he cannot do otherwise than serve his family members. If he intends to serve his family members, he cannot do otherwise than know men. If he intends to know men, he cannot do otherwise than know Heaven." **[7]**

There are five [components] to the world's all-pervading Way and three [components] to putting it into practice. I say [the five are the relationships between] ruler and minister, father and son, husband and wife, older and younger brother, and friend and friend. The five [relationships] are the all-pervading Way of Heaven. Three things—*zhi* 知 (knowledge, wisdom), *ren* 仁 and *yong* 勇 (courage, bravery)—are [the components of] the world's all-pervading virtue. The way in which to put them into practice is one. Some are born and know these things, some study and know them, and some have difficulties and know them, but when it comes to their knowing them, it is one and the same thing. **[8]** Some practise them with a natural ease, some practise them for the benefits they bring, and some practise them through great effort, but when it comes to their succeeding, it is one and the same thing. **[9]**

Notes ZY20.1 (Zhu Xi)

[1] Duke Ai was the ruler of Lu; Jiang was his name.
[2] *Fang* 方 is equivalent to *ban* 版 (i.e. wooden tablet). *Ce* 策 is equivalent to *jian* 簡 (i.e. bamboo slip). *Xi* 息 is like *mie* 滅 (to destroy, extinguish). If there are these rulers and these ministers, then there is this government.

[3] {夫，音扶。} 敏，速也。蒲盧，<u>沈括</u>[24] 以為蒲葦是也。以人立政，猶以地種樹，其成速矣，而蒲葦又易生之物，其成尤速也。言人存政舉，其易如此。

[4] 此承上文人道敏政而言也。為政在人，《家語》作「為政在於得人」，[25] 語意尤備。人，謂賢臣。身，指君身。道者，天下之達道。仁者，天地生物之心，而人得以生者，所謂元者善之長也。言人君為政在於得人，而取人之則又在脩身。能脩其身，則有君有臣，而政無不舉矣。

[5] {殺，去聲。} 人，指人身而言。具此生理，自然便有惻怛慈愛之意，深體味之可見。宜者，分別事理，各有所宜也。禮，則節文斯二者而已。

[6] <u>鄭氏</u>曰：「此句在下，誤重在此。」[26]

[7] 為政在人，取人以身，故不可以不脩身。脩身以道，脩道以仁，故思脩身不可以不事親。欲盡親親之仁，必由尊賢之義，故又當知人。親親之殺，尊賢之等，皆天理也，故又當知天。

[8] {知，去聲。} 達道者，天下古今所共由之路，即《書》所謂「五典」，[27] 孟子所謂「父子有親、君臣有義、夫婦有別、長幼有序、朋友有信」[28] 是也。知，所以知此也；仁，所以體此也；勇，所以強此也；謂之達德者，天下古今所同得之理也。一則誠而已矣。達道雖人所共由，然無是三德，則無以行之；

24 Shen Kuo 沈括 (1031–1095) was a noted scholar and scientist of the Song period and one time Chancellor of the Hanlin Academy—see, for example, SB, 226–28, 247–48.
25 *Kongzi jiayu* 孔子家語 17 (*Xinyi Kongzi jiayu*, ed. Yang Chunqiu 羊春秋 [Taipei: San-min shuju, 1998], 266).
26 See *Li ji* version, ZY14, Zheng Xuan, note 7.
27 See, for example, the *Documents*, "Canon of Shun," LCC, 3:31.
28 See *Mencius* IIIA.4(8), LCC, 2:251–52, Lau, *Mencius*, 114–17.

[3] . . . *Min* 敏 is equivalent to *su* 速 (swift, rapid). [As for] *pu lu* 蒲盧, Shen Kuo (see note 24 above) takes this to be *pu wei* 蒲葦 (rushes and reeds). Using men to establish government is like using the earth to grow plants in that their completion is swift. Also rushes and reeds are things that readily grow and their completion is particularly swift, which is to say that, if such men exist, government goes forward easily like this.

[4] This continues the previous text's discussion of the Way of man facilitating government. In taking government to lie in men, the *Jiayu* has: "Conducting government lies in getting [the right] men." This meaning is particularly apposite. *Ren* 人 refers to worthy ministers. *Shen* 身 indicates the ruler himself. *Dao* 道 is the all-pervading Way of the world. *Ren* 仁 is the mind-heart of Heaven and Earth, that which gives birth to things, what people acquire by being born, and what is spoken of as the origin of the growth of goodness. This says that the ruler's conduct of government lies in getting the [right] men, and the rule for choosing men also lies in [the ruler] cultivating himself. If he is able to cultivate himself, then there is the ruler and there are ministers, and government inevitably flourishes.

[5] . . . *Ren* 人 indicates the man himself (i.e. the ruler) and speaks of him. All these principles of life will naturally lead to commiseration and compassion, and the sense of their deep embodiment can be seen. "Being appropriate" is to distinguish the principles of affairs, each having that which is appropriate. *Li* 禮, then, is nothing more than the two things mentioned in this chapter.

[6] Zheng [Xuan] says: "This sentence appears below; it is repeated here by mistake."

[7] Conducting government lies in men, and choosing men is by the (ruler) himself, therefore he cannot do otherwise than cultivate himself. He cultivates himself through the Way, and he cultivates the Way through *ren* 仁. Therefore, in intending to cultivate himself, he cannot do otherwise than serve his family members. If he wishes to complete the *ren* 仁 of loving his family members, it must be through the *yi* 義 of honouring worthiness; therefore, it is also right to know men. The hierarchy of love for family members and the gradations of honouring worthiness are both principles of Heaven. Therefore, it is also right to know Heaven.

[8] . . . The all-pervading Way (*da dao* 達道) is the path which the world, both ancient and modern, collectively follows and is what the *Book of Documents* calls "The Five Relationships" (*wu dian* 五典). This is what Mencius spoke of [when he wrote]: "There should be love between father and son, right action between ruler and subject, differentiation between husband and wife, proper order between old and young, and trust between friends." *Zhi* 知 is the means of knowing this; *ren* 仁 is the means of embodying this; *yong* 勇 is the means of strengthening this. What is called all-pervading virtue is a principle which all under Heaven, both ancient and modern, can equally attain. The one principle is *cheng* 誠, and that is all. Although the all-pervading Way is what people collectively follow, nevertheless, if there are not these three virtues, then there is no means to put it into practice.

達德雖人所同得，然一有不誠，則人欲間之，而德非其德矣。<u>程子</u>曰：「所謂誠者，止是誠實此三者。三者之外，更別無誠。」[29]

[9]｛強，上聲。｝知之者之所知，行之者之所行，謂達道也。以其分而言：則所以知者知也，所以行者仁也，所以至於知之成功而一者勇也。以其等而言：則生知安行者知也，學知利行者仁也，困知勉行者勇也。蓋人性雖無不善，而氣稟有不同者，故聞道有蚤莫，行道有難易，然能自強不息，則其至一也。<u>呂氏</u>曰：「所入之塗雖異，而所至之域則同，此所以為中庸。若乃企生知安行之資為不可幾及，輕困知勉行謂不能有成，此道之所以不明不行也。」[30]

ZY20.2: 子曰：「好學近乎知，力行近乎仁，知恥近乎勇。[10]知斯三者，則知所以脩身；知所以脩身，則知所以治人；知所以治人，則知所以治天下國家矣。」[11]凡為天下國家有九經，曰：脩身也，尊賢也，親親也，敬大臣也，體群臣也，子庶民也，來百工也，柔遠人也，懷諸侯也。[12]脩身則道立，尊賢則不惑，親親則諸父昆弟不怨，敬大臣則不眩，體群臣則士之報禮重，子庶民則百姓勸，來百工則財用足，柔遠人則四方歸之，懷諸侯則天下畏之。[13]

---

29   Cheng Hao 程顥—see the *Er Cheng quanshu*, 1:135. This text has *ze* 則 instead of *suo*
     所 and continues "三者之外更別無誠."
30   Lü Dalin 呂大臨 (1044–1093): a brief biography is given in the *Song shi* 340, 31:10848.
     See also the *Song Yuan xue'an* 30. For the quotation, see the *Zhongyong jie* 中庸解 in the
     Er Cheng quanshu, 2:1818. Zhu Xi considered Lü Dalin to be the author of this work
     included in the *Yichuan jingshuo* 伊川經說—see SB, 50.

Although all-pervading virtue is what people can equally attain, nevertheless, if there is no *cheng* 誠, the virtue will no longer be the true virtue as it will be obstructed by human desires. Master Cheng said: "That which is called *cheng* 誠 is only truly this *cheng* 誠 in these three things. Beyond these three things there is no other *cheng* 誠."

[9] ... What the one knowing it knows, and what the one practising it practises is called the all-pervading Way. To speak of its divisions, then the means by which it is known is *zhi* 知, the means by which it is practised is *ren* 仁, and the means by which it comes to the successful realisation of knowledge and is one, is *yong* 勇. To speak of its grades, then being born with knowledge and practising with a natural ease is *zhi* 知; to know through study and to practise for benefit is *ren* 仁; to know through difficulties and to practise with diligent effort is *yong* 勇. Thus, although human nature is undoubtedly good, there are still differences in natural endowment. Therefore, in terms of hearing of the Way, there is early and late; in terms of practising the Way, there is difficult and easy. Nevertheless, if one can be naturally strong without ceasing, then the same result is achieved. Lü Shi said: "The ways of entering the path are different, and yet the place that is reached is the same, and this is what is deemed central and constant (undeviating and unchanging). With regard to being anxious about a disposition of innate knowledge and ease of action, and deeming it impossible to come close to, and making light of knowledge acquired through difficulty and assiduous application, saying this cannot be achieved, these are the reasons why the Way is not clear and not practised.

ZY20.2: The Master said: "To love learning comes close to *zhi* 知 (wisdom, knowledge); to practise with diligent effort comes close to *ren* 仁; to know shame comes close to *yong* 勇 (courage, bravery). **[10]** To know these three things is, then, to know how to cultivate the self. To know how to cultivate the self is, then, to know how to bring good order to people. To know how to bring good order to people is, then, to know how to bring good order to the world, states and households." **[11]** In general, for the world, states and households, there are nine canons as follows: cultivate the self, honour worthiness, love one's family members, respect great officials, have consideration for the great mass of officials, treat the people like one's children, encourage the hundred artisans, be kind to those from afar, and cherish the feudal lords. **[12]** If there is cultivation of the self, then the Way is established. If worthiness is honoured, then there is no doubt. If there is love for family members, then there is no resentment between uncles and older and younger brothers. If there is respect for great officials, then there is no confusion. If there is consideration for the great mass of officials, then officers will repay the *li* 禮 many times over. If people are treated like one's children, then the ordinary people will be urged on. If there is encouragement for the hundred artisans, then the materials for use will be sufficient. If there is kindness towards those from afar, then the four regions will return to the fold. If the feudal lords are cherished, then the world will be in awe of [the ruler]. **[13]**

Comment: This corresponds to ZY15 in the *Li ji* arrangement. There are only minor differences in the interpretations of the two versions. First, Zhu Xi regards the opening *zi yue* 子曰 as superfluous, taking this to continue straight on from ZY20.1 with the three "knowings" being *zhi* 知 and the three "actings" being *ren* 仁. It is noted in the comment to the *Li ji* version that the *Kongzi jiayu* text has a reply from Duke Ai prior to the statement in this section, hence the repetition of 子曰. Second, whilst Zheng Xuan (and Kong Yingda) understand *ti* 體 in the sense of *jiena* 接納 (to accept, receive), Zhu Xi explains this as "someone putting himself in another person's place and examining his mind-heart." Third, Zhu Xi takes *yuan ren* 遠人 as guests or travelers, whereas the *Li ji* commentators take them to be feudal lords of foreign states specifically. As can be seen, these variations do not alter the essential meaning of the section. Zhu Xi also includes two substantial quotes from Lü Dalin in his notes.

注 ZY20.2 (朱熹)

[10]「子曰」二字衍文。{好近乎知之知，並去聲。}此言未及乎達德而求以入德之事。通上文三知為知，三行為仁，則此三近者，勇之次也。呂氏曰：「愚者自是而不求，自私者殉人欲而忘反，懦者甘為人下而不辭。故好學非知，然足以破愚；力行非仁，然足以忘私；知恥非勇，然足以起懦。」[31]

[11] 斯三者，指三近而言。人者，對己之稱。天下國家，則盡乎人矣。言此以結上文脩身之意，起下文九經之端也。

[12] 經，常也。體，謂設以身處其地而察其心也。子，如父母之愛其子也。柔遠人，所謂無忘賓旅者也。此列九經之目也。呂氏曰：「天下國家之本在身，故脩身為九經之本。然必親師取友，然後脩身之道進，故尊賢次之。道之所進，莫先其家，故親親次之。由家以及朝廷，故敬大臣、體群臣次之。由朝廷以及其國，故子庶民、來百工次之。由其國以及天下，故柔遠人、懷諸侯次之。此九經之序也。」視群臣猶吾四體，視百姓猶吾子，此視臣視民之別也。

[13] 此言九經之效也。道立，謂道成於己而可為民表，所謂皇建其有極是也。不惑，謂不疑於理。不眩，謂不迷於事。敬大臣則信任專，而小臣不得以間之，故臨事而不眩也。來百工則通功易事，農末相資，故財用足。柔遠人，則天下之旅皆悅而願出於其塗，故四方歸。懷諸侯，則德之所施者博，而威之所制者廣矣，故曰天下畏之。

---

[31]   Lü Dalin: The reference is to the *Zhongyong jie*, 1818–19—see note 30 above.

Notes ZY20.2 (Zhu Xi)

[10] The two characters *zi yue* 子曰 are superfluous. . . . This [section] says he has not yet reached thoroughgoing virtue and seeks a way of gaining entry to the matter of virtue. This connects with the previous text, the three "knowings" being *zhi* 知 and the three "actings" being *ren* 仁 so then, of the three instances of "coming close to," *yong* 勇 is the next. Lü Shi (Lü Dalin) says: "One who is foolish is self-satisfied and does not seek; one who is selfish is obsessed with human desires and forgets to reflect; one who is weak voluntarily places himself in an inferior position and does not resign. Therefore, to love to learn is not *zhi* 知 (wisdom, knowledge); nevertheless, it is enough to get rid of foolishness. To practise with diligent effort is not *ren* 仁; nevertheless, it is enough to forget selfishness. To know shame is not *yong* 勇 (courage, bravery); nevertheless, it is enough to get rid of weakness."

[11] "These three things" indicate the instances of "coming close to" and speak of them. "Others" (*ren* 人) stands in opposition to the self (*ji* 己); "The world, states and households" is, then, all others. These things are spoken of in order to continue the idea of cultivating the self from the previous text and to introduce the beginning of the nine canons that follow.

[12] *Jing* 經 is equivalent to *chang* 常 (rule, principle). *Ti* 體 refers to someone putting himself in another person's place and examining his mind-heart. *Zi* 子 is like parents' love for their children. *Rou yuan ren* 柔遠人 refers to not neglecting a guest or traveller. This sets out the list of the nine canons. Lü Shi says: "The basis of the world, states and households lies in the self. Therefore, the cultivation of the self may be taken as the basis of the nine canons. Certainly, one must love one's teacher and choose one's friends, and afterwards approach the Way of cultivating the self. Thus, honouring worthiness comes after this. How the Way progresses is to start from one's family, therefore devotion to family members comes next. From the family it extends to the court, therefore respecting high ministers and accepting the great mass of officials comes next. From the court, it extends to one's state, therefore loving the people like one's children and encouraging the hundred artisans comes next. From one's state it extends to the whole world, therefore being kind to those from afar and cherishing the feudal lords comes next. This is the sequence of the nine canons." [There is] regarding the great mass of officials as one's own four limbs [and there is] regarding the ordinary people as one's own children. This is the difference in how officials and the ordinary people are regarded.

[13] This speaks of the efficacy of the nine canons. *Dao li* 道立 (the Way is established) refers to the Way being completed in oneself and so being able to act as a model for the people; this is how the sovereign is said to establish himself as being complete. *Bu huo* 不惑 refers to there being no doubt regarding principle. *Bu xuan* 不眩 refers to there being no confusion in affairs. If there is respect for great ministers, then there is absolute confidence, and minor officials are not able to come between them. Therefore, in a crisis, there is no confusion. If there is encouragement for the hundred artisans, then there is a satisfactory interplay between labour and production, farming and other occupations mutually aid each other, and so materials are sufficient for use. If there is kindness towards those from afar, then the world's travellers are all happy and wish to go forth on his roads, so the four regions return to the fold. If there is cherishing of the feudal lords, then virtue will spread widely, and his power will extend widely, therefore it is said that the world is in awe of him.

ZY20.3: 齊明盛服，非禮不動，所以脩身也；去讒遠色，賤貨而貴德，所以勸賢也；尊其位，重其祿，同其好惡，所以勸親親也；官盛任使，所以勸大臣也；忠信重祿，所以勸士也；時使薄斂，所以勸百姓也；日省月試，既稟稱事，所以勸百工也；送往迎來，嘉善而矜不能，所以柔遠人也；繼絕世，舉廢國，治亂持危，朝聘以時，厚往而薄來，所以懷諸侯也。[14]

Comment: This corresponds to ZY16 in the *Li ji* arrangement. It is, as Zhu Xi points out, further elaboration on how to follow the "nine canons." Apart from a minor variation in the reading of the opening phrase, there is no difference in interpretation from the *Li ji* commentators. Zhu Xi's note adds a little detail to several of the points with reference to the *Zhou li* and the *Li ji*.

注 ZY20.3 (朱熹)

[14] {齊，側皆反。去，上聲。遠、好、惡、斂，並去聲。既，許氣反。稟，彼錦、力錦二反。稱，去聲。朝，音潮。}此言九經之事也。官盛任使，謂官屬眾盛，足任使令也，蓋大臣不當親細事，故所以優之者如此。忠信重祿，謂待之誠而養之厚，蓋以身體之，而知其所賴乎上者如此也。既，讀曰餼。餼稟，稍食也。稱事，如《周禮‧稟人職》，曰「考其弓弩，以上下其食」[32] 是也。往則為之授節以送之，來則豐其委積以迎之。朝，謂諸侯見於天子。聘，謂諸侯使大夫來獻。〈王制〉「比年一小聘，三年一大聘，五年一朝」。[33] 厚往薄來，謂燕賜厚而納貢薄。

---

[32] See the *Zhou li*, "Gaoren zhi," SSJZS, 3:487–88.
[33] See the *Li ji*, "Wang zhi," SSJZS, 5:225.

ZY20.3: Fasting, purification and donning fine garments, as well as not making movements contrary to *li* 禮 are ways to cultivate the self. Keeping away from flatterers and distancing oneself from beauties, despising worldly goods and valuing virtue are ways to encourage worthiness. Honouring their status, making their salary substantial and sharing their likes and dislikes are ways to persuade family members to be devoted to each other. Providing them with numerous officers and letting them discharge their responsibilities are ways to encourage great ministers. Loyalty, trust, and a substantial salary are ways to encourage officers. Using them at appropriate times and making tax levies light are ways to encourage the ordinary people. Daily examinations and monthly trials, and making the grain allowance commensurate with work done are ways to encourage the hundred artisans. To give those departing a send-off and those arriving a welcome, and to praise the good and be compassionate towards the incompetent are ways to be kind to those from afar. To restore continuity to lineages that have been broken and to raise states that have fallen, to bring order where there is disorder and give support where there is danger, to have proper times for court invitations, and to be generous when sending them away but requiring little when they come are ways to cherish the feudal lords. **[14]**

Notes ZY20.3 (Zhu Xi)

[14] . . . This speaks of the matter of the "nine canons." *Providing them with numerous officers and letting them discharge their responsibilities* refers to the various officials being in abundance, sufficient to allow them to carry out their responsibilities. Since it is not appropriate for great ministers to devote themselves to minor matters, so [the various officials] are made abundant like this. *Loyalty, trust, and a substantial salary* refers to treating them with *cheng* 誠 and looking after them generously through oneself giving substance to these things and knowing that what is relied upon in superiors is like this. *Ji* 既 is read as *xi* 餼 (to give a supply of grain). *Xi bing* 餼稟 is equivalent to grain rations. *Cheng shi* 稱事 is as in the *Zhou li*, "Gaoren zhi," which says: "Examine his cross-bows [to determine whether] to increase or decrease his rations." If they are departing, then make it so they are sent off with credentials, and if they are arriving, then enrich them with stores as a welcome. *Chao* 朝 refers to feudal lords being seen by the Son of Heaven. *Pin* 聘 refers to feudal lords sending great officers to make a presentation. [For example] in the [*Li ji*,] "Wang zhi," [there is]: "Every year a minor mission; every three years a major mission, and every five years a mission in person." *To be generous when sending them away but requiring little when they come* refers to the feasts given being substantial and the tribute paid being slight.

ZY20.4: 凡為天下國家有九經，所以行之者一也。[15]凡事豫則立，不豫則廢。言前定則不跲，事前定則不困，行前定則不疚，道前定則不窮。[16]

Comment: This corresponds to ZY17 of the *Li ji* arrangement. The only notable point of difference in the two interpretations (which does not come out in the translation itself) is what "the one way" of putting the "nine canons" into practice is. For Zhu Xi, it is *cheng* 誠, which in subsequent sections is the focus of discussion and analysis. Zhu Xi specifically accepts two of the three glosses offered by the *Li ji* commentators (for *jia* 跲 and *jiu* 疚), but is silent on *kun* 困.

注 ZY20.4 (朱熹)

[15] 一者，誠也。一有不誠，則是九者皆為虛文矣，此九經之實也。
[16] {跲，其劫反。行，去聲。}凡事，指達道達德九經之屬。豫，素定也。跲，躓也。疚，病也。此承上文，言凡事皆欲先立乎誠，如下文所推是也。

ZY20.5:在下位不獲乎上，民不可得而治矣；獲乎上有道：不信乎朋友，不獲乎上矣；信乎朋友有道：不順乎親，不信乎朋友矣；順乎親有道：反諸身不誠，不順乎親矣；誠身有道：不明乎善，不誠乎身矣。[17]誠者，天之道也；誠之者，人之道也。誠者不勉而中，不思而得，從容中道，聖人也。誠之者，擇善而固執之者也。[18]

Comment: This corresponds to sections ZY18 & 19 in the *Li ji* arrangement and to the complete section IVA.12(6) in the *Mencius*. As noted in the comment to the former, there are some issues regarding interpretation of characters which pertain to the translation, but Zhu Xi does not address these. His notes are entirely about content. This is the section that introduces the term *cheng* 誠, variously translated as "sincerity," "integrity," "creativity," "truthfulness," etc, which Zhu Xi himself defines as "being true and genuine without falseness" (*zhen shi wu wang* 真實無妄). Essentially, there are two ways of attaining a state of *cheng* 誠. The first is to "possess" *cheng* 誠 (to be *cheng* 誠) innately. This requires no effort on the part of the person concerned and is characteristic of the sage—this is the Way of Heaven. The second is to "acquire" *cheng* 誠 (to become *cheng* 誠) by diligent effort through study and self-cultivation, characterised elsewhere as the course of the worthy man—this is the Way of mankind.

ZY20.4: All in all, for the world, states and households, there are nine canons, [but] there is just the one way of putting them into practice. [15] In all matters, if there is prior preparation, there is success; if there is no prior preparation, there is failure. If words are determined beforehand, then there is no stumbling. If affairs are determined beforehand, then there are no difficulties. If actions are determined beforehand, then there are no faults. If the Way is determined beforehand, then there is no limit. [16]

Notes ZY20.4 (Zhu Xi)

[15] The one way is *cheng* 誠. If the one way is not *cheng* 誠, then the nine [canons] are all just empty words—this is the reality of the nine canons.

[16] . . . "In all matters" indicates the all-pervading Way, all-pervading virtue and the nine canons collectively. *Yu* 豫 is to establish beforehand. *Jia* 跲 is equivalent to *zhi* 躓 (to stumble). *Jiu* 疚 is equivalent to *bing* 病 (fault, defect). This continues the previous text and says that all matters first require establishment of *cheng* 誠, as is elaborated in the following text.

ZY20.5: When those in inferior positions do not gain the confidence of superiors, the people cannot be won over and brought to good order. To gain the confidence of superiors, there is the Way. One who is not trusted by friends will not gain the confidence of superiors. To be trusted by friends, there is the Way. One who is not compliant towards family members will not be trusted by friends. To be compliant towards family members, there is the Way. If a man examines himself and finds he is not *cheng* 誠, he will not be compliant towards family members. To become *cheng* 誠 in oneself, there is the Way. One who is not clear about goodness will not become *cheng* 誠 in himself. [17] Being *cheng* 誠 is the Way of Heaven. Becoming *cheng* 誠 is the Way of mankind. Being *cheng* 誠 is to be in the centre (undeviating) without effort, to attain without thinking, to follow the Way with a natural ease, and is to be a sage. Becoming *cheng* 誠 is to choose what is good and hold on to it. [18]

注 ZY20.5 (朱熹)

[17] 此又以在下位者,推言素定之意。反諸身不誠,謂反求諸身而所存所發,未能真實而無妄也。不明乎善,謂未能察於人心天命之本然,而真知至善之所在也。

[18] {中,並去聲。從,七容反。}此承上文誠身而言。誠者,真實無妄之謂,天理之本然也。誠之者,未能真實無妄,而欲其真實無妄之謂,人事之當然也。聖人之德,渾然天理,真實無妄,不待思勉而從容中道,則亦天之道也。未至於聖,則不能無人欲之私,而其為德不能皆實。故未能不思而得,則必擇善,然後可以明善;未能不勉而中,則必固執,然後可以誠身,此則所謂人之道也。不思而得,生知也。不勉而中,安行也。擇善,學知以下之事。固執,利行以下之事也。

ZY20.6: 博學之,審問之,慎思之,明辨之,篤行之。[19]有弗學,學之弗能,弗措也;有弗問,問之弗知,弗措也;有弗思,思之弗得,弗措也;有弗辨,辨之弗明,弗措也;有弗行,行之弗篤,弗措也;人一能之己百之,人十能之己千之。[20]果能此道矣,雖愚必明,雖柔必強。[21]

Notes ZY20.5 (Zhu Xi)

[17] This also, from the perspective of someone in a lowly position, elaborates on and speaks of the meaning of "determining beforehand." Reflecting back on oneself as not *cheng* 誠 refers to one turning and seeking in oneself what is preserved and what is cast off, and what cannot be true and genuine and not false. Not being enlightened by goodness refers to being unable to look into the human heart, the natural basis of Heaven's decree, and truly know where perfect goodness exists.

[18] . . . This continues the previous section in speaking about making the self *cheng* 誠. "Being *cheng* 誠" is a term signifying being true and genuine without falseness; the foundation of Heavenly principle is such. "Becoming *cheng* 誠" refers to someone who is not yet true and genuine without falseness, but wishes to be true and genuine without falseness, which is appropriate for human affairs. The virtue of the sage is entirely in accord with Heavenly principle, is true and genuine without falseness, does not depend on thought and exertion, and is naturally and easily centred in the Way. Then it is also the Way of Heaven. If one has not yet reached sagehood, then one cannot be without the selfishness of human desires, and one's being virtuous cannot be altogether genuine. Therefore, if one is not yet able to "attain without thinking," then one must choose goodness and subsequently one can be enlightened and good. If one is not yet able to be in the centre without effort, then one must hold fast and subsequently one can make oneself *cheng* 誠. This, then, is what is called the Way of mankind. To attain without thinking equates with innate knowledge. To be in the centre without effort equates with ease in actions. "Choosing goodness" is to learn and know through lesser matters. "Holding fast" is to benefit and practise through lesser matters.

ZY20.6: Extensively study, judiciously enquire, carefully think, be clear about distinctions, and sincerely practise. **[19]** If there is that which has not been studied, or has been studied but not to mastery, do not stop. If there is that which has not been enquired into, or has been enquired into but not to the point of understanding, do not stop. If there is that which has not been thought about, or has been thought about but not to the point of full apprehension, do not stop. If there are distinctions that have not been made, or have been made but not clearly, do not stop. If there is that which has not been put into practice, or has been put into practice but not sincerely, do not stop. Even if others can do it with one attempt, you must make a hundred attempts. Even if others can do it with ten attempts, you must make a thousand attempts. **[20]** If someone is resolutely able to follow this Way, even if he is dull, he will inevitably become bright; even if he is weak, he will inevitably become strong. **[21]**

右第二十章。(此引<u>孔子</u>之言，以繼大<u>舜</u>、<u>文</u>、<u>武</u>、<u>周公</u>之緒，明其所傳之一致，舉而措之，亦猶是耳。蓋包費隱、兼小大，以終十二章之意。章內語誠始詳，而所謂誠者，實此篇之樞紐也。又按：《孔子家語》，亦載此章，而其文尤詳。「成功一也」之下，有「公曰：子之言美矣！至矣！寡人實固，不足以成之也」。故其下復以「子曰」起答辭。今無此問辭，而猶有「子曰」二字；蓋<u>子思</u>刪其繁文以附于篇，而所刪有不盡者，今當為衍文也。「博學之」以下，《家語》無之，意彼有闕文，抑此或<u>子思</u>所補也歟？)

Comment: This final section of Zhu Xi's chapter 20 corresponds to ZY20 of the *Li ji* arrangement. Although in Zhu Xi's notes no specific points are made about the readings of individual characters, a slightly different translation is given, revolving around the readings of *zhi* 之 and *you* 有. Thus, nothing specific is identified to which *zhi* 之 refers. As Legge states in his note (p. 414): "Rather it seems to me, that the *zhi* 之, according to the idiom pointed out several times in the *Analects*, simply intensifies the meaning of the different verbs, whose regimen it is." Also, as note 20 indicates, *you* 有 does not indicate "something/anything." The noble man either does not do each of the five things, or he does them to completion. The quotation from Lü Dalin states an important basic position for Zhu Xi—human nature is uniformly good, but people differ in their dispositions. It is the dispositions that can be changed, particularly through the five activities listed.

注 ZY20.6 (朱熹)

[19] 此誠之之目也。學、問、思、辨，所以擇善而為知，學而知也。篤行，所以固執而為仁，利而行也。<u>程子</u>曰：「五者廢其一，非學也。」[34]

[20] 君子之學，不為則已，為則必要其成，故常百倍其功。此困而知，勉而行者也，勇之事也。

[21] 明者擇善之功，強者固執之效。<u>呂氏</u>曰：「君子所以學者，為能變化氣質而已。德勝氣質，則愚者可進於明，柔者可進於強。不能勝之，則雖有志於學，亦愚不能明，柔不能立而已矣。蓋均善而無惡者，性也，人所同也。昏明強弱之稟不齊者，才也，人所異也。誠之者所以反其同而變其異也。夫以不美之質，求變而美，非百倍其功，不足以致之。今以鹵莽滅裂之學，或作或輟，以變其不美之質，及不能變，則曰天質不美，非學所能變。是果於自棄，其為不仁甚矣！」[35]

---

34   We have not been able to locate the Cheng Yi 程頤 reference.
35   Lü Dalin—see note 30 above. This long quotation does not appear in the *Zhongyong jie* as the others by Lü Dalin do. We have been unable to locate its source.

To the right (above) is the twentieth chapter. (This quotes the words of Confucius to continue the thread of the great Shun, Wen, Wu, and the Duke of Zhou, to make it clear that what is transmitted is consistent, and to bring it forward and arrange it like this. Now the far-reaching and the subtle are embraced, and the small and the large are linked through the meaning of the last twelve chapters. Within this chapter, the word *cheng* 誠 is first examined. What is termed *cheng* 誠 is truly the pivotal point of this work. The *Kongzi jiayu* also records this chapter, but in a more detailed form. Following "when it comes to their success, it is one and the same thing," there is "the Duke said: 'The Master's words are excellent! They are perfect! But I am a poor stubborn fellow and am not up to achieving it.'" That is why it is followed by a reply starting with "the Master said." But here (in this chapter) the implied question is absent, although there are still the two characters *zi yue* 子曰 (the Master said). Presumably Zisi cut out what was superfluously added to the work, but the deletion here is incomplete. This must be a case of redundancy (due to miscopying) and now ought to be considered a corruption. What follows "博學之" is not in the *Jiayu*. I suspect it is either omitted there, or is it possible that Zisi added this part here?)

Notes ZY20.6 (Zhu Xi)

[19] These are the key points of becoming *cheng* 誠. Studying, enquiring, thinking, and distinguishing are the ways of choosing goodness and being knowledgeable. [This is] to study and know. To sincerely practise is how to hold fast and be *ren* 仁, to be benefitted and practise. Master Cheng said: "All five [are indispensable]. If you do away with one, it is not *xue* 學 (studying)."
[20] In the study of the noble man, he either does not do it at all, or he does it and must inevitably seek its completion. Therefore, he will constantly increase his effort a hundredfold. These things, encountering difficulty and knowing, being diligent and practising, are the actions of *yong* 勇.
[21] Enlightenment is the result of choosing the good. Strength is the outcome of resolutely persevering. Lü Shi said: "The reason why the noble man studies is to be able to change [his] disposition (*qizhi* 氣質) and that is all. If virtue overcomes disposition, then even a fool can progress to enlightenment, even a weakling can progress to strength. If it cannot overcome disposition, then although there is the will to study, not only will a fool be unable to gain enlightenment, but also a weakling cannot become strong. What is uniformly good and without evil is nature, and people are the same in this respect. The unequal endowment of dullness and clarity, strength and weakness, is ability, and this is where people differ. Becoming *cheng* 誠 is how this sameness is reflected and how this difference is changed. If you take a disposition that is not good and seek to change it to one that is good, unless you make a hundredfold effort, it is not enough to achieve it. Now to be careless and haphazard in one's studies, sometimes working and sometimes stopping, in trying to change a disposition that is not good, and to come to a point where it cannot be changed, and then say Heavenly disposition not being good is not something which study is able to change, is to give oneself up as hopeless. This is to be non-*ren* 仁 in the extreme."

ZY21: 自誠明，謂之性；自明誠，謂之教。誠則明矣，明則誠矣。**[1]**

右第二十一章。子思承上章夫子天道、人道之意而立言也。自此以下十二章，皆子思之言，以反覆推明此章之意。

注 ZY21 (朱熹)

[1] 自，由也。德無不實而明無不照者，聖人之德。所性而有者也，天道也。先明乎善，而後能實其善者，賢人之學。由教而入者也，人道也。誠則無不明矣，明則可以至於誠矣。

ZY22: 唯天下至誠，為能盡其性；能盡其性，則能盡人之性；能盡人之性，則能盡物之性；能盡物之性，則可以贊天地之化育；可以贊天地之化育，則可以與天地參矣。**[1]**

右第二十二章。(言天道也。)

Comment: These two chapters, which correspond to ZY21 & ZY22 of the *Li ji* arrangement, are identified by Zhu Xi as beginning the final part of the work, which he describes as Zisi's elaboration and clarification of Confucius' meaning on the Ways of Heaven and mankind respectively. In each case the attainment of *cheng* 誠 is the realisation of perfection in the Way. *Cheng* 誠 itself, as argued in the introductory section on terminology, has no satisfactory English equivalent. As Legge says: " . . . we have no single term in English which can be considered as the complete equivalent of this character." The sage follows the Way of Heaven, is naturally endowed with *cheng* 誠, and is enlightened. Among others, those who are worthy achieve enlightenment through diligent study and so become *cheng* 誠.

ZY21: *Ming* 明 (enlightenment, clarity, understanding) from *cheng* 誠 (purity, genuineness, sincerity) is referred to as nature. *Cheng* 誠 from *ming* 明 is referred to as teaching. If there is *cheng* 誠, there is *ming* 明. If there is *ming* 明, there is *cheng* 誠. [1]

To the right (above) is the twenty-first chapter. Zisi continues the Master's meaning and establishes [these] words on the Way of Heaven and the Way of mankind from the previous chapter. The twelve chapters following this are all Zisi's words, reflecting on, reiterating, enlarging on, and clarifying the meaning of this chapter.

Notes ZY21 (Zhu Xi)

[1] *Zi* 自 is equivalent to *you* 由 (from). Virtue that is undoubtedly genuine and enlightenment that is undoubtedly illuminating constitute the virtue of the sage. What is nature and is this, is the Way of Heaven. If first there is enlightenment through goodness, and afterwards the ability to realise this goodness; this is the learning of the worthy man. To gain entry through teaching is the Way of mankind. If there is *cheng* 誠, then undoubtedly there is enlightenment; if there is enlightenment, then one can advance to *cheng* 誠.

ZY22: In the world only someone of perfect *cheng* 誠 is considered able to complete his nature. Someone who is able to complete his nature is then able to complete the natures of others. Someone who is able to complete the natures of others is then able to complete the natures of things. Someone who is able to complete the natures of things can then assist the transforming and nourishing [functions] of Heaven and Earth. Someone who can assist the transforming and nourishing [functions] of Heaven and Earth can then join with Heaven and Earth as a triad. [1]

To the right (above) is the twenty-second chapter. (This speaks of the Way of Heaven.)

注 ZY22 (朱熹)

[1] 天下至誠，謂聖人之德之實，天下莫能加也。盡其性者德無不實，故無人欲之私，而天命之在我者，察之由之，巨細精粗，無毫髮之不盡也。人物之性，亦我之性，但以所賦形氣不同而有異耳。能盡之者，謂知之無不明而處之無不當也。贊，猶助也。與天地參，謂與天地並立為三也。此自誠而明者之事也。

ZY23: 其次致曲，曲能有誠，誠則形，形則著，著則明，明則動，動則變，變則化，唯天下至誠為能化。**[1]**

右第二十三章。(言人道也。)

注 ZY23 (朱熹)

[1] 其次，通大賢以下凡誠有未至者而言也。致，推致也。曲，一偏也。形者，積中而發外。著，則又加顯矣。明，則又有光輝發越之盛也。動者，誠能動物。變者，物從而變。化，則有不知其所以然者。蓋人之性無不同，而氣則有異，故惟聖人能舉其性之全體而盡之。其次則必自其善端發見之偏，而悉推致之，以各造其極也。曲無不致，則德無不實，而形、著、動、變之功自不能已。積而至於能化，則其至誠之妙，亦不異於聖人矣。

Notes ZY22 (Zhu Xi)

[1] In the world, perfect *cheng* 誠 is referred to as the genuineness of the sage's virtue; nothing in the world can add to [it]. In the case of someone who is able to complete his nature, his virtue is undoubtedly genuine, therefore he is without the selfishness of human desire. When the decree of Heaven exists in myself, I observe it and follow it, both great and small, both fine and coarse, and there is not one iota of it that is not complete. The natures of other people and things are also my nature, but the form and spirit with which they are bestowed is not the same; there are differences. In the case of someone who is able to complete it, he is spoken of as knowing with unquestioned enlightenment and resting in unquestioned correctness. *Zan* 贊 is like *zhu* 助 (to help, assist). *Yu tian di can* 與天地參 refers to joining Heaven and Earth to establish a triad. This is the matter of enlightenment from *cheng* 誠.

ZY23: The next level pertains to the partial. If *cheng* 誠 can exist partially, then *cheng* 誠 has a form; if it has a form, then it is manifest; if it is manifest, then it is clearly apparent; if it is clearly apparent, then it acts; if it acts, then it effects change; if it effects change, then it transforms. In the world, there is only perfect *cheng* 誠 that can transform. [1]

To the right (above) is the twenty-third chapter. (This speaks of the Way of mankind.)

Notes ZY23 (Zhu Xi)

[1] *Qi ci* 其次 refers to all those below the level of great worthiness; those whose *cheng* 誠 has not yet reached perfection. *Zhi* 致 is equivalent to *tui zhi* 推致 (to extend to, reach). *Qu* 曲 is equivalent to *yi pian* 一偏 (partial). *Xing* 形 is what accumulates within and is manifest without. *Zhu* 著, then, is also to be increasingly obvious. *Ming* 明, then, is also the abundance of glorious display. *Dong* 動 means *cheng* 誠 can move things. *Bian* 變 means things follow and change. *Hua* 化 speaks of there being no knowledge of how this is so. Because the nature of people is always the same but the *qi* 氣 (spirit) is different, only the sage can raise his nature's whole substance and complete it. The next level must take its origin from this good, the part which comes forth and is seen, and expand and extend it in order to create its perfection in each case. If *Qu* 曲 (the partial) does not do otherwise than extend, then virtue is not otherwise than genuine, and the functions of form, manifestation, movement, and change are not able to end of themselves. If it accumulates and reaches the point of being able to transform, then this wondrous subtlety of perfect *cheng* 誠 is also no different from a sage.

ZY24: 至誠之道，可以前知。國家將興，必有禎祥；國家將亡，必有妖孽；見乎蓍龜，動乎四體。禍福將至：善，必先知之；不善，必先知之。故至誠如神。**[1]**

右第二十四章。(言天道也。)

Comment: Both ZY23 and ZY24 above correspond to the similarly numbered sections in the *Li ji* arrangement. In the first, Zhu Xi takes a somewhat different position from the *Li ji* commentators on the two contentious terms, *qi ci* 其次 and *qu* 曲. *Qi ci* 其次, according to Zhu Xi, indicates the next level to the sage, that is, people who have not yet achieved perfect *cheng* 誠, people whose *cheng* 誠 is partial (*qu* 曲). Nonetheless, partial *cheng* 誠 can be as effective as the perfect *cheng* 誠 of the sage, if it accumulates sufficiently. In ZY24 the only minor difference is that Zhu Xi takes the four limbs to be those of men rather than those of tortoises.

注 ZY24 (朱熹)

[1] {見，音現。}禎祥者，福之兆。妖孽者，禍之萌。蓍，所以筮。龜，所以卜。四體，謂動作威儀之間，如執玉高卑，其容俯仰之類。凡此皆理之先見者也。然惟誠之至極，而無一毫私偽留於心目之間者，乃能有以察其幾焉。神，謂鬼神。

ZY25: 誠者自成也，而道自道也。**[1]**誠者物之終始，不誠無物。是故君子誠之為貴。**[2]**誠者非自成己而已也，所以成物也。成己，仁也；成物，知也。性之德也，合外內之道也，故時措之宜也。**[3]**

右第二十五章。(言人道也。)

Comment: Zhu Xi makes this section, which corresponds to the opening part of section ZY25 in the *Li ji* arrangement, a separate section and has the main part of the *Li ji* ZY25 as his ZY26. The section as above is a further elaboration of the Way of mankind. The distinction he makes between *cheng* 誠 and *dao* 道 is that the former is what perfects (completes) the mind-heart within, whilst the latter is the outward and practical manifestation of this perfected mind-heart. The dichotomy is pursued in the distinction between *ren* 仁 and *zhi* 知; that is, what exists within the substance of the self and what is manifest in the self-in-action. But a warning note is sounded to the effect that this does not simply correspond to internal and external.

ZY24: The Way of perfect *cheng* 誠 carries the possibility of prior knowledge. When a state or house is about to flourish, there are inevitably omens of good fortune. When a state or house is about to perish, there are invariably omens of misfortune. These are manifest in the milfoil and tortoise and affect the movements of the four limbs. When misfortune or good fortune is about to come, the good will certainly be known beforehand as will the bad. Thus perfect *cheng* 誠 is like a spirit. **[1]**

To the right (above) is the twenty-fourth chapter. (This speaks of the Way of Heaven.)

Notes ZY24 (Zhu Xi)

[1] . . . *Zhen xiang* 禎祥 are omens of good fortune. *Yao nie* 妖孽 are the first signs of misfortune. *Shi* 蓍 (the milfoil) is a means of divining by plant stalks. *Gui* 龜 (the tortoise) is a means of divining. "The four limbs" refers to the dignity of movements, like grasping the jade high or low, and the countenance looking up or down, and so on. In general, these are all the first manifestations of principle. Nevertheless, only if *cheng* 誠 reaches its highest point, and there is not one speck of selfishness or deceit left between mind and eye, is one able to see into its subtlety. *Shen* 神 refers to *gui shen* 鬼神 (ghosts and spirits).

ZY25: *Cheng* 誠 completes the self and the Way directs the self. **[1]** Being *cheng* 誠 is the end and beginning of things; without *cheng* 誠 there would be no things. For this reason the noble man regards *cheng* 誠 as prized. **[2]** But being *cheng* 誠 is not just the self completing the self and nothing more—it is the way of completing things. Completing the self is *ren* 仁. Completing things is *zhi* 知 (wisdom, knowledge). These are virtues of nature and combine the external and internal [components] of the Way. Therefore, whenever you put them to use it is fitting. **[3]**

To the right (above) is the twenty-fifth chapter. (This speaks of the Way of mankind.)

注 ZY25 (朱熹)

[1]{道也之道，音導。}言誠者物之所以自成，而道者人之所當自行也。誠以心言，本也；道以理言，用也。

[2]天下之物，皆實理之所為，故必得是理，然後有是物。所得之理既盡，則是物亦盡而無有矣。故人之心一有不實，則雖有所為亦如無有，而君子必以誠為貴也。蓋人之心能無不實，乃為有以自成，而道之在我者亦無不行矣。

[3]{知，去聲。}誠雖所以成己，然既有以自成，則自然及物，而道亦行於彼矣。仁者體之存，知者用之發，是皆吾性之固有，而無內外之殊。既得於己，則見於事者，以時措之，而皆得其宜也。

ZY26: 故至誠無息。[1]不息則久，久則徵。[2]徵則悠遠，悠遠則博厚，博厚則高明。[3]博厚，所以載物也；高明，所以覆物也；悠久，所以成物也。[4]博厚配地，高明配天，悠久無疆。[5]如此者，不見而章，不動而變，無為而成。[6]天地之道，可一言而盡也：其為物不貳，則其生物不測。[7]天地之道：博也，厚也，高也，明也，悠也，久也。[8]今夫天，斯昭昭之多，及其無窮也，日月星辰繫焉，萬物覆焉。今夫地，一撮土之多，及其廣厚，載華嶽而不重，振河海而不洩，萬物載焉。今夫山，一卷石之多，

Notes ZY25 (Zhu Xi)

[1] . . . This says that *cheng* 誠 is how things complete themselves and the Way is what people should follow themselves. *Cheng* 誠 is to speak in terms of the mind-heart, and is the foundation. The Way is to speak in terms of principle, and is the application.

[2] The things of the world are all truly what principle creates. Therefore, they inevitably acquire this principle and afterwards they are this thing. If the principle which is acquired is already complete, then this thing is also complete and lacks nothing. Therefore, once a person's mind-heart is not true, then although he acts, it amounts to nothing. That is why the noble man must take *cheng* 誠 to be prized. This is because, if a man's mind-heart cannot be other than true, then it creates the means whereby he completes the self, and the Way that exists for himself also cannot but be practised.

[3] . . . Although *cheng* 誠 is the means of completing the self, nevertheless, since it is the means of self-completing, then it naturally extends to things, and the Way also acts on others. *Ren* 仁 exists in the substance; knowledge is the display of its use; these are both what my nature originally has and are not differentiated into internal and external. Since they are acquired by the self, they are manifest in affairs. When you use them at all times, they both acquire their appropriateness.

ZY26: Therefore, perfect *cheng* 誠 is unceasing. [1] Being unceasing, it is long-lasting. Being long-lasting, it is efficacious. [2] Being efficacious, it is far-reaching. Being far-reaching, it is broad and thick. Being broad and thick, it is high and bright. [3] Being broad and thick is how it contains things. Being high and bright is how it spreads over things. Being far-reaching and long-lasting is how it completes things. [4] In being broad and thick, it matches Earth. In being high and bright, it matches Heaven. In being far-reaching and long-lasting, it is boundless. [5] Being like this, it is not seen, and yet is manifest; it does not move, and yet it effects change; it does not act, and yet it brings about completion. [6] The Ways of Heaven and Earth can be completely encapsulated in a single word. Since the things they create are never duplicated, then their giving rise to things is unfathomable. [7] The Way of Heaven is broad; it is thick; it is high; it is bright; it is far-reaching; and it is long-lasting. [8] Now Heaven is this multiplicity of small points of light, yet such is its limitlessness that the sun, moon, and stars are suspended in it, and the ten thousand things are covered by it. Now Earth is a multiplicity of handfuls of soil, yet such is its breadth and thickness, it supports the holy peaks of Hua and Yue and is not weighed down, it collects the rivers and seas and they do not leak away, and the ten thousand things are contained in it. Now the mountains are a multiplicity of single little stones, yet such is

及其廣大，草木生之，禽獸居之，寶藏興焉。今夫水，一勺之多，及其不測，黿鼉、蛟龍、魚鼈生焉，貨財殖焉。**[9]**《詩》云：「維天之命，於穆不已！」蓋曰天之所以為天也。「於乎不顯！<u>文王</u>之德之純！」蓋曰<u>文王</u>之所以為文也，純亦不已。**[10]**

右第二十六章。(言天道也。)

Comment: Zhu Xi's chapter ZY26 comprises the second part of ZY25 and all of ZY26 in the *Li ji* arrangement. The important distinction is, then, that whilst his ZY25 is about the Way of man insofar as it is *cheng* 誠, so the first part (i.e. down to note [8]) is not an explanation/clarification of the opening statement, but a specific statement about the Way of Heaven, and the one word which can completely describe this Way is, in fact, *cheng* 誠. A further issue is how the second *wen* 文 is to be taken in the concluding quote from the *Odes*—whether in the general sense or as referring to King Wen specifically. In our interpretation the point is that the reason King Wen is King Wen (or *wen* 文) is because his virtue is so pure and everlasting (i.e. the "culture" aspect of *wen* 文). Hence, the emphasis is on man in the Heaven-Earth-man relationship.

注 ZY26 (朱熹)

[1] 既無虛假，自無間斷。

[2] 久，常於中也。徵，驗於外也。

[3] 此皆以其驗於外者言之。<u>鄭氏</u>所謂：「至誠之德，著於四方」者是也。存諸中者既久，則驗於外者益悠遠而無窮矣。悠遠，故其積也廣博而深厚；博厚，故其發也高大而光明。

[4] 悠久，即悠遠，兼內外而言之也。本以悠遠致高厚，而高厚又悠久也。此言聖人與天地同用。

[5] 此言聖人與天地同體。

[6] {見，音現。}見，猶示也。不見而章，以配地而言也。不動而變，以配天而言也。無為而成，以無疆而言也。

[7] 此以下，復以天地明至誠無息之功用。天地之道，可一言而盡，不過曰誠而已。不貳，所以誠也。誠故不息，而生物之多，有莫知其所以然者。

[8] 言天地之道，誠一不貳，故能各極所盛，而有下文生物之功。

their breadth and height that grasses and trees grow on them, birds and beasts dwell in them, and precious things are stored and flourish in them. Now the waters are a multiplicity of single scoops, yet such is their unfathomableness that soft-shelled turtles, alligators, flood dragons, dragons, fish and freshwater turtles all arise in them, and goods and materials flourish in them. **[9]** The *Odes* says: "The decree of Heaven—Ah! How profound and unending!" This tells why Heaven is Heaven. [The *Odes* also says:] "Ah! How brilliant it was, the purity of King Wen's virtue!" This tells why King Wen was *wen* 文 (cultured) and that his purity also was unending. **[10]**

To the right (above) is the twenty-sixth chapter. (This speaks of the Way of Heaven.)

Notes ZY26 (Zhu Xi)

[1] Since there is nothing false, naturally there is no interruption.

[2] *Jiu* 久 is being constant within; *Zheng* 徵 is being efficacious without.

[3] These all speak about how it is efficacious externally. Zheng Shi saying, "The virtue of perfect *cheng* 誠 is manifest in the four directions" is this. The longer it is preserved within, then the more the efficacy in the external is far-reaching and without limit. It is far-reaching, therefore its accumulation is broad and extensive, deep and thick. It is broad and thick, therefore its manifestations are high and great, bright and clear.

[4] Long-lasting then far-reaching joins internal and external and speaks of these. Originally, it is by being far-reaching that it reaches high and thick, yet what is high and thick is also long-lasting. This refers to the sage joining Heaven and Earth in the same functions.

[5] This refers to the sage joining Heaven and Earth as a whole.

[6] ... *Jian* 見 is like *shi* 示 (to display, to be seen). *It is not seen, and yet is manifest* speaks of how it matches Earth. *It does not move, and yet it effects change* speaks of how it matches Heaven. *It does not act, and yet it brings about completion* speaks of how it is without limit.

[7] From this point on, [the text] again takes Heaven and Earth to clarify the beneficial results of perfect *cheng* 誠 being unceasing. *The Ways of Heaven and Earth can be completely encapsulated in a single word* is just to say "*cheng* 誠" and nothing more. *Never duplicated* is what *cheng* 誠 is. *Cheng* 誠, therefore, is unceasing and gives rise to the multiplicity of things, although there is no knowledge of how this is so.

[8] This speaks of the Way of Heaven and Earth and *cheng* 誠 as being one without duplication, and as having efficacy in giving rise to things, as discussed in the following chapter.

[9]｛夫，音扶。華、藏，並去聲。卷，平聲。勺，市若反。｝昭昭，猶耿耿，小明也。此指其一處而言之。及其無窮，猶十二章及其至也之意，蓋舉全體而言也。振，收也。卷，區也。此四條，皆以發明由其不貳不息以致盛大而能生物之意。然天、地、山、川，實非由積累而後大，讀者不以辭害意可也。

[10]｛於，音烏。乎，音呼。｝《詩 • 周頌 • 維天之命》篇。[36] 於，歎辭。穆，深遠也。不顯，猶言豈不顯也。純，純一不雜也。引此以明至誠無息之意。程子曰：「天道不已，<u>文王</u>純於天道，亦不已。純則無二無雜，不已則無間斷先後。」[37]

ZY27: 大哉聖人之道！[1]洋洋乎！發育萬物，峻極于天。[2]優優大哉！禮儀三百，威儀三千。[3]待其人而後行。[4]故曰苟不至德，至道不凝焉。[5]故君子尊德性而道問學，致廣大而盡精微，極高明而道中庸。溫故而知新，敦厚以崇禮。[6]是故居上不驕，為下不倍，國有道其言足以興，國無道其默足以容。《詩》曰：「既明且哲，以保其身」，其此之謂與！[7]

右第二十七章。(言人道也。)

Comment: Zhu Xi groups what are given as three separate sections in the *Li ji* arrangement (ZY27–29) as a single section. As mentioned in relation to the *Li ji* version, there are only minor variations in the readings (or emendations) of certain characters. Zhu Xi's notes are brief other than his note 6 in which he elaborates on the "the path of enquiry and study," which is the road all those who are not sages must travel to acquire *cheng* 誠.

---

36 See the *Odes*, Mao 267, LCC, 4:570.

37 Cheng Hao 程顥—see the *Er Cheng quanshu*, 1:287. In that text there is *ming* 命 instead of *dao* 道.

[9] . . . *Zhao zhao* 昭昭 is like *geng geng* 耿耿, that is, a small light. Here it indicates this one spot only and speaks of it. When it comes to its being limitless, it is like "reaching to its extreme" in chapter 12 bringing up the whole substance and talking about it. *Zhen* 振 is equivalent to *shou* 收 (to receive, collect). *Juan* 卷 is equivalent to *qu* 區 (small). These four clauses all explain the meaning of how it is unduplicated and unceasing, comes to reach abundance and greatness, and is able to give rise to things. Nevertheless, Heaven, Earth, mountains and rivers do not, in reality, come about by gradual accumulation and are afterwards large—the reader cannot let the words harm the meaning.

[10] . . . The ode in question is the "Wei tian zhi ming" from the "Zhou song." *Wu* 於 is an interjection. *Mu* 穆 is equivalent to *shenyuan* 深遠 (profound, far-reaching). *Bu xian* 不顯 is like saying "how is it not manifest?" *Chun* 純 is equivalent to single/pure and unmixed/unalloyed. This is quoted in order to make clear the meaning of *perfect cheng* 誠 *is unceasing*. Master Cheng said: "The Way of Heaven is without end, and King Wen's purity in the Way of Heaven was also unending. *Chun* 純, then, is single and unmixed; it is unending, and remains so from beginning to end."

ZY27: Great, indeed, is the Way of the sage! **[1]** Vast and extensive, it brings forth and nourishes the ten thousand things; lofty and great, it reaches to Heaven. **[2]** Great, indeed, is its abundance. Its major forms of ceremony number three hundred and its minor forms of ritual number three thousand. **[3]** They await this man and afterwards can be put into practice. **[4]** Therefore, it is said: "Without perfect virtue, the perfect Way cannot be realised." **[5]** Therefore, the noble man honours a virtuous nature and the path of enquiry and study. He reaches to the broad and great and exhausts the subtle and minute. He reaches to the high and bright and penetrates to the central and constant (undeviating and unchanging). He revives the old and understands the new; he is honest and genuine through his respect for *li* 禮. **[6]** For this reason, when occupying a superior position, he is not arrogant; when he is an inferior, he is not refractory. When the state has the Way, his words are sufficient for him to rise. When the state does not have the Way, his silence is enough for him to be tolerated. The *Odes* says: "Since he is enlightened and wise, so he protects himself." Surely this is what it refers to? **[7]**

To the right (above) is the twenty-seventh chapter. (This speaks of the Way of mankind.)

注 ZY27 (朱熹)

[1] 包下文兩節而言。

[2] 峻，高大也。此言道之極於至大而無外也。

[3] 優優，充足有餘之意。禮儀，經禮也。威儀，曲禮也。此言道之入於至小而無閒也。

[4] 總結上兩節。

[5] 至德，謂其人。至道，指上兩節而言也。凝，聚也，成也。

[6] 尊者，恭敬奉持之意。德性者，吾所受於天之正理。道，由也。溫，猶燖溫之溫，謂故學之矣，復時習之也。敦，加厚也。尊德性，所以存心而極乎道體之大也。道問學，所以致知而盡乎道體之細也。二者修德凝道之大端也。不以一毫私意自蔽，不以一毫私欲自累，涵泳乎其所已知，敦篤乎其所已能，此皆存心之屬也。析理則不使有毫釐之差，處事則不使有過不及之謬，理義則日知其所未知，節文則日謹其所未謹，此皆致知之屬也。蓋非存心無以致知，而存心者又不可以不致知。故此五句，大小相資，首尾相應，聖賢所示入德之方，莫詳於此，學者宜盡心焉。

[7] {倍，與背同。與，平聲。}興，謂興起在位也。《詩‧大雅‧烝民》[38]之篇。

Notes ZY27 (Zhu Xi)

[1] This statement embraces the two following statements and speaks [of them].

[2] *Jun* 峻 is equivalent to *gaoda* 高大 (lofty and great). This speaks of the Way reaching to extreme greatness and having nothing outside it.

[3] *You you* 優優 has the meaning of "more than sufficient." *Li yi* 禮儀 equates with *jing li* 經禮 (principal forms of etiquette). *Wei yi* 威儀 equates with *qu li* 曲禮 (the minutiae of etiquette). This speaks of the Way entering into the extremely small and being without interruption.

[4] This summarises the two previous statements.

[5] "Perfect virtue" refers to this man (i.e. right man). The "perfect Way" points back to the previous two statements and speaks of them. *Ning* 凝 is equivalent to *ju* 聚 (to assemble, collect, gather) or *cheng* 成 (to complete, realise).

[6] *Zun* 尊 has the meaning of "reverentially and respectfully hold." *De xing* 德性 (a virtuous nature) is the correct principle which I receive from Heaven. *Dao* 道 (here) equates with *you* 由 (follow, by way of). *Wen* 溫 is like the *wen* of *xunwen* 燖溫 (to warm up). It speaks of what was previously studied and again frequently practised. *Dun* 敦 equates with *jia hou* 加厚 (increased honesty). "Honouring a virtuous nature" is the way of preserving the mind-heart and reaching to the greatness of the Way's substance. "The path of enquiry and study" is the way of extending knowledge and thoroughly exhausting the fine points of the Way's substance. These two things are the great principles of cultivating virtue and realising the Way. Do not darken yourself with one iota of self-interest. Do not involve yourself in one iota of selfish desire. Immerse yourself in what is already known. Consolidate yourself with what you are already capable of. These are all forms of preserving the mind-heart. In distinguishing principle, do not allow the slightest error. In attending to affairs, do not allow the faults of going beyond and failing to reach. With *li* 理 (principle) and *yi* 義 (right action), each day understand what you do not yet know. In attending to details, each day give careful attention to what you have not yet given attention to. These are all forms of extending knowledge. Unless you preserve the mind-heart, there is no way to extend knowledge, and in preserving the mind-heart, it is not possible to do otherwise than extend knowledge. Therefore, in these five sentences, great and small are mutually interdependent, head and tail are mutually corresponding, and the way to enter virtue as directed by the sage and worthy cannot be more detailed. It is proper for the learner to exhaust his mind-heart in this.

[7] . . . *Xing* 興 refers to rising in position. The ode is the "Zheng min" from the "Da ya."

ZY28: 子曰：「愚而好自用，賤而好自專，生乎今之世，反古之道。如此者，烖及其身者也。」[1]非天子，不議禮，不制度，不考文。[2]今天下車同軌，書同文，行同倫。[3]雖有其位，苟無其德，不敢作禮樂焉；雖有其德，苟無其位，亦不敢作禮樂焉。[4]子曰：「吾說夏禮，杞不足徵也；吾學殷禮，有宋存焉；吾學周禮，今用之，吾從周。」[5]

右第二十八章。(承上章為下不倍而言，亦人道也。)

Comment: Zhu Xi combines what are ZY30 and the first sentence of ZY31 in the *Li ji* arrangement and takes a somewhat different position on what the actual words of Confucius are. In his notes, he makes clear what he thinks the words of Zisi are. On the issue of *fan* 反, considered in the Comment to the *Li ji* ZY30, he explicitly equates this with *fu* 復, as reflected in the translation. In including the second quotation, he ends it with Confucius' statement about following Zhou. In the *Li ji*, all of ZY31 is taken as a statement by Confucius with an added internal quotation.

注 ZY28 (朱熹)

[1] {好，去聲。烖，古災字}。以上孔子之言，子思引之。反，復也。

[2] 此以下，子思之言。禮，親疏貴賤相接之體也。度，品制。文，書名。

[3] {行，去聲}。今，子思自謂當時也。軌，轍迹之度。倫，次序之體。三者皆同，言天下一統也。

[4] 鄭氏曰：「言作禮樂者，必聖人在天子之位。」

[5] 此又引孔子之言。杞，夏之後。徵，證也。宋，殷之後。三代之禮，孔子皆嘗學之而能言其意；但夏禮既不可考證，殷禮雖存，又非當世之法，惟周禮乃時王之制，今日所用。孔子既不得位，則從周而已。

ZY28: The Master said: "To be foolish and yet to like to use one's own judgement; to be lowly and yet to like to act on one's own authority; to be born into the present age and yet to return to the ways of the past—it is things like these that bring disaster down on oneself." **[1]** Nobody but the Son of Heaven determines the rites, or establishes standards, or verifies the written script. **[2]** Nowadays, in the world, carriages run in the same wheel-tracks, writing has the same script, and conduct has the same principles. **[3]** Although he has his position [of ruler], if he does not have his virtue, he dare not create rites and music. Although he has his virtue, if he does not have his position [of ruler], he also dare not create rites and music. **[4]** The Master said: "I have spoken of the rites of Xia but Qi is not enough to verify them. I have studied the rites of Yin but only Song has preserved them. I have studied the rites of Zhou and they are now used. I follow Zhou." **[5]**

To the right (above) is the twenty-eighth chapter. ([This] continues the previous chapter and is not at odds with what follows, also speaking of the Way of mankind.)

Notes ZY28 (Zhu Xi)

[1] . . . Zisi quotes Confucius' words above. *Fan* 反 equates with *fu* 復.

[2] From here on are Zisi's words. *Li* 禮 is the essential element of the interaction between near and distant, noble and base. *Du* 度 is the regulation of measures. *Wen* 文 is the name for the written script.

[3] . . . *Jin* 今 is Zisi himself speaking of his own time. *Gui* 軌 is the measure of wheel tracks. *Lun* 倫 are the essentials of order and sequence. If these three things are all the same, this speaks of the world being unified.

[4] Zheng Shi said: "This says that the one who creates rites and music must be a sage occupying the position of Son of Heaven."

[5] This also quotes Confucius' words. Qi was after Xia. *Zheng* 徵 is equivalent to *zheng* 證 (to verify). Song was after Yin. Confucius had already studied the rites of all three dynasties and was able to state their meaning. But the Xia rites, since they could not be verified, and the Yin rites, although they were preserved, were not methods for the present age. Only the Zhou rites were, then, regulations for kings of the time, so at the time in question, they were what was being used. Confucius, since he did not gain a position, then followed Zhou and that was all.

ZY29: 王天下有三重焉，其寡過矣乎！**[1]**上焉者雖善無徵，無徵不信，不信民弗從；下焉者雖善不尊，不尊不信，不信民弗從。**[2]**故君子之道：本諸身，徵諸庶民，考諸三王而不繆，建諸天地而不悖，質諸鬼神而無疑，百世以俟聖人而不惑。**[3]**質諸鬼神而無疑，知天也；百世以俟聖人而不惑，知人也。**[4]**是故君子動而世為天下道，行而世為天下法，言而世為天下則。遠之則有望，近之則不厭。**[5]**《詩》曰：「在彼無惡，在此無射；庶幾夙夜，以永終譽！」君子未有不如此而蚤有譽於天下者也。**[6]**

右第二十九章。(承上章居上不驕而言，亦人道也。)

Comment: This corresponds to ZY31 minus the opening sentence (which concludes Zhu Xi's ZY28) in the *Li ji* arrangement. This difference relates directly to the different interpretations in that the "three important things" are identified by Zhu Xi (following Lü Dalin) as "determining *li* 禮," "establishing standards," and "verifying the script" listed in the previous chapter rather than the *li* 禮 of the Three Kings as suggested by Zheng Xuan. Also, *shang yan zhe* 上焉者 and *xia yan zhe* 下焉者 are taken as referring to what has gone before and what has come after respectively, rather than rulers and ministers. As Legge points out, this reading in reality gives the terms a reference to both time and rank. In other respects, the interpretations are the same. The two alternatives given are, however, not the only possibilities—see, for example, Haloun, p. 105 and Ames & Hall, note 87, p. 129.

注 ZY29 (朱熹)

[1] {王，去聲。}呂氏曰：「三重，謂議禮、制度、考文。惟天子得以行之，則國不異政，家不殊俗，而人得寡過矣。」[39]

[2] 上焉者，謂時王以前，如夏、商之禮雖善，而皆不可考。下焉者，謂聖人在下，如孔子雖善於禮，而不在尊位也。

---

[39] Lü Dalin—see note 30 above. For the quotation, see *Er Cheng quanshu*, "Zhongyong jie," 2:1835. This is not an exact quotation.

ZY29: In ruling all under Heaven, there are three important things which will surely minimise mistakes. **[1]** What has gone before, although it may have been good, may be unattested. If it is unattested, it is not trusted. If it is not trusted, the people will not follow it. What has come after, although it may be good, may not be honoured. If it is not honoured, it is not trusted. If it is not trusted, the people will not follow it. **[2]** Therefore, the Way of the noble man (ruler) has its foundation in his own person, is attested by the common people, and is verified in relation to the Three Kings, so there is no mistake. It is established in Heaven and on Earth, and is not contrary to what is right. It is rectified by ghosts and spirits, and is without doubt. There is a preparedness to wait a hundred generations for a sage and be without misgivings. **[3]** To be rectified by ghosts and spirits and be without doubt is to know Heaven. To be prepared to wait a hundred generations for a sage and be without misgivings is to know man. **[4]** This is why, when the ruler moves, the age takes this to be the Way of the world. When he acts, the world takes this to be the world's laws. When he speaks, the age takes this to set the world's standards. Those who are distant are then hopeful; those who are near are then without dissatisfaction. **[5]** The *Odes* says: "There, he is not disliked; here, he is not wearied of. Day after day, night after night, there is perpetual praise." There has never been a noble man (ruler) like this who was not quick to find praise in the world. **[6]**

To the right (above) is the twenty-ninth chapter. (This continues the discussion from the previous chapter of occupying a superior position without arrogance, and is about the Way of mankind.)

Notes ZY29 (Zhu Xi)

[1] . . . Lü Shi said: "The 'three important things' refer to determining *li* 禮, establishing standards, and verifying the script. If only the Son of Heaven has the power to do these things, then the kingdom will not have a heterodox administration, families will not have strange customs, and the people will acquire few faults."
[2] *Shang yan zhe* 上焉者 indicates what preceded the king of the present time. For example, the rites of Xia and Shang which, although good, cannot all be attested. *Xia yan zhe* 下焉者 refers to the sages who came after, like Confucius who, although well-versed in *li* 禮, did not occupy an eminent position.

[3] 此君子，指王天下者而言。其道，即議禮、制度、考文之事也。本諸身，有其德也。徵諸庶民，驗其所信從也。建，立也，立於此而參於彼也。天地者，道也。鬼神者，造化之迹也。百世以俟聖人而不惑，所謂聖人復起，不易吾言者也。

[4] 知天知人，知其理也。

[5] 動，兼言行而言。道，兼法則而言。法，法度也。則，準則也。

[6] {惡，去聲。射，音妬。詩作斁。}《詩•周頌•振鷺》之篇。[40] 射，厭也。所謂此者，指本諸身以下六事而言。

ZY30: <u>仲尼祖述堯舜</u>，憲章<u>文</u>武；上律天時，下襲水土。[1]辟如天地之無不持載，無不覆幬，辟如四時之錯行，如日月之代明。[2]萬物並育而不相害，道並行而不相悖，小德川流，大德敦化，此天地之所以為大也。[3]

右第三十章。(言天道也。)

Comment: This corresponds to the opening sentences of the long section ZY32 in the *Li ji* arrangement. It is generally taken to be the first of three chapters (in Zhu Xi's arrangement) constituting an encomium for Confucius. The opening sentence is something of a problem and Zhu Xi's interpretation is somewhat different from that of the *Li ji* commentators. The essential meaning is clear enough—Confucius was fully cognisant of the greatness of the ancient kings and was in harmony with the forces of nature, specifically Heaven and Earth personified. This, then, is a statement about the "Way of Heaven," exemplified by Confucius as a sage. A distinction is made between "small virtue" and "large virtue" which Zhu Xi equates with "perfect sagacity" (*zhi sheng* 至聖) and "perfect *cheng*" (*zhi cheng* 至誠) respectively and elaborates on in the following two sections.

---

[40] See the *Odes*, Mao 278, LCC, 4:585.

[3] This *junzi* 君子 refers to the one who rules all under Heaven. His Way includes the matters of determining *li* 禮, establishing standards, and verifying the script. The *foundation in his own person* is his virtue. *Attested by the common people* is the proof of what is trustworthy and is followed. *Jian* 建 equates with *li* 立 (to set up, establish), as in set up in this and consider in that. *Tiandi* 天地 is the Way. Ghosts and spirits are the traces of creation. *There is a preparedness to wait a hundred generations for a sage and be without misgivings* is to say that when a sage again arises he will not be someone who changes my words.

[4] Knowing Heaven and knowing man is to know their principles.

[5] *Dong* 動 refers to both words and deeds. *Dao* 道 refers to both laws and standards. *Fa* 法 equates with *fadu* 法度 (laws, regulations). *Ze* 則 equates with *zhunze* 準則 (standards, criteria).

[6] . . . The ode is the "Zhen lu" from the "Zhou song." *Yi* 射 equates with *yan* 厭 (to be weary of, to detest). What is referred to as "these" are the six things that follow "are rooted in oneself" (*ben zhu shen* 本諸身), i.e. *has its foundation in his own person*.

ZY30: Zhongni (Confucius) honoured [the Way of] Yao and Shun from remote times. He took as a model the decrees of Wen and Wu from more recent times. Above, he followed the times of Heaven. Below, he was in accord with water and soil. [1] He was comparable to the unfailing supporting and containing, the unfailing cover and canopy of Heaven and Earth. He was comparable to the alternating advance of the four seasons, and like the successive brightness of the sun and moon. [2] The ten thousand things are nurtured at the same time, and yet do not harm each other. The Ways are travelled at the same time, and yet are not contrary to each other. Small virtue flows like a stream; large virtue is genuinely transforming. These things are what make Heaven and Earth great. [3]

To the right (above) is the thirtieth chapter. (This speaks of the Way of Heaven.)

注 ZY30 (朱熹)

[1] 祖述者，遠宗其道。憲章者，近守其法。律天時者，法其自然之運。襲水土者，因其一定之理。皆兼內外該本末而言也。

[2] {辟，音譬。幬，徒報反。} 錯，猶迭也。此言聖人之德。

[3] 悖，猶背也。天覆地載，萬物並育於其間而不相害；四時日月，錯行代明而不相悖。所以不害不悖者，小德之川流；所以並育並行者，大德之敦化。小德者，全體之分；大德者，萬殊之本。川流者，如川之流，脈絡分明而往不息也。敦化者，敦厚其化，根本盛大而出無窮也。此言天地之道，以見上文取辟之意也。

ZY31: 唯天下至聖，為能聰明睿知，足以有臨也；寬裕溫柔，足以有容也；發強剛毅，足以有執也；齊莊中正，足以有敬也；文理密察，足以有別也。[1]溥博淵泉，而時出之。[2]溥博如天，淵泉如淵。見而民莫不敬，言而民莫不信，行而民莫不說。[3]是以聲名洋溢乎中國，施及蠻貊；舟車所至，人力所通；天之所覆，地之所載，日月所照，霜露所隊；凡有血氣者，莫不尊親，故曰配天。[4]

右第三十一章。(承上章而言小德之川流，亦天道也。)

Comment: This chapter corresponds to the second part of section ZY32 in the *Li ji* arrangement and details the qualities and manifestations of "perfect sagacity" (*zhi sheng* 至聖), relating this to the "small virtue" identified in the previous chapter. Although a number of translators (e.g. Legge—see his note to ZY31, pp. 428–29) take this to refer to Confucius, there is no mention of a specific individual in Zhu Xi's notes. Riegel remarks that "it is possible that here we have shifted from a hymn in praise of Confucius to one in praise of the ruling Han emperor" (n. 208, p. 251). In fact, the passage could quite well be translated impersonally—"In the world, only perfect sagacity etc." with "it" instead of "his" in the succeeding sentences. Whatever option is chosen, it is, according to Zhu Xi, a continuation of the description of the "Way of Heaven."

Notes ZY30 (Zhu Xi)

[1] *Zu shu* 祖述 is the Way of distant ancestors. *Xian zhang* 憲章 is nearer at hand, preserving their model. *Lü tian shi* 律天時 means to take as a model its natural revolutions. *Xi shui tu* 襲水土 means to follow their established principles. All these combine what are properly the essential elements (root and branches) of internal and external and speak [of them].

[2] ... *Cuo* 錯 is like *die* 迭 (alternate, change). This speaks of the virtue of the sage.

[3] *Bei* 悖 is like *bei* 背 (to act contrary to, violate). Heaven covers, Earth contains, and the ten thousand things are all nurtured between them and do not harm each other. The four seasons, and the sun and moon alternate in movement, succeed one another in brightness, and are not in opposition to each other. That by which they do not harm and do no act contrary [to each other is that] small virtue flows like a stream. That by which they unite in nurturing and unite in acting [is that] large virtue is genuinely transforming. Small virtue is part of the complete whole. Large virtue is the basis of the ten thousand differences. The "stream flowing" is like the flow of a stream, a clear progression going forward and not stopping. *Dun hua* 敦化 means being genuine in transformation, fundamentally abundant and great, and coming forth without limit. This refers to the Ways of Heaven and Earth in order to reveal the meaning of the examples of the preceding text.

ZY31: In the world, only [someone with] perfect sagacity is deemed able to be intelligent, perspicacious, astute and knowledgeable enough to look down from above; to be liberal, genuine, gentle and compliant enough to be tolerant; to be outgoing, strong, steadfast and resolute enough to maintain control; to be regular, honourable, central and upright enough to be reverential; to be orderly, principled, careful and discerning enough to be discriminating. **[1]** All-encompassing and wide-ranging, still and deep he is, and at the right time brings this forth. **[2]** All-encompassing and wide-ranging he is, like Heaven; still and deep he is, like an abyss. He is seen and the people cannot but respect [him]; he speaks and the people cannot but trust [him]; he acts and the people cannot but be pleased. **[3]** This is why his great name spreads throughout the Central States and reaches to the Man and Mo [barbarians]. As far as boats and carriages travel, as far as human strength extends, whatever Heaven covers, whatever Earth contains, wherever the sun and moon shine, wherever frost and dew fall, of all creatures that have blood and spirit, there is none that does not respect and love him. Therefore, he is said to match Heaven. **[4]**

To the right (above) is the thirty-first chapter. (This continues the previous section and speaks of small virtues flowing like a river, which is also the Way of Heaven.)

注 ZY31 (朱熹)

[1] {知，去聲。齊，側皆反。別，彼列反。}聰明睿知，生知之質。臨，謂居上而臨下也。其下四者，乃仁義禮知之德。文，文章也。理，條理也。密，詳細也。察，明辯也。

[2] 溥博，周徧而廣闊也。淵泉，靜深而有本也。出，發見也。言五者之德，充積於中，而以時發見於外也。

[3] {見，音現。説，音悦。}言其充積極其盛，而發見當其可也。

[4] {施，去聲。隊，音墜。}舟車所至以下，蓋極言之。配天，言其德之所及，廣大如天也。

ZY32: 唯天下至誠，為能經綸天下之大經，立天下之大本，知天地之化育。夫焉有所倚？**[1]**肫肫其仁！淵淵其淵！浩浩其天！**[2]**苟不固聰明聖知達天德者，其孰能知之？**[3]**

右第三十二章。(承上章而言大德之敦化，亦天道也。前章言至聖之德，此章言至誠之道。然至誠之道，非至聖不能知；至聖之德，非至誠不能為，則亦非二物矣。此篇言聖人天道之極致，至此而無以加矣。)

Comment: This corresponds to the third part of section ZY32 of the *Li ji* arrangement and is a consideration of perfect *cheng* (*zhi cheng* 至誠), identified as the "large virtue" of chapter ZY30 by Zhu Xi. Again, there is no mention in the notes of any specific individual, so that while it may be a continuation of the encomium for Confucius (e.g. Legge), it may also be for the Han emperor at the time of its composition (e.g. Riegel), or non-specific, or impersonal. If the last, on Zhu Xi's interpretation of chapters ZY30–32 inclusive, this concludes the consideration of the Way of Heaven which begins with a statement of praise of Zhongni, then considers the greatness of Heaven and Earth in their nurturing of the ten thousand things, recognising a "small virtue" which flows like a river and a "large virtue" which is genuinely transforming. The former is identified as "perfect sagacity" and is elaborated on in ZY31 whilst the latter is identified as "perfect *cheng*" and is elaborated on in this present chapter.

Notes ZY31 (Zhu Xi)

[1] . . . *Cong ming rui zhi* 聰明睿知 is a disposition that gives rise to knowledge. *Lin* 臨 refers to those occupying a high position looking down on what is below. The four things below are, then, the virtues of *ren* 仁, *yi* 義, *li* 禮, and *zhi* 知. *Wen* 文 equates with *wen-zhang* 文章 (figured and brilliant, orderly and defined). *Li* 理 equates with *tiao li* 條理 (orderliness). *Mi* 密 equates with *xiangxi* 詳細 (detailed). *Cha* 察 equates with *ming bian* 明辯 (clearly discriminating).

[2] *Pu bo* 溥博 equates with *zhou bian* 周偏 (all around) and *guang kuo* 廣闊 (broad and extensive). *Yuan quan* 淵泉 equates with *jing shen* 靜深 (serene and deep) and *you ben* (having a source). *Chu* 出 equates with *fa xian* 發見 (to discover, reveal). This speaks of the virtue of these five things filling up and accumulating within (in the centre), and at the appropriate time revealing itself in what is external.

[3] . . . This speaks of its filling up and accumulating to extend its greatness and revealing at the right time its possibilities.

[4] . . . From "as far as boats and carriages travel" onward, talks about the extreme. *Pei tian* 配天 says that what his virtue reaches to is broad and great like Heaven.

ZY32: In the world, only [someone with] perfect *cheng* 誠 is deemed able to bring order to the great fabric of the social structure of the world, to establish the great foundation of the world, and to comprehend the transformations and nurturings of Heaven and Earth. Indeed, is there anything on which he depends? **[1]** Honest and sincere is his *ren* 仁; deep and still is his profundity; great and wide is his [understanding of] Heaven. **[2]** Other than one who is genuinely perspicacious, enlightened, wise, and knowledgeable, and understands Heavenly virtue, who can know him (i.e. the sage)? **[3]**

To the right (above) is the thirty-second chapter. (This continues the previous chapter and speaks of the genuine transformations of great virtue, which is also the Way of Heaven. The previous chapter speaks of the virtue of [one with] perfect sagacity; this chapter speaks of the Way of [one with] perfect *cheng* 誠. Nevertheless, the Way of perfect *cheng* 誠 cannot be known without perfect sagacity [just as] the virtue of perfect sagacity cannot be practised without perfect *cheng* 誠, so they are not two [separate] things. This section speaks of the extreme extension of the Heavenly Way of the sage reaching to this and having no room for increase.)

注 ZY32 (朱熹)

[1] {夫，音扶。焉，於虔反。}經、綸，皆治絲之事。經者，理其緒而分之；綸者，比其類而合之也。經，常也。大經者，五品之人倫。大本者，所性之全體也。惟聖人之德極誠無妄，故於人倫各盡其當然之實，而皆可以為天下後世法，所謂經綸之也。其於所性之全體，無一毫人欲之偽以雜之，而天下之道千變萬化皆由此出，所謂立之也。其於天地之化育，則亦其極誠無妄者有默契焉，非但聞見之知而已。此皆至誠無妄，自然之功用，夫豈有所倚著於物而後能哉。

[2] {肫，之純反。}肫肫，懇至貌，以經綸而言也。淵淵，靜深貌，以立本而言也。浩浩，廣大貌，以知化而言也。其淵其天，則非特如之而已。

[3] {聖知之知，去聲。}固，猶實也。鄭氏曰：「惟聖人能知聖人也。」

ZY33:《詩》曰「衣錦尚絅」，惡其文之著也。故君子之道，闇然而日章；小人之道，的然而日亡。君子之道：淡而不厭，簡而文，溫而理，知遠之近，知風之自，知微之顯，可與入德矣。[1]

《詩》云：「潛雖伏矣，亦孔之昭！」故君子內省不疚，無惡於志。君子之所不可及者，其唯人之所不見乎。[2]

《詩》云：「相在爾室，尚不愧于屋漏。」故君子不動而敬，不言而信。[3]

Notes ZY32 (Zhu Xi)

[1] . . . *Jing* 經 and *lun* 綸 are both matters pertaining to silk thread. *Jing* 經 is to arrange the threads and separate them. *Lun* 綸 is to categorize and combine them. *Jing* 經 equates with *chang* 常. *Da jing* 大經 are the five grades of relationships between people. *Da ben* 大本 is the complete substance of nature. Only the virtue of the sage reaches utmost *cheng* 誠 without falseness. Therefore, in the relationships between people, each exhausts their proper genuineness and all can be considered as models for later generations of the world—this is what is referred to as "bringing order to the fabric" (*jing lun* 經綸). In what is the whole substance of his nature, there is not one iota of the falsity of human desire mixed with it, and the thousand changes and ten thousand transformations of the world all come forth from this—this is what is referred to as "establishing it." In the transformings and nurturings of Heaven and Earth, as also in his extreme *cheng* 誠 without falseness, there is a silent understanding, and not just knowledge which comes from hearing and seeing. These are all the naturally occurring beneficial results of perfect *cheng* 誠 without falseness, so how is he only able to achieve these if there are things he must rely on?

[2] . . . *Zhun zhun* 肫肫 is the appearance of extreme earnestness, and pertains to the discussion of *jing lun* 經綸 (bringing order to the fabric). *Yuan yuan* 淵淵 is the appearance of being still and deep, and pertains to the discussion of establishing the foundation. *Hao hao* 浩浩 is the appearance of being broad and great, and refers to comprehending transformations. *Qi yuan* 其淵 and *qi tian* 其天 are, then, not specifically like this and nothing more.

[3] . . . *Gu* 固 is like *shi* 實 (true, genuine, sincere). Zheng Shi said: "Only a sage is able to know a sage."

ZY33: The *Odes* says: "Over her brocade garments she wore a plain, unlined coat"—she did not like to display her elegance. Thus, the Way of the noble man is veiled, and yet each day is more clearly apparent whereas the Way of the lesser man is clearly apparent, and yet each day fades further away. The Way of the noble man [is this]: He is plain but not tiresome, simple but refined, gentle but principled. He knows the nearness of the distant, the source of the wind, the manifestations of the subtle. With these can he enter virtue. **[1]**

The *Odes* says: "Although [the fish] lie on the bottom to hide, they are still clearly visible." Thus the noble man, when he looks within himself, finds no fault and no evil in his intentions. That in the noble man which cannot be reached is just that which others do not see. **[2]**

The *Odes* says: "When you are seen in your own house, still be without shame even in the farthest corner." Thus the noble man does not act and yet is revered, does not speak and yet is trusted. **[3]**

《詩》曰:「奏假無言,時靡有爭。」是故君子不賞而民勸,不怒而民威
於鈇鉞。[4]

《詩》曰:「不顯惟德!百辟其刑之。」是故君子篤恭而天下平。[5]

《詩》云:「予懷明德,不大聲以色。」子曰:「聲色之於以化民,末也。」
《詩》曰「德輶如毛」,毛猶有倫。「上天之載,無聲無臭」,至矣![6]

右第三十三章。子思因前章極致之言,反求其本,復自下學為己謹獨之
事,推而言之,以馴致乎篤恭而天下平之盛。又贊其妙,至於無聲無臭
而後已焉。蓋舉一篇之要而約言之,其反復丁寧示人之意,至深切矣,
學者其可不盡心乎!

Comment: This chapter corresponds to the final part of ZY32 and all of ZY33 in the *Li ji*
arrangement. It comprises eight quotations from the *Odes* together with a single statement
from Confucius elaborating on one of the quotations. Zhu Xi, unlike the *Li ji* commentators, attributes the whole chapter to Zisi and takes the section to be a review of the qualities of the noble man previously considered in the earlier chapters.

The *Odes* says: "Silently and without a word he enters and makes the offering; at the time there is no contention." This is why the noble man does not give rewards and yet the people are encouraged, why he shows no anger and yet the people fear him more than blade or axe. [4]

The *Odes* says: "He makes no display of his virtue, yet the hundred princes take him as an exemplar." This is why the noble man is genuine and reverential, and the world is at peace. [5]

The *Odes* says: "I cherish your enlightened virtue; it is not loudly proclaimed by outward show."

The Master said: "In transforming the people, sights and sounds are of little importance." The *Odes* says: "Virtue is light, like a feather." But a feather can still be used as a comparison.

[The *Odes* also says:] "Above, what Heaven contains has neither sound nor smell"—how perfect! [6]

To the right (above) is the thirty-third chapter. Zisi, having followed the words of the previous chapters to their furthest point, turns back to seek their foundation. Again, following on from the matter of the scholar being attentive to himself even when he is alone, he extends the discussion to proceed gradually to genuineness and reverence, and the greatness of the world being at peace. He also praises its mysterious subtlety to the point of it being without sound or smell, and afterwards ends with this. So he raises the central point of the whole work and summarises it, and his repeated attempts to show what it means to people are of great depth and profundity. How can the scholar not exert his mind to the utmost!

注 ZY33 (朱熹)

[1] {衣，去聲。絅，口迴反。惡，去聲。闇，於感反。}前章言聖人之德，極其盛矣。此復自下學立心之始言之，而下文又推之以至其極也。《詩•國風•衛•碩人》、〈鄭〉之〈丰〉，皆作「衣錦褧衣」。[41]褧，絅同，禪衣也。尚，加也。古之學者為己，故其立心如此。尚絅故闇然，衣錦故有日章之實。淡、簡、溫，絅之襲於外也；不厭而文且理焉，錦之美在中也。小人反是，則暴於外而無實以繼之，是以的然而日亡也。遠之近，見於彼者由於此也。風之自，著乎外者本乎內也。微之顯，有諸內者形諸外也。有為己之心，而又知此三者，則知所謹而可入德矣。故下文引詩言謹獨之事。

[2] {惡，去聲。}《詩•小雅•正月》之篇。[42]承上文言「莫見乎隱、莫顯乎微」也。疚，病也。無惡於志，猶言無愧於心，此君子謹獨之事也。

[3] {相，去聲。}《詩•大雅•抑》之篇。[43]相，視也。屋漏，室西北隅也。承上文又言君子之戒謹恐懼，無時不然，不待言動而後敬信，則其為己之功益加密矣。故下文引詩并言其效。

[4] {假，格同。鈇，音夫。}《詩•商頌•烈祖》之篇。[44]奏，進也。承上文而遂及其效，言進而感格於神明之際，極其誠敬，無有言説而人自化之也。威，畏也，鈇，莝斫刀也。鉞，斧也。

---

[41] See, respectively, Mao 57, verse 1, LCC, 4:94, and Mao 88, verse 3, LCC, 4:141.
[42] See the *Odes*, Mao 192, verse 11, LCC, 4:319.
[43] See the *Odes*, Mao 256, verse 7, LCC, 4:514.
[44] See the *Odes*, Mao 302, verse 2, LCC, 4:635.

Notes ZY33 (Zhu Xi)

[1] . . . The previous chapter speaks of the virtue of the sage and the extent of his great-ness. This [chapter] goes on from the scholar establishing the beginning of the mind-heart and discusses this, whilst the following section also elaborates on it in order to reach its far-thest point. The ode is the "Shuo ren" from the "Guo feng" (Wei). This and the ode "Feng" from the "Guo feng" (Zheng) both have "衣錦褧衣." *Jiong* 褧 is the same as *jiong* 絅—a garment without a lining. *Shang* 尚 is equivalent to *jia* 加 (to add). The scholars of ancient times applied this to themselves. Therefore, in establishing their minds, they were like this. "Adding a plain (unlined) coat" is therefore concealment, whilst the elegant garments are the reality of "each day more clearly apparent." *Dan* 淡 (plain, dull), *jian* 簡 (simple) and *wen* 溫 (gentle) are the plain coat (*jiong* 絅) worn on the outside. *Bu yan* 不厭 (not tire-some), *wen* 文 (refined) and *li* 理 (principled) are the beauty of the brocade garments that lie within. The lesser man, being the opposite of this, makes a display on the outside but has no substance to back it up; this is being "clearly apparent yet each day fading further away." The "nearness of the distant" is to see in "that" through what is in "this." The "source of the wind" refers to what is displayed on the outside being based on what is within. The "manifestations of the subtle" is all that is within informing all that is without. The one who has the mind-heart to apply this to himself and also knows these three things, then knows what to be careful about and can enter virtue. Therefore, the text quotes the *Odes* to speak of the matter of being careful when alone.

[2] . . . The ode is the "Zheng yue" of the "Xiao ya." This continues the statement in the previous text that "there is nothing more visible than what is hidden; there is nothing more apparent than what is obscure" (ZY1). *Jiu* 疚 is equivalent to *bing* 病 (fault, defect). Hav-ing nothing bad in his intentions is like saying having nothing to be ashamed of in one's mind-heart. This is the matter of the noble man being careful when alone.

[3] . . . The ode is the "Yi" from the "Da ya." *Xiang* 相 is equivalent to *shi* 視 (to be seen). *Wu lou* 屋漏 is the north-west corner of the house. This continues the discussion in the previous text, speaking about the noble man being cautious, attentive, apprehensive, and fearful, and having no times when he is not so, and that his being respected and trusted does not depend on prior words and actions, so the efficacy of applying it to himself is se-cretly increased. Therefore, the text quotes the *Odes* to stress the beneficial effects of this.

[4] . . . The ode is the "Lie zu" from the "Shang song." *Zou* 奏 is equivalent to *jin* 進 (to enter). This continues the previous text and goes on to extend its examples. It speaks of his extreme *cheng* 誠 and reverence on the occasion of entering and giving thanks to the gods. He does not need to say anything and yet people transform themselves. *Wei* 威 is equiva-lent to *wei* 畏 (to fear, be in awe). *Fu* 鈇 is a chopping knife. *Yue* 鉞 is an axe.

[5]《詩•周頌•烈文》之篇。[45] 不顯，説見二十六章，此借引以為幽深玄遠之意。承上文言天子有不顯之德，而諸侯法之，則其德愈深而效愈遠矣。篤，厚也。篤恭，言不顯其敬也。篤恭而天下平，乃聖人至德淵微，自然之應，中庸之極功也。

[6] {輶，由、酉二音}。《詩•大雅•皇矣》之篇。[46] 引之以明上文所謂不顯之德者，正以其不大聲與色也。又引孔子之言，以為聲色乃化民之末務，今但言不大之而已，則猶有聲色者存，是未足以形容不顯之妙。不若〈烝民〉之詩所言「德輶如毛」，則庶乎可以形容矣，而又自以為謂之毛，則猶有可比者，是亦未盡其妙。不若文王之詩所言「上天之事，無聲無臭」，[47] 然後乃為不顯之至耳。蓋聲臭有氣無形，在物最為微妙，而猶曰無之，故惟此可以形容不顯篤恭之妙。非此德之外，又別有是三等，然後為至也。

---

45   See the *Odes*, Mao 269, verse 2, LCC, 4:573.

46   See the *Odes*, Mao 241, verse 7, LCC, 4:454.

47   See the *Odes*, Mao 235, verse 7, LCC, 4:431.

[5] The ode is the "Lie wen" from the "Zhou song." *Bu xian* 不顯 refers to chapter 26 and is quoted here to suggest a deep and far-reaching meaning. It continues the statement of the previous text about the Son of Heaven having virtue which he does not display, and yet the feudal lords take him as a model. Then his virtue is increasingly deep and its effects increasingly far-reaching. *Du* 篤 is equivalent to *hou* 厚 (substantial, generous). *Du gong* 篤恭 refers to the absence of display in his reverence. If he is genuine and reverential and the world is at peace, then the sage's perfect virtue is deep and subtle, and is the natural outcome and ultimate achievement of using the Way of central and constant (undeviating and unchanging).

[6] . . . The ode is the "Huang yi" from the "Da ya." It is quoted in order to make clear what the previous text calls "virtue without display," correct in its being devoid of great sounds and sights. It also quotes Confucius' words to the effect that sounds and sights are only an insignificant component (a mere branch) in transforming the people. But now, if he only emphasises the aspect of greatness, then there is still the existence of sounds and sights, and this is not good enough to describe the mystery of non-displaying. What is said in the ode "Zheng min"—that virtue is like a feather—seems to be a better description. But also, by taking it to be referred to as a feather, then it is still possible to compare it, which also does not exhaust its mystery. It is not as good as what was said in the poem on King Wen—"Above, what Heaven contains is without sound or smell." Afterwards, then, this is the perfection of non-displaying. For sounds and smells have "spirit" (*qi* 氣) but no form, and among things, these are the most subtle and mysterious. It is like saying that they do not exist, so only this can describe the mystery of genuineness and reverence which is not displayed. When there is nothing outside this virtue, and there is also the separation of the three grades, there is perfection.

Appendices

Appendix 1—The Origin of the *Li ji* 禮記

The standard edition of the *Li ji* is that included in the *Shisanjing zhushu* 十三經注疏 (SSJZS) prepared in the early nineteenth century by Ruan Yuan 阮元 (1764–1849) from Song editions and containing commentary material by Zheng Xuan 鄭玄 (127–200), Lu Deming 陸德明 (556–627) and Kong Yingda 孔穎達 (574–648). The 49 chapters are a miscellany both in subject matter and origin. Indeed, the precise authorship and origin of all of them are more or less uncertain although there is a group of four, which includes the *Zhongyong* 中庸, attributed to Kong Ji 孔伋 (Zisi 子思, c. 483–422 BCE) and another group of four, which includes the *Daxue* 大學, attributed to Zeng Shen 曾參 (Zengzi 曾子, c. 505–437 BCE). It is not clear how these relate to the material attributed to both Confucian disciples in the *Han shu*, "Yiwenzhi."[1] Not only is the origin of the individual chapters obscure; so too is the redaction of the *li* 禮 material from the pre-Qin period to create the three *li* 禮 texts, the *Yi li* 儀禮, the *Zhou li* 周禮, and the *Li ji* 禮記. When did these texts come to their present form and who was responsible? There are, then, unresolved issues about the the origin of each of the chapters of the *Li ji*, and there are issues about the time and mechanism of the compilation of the work as a whole.

The traditional view is that the *li* 禮 material originated to a large extent from the state of Zhou 周 and dates back to the Duke of Zhou 周公 and to Confucius and his disciples. This material was thought to have suffered particularly during the Qin period and to have been in a sorry state at the start of the Han dynasty (206 BCE). Beginning during the Western Han, the body of *li* 禮 material recovered at that time was worked on by Gao Tang 高堂 (fl. 2nd century BCE) who produced a work, the *Shi li* 士禮, now lost. From this *li* 禮 material the three existing texts were fashioned, with the addition of an unknown amount of further material attributed to Han scholars. Work on all this *li* 禮 material was continued by the noted Han scholar, Hou Cang 后

---

[1]   *Han shu* 30, 6:1724.

蒼 (fl. 1ˢᵗ century BCE) and subsequently by two of Hou Cang's students, Dai De 戴德 (fl. 1ˢᵗ century BCE) and Dai Sheng 戴聖 (fl. 1ˢᵗ century BCE), commonly referred to as "big Dai" (Da Dai 大戴) and "Little Dai" (Xiao Dai 小戴) respectively (they were, in fact, cousins). Work was also done on this material by Liu Xiang 劉向 (c. 79–6 BCE) and his son, Liu Xin 劉歆 (c. 46 BCE–23 CE), in whose catalogue were listed the *Yi li*, the *Zhou li* and 199 *pian* of *li* 禮 treatises. It is said that both Liu Xiang and Dai Sheng were present at the Stone Conduit Cloister assembly of scholars in 51 BCE, an important milestone in the restoration of Confucian texts.

Ultimately, it is said, a work in 85 sections was created by Dai De ("Big Dai") and was distilled down to 46 *pian* by Dai Sheng ("Little Dai"), this revision being the basis of what we now have as the *Li ji* (the *Xiao Dai Li ji* 小戴禮記). Also extant is the *Da Dai Li ji* 大戴禮記, which probably comprises the material edited out by Dai Sheng. There was also a work in 12 *pian* by Dai Sheng entitled *Discussion of the Doubts of Scholars about the Li ji*—sadly no longer extant, although it was still in existence during the Sui dynasty. Three chapters were added to the 46 of the *Xiao Dai Li ji*, as indicated in the excerpt from the *Sui shu* 隋書 below, to create what has remained unchanged for close on two millennia as the *Li ji*. Two other notable scholars involved in the preparation of the classic were Ma Rong 馬融 (79–166) and his student, Zheng Xuan 鄭玄 (127–200) whose commentary is preserved in current editions of the *Li ji* and is included in the present translations. The relevant section in the *Sui shu* 隋書, which also offers a statement about commentaries available at the time, is as follows:

> At the beginning of the Han, King Xian 獻王 of Hejian 河間 also acquired what had been recorded by Confucius' disciples and later scholars, a total of 131 *pian*, and submitted it, at the time there being no transmission of this. When it came to Liu Xiang, he examined and collated their works and reduced them to 130 *pian* which he arranged and put into sequence. He also acquired the *Mingtang yinyang ji* 明堂陰陽記 (33 *pian*), the *Kongzi sanchao ji* 孔子三朝記 (7 *pian*), the *Wang Shi shiji* 王氏史記 (21 *pian*), and the *Yue ji* 樂記 (23 *pian*), five volumes in all, which he combined [with the original material] to give 214 *pian*. Dai De edited out their troublesome repetitions and combined and recorded them to make 85 *pian* which was called the *Da Dai ji* 大戴記. Dai Sheng made further excisions from Da Dai's book to create 46 *pian* which was called the *Xiao Dai ji* 小戴記. Towards the end of the Han, Ma Rong subsequently transmitted Xiao Dai's studies. Rong further established the "Yue ling" 月令 (1 *pian*), the "Mingtang wei" 明堂位 (1 *pian*) and the "Yue ji" 樂記 (1 *pian*) to give a combined total of 49 *pian*. Zheng Xuan received the work from Rong and made notes for it. Now there are the *Zhou guan* 周官 (6

pian), the ancient classic (17 *pian*), and the *Xiao Dai ji* 小戴記 (49 *pian*), three volumes in all. Only Zheng's commentary is established in the nation's studies—all the rest, and there are many, are either lost or destroyed, and also there are no "teacher's explanations."[2]

Riegel, in Loewe's handbook of early Chinese texts,[3] has this to say on the traditional account:

> It is for the most part a fabulation constructed to reconcile various works mentioned in the section on *li* in the *Han shu* 30, 1709–10, with the text in 49 *p'ien* [*pian*], which is not listed there, and to show how these works preceded and led in rational fashion to the contemporary redaction. There is little in the account that is reliable; some of it is to be rejected outright.

It is also pointed out by Riegel that the earliest evidence for the involvement of Big and Little Dai in editing the *Li ji* derives from Zheng Xuan's *Liuyi lun* 六藝論 of which only fragments remain. As an alternative view, he suggests that as late as the White Tiger Hall debates of 79 the definitive editing to create the work of 49 *pian* had not yet taken place and that Cao Bao 曹褒 (d. 102) of the Qing Pu 慶普 (1st century BCE) school may have been responsible for the transmission of the work in its present form.[4]

In summary, it seems reasonable to assume on available evidence that the *Li ji* reached its present form at some time during the Eastern Han dynasty in the first or second century CE and quite soon after this was inscribed onto stone under the direction of Cai Yong 蔡邕 (133–192). How much was original material and how much was added, what the added material was, who added it, and to what extent it was based on pre-existing material—all questions of particular relevance for the *Daxue* and the *Zhongyong*—are as yet unresolved issues.

---

2   See the *Sui shu* 隋書, 2:925–26.

3   Michael Loewe, ed., *Early Chinese Texts: A Bibliographical Guide* (Berkeley: The Institute of East Asian Studies, University of California, 1993), 293–97.

4   For Cao Bao's biography, see the *Hou Han shu* 35, 5:1201–7.

Appendix 2—Commentaries and Translations

The first part of this appendix (I) will list the most significant commentators on both the *Daxue* and the *Zhongyong* from Zheng Xuan to the end of the Qing period along with brief biographical information on each person (Ia), and then will list the most important commentaries and analyses (Ib). The first list will be subdivided into three periods: Han to Song, Song, and post-Song. The second list will be subdivided according to sources: the *Han shu*, "Yiwen zhi," the *Sui shu*, "Jingji zhi," the SKQS Catalogue (*Zongmu tiyao* 總目提要), and other sources. The second part of the Appendix (II) will provide details of previous translations of both works into European languages.

Ia. Commentators

(1) Han to Song (206 BCE–960 CE)

Ma Rong 馬融 (79–166): Known as the "universal scholar" (*tong ru* 通儒), Ma was a major classical scholar of the Eastern Han period and was particularly renowned as a teacher. He is credited with the introduction of the double column interlinear commentary and prepared such commentaries for a variety of works including the *San li* 三禮 (the Three Li). None is extant in full although fragments do survive. He is also remembered as Zheng Xuan's teacher.

Zheng Xuan 鄭玄 (127–200): Undoubtedly the most notable of the pre-Tang commentators and Ma Rong's most famous student, Zheng provided commentaries for most of the classical works. These are preserved today in the SSJZS. An interesting issue is the matter of his borrowings from other commentaries, now no longer extant. On this point, and with particular reference to the *Lunyu*, Makeham has the following note: "Since Zheng Xuan 'borrowed' significantly from earlier commentators, especially Kong and Bao, even though he never acknowledged these sources, this claim (i.e. of his preeminence) may seem unfounded. If, however, it is accepted that the commentaries which Zheng Xuan modified and appropriated as his own were traditionally attributed to Zheng Xuan, then the claim is still defensible."[5]

Wang Su 王肅 **(196–256):** Regarded as a major classical scholar, but also described as a "celebrated forger," Wang rose to high office in Wei and is particularly remembered as the "discoverer" of the *Kongzi jiayu* 孔子家語—a work now considered to be one of his forgeries. Apparently, he was critical of many of Zheng Xuan's interpretations but nothing of his work remains. There is, however, one reference to Wang in the *Li ji* "Daxue" commentary.

Dai Yong 戴顒 **(5th century):** A work, no longer extant, is listed under the name of Dai Yong in the *Sui shu* (vide infra). Biographical details may be found in the *Song shu* 93 and the *Nan shi* 75.

Lu Deming 陸德明 **(556–627):** A classical scholar of particular note, Lu served at one point as imperial librarian to Emperor Yang of the Sui. Later, he is said to have distinguished himself at the *Wenxueguan* 文學館 for his defence of Confucianism against the rival doctrines of Daoism and Buddhism. His best known work is an explanation of phrases in classical and other writings titled *Jingdian shiwen* 經典釋文 which can be found in the CSJC, n.s., 38:696–719 and 39:1–195.

Kong Yingda 孔穎達 **(574–648):** Kong is said to have been a direct descendant of Confucius of the 32nd degree. At the command of the Emperor Taizong (r. 627–649), and under the overall direction of Yan Shigu 顏師古 (581–645), Kong and other scholars prepared detailed commentaries on the Confucian Classics, the aim being to establish "correct" editions of these works. This endeavour resulted in the *Wujing zhengyi* 五經正義 (The Correct Meanings of the Five Classics) in 180 *juan*. This commentary, or subcommentary as it is often called, is preserved in the SSJZS along with Zheng Xuan's much briefer annotations.

---

5   John T. Makeham, *Transmitters and Creators* (Cambridge, MA: Harvard University Press, 2003), 23–24n3: the two men referred to are Kong Anguo 孔安國 (d. ca. 100 BCE) and Bao Xian 包咸 (6 BCE–65 CE).

Han Yu 韓愈 (768–824) and Li Ao 李翱 (774–826): These two men, almost exact contemporaries, are seen as relevant to the origins of the Neo-Confucian philosophy that developed to counter, at least in part, the perceived pernicious effects of the then burgeoning Buddhist and Daoist ways of thought. With respect to the *Daxue* and *Zhongyong*, the importance of these two men lies particularly in three essays, two by Han Yu and one by Li Ao, which focussed on the two tracts and began the process of identifying each of them as being of critical importance in the development of Neo-Confucian concepts. Han Yu's essays are his "Yuan Dao" 原道 (The Original Way) and "Yuan xing" 原性 (Original Nature), which draw on the *Daxue* to a significant extent, exploring and developing certain aspects of that text, especially the key terms. Li Ao's essay is his "Fu xing shu" 復性書 (Restoring Nature), which focuses primarily on the *Zhongyong* and the concept of *cheng* 誠, so crucial in that work.[6]

(2) Song (960–1279)

Sima Guang 司馬光 (1019–1086): A noted scholar with wide-ranging interests, Sima Guang's most famous works are his studies of history, the *Jigu lu* 稽古錄 and the *Sima Shi shuyi* 司馬氏書儀, the latter a work particularly admired by Zhu Xi.[7] His relevance here is that he prepared commentaries on both the *Daxue* and the *Zhongyong*, neither of which is extant. Still extant, however, is an essay by the same author on the line "*zhi zhi zai ge wu*" 致知在格物 (extending knowledge lies in the investigation of things) from the *Daxue*. Sima Guang's contribution, specifically referring to the *Daxue*, has been summarised by Gardner as follows: "Sima's contribution to the history of the *Daxue* then is twofold. He began the tradition of writing commentaries on the *Daxue* as a separate work. And, following in the steps of Li Ao, he elevated the line *zhi zhi zai ge wu* 致知在格物."[8]

Zhang Zai 張載 (1020–1077): Zhang was one of the most important of the Neo-Confucians, now remembered particularly for his *Zhengmeng* 正蒙

---

6 See Li Ao, *Li Wengong ji* 2, in SBCK, 35:8–12 and also Chan, *A Source Book in Chinese Philosophy*, 456–59 for a partial translation. T. H. Barrett's unpublished PhD thesis contains a full, annotated translation of this essay. Timothy H. Barrett, "Buddhism, Taoism and Confucianism in the Thought of Li Ao" (PhD diss., Yale University, 1978).

7 See the SB, 183.

8 See Gardner, *Chu Hsi and the Ta-hsueh*, 23. Romanisations have been changed to *pinyin* and characters added.

(Correcting Youthful Ignorance). Initially interested in military matters, at the age of twenty-one, he came under the influence of Fan Zhongyan 范仲淹 (989–1052) and was encouraged to study the *Zhongyong*. Fan is reported to have advised him thus: "Since the scholar has morals and institutions in which to find his pleasure, why should he concern himself with military matters?"[9] Gardner quotes as follows from Zhang Zai as evidence for the developing independence of the *Daxue* and the *Zhongyong* from the *Li ji* as a whole: "Scholars—those who put their trust in the written word—should put their trust in the *Lunyu*, the *Mengzi*, the *Shi* (*Odes*), and the *Shu* (*Documents*), for they are free from heterodox principles. Even though each of these texts comes from the hands of many different Confucians, still they contain no passage injurious to what is right. As for the *Zhongyong* and the *Daxue*, there can be no doubt that they come from the school of Confucius."[10] Zhu Xi includes several quotations from Zhang Zai in his commentary on the *Zhongyong*.

Yang Shi 楊時 (1053–1135): Yang studied first with Cheng Hao, and then, after the elder Cheng's death, with Cheng Yi. By way of Luo Congyan 羅從 彥 (1072–1135) and Li Tong 李侗 (1088–1158), he was in the direct line of teachers leading to Zhu Xi. He is included in the *Yiluo yuanyuan lu* 伊洛淵源 錄 (see the SB, 222) and is referred to by Zhu Xi in his commentary on the *Zhongyong*.

Cheng Hao 程顥 (1032–1085) and Cheng Yi 程頤 (1033–1107): The Cheng brothers are generally acknowledged to have been of primary importance in the development of Neo-Confucianism and were especially important as influences on Zhu Xi. Cheng Yi, in particular, gave close attention to the *Daxue* and the *Zhongyong*. Fung Yu-lan quotes from the *Song shi* 宋史 as follows: "Cheng Yi was styled Zhengshu 正叔. . . . He was an omnivorous reader whose learning was rooted in *cheng* 誠. He took the *Great Learning*, *Analects*, *Mencius*, and *Doctrine of the Mean* as his guides, and delved into the Six Classics. Whether active or still, speaking or silent, he always took the Sage (Confucius) as his teacher, and refused to remain idle as long as he failed to attain to him."[11] Although neither brother wrote a specific commentary on either of the two works in question, they did express views on both works,

---

[9]   See Fung, *A History of Chinese Philosophy*, 2:477.

[10]   Gardner, *Chu Hsi and the Ta-hsueh*, 23.

[11]   See Fung, *A History of Chinese Philosophy*, 2:499 (with minor modifications).

with the thoughts of the younger brother being notably influential in Zhu Xi's rearrangement of the *Daxue*.

Lü Dalin 呂大臨 (1044–1093): Lü was one of the *Si Xiansheng* 四先生 who studied under Cheng Yi, the others being Yang Shi (vide supra), You Zuo 游酢, who wrote on the *Zhongyong*,[12] and Xie Liangzuo 謝良佐 who wrote a commentary on the *Lunyu*. Perhaps most noted for his work on bronze vessels, the *Kaogu tu* 考古圖, he was credited by Zhu Xi with the *Zhongyong jie* 中庸解, which appears in the *Er Cheng quanshu* 二程全書 and is quoted a number of times by Zhu Xi in his own commentary to that work.

Zhang Jiucheng 張九成 (1092–1159): An outstanding scholar with early examination success, Zhang later encountered considerable difficulty in his official career. He wrote a work on the *Zhongyong*—the *Zhongyong shuocan* 中庸説殘 in three *juan*—which suffered criticism from Zhu Xi and resultant neglect. It is not listed in the SKQS, although it is found in the SBCK.[13]

Zhu Xi 朱熹 (1130–1200): Nothing additional will be said here about Zhu Xi as a person. Arguably his most important work, the *Sishu zhangju jizhu* 四書章句集注, from which the commentaries to the *Daxue* and *Zhongyong* in the present work have been taken, was profoundly influential, as has been described. For further details see the SB, 44–45 where it is noted that, "all in all, the four commentaries cited fifty-six people in 923 quotations and references." Those quoted in the two works translated here are, in chronological order, Zheng Xuan (7), Zhang Zai (4), Yang Shi (1), You Zuo (1), Cheng Hao (6), Cheng Yi (14), Lü Dalin (6), and Hou Zhongliang (1).

Zhen Dexiu 真德秀 (1178–1235): Rising to high office during the Southern Song, Zhen was ultimately appointed president of the Board of Ceremonies. In the present context, his most influential work was his *Daxue yanyi* 大學衍義, which expanded on the teachings of the *Daxue* as they applied to administration. This work spawned a series of further works by later scholars—the *Daxue yanyi bu* 大學衍義補 by Qiu Jun (vide infra), the *Daxue yanyi tonglüe* 大學衍義通略 by Wang Zheng 王諍 (fl. 1550) and two works by Chen Hongmou 陳弘謀 (1696–1771), the *Daxue yanyi jiyao* 大學衍義輯要

---

12   See the *Sikuquanshu zongmutiyao*, 4:163.
13   See the SB, 43–44.

and the *Daxue yanyi bu jiyao* 大學衍義補輯要.[14] Zhen also wrote the *Sishu jibian* 四書集編, the *Du shu ji* 讀書記, which considers the actions of ancient worthies, and the *San Li kao* 三禮考.[15]

Wang Bo 王柏 (1197–1274): Another notable contributor to the literature on the two texts in the Song dynasty, Wang Bo is particularly remembered for his views on the authorship of the *Zhongyong* which are discussed in the introduction to that work and have been given prominence in recent times by Fung Yu-lan and by Riegel. The essays expressing his views on both the *Daxue* and the *Zhongyong* are to be found in the *Luzhai Wang Wenxian Gong wenji* 魯齋王文憲公文集.[16]

(3) Post-Song (after 1279)

Qiu Jun 邱濬 (1420–1495): Qiu was a prolific author who served in a number of important posts. Probably his most noteworthy work was the *Daxue yanyi bu* 大學衍義補, which is avowedly a supplement to Zhen Dexiu's work referred to above. The following excerpt from the *Dictionary of Ming Biography* (DMB) summarises the nature and content of this work:

> In his introduction Qiu indicates that his purpose is to supplement the *Daxue yanyi* written by Zhen Dexiu (1178–1235). Zhen's work set the standard for righteous living, the scope of the book applying only to individuals and households, while Qiu's book, imitating Zhen's plan, extends the coverage to public affairs. In reality, however, the two works bear no resemblance to each other except in form. Whereas Zhen concentrates on philosophy and ethics, Qiu's compilation is by and large a comprehensive handbook on public administration, dealing with every aspect of government function including military defence, public finance, personnel management, transportation, water control, etc. Under each entry the historical background is presented, different approaches to every problem are discussed, the author's own opinion is enunciated, and, whenever possible, considerable numerical data are appended. Aside from its practical use, the work is noted for the painstaking research behind it and for its historical value. Being widely read, it exercised a genuine impact on Ming scholarship.[17]

---

[14] See the SB, 215–16.
[15] The first and third of these works are to be found in the CSJC, 32:359 and the CSJC, n.s., 9:534 respectively.
[16] See the CSJC, 132:203–374, *juan* 9, 10, 11, and 13.
[17] See DMB, 1:250.

Wang Yangming 王陽明 (1472–1529): Wang Yangming (Wang Shouren 王守仁) was not only a major philosopher during the Ming period but also a major figure in the political and military activities of his time. In his collected works (e.g. *Wang Yangming quanji* 王陽明全集) there are four writings specifically on the *Daxue*: the *Daxue wen* 大學問, the *Daxue guben xu* 大學古本序, the *Daxue guben bangshi* 大學古本傍釋, and the *Daxue guben yuanxu* 大學古本原序.[18] On the first and most important of the four, Fung Yu-lan has this to say:

> The leading concept in Wang Shou-jen's philosophy appears in his treatise known as the *Ta Hsüeh Wen* or *Questions on the Great Learning*. Wang's disciple, Ch'ien Te-hung (1496–1574), in a comment appended to this treatise, writes: "The *Questions on the Great Learning* is the textbook used by the students of the Teacher. When students first came to him, they were initially given the ideas (in his treatise). . . . (Before its formal compilation, however), when some students requested to record it in writing, he said: 'This (teaching) has to be transmitted verbally by you gentlemen. For if it were set down in writing, then people would consider it simply as some kind of literary document, and it would be of no benefit.' In the eighth month of the *ting-hai* year of Chia-ching (1527), however, when the Teacher was about to start forth on his Ssu-t'ien campaign, the students renewed their request and the Teacher gave his consent." This was hardly more than a year before Wang's death. Hence what is recorded in the *Questions on the Great Learning* may truly be said to represent his final views.[19]

The essay is set out as a series of questions on various passages in the *Daxue* posed to Wang by one of his students.[20]

Zhang Juzheng 張居正 (1525–1582): Zhang is included here not because of his absolute importance as a scholar in relation to the *Daxue* and the *Zhongyong*, but because his work, the *Sishu zhijie* 四書直解, was apparently the basis for the early Jesuit translations of these texts. Zhang was a major political figure, and at one time Imperial Tutor to the Wanli Emperor. Pfister writes: "His commentaries on the Four Books were written in a simpler style for the young emperor, and so were accessible as well as culturally more open

---

18 See the *Wang Yangming quanji* 王陽明全集, 2 vols. (Shanghai: Shanghai guji chubanshe, 1992), 967–73, 242–43, 1192–97 and 1197 respectively.

19 Fung, *The History of Chinese Philosophy*, 2:598–99.

20 For an English translation see F. G. Henke, *The Philosophy of Wang Yang-ming* (Chicago: Open Court, 1916), 204–20.

to political and cosmological positions the Jesuits could also affirm."[21] Jensen describes the *Confucius Sinarum Philosophus* as " . . . an incomplete translation of a recension of the Four Books by Zhang Juzheng, the *Sishu zhijie* 四書直解 . . . "[22] We have not examined this work which is not listed in the SKQS Catalogue.

Zhao Nanxing 趙南星 (1550–1628): Zhao was the precocious offspring of a family of officials and he himself enjoyed examination success and official advancement. However, like so many officials, his career was marked by reverses, and after several of these he returned home in 1593 where he remained for almost 30 years. He prepared a number of essays and works providing relatively straightforward explanations of the Classics, including both the *Daxue* and the *Zhongyong*. He did return to official life only to suffer his most severe reverse late in life (aged 75), after which he returned to live in a small adobe house which he named the "Studio of Tasting the Yellow Bark (bitter remedy)." He was pardoned, but died before receiving notification of this, which was delayed on some bureaucratic pretext.

Chen Que 陳確 (1604–1677): According to Chow, Chen Que's " . . . philosophy was informed by two powerful currents in the early Qing: ritualistic ethics and Confucian purism." One of his most important works was the *Daxue bian* 大學辯 in which he argues against the authenticity of the *Daxue* as a genuine early Confucian work and altogether questions its value.[23] The *Daxue bian* 大學辯, included in the *Chen Que ji* 陳確集, provides a general consideration of the work and a consideration also of other writings on it. Chen's "attack" on the *Daxue* apparently received relatively little attention, although there has been a recent study of it.[24]

---

[21]   See Lauren F. Pfister, *Striving for "The Whole Duty of Man,"* 2 vols. (Frankfurt-am-Main: Peter Lang, 2004), 2:343n426 which gives further references on this matter.

[22]   See Lionel M. Jensen, *Manufacturing Confucianism* (Durham and London: Duke University Press, 1997), 121.

[23]   Chow's comment, part of a synopsis of Chen Que's life and philosophical relevance, appears in Antonio S. Cua, ed., *Encyclopedia of Chinese Philosophy* (New York: Routledge, 2003), 32. Chen's *Daxue bian* 大學辯 comprises *juan* 14–17 of the *Chen Que ji* 陳確集 (2:552–624).

[24]   The *Chen Qianchu Daxue bian yanjiu* 陳乾初大學辯研究 by Zhan Haiyun 詹海雲 (Taipei: Mingwen shuju, 1986).

Wang Fuzhi 王夫之 **(1619–1692):** Two works by this author are of particular importance in relation to the *Daxue* and the *Zhongyong*. The more important is his *Du Sishu daquan shuo* 讀四書大全説 in which the section devoted to the two texts totals 192 pages (59 pages for the *Daxue* and 133 pages for the *Zhongyong*). For each text there is a relatively brief introduction followed by a detailed analysis of each section based on Zhu Xi's numeration. The actual text itself is not given other than as the excerpts being considered. There is also his *Li ji zhengyu* 禮記正語 in two volumes, which is a complete commentary on that work. For the two chapters in question, he follows the *Sishu zhangju* 四書章句 text, including Zhu Xi's notes, to which he appends his own, supplementary notes.

Mao Qiling 毛奇齡 **(1623–1716):** A man of strong opinions strongly expressed, Mao encountered significant difficulties in his life, and evoked severe criticism with his writings. He has been described as "a man of outstanding ability, but tenacious and dogmatic in his opinions" who was "often subjected to severe criticism when he engaged in controversy with the scholars of his time."[25] He was certainly a prolific writer on a variety of subjects—no fewer than 63 works are listed under his name in the SKQS Catalogue. Legge, for one, clearly held him in high regard as the following statement attests:

> The scholars of the present dynasty, however, seem inclined to question the correctness of his (i.e. Zhu Xi's) views and interpretations of the Classics and the chief place among them is due to Mao Qiling, known by the local name of Xihe 西河. His writings, under the name of "The Collected Works of Xihe," have been published in eighty volumes, containing between three and four hundred books or sections. He has nine treatises on the Four Books, or parts of them, and deserves to rank with Zheng Xuan 鄭玄 and Zhu Xi 朱熹 at the head of Chinese scholars, though he is a vehement opponent of the latter. Most of his writings are to be found also in the great work called "A Collection of Works on the Classics, under the Imperial Dynasty of Qing" 皇清經解, which contains 1,400 sections, and is a noble contribution by the scholars of the present dynasty to the illustration of its ancient literature.[26]

---

[25] ECCP, 564.
[26] See proleg. in LCC, 1:20.

In the list of works under Mao's name in the SKQS Catalogue, there are three devoted to the *Daxue* (the *Daxue zhiben tushuo* 大學知本圖説, the *Daxue wen* 大學問 and the *Daxue zhengwen* 大學證問), one to the *Zhongyong* (the *Zhongyong shuo* 中庸説) and two to the Four Books (the *Sishu suojie* 四書索解 and the *Sishu shengyan bu* 四書賸言補).

Hu Wei 胡渭 (1633–1714): Hu came from a family of officials. He studied at the Imperial Academy in Beijing and later worked as private tutor. He was particularly renowned for his work on the *Documents* and the *Changes*, in the latter work opposing in part some of the Song Neo-Confucian interpretations and formulations. He wrote a work on the *Daxue* in seven *juan*, which was included in the SKQS.

Yan Ruoqu 閻若璩 (1636–1704): A brief mention only is made of Yan Ruoqu, recogised as an important scholar—indeed, identified by Wang Zheng as one of the "six great scholars of the Qing"—most renowned for his work on the *Documents*. His relevance to the present texts is that he added his authority to the questioning of Zeng Shen as author of the *Daxue*.

Li Guangdi 李光地 (1642–1718): Li rose to high office, becoming grand secretary in 1705 and retaining this post until his death in 1718. During this time, he headed several commissions for the official compilation of works expounding Song philosophy, including the complete works of Zhu Xi and a synthesis of Neo-Confucian doctrines, the *Xingli jingyi* 性理精義. His works on the two texts listed in the SKQS Catalogue include the *Daxue guben shuo* 大學古本説, the *Zhongyong yulun* 中庸餘論 and the *Zhongyong zhangduan* 中庸章段.[27]

Li Gong 李塨 (1659–1733): Also from the early Qing, and at one time a pupil of Mao Qiling, Li Gong is more closely associated with Yan Yuan. He is said to have used the *Zhongyong* as the basis for lectures to his students. Yang states that " . . . the substance of these lectures was later brought together by Chen Rui'an 陳叡庵 in the *Shugu Zhongyong jiangyu* 恕谷中庸講語."[28] Three works specifically on the *Daxue* and the *Zhongyong* are listed under his name

---

[27]   For a detailed consideration of Li Guangdi's studies on the two texts see On-cho Ng in *Imagining Boundaries: Changing Confucian Doctrines, Texts, and Hermeneutics*, eds. Kai-wing Chow, On-cho Ng and John B. Henderson (New York: State University of New York Press, 1999), 165–93.

[28]   See ECCP, 477.

in the SKQS Catalogue as follows: the *Daxue zhuanzhu* 大學傳注, the *Daxue bianye* 大學辯業 and the *Zhongyong zhuanzhu* 中庸傳注.[29]

Luo Zhongfan 羅仲藩 (died ca. 1850): A late Qing scholar, personally known to Legge, Luo prepared commentaries on the Classics, including one on the *Daxue*—the *Guben Daxue zhubian* 古本大學註辨. In this he strongly opposes the views of Zhu Xi. Luo, and his relationship to Legge and Christianity, has been the subject of a specific study by Lauren Pfister.[30]

Ib. Commentaries & Other Works

(a) *Han shu*, "Yiwenzhi": In this chapter, there are 13 works comprising 555 *pian* on *li* 禮, including one on the *Zhongyong* and also two works named for the putative authors of the *Daxue* and *Zhongyong*—Zengzi and Zisi respectively.[31]

Zhongyong shuo 中庸説 (2 *pian*): no longer extant.
Zisi 子思 (23 *pian*): no longer extant. Zisi (Kong Ji), a grandson of Confucius, is by tradition the author of the *Zhongyong*.
Zengzi 曾子 (18 *pian*): no longer extant. Zengzi (Zeng Shen) was a first generation disciple and putative author of the *Daxue*.

(b) *Sui shu*, "Jingji": In the *Sui shu* bibliography there are, in all, 136 works comprising 1622 *juan* on *li* 禮. Of these, 82 are about the *Li ji* or chapters therein. Again, works by Zengzi and Zisi are listed.

Zengzi 曾子 (2 *juan*): no longer extant.
Zisi 子思 (7 *juan*): no longer extant.
Li ji Zhongyong zhuan 禮記中庸傳 (2 *juan*): attributed to Dai Yong 戴顒 of the Song (5th century). The work is also mentioned in both his biographies (*Song shu* 93 and *Nan shi* 75).[32] It is no longer extant.
Zhongyong jiangshu 中庸講疏 (1 *juan*): attributed to Emperor Wu of Liang 梁武帝 (reigned 502–549); no longer extant.
Siji zhizhi Zhongyong yi 私記制旨中庸義 (5 *juan*): no author indicated; no longer extant.

---

29   For the *Daxue bianye* see CSJC, n.s., 17:419.
30   Lauren Pfister, "Discovering Monotheistic Metaphysics," in *Imagining Boundaries*, eds. Kai-Wing Chow et al, 213–54.
31   See the *Han shu* 30, 6:1709 and 1724.
32   *Song shu* 宋書 93, 8:2276–78 and *Nan shi* 南史 75, 6:1866–67.

(c) SKQS Catalogue (*Sikuquanshu zongmu tiyao*): As detailed below, there are 30 works listed under *Daxue* and 17 under *Zhongyong*. In addition, there are 64 works listed under *Sishu* and 34 under *Li ji* which are not included in the following list.

Daxue benwen 大學本文: Wang Shu 王澍
Daxue benzhi 大學本旨: Li Liwu 黎立武, CSJC, n.s., 17:407–11.
Daxue bianye 大學辨業: Li Gong 李塨, CSJC, n.s., 17:419–31.
Daxue fawei 大學發微: Li Liwu 黎立武 , CSJC, n.s., 17:405–6.
Daxue guankui 大學管窺: Liao Ji 廖紀
Daxue guben 大學古本: Wang Shu 王澍
Daxue guben shuo 大學古本説: Li Guangdi 李光地
Daxue gujin tongkao 大學古今通考: Liu Siyuan 劉斯源
Daxue jiangyi 大學講議: Yang Mingshi 楊名時
Daxue jizhong zhuan 大學稽中傳: Li Jinglun 李經綸
Daxue ouyan 大學偶言: Zhang Wenfeng 張文薑
Daxue qianlü 大學千慮: Mu Konghui 穆孔暉
Daxue shuyi 大學疏義: Jin Lüxiang 金履祥: This work, in 1 *juan*, is described in the *Song Bibliography*, 47–48 and is available in the CSJC, n.s., 17:394–404.
Daxue wen 大學問: Mao Qiling 毛奇齡
Daxue xinbian 大學新編: Liu Yuanqing 劉元卿
Daxue yanyi 大學衍義: Zhen Dexiu 真德秀
Daxue yanyi bu 大學衍義補: Qiu Jun 丘濬
Daxue yanyi bu jiyao 大學衍義補輯要: Chen Hongmou 陳弘謀
Daxue yanyi jiyao 大學衍義輯要: Chen Hongmou 陳弘謀
Daxue yanyi tonglüe 大學衍義通略: Wang Zheng 王諍
Daxue yinxuelu 大學因學錄: Wang Shu 王澍
Daxue yizhen 大學翼真: Hu Wei 胡渭
Daxue zhangju 大學章句: Zhu Xi 朱熹
Daxue zhengwen 大學證文: Mao Qiling 毛奇齡, CSJC, n.s., 17:414–18.
Daxue zhiben tushuo 大學知本圖説: Mao Qiling 毛奇齡
Daxue zhigui 大學指歸: Wei Jiao 魏校
Daxue Zhongyong du 大學中庸讀: Yao Yingren 姚應仁
Daxue Zhongyong jishuo qimeng 大學中庸集説啟蒙: Jing Xing 景星
Daxue zhu 大學註: Cai Xi 蔡悉
Daxue zhuanzhu 大學傳註: Li Gong 李塨
Zhongyong benwen 中庸本文: Wang Shu 王澍

Zhongyong benzhi 中庸本旨: Zhu Jin 朱謹
Zhongyong dianzhui 中庸點綴: Fang Shihua 方時化
Zhongyong fenzhang 中庸分章: Li Liwu 黎立武 , CSJC, n.s., 17:474–79.
Zhongyong guankui 中庸管窺: Liao Ji 廖紀
Zhongyong hezhu 中庸合注: no author
Zhongyong jiangyi 中庸講議: Yang Mingshi 楊名時
Zhongyong jie 中庸解: Ren Daren 任大任
Zhongyong jilüe 中庸輯略: Zhu Xi 朱熹
Zhongyong shuo 中庸說: Mao Qiling 毛奇齡
Zhongyong yanyi 中庸衍義: Xia Liangsheng 夏良勝
Zhongyong yinxuelu 中庸因學錄: Wang Shu 王澍
Zhongyong yulun 中庸餘論: Li Guangdi 李光地
Zhongyong zhangduan 中庸章段: Li Guangdi 李光地
Zhongyong zhangju 中庸章句: Zhu Xi 朱熹
Zhongyong zhigui 中庸指歸: Li Liwu 黎立武, CSJC, n.s., 17:466–69.
Zhongyong zhuanzhu 中庸傳註: Li Gong 李塨

(d) Other Sources:
Daxue guben 大學古本: Zeng Shen 曾參, CSJC, n.s., 17:385–89.
Daxue guben bangzhu 大學古本傍註: Wang Yangming 王陽明, *Wang Yang-
ming quanji*, 2:1192–97.
Daxue guben xu 大學古本序: Wang Yangming 王陽明, *Wang Yangming quanji*,
1:242–43.
Daxue guben yuanxu 大學古本原序: Wang Yangming 王陽明, *Wang Yangming
quanji*, 2:1197.
Daxue jibian 大學集編: Zhen Dexiu 真德秀, CSJC, 32:365–92.
Daxue jiexun 大學節訓: Lü Diaoyang 呂調陽, CSJC, 6:601–6.
Daxue shijing guben 大學石經古本: Zeng Shen 曾參, CSJC, n.s., 17:390–93.
Daxue wen 大學問: Wang Yangming 王陽明, *Wang Yangming quanji*, 2:967–73.
Du Sishu daquan shuo 讀四書大全說: Wang Fuzhi 王夫之 (Beijing: Zhonghua
shuju, 2009).
Gaizheng Daxue 改正大學: Cheng Yi 程頤. This was a work of particular
influence on Zhu Xi. It is included in the *Yichuan jingshuo* 伊川經說 (*juan*
6) and the *Er Cheng quanshu* 二程全書 (*juan* 50). See also the SB, 50.
Guben Daxue jijie 古本大學輯解, Yang Danhua 楊亶驊, CSJC, n.s., 17:432–52.
Guben Daxue zhubian 古本大學註辨, Luo Zhongfan 羅仲藩, available at the
New York Public Library.
Mengzhai Zhongyong Jiangyi 蒙齋中庸講義: Yuan Fu 袁甫, CSJC, 34:299–370.
Xue Yong jiangyi 學庸講義: Zhu Bailu 朱柏盧, CSJC, 34:371–408.

Zhongyong benjie 中庸本解: Yang Danhua 楊亶驊, CSJC, n.s., 17:480–93.

Zhongyong buzhu 中庸補注: Dai Zhen 戴震, CSJC, 34:409–28.

Zhongyong guben 中庸古本: Zisi 子思, CSJC, n.s., 17:453–60.

Zhongyong jibian 中庸集編: Zhen Dexiu 真德秀, CSJC, 32:393–433.

Zhongyong jie 中庸解: Lü Dalin 呂大臨, included in the *Yichuan jingshuo* 伊川經説 (*juan* 8) and the *Er Cheng quanshu* 二程全書 (*juan* 53) but attributed by Zhu Xi to Lü Dalin—see the SB, 50.

Zhongyong jiexun 中庸節訓: Lü Diaoyang 呂調陽, CSJC, 6:606–29.

Zhongyong pianyi 中庸篇義: CSJC, 34:489–98.

Zhongyong qianshuo 中庸淺説: CSJC, 34:499–504.

Zhongyong qieyilu 中庸切已錄: Xie Wenjian 謝文洊, CSJC, 34:429–87.

Zhongyong shuo 中庸説: Zhang Jiucheng 張九成, CSJC, 34:275–98.

Zhongyong shuocan 中庸説殘: Zhang Jiucheng 張九成, listed in the SB and included in the SBCK.

Zhongyong zhiguitu 中庸旨歸圖: Li Liwu 黎立武, CSJC, n.s., 17:470–73.

Zhongyong zhuan 中庸傳: Chao Yuezhi 晁説之, CSJC, n.s., 17:461–65.

II. Translators and Translations

Translations of these two texts into Western languages, either singly or together, or as two components of the Four Books, have been produced intermittently for over four hundred years, beginning with the work of the Jesuits in the 16th and 17th centuries and continuing to the present day. Here we shall confine ourselves to a brief consideration of some aspects of this on-going translation "project." Table 1 lists, in chronological order, the translations we have identified and, for the most part, been able to obtain. For convenience, we shall consider these under three headings: (i) the Jesuits; (ii) 18th and 19th century translations; and (iii) 20th/21st century translations.

(i) The Jesuits: The process of translation of the key Confucian texts (into Latin) began with the first Jesuit missionaries who arrived in China late in the 16th century—Michele Ruggieri (1543–1607) and Matteo Ricci (1552–1610). Among these texts were the *Daxue* and the *Zhongyong*, works which according to Jensen, the Jesuits " . . . found to be particularly inspiring: as many as six partial and complete translations of them were produced by the missionaries between 1588 and 1687" and " . . . not unlike the 20th century Chinese intellectual historians and philosophers in the West, the Jesuits were spiritually aroused by the mystical vision of sociocosmic harmony found in the *Daxue* and the *Zhongyong*."[33]

Of the several compendia of Confucian texts translated into Latin by the Jesuits, the last and most comprehensive was the *Confucius Sinarum Philosophus* which appeared in 1687 under the joint authorship of Intorcetta, Herdtrich, Rougemont and Couplet, and included both the *Daxue* and *Zhongyong* in Latin translation along with a detailed interpretative commentary, as well as a similar translation of the *Lunyu* and other largely historical material. Such was the reception of this work in Europe that abridgements in French and English quickly appeared, the latter under the title of *The Morals of Confucius*.[34] The role of the Jesuits in creating the concept of Confucianism in the West has recently been examined in detail by Jensen in the work referred to above. As for the translations themselves, they are still of interest, based as they are on the commentaries of Zhu Xi and Zhang Juzheng, although both translation and commentary inevitably reflect the Christian religious background and motivations of the translators, as do the later translations of the British Protestant missionaries.

---

[33]   See Jensen, *Manufacturing Confucianism*, 59–61.
[34]   Randal Taylor, *The Morals of Confucius a Chinese Philosopher* (London: J. Fraser, 1691).

Table 1: Translations of the *Daxue* and *Zhongyong* into European Languages

Translator	*Daxue* 大學	*Zhongyong* 中庸
Intorcetta et al (1687)	Magnae Scientiae	De medio sempiterno
Noël (1784)	La Grande Science, ou la Science des Adults	Le Juste Milieu, ou Le Milieu Immuable
Abel-Rémusat (1817)		L'Invariable Milieu
Collie (1828)	Superior Learning	The Golden Medium
Pauthier (1837)	La Grande Étude	L'Invariabilité dans la Milieu
Legge (1861)	The Great Learning	The Doctrine of the Mean
Legge (1885)	The Great Learning	The State of Equilibrium & Harmony
Couvreur (1895)	La Grande Étude	L'Invariable Milieu
Gu Hongming (1906)		The Conduct of Life
Lyall & King Chien-kün (1927)		The Centre, The Common
Wilhelm (1930)	Die Grosse Wissenschaft	Mass und Mitte
Haloun (no date)		Untitled
Hughes (1943)	The Great Learning	The Mean in Action
Chan Wing-tsit (1963)	The Great Learning	The Doctrine of the Mean
Weber-Schäfer (1968)	Die Grosse Lehre	Anwendung der Mitte
Pound (1969)	The Great Digest	The Unwobbling Pivot
Bahm (1969)	Great Wisdom	Genuine Living
Riegel (1978)		Application of the Inner
Hasse (1984)	La Grande Étude	
Gardner (1986)/(2007)	The Greater Learning/The Great Learning	Maintaining Perfect Balance
Tu Wei-ming (1989)* (many passages translated but not a complete translation)		Centrality & Commonality
Moran (1993)	The Great Learning	The Doctrine of the Mean
Jullien (1993)		La Regulation à Usage Ordinaire
Fu Yunlong & He Zuokang (1996)	The Great Learning	The Doctrine of the Mean
Ames & Hall (2001)		Focusing the Familiar
Plaks (2003)	The Highest Order of Cultivation	On the Practice of the Mean
Sanderson Beck (2007)		The Center of Harmony

(ii) 18th & 19th Century Translations: The translations from this period were predominantly those of missionaries working in China itself or nearby countries. The first of these was the seven volume work by F. Noël, *Les Livres Classiques de l'Empire de la Chine* which included the *Daxue* and the *Zhongyong* in volume 2. There were also the first contributions from academic Sinology to the translation of classical Chinese texts, beginning with the French school and including the later work of Legge after his transition from missionary work to academia. The two early French academic works, those of J-P Abel-Rémusat and of Guillaume Pauthier, are of particular interest, and are quite different in nature.[35] In form, at least, Abel-Rémusat's translation of the *Zhongyong* alone, published in 1817, is an outstanding work, providing a substantial introduction, the Chinese text, both French and Latin translations, a Manchu translation as an appendix, and detailed end-notes. Pauthier, whose translation of the Four Books was first published in 1837, offered a French translation with relatively detailed notes, but no Chinese text. Legge, in the introduction to his own translation of the *Daxue*, recoils somewhat from Pauthier's unequivocally expressed admiration for that text: " . . . my readers will probably conclude that the Work before us is far from developing, as Pauthier asserts, 'a system of social perfectionating which has never been equalled.'"[36]

In the next wave of missionary translations the baton passed to the British Protestant missionaries, Robert Morrison (1785–1834) and Joshua Marshman (1768–1837), and their work on the Four Books. The first complete English translation of the *Daxue* and the *Zhongyong* would appear to be that by another British Protestant missionary, David Collie in his work entitled *The Chinese Classical Work Commonly Called the Four Books*, first published in 1828 (the year of Collie's death), but reprinted as recently as 1970. Collie remarks, in a note to his preface, that he had " . . . seen two English Translations of the Ta Heo (i.e. the *Daxue*)—one by Dr. Morrison, and another published in Serampore in 1814,

---

[35] Pfister has the following comment on these two early French sinologists: "During the first half of the 19th century, the sinological works of the French Academy by Abel-Rémusat, Pauthier and Julien sought to place many kinds of Chinese literature into the broader spectrum of cross-cultural literatures. This included philological, religious, and philosophical studies of the Ruist canon. The results varied in their degree of accuracy and insight, ensuing in one lifelong battle over mistranslations and misrepresentations between Stanislaus Julien, the critical and eccentric scholar, and Guillaume Pauthier, the sinological popularist" (Pfister, *Striving for the "Whole Duty of Man,"* 2:151).

[36] See proleg. in LCC, 1:33.

and ascribed to Mr. John Marshman, Son of the Rev. Dr. Marshman . . . "[37]
Collie's work itself has been severely criticised by Pfister who remarks, *vis-à-vis*
the translation, that it " . . . was flawed by some elementary linguistic mistakes,
showed little contact with Chinese traditions of commentary, and was at times,
in footnotes aggressive in criticizing these ancient Chinese teachings from the
perspective of Christian theology."[38] Whilst the third limb of the criticism
is doubtless deserved, at least up to a point, the first perceived failing might
be forgiven in view of the pioneering nature of the work and the translator's
own remarks on his efforts.[39] On the question of commentary, there are, in
fact, detailed footnotes which include quite extensive translations from the
commentaries of Zhu Xi (in particular) and others.

The high point of the missionary endeavours in English translation was,
of course, the remarkable work of James Legge (1815–1897) who came to his
missionary work from a background of high academic achievement in ancient
languages and whose obvious Christian bias suffered a steady attrition over
several decades with his increasing immersion in early Chinese literature and
contact with native Chinese scholars. His translations of the *Daxue* and the

---

[37]   See David Collie, *The Chinese Classical Work Commonly Called the Four Books (1828)* (1828;
      repr., Gainsville, FL: Scholars' Facsimiles & Reprints, 1970), preface, p. iii.

[38]   Pfister provides a brief but interesting, historically based consideration of the problems
      of translation with particular reference to the Chinese classics in Cua, *Encyclopedia of
      Chinese Philosophy*, 734–39. For his comments on Collie see p. 735.

[39]   We include the following somewhat lengthy quotation from Collie's preface, allowing
      him to speak in his own defence: " . . . for nothing we can urge will afford any sufficient
      apology for the faults and defects with which we are well aware the work abounds. Some
      will say, that in many instances the rendering is too literal and in others too free, and
      in many cases the spirit and force of the original have been lost. Others may observe
      so many Chinesisms and Scotticisms in the style that they will be apt to say that it
      does not deserve the name of an *English* version. To such charges we are ready to plead
      guilty; but trust that the frequent obscurity and uniform conciseness of the original, will,
      in some degree, be admitted as our apology. At least if such considerations as those do
      not tend to soften the severity of criticism, we have no other to offer, for the translation
      was written with due deliberation and with good native assistance, and with the same
      assistance every page of it has again been carefully compared with the original; nor has
      the translator failed to avail himself of the aid to be derived from the English and Latin
      Versions of the Four Books to which he had access, and although he has often taken the
      liberty to differ from his highly respectable Predecessors and been guided principally by
      native Commentators, still he has frequently received considerable assistance from the
      former. So that either the difficulty of the task, or the ignorance of the Translator, or
      both, can form the only apology for the faults of the version." See Collie, *The Chinese
      Classical Work Commonly Called the Four Books (1828)*, pp. v–vi.

Zhongyong appeared in the first volume of *The Chinese Classics*, published in 1861, where the order of the Four Books was changed from that established by Zhu Xi, with the *Lunyu* being placed first, the *Mencius* last (in a second volume), and the *Daxue* and *Zhongyong* second and third respectively. These works by Legge are exemplary works, allowing for their inevitable Christian bias (which translator is entirely free of some form of bias!) and what might now seem somewhat dated phraseology. Quite apart from the quality of the actual translations, the arrangement is excellent for anyone with a serious interest in the texts: the Chinese text is available in direct apposition to the translation and detailed, helpful notes, drawing heavily on the two main Chinese commentarial traditions, as well as the work of earlier translators are provided, also on the same page. Legge's second version of the two tracts appeared in his complete translation of the *Li ji* published in 1885 after his resignation from the missionary service and appointment to the Chair of Chinese at Oxford in 1876. The translations are very similar, although by no means identical, but there is no Chinese text and the notes are much reduced.

Finally, there is the work of the Catholic missionary, F. Seraphin Couvreur whose translations of both texts appeared in his *Quatre Livres* (1895) and in his *Li Ki ou Mémoires sur les bienséances et les cérémonies* (1899–1913). Couvreur arranges his material in a manner somewhat similar to Legge in his *Chinese Classics*, each page containing the Chinese text, French and Latin translations, notes and commentary.

(iii) 20th/21st century translations: In all, we examined 19 translations of one or other or both of the texts published between 1906 and the present (Tu Wei-ming's work, marked with an asterisk in Table 1, is not a continuous translation). Of these, fourteen were into English, two into French, and two into German, and include all the translations listed in Vittinghof's recent bibliography.[40] Considering the English translations first, eight were of both works together. In chronological order, the first were those by Hughes and Wing-tsit Chan in 1943 and 1963 respectively. Both were contained within much larger compendia of Chinese philosophical writing although Hughes' translations were subsequently published separately with a general introduction on the history of Chinese philosophy. Next were the translations by Pound and Bahm. In Pound's case the translation is incomplete and far from literal.

---

[40]   Helmolt Vittinghoff, "Recent Bibliography in Classical Chinese Philosophy," *Journal of Chinese Philosophy* (2001): 28.

Nevertheless, it is highly readable, captures the spirit of the works, and contains some arresting formulations, as one might expect. Bahm's translations, which include a short introduction and brief notes, clearly have the primary aim of making the works accessible to the general reader. Moran places the two Confucian works in somewhat uneasy juxtaposition with the *Laozi*, although some might argue that they are not altogether mismatched bedfellows. Moran does include the Chinese text but his notes are absolutely minimal. His introduction, which covers both texts, is brief but to the point. Next was the bilingual version by Fu Yunlong and He Zuokang published in Beijing in 1996. This provides the original Chinese text together with a modern Chinese version and an English translation without notes, following a brief introduction for each book. Of the two most recent translations of both works together, that by Plaks includes a relatively detailed analysis of the background of the two works and the issues within them that have been the focus of commentators over the centuries. Plaks offers a somewhat unusual, but very readable, translation of the two works, but as he himself readily acknowledges, the English version certainly departs to a notable extent from the Chinese original in a number of places.[41] Gardner's translations include the other two of the Four Books. The translations are of high quality, both accurate and highly readable, and he also gives a good deal of attention to Zhu Xi's commentary. He does, however, offer only selected passages from both texts.

Of the seven English translations of single works, four were detailed studies: those of Haloun, Riegel, and Ames and Hall for the *Zhongyong* and that of Gardner for the *Daxue*. Two of the *Zhongyong* translations also contain the Chinese text, whilst Gardner's translation of the *Daxue* gives particularly detailed consideration to Zhu Xi's commentary, both that in the *Sishu zhangju* and in other works such as the *Yulei*, and includes the Chinese text as an appendix. Unfortunately, two of these works, both of which we found most helpful in our own translations, are not generally available: one is the unpublished MS by Gustav Haloun presently held in the Needham Research Institute, Cambridge,[42] and the other is Riegel's PhD thesis. The other version of the *Zhongyong*, that of Ames & Hall, is also of considerable interest but presents a deliberately idiosyncratic view of a number of the key elements.

---

[41]   Plaks writes, in his introduction, " . . . I frequently allow myself considerable leeway in my formulations, for example, inserting additional words to convey loaded Chinese concepts, or combining Chinese stylistic redundancies into single propositions . . . " (p. xxxvi).

[42]   Our considerable gratitude is due to Sue Bennett and John Moffett of the Needham Research Institute, Cambridge for providing a CD of this manuscript.

It is a translation fashioned in the light of modern Western philosophy, notably that of A. N. Whitehead, rather than one based principally on the Chinese commentarial tradition.

The three other translations in this group are of the *Zhongyong* only. The first of these, by Gu Hongming (Ku Hung-ming), was initially published in 1906 under the title of "The Conduct of Life," but is now preserved in Lin Yutang's *The Wisdom of Confucius* where it is the only translation not by the author himself. As the title indicates, it is a somewhat imaginative translation. The translation by Lyall and King Chien-kün, published in 1927, has a short introduction and very little in the way of notes, whilst that of Beck is a translation available on the internet, with virtually no accompanying material.

The two recent French translations are of single works. That of Hasse, of the *Daxue*, is unique among the works examined both in giving separate translations of the *Li ji* and the *Sishu zhangju* texts and in providing a full translation of Zhu Xi's notes in the latter. However, no Chinese text is given in either case and the focus is particularly on Zhu Xi's version, there being no notes for the *Li ji* version, which is termed the "version ancienne." Jullien's translation is of the *Zhongyong* and is based on Zhu Xi's text. The translation is preceded by a short but informative introduction (particularly on the question of how the title should be rendered) and supplemented for each section by the translator's notes. We have not examined the two German works cited, the first being Richard Wilhelm's translation of the *Li ji* and the second, Weber-Schäfer's study of the two works. Also we have not explored the extensive literature in other Asian languages, especially Japanese, Korean and Manchu, which might well be the subject of a separate study.

Finally, mention should also be made of the analyses by Tu Wei-ming and Fung Yu-lan (Feng Youlan). The former, confined to the *Zhongyong*, is a separate monograph of some 165 pages, which not only presents a detailed and informative consideration of the work as a whole, but also contains translations of many passages scattered throughout the discussion. In addition, it is an excellent source of reference to modern Chinese studies of the work. Fung Yu-lan's contribution, necessarily much shorter in the context of a general work on Chinese philosophy, is nonetheless informative in respect to both works and also has translations of several key passages.

Appendix 3—Terminology

Three groups of terms common (in most instances) to both works will be considered here:

1. Terms on which there is general agreement as to the appropriate English rendering—a brief comment only will be made on each of these.
2. Terms for which, we would argue, there is no satisfactory English equivalent—for these, a list of the various attempts at translation will be given, focussing mainly on the two books in question, then a series of quotations from relevant Chinese and Western sources arranged in chronological order. There are four such terms: *cheng* 誠, *ren* 仁, *yi* 義, and *li* 禮.
3. Terms relatively specific to the two treatises and subsequent discussions of them. These are: *ge wu* 格物; *guo/wu ji* 過/無及; *xie ju zhi dao* 絜矩之道; *zhong yong/zhong he* 中庸/中和; and *zi qi* 自欺. Again, a series of quotations in chronological order will be give for each term, followed by a concluding statement.

1. Terms on Which There is General Agreement

Dao 道—the Way: This is the widely accepted translation of *dao* 道 in the nominal form. The *Li ji* commentators make specific mention of the use of *dao* 道 in the verbal sense ("to say") whenever it occurs as such in these texts. The *Shuowen jiezi* 説文解字 definition is: "That which is travelled is the *dao* 道 (way); one who attains it calls it the *Dao* 道 (Way)." The only real alternative is to romanise the term, but this carries the risk here of some implied connection with Daoism.

De 德—virtue: In the majority of instances in the present texts *de* 德 is used alone rather than in conjunction with *dao* 道, an association particularly characteristic of the *Laozi*. The following statement is from Ryden's translation of Zhang Dainian's 張岱年 work *Zhongguo gudian zhexue gainian fanchou yaolun* 中國古典哲學概念範疇要論 (*Key Concepts in Chinese Philosophy*): "The original meaning of the term *de* 德 is difficult to determine. Some guesses have been made by scholars of early writing but no reliable conclusion has been reached. The modern meaning of the term is 'morally praiseworthy behaviour,' 'high moral character.' *The Explanation of the Characters* (i.e. the *Shouwen jiezi*) says, '*De* 德 is what is won from others outside and from the self inside.' In other words, it refers to the proper means of dealing with social relations between the self and others."[43] We have taken *de* 德 as a general term for virtue which includes the specific virtues such as *ren* 仁, *yi* 義, *li* 禮, etc. Where it is used in conjunction with *dao* 道, we have rendered this "the Way of virtue" rather than introduce the other possibility, "power."

He 和—harmony: Although this is the common translation of *he* 和, it is by no means the only one possible. For example, in a key *Lunyu* passage (XIII.23)—子曰，君子和而不同，小人同而不和—which Watson translates as "The gentleman acts in harmony with others but does not ape them. The petty man apes others but is not in harmony with them," Waley uses "conciliatory" and Legge "affable." Indeed, in the four uses of *he* 和 in the *Lunyu* listed in his index, Legge uses four different translations: natural ease, affable, harmony and harmonious.[44] Ryden quotes the commentary of He Yan et al on this passage, and adds the following: "The sage is able to accept difference and so produce harmony, whereas the mean man can only choose one thing and hence different things compete for his attention; he is not at harmony. He Yan has moved the focus from the degree of assent with another . . . and concentrated on the state of mind of the *speaker*."[45] This clearly relates to the use in the *Zhongyong* (vide infra).

Junzi 君子—noble man: *Jun* 君 is a general term for a ruler and therefore *junzi* 君子, the son of a *jun* 君, is a person of high birth. The term as used

---

[43] See E. Ryden, *Key Concepts in Chinese Philosophy* (Beijing: Foreign Languages Press, 2002), 338.

[44] See Burton Watson, *The Analects of Confucius* (New York: Columbia University Press, 2007), 93, Arthur Waley, *The Analects of Confucius* (London: George Allen & Unwin, 1971), 177 and LCC, 1:273. The other three passages in the *Lunyu* are, respectively, I.12 (LCC, 1:143), XVI.1/10 (LCC, 1:308 and XIX.24/4 (LCC, 1:349).

[45] Ryden, *Key Concepts in Chinese Philosophy*, 272.

in the present texts (and in other early writing including the *Lunyu*) means rather more than that. Included is the meaning of high moral character, whilst the connection to ruling is by no means lost. The most common translations are "superior man" (which, in English, can have a pejorative sense) and "gentleman" (which seems to lack the required weight). In addition, both lack the connection to ruling. More elaborate renderings such as exemplary or paradigmatic person, while capturing the force of the term more satisfactorily, are rather cumbersome. The opposite term, *xiao ren* 小人, commonly used in conjuction with *junzi* 君子, also presents something of a problem. The usual translations as "petty," "mean" or "small" appear to identify a sub-class of all those who are not *junzi* 君子, whereas what seems to be meant, in most instances, is all those who have not attained the status of *junzi* 君子. For *xiaoren* 小人, we have settled for "lesser men," i.e. less than a *junzi* 君子, although simply "other men" might be a reasonable alternative. For *junzi* itself we have settled on "noble man."

Qing 情—emotions, feelings: These usual translations of *qing* 情 are relatively uncontentious. A specific instance where this translation is appropriate is the list of "emotions" given by Xun Zi—"the love, hate, joy, anger, sadness and happiness of human nature are what are called *qing* 情 (emotions)."[46] The contrast between *qing* 情 and *xing* 性 (nature) is brought out in the following quotation from Liu Xiang: "Nature is what one is born with. It is just so. It is in the person and does not develop out. The emotions reach out to things and are so. They go out of the bodily form and encounter the outside."[47] The term is, however, somewhat more wide-ranging than "emotions" alone. It appears only once in the *Daxue* and there is equated with *shi* 實 in the sense of "truth" by both *Li ji* commentators. It does not appear at all in the text of the *Zhongyong* but is important in the commentary, particularly in relation to *xing* 性. In considering the wider meaning of the term, Ames and Hall write: "Since feelings define the quality of one's interactions, the proper expression of such feelings is a singularly important element in the early Confucian conception of a person. *Qing* 情 is 'what something really is' in the sense that the unmediated experience itself resides in affective transactions that become selective and abstract when reduced to the cognitive structures of language."[48]

---

[46] See the *Xunzi* 22.
[47] Ryden, *Key Concepts in Chinese Philosophy*, 384.
[48] Ames and Hall, *Focusing the Familiar: A Translation and Philosophical Interpretation of the Zhongyong*, 73.

Tian 天—Heaven: This is a complex term. First, it is an objective reality—the sky. Second, it is the embodiment of a supramundane force capable of direct intervention in human affairs specifically, and in worldly affairs generally. Third, it is paired with Earth and, indeed, in the *Zhongyong*, can be one component of a triad comprising also Earth and the sage to effect and control the necessary creations and transformations of life. The problem with anthropomorphising Heaven, as we and others have done, is that it introduces unwanted associations with the Judaeo-Christian tradition. As Ames & Hall (who favour direct romanisation) point out in defence of their decision, these theological associations are " . . . largely irrelevant to the Chinese experience but, nonetheless, have often overwritten Chinese cultural practices with presuppositions that are alien to them. In any case, we must extricate the term from these unfortunate associations if we are to develop an understanding of *tian* 天."[49] We have settled on "Heaven" as a translation, these difficulties notwithstanding.

Xin 心—heart and mind: The options are to choose one or other of the components of this somewhat cumbersome compound, either consistently or variably according to context, or to accept the compound term. The grounds for doing the latter are well stated by Ames & Hall—" . . . there are many passages in these classical texts that would not make sense in English unless xin thinks as well as feels. The point, of course, is that in this classical Chinese world view, the mind cannot be divorced from the heart. To avoid such a dichotomy, we have translated xin rather inelegantly as 'heart and mind' with the intention of reminding the reader that there are no rational thoughts devoid of feeling, nor any raw feelings altogether lacking in cognitive content."[50] We have used "mind-heart" in some instances, on the ground that "mind" is undoubtedly the dominant sense in most cases in the two texts being translated, but have also used the individual components separately where context seems to dictate.

Xing 性—(human) nature: There is general acceptance of this translation. Ryden (Zhang Dainian) opens his consideration of the term as follows: "Theories of human nature in ancient Chinese philosophy abound and are

---

[49]   See Ames and Hall, *Focusing the Familiar: A Translation and Philosophical Interpretation of the Zhongyong*, 79.

[50]   Ames and Hall, *Focusing the Familiar: A Translation and Philosophical Interpretation of the Zhongyong*, 82.

very complicated. . . . By and large two trends of interpretation are to be found. On one hand 'human nature' refers to what is innate; on the other, it refers to what distinguishes human beings from animals and is thus specific to humans."[51] Han Yu has the following to say in the opening sentences of his "Yuan xing" 原性 (Original Nature) which is particularly relevant to the *Daxue* and *Zhongyong*:

> [Human] nature is born at the time of birth; emotion is born when there is contact with things. Nature has three grades and five components by which it is nature; emotion has three grades and seven components by which it is emotion. "What are these?" you say. I say the three grades of nature are superior, middle and inferior. The superior is entirely good; the middle can be led to become either superior or inferior; the inferior is entirely bad. As to what the five components are, I say they are *ren* 仁, *li* 禮, *xin* 信, *yi* 義 and *zhi* 智.[52]

Yi 意—intentions: Basically, *yi* 意 can have the meaning of either intentions or ideas; that is, it can apply to volition or to mentation (conceptualisation). Purpose (in effect, a variant of intention) can also be used. In modern usage, *yi* 意 is combined with *zhi* 志 to refer to "will." Zhu Xi (DX1.4) offers the definition that *yi* 意 are what the mind-heart sends forth (意者，心之所發也) which could apply equally well to intentions and ideas (thoughts). Quite a few translators do, in fact, use the latter. We have settled for the former.

Yong 勇—courage: Bravery and valour are also suitable. The important point in the two texts is to understand a significant mental or moral component to the courage in addition to the physical. For example: "The Master said: ' . . . To see what is *yi* 義 and not do it is to be without courage (*yong* 勇).'"[53]

Zhi 知/智—knowledge, wisdom: these are the widely accepted translations, although in the case of the first graph, only when it is used in the sense of the second. The two were used to a definite extent interchangeably in early literature. One of the most detailed early analyses is that in the Later Mohist Canons. Here *zhi* 知 is equated with both *cai* 材 (capacity) and *jie* 接 (contacting), and in a more extended statement, "*zhi* 知 (knowing) [is by] hearing (*wen* 聞), explaining (*shuo* 説) and personally experiencing (*qin* 親); (it is about) names

---

51   See Ryden, *Key Concepts in Chinese Philosophy*, 367–68.
52   *Xinyi Changli Xiansheng wenji* 新譯昌黎先生文集, 1:13–14.
53   *Lunyu* II.24(2), LCC, 1:154.

(*ming* 名), entities (*shi* 實), correlations (*he* 合) and actions (*wei* 為)."[54] In our translations both "knowledge" and "wisdom" are used, either together or separately, according to context.

***Zhi* 志**—will: Chen Chun 陳淳 (1159–1223) has the following statement on *zhi* 志: "*Zhi* 志 means where the mind wants to go. To go means to proceed in a certain direction. It means that the heart and mind face the front and go completely in that direction. Take the saying, 'Set your *zhi* 志 on the Way.' That means that the heart and mind are completely directed toward the Way. Or take the saying, 'Set your *zhi* 志 on learning.' That means the heart and mind are completely directed toward learning. One must go straight in the search and be strongly determined to achieve the objective—that is *zhi* 志. If in the process there is any interruption or deviation, that cannot be called *zhi* 志."[55] *Zhi* 志 as "will" is infrequent in the two texts translated here.

2. Terms without a Satisfactory English Equivalent

Cheng 誠

English Translations: sincerity (Collie, Legge, Pound, Fu Yunlong); being true (to oneself) (Lau, Gardner, Gu Hongming); creativity (Ames & Hall); real/realness (Chan); integral wholeness (Plaks); integrity (Moran); authenticity (Ryden).

Mencius:[56] Mencius said: "If those in subordinate positions do not gain the confidence of superiors, the people cannot be won over and brought to good order. There is a way to gain the confidence of superiors. If he is not trusted by friends, he will not gain the confidence of superiors. There is a way to be trusted by friends. If, in serving his parents, he does not please them, he will not be trusted by friends. There is a way to please his parents. If he looks at himself and finds he is not *cheng* 誠, he will not please his parents. To make himself *cheng* 誠, there is the Way. If he is not transparently good, he will not make himself *cheng* 誠. Therefore, to be *cheng* 誠 is the Way of Heaven; to

---

54 See Ian Johnston, *The Mozi: A Complete Translation* (Hong Kong: Chinese University Press, 2010), Canons A3, A5 and A80.

55 See Chan, *Neo-Confucian Terms Explained (The Pei-hsi tzu-i)*, 64–65. The translation follows Chan with minor modifications. The first sentence is a quotation from Zhu Xi's *Zhu Zi yulei* 朱子語類, whilst the two "sayings" are from the *Lunyu* VII.6 and II.5 respectively.

56 *Mencius* IVA.12, Lau, *Mencius*, 160–61. This passage is very similar, indeed almost identical to ZY18 (*Li ji*), ZY20.5 (Zhu Xi).

think about *cheng* 誠 is the Way of man. There has never been anyone with perfect *cheng* 誠 who did not influence others; conversely, there has never been anyone who was able to influence others who was not *cheng* 誠."

Xun Zi:[57] If the mind-heart that is *cheng* 誠 puts into practice *yi* 義, then there is principle (*li* 理); if there is principle, then there is enlightenment; if there is enlightment, then there can be change. If there is change and transformation repeatedly flourishing, it is called Heavenly virtue. Heaven does not speak and yet people praise it as high. Earth does not speak and yet people praise it as bounteous. The four seasons do not speak and yet the ordinary people know their times. Their having this constancy is through the perfection of their *cheng* 誠. When the noble man has perfect virtue, he is silent and yet he is loved, he is not angry and yet he is held in awe. Now this is to follow [Heaven's] decree by being *cheng* 誠 in his inner self (when he is alone). One who is good at carrying out the Way, if he is not *cheng* 誠, then he is not 'alone'; if he is not alone, then he has no form. If he has no form, then although he creates with his heart and mind, reveals with his countenance, and expresses himself with words, the people, nonetheless, will never follow him. Or if they do, it will certainly be with suspicion. Heaven and Earth are great indeed, but if they are without *cheng* 誠, then they are not able to transform the ten thousand things. Sages are knowledgeable indeed, but if they are without *cheng* 誠, then they are not able to transform the ten thousand people. Fathers and sons are loving indeed, but if they are not *cheng* 誠, then they are distant [from each other]. Rulers and superiors are honoured indeed, but if they are not *cheng* 誠, then they are base. *Cheng* 誠, then, is what the noble man preserves and is the foundation of government and affairs . . . For the noble man there is nothing better than *cheng* 誠 in nourishing the mind. If there is perfect *cheng* 誠, nothing else is required. With it, *ren* 仁 is maintained and *yi* 義 is put into practice. If the mind is made *cheng* 誠 and *ren* 仁 is maintained, then there is form.

Li Ao:[58] *Cheng* 誠 is the nature of the sage. It is "docile and unmoving," broad and great, clear and bright, illuminating Heaven and Earth. "When influenced, it reaches out to all phenomena under Heaven." In their going and resting, their speaking and silence, there is nowhere they do not attain to the peak.

---

57   *Xunzi 3, Xunzi jianshi,* 29–30.
58   Li Ao, "Restoring Nature," see Ryden, *Key Concepts in Chinese Philosophy,* 143.

Zhou Dunyi:[59] *Cheng* 誠 is the foundation of the sage. "Great is *qian* 乾, the originator! All things obtain their beginning from it." It is the source of *cheng* 誠. "The way of *qian* 乾 is to change and transform so that everything will obtain its correct nature and destiny." In this way, *cheng* 誠 is established. It is pure and perfectly good. Therefore "the successive movement of *yin* and *yang* constitutes the Way. What issues from the Way is good, and that which realizes it is the individual nature." Origination and flourish characterise the penetration of *cheng* 誠, and advantage and firmness are its completion (or recovery). Great is the *Changes*, the source of nature and destiny!

Sagehood is nothing but *cheng* 誠. It is the foundation of the Five Constant Virtues (*ren* 仁, *yi* 義, *li* 禮, *zhi* 智, and *xin* 信) and the source of all activities. When tranquil, it is in the state of non-being, and when active, it is in the state of being. It is perfectly correct and clearly penetrating. Without *cheng* 誠, the Five Constant Virtues and all activities will be wrong. They will be depraved and obstructed. Therefore, with *cheng* 誠, very little effort is needed [to achieve the Mean]. [In itself] it is perfectly easy yet it is difficult to put into practice. But with determination and firmness, there will be no difficulty. Therefore it is said, "If a man can for one day master himself and return to *li* 禮, all under Heaven will return to *ren* 仁."

Cheng 誠 [in its original substance] engages in no activity, but is the subtle, incipient, activating force giving rise to good and evil. The virtue of loving is called *ren* 仁, that of doing what is proper is called *yi* 義, that of putting things in order is called *li* 禮, that of penetration is called *zhi* 智, and that of abiding by one's commitments is called *xin* 信. One who is in accord with his nature and acts with ease is a sage. One who returns to his nature and adheres to it is a worthy. And one whose subtle emanation cannot be seen and whose [goodness] is abundant and all-pervasive without limit is a man of the spirit.

Chen Chun:[60] *Cheng* 誠 is similar in meaning to loyalty and faithfulness, and yet they must be distinguished. *Cheng* 誠 is a description of natural principles, whereas loyalty and faithfulness have to do with human effort. Latter-day scholars were all wrong about *cheng* 誠. It was not until Yichuan (Cheng Yi) who said that "*cheng* 誠 is freedom from error" that its meaning became clear. Later Huian (Zhu Xi) added two words to say that "*cheng* 誠 means reality, truth, and freedom from error" and thus the principle became especially

---

59 From "Penetrating the *Book of Changes*"—see Chan, *A Source Book in Chinese Philosophy*, 465–66.
60 From Chan, *Neo-Confucian Terms Explained (The Pei-hsi tzu-i)*, 97.

transparent. In talking about perfect *cheng* 誠, latter-day scholars have been apt to expect it of ordinary people, making it merely mean respect, modesty, and sincerity, without realizing that it denotes reality, truth, and freedom from error. Perfect *cheng* 誠 means being real and true to the highest degree without the slightest deficiency. Only a sage can measure up to this. How can it easily be expected of ordinary people? . . .

Wang Fuzhi:[61] *Cheng* 誠 binds together the principles under Heaven and does not exclude anything. It threads through the centre of everything and there is nothing it does not penetrate.

Speaking of *cheng* 誠, it is a key word and no other word can replace it or explain it. Even more, there is no manner of speech that can oppose its form. It is said of all that is good in the world. It is said of all that penetrates my body, mind, will and knowledge and is not not one with goodness.

Cheng 誠 depends on things to make its efforts apparent. Things take *cheng* 誠 as their stem.

Cheng 誠 is what really exists. What is at the beginning has that where it begins; what is at the end has that where it ends. What really is, is what is held in common by all the world. It is what those with eyes can all see and those with ears can all hear.

Legge:[62] The ideal of humanity—the perfect character belonging to the sage, which ranks him on a level with Heaven—is indicated by *cheng* 誠, and we have no single term in English, which can be considered as the complete equivalent of that character. The Chinese themselves had great difficulty in arriving at that definition of it which is now generally acquiesced in. In the *Sishu tong* 四書通 (quoted in the *Huican* 匯參, *Zhongyong* 中庸, xvi.5), we are told that "the Han scholars were all ignorant of its meaning. Under the Song dynasty, first came Li Bangzhi 李邦直, who defined it by *bu qi* 不欺 (freedom from all deception). After him, Xu Zhongche 徐仲車 said that it meant *bu xi* 不息 (ceaselessness). Then, one of the Cheng (brothers) called it *wu wang* 無妄 (freedom from all moral error); and finally, Zhu Xi added to this the positive element of *zhenshi* 真實 (truth and reality), on which the definition of *cheng* 誠 was complete." Rémusat calls it *la perfection*, and *la perfection morale*. Intorcetta and his friends call it *vera solidaque perfectio*. Simplicity or singleness

61 The following quotations are all taken from Ryden, *Key Concepts in Chinese Philosophy*, 145–46.
62 LCC, 1:414–15n21.

of soul seems to be what is chiefly intended by the term—the disposition to, and the capacity of, what is good, without any deteriorating element, with no defect of intelligence, or intromission of selfish thoughts. This belongs to Heaven, to Heaven and Earth, and to the Sage. Men, not naturally sages, may, by cultivating the intelligence of what is good, raise themselves to this elevation.

Ivanhoe:[63] I follow the standard practice of translating the Chinese character *cheng* 誠 as "sincere" with the qualification that this means "true to one's innate moral mind." A. C. Graham sought to bring out this sense of the word by translating it as "integrity." . . . The idea is that a thing is *cheng* when it is as it ought to be, i.e. when it follows its *li*. And so being sincere for Wang means realising or bringing into being the true state of one's nature. This is appropriately thought of as "integrity."

Ren 仁

Translations Used: perfect virtue (Legge, *Lunyu*); Goodness (Waley); humaneness (Watson); benevolence (Legge, *Zhongyong*); magnanimity (Legge, *Zhongyong*); authoritative conduct (Ames & Hall); human kindness (Plaks); human heartedness; true goodness (Gardner); altruism (Chan); humane behaviour (Knoblock); humanity (Chan).

Zuo zhuan:[64] Zhongni said: "In ancient times it was in the annals that to subdue the self and return to *li* 禮 was *ren* 仁."

Confucius:[65] Yan Yuan asked about *ren* 仁. The Master said: "To master yourself and return to *li* 禮 is to be *ren* 仁. Master yourself for one day and all under Heaven will ascribe *ren* 仁 to you. Being *ren* 仁 comes from yourself; how could it come from others?"

Zhonggong asked about *ren* 仁. The Master said: "When you go out the door act as if you were meeting an important guest. Deal with the people as if you were undertaking an important sacrifice. Do not do to others what you would not wish done to yourself. Let there be no resentment in either the country or the household." . . .

Sima Niu asked about *ren* 仁. The Master said: "One who is *ren* 仁 is cautious (*ren* 訒) in his words." . . .

---

63 P. J. Ivanhoe, *Confucian Moral Self Cultivation* (Indianapolis: Hackett, 2000), 72n22.
64 *Zuo zhuan* for the 12ᵗʰ year of Zhao, LCC, 5:638.
65 *Lunyu* XII.1–3, LCC, 1:250–51.

Confucius:[66] Zigong said: "Suppose there were [a ruler] who was liberal in his bounty towards the people and was able to save the masses—what would you say about that? Could he be called *ren* 仁? The Master said: How would that be a matter of *ren* 仁? Certainly, he would be a sage. Even Yao and Shun could not fault him. One who is *ren* 仁, in wishing to establish himself, establishes others; in wishing to make himself successful, he makes others successful. To be able to take one's examples from what is near at hand can be called the direction of *ren* 仁."

Confucius:[67] Fan Chi asked about *ren* 仁. [The Master] said: "First overcome difficulties and afterwards think about achievement—this can be called *ren* 仁." . . . Fan Chi asked about *ren* 仁. The Master said: "It is to love others."

Mencius:[68] Mencius said: "All men have a heart and mind that cannot bear [the suffering of] others. . . . Why I say that all men have a heart and mind that cannot bear [the suffering of] others is that now, when they suddenly see a young child about to fall into a well, they will all have a heart and mind that is fearful and sympathetic. This is not because they wish to ingratiate themselves with the child's parents; it is not because they wish to gain the praises of their fellow-villagers and friends; it is not even because they dislike the sound [of the child's cry]. From this we can see that a heart and mind without compassion is not human, a heart and mind without a sense of shame and distaste is not human, a heart and mind without modesty and complaisance is not human, a heart and mind without a sense of right and wrong is not human. A heart and mind of compassion is the beginning of *ren* 仁; a heart and mind with a sense of shame and distaste is the beginning of *yi* 義; a heart and mind of modesty and complaisance is the beginning of *li* 禮; a heart and mind with a sense of right and wrong is the beginning of *zhi* 智. Men have these 'four beginnings' just as they have their four limbs. For a man to say that he has these 'four beginnings' but that he cannot [develop them] is to injure himself. For him to say that his prince has them but cannot [develop them] is to injure his prince. In general, if I have these 'four beginnings' in myself, and I know they can all be developed and realised, it will be like a fire starting to burn or a spring first finding its course. If their realisation is complete, it is enough to

---

[66]   *Lunyu* VI.28, LCC, 1:194.
[67]   *Lunyu* VI.20 and XII.22, LCC, 1:191, 260.
[68]   *Mencius* IIA.6, LCC, 2:201–4.

protect all within the Four Seas; if it is not, it is not enough to serve one's parents."

Xun Zi:[69] *Ren* 仁 is love, therefore it is about relationships. *Yi* 義 is order, therefore it is about conduct. *Li* 禮 is moderation, therefore it is about accomplishment. *Ren* 仁 is the village and *yi* 義 is the gate. If *ren* 仁 is not the village in which one dwells, there is no *ren* 仁. If *yi* 義 is not the gate one uses, there is no *yi* 義. . . . Only when the noble man dwells in *ren* 仁 through *yi* 義 is there subsequently *ren* 仁; only when he practises *yi* 義 through *li* 禮 is there subsequently *yi* 義. Regulating *li* 禮, he returns to the root and completes the branches and subsequently there is *li* 禮. When these three things are all interconnected, subsequently there is the Way.

Han Yu:[70] Extensive love is what is meant by *ren* 仁. To practise this in accordance with what ought to be done is what is meant by *yi* 義. To act according to these is what is meant by the Way. To have enough in oneself and not to depend on what is without is what is meant by virtue. *Ren* 仁 and *yi* 義 are terms with a definite content; the Way and virtue are abstract terms.

Dong Zhongshu:[71] What is meant by *ren* 仁? *Ren* 仁 is loving others with compassion, living in concord and not competing. It has no mind to hurt or wrong others; it has no will to scheme behind someone else's back. It has no *qi* 氣 to be jealous. It has no desire for making others sad. It does not engage in backbiting and flattery. It does not act against others. Therefore its mind is at ease; its will is at peace; its *qi* 氣 harmonious; its desires moderated; its affairs easy; its conduct according to the Way. Therefore it is able to be at peace and in accord with principle and not to compete. Such as this is what is meant by *ren* 仁.

Cheng Hao:[72] The scholar must first recognise *ren* 仁. The person of *ren* 仁 is thoroughly involved and forms one with things. *Yi* 義, *li* 禮, wisdom, and trust are all aspects of *ren* 仁. . . . This way cannot be compared to things.

---

69 *Xunzi* 27, *Xunzi jianyi*, 367–68.
70 See Ryden, *Key Concepts in Chinese Philosophy*, 302. The quotation is from Han Yu's "Yuan Dao" 原道, in *Xinyi Changli Xiansheng wenji*, 1:1.
71 From the *Luxuriant Gems of the Spring and Autumn Annals* 30—see Ryden, *Key Concepts in Chinese Philosophy*, 301–2.
72 Ryden, *Key Concepts in Chinese Philosophy*, 304.

Even the greatest thing is not big enough to name it. The use that Heaven and Earth make of it is the use I make of it. Mencius spoke about the myriad things all being present in the self. One must turn back on oneself and be sincere and then one truly attains great joy.

Zhu Xi:[73] Whenever and wherever *ren* 仁 flows and operates, *yi* 義 will fully be *yi* 義 and *li* 禮 and *zhi* 智 will fully be *li* 禮 and *zhi* 智. It is like the ten thousand things being stored and preserved. There is not a moment of cessation for in all of these things there is the spirit of life. Take for example such things as seeds of grain or the peach and apricot kernels. When sown they will grow. They are not dead things. For this reason they are called *ren* 仁. This shows that *ren* 仁 implies the spirit of life.

Ren 仁 is spontaneous, *shu* 恕 is cultivated. *Ren* 仁 is natural, *shu* 恕 is by effort. *Ren* 仁 is uncalculating and has nothing in view, *shu* 恕 is calculating and has an object in view.

Ren 仁 is the principle of love, and impartiality is the principle of *ren* 仁. Therefore, if there is impartiality, there is *ren* 仁, and if there is *ren* 仁, there is love.

Chen Chun:[74] The principle of *ren* 仁 is vast, refined and subtle. Why is its application limited to love, and why is the beginning of its manifestation the feeling of commiseration? *Ren* 仁 is the totality of the mind's principle of production. It is always producing and reproducing without cease. Its clue becomes active in the mind. When it issues forth, naturally there is the feeling of commiseration. As the feeling of commiseration grows in abundance to reach a thing, it becomes love. Therefore *ren* 仁 is the root of love, commiseration is the sprout from the root, and love the sprout reaching its maturity and completion. Looking at it this way, we can easily see the vital connection between *ren* 仁 as the principle of love and love as the function of *ren* 仁.

Waley:[75] It seems to me that "good" is the only possible translation of the term *ren* 仁 as it occurs in the *Analects*. No other word is sufficiently general to cover the whole range of meaning; indeed terms such as "humane," "altruistic," "benevolent" are in almost every instance inappropriate, often

[73] Chan, *A Source Book in Chinese Philosophy*, 632–33 (translation slightly modified).
[74] Chan, *Neo-Confucian Terms Explained (The Pei-hsi tzu-i)*, 71–72.
[75] Waley, *The Analects of Confucius*, 29.

ludicrously so. But there is another word, *shan* 善, which though it wholly lacks the mystical and transcendental implications of *ren* 仁, cannot conveniently be translated by any other word but "good." For that reason I shall henceforward translate *ren* 仁 by Good (Goodness, etc.) with a capital; and *shan* 善 by good, with a small g.

Chong:[76] For Confucius, *ren* 仁 connotes an ideal ethical orientation from which one sees the ethical life as a never-ending task. In different contexts, being a *ren* 仁 person connotes having emotions, attitudes, and values such as affection and reverence for elders, earnestness or the doing of one's best for others, sincerity, genuine feeling, cautiousness in speech and action. In this regard, I refer to the internal relation between *ren* 仁 and *li* 禮. There are two aspects to this relation. First, learning to be a *ren* 仁 person involves the institutional and educational structures of *li* 禮. Second, the emotions, attitudes, and values that *ren* 仁 encompasses are more or less similar to those that have been spelled out independently as the spirit of *li* 禮 in chapter 1.

Yi 義

Translations Used: righteousness (Legge, Chan, Gardner); justice (Ryden): appropriateness (Ames & Hall); what is right (Waley, Legge); rightness (Lau, Watson); rectitude (Plaks); morality (Knoblock).

Confucius:[77] Truthfulness (*xin* 信) is close to *yi* 義; what is said can be relied upon.

To see what is *yi* 義 and not to do it is to be without courage.

The Master said: "The noble man takes *yi* 義 to be foundational and *li* 禮 the means to implement it. Humility is the way to bring it forth; truthfulness is the way to complete it."

Zilu asked: "Does the noble man hold courage in high regard?" The Master replied: "The noble man gives *yi* 義 the highest place. A noble man who has courage but not *yi* 義 is disorderly; a lesser man who has courage but not *yi* 義 is a robber."

Mencius:[78] Gaozi said: "Appetite for food and sex is nature. *Ren* 仁 is internal, not external; *yi* 義 is external, not internal."

---

[76] Kim-chong Chong, *Early Confucian Ethics*, intro., p. xiii.
[77] The references to the *Lunyu* are as follows: I.13 (LCC, 1:143), II.24 (LCC, 1:154), XV.17 (LCC, 1:299), XVII.23 (LCC, 1:329).
[78] The references to the *Mencius* are to VIA.4 and 5, Lau, *Mencius*, 243–45 (translation follows Lau apart from substituting *yi* 義 for "rightness."

"Why do you say," said Mencius, "that *ren* 仁 is internal and *yi* 義 is external?"

"That man there is old and I treat him as an elder. He owes nothing of his elderliness to me, just as in treating him as white because he is white I only do so because of his whiteness which is external to me. That is why I call it external."

"The case of *yi* 義 is different from that of whiteness. 'Treating as white' is the same whether one is treating a horse as white or a man as white. But I wonder if you would think that 'treating as old' is the same whether one is treating a horse as old or a man as an elder? Furthermore, is it the one who is old that is dutiful, or is it the one who treats him as an elder that is dutiful?"

"My brother I love, but the brother of a man from Qin I do not love. This means that the explanation lies in me. Hence I call it internal. Treating an elder of the Qin people as an elder is the same as treating an elder of mine as an elder. We use elderliness as explanation. Hence I call it external."

Meng Jizi asked Kongdu Zi, "Why do you say that *yi* 義 is internal?"

"It is the respect in me that is being put into effect. That is why I say it is internal."

"If a man from your village is a year older than your eldest brother, which do you respect?"

"My brother."

"In filling their cups with wine, which do you give precedence to?'

"The man from my village."

"The one you respect is the former; the one you treat as an elder is the latter. This shows that in fact it is external, not internal."

Kongdu Zi was unable to find an answer and gave an account of the discussion to Mencius.

Xun Zi:[79] Now what about the Way (*Dao*) of the former Kings, the unifying principles of *ren* 仁 and *yi* 義, the function of the *History*, the *Odes*, the *Rites* (*Li*), and the *Music*? They are certainly the greatest thoughts of the world; they will make all people who are born into the world think far into the future, and they will protect all generations forever. Their influence is vast; their accumulated virtue is great; their effects reach out very far. . . . Hence the

---

[79] *Xunzi 4, Xunzi jianyi*, 44. The translation follows Dubs (Homer H. Dubs, *The Works of Hsüntze* [London: Arthur Probsthain, 1928], 64–65), who supplies the romanisation for the characters *ren* 仁, *yi* 義 and *li* 禮; we have added the characters.

ancient Kings invented the rules of proper conduct (*li* 禮) and justice (*yi* 義) for men in order to divide them; causing them to have the classes of noble and base, the disparity between the aged and the young, and the distinction between the wise and the stupid, the able and the powerless; all to cause men to assume their duties and each one to get his proper position; then only can the amount and grade of their emoluments be made fitting to their positions. This is the way (*Dao*) of living in society and having harmony and unity.

Han Fei Zi:[80] *Yi* 義 informs the affairs of princes and ministers, superiors and inferiors; it informs the distinctions between fathers and sons, noble and base; it informs the associations between intimates and friends; it informs the differentiation of close and distant, "internal" and "external." A minister should serve the prince properly; inferiors should serve superiors properly; sons should serve fathers properly; the base should respect the noble appropriately; intimates and friends should help one another appropriately; the close should be appropriately "internal"; the distant should be appropriately "external." *Yi* 義 refers to something being proper or appropriate. If it is proper or appropriate, do it. Therefore it is said: "The highest *yi* 義 takes action and has the means to act."

Li ji:[81] What is it that is called *yi* 義 in men? It is a father's compassion, a son's filial piety, an older brother's goodness, a younger brother's respect for elders, a husband's *yi* 義, a wife's compliance, an elder's kindness, a youth's deference, a ruler's *ren* 仁, a minister's loyalty—it is these ten things that men call *yi* 義.

Chen Chun:[82] In terms of the mind, *yi* 義 is the mind's decision and judgement. What is right comes after the decision. When the decision is in accord with principle it is right. In anything, at the very start, there must be judgement as to whether it should or should not be done. Wen Gong (Zhu Xi) said, "*Yi* 義 in the mind is like a sharp knife. When a thing comes in contact with it, the thing will split into two pieces." If one cannot even judge whether a thing should or should not be done, it means the mind is dull and devoid of *yi* 義. Suppose someone comes to invite me to go out with him. I must be able to judge whether I should or should not go. If I want to go and yet do

---

[80]   See the *Xinyi Hanfeizi*, 178. The final quotation is from the *Laozi* 38.
[81]   *Li ji* 禮記 9 ("Li yun" 禮運), *Xinyi Li ji duben*, 335.
[82]   Chan, *Neo-Confucian Terms Explained (The Pei-hsi tzu-i)*, 71–72.

not want to go, hesitate in the matter and cannot decide, what have I to do with *yi* 義? In such matters one must see it through by oneself. When Han Wengong (Han Yu) said, "To practise *ren* 仁 in the right manner is *yi* 義," he is speaking about the external aspect and has made *yi* 義 external.

Cua:[83] The ethical significance of *yi* 義, in part, is an attempt to provide a rationale for the acceptance of *li* 禮. *Yi* 義 focuses principally on what is right or fitting. The equation of *yi* 義 with its homophone meaning "appropriateness" is explicit in *Zhongyong* (Sec. 20) and generally accepted by Confucian thinkers . . . However, what is right or fitting depends on reasoned judgement concerning the right thing to do in particular exigencies. . . . In contemporary idiom, *yi* 義 as an ethical notion can be explicated as a deontic, an aretaic, an epistemic, or a psychological term. Thus *yi* 義 is a distinct plurisign adaptable to a range of meaning or significance in the various contexts of discourse.

Chong/Lau:[84] According to Lau, *yi* 義 has the following more specific meanings: (1) "right" as a moral quality of an act; (2) "duty" as an act one ought to perform; (3) "righteous" or "dutiful" as descriptive of an agent. Lau takes it as distinctive of *yi* 義, however, that it is act-based, i.e. the rightness of an action depends on its "being morally fitting in the circumstances and has little to do with the disposition or motive of the agent." An agent is described as "righteous" or "dutiful," derivatively, in this regard: "rightness is basically a character of acts and its application to agents is derivative. A person is righteous only insofar as he consistently does what is right." *Yi* 義, according to Lau, is the underpinning of Confucius' moral system . . . In effect, *yi* 義 is the *zhi* 質 or the basic stuff that comes before *li* 禮 or *wen* 文.

Li 禮

Translations Used: propriety (Collie, Legge, Liao); courtesies (Legge, *Zhongyong*); rites (Pound); what is proper (Legge); rules of propriety (Legge); ceremony; ritual propriety (Ames & Hall, Plaks); ritual observances; ritual (Waley, Watson); ritual requirements (Moran); ritual principles (Knoblock).

Confucius:[85] Respect is close to *li* 禮; it is to be distant from shame and disgrace.

---

[83] Cua, *Encyclopedia of Chinese Philosophy*, 842–43.
[84] Chong, *Early Confucian Ethics*, 3.
[85] The references to the *Lunyu* are as follows: I.13 (LCC, 1:143), VI.25 (LCC, 1:193), VIII.2 (LCC, 1:208), XII.1 (LCC, 1:250).

A noble man has wide learning in literature but moderates this with *li* 禮; how can he stray from the path?

The Master said: "If there is respect without *li* 禮, then it is tiresome; if there is prudence without *li* 禮, then it is timidity; if there is courage without *li* 禮, then it is recklessness; if there is straightforwardness without *li* 禮, then it is rudeness."

Yan Yuan said: "May I ask you about its (i.e. *ren*'s 仁) objectives?"

The Master said: "If something is contrary to *li* 禮, do not look at it. If something is contrary to *li* 禮, do not listen to it; if something is contrary to *li* 禮, do not talk about it; if something is contrary to *li* 禮, do not do it." . . .

Mencius:[86] The feeling of modesty and complaisance is the principle of *li* 禮.

Xun Zi:[87] How was it that *li* 禮 arose? I say that men are born and have desires. If these desires are not satisfied, then they cannot do otherwise than seek. If this seeking is not contained within limits and measures, then there cannot but be contention. If there is contention, then there is disorder and if there is disorder, then there is impoverishment. The Former Kings detested this disorder so they established *li* 禮 and *yi* 義 to divide things and provide for their satisfaction. They made it so that desires certainly did not exhaust things and things were certainly not exhausted by these desires. These two [measures] mutually supported each other and this was maintained over time. This is how *li* 禮 arose. Thus, *li* 禮 is a caring for.

Li 禮 is what men "stand" on. If they lose what they "stand" on, then inevitably they stumble and fall, sink and drown. If you lose sight of small matters, then great disorder follows—this is *li* 禮.

In rectifying a kingdom, *li* 禮 is like the weight and beam (steelyard) in determining whether something is light or heavy; it is like the marking line in determining whether something is crooked or straight. Therefore, men without *li* 禮 will not survive, affairs without *li* 禮 will not succeed, and a kingdom without *li* 禮 will not be at peace.

Li ji:[88] *Li* 禮 is the instrument of a settled existence and that by which all forms of conduct are perfected. The perfection of conduct is the acme of

---

86   *Mencius* IIA.6, LCC, 2:202–3 and Lau, *Mencius*, 72–73 (translation after Legge).
87   See *Xunzi* 19 (*Xunzi jianyi*, 253) and *Xunzi* 27 (*Xunzi jianyi*, 371).
88   *Li ji* 禮記 10 ("Li qi"), *Xinyi Li ji duben*, 345–46.

virtue. *Li* 禮 casts out depravity and increases the goodness [of a man's] disposition. When *li* 禮 is in place, there is rectitude; when *li* 禮 is put into practice,
there is conduct. In a man, *li* 禮 is like the green covering of the bamboo; it is
like the heart of the pine or cypress. These two things exist as the world's great
principles, therefore they endure throughout the four seasons and there is no
change to either branch or leaf. Therefore, if the noble man has *li* 禮, then
without there is accord and within there is no resentment. Therefore, there is
nothing that does not cherish *ren* 仁 and ghosts and spirits receive his virtue.
As established by the former kings, *li* 禮 had a foundation and it had outward
adornments. Loyalty and fidelity (*zhong* 忠 and *xin* 信) were its foundation;
yi 義 and *li* 禮 were its outward adornments. Without this foundation, there
would be no rectitude; without the outward adornments, there would be no
putting it into practice.

Han Fei Zi:[89] *Li* 禮 is the means whereby emotions are given form. It is the
outward adornment of all *yi* 義, the intercourse between prince and minister,
father and son, the way in which noble and base, worthy and unworthy are
distiguished. Thus, if someone holds another dear and yet this is not clear, he
runs forward and bows low to make it clear. If someone loves another and yet
it is not known, he uses fine words and elaborate phrases to express this. *Li* 禮
is the external [expression] of what is felt within. Therefore it is said, *li* 禮 is
the means of giving form to feelings.

Chen Chun:[90] *Li* 禮 (propriety, rites) is the seriousness of the mind and
restraint and beautiful ornament (*wen* 文) are according to the Principle of
Heaven. When the seriousness of the mind arises abundantly and naturally,
there is *li* 禮. As expressed in responses to and dealings with things, there will
naturally be restraint and beautiful ornament, there will be no deficiency. For
instance, in doing a thing, if one is too simple and lacks beautiful ornament,
one is mistaken in being deficient but, if one lacks restraint and adds too
much superfluous ornament, one will degenerate into excess. Restraint and
beautiful ornament according to the Principle of Heaven mean the proper
degree, that is, what is correct according to principle. When there is no more
excess or deficiency and the act is as it should be, there will be *zhong* 中. That
is why Zhou Dunyi (Lianxi) talked about *ren* 仁, *yi* 義, *zhong* 中 and *zheng* 正

89 *Hanfeizi, juan* 6 ("Jie Lao"), *Xinyi Hanfeizi*, 178.
90 Chan, *Neo-Confucian Terms Explained (The Pei-hsi tzu-i)*, 72.

in his *Explanation of the Diagram of the Great Ultimate* and substituted *zhong* 中 for *li* 禮. In doing so, he was particularly to the point.

Hsü:[91] The word *li* 禮 has no English equivalent. It has been erroneously translated as "rites" or "propriety." It has been suggested that the term "civilisation" is its nearest English equivalent; but "civilisation" is a broader term, without necessarily implying ethical values, while *li* 禮 is essentially a term suggesting such values. . . . The practical programme of *li* 禮 in achieving the ideal of a harmonious moral order consists of three steps. In the first place, *li* 禮 provided principles for the establishment of a social fabric in which people are ranked in a consistent order of superiority and inferiority. In other words, *li* 禮 is an applied doctrine of rectification. . . . In the second place, *li* 禮 provides a code of morality for social control. It defines clearly, the social and political duties of the individual. . . . In the third place, *li* 禮 provides an ideal of social harmony emphasizing the individual's obligation to the society. *Li* 禮 is a principle of socialistic moral idealism and gives a new set of social values to be cultivated in the practical world in which we live.

Cheng:[92] The tradition of *li* 禮 is inner-orientated and society-centered, and opens an order of social interdependencies and human subjectivity, a life-world of human values and telos, which culminates in the belief in and awareness of Heaven and its mandate. . . . Zi Dashu quotes Zi Zhan as saying: "*Li* 禮 is the canon of Heaven, the norm of Earth, and the principle which people follow in their action" and then suggested that all the rules of *li* 禮 which govern human relationships and behaviours are introduced to match, symbolise, follow and accord with natural events, natural phenomena, and natural processes and thus to control or balance and edify human emotions and actions and consequently to harmonise with the nature of Heaven and Earth, and to endure . . . This view led to the reformulation of *li* 禮 as embodying and reflecting patterns (*li* 禮) of nature or Heaven and Earth in the *Li ji* and the *Guan Zi* ("Neiye" chapter).

---

91   Leonard Shihlien Hsü, *The Political Philosophy of Confucianism: An Interpretation of the Social and Political Ideas of Confucius, His Forerunners and His Early Disciples* (London: Routledge, 2005), 93–96.
92   Chung-ying Cheng, *Companion Encyclopedia of Asian Philosophy*, eds. Brian Carr and Indira Mahalingam (London: Routledge, 1997), 514–15.

Lai:[93] While the paradigmatic person (*junzi* 君子) is no longer restricted by the dictates of existing *li* 禮, he nevertheless abides by them where appropriate. The fluidity and overlap in the different functions of *li* 禮 in moral cultivation is brilliantly captured by an analogy Philip Ivanhoe sets up between *li* 禮 and juggling: "The *li* 禮 are the best means for developing virtue and the best way in which to display the perfected virtue. In this regard, they are not unlike juggling which is both an excellent way to develop dexterity and an excellent way to display it." The received *li* 禮 engender and support an environment of shared expectations within which the expressions of individuals are properly understood. Within this ethical and social context the paradigmatic individual expresses herself in creative and novel ways.

In summary, these chronologically arranged examples, ranging from the ancient classics to modern analyses, are presented to give some idea of the range of meaning of these four critically important ethical terms, central to the two texts being translated. The intention is to make apparent the evolution of their meanings over time, and to underscore the argument, advanced in the General Introduction, that they are essentially untranslatable without critical loss of meaning for the text in question.

3. Terms Relatively Restricted to the Two Treatises

There are five terms included under this heading, three from the *Daxue* and two from the *Zhongyong*. The three from the *Daxue* are *ge wu* 格物, *xie ju zhi dao* 絜矩之道, and *zi qi* 自欺.

Ge wu 格物: This phrase, and its meaning in the statement "致知在格物," has been a matter of considerable controversy since the Neo-Confucian elevation of the *Daxue* to its position as a key Confucian text. To the early *Li ji* commentators, Zheng Xuan and Kong Yingda, *ge* 格 was equivalent to *lai* 來 (to come) and *wu* 物 to *shi* 事 (matters, affairs). Zhang Dainian is quite dismissive of this view, saying: "This explanation is very superficial and does not fit the original context of the phrase."[94] Kong Yingda, while accepting Zheng Xuan's glosses of the individual characters, puts a somewhat different construction on the phrase as a whole—"knowledge is extended by study and

---

93 Karyn Lai, "*Li* in the Analects: Training in Moral Competence and the Question of Flexibility," *Philosophy East and West* 56 (2006): 69–83, p. 77.

94 Ryden, *Key Concepts in Chinese Philosophy*, 453.

practice; to come to good things is to extend one's knowledge of good and the more profound one's knowledge of good, the more good things one does in practice." For the Song Neo-Confucians, a more philosophically elaborate meaning was to be found in the phrase. Thus, for Cheng Yi, *ge* 格 was taken to mean "arrive" and what is "arrived" at is the principle in things:

> The perfection of knowledge lies in arriving at things. *Ge* is "arriving at" as when one says that the ancestors "arrive" [at the sacrificial offerings]. Over and above every thing is a principle. One must fully comprehend and arrive at their principles. There are many starting points to reach to a full comprehension of principles. Some may read books and discourse clearly on justice and principle. Some may discuss people and things of past and present and discriminate what is right and wrong about them. Some respond to affairs and come into contact with things and stick with what ought to be done. These are all cases of fully comprehending principles. . . . One must arrive at one thing today and another thing tomorrow, accumulate one's experience and gather it all and then one can synthesize it all.[95]

Zhu Xi's interpretation follows this line and is set out in his detailed commentary to DX Comm. 5 which he takes to be the remnant of a section of the original that has been largely lost. Subsequently, further different views were expressed, notably by Wang Yangming who read *ge* 格 as "to rectify," based on Mencius. The following rather more down-to-earth interpretation was offered by Yan Yuan 顏元 (1635–1704):

> Knowledge has no substance of its own. Its substance consists of things. It is similar to the fact that the eye has no substance of its own; its substance consists of physical forms and colours. Therefore, although the human eye has vision, if it does not see black or white, its vision cannot function. Although the human mind is intelligent, if it does not ponder over this or that, its intelligence will find no application. Those who talk about the extension of knowledge today mean no more than reading, discussion, questioning, thinking and sifting, without realising that the extension of one's knowledge does not lie in these at all. Take, for example, one who desires to understand the rules of propriety (*li* 禮). Even if he reads a book on the rules of propriety hundreds of times, discusses and asks scores of times, thinks and sifts scores of times, he cannot be considered to know them at all. He simply has to kneel down, bow, and otherwise move, hold up the jade wine-cup with both hands, hold the present of silk, and go through all these himself before he knows what the rules of propriety really are. Those who know the rules of propriety in this way know them perfectly. Or take, for example, one who desires to know music (*yue* 樂). Even if he

---

Ryden, *Key Concepts in Chinese Philosophy,* 453–54.

reads a music score hundreds of times, and discusses, asks, thinks and sifts scores of times, he cannot know music at all. He simply has to strike and blow musical instruments, sing with his own voice, dance with his own body, and go through all these himself before he knows what music really is. Those who know music in this way know it perfectly. This is what is meant by "when things are *ge* 格 (investigated, reached etc.), true knowledge is extended." . . . The word *ge* 格 is the same as that in the expression, *ge* 格 (submit and kill) fierce animals with one's own hands.[96]

Fung Yu-lan has this to say on the view of Yan's disciple, Li Gong:

> As to the *Great Learning*'s famous phrase, *ge wu*, this, Li asserts, means nothing more than the concrete practising of such activities. It does not mean, as interpreted by Zhu Xi, the 'investigation of things.' Thus the word *ge* (lit. "to reach into") means, in Li's own words, "to practise a thing with one's own hand," while the word *wu* (things) has reference to such matters as "the exemplification of illustrious virtue, loving of people, (making) one's thoughts (sincere), (rectifying) the mind, (cultivating) the self, (regulating) the family, (giving good government to) the state, and (bringing peace to) the world. That these (acts) are referred to (in the *Great Learning*) as 'things' is because the acts of making sincere (the thoughts), rectifying (the mind), cultivating (the self), regulating (the family), giving good government (to the state), and bringing peace (to the world), are all tasks, for the learning of which certain 'things' (*wu*) are necessary. These, namely, are the rituals, music, etc., which in the *Zhou Rituals* are spoken of as 'things.'[97]

Ryden (Zhang Dainian), in summarising his review of the various more or less disparate readings of this phrase, concludes that " . . . none . . . would seem to fit the context of the *Daxue*. Here it would seem that the meaning of the phrase *zhi zhi* 致知 (perfecting knowledge) is a matter of knowing the root and what comes first and what last. Thus *ge wu* 格物 is a matter of being able to discriminate between the root and the branches, between what is first and what last."[98]

An interesting recent analysis of the phrase, linking it to certain Western philosophical concepts, has been presented by Haiyu Wang, who says:

> As I see it, the knowing that arrives from *ge wu* is not the universal principle acquired through the investigation of external things, but an understanding of one's own most

---

96 See Yan Yuan 顏元, *Sishu zhengwu* 四書正誤, 1.2b in *Yan-Li congshu* 顏李叢書—translation after Chan, *A Source Book in Chinese Philosophy*, 707–8.
97 See Fung, *A History of Chinese Philosophy*, 2:634.
98 See Ryden, *Key Concepts in Chinese Philosophy*, 460.

internal self—an understanding that can only originate in one's own heart. Such knowing compares well with what Heidegger describes as the understanding of the truth (*alethia*) of situated human existence (*Existenz*) in the world.[99]

Finally, then, it is clear that there is by no means consensus on this phrase which continues to exercise scholars and readers alike. From the standpoint of the translation, the views of the respective commentators have been followed. From the standpoint of the reader, the matter remains open.

Xie ju zhi dao 絜矩之道: The *locus classicus* for this phrase, which occurs twice only in the same section of the *Daxue* (TX11, DX Comm. 10), as given in the ZWDCD, is that section, and the explanation given follows Zheng Xuan's commentary—"The Way of measuring and squaring/modelling is to skillfully maintain that which you have in order to show reciprocity towards others." In terms of translation, one difficulty is whether to take *xie* and *ju* as nominal or verbal. Three comments by other translators follow:

Legge, who has for the whole sentence, "Thus the ruler has 'a principle with which, as with the measuring square, he may regulate his conduct," quotes at some length from the *Sishu jiyao* 四書輯要 and concludes that "the greatest stress is to be laid on the phrase—*the measuring square.*"

Gardner quotes Zhu Xi as follows: "The superior man perceives that the minds of others and his own are similar. Hence he always uses his own mind to measure the minds of others so that all will become tranquil." The expression is explained by what immediately follows.[100]

Plaks, who renders the phrase "measuring by the carpenter's square," writes: "This crucial term is used metaphorically to express the taking of one's own moral measure and then using this as a basis of one's interactions with others."

Zi qi 自欺: Interestingly, Zheng Xuan makes no comment on *zi qi* 自欺. Kong Yingda, however, explains the phrase as follows: "In wishing to make one's intentions *cheng* 誠, one should not cheat and deceive oneself (*qi* 欺 and *kuang* 誑); that is to say, in oneself, one must be true and genuine (*cheng* 誠 and *shi* 實)." Zhu Xi's explanation carries more outwardly directed implications: "What self-deception (*zi qi* 自欺) means is knowing to be good by

99   Haiyu Wang, "On *Ge Wu*: Recovering the Way of the Great Learning," 204–26.
100 See Gardner, *Chu Hsi and the Ta-hsueh*, 114n135—the reference is to the *Yulei* 16.449.

getting rid of evil, and yet what the mind-heart brings forth is not yet true/genuine." Gardner quotes two further comments by Zhu Xi from the *Yulei* as follows: "It may be likened to something that is silver on the outside and iron on the inside—this is self-deception" and "Outwardly doing good things but inwardly in fact feeling quite different is 'self-deception.' It may be compared to a piece of copper that is coated with gold on the outside—inside it is not true gold."[101]

The *Zhongwen da cidian*, which gives the *Daxue* passage as the *locus classicus*, has the following definition, "自昧其心也," and also gives consideration to the phrase, "自欺欺人"[102] both of which, like Zhu Xi's comments, suggest an "other-related" component. A detailed and informative recent treatment of the concept of "self-deception" (*zi qi* 自欺) in relation to the *Daxue* and, more particularly, the *Xunzi*, is provided by Cua. His conclusion is, in part, as follows:

> In the Confucian perspective, avoidance of self-deception is required in personal cultivation or character formation, especially in the task of attaining sincerity of thought (*cheng qi yi* 誠其意). Indispensible to the success of this task is constant engagement in self-cultivation, a process partially exemplified in the diagnostic use of reflexive *zi*-locutions.[103]

The two phrases from the *Zhongyong* are the interrelated pairs *zhong he* 中和 / *yong* 庸 and *guo* 過 / *bu ji* 不及.

Zhong he 中和 and zhong yong 中庸: The complexities of the term *zhong yong* 中庸, used as a title for the *Li ji* chapter 31 and in the body of the work, are considered in some detail in the introduction to that work. Here the focus is on *zhong he* 中和, used only in the first section of the ZY, and this involves consideration of its relation to *zhong yong* 中庸. At first glance, the distinction being made in ZY1 seems clear. Thus there are three states of human nature: the first is an emotionless state when, as Kong Yingda says, "there is tranquility and abstraction, the mind has nothing to think about, and is properly in accord with principle"—this is *zhong* 中. The second is when emotions do arise but are properly restrained, regulated and controlled, when,

---

[101] See Gardner, *Chu Hsi and the Ta-hsueh*, 105n106.

[102] Reference is made to Zhang Zhidong's 張之洞 *Youxuan yu* 輶軒語—see ZWDCD, 7:1186.

[103] See Cua, *Encyclopedia of Chinese Philosophy*, 670–77.

as Kong Yingda says, "nature and conduct are in harmonious concert"—this is *he* 和. The third state, which is implied but not specifically mentioned, and is therefore without a specific term, is when emotions arise but are not properly regulated—that is, when they are not in harmony.

Is *he* 和 equivalent to *yong* 庸? For the *Li ji* commentators the answer is clearly no. *He* 和 is not seen as requiring further elaboration and may be taken as "harmony" in the sense of an harmonious balance in one's emotional state as above. *Yong* 庸, however, is equated with *chang* 常 by both Zheng Xuan and Kong Yingda, apparently in the sense of "constant" so *zhong he* 中和 and *zhong yong* 中庸 are quite different. The situation becomes more complex with Zhu Xi and other Song commentators. Two quotations from Chen Chun reveal this. In the first, on *zhong he* 中和, he writes:

> Centrality has two meanings. There is centrality after manifestation and there is centrality before manifestation. Centrality before manifestation refers to nature, while centrality after manifestation refers to affairs. In the centrality after manifestation, there is pleasure when there should be pleasure and there is anger when there should be anger. When the proper degree is attained without any excess of deficiency, that is centrality. This centrality is the same as harmony. That is why Master Chou (Zhou Dunyi) in his *T'ung-shu* (Penetrating the *Book of Changes*) said: "Centrality is harmony." He was talking about the centrality that has been manifested.[104]

In the second, on *zhong yong* 中庸, he has this to say, also quoting You Zuo as Zhu Xi himself does:

> Master Ch'eng (Cheng Yi) said, "By *yong* 庸 (ordinary) is meant what is unchangeable." What he said was of course good but does not fully express the meaning. It is not as clear and complete as Wen Kung's (Zhu Xi's) interpretation of it as what is ordinary. The idea of the ordinary includes that of unchangeability but unchangeability does not include the idea of the ordinary. In reality, they are but one principle. Yu Ting-fu (You Zuo) said that "*zhong he* refers to nature and feelings, thus making the distinction between substance and function and between activity and tranquility, while *zhong yong* 中庸 refers to moral activity, combining both action and affairs.[105]

Finally, Wang Fuzhi states:

> As for the meaning of this *yong* 庸, in the *Explanation of the Characters* it says that

---

104 Chan, *Neo-Confucian Terms Explained (The Pei-hsi tzu-i)*, 123.
105 Chan, *Neo-Confucian Terms Explained (The Pei-hsi tzu-i)*, 126.

yong (harmony) is *yong* (use). In the *Book of History* the use of *yong* 庸 is never inconsistent with its meaning *yong* 用 (use). Before Master Zhu no one ever read this character as meaning ordinary. . . . Hence one who knows how to talk about moderation and harmony is speaking about the use of moderation.[106]

The conclusion would seem to be that there is a definite distinction between *he* 和 and *yong* 庸 in the phrases *zhong he* 中和 and *zhong yong* 中庸. Whilst *he* 和 may be taken as "harmony" by general agreement, the meaning of *yong* 庸 is far from consensus—should it be understood as "use," or "constant," or "ordinary"? It seems probable also that, as Chen Chun claims, the meaning of *zhong* 中 differs somewhat in the two phrases.

Guo 過 / bu ji 不及: These two terms are opposed to each other twice in the early sections of the *Zhongyong*: in the first instance the opposition is equated to that between the wise and the foolish and, in the second instance, to that between the worthy (*xian* 賢) and the unworthy (*bu xiao* 不肖). The reference in both instances is to the Way (of using the centre/central and constant). Both terms are taken as having a pejorative sense. The use of *bu ji* 不及 is readily understood in the case of the foolish and unworthy—they are simply unable to reach (achieve) the Way of using the centre/central and constant. The use of *guo* 過 is, however, less easily understood in the case of the wise and worthy. How do they "go beyond" the Way and in what respect is this a fault?

Wang Fuzhi, for one, expressed dissatisfaction with these terms:

> Wickedness will always be a matter of falling short. How can it be to go beyond? The sagely Way is the peak of majesty, the best, what is so lofty it is like Heaven. How can one go beyond it? . . . One must take moderation as the utmost, be a partner of Heaven and Earth, praise transformation and generation and there can be nothing that can be exceeded. Do not want to let people say that the Way has limits and boundaries and thus take refuge in the vale of wrong. It is not that originally there were three roads: one of excess, one in the centre and one of falling short. . . . The separation into these three roads of excess, the centre and falling short does not even hold water when applied to children's games.[107]

---

[106] Ryden, *Key Concepts in Chinese Philosophy*, 335–36.
[107] Ryden, *Key Concepts in Chinese Philosophy*, 336.

The *Li ji* commentators have little to say on the matter. Zheng Xuan merely identifies "going beyond" and "not reaching" as reasons why the Way is not practised whilst Kong Yingda, who is somewhat more forthcoming, equates "going beyond" with being careless towards the Way and "not reaching" with being distant from the Way. Zhu Xi is more explicit: "The wise go beyond it because they think that it is not enough to practise the Way. The foolish do not attain wisdom and also do not know how to practise it." Legge offers the following explanation referring respectively to the wise and the worthy: "The former thought the course of the Mean not worth their study and the latter thought it not sufficiently exalted for their practice."[108]

In summary, with these five phrases the issue is not one of finding a suitable English translation, although this is, to some extent, a problem with *bu qi* 不欺 and *zhong yong* 中庸. The difficulty is understanding the true meaning, whether in Chinese or any other language—a meaning that must be grasped fully at a practical level if one is to carry out the programme of self-cultivation and ethical development put forward in these texts.

---

[108] LCC, 1:387n3.

Bibliography

Primary Texts Used

Li ji zhengyi 禮記正義, vols. 21–28, *Shisanjing zhushu* 十三經注疏. 46 vols. Taipei: Taiwan guji, 2002.

Shisanjing zhushu 十三經注疏. 8 vols. Taipei: Yiwen yinshu guan, 1982.

Zhu Xi 朱熹. *Sishu zhangju jizhu* 四書章句集注. 2 vols. Shanghai: Shanghai guji chubanshe, 2006.

———. *Sishu zhangju jizhu* 四書章句集注. Taipei: Da'an chubanshe, 1999.

———. *Sishu jizhu* 四書集註. Hong Kong: Taiping shuju, 1968.

Chinese Works on the *Daxue* 大學 and *Zhongyong* 中庸

Chao Yuezhi 晁説之. *Zhongyong zhuan* 中庸傳. CSJC, n.s., 17:461–65.

Chen Pan 陳槃. "*Zhongyong* bianyi" 中庸辯疑. *Minzhu pinglun* 民主評論 5 (1954): 3–7.

Chen Que 陳確. *Daxue bian* 大學辨. In *Chen Que ji* 陳確集. 2 vols. Taipei: Hanjing wenhua shiye, 1984.

Jiang Yihua 姜義華. *Xinyi Li ji duben* 新譯禮記讀本. Taipei: Sanmin Publishing Co., 2000.

Jin Lüxiang 金履祥. *Daxue shuyi* 大學疏義. CSJC, n.s., 17:394–404.

Kong Ji 孔伋. *Zhongyong guben* 中庸古本. CSJC, n.s., 17:453–60.

Lai Kehong 來可泓. *Daxue zhijie Zhongyong zhijie* 大學直解中庸直解. Shanghai: Fudan daxue, 1998.

Lao Siguang (Lao Sze-kwang) 勞思光. *Daxue Zhongyong yizhu xinbian* 大學中庸譯註新編. Hong Kong: Chinese University Press, 2000.

Li Gong 李塨. *Daxue bianye* 大學辨業. CSJC, n.s., 17:419–31.

Li Liwu 黎立武. *Daxue benzhi* 大學本旨. CSJC, n.s., 17:407–11.

———. *Daxue fawei* 大學發微. CSJC, n.s., 17:405–6.

———. *Zhongyong fenzhang* 中庸分章. CSJC, n.s., 17:474–79.

———. *Zhongyong zhigui* 中庸指歸. CSJC, n.s., 17:466–69.

———. *Zhongyong zhiguitu* 中庸指歸圖. CSJC, n.s., 17:470–73.

Mao Qiling 毛奇齡. *Daxue zhengwen* 大學證文. CSJC, n.s., 17:414–18.

Nan Huaijin 南懷瑾. *Yuanben Daxue weiyan* 原本大學微言. 2 vols. Taipei: Laogu Wenhua Publishing Co., 2005.

Song Tianzheng 宋天正. *Daxue jinzhu jinyi* 大學今註今譯. Taipei: Taiwan Shangwu, 1977.

———. *Zhongyong jinzhu jinyi* 中庸今註今譯. Taipei: Taiwan Shangwu, 1977.

Wang Bo 王柏. *Luzhai Wang Wenxian Gong wenji* 魯齋王文憲公文集. CSJC, n.s., 132: 203–381.

Wang Fuzhi 王夫之. *Du Sishu daquan shuo* 讀四書大全說. Beijing: Zhonghua shuju, 1975.

———. *Li ji zhangju* 禮記章句. Taipei: Huangwen shuju, 1977.

Wang Shouren 王守仁 (Wang Yangming 王陽明). *Daxue guben pangzhu* 大學古本旁注. CSJC, n.s., 17:412–13.

Wang Yangming 王陽明. *Daxue guben xu* 大學古本序. SBCK, 75, 240.

———. *Daxue wen* 大學問. SBCK, 75:733–38.

Wang Zeying 王澤應. *Xinyi Xue Yong duben* 新譯學庸讀本. Taipei: Sanmin Publishing Co., 2004.

Xie Bingying 謝冰瑩 et al. *Xinyi Sishu duben* 新譯四書讀本. Taipei: Sanmin Publishing Co., 2006.

Yang Danhua 楊亶驊. *Guben Daxue jijie* 古本大學輯解. CSJC, n.s., 17:432–52.

———. *Zhongyong benjie* 中庸本解. CSJC, n.s., 17:480–93.

Zeng Shen 曾參. *Daxue guben* 大學古本. CSJC, n.s., 17:385–89.

———. *Daxue shijing guben* 大學石經古本. CSJC, n.s., 17:390–93.

Zhang Juzheng 張居正. *Zhang Taiyue ji* 張太岳集. Shanghai: Shanghai guji chubanshe, 1984.

Western Translations and Works on the *Daxue* 大學 and *Zhongyong* 中庸

Abel-Rémusat, J-P. *L'Invariable Milieu. Ouvrage Moral de Tseu-sse.* Paris: De L'Imprimerie Royale, 1817.

Ames, Roger T. and David L. Hall. *Focusing the Familiar: A Translation and Philosophical Interpretation of the Zhongyong.* Honolulu: University of Hawai'i Press, 2001.

Bahm, Archie J. *The Heart of Confucius: Interpretations of "Genuine Living" and "Great Wisdom."* Fremont, CA: Jain Publishing Company, 1992.

Beck, Sanderson. *Zhong Yong. The Center of Harmony.* Terebess Asia Online (TAO), http://www.terebess.hu/english/zisi.html, 2007.

Chan, Wing-tsit. *A Source Book in Chinese Philosophy.* Princeton: Princeton University Press, 1963.

Collie, David. *The Chinese Classical Work Commonly Called the Four Books (1828).* Gainsville, FL: Scholars' Facsimiles and Reprints, 1970.

Couvreur, F. Seraphin. *Les Quatre Livres avec un commentaire abrégé en chinois, une double traduction en français et en latin, et un vocabulaire des lettres et des noms propres.* Sien Hsien: Imprimerie de la Mission Catholique, 1930 reprint.

———. *Li Ki ou Mémoires sur les bienséances et les cérémonies: Texte chinoise avec une double traduction en français et en latin.* Reprint in 2 volumes, Paris: Les Belles Lettres, 1950.

Fu Yunlong and He Zuokang. *The Great Learning, The Doctrine of the Mean*. Beijing: Sinolingua, 1996.

Gardner, Daniel K. *Chu Hsi and the Ta-hsueh*. Cambridge, MA: Harvard University Press, 1986.

————. *The Four Books*. Indianapolis: Hackett Publishing Co., 2007.

Gu Hongming (Ku Hungming). *Central Harmony*. In *The Wisdom of Confucius*, Lin Yutang, 102–134. New York: The Modern Library, 1966.

Haloun, Gustav. *The Zhongyong*. Unpublished manuscript. Library of the Needham Research Institute, Cambridge.

Hasse, Martine. *Tseng-tseu, la grande etude (avec le commentaire traditionnel de Tchou Hi)*. Paris: Les Editions du Cerf, 1984.

Hughes, Ernest R. *The Great Learning and The Mean-in-Action*. New York: E. P. Dutton & Co., 1943.

Intorcetta, Prosperi, Christiani Herdtrich, Francisci Rougemont, and Philippi Couplet. *Confucius Sinarum Philosophus*. Paris: Danielem Horthemels, 1687.

Jullien, François. *Zhong Yong: La régulation à usage ordinaire*. Paris: Imprimerie Nationale, 1993.

Legge, James. *Li Chi: Book of Rites*. 2 vols. New York: University Books, 1967.

————. *The Great Learning, The Doctrine of the Mean*. Vol. 1, *The Chinese Classics*. Hong Kong: Hong Kong University Press, 1960.

Lyall, Leonard A. and King Chien-kün. *The Chung-Yung or The Centre, The Common*. London: Longmans, Green and Co. Ltd., 1927.

Marshman, J. *Ta-Hyoh of Confucius*. In *Elements of Chinese Grammar*. Serampore: Mission Press, 1814.

Moran, Patrick E. *Three Smaller Wisdom Books: Lao Zi's 'Dao De Jing', The Great Learning (Da Xue), and the Doctrine of the Mean (Zhong Yong)*. New York: University Press of America, 1993.

Morrison, Robert. *To-hiu: The Great Science*. In *Horae Sinicae; Translations from Popular Literature*. London: Black and Parry, 1812.

Noël, F. *Les Livres Classique de l'Empire de la Chine*. Paris: de Bure, Barrois aîné S. Barrois jeune, 1784.

Pauthier, Guillaume. *Confucius et Mencius: Les Quatres Livres de Philosophie Morale et Politique de la Chine*. Paris: Charpentier, 1854.

Plaks, Andrew. *Ta Hsüeh and Chung Yung (The Highest Order of Cultivation and On the Practice of the Mean)*. London: Penguin Books, 2003.

Pound, Ezra. *Confucius: The Unwobbling Pivot, The Great Digest, The Analects*. New York: New Directions, 1969.

Riegel, Jeffrey. "The Four 'Tzu Ssu' Chapters of the 'Li Chi': An Analysis and Translation of the *Fang Chi, Chung Yung, Piao Chi*, and *Tzu I*." PhD diss., Stanford University, 1978.

Tu Wei-ming. *Centrality and Commonality: An Essay on Confucian Religiousness*. Albany: State University of New York Press, 1989.

Weber-Schäfer, Peter. *Die "Grosse Lehre" und die "Anwendung der Mitte."* In Peter J. Opitz, *Chinesisches Altertum und konfuzionische Klassik.* München, 1968, pp. 141–168.

Wilhelm, Richard. *Li Gi: Das Buch der Sitte des älteren und jüngeren Dai. Aufzeichnungen über Kultur und Religion des alten China.* 1930. Reprint, Köln: Anaconda, 2007.

Secondary Sources (Chinese)

Chen Chun 陳淳. *Beixi ziyi* 北溪字義. CSJC, n.s., 22:509.

Cheng Hao 程顥 and Cheng Yi 程頤. *Er Cheng quanshu* 二程全書. 2 vols. Taipei: Zhongwen chubanshe, 1969.

Duan Yucai 段玉裁. *Shuo wen jiezi zhu* 說文解字注. Taipei: Yiwen yinshu guan, 2005.

Han Yu 韓愈. *Xinyi Changli Xiansheng wenji* 新譯昌黎先生文集. Edited by Zhou Qicheng 周啟成 et al. 2 vols. Taipei: Sanmin shuju, 1999.

He Yan 何晏 and Huang Kan 皇侃. *Lunyu jijie yishu* 論語集解義疏. CSJC, n.s., 17: 494–567.

Liang Qixiong 梁啟雄, ed. *Xunzi jianshi* 荀子簡釋. Beijing, Zhonghua shuju, 1983.

Zhan Haiyun 詹海雲. *Chen Qianchu Daxue bian yanjiu* 陳乾初大學辨研究. Taipei: Mingwen shuju, 1986.

Zhang Zai 張載. *Zhang Zai ji* 張載集. Taipei: Hanjing wenhua shiye, 2004.

Zhu Xi 朱熹. *Zhu Zi wenji* 朱子文集. 10 vols. Taipei: Defu wenjiao jijin hui, 2000.

———. *Zhu Zi yulei* 朱子語類. 8 vols. Taipei: Wenjin Publishing Co., 1986.

Secondary Sources (Western)

Barrett, Timothy H. "Buddhism, Taoism and Confucianism in the Thought of Li Ao." Unpublished PhD diss. Yale University, 1978.

Bol, Peter K. *Neo-Confucianism in History.* Cambridge, MA: Harvard University Press, 2008.

Carr, Brian and Indira Mahalingam, eds. *Companion Encyclopedia of Asian Philosophy.* London, Routledge, 1997.

Chan Wing-tsit. *Neo-Confucian Terms Explained (The Pei-hsi tzu-i).* New York: Columbia University Press, 1986.

———. *Reflections on Things at Hand: The Neo-Confucian Anthology Compiled by Chu Hsi and Lü Tsu-Ch'ien.* New York: Columbia University Press, 1967.

———. *A Source Book in Chinese Philosophy.* Princeton, NJ: Princeton University Press, 1963.

Chang, Carson. *The Development of Neo-Confucian Thought.* New York: Bookman Associates, 1957.

Chong Kim-chong. *Early Confucian Ethics.* Chicago: Open Court, 2007.

Chow Kai-wing. "Between Canonicity and Heterodoxy: Hermeneutical Moments of the *Great Learning* (Ta-hsueh)." In *Imagining Boundaries,* edited by Chow Kai-wing et al. Albany: State University of New York Press, 1999.

Chow Kai-wing, Ng On-cho and J. B. Henderson. *Imagining Boundaries: Changing Confucian Doctrines, Texts, and Hermeneutics.* Albany: State University of New York Press, 1999.

Csikszentmihalyi, Mark. *Material Virtue: Ethics and the Body in Early China.* Leiden: Brill, 2003.

Cua, Anthony S., ed. *Encyclopedia of Chinese Philosophy.* New York: Routledge, 2003.

Dubs, Homer H. *The Works of Hsüntze.* London: Arthur Probsthain, 1928.

Fung Yu-lan (Feng Youlan). *A History of Chinese Philosophy.* 2 vols. Translated by D. Bodde. Princeton: Princeton University Press, 1952.

Goodrich, L. C., and Fang Chaoying, eds. *Dictionary of Ming Biography 1368–1644.* 2 vols. New York: Columbia University Press, 1970.

Henke, F. G. *The Philosophy of Wang Yang-ming.* Chicago: Open Court, 1916.

Holloway, Kenneth W. *Guodian: The Newly Discovered Seeds of Chinese Religious and Political Philosophy.* New York: Oxford University Press, 2009.

Hsü, Leonard Shihlien. *The Political Philosophy of Confucianisn: An Interpretation of the Social and Political Ideas of Confucius, His Forerunners and His Early Disciples.* London: Routledge, 2005.

Hughes, Ernest R. *Chinese Philosophy in Classical Times.* London: Dent, 1942.

Hummel, A. W., ed. *Eminent Chinese of the Ch'ing Period.* 1943. Reprint, Taipei: Ch'eng Wen Publishing Co., 1970.

Ivanhoe, P. J. *Confucian Moral Self Cultivation.* Indianapolis: Hackett, 2000.

Jensen, Lionel M. *Manufacturing Confucianism.* Durham and London: Duke University Press, 1997.

Knoblock, John. *Xunzi: A Translation and Study of the Complete Works.* 3 vols. Stanford: Stanford University Press, 1988–1994.

Lai, Karyn. "*Li* in the Analects: Training in Moral Competence and the Question of Flexibility." *Philosophy East and West,* 56 (2006): 69–83.

Lau, D. C. *Mencius: A Bilingual Edition.* Hong Kong: Chinese University Press, 2003.

Legge, James. *The Chinese Classics.* 5 vols. Hong Kong: Hong Kong University Press, 1960.

Loewe, Michael. *Early Chinese Texts: A Bibliographical Guide.* Berkeley: The Institute of East Asian Studies, University of California, 1993.

Makeham, John T. *Transmitters and Creators.* Cambridge, MA: Harvard University Press, 2003.

Ng, On-chong. "Negotiating the Boundary between Hermeneutics and Philosophy in Early Ch'ing Ch'eng-Chu Confucianism: Li Kuang-ti's (1642–1718) Study of the *Doctrine of the Mean* (Chung-yung) and *Great Learning* (Ta-hsueh)." In *Imagining Boundaries,* edited by Chow Kai-wing et al. Albany: State University of New York Press, 1999.

Nylan, Michael. *The Five "Confucian" Classics.* New Haven: Yale University Press, 2001.

Pfister, Lauren F. *Striving for "The Whole Duty of Man."* 2 vols. Frankfurt-am-Main: Peter Lang, 2004.

Ryden, E. *Key Concepts in Chinese Philosophy.* Beijing: Foreign Languages Press, 2002.

Taylor, Randal. *The Morals of Confucius a Chinese Philosopher.* London: J. Fraser, 1691.

Van Nordern, Bryan W. *Virtue Ethics and Consequentialism in Early China.* Cambridge: Cambridge University Press, 2007.

Vittinghoff, Helmolt. "Recent Bibliography in Classical Chinese Philosophy." *Journal of Chinese Philosophy* (2001): 28.

Waley, Arthur. *The Analects of Confucius.* London: George Allen and Unwin, 1971.

Wang, Haiyu. "On *Ge Wu*: Recovering the Way of the Great Learning." *Philosophy East and West* 57 (2007): 204–26.

Wang Hui. *Translating Chinese Classics in a Colonial Context: James Legge and His Two Translations of the Zhongyong.* Bern: Peter Lang, 2008.

Watson, Burton. *The Analects of Confucius.* New York: Columbia University Press, 2007.

Index[*]

(i) Personal Names

Abel-Rémusat, J-P, 183, 184, 322c, 515, 529

Ban Gu 班固, 2, 185, 187
Bao Xian 包咸, 500, 500n5
Boyang Fu 伯陽父, 335

Cai Shu 蔡叔, 69
Cai Yong 蔡邕, 497
Cao Bao 曹褒, 497
Chan, Wing-tsit, 181, 182n3, 292c, 517
Chen Chun 陳淳, 182n3, 185, 526, 528, 533, 536, 539, 546, 547
Chen Hongmou 陳弘謀, 503
Chen Que 陳確, 13, 19, 40, 506
Chen Rui'an 陳叡庵, 508
Cheng Hao 程顥, 4, 29, 131, 132n16, 133, 150c, 174n49, 199, 405, 408n2, 451, 473, 502, 503
Cheng Yi 程頤, 4, 19, 26, 66c, 131, 132n16, 133, 136c, 137, 142c, 150c, 150n32, 151, 156c, 157, 173, 174n49, 182, 182n3, 183, 184, 198, 201, 405, 407, 408n2, 412c, 413, 429, 436c, 437, 446c, 461, 502, 503, 528, 542, 546

Chong'er 重耳, 99, 103. *See also* King (Duke) Wen 文王
Collie, David, 184, 515–6
Confucius, 1, 2, 5, 6, 7, 10, 15, 21, 22, 26, 27, 28, 34, 39, 71, 73, 129, 131n15, 133, 136c, 137, 145, 181, 185, 187, 188, 189, 191–95, 198–208, 213, 221, 224c, 237, 240c, 250c, 264c, 270c, 273, 295, 302c, 312c, 318c, 320c, 347, 349, 356c, 357, 359, 360c, 363, 372c, 373–79, 383, 385, 394c, 397, 407, 414c, 420c, 427, 432c, 434c, 435, 437, 446c, 461, 462c, 476c, 477, 479, 480c, 482c, 484c, 488c, 493, 495, 496, 502, 530–31, 534, 537; as the Master, 149, 223–43, 251, 257, 261, 265, 269, 291, 301–5, 306c, 357, 359, 377, 385, 387, 395, 403, 409, 415–21, 425, 429, 433, 437, 439, 441, 443, 447, 451, 463, 477, 489; as Zhongni 仲尼, 223, 372c, 377, 413, 481
Couvreur, F. Seraphin, 426c, 517

Dai De 戴德 (Da Dai 大戴), 496, 497
Dai Sheng 戴聖 (Xiao Dai 小戴), 187, 496, 497

---

[*] References are given for the English text only; those for the Comments and footnotes are indicated by a "c" or "n" (respectively) that directly follows the page number.

Dai Yong 戴顒, 500

Dong Zhongshu 董仲舒, 532

Du Bo 杜伯, 335

Du Yuankai 杜元凱, 382n109, 383

Duan Yucai 段玉裁, 80n21

Duke Ai of Lu 魯哀公, 6, 11, 188, 189,
    191, 192, 194, 195, 202, 291, 292c,
    295, 302c, 303, 305, 306c, 312c,
    318c, 320c, 353, 379, 381, 446c,
    447

Duke Chen Hu 陳胡公, 438c, 439, 439n18

Duke Ding 定公, 103

Duke Miu of Lu 魯繆公, 186

Duke Mu of Qin 秦穆公, 99, 103, 105,
    107, 109, 111

Duke of Shao 召公, 403

Duke of Zhou 周公, 65, 119, 191, 201,
    255, 275, 279, 283, 284c, 285, 287,
    289, 292c, 403, 440c, 441, 442c,
    443, 461, 495

Duke Xi 僖公, 111

Duke Xian 獻公, 105

Duke (King) Xiang of Jin 晉襄公, 111,
    365

Duke Yin 隱公, 89

Duke Zhao 昭公, 121, 281

Earl of Mao 毛伯, 381

Fan Zhongyan 范仲淹, 502

Fu Lang 茯朗, 228n18, 229

Fu Xi 伏羲, 127

Fu Yue 傅説, 403

Fung Yu-lan (Feng Youlan), 187, 502, 504,
    505, 519, 543

Gao Tang 高堂, 495

Gao Yao 皋陶, 403

Gardner, Daniel K., 143n26, 144n30,
    160nn39–40, 502, 518, 544–45

Grand Master Yin 師尹, 36, 90c, 91, 93,
    95, 97, 164c, 165, 167

Guan Shefu 觀射父, 99, 103, 105

Guan Shu 管叔, 69

Haloun, Gustav, 212c, 214c, 292c, 314c,
    320c, 326c, 348c, 436c, 478c, 518

Han Yu 韓愈, 3, 39, 501, 525, 532

He Xiu 何休, 106n46, 107, 378n105, 379,
    381

He Yan 何晏, 218n6, 238n23, 522

He Yang 賀瑒, 218n8, 219

He Yin 何胤, 331, 332n78

Hou Cang 后蒼, 495, 496

Hou Ji 后稷, 277, 283, 441

Hou Zhongliang 候仲良, 426c, 426n8,
    427, 503

Hu Wei 胡渭, 508

Hu Yan 狐偃, 99, 105, 171. *See also* Jiu
    Fan 舅犯

Huang Di 皇帝, 127

Huang Kan 皇侃, 218n6, 219, 300n66,
    301, 364n97, 365

Hui Lu 回祿 (god of fire), 335

Intorcetta, P., 184, 336c, 513

Jia Kui 賈逵, 21, 353

Jian Shu 蹇叔, 111

Jiang Rong 姜戎, 111

Jie 桀 (Jie Gui 桀癸), 81, 82c, 97, 160c,
    161, 273

Jiu Fan 舅犯, 37, 97, 99, 103, 105, 169,
    171

Kang Shu 康叔, 35, 60n7, 61, 65, 69, 85,
    142c

King Cheng 成王, 69, 85, 89, 90c, 95, 99,
    142c, 164c, 275, 279

King Hui of Zhou 周惠王, 335

King Ji 王季, 275, 276c, 279, 283, 441,
    443

King Li 厲王, 267, 387, 391

King (Duke) Wen 文王, 58c, 63, 64n8, 66c, 67, 71, 89, 99, 105, 138n18, 140c, 142c, 143, 144c, 147, 171, 201, 207, 249, 263, 271–91, 292c, 295, 331, 345, 349, 360c, 365, 369, 372c, 373, 377–81, 393, 397, 403, 440c, 441, 443, 461, 470c, 471, 473, 481, 493

King (Duke) Wu 武王, 34–35, 58c, 61, 63, 144c, 147, 191, 201, 207, 275, 276c, 279–91, 292c, 295, 369, 372c, 373, 379, 381, 403, 440c, 441, 442c, 443, 461, 481

King Xian of Hejian 河間獻王, 496

King Xiang of Zhou 周襄王, 379

King Xuan 宣王, 335, 355, 395

King You 幽王, 36, 71, 90c, 95, 335, 389, 393

King Zhao of Chu 楚昭王, 99, 103

Kong Anguo 孔安國, 500, 500n5

Kong Ji 孔伋. *See* Zisi 子思

Kong Yingda 孔穎達, 3, 7, 9, 12, 19–20, 24, 43, 46c, 51n2, 58c, 64c, 66c, 72c, 90c, 96c, 118c, 160n39, 164c, 196–208, 230c, 250c, 260c, 276c, 292c, 320c, 344c, 356c, 452c, 495, 500, 541, 544–48; on interpretation of *Daxue*, 29–38; on interpretation of *Zhongyong*, 196–207

Lao Zi 老子, 217, 405

Legge, James, 1, 10, 12, 15, 40, 66n11, 72n18, 88n27, 91n30, 106c, 136c, 138n20, 142c, 144n29, 160c, 160n40, 164nn44–45, 190n8, 214c, 250c, 276c, 292c, 300n65, 320c, 330c, 336c, 391n115, 426c, 460c, 462c, 478c, 482c, 484c, 507, 509, 515, 516–17, 529–30, 544, 548; on title of the *Daxue*, 21; on title of the *Zhongyong*, 183

Li Ao 李翱, 3, 39, 501, 527

Li Gong 李塨, 508, 543

Li Guangdi 李光地, 508

Li Ji 驪姬, 99, 105

Li Tong 李侗, 502

Liu Xiang 劉向, 43n1, 213n3, 496, 523

Liu Xin 劉歆, 213n3, 496

Lü Dalin 呂大臨, 4, 174n49, 175, 203, 206, 446c, 450n30, 451, 452c, 453, 460c, 461, 478c, 479, 503

Lu Deming 陸德明, 3, 20, 43, 198, 212n1, 213, 495, 500

Luo Congyan 羅從彥, 502

Luo Zhongfan 羅仲藩, 13, 509

Ma Rong 馬融, 2, 496, 499

Mao Qiling 毛奇齡, 21, 40, 507, 508

Marshman, Joshua, 515

Master Kuang 師曠, 228n18, 229

Mencius, 129, 131, 187, 188, 203, 314c, 403, 407, 443, 446c, 449, 526, 531, 533, 534–35, 538, 542

Meng Xianzi 孟獻子, 36–38, 118c, 119, 121, 164c, 177

Morrison, Robert, 515

Noël, F., 515

Pauthier, Guillaume, 515

Pfister, Lauren F., 505, 509, 515n35, 516

Plaks, Andrew, 13, 20, 72c, 160n40, 518, 518n41, 544

Qiu Jun 邱濬, 503, 504

Queen Mu 穆后, 281

Ricci, Matteo, 513

Riegel, Jeffrey, 182n4, 186n12, 190n18, 230c, 234c, 250c, 320c, 414c, 426c, 482c, 497, 504, 518

Ruan Yuan 阮元, 3, 495

Ruggieri, Michele, 513

Shangdi 上帝, 97, 169

Shen Nong 神農, 127

Shun 舜, 81, 82c, 113, 127, 161, 191,
    198, 199, 207, 230c, 230n19, 231,
    243, 245, 269–77, 292c, 369, 372c,
    373–79, 383, 387, 401, 403, 417,
    419, 424c, 425, 427, 438c, 439, 461,
    481

Shuxiang 叔向. *See* Yangshe Xi 羊舌肸

Sima Guang 司馬光, 131n14, 501

Sima Qian 司馬遷, 2, 185

Sima Rangju 司馬穰苴, 244n25

Sima Zifa 司馬子發, 103, 105

Tai Jia 太甲, 65

Tai Wang 大王 191, 275–83, 441, 443

Tang 湯 (Cheng Tang 成湯), 64n9, 67, 69,
    138n19, 140c, 141, 143, 277, 360c,
    393, 403

Tu Wei-ming, 183, 517, 519

Wang Bo 王柏, 10, 186, 187, 208, 214c,
    504

Wang Fuzhi 王夫之, 40, 184, 184n6, 507,
    529, 546, 547

Wang Su 王肅, 6n11, 225n16, 412n4, 413,
    500

Wang Yangming 王陽明 (Wang Shouren
    王守仁), 9n12, 10, 13, 39, 505, 542

Wang Zheng 王諍, 503, 508

Wangsun Yu 王孫圉, 103

Xian Diao 顯弔, 105

Xie Liangzuo 謝良佐, 503

Xiong Shi 熊氏, 283, 285

Xu You 許由, 244n25, 245

Xun Zi 荀子 (Xun Kuang 荀況), 523,
    527, 532, 535, 538

Yan Hui 顏回. *See* Yan Yuan 顏淵 (Yan
    Hui 顏回)

Yan Ruoqu 閻若璩, 508

Yan Shigu 顏師古, 500

Yan Yuan 顏元, 508, 542

Yan Yuan 顏淵 (Yan Hui 顏回), 198,
    234c, 235, 237, 403, 420c, 421,
    424c, 425, 530, 538

Yang Shi 楊時, 408n2, 409, 412c, 502

Yangshe Xi 羊舌肸, 280n51, 281

Yao 堯, 65, 81, 82c, 127, 140c, 161, 199,
    207, 244n25, 277, 292c, 369, 372c,
    373–79, 383, 387, 401, 403, 427,
    481

Yi Yang 夷羊, 335

Yi Yin 伊尹, 65, 403

Yin Shi 尹氏, 167

You Zuo 游酢, 183, 191, 198, 412c, 413,
    503, 546

Yu 禹 (Da Yu 大禹), 127n5, 230n19, 271,
    273, 277, 360c, 401, 403

Yu Shi 庾氏, 236n21, 237

Yu Si 虞思, 438c, 439, 439n18

Zeng Shen 曾參 (Zengzi 曾子), 2, 4, 7,
    21, 24, 26, 27, 52c, 53, 129, 131n15,
    136c, 137, 152c, 153, 403, 495, 508,
    509

Zengzi 曾子. *See* Zeng Shen 曾參 (Zengzi
    曾子)

Zhang Hua 張華, 228n18, 229

Zhang Jiucheng 張九成, 503

Zhang Juzheng 張居正, 505, 506, 513

Zhang Zai 張載, 430n11, 431, 433, 436c,
    437, 501, 502, 503

Zhao Jianzi 趙簡子, 103

Zhao Nanxing 趙南星, 506

Zhao Shang 趙商, 362n95, 363

Zhao Xixu 昭奚恤, 99, 103, 105

Zhen Dexiu 真德秀, 503, 504

Zheng Bo 鄭伯, 83, 89

Zheng Chong 鄭沖, 238n23, 239

Zheng Xuan 鄭玄, 3, 4, 7, 9, 12, 24, 43,
    44c, 46c, 63, 64c, 72c, 89, 106n45,
    118c, 121, 147, 155, 160n39, 173,

183, 212c, 213, 230c, 260c, 276c, 281, 292c, 314c, 320c, 324c, 326c, 335, 354c, 356c, 428c, 446c, 449, 452c, 471, 477, 478c, 487, 495, 496, 499, 500, 503, 507, 541, 544–48; on interpretation of *Daxue*, 28–38; on interpretation of *Zhongyong*, 195–208; on title of *Daxue*, 20–21; on title of *Zhongyong*, 183

Zhongni 仲尼. *See* Confucius

Zhongshan Fu 仲山甫, 355

Zhongsun Mie 仲孫蔑. *See* Meng Xianzi 孟獻子

Zhou Dunyi 周敦頤, 528, 539, 546

Zhou 紂 (Zhou Xin 紂辛), 81, 82c, 97, 99, 160c, 161, 273

Zhu Xi 朱熹, 1, 2, 3, 4n8, 5, 7–13, 19, 22–23, 46c, 64c, 65c, 72c, 74c, 136c, 140c, 142c, 144c, 148c, 152c, 158c, 160c, 224c, 240c, 260c, 306c, 312c, 336c, 408c, 412c, 501–3, 507–8, 513, 516, 525, 528, 533, 536, 542, 544–48; on arrangement of *Daxue*, 26–28; on authorship of *Daxue*, 21; on authorship of *Zhongyong*, 185–89; on interpretation of *Daxue*, 29–38; on interpretation of *Zhongyong*, 196–207; on title of *Daxue*, 20–21; on title of *Zhongyong*, 182–95

Zhuang Jiang 莊姜, 387

Zi Xian 子顯, 99

Zigong 子貢, 353

Zilu 子路, 191, 236c, 237, 239, 422c, 423, 424c, 425

Zisi 子思, 2, 3, 4, 5, 7, 11, 21, 22n9, 185–89, 194, 199, 206–8, 213, 217, 377, 394c, 401–9, 424c, 425–29, 432c, 433, 435, 461, 462c, 463, 476c, 477, 488c, 489, 495, 509

Zixia 子夏, 126n3

Zu Gan 組紺, 277, 283, 441

(ii) General

an 安 (peace/tranquility), 29, 30, 45, 135, 137

Analects. See Lunyu 論語 (*Analects*)

"Announcement to Kang" 康誥, 35, 65, 67, 81, 85, 97, 103, 139, 141, 159, 169, 173

archery (as metaphor for the Way of the noble man), 261–63, 433

barbarians: Yi 夷 and Di 狄, 251, 259, 433; Man 蠻 and Mo 貊, 371, 483

Beixi ziyi 北溪字義 (*Neo-Confucian Terms Explained*), 182n3, 185

ben 本/*mo* 末 (root/branch), 35, 45, 47, 49, 51, 55, 71, 73, 97, 101, 135, 139, 149, 151, 169, 171, 175, 299, 483

Bielu 別錄, 43, 213

Buddhism, 405, 500–501

cart tracks (*che gui* 車軌), 357–59, 477

central and constant (*zhongyong* 中庸), 413, 415, 419, 421, 423, 425; Way of, 415, 421, 425, 493

chang 常 (constant), 198–200. *See also yong* 庸 (to use, constant, ordinary)

Chen 陳 (state), 271

cheng 誠, 6, 7–11, 13, 14, 23–26, 31–35, 43, 49, 51, 52c, 53–57, 63, 115, 117, 139, 152c, 153, 186, 189, 192–94, 201–2, 203–5, 207, 209, 264c, 265–69, 292c, 303, 314c, 315–19, 320c, 321–23, 326c, 337–43, 437, 449–51, 456c, 457, 461–71, 487; as transforming, 327–29; being and becoming *cheng* 誠, 457; in completing nature, 325–27; in relation to *ming* 明 (enlightenment), 323–25, 329, 463–65; meaning and translation, 336c, 526–30; perfect,

324c, 327–29, 330c, 331–35, 337, 353–57, 372c, 375, 465–69, 480c, 484c, 485, 491. *See also cheng yi* 誠意 (making intentions *cheng* 誠)

cheng yi 誠意 (making intentions *cheng* 誠), 9, 23, 26, 28, 30, 43, 47, 49, 51, 53, 55, 61, 63, 65, 69, 72c, 73, 135, 145, 152c, 153, 155, 157, 177. *See also cheng* 誠

Chu 楚 (state), 97, 103, 105

Chunqiu 春秋 (*Spring and Autumn Annals*), 3n6, 83, 89, 207, 371–83

ci 慈. *See* compassion (*ci* 慈)

Classic of Filial Piety (*Xiaojing* 孝經), 3n6, 129n9, 195, 207, 215, 371–77

coming to rest (*zhi* 止), 44c, 45, 49, 66c, 67, 71, 135, 137, 143, 144c, 145

coming to things. *See ge wu* 格物 (coming to/investigating things)

compassion (*ci* 慈), 66c, 67, 81, 82c, 143, 159, 163

Confucian canon, 5, 28, 181, 500

Confucians/Confucianism, 1, 19, 131, 513

cultivation of the self (*xiu shen* 脩(修)身), 5, 10, 23, 24, 30, 44c, 46c, 47, 49, 58c, 59, 61, 74c, 75, 76c, 77, 81, 89, 127, 135, 139, 145, 147, 155, 156c, 157, 159, 163, 203, 209, 291, 299, 301, 302c, 303, 306c, 433, 447, 451–53. *See also* Way (*dao* 道)

dao 道: as a road, 221, 409; translation of, 521. *See also* Way (*dao* 道)

Daoism, 405, 500–501

Daxue 大學 (the book), 1, 2, 5–8, 10, 11–13, 19, 133, 200, 208; arrangement of, 24–28; authorship and date, 21–22; commentaries on, 509–12; commentators on, 499–509; components of text, 22–24; in the *Li ji*, 495; interpretation of, 28–38;

quotations in, 34–37; title of, 20–21, 44; translations of, 513–19. *See also* highest/greater learning

de 得 (to attain), 29, 30, 45, 47, 135, 137

de 德 (virtue), 26, 37, 53, 57, 58c, 63, 65, 66c, 67, 69, 71, 77, 96c, 97, 101, 117, 135, 139, 141, 143, 145, 153, 155, 164c, 169, 171, 264c, 295, 299, 349, 436c, 447–51, 455, 457, 463, 473, 485, 489, 493; and virtuous nature, 351–53, 473–75; as light as a feather, 395–97, 489, 493; as nature, 351–53; of Confucius, 273, 377, 383–85; of ghosts and spirits, 265, 437; of Heaven, 353, 387; of Kings Wen 文 and/or Wu 武, 349, 441, 471; of noble man (*junzi* 君子), 395; of sages (*shengren* 聖人), 249, 375, 463; of Shun, 269, 273, 439; perfect, 349–51, 473–75; small and large, 369, 375, 383, 481–83; translation of, 521–22

deception/self-deception (*zi qi* 自欺), 53, 55, 152c, 153, 155; meaning and translation of, 544–45

"Declaration of Qin" 秦誓, 36, 106c, 107, 109, 171, 173

di 弟 (fraternal respect). *See ti* 悌 (fraternal respect)

"Di dian" 帝典, 65, 139, 141

ding 定 (stability), 29, 30, 45, 135, 137

displaying enlightened virtue (*ming ming de* 明明德), 30, 40, 43, 44c, 45, 46c, 47, 49, 51, 65, 72c, 135, 137, 139, 141, 149, 169

divination and omens, 331–35, 467

Doctrine of the Mean. See Zhongyong 中庸

Documents (*Shang shu* 尚書), 3n6, 5, 7, 24, 26, 34–37, 64c, 66c, 82c, 103, 106c, 109, 111, 140c, 141, 142c, 163, 164c, 188, 207, 333, 381, 446c, 449, 502, 508

Documents of Chu (*Chu shu* 楚書), 37, 64c, 82c, 97, 99, 106c, 169

du 獨 (alone), 32, 52c, 53, 152c, 153, 155, 197, 408c; in relation to noble man (*junzi* 君子), 215–23, 407, 409, 491; meaning of in *Zhongyong*, 214c, 411

Earth (*di* 地), 344c, 353, 371, 445, 469, 473, 483; nature of, 345–47. *See also* Heaven and Earth

emotions (*qing* 情), 46c, 196, 411. *See also qing* 情 (emotions, feelings)

Er ya 爾雅, 3n6, 61, 111, 391

extending knowledge (*zhi zhi* 致知), 30–31, 135, 151, 475, 543. *See also* perfecting knowledge (*zhi zhi* 至知)

Five Constant Virtues (*wu chang* 五常), 196, 219–21, 339

Five Phases/Elements (*wu xing* 五行), 196, 219–21

foreknowledge (*qian zhi* 前知), 331–35, 467

Four Books, 1, 4, 5, 8, 19, 28, 39, 181, 207, 505–6, 513

ge wu 格物 (coming to/investigating things), 9, 23, 30–31, 39, 46c, 47, 49, 51, 127, 135, 139, 151; meaning and translation of, 541–44

ghosts and spirits (*gui shen* 鬼神), 191, 201, 265–69, 361, 367, 409, 436c, 437, 467, 479, 481

going beyond/not reaching (*guo/bu ji* 過/不及), 184, 198–99, 212, 230c, 231, 401, 415, 416c, 421; meaning and translation of, 547–48

Gongyang zhuan 公羊傳 (*Gongyang Commentary*), 3n6, 89, 107, 379, 381, 387

good/goodness. *See shan* 善 (good/goodness)

good order to the state/country (*zhi guo* 治國), 23, 24, 43, 49, 51, 135, 159, 161, 165, 177, 303–5
government. *See zheng* 政 (government)
Guliang zhuan 穀梁傳 (*Guliang Commentary*), 3n6, 383
Guodian, 2, 22, 189

Han 漢 (dynasty/period), 1, 3, 22, 38, 208, 484c, 495, 497, 499
Han shu 漢書, 479; "Yiwenzhi," 2, 185, 208, 218n7, 495, 499, 507
he 和 (harmony), 215, 223, 407, 411, 423; in relation to *yong* 庸, 413; in *zhong he* 中和, 545–47; translation of, 522
Heaven (*tian* 天), 6, 11, 99, 103, 127, 173, 190, 201, 206 214c, 215, 251, 259, 269, 273, 275, 331, 349, 353, 361, 369, 371, 381, 397, 407, 408c, 433, 439, 445, 471, 473; decree of, 137, 141, 205, 215–19, 295, 345, 413, 459, 465, 471, 481–83, 487–93; mandate of, 69, 96c, 97, 143, 269, 271, 275; nature of, 345–47
Heaven and Earth, 198, 203, 207, 215, 223, 241, 247, 249, 269, 285, 303, 324c, 325–27, 331, 361ff, 369, 375–77, 383, 397, 411, 427, 437, 443, 463–65, 469, 479, 481, 484c, 485, 487; Ways of, 337–43, 343, 469
highest/greater learning, 127, 129, 131, 151. *See also Daxue* 大學 (the book)

investigating things. *See ge wu* 格物 (coming to/investigating things)

Ji 濟 (river), 89
jiao 教 (teaching), 81, 159, 190, 215–17, 323–25, 407–11, 463
jing 敬 (respect), 66c, 67, 143, 143n26
jing 靜 (tranquility), 29, 30, 45, 47, 135
junzi 君子 (noble man), 40, 46c, 53, 59, 76c, 81, 83, 87, 91, 95, 107, 113, 145, 147, 153, 155, 159, 165, 169, 190, 198, 209, 369, 407, 460c, 473, 479; conduct of, 215–23, 241–45, 251, 259, 351–53, 371, 373–75, 387, 391–93, 407–11, 423, 425, 429, 433–35, 487–93; equivalent to Confucius, 379; examples of, 292c; in relation to *cheng* 誠, 337; in relation to lesser man (*xiaoren* 小人), 53, 59, 145–47, 153, 215, 223–29, 261, 413; in relation to ordinary men and women, 241–45, 427; in relation to strength (*qiang* 強), 237–39, 423; like an archer, 433; translation of, 522–23; Way of, 251, 361–65, 427, 429

Kongzi jiayu 孔子家語 (*The Family Sayings of Confucius*), 191–92, 195, 202, 225n16, 292c, 302c, 306c, 318c, 449, 461, 500

Laozi, 99, 103, 216n4
lawsuits, hearing of (*ting song* 聽訟), 71, 72c, 73, 149
le 樂 (happiness), 67, 71, 144c, 145
learning. *See jiao* 教 (teaching)
li 利 (benefit/profit), 24, 38, 61–63, 107, 111, 121, 144c; in relation to *yi* 義 (right action), 118c, 119, 121, 123, 164c, 177
li 理 (principle, pattern), 9, 10, 39, 137, 151, 196, 197, 247, 403, 419, 429, 469, 475; heavenly (*tian li* 天理), 401, 417, 459, 485; in relation to the Way, 469
li 禮 (propriety/rites), 6, 13, 14, 15, 23, 24, 26, 29, 67, 71, 127, 189–93, 195, 197, 202, 205–6, 215–19, 225, 301–9, 339, 446c, 451, 455, 473, 475, 477, 479, 485; forms

of ceremony, 349–51, 353; in conjunction with music (*yue* 樂), 357–59, 477; in conjunction with *ren* 仁 and *yi* 義, 446c; meaning and translation of, 537–41; noble man's respect for, 351–53; of different states, 359–65, 477

Li ji 禮記 (*Book of Rites/Rites Record*), 1, 2, 3, 7, 9, 12, 19, 21, 22, 57, 72c, 181–83, 284c, 348c, *et passim*; arrangement of *Daxue* in, 24–26; arrangement of *Zhongyong* in, 192–93; origin of, 495–97; translation of, 517

Li ji zhengyi 禮記正義, 12, 39, 208

love/hate (*ai/e* 愛/惡), 81, 95, 107, 113, 165, 171, 173

loving the people (*qin min* 親民), 44c, 45, 49

lü 慮 (contemplation), 29, 30, 45, 47, 135, 137

Lu 魯 (state), 118c, 119, 121, 333

Lunyu 論語 (*Analects*), 1, 3, 5, 11, 24, 26, 34–36, 58c, 67, 71, 72c, 119, 121, 133, 148c, 181, 191, 200, 208, 221, 253, 259, 261, 284c, 301, 302c, 350c, 363, 415, 445, 460c, 499, 502–3, 517

Mawangdui, 2, 189, 216n4

Mencius, 1, 3, 5, 6n11, 11, 90c, 133, 181, 192, 202, 208, 314c, 318c, 502, 517

mind. *See xin* 心 (mind/heart)

ming 明 (enlightenment): in relation to *cheng* 誠 322c, 323–25, 461, 463–65, 473

ming de 明德. *See* displaying enlightened virtue (*ming ming de* 明明德)

mourning practices, 275–85, 441

nature. *See xing* 性 (nature)

Neo-Confucianism 3, 8, 501–2, 508

"nine canons" (*jiu jing* 九經) 301–13, 451–57

Noble man. *See junzi* 君子 (noble man)

Odes (*Shi jing* 詩經) 3n6, 5, 7, 24, 26, 34–36, 58c, 59, 61, 63, 66c, 67, 69, 71, 82c, 83, 87, 89, 91, 95, 97, 99, 121, 141, 142c, 143, 145, 147, 152c, 161, 163, 164c, 165, 167, 169, 186, 188, 193, 195, 199–201, 207, 241, 249, 261, 263, 265, 269, 275, 344c, 361, 369, 371–73, 387–91, 395–97, 423, 427, 431, 435, 437, 470c, 471, 473, 479, 487–93, 502 *et passim*

peace to the world/all under Heaven (*ping tianxia* 平天下), 23, 47, 51, 91, 93, 96c, 135, 165, 167, 177

perfecting knowledge (*zhi zhi* 至知), 9, 23, 26, 27, 30, 47, 49, 51, 53, 135, 151, 153. *See also* extending knowledge (*zhi zhi* 致知)

Protestant missionaries: translation by, 515–17

Qi 齊 (state), 277–79

Qi 杞 (state): rites of, 359–63, 477

qi 氣 & *qizhi* 氣質 (vital spirit/disposition), 137, 196, 198, 205, 219, 411, 436c, 461, 465, 493; of ghosts and spirits, 201

qiang 強 (strength), 422c; Zilu's question about, 237–41, 423

Qin 秦 (dynasty/state), 103, 105, 109, 111, 208, 495

qin 親 (to love), 8, 29, 35, 66c, 144c; as *xin* 新 (to restore/renew), 29, 66c, 135, 136c, 137, 142c

Qing 清 (dynasty/period), 3, 187, 208, 499, 506–9

qing 情 (emotions, feelings): translation of, 523

rang 讓 (complaisance): in conjunction with *ren* 仁, 35, 81, 82c, 83–87, 161

reciprocity, principle of, 90c, 91. *See also*
    shu 恕 (reciprocity); Way (*dao* 道):
    of measuring and modeling/
    squaring (*xieju zhi dao* 絜矩之道)
rectifying the mind (*zheng xin* 正心), 23,
    47, 49, 74c, 75, 135, 139, 156c, 157,
    158c
regulating the household (*qi jia* 齊家), 23,
    24, 47, 49, 77–89, 117, 135, 139,
    159, 161, 165
ren 仁 (loving kindness/benevolence),
    6, 13, 14, 23, 24, 26, 29, 38, 66c,
    67, 81, 99, 107, 109, 113, 114c,
    115, 117, 127, 131, 161, 164c,
    171, 173, 186, 191, 195, 202–4,
    215–19, 291, 297, 301–5, 339, 371,
    421, 424c, 425, 446c, 447–53, 461,
    467–69, 485; definition of, 291,
    297, 447, 449; in conjunction with
    li 禮 (propriety/rites), 292c, 447;
    in conjunction with *rang* 讓, 35,
    81, 82c, 83, 85, 87, 96c, 161; in
    conjunction with *yi* 義, 115, 175,
    231, 291, 292c, 297, 447; meaning
    and translation of, 530–34; of
    Confucius, 385
renewing the people (*xin min* 新民—
    also given as "restore the original
    brightness of their innate virtue"),
    29–30, 135–39, 141, 142c

sacrificial practices, 285–91, 441–45
San li 三禮, 3, 218n8, 499
Sun li mulu 二禮目錄, 43
shan 善 (good/goodness), 26, 58c, 96c,
    113, 123, 137, 143, 145, 147, 155,
    161, 163, 177, 403, 421, 457, 461
Shang 商 (dynasty), 127n6, 277. *See also*
    Yin 殷 (dynasty/people)
self-cultivation. *See* cultivation of the self
    (*xiu shen* 脩(修)身)
sheng 聖 (sagacity/sagehood), 7; perfect,
    193, 207, 369, 372c, 480c, 482c,

483, 484c, 485; sages (*shengren* 聖人),
    241, 247, 249, 303, 319, 403, 409,
    425, 427, 465, 479, 487; Shun as
    sage, 269, 439; virtue of sages, 249,
    483. *See also* Way (*dao* 道): of the
    sage
Shi li 士禮, 495
Shiji 史記, 105, 130n11, 245
Shisanjing zhushu 十三經注疏 (SSJZS), 3, 4,
    11, 12, 15, 39, 495
shu 恕 (reciprocity), 82c, 83, 87, 114c,
    161, 163, 164c, 200 250c, 251, 257,
    428c, 429–31
Shuowen 説文, 182, 198, 212, 521
Sima fa 司馬法, 244n25, 245
Sishu zhangju 四書章句 (SSZJ, also *Sishu
    zhangju jizhu* 四書章句集注), 3, 4,
    7, 11, 12, 15, 27n11, 39, 182, 187,
    507; arrangement of *Daxue* in,
    25–28; arrangement of *Zhongyong*
    in, 194–95
Spring and Autumn Annals. *See Chunqiu* 春
    秋 (*Spring and Autumn Annals*)
Son of Heaven (*Tianzi* 天子), 47, 69, 93,
    97, 127, 135, 235, 269, 275–83,
    357–59, 439, 441, 455, 477, 493
Song 宋 (dynasty/period), 4, 131, 499, 501
Song 宋 (state): rites of, 359–63, 477
SSZJ. *See Sishu zhangju* 四書章句 (SSZJ)
SSJZS. *See Shisanjing zhushu* 十三經注疏
    (SSJZS)
Sui shu 隨書 (*Sui History*), 3, 496–97, 499,
    509
superiors/inferiors, 91, 93, 95, 117, 165,
    255, 297, 315–17, 355, 433, 447,
    473

"Tai Jia" 太甲, 65, 139, 141
Tang 堂 (place), 89
Taixue 太學. *See Daxue* 大學 (the book)
Tang 唐 dynasty/period, 3, 499
teaching. *See jiao* 教 (teaching)
Three Dynasties 三代, 127

ti 悌 (fraternal respect—also written as *di* 弟), 81, 82c, 91, 113, 115, 159, 163, 165

tian 天 (Heaven): translation of, 524. *See also* Heaven (*tian* 天); Heaven and Earth (*tiandi* 天地; Way of Heaven (*tian dao* 天道)

trustworthiness. *See xin* 信 (trustworthiness)

using the centre. *See zhong* 中 (the centre/ central)

Way (*dao* 道), 6, 11, 47, 85, 93, 97, 99, 103, 107, 109, 113, 115, 131, 135, 175, 190, 196, 205, 215, 217, 221–29, 237, 240c, 241–49, 291, 301, 311, 315–17, 353, 407–11, 417, 439, 475; compared to cutting an axe handle, 251–55, 429–33; in relation to government, 291–319; learning of, 401; of cultivating the self, 453; of Earth, 291, 297, 361, 446c, 447; of former kings, 243, 249; of goodness, 113; of Heaven (*tian dao* 天道), 7, 194, 204, 291, 317–19, 327, 337, 361, 456c, 457, 463, 467, 473, 481; of highest/greater learning, 44c, 45, 135; of mankind (*ren dao* 人道), 7, 193, 204–6, 250c, 253, 291, 317–19, 446c, 447–49, 456c, 457, 463–65, 466c, 467, 479; of measuring and modeling/ squaring (*xieju zhi dao* 絜矩之道), 36–37, 90c, 91–95, 165, 167, 169, 171, 177; of the noble man (*junzi* 君子), 251, 260c, 261, 263, 387, 435, 479, 487; of perfect *cheng* 誠, 331, 485; of *ren* 仁, 97, 99, 103, 115, 123; of the sage (*shengren* 聖人), 193, 325, 349, 353, 367–69, 473; of Wen 文 and Wu 武, 369–73, 377; of the worthy man (*xian ren* 賢人),

327–29; of Yao and Shun, 207, 369–73, 377, 481; practising/not practising the Way, 241–47, 414c, 417, 419, 451; state does/does not possess the Way, 237, 239, 423; the perfect Way, 349–51, 473–75; thoroughgoing/all-pervading, 446c, 447–51, 457

written script (*shu wen* 書文), 357–59, 477

Wujing zhengyi 五經正義 (The Correct Meanings of the Five Classics), 3, 11, 500

Xia (dynasty), 127nn5–6, 277, 360c; rites of, 359–63, 477

xian 賢 (worthiness), 69, 107, 113, 144c, 177, 297, 306c, 307, 455; compared to unworthiness, 417; worthy man (*xian ren* 賢人), 295, 305, 319, 327–29, 463

xiao 孝 (filial piety), 66c, 67, 81, 82c, 91, 113, 115, 143, 159, 163, 165, 284c, 285, 439, 443

Xiao 崤 (place), 107, 109, 111

Xiaojing 孝經. *See Classic of Filial Piety* (*Xiaojing* 孝經)

xiaoren 小人 (lesser man), 113, 119, 123, 147, 153, 155, 177, 217, 233; in relation to *junzi* 君子 (noble man), 53, 59, 145, 215, 223–29, 261, 387, 413

xiaoxue 小學 (lesser learning), 20, 127, 128n7, 129, 131

xin 心 (mind/heart), 49, 53, 57, 69, 75, 76c, 77, 85, 139, 155, 156c, 157, 159, 165, 167, 453, 469, 475; of Heaven and Earth, 449; of man (*ren xin* 人心), 401; of the Way (*dao xin* 道心), 401; original (*ben xin* 本心), 401; translation of, 524

xin 新 (to renew), 66c, 67, 69, 72c, 141, 142c, 143; as *qin* 親, 136c, 137, 142c *xin* 信 (trustworthiness), 6, 14, 38, 66c, 67, 107, 113, 143, 173, 195, 201, 202, 215–19, 307, 339, 455

xing 性 (nature), 107, 113, 127, 173, 190, 196, 214c, 215–17, 325–27, 401, 407, 431, 451, 460c, 501, 523; as principle (*li* 理), 409; completing, 325–27; Heaven-decreed, 324c, 408c; in relation to *cheng* 誠 and *ming* 明, 323–25; in relation to teaching, 323–25; translation of, 524–25

xiu 脩(修) (to regulate/cultivate), 214c, 215. *See also* cultivation of the self (*xiu shen* 脩(修)身)

xue 學 (study, learning), 5, 6, 59, 81, 159, 163, 323–25, 403, 409, 411, 459, 461, 473; to love to learn, 301, 451

"Yao Dian" 堯典, 65, 138n20

yi 意 (intentions/thoughts), 47–49, 52c, 53–57, 139, 152c, 153–57; translation of, 525. *See also cheng yi* 誠意 (making intentions *cheng* 誠)

yi 義 (right action/righteousness), 6, 13, 14–15, 23, 24, 26, 29, 38, 67, 71, 113, 114c, 115, 127, 131, 164c, 191, 195, 202–4, 206, 215–19, 291, 339, 446c, 475, 485; in relation to *li* 禮, 118c, 119, 121, 123, 164c, 177, 291, 292c, 447; in relation to *ren* 仁, 131, 175, 231, 291, 292c, 447; meaning and translation of, 534–37

Yi li 儀禮, 3, 205, 247, 495–96

Yijing 易經 (*Classic of Change*, also *Zhou yi* 周易), 3n6, 219, 269, 344c, 349, 361, 508

Yin 殷 (dynasty/people), 66n11, 69, 97, 99, 140n21, 169, 275–79, 360c, 477. *See also* Shang 商 (dynasty)

yong 勇 (courage/bravery), 6, 13, 186, 191, 202, 291, 292c, 299, 301–3,

421, 424c, 425, 446c, 447–53, 461; translation of, 525

yong 庸 (to use, constant/ordinary), 10, 181–85, 191, 198; as unchanging (*bu yi* 不易), 407, 412c, in relation to *chang* 常 (constant), 224c, 225, 227, 229, 253, 257; in relation to *yong* 用, 212c, 213, 224c; meaning of, 250c, 412c, 428c, 433

yue 樂 (music): in conjunction with *li* 禮 (propriety/rites), 357–59, 477

zheng 政 (government): Duke Ai's question on, 291–319, 447–61; of Wen 文 and Wu 武, 291–95, 447

zheng 正 (rectifying, correcting), 76c, 89, 127. *See also* rectifying the mind (*zheng xin* 正心)

Zheng 鄭 (state), 109, 111

zhi 止 (coming to rest). *See* coming to rest (*zhi* 止)

zhi 知/智 (knowledge/wisdom), 6, 14, 127, 127n4, 139, 186, 191, 195, 202–4, 215–19, 291, 292c, 299, 337, 339, 421, 424c, 425, 446c, 447–53, 467, 485; translation of, 525–26

zhi 志 (will): translation of, 526

zhong 忠 (loyalty), 38, 107, 113, 173, 200, 202, 250c, 251, 257, 307, 428c, 429–31, 455

zhong 中 (the centre/central), 10, 181–85, 191, 197, 215, 217, 223, 230c, 413; as not deviating (*bu pian* 不偏), 407, 412c; using the centre (*zhongyong* 中庸), 223–29, 231, 232c, 233, 235, 243, 265, 351–53

Zhongyong 中庸, 1, 5, 6, 10, 11, 12, 15, 19, 21; arrangement of, 192–95; authorship and date, 188–89, 354c; commentaries on, 509–12; commentators on, 499–509; composition of text, 189–92; in the *Li ji*, 495; interpretation of, 195–207; meaning of, 234c; on title of, 181–85, 212–13; term in relation to *zhonghe* 中和, 413, 545–47; translations of, 513–19; purpose of writing, 401

Zhou 周 (state/dynasty), 90c, 99, 127n6, 129, 141, 271, 277, 445; rites of, 359–63, 360c, 477, 495

Zhou li 周禮 (*Rites of Zhou*), 3, 203, 205, 311, 455, 495–96

Zuo zhuan 左傳 (*The Zuo Commentary*), 3n6, 88n27, 89, 105, 121, 263, 281, 333, 353